Integrated Marketing Communications

Integrated Marketing Communications

THIRD EDITION **STRATEGIC PLANNING PERSPECTIVES** KEITH J. TUCKWELL

St. Lawrence College

Pearson Canada
Toronto

Library and Archives Canada Cataloguing in Publication

Tuckwell, Keith J. (Keith John), 1950–
        Integrated marketing communications / Keith J. Tuckwell. — 3rd ed.

Includes bibliographical references and index.
ISBN 978-0-13-714074-9

1. Communication in marketing—Textbooks. I. Title.

HF5415.123 T82 2011   658.8'02   C2009-906673-4

ISBN 978-0-13-714074-9

Vice-President, Editorial Director: Gary Bennett
Editor-in-Chief: Nicole Lukach
Acquisitions Editor: Nick Durie
Marketing Manager: Leigh-Anne Graham
Developmental Editor: Christina Lee
Production Editor: Cheryl Jackson
Copy Editor: Susan Bindernagel
Proofreader: Linda Cahill
Production Coordinator: Patricia Ciardullo
Compositor: Christine Velakis
Photo and Permissions Researcher: Heather Jackson
Art Director: Julia Hall
Cover Designer: Anthony Leung
Interior Designer: Miguel Acevedo
Cover Image: Corbis Images

1 2 3 4 5   14 13 12 11 10

Printed and bound in the United States of America.

To Esther...and our children, Marnie, Graham, and Gordon

Brief Contents

Contents

PART 2   PLANNING FOR INTEGRATED MEDIA   95

PART 3   PLANNING FOR INTEGRATED MARKETING   219

Preface

Teachers face many challenges in the classroom. It is difficult to get students to read a textbook; multicultural classrooms present language problems; and it is often difficult to cover course material in the time allotted. This textbook is designed to conquer these problems. My primary goal is to present essential elements of integrated marketing communications in a clear, concise, and informative manner. Many students who have read previous editions comment that this book is an "enjoyable" book to read!

Keeping content current in such a rapidly changing environment is a constant challenge. The impact of new technologies makes it difficult for educators and practitioners to keep pace. Finding the right balance between traditional media and emerging digital media alternatives is a key concern since practitioners must recommend the most effective and efficient marketing communications mix to their clients. Students have to appreciate the challenges associated with this task. In a rapidly changing environment, I have done my very best to ensure the content reflects contemporary practice.

From a teaching perspective, textbook readability has always been an issue with me. Readability is a primary strength of *Integrated Marketing Communications: Strategic Planning Perspectives*. The book is written in a straightforward, easy-to-understand manner and is full of examples and illustrations that students will quickly identify with. If you accept the notion that being familiar with something makes it easier to understand and apply, then your students will be better equipped to develop a marketing communications plan once they have read this book.

Most courses in marketing communications are one semester (14 to 15 weeks) in length with only 45 to 60 course hours available for teaching. You will find the format of this textbook ideal for such a course. The **primary strength** of this book is that it is truly a marketing communications book. It is not an advertising book with additional chapters devoted to IMC content. This book offers balance across the various components of marketing communications. Current users of the book have identified **other strengths** which are:

- It is the only Canadian IMC book available—a Canadian perspective on media and marketing communications practice instead of an American perspective.

- There is an emphasis on strategic planning—a separate chapter is devoted to the subject and it is also discussed throughout the text. The concept of "integration" is stressed and demonstrated continually.

- The lead-in chapter on branding is a natural starting point for marketing communications planning—all plans start with a sound understanding of the brand.

- There is always ample discussion of all recent trends and issues facing the industry—the challenges faced by practitioners are identified.

- It is the only text on the market offering an illustration of a strategic plan. The plan demonstrates how an organization applies planning principles and concepts.

- Material is presented in an "easy-to-understand" writing style—practical, friendly, and student-oriented.

The textbook includes four parts and 12 core chapters that cover all aspects of integrated marketing communications. A common planning model is presented in relevant chapters that bind the various components of marketing communications together. Each chapter includes two **IMC Highlight boxes** that show how organizations apply marketing communications concepts. Approximately 80 percent of these boxes are new.

Appendix 1 offers information about how to plan and buy media time and is an ideal supplement to all media-related chapters. **Appendix 2** presents an integrated marketing communications plan, something you will not find in any other textbook.

Some of the key issues and trends addressed in this edition of the text include:

- The integration of long-term strategic plans (traditional media and other forms of marketing communications) with short-term tactical plans (experiential, buzz, street, and viral tactics).

- The control of brands and marketing communications has shifted from the marketer to the customer, a process referred to as brand democratization.

- Consumers' media habits are constantly changing and such a dynamic situation presents new challenges and opportunities for reaching target markets.

- New technologies are changing the communications playing field (video-on-demand, video games, mobile devices, and social networks).

- Database management techniques and customer relationship management programs are influencing the direction of marketing communications strategies from being macro-based (mass appeal or traditional forms of targeting) to micro-based (individual targeting).

- New insights are offered into the expanding role of public relations and experiential marketing in the IMC mix.

Organization of the Text

The book is divided into four essential parts.

PART 1: UNDERSTANDING INTEGRATED MARKETING COMMUNICATIONS

This section presents an overview of essential inputs that a manager would consider when developing a marketing communications plan. The content included in Chapter 1, Integrated Marketing Communications: An Overview, introduces the various components of the marketing communications mix and summarizes the essential concepts dealing with consumer behaviour and organizational behaviour. Discussion of ethical issues associated with the practice of marketing communications has been added to this edition.

Chapter 2 shifts the focus to strategic planning. Relationships are drawn between plans and planning at various levels of an organization and how they are integrated. The structure and content of a marketing plan and a marketing communications plan are examined in order to show how plans work together to resolve marketing problems.

Chapter 3 introduces the concept of branding and branding strategy. Discussion about branding is strategically located in the textbook to precede detailed coverage of the components of the marketing communications mix. Branding strategies and brand positioning strategies are often the foundation upon which marketing communications strategies are devised.

PART 2: PLANNING FOR INTEGRATED MEDIA

This section examines planning considerations for traditional media choices and new media choices. Chapter 4, Advertising Planning: Creative, introduces the communications process and the various planning concepts that are considered when briefing an agency about message requirements. The role of strategies and tactics—and the distinctions between them and creative objectives—is considered. Chapter 5, Advertising Planning: Traditional Media, presents the media planning process and stresses the importance of planning an effective yet efficient media plan. The various strategic decisions that apply to using traditional media alternatives are presented in detail.

Chapter 6 introduces the rapidly expanding field of direct-response communications. Since direct response relies on database management techniques, there is considerable emphasis on customer relationship management practices and the key role played by individualized marketing communications strategies in fostering solid customer relationships. Chapter 7, Planning for Online and Interactive Communications, examines the expanding role of web-based communications, mobile communications, and social networks in the marketing communications mix. The chapter offers expanded coverage of all forms of digital communications.

PART 3: PLANNING FOR INTEGRATED MARKETING

Because organizations look for synergy, the objective is to integrate related marketing and marketing communications practices with the media strategies already presented in the book. Chapter 8 introduces the various sales promotion alternatives that are frequently employed in integrated marketing communications plans. The roles of consumer promotions and trade promotions are examined in detail. Chapter 9 examines the role of public relations in communications. The content focuses on the various techniques that are available, planning procedures, and measurement techniques.

Chapter 10 examines the expanding role of experiential marketing, event marketing, and sponsorships in contemporary marketing. It introduces the criteria for participating in events and the steps and procedures for planning an event. Chapter 11 covers the role of personal selling in a variety of business settings. Personal selling adds a human component to the integrated marketing communications mix, and for this reason plays a very important role in establishing and building solid customer relationships.

PART 4: MEASURING PLAN PERFORMANCE

This section examines the role of various research procedures for evaluating the effectiveness of marketing communications programs. Chapter 12 introduces some fundamental methodologies for collecting and analyzing primary research data and distinguishes between qualitative and quantitative data. The role and influence of collecting and interpreting information on the development of marketing communications strategies are considered.

Additional Content

Each chapter includes at least two **IMC Highlight boxes**. These short inserts reflect important aspects of marketing communications planning or provide actual illustrations of how organizations apply marketing communications concepts. Among the featured organizations and brands are familiar names such as Levi-Strauss, Audi, Pepsi-Cola, Metro, Shreddies, Toyota, BMW, Coors Light, Canadian Tire, Maple Leaf Foods, A&W, and Procter & Gamble.

Appendix 1, Media Buying Principles and Media Information Resources, is a supplement that provides additional media details, and shows students some fundamental procedures for estimating costs and buying media time and space in a variety of media and other components or the marketing communications mix. Students can quickly refer to media-buying information in this specific section of the book. Review questions will challenge the students to understand and apply rate card information.

Appendix 2, Integrated Marketing Communications Plan: Mr. Sub, provides an example of a marketing communications plan so that students can quickly see the relationship between various planning principles such as objectives, strategies, and execution and between the various components of the marketing communications mix with respect to how each contributes to achieving objectives. No other textbook offers an illustrative marketing communications plan.

Pedagogy

Learning Objectives. Each chapter starts with a list of learning objectives directly related to the key concepts contained in the chapter.

Advertisements, Figures, and Charts. Throughout each chapter, key concepts and applications are illustrated with strong visual material. Sample advertisements and other forms of marketing communications augment the Canadian perspective and demonstrate key aspects of marketing communications strategy and execution.

Key Terms. Key terms are highlighted in boldface in the text and in colour in page margins, where they are accompanied by definitions. Students also have quick access to key terms and definitions in the glossary at the end of the book.

Chapter Summaries. The summary at the end of each chapter reinforces major points and concepts.

Review Questions and Discussion and Application Questions. Both sets of questions allow students to review material and apply concepts learned in the chapter.

Appendix 1, Media Buying Principles and Media Information Resources. The essentials of buying media time and space in various media outlets are covered in this section. Review questions that test students' understanding of and ability to apply rate card information are included.

Appendix 2, Integrated Marketing Communications Plan: Mr. Sub. This plan shows how various elements of marketing communications combine to form an integrated marketing communications plan. A variety of charts and figures are included to show how media and marketing communications budget allocations are presented in a plan.

Glossary. A glossary of all key terms and definitions appears at the end of the textbook.

Supplements

INSTRUCTOR'S RESOURCE CD-ROM

This valuable tool is an all-in-one resource package that provides quick and easy access to the following supplements.

INSTRUCTOR'S RESOURCE MANUAL

The Instructor's Resource Manual includes learning objectives, chapter highlights that can act as lecture outlines, additional illustrations of key concepts that can be built into lectures, and answers to review and discussion questions.

TESTGEN

A series of questions for each chapter has been prepared to test students on the material they have studied. The mix of questions will challenge the student's ability to understand concepts and apply concepts. The TestGen software enables instructors to view and edit questions, generate tests, and print the tests in a variety of formats. It also allows instructors to administer tests on a local area network, have tests graded electronically, and have their results prepared in electronic or printed reports.

POWERPOINT® SLIDES

A complete set of slides that are specifically designed or culled from the textbook is available electronically. Full-colour versions of ads, photos, and figures from the textbook, found in the Image Library, can be inserted into your presentations.

IMAGE LIBRARY

The Image Library contains various full-colour images from the textbook such as photos, ads, and figures. Instructors can integrate these images in their own presentations.

Acknowledgments

Many organizations and individuals have contributed to the development of this book. I would like to sincerely thank the following organizations for their cooperation and contribution:

3M Canada
Advertising Age
Apple Computer, Inc
BBM Canada
Biotherm Canada
Blue Mountain Resorts Limited
BMO Financial Group
BMW Group Canada
Canadian Advertising Rates and Data (CARDonline)
Canadian Business Magazine
Canadian Curling Association
Canadian Geographic
Canadian National Sportsmen's Shows
Cara Operations Limited
CBS Outdoor Canada
CKCO-TV
Cornerstone Group of Companies
Coupon Industry Association of Canada
Diesel
Frito Lay Canada
Gay Lea Foods Co-operative Ltd.
General Motors

Gillette
Grocery Gateway Inc.
Harley-Davidson Motor Company
Harry Rosen Inc.
Honda Canada Inc.
Hyundai Auto Canada Corp.
IEG, LLC
Interactive Advertising Bureau of Canada
Interbrand
JM Intimode Canada Inc.
john st. advertising
Johnson & Johnson Inc.
KAO Brands Canada
Kruger Producers/Kimberley-Clark Worldwide Inc.
Leger Marketing
Mark's Work Wearhouse
Mazda Canada Inc.
McNeil Consumer Healthcare
Media in Canada
Melitta Coffee
Metro Supermarkets
Mountain Equipment Co-op
Open&Save, Qponz Inc.
PepsiCo Canada ULC
Print Measurement Bureau

Procter & Gamble Canada
Royal Bank of Canada
Reader's Digest
Revenues From Sports Venues
Rogers Publishing Limited
Rolex Canada Ltd.
Royal Canadian Golf Association
Samsung Electronics Canada
Sears Canada
Shell Canada Limited
Shoppers Drug Mart
Statistics Canada
Suzuki Canada
TaylorMade-adidas Golf
TDL Group Corp.
The Clorox Company
The Globe and Mail
The Hockey News
The Martin Agency
The Old Mill Inn & Spa
Unilever Canada Inc.
United Way of Halifax Region
UPS
Via Rail Canada
Viceroy
Visa Canada
Volvo Cars of Canada Corp.

From Pearson Canada Inc., I would like to thank Nick Durie, Christina Lee, Cheryl Jackson, Susan Bindernagel, Linda Cahill, Heather Jackson, Deborah Starks, Miguel Acevedo, and Joan Wilson.
As always, a very special thank you goes to my wife, Esther, for her patience, understanding, support, and guidance!

Keith J. Tuckwell
2010

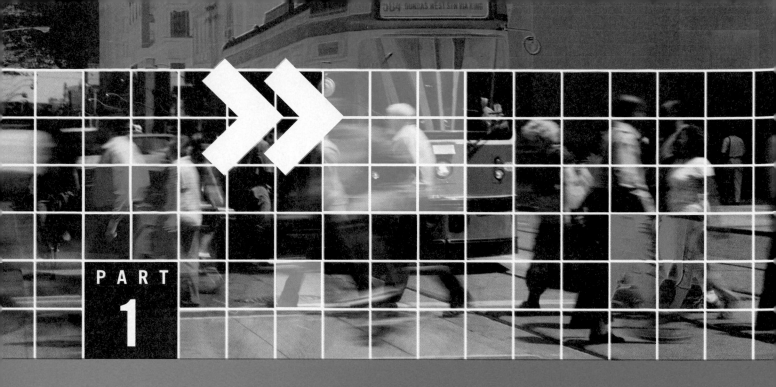

Understanding Integrated Marketing Communications

Part 1 focuses on several introductory issues that are associated with the development of integrated marketing communications programs. Chapter 1 introduces the components of the integrated marketing communications mix and the factors that encourage their use. The latter part of the chapter introduces the reader to a variety of ethical issues that confront marketing communications practitioners.

Chapter 2 introduces the student to essential strategic planning principles while drawing relationships between planning at various levels of an organization. The various inputs for marketing and marketing communications planning are presented along with the content of typical marketing and marketing communications plans. The intent is to show how integrated planning provides solutions to marketing problems.

Chapter 3 concentrates on issues related to branding strategy. Marketing communications strategies are the primary vehicle for building the image of a brand or company. Since brand positioning is the focal point of most marketing communications strategies, the role that positioning strategy statements play in the development of communications campaigns is examined in detail. The role and influence of packaging and product design strategies and their effect on brand image are also examined.

Integrated Marketing Communications: An Overview

Learning Objectives

After studying this chapter, you will be able to

1. Appreciate the role of integrated marketing communications planning in business today

2. Identify the components of the integrated marketing communications mix

3. Identify the conditions that have led to the emergence of integrated marketing communications

4. Assess the information needed to identify and select target markets

5. Explain how unique characteristics of organizational buying behaviour influence marketing communications

6. Identify basic ethical issues confronting marketing communications practice

7. Describe the role that laws and regulations play in guiding marketing communications in Canada.

Organizations today are searching for complete solutions to their communications needs and in that respect are calling upon experts in various marketing communications areas to get the job done. The challenge for organizations today is to successfully combine various communications disciplines into an effective marketing communications strategy and plan. This often requires specialists from various external agencies to collaborate on projects—that too is a challenge for organizations to coordinate.

The environment that businesses operate in today continues to change at a very rapid pace. The influence of technology alone has forced business organizations to examine how they deliver messages to their target markets. Generally speaking, there has been a movement toward targeted media and away from mass media. People's media habits have changed. The average consumer relies less on newspapers and television and more on computers and telephones for receiving news and commercial messages. Consequently, marketing organizations are experimenting with new communications concepts such as *branded content* and *product seeding* to create a "buzz" for new products. They are also placing more ads on the Internet and are looking at ways to deliver advertising messages via social media outlets like Facebook and MySpace. Their objective is to deliver messages where their customers are.

The nature of marketing communications planning has changed dramatically. No longer do companies rely on disjointed strategies from a variety of sources, even though those sources are experts at what they do. The overall goal of communications now is to deliver the same message through a variety of media in order to have a synergistic impact on the target. Furthermore, the development of message strategy is now in the hands of fewer external suppliers. Many traditional advertising agencies have evolved into full-fledged marketing communications agencies and offer services in areas such as public relations, sales promotion, and direct response and online communications. The range of services and the level of specialization that agencies provide are much greater than before. In effect, these agencies are changing with their clients' needs and are providing integrated marketing communications solutions.

The Integrated Marketing Communications Mix

Integrated marketing communications involves the coordination of all forms of marketing communications in a unified program that maximizes the impact on consumers and other types of customers. It embraces many unique yet complementary forms of communication: media advertising (a focus on message strategies and media strategies

integrated marketing communications
The coordination of all marketing communications in a unified program that maximizes the impact on the intended target audience.

3

in a traditional media environment); direct response communications (communications that encourage immediate action); digital communications that include online, mobile (cell phone), and CD-DVD communications; sales promotion (both consumer and trade promotions); public relations; experiential marketing; and personal selling (see Figure 1.1). Effective communications integration also considers the role of packaging and its impact on consumers at point-of-purchase and the role that all employees of an organization play in communicating a positive attitude about a company to its various publics. Any customer touch-point is part of integrated marketing communications.

How an organization plans and manages the various components of the mix is important. Rarely does an organization employ all components at one time, but rather selects and uses those components that are deemed appropriate for the situation at hand. For the components used, the message delivered by each must be complementary. Integration of message strategy, regardless of the medium, is crucial to generating maximum impact on the target audience.

Clients look for a "total solutions" communications approach to resolve their business problems. There is a demand for comprehensively planned, seamless campaigns. However, since the communications industry is structured in a rather fragmented manner, with specialized agencies competing for a client's attention, a total solutions approach is not always feasible. The industry is restructuring itself, however, and as the concept of integrated marketing communications takes hold, the "total solutions" approach will be more available.

Let's start the discussion about integrated marketing communications by clearly explaining the fundamental nature of each form of marketing communication.

ADVERTISING

advertising
A form of marketing communications designed to stimulate a positive response from a defined target market.

Advertising is the placement of persuasive messages in time or space purchased in any of the mass media by organizations that seek to inform and persuade members of a target market about their products, services, organization, or ideas. In the context of the integrated marketing communications mix, good advertising (advertising that has an impact on the audience) will influence the behaviour of that audience—that is its

FIGURE
1.1

The Integrated Marketing Communications Mix

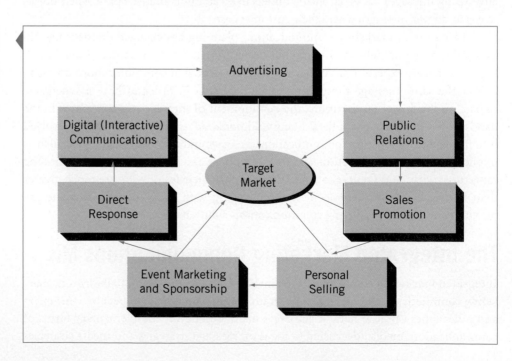

primary function. Once a positive attitude toward a specific product or company is created in the customer's mind, that customer may be motivated to purchase the product or look favourably upon it.

Advertising can be either product oriented or promotion oriented. Product advertising provides information and helps build an image for the product, whether it's a brand or a company. In doing so, the features, attributes, and benefits of the product are presented in a persuasive manner. An ad for Kellogg's Special K stresses essential benefits that consumers are looking for—nutritious food that tastes good. Special K has always advertised that it should be part of a healthy eating regimen. That is a compelling argument for buying this product. With reference to Figure 1.2, the ad for SpongeTowels stresses one key benefit to potential users: the product truly soaks up big spills (like a sponge!). That is a compelling argument for buying this product.

Among the leading advertisers in Canada are Procter & Gamble, Rogers, General Motors, Telus, Bell Canada, L'Oreal, and Sony. These companies are also among the leaders in integrated marketing communications. Bell Canada, for example, communicates online through its company website, is active in direct response communications

product advertising
Advertising that provides information about a branded product to help build its image in the minds of customers.

FIGURE
1.2

A Benefit-Oriented Advertisement for SpongeTowels

Source: ® Registered trademarks and TM trademarks of Kruger Products. © 2005 Kruger Products. Registered trademark of Kimberly-Clark Worldwide Inc. Used under licence.

with current and prospective customers, uses sales promotions to offer more attractive prices to customers, employs personal selling in its retail stores, and is constantly in the news thanks to the success of its public relations program.

Promotional advertising is designed to accomplish a specific task—usually to communicate a specific offer in order to elicit some kind of immediate response from the customer. Including some kind of coupon or contest promotion with a print advertisement, for example, is a form of promotional advertising. In this case, the content of the ad presents the features and primary benefit to help build the image, and the coupon provides an incentive for customers to buy. Automobile manufacturers, for example, are well known for their rebate programs and low-cost financing programs, both of which are advertised heavily to attract customers. Packaged goods manufacturers use coupons and other incentives to encourage more immediate action by consumers. Offering a promotion incentive could be the entire focus of an integrated marketing communications campaign.

DIRECT RESPONSE COMMUNICATIONS

Direct response communications involves the delivery of a message to a target audience of one. As the term implies, "direct" means direct from the marketing company to a specific user or prospective user of a company's product. Direct mail is a common form of direct response communications. Other forms of direct response include direct response television (DRTV), telemarketing, and cell phone communications. This segment of the communications industry is growing at a much faster pace than traditional forms of advertising. Time-pressed consumers, for example, find the convenience of direct response appealing. They can learn of a product's benefit and actually buy it, if they so desire, all in one stage.

Figure 1.3 includes the content of a direct mail package that was used as part of the launch strategy for Tylenol 8 Hour tablets. The mailing includes product information, sample tablets, and a $2.00 coupon on the first purchase of the product. The direct mail execution was a key element of the launch campaign since it was designed to encourage trial purchase. A television and print advertising campaign was implemented to generate awareness and interest for the brand, another example of successful integration.

DIGITAL (INTERACTIVE) COMMUNICATIONS

In an integrated marketing communications context, **digital (interactive) communications** are commercial messages for an organization placed on the Internet, a cell phone, other personal electronic device, or a DVD. Technology is changing so rapidly that there is little doubt that communications by way of electronic devices will be the future of marketing communications. In fact, investment in online communications by Canadian advertisers is growing steadily. In 2007 (latest year that statistics were available) revenue from online advertising climbed to $1.2 billion, a 36% increase over 2006. Investment has quadrupled over a five-year period. "The growth of online advertising speaks volumes about the importance of the medium to marketers in terms of its ability to reach, target, engage, and dialogue with consumers," says Paula Gignac, President, IAB Canada.[1] Right now the Internet is the number one medium among Canadians 18 to 34 years old in terms of time spent with a medium.

Consumers remain somewhat skeptical of online and cell phone advertising, viewing it as an invasion of privacy or something that gets in the way of what they are doing. For many consumers it is not a medium like television or radio; advertising online is seen as somewhat of an interruption or intrusion. Consumers must realize that the online services they take for granted have to be paid for by someone. Advertising revenue is vital for the survival of Internet service providers.

---

promotional advertising
Advertising that communicates a specific offer to encourage an immediate response from the target audience

direct response communications
The delivery of a message to a target audience of one; the message can be distributed by direct mail, direct response television, or telemarketing.

digital (interactive) communications
The placement of an advertising message on a website, or an ad delivered by email or through mobile communications devices.

FIGURE 1.3   A Direct Mail Package Containing Product Information and Trial Purchase Incentives

Source: Provided by McNeil Consumer Healthcare.

The new emphasis that business organizations place on **customer relationship management (CRM)**, combined with their ability to manage internal databases, is forcing them to move toward direct-response and interactive communications. At present, organizations communicate through their own websites and through various forms of online advertising such as display ads, video, search advertising, and classified directories. These and other new forms of communications will play an increasing role in the communications mix in the future.

customer relationship management (CRM)
A process that enables an organization to develop an ongoing relationship with valued customers; the organization captures and uses information about its customers to its advantage in developing the relationship.

SALES PROMOTION

Sales promotion involves special incentives to stimulate an immediate reaction from consumers and distributors. An organization's promotion expenditures tend to be divided between consumers and distributors. Strategies that include coupons, free samples, contests, and cash refunds are classified as consumer promotions. The direct mail campaign included in Figure 1.3 is a good example of how sales promotions are integrated with media advertising. Offering price discounts to distributors for purchasing goods in large quantities or for performing some kind of marketing or merchandising task on behalf of a marketing organization is classified as a trade promotion.

sales promotion
An activity that provides incentives to bring about immediate response from customers, distributors, and an organization's sales force.

The marketing organization is constantly challenged on how to divide the sales promotion budget between consumers and trade customers. Regardless of how the budget is allocated, it is imperative that consumer promotion strategies be aligned effectively with consumer advertising programs (to pull the product through the channel of distribution) and that trade promotions be aligned effectively with personal selling programs (to push the product through the channel of distribution). In business, it is the integration of various marketing communications programs that pays off for the organization.

PUBLIC RELATIONS

public relations
A form of communications designed to
gain public understanding and
acceptance.

Public relations communications are primarily directed toward gaining public understanding and acceptance. Public relations (PR) messages influence the attitudes and opinions of interest groups to an organization. Consequently, progressive-minded marketing organizations fully appreciate the role that public relations campaigns can play in generating positive attitudes toward products.

Public relations involve placing messages in the media that require no payment. In effect, they can generate "free" exposure. For example, a company issues a press release announcing a new product. The release includes all the virtues of the product, where it will be available, and how it will be advertised. Stories about the new product will appear on television newscasts and in newspaper and magazine articles. Such exposure offers a legitimacy that advertising does not have. To demonstrate, Hollywood movie producers rely heavily on public relations to generate publicity for new movie releases—this helps create the necessary hype they desire!

Public relations also play a major role when a company finds itself in a crisis. Senior managers of an organization must be prepared to deal with the media and issue effective communications when unpleasant circumstances arise, for instance, a product recall or a matter of public safety involving the company. Such was the case when Maple Leaf Foods was forced to recall tainted meat products in August 2008. Various Maple Leaf meats products were linked to an outbreak of listeria which caused 11 deaths. Maple Leaf responded quickly and earnestly by closing down the plant from which the meats came and recalling some 220 products. Company president Michael McCain offered a candid apology saying, "We have an unwavering commitment to keeping our food safe with standards well beyond regulatory requirements, but our best efforts failed and we are deeply sorry."[2] Full-page ads that included the apology and details of what action the company was taking appeared in daily newspapers across Canada. The company's quick and thorough response to the outbreak helped ensure the company wouldn't suffer serious long-term damage.

Traditional public relations are changing rapidly due to the popularity of social media. Communications tools such as Facebook and Twitter get regular people communicating information (positive and negative) about products and companies. In such an advanced technological age the comments of one online dissenter can spread quickly.[3] Discussions that start online can be tomorrow's front-page headline. Online tools are now part of good PR strategy.

EXPERIENTIAL MARKETING

experiential marketing
A form of marketing that creates an
emotional connection with the consumer in personally relevant and memorable ways.

Experiential marketing is a blend of marketing communications disciplines that engage people with a brand in a more personal way. The core of experiential marketing is event marketing where consumers are immersed in a branded experience.[4] The experience could be anything from attending an event where a sponsor's product is freely distributed to devising a specific branded event that becomes the focal point of an entire integrated marketing communications campaign. Budweiser's Bud Camp contest

(Labatt) and the Coors Light Maxim Golf Experience weekend (Molson Coors) are examples. In both cases the event is the core experience. Integrated campaigns are implemented by each company to attract and engage its target market with the brand. **Event marketing**, therefore, involves planning, organizing, and marketing an event, whether it is an event for a company or a brand of a company, that integrates a variety of communications elements.

Sponsorship simply means that a company provides money to an event in return for specified marketing privileges for being associated with the event. Rogers, for example, is involved in event marketing as the title sponsor of the men's and women's Rogers Cup, a major tennis championship held annually in Toronto and Montreal. Rogers defrays the cost of holding such events by selling sponsorships to other companies. Those companies have advertising and on-site signage privileges at the event and can use the event logo to help market their product to the public.

Experiential marketing is a growing component of the marketing communications mix. Marketers are attracted to events because they reach their target market directly and improve brand awareness when associated with the right event. At events, people expect to see branded content; they are generally more receptive to brand messages and therefore more engaged with the experience. Scotiabank has significantly increased its sponsorship spending by 50 percent over a two-year period and has associated its brand with the NHL and the NHLPA (player's association).[5] Scotiabank believes such a partnership will raise its profile with consumers more efficiently than traditional advertising, where competition among major banks is intense.

event marketing
The process, planned by a sponsoring organization, of integrating a variety of communications elements with a single event theme.

sponsorship
The act of financially supporting an event in return for certain advertising rights and privileges.

PERSONAL SELLING

As the term implies, **personal selling** involves the delivery of a personalized message from a seller to a buyer. That message presents the features, attributes, and benefits of a product or service. Personal selling is important in so many situations, whether the seller is a car salesperson in a Toyota showroom, a store clerk in Best Buy, or the Kraft sales representative presenting a new product to a buyer at the head office of Loblaws.

personal selling
Face-to-face communication involving the presentation of features and benefits of a product or service to a buyer; the objective is to make a sale.

Compelling advertising campaigns for new automobiles encourage consumers to visit dealer showrooms. That money can go to waste if a salesperson at a dealership is unprepared to handle customer inquiries effectively. The same can be said if Kraft is launching a new line of cereal with a big advertising campaign. If the salesperson does not successfully sell the new cereal to head office buyers at major chains like Loblaws or Safeway, Kraft faces a significant setback. No amount of advertising will help sell the product—it simply will not be available at Loblaws or Safeway. The job of the sales representative is to secure distribution of the product in a timely manner. The availability of the product in stores must coincide with the scheduling of media advertising. If that is not the case, a lot of advertising money could be wasted.

In summary, contemporary organizations realize there are significant benefits to be achieved if all forms of marketing communications they choose to use are integrated successfully. For certain, integration fosters a cooperative approach to communications planning, presents a unified message, and creates a higher level of impact on the target audience.

Factors Encouraging Integrated Marketing Communications

Selecting the right combination of marketing communications alternatives to solve unique business problems is the key to success today. And that is a difficult challenge. In the past, strategies for the various forms of marketing communications (advertising, sales promotions, public relations, and so on) were implemented independently of each other. Each alternative was a silo. Contemporary thinking suggests a different approach, an approach in which each communications alternative is an equal partner; an approach where there is media neutrality; an approach in which creative solutions are recommended to solve business problems. This way of thinking is the foundation on which integrated marketing communications strategies are built.

Several key issues and trends continue to affect marketing and marketing communications practice. Among these issues and trends are the following:

- Consumers' media habits are changing in a manner that makes them more difficult to reach.

- The strategic focus on relationship marketing, commonly referred to as customer relationship management (CRM).

- The expanding role of database marketing.

- The dramatic impact of the Internet and other communications technologies.

- The greater demand for efficiency and accountability in organizations.

MEDIA CONSUMPTION TRENDS

There is definitely a trend moving toward newer, electronic forms of communication and away from traditional forms of communication. Canadian consumers are spending less time with television and radio each week and more time with the Internet (see Figure 1.4 for details). In 2008, advertising revenues generated by the Internet were $1.6 billion in Canada and surpassed all forms of media advertising except for television.[6] As well, consumers tend to multi-task with the media. They will watch television while reading the newspaper or they will view a downloaded television show online while talking on a cell phone. Cell phones, commonly referred to as the "third screen," are extremely popular with younger consumers and are used for text messaging, playing video games, and downloading video content.

These trends create interesting challenges and opportunities for media planners who make recommendations to clients on how best to spend their advertising dollars. To demonstrate, General Motors, one of the largest advertisers in North America, will shift half of its $3 billion advertising budget into digital and direct marketing within the next three years (by 2011).[7] Undoubtedly, many automotive competitors will follow.

For additional insight into how media consumption trends are influencing communications strategies, refer to the IMC Highlight: **Change is Fast and Furious!**

FIGURE 1.4

Media Consumption in Canada—Share of Time Spent with Media

Source: Interactive Advertising Bureau of Canada, 2008 Canadian Media Usage Trend Study.

Medium	2001 Minutes	2001 Share	2007 Minutes	2007 Share
Television	818	36	818	35
Radio	763	33	678	29
Internet	309	14	543	23
Newspaper	240	11	223	9
Magazine	120	5	99	4
Total	2250	100	2361	100

Data is for all adults 18+

Change Is Fast and Furious!

The ability of the traditional mass media (television, radio, newspapers, magazines, and outdoor advertising) to reach consumers is dwindling, and for good reason. In the 1950s, the placement of one, 60-second TV commercial would reach 80 percent of North America's population. Today, to reach that many people would take more than 100 commercials!

The media landscape has changed, and how people use the media has also changed. Today, consumers are using technology to avoid watching commercials, and consumers, particularly young ones, are talking on their cell phones, surfing the web, and watching TV all at once. Therefore, marketers that cling to traditional media strategies are doomed to failure.

For certain, television advertising is not as dominant as it was. The proliferation of new technologies such as the Internet, digital TV, cell phones, smart phones, and iPods has resulted in a variety of new ways of reaching consumers. Now consumers can download TV shows, pass over regular radio for streamed music, and generally watch and listen when they want to. The media no longer control when and where people watch and listen, the people do!

It's been tough for the media experts employed by ad agencies to keep up with the changes. Traditional full-service agencies have given way to boutique-style agencies specializing in new media such as online communications, word of mouth, viral campaigns, and experiential marketing. Any agency clinging to the old business model is stumbling while those that have learned to manipulate new technologies are profiting.

There was also a time when "message" issues dominated communications strategies, but now the medium is the message. Traditional media buyers must alter their approach in this new environment. Today, media strategists are expected to understand and make recommendations about all media channels. They must find ways of blending traditional media with new media to reach and influence the target market. In that respect, communications dollars are moving online. In the auto sector alone as much as 20 percent of all spending is now devoted to online communications.

The popularity of social media is also an influence causing change. Social applications such as networks, blogs, video, and photo-sharing sites are proving useful for sending branded messages. Companies are blogging. Coca-Cola blogs about the brand's role in pop culture, its brand history, and Coke collectables.

Sites such as Facebook and Twitter are used to create a fan following. Once you create awareness in these media, a company can launch applications and fan pages to engage with its customers better. Harley-Davidson, among many other companies, has a Facebook page and Twitter account to connect with its customers. Talk about change . . . these practices were unheard of just a few short years ago!

Adapted from Vaibhav Kalamdan, "Using Corporate Blogs and Social Networks to Save Communications Costs," *SocialNetBuzz*, May 19, 2009, www.socialnetbuzz. wordpress.com and Laura Bogomolny, "Advolution: The ad industry's struggle to keep up," *Canadian Business*, February 13–26, 2006, pp. 61–64.

DATABASE MANAGEMENT TECHNIQUES AND CUSTOMER RELATIONSHIP MARKETING

Database management systems involve the continuous collection and analysis of information about customers. Companies that embrace database management can predict how likely the customer is to buy, and then develop a message precisely designed to meet that customer's unique needs. Technological advances allow a company to zero in on extremely small segments of the population, often referred to as niches. The ultimate goal is to aim directly at the smallest segment—the individual. The database is the internal vehicle that facilitates implementation of customer relationship management programs.

Business today is all about relationships: the relationships that an organization has with its customers, distributors, and suppliers. Customer relationship marketing may

database management system
A system that collects information about customers for analysis by managers to facilitate sound business decisions.

involve numerous companies working together to achieve common goals, or it may only involve one company trying to build a meaningful relationship with its consumers. Customer relationship management (CRM) programs are concerned with establishing, maintaining, and enhancing long-term relationships. These programs call for marketing and marketing communications programs that are designed to approach customer groups (targets) collectively and each customer individually, when applicable.

To demonstrate CRM, let's examine the marketing communications used by Shoppers Drug Mart. Shoppers Drug Mart has amassed information about its customer demographics and shopping patterns, so it can identify items customers are "likely" to buy. Through its Optimum Rewards program Shoppers has one of the largest customer databases in Canada, and it provides a means to communicate information and offers directly to loyal customers. Consequently, Shoppers now spends much less on traditional media such as television and weekly flyers (formerly staple means of communication in its mix) and more on direct communications via mail and email. It is also common for Shoppers to send loyal customers free samples of branded items in the mail that customers are likely to be interested in. A sample of Shoppers's marketing communications appears in Figure 1.5.

In today's very competitive business environment, equal consideration must be given to attracting new customers and to retaining existing customers. Typically, the

FIGURE 1.5   An Example of Direct Communications between Shoppers Drug Mart and Its Loyal Customers

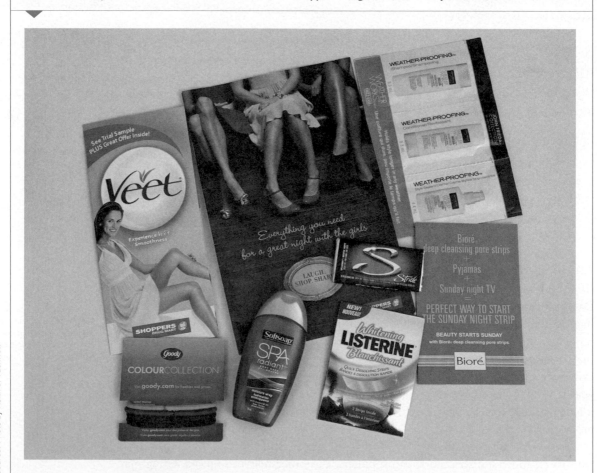

Source: Photo by Keith J. Tuckwell

more traditional means of communications are used to pursue new customers, and non-traditional media such as telemarketing, online communications, social networks, and loyalty programs are used to retain and enhance the customer relationship.

DIGITAL COMMUNICATIONS TECHNOLOGIES

The Internet and mobile communications devices are now a vital means for communicating information about goods and services and conducting business transactions with customers. With consumers' eyeballs shifting from the "big screen" (television) to the "small screen" (computers and mobile devices), companies are reacting and are experimenting with new media communications mixes to more effectively reach and have an impact on their target audiences.

A report issued by the Canadian Radio-television and Telecommunications Commission (CRTC) reveals that 70 percent of Canadian households subscribe to the Internet and 60 percent have high-speed access. As a result, the demand for video content online has skyrocketed and networks have begun streaming their most popular shows so consumers can view them any time they like. CTV streams *Mad Men* and *Canadian Idol*, among others, and Global streams *The Office* and *Heroes,* among others. The streaming of video content presents new advertising opportunities for marketing organizations.

These trends, along with the growing popularity of user-generated social network sites such as YouTube, Facebook, and MySpace, are forcing change in media strategy. Strategically thinking managers now realize that online and other forms of interactive communications are complementary to traditional media and, when used together, improve awareness levels and stimulate more action.

On the mobile communications front, Canadians are avid cell phone users—70 percent of the population aged 16 to 60 has a cell phone. Cell phones have become ubiquitous in today's society and are now an important part of most Canadians' communications activities. While all ages use cell phones, younger consumers spend almost twice as much time on the phone as those 55 years and over.[8] Given these data, the medium offers significant potential to reach consumers with multimedia advertising messages. Further, marketers have a personal link to consumers at any time wherever they are!

THE DEMAND FOR EFFICIENCY AND ACCOUNTABILITY

Organizations now understand that scarce resources can be put to better use if the efforts of individual activities are coordinated. A coordinated effort encourages synergy, which in turn should have a stronger impact on the target audience. There is intense pressure on managers today to be more accountable for producing tangible results for their marketing communications investment. Therefore, communications strategies that are efficient are popular, as are strategies that can be measured easily in terms of return on investment. Senior management likes the idea of tangible results. Such a demand is fuelling interest in electronic communications because consumer responses to the communications can be tracked electronically and without cost. Similar measurements are not possible when traditional forms of communications are employed.

Toyota Canada was quick to recognize how integrated media and marketing strategies produce efficient communications. At Toyota all communications departments now work together in one integrated group. "We combined all departments in order to ensure that we were speaking with a consistent voice and were sending out a consistent message all the time. It's given us an opportunity to think more 'out of the box' in terms of ideas. With all disciplines working together there are tremendous efficiencies," says Peter Renz, national director of public relations and advertising at Toyota Canada.[9]

Levi Strauss & Co. launched its first integrated marketing campaign in August 2008 to celebrate its 501 jeans. The "Live Unbuttoned" campaign embraced television, print, outdoor, online, and viral components. For more insight into the Levi's campaign read the IMC Highlight: **Multiple Channels Deliver Levi's Message**.

IMC HIGHLIGHT »

Multiple Channels Deliver Levi's Message

How does Levi's and its Levi 501 tight-fitting jeans grab the attention of a 16-to-21-year-old demographic that has grown up wearing loose and baggy jeans? By understanding and using to advantage what's on the mind of this age group. Levi's sense of "realness" would be presented in a way the millennial generation would understand. Today's younger generation is empowered to broadcast every detail of their life, and they do so online. In a word, they are "unbuttoned"—a word that would become the focus of the campaign.

Levi's launched its biggest global campaign ever with the theme "Live Unbuttoned" in 2008. The "Live Unbuttoned" campaign centres on the experience of "unbuttoning" yourself and breaking free from inhibitions and convention. "Live Unbuttoned" embraces the unrestrained, free-spirited, and self-expressive attitude behind the world's most perfect, timeless, and quintessential straight-leg, button-fly jean.

Business-wise, the campaign represents an opportunity to let a new generation of jeans consumers around the world know that the original 501 jean is relevant to their lifestyle. No other jeans brand can do this—the 501 is an icon in the industry! Being sold in 110 countries, Levi's is the biggest marketer of jeans in the world.

The "Unbuttoned" campaign is a great example of effective brand integration across all media platforms. Message-wise, the act of a young male unbuttoning his 501 jeans is a symbol of personal expression and

revelation. Media-wise, the campaign included viral videos, print ads, TV ads, digital campaigns, outdoor, button covers, and in-store activation.

A series of viral videos created initial brand excitement prior to the official launch of the campaign. The videos gave the target an opportunity to engage with the brand. Three videos, "Jeans Jump," "Hollywood Jungle," and "Moon Walker" generated more than 5 million views online and were recognized as a viral phenomenon.

Print ads which ran in magazines like *Maxim, Details, Rolling Stone, Paper,* and *Sports Illustrated* featured unrestrained, youthful, and artistic shots of men wearing their 501 jeans. The models in the ads conjure up images of movie icons Marlon Brando, James Dean, and Paul Newman to convey a self-expressive and free-spirited attitude.

A television ad titled "Secrets and Lies" ran in Canada. It features two young males confessing to a series of white lies as they unbutton their Levi's 501 jeans. Their unveilings, along with the physical unbuttoning of their jeans, captures the provoking theme of self-expression—for some viewers it may be too expressive and provoking!

The digital campaign was designed to create dialogue between consumers and the brand. The initial component features up-and-coming pop culture icons that contribute to the world's cultural landscape in unique ways and represent the spirit of living an "unbuttoned" life. The program invites consumers to literally "unbutton" each person online to obtain exclusive content they can only get from Levi's. A second component features a user-generated viral concept to harness the power of social media to invite consumers to playfully interact with their friends and the Levi's brand online.

Rounding out the Canadian portion of the campaign were over-sized outdoor boards, wild postings, and transit shelter ads in Toronto, Montreal, and Vancouver. As well, a collection of limited-edition button-fly button covers were given away as a fun and whimsical outlet for self-expression.

The Levis campaign clearly demonstrates the concept of integrated marketing communications as well as the importance of delivering a clear and consistent brand message across all media outlets. The campaign created a lot of buzz for the brand and Levi's is very satisfied with the sales it has achieved.

Adapted from "Live Unbuttoned with Global Launch of New, Innovative Levi's 501® Marketing Campaign," press release, Levi Strauss, July 21, 2008, www.levistrauss. com/news and "Levi's to launch button-fly covers to support Live Unbuttoned," press release, *Fibre2Fashion*, July 23, 2008, www.fibre2fashion.com/news.

Input for Marketing Communications Planning: Consumer Behaviour Essentials

A basic understanding of some important behavioural concepts is essential, because such knowledge is applied directly in the development of marketing communications strategies. Knowledge in the areas of needs and motives, personality and self-concept, attitudes and perceptions, reference groups, and families is considered when an organization plans its marketing communications strategies.

Consumer behaviour is the study of how people buy, what they buy, when they buy, and why they buy. Essentially, consumer behaviour is the psychology behind marketing and the behaviour of consumers in the marketing environment. In the context of marketing and marketing communications, it is imperative that organizations understand what influences consumers' behaviour. Consequently, organizations invest considerable sums of money on marketing research to understand consumers better. Information is power, as they say.

consumer behaviour
The combined acts carried out by individuals choosing and using goods and services, including the decision-making processes that determine these acts.

NEEDS AND MOTIVES

There is a direct link between needs and motives. Individuals have a **need** when they perceive the absence of something that is useful to them. A **motive** is a condition that prompts the individual to take action to satisfy the need. Consumers are motivated by friends and family members (word of mouth), or they can be influenced by what they see and read in the media, or by broadcast messages on radio and television. An appealing presentation of a product's features and benefits as they relate to a target's needs is often good enough to stimulate action—a purchase decision. For example, you might say to yourself, "I need (want) a fresh meat sandwich for lunch, so I'm going to a SUBWAY restaurant. 'SUBWAY...Think Fresh. Eat Fresh!'" That's the power of advertising!

Maslow's *hierarchy of needs* and *theory of motivation* have had a significant impact on marketing and marketing communications strategies. Maslow classified needs from lower level to higher level. His theory is based on two assumptions. First, when lower-level needs are satisfied a person moves up to higher-level needs. Second, satisfied needs do not motivate; behaviour is influenced by needs yet to be satisfied.

Maslow states that individuals move through five levels of needs, as shown in Figure 1.6. Numerous advertising examples can be cited to show how needs theory is

need
The perception of the absence of something useful.

motive
A condition that prompts an individual to take action to satisfy a need.

FIGURE
1.6   **The Hierarchy of Needs**

Self-Actualization	→ Fulfillment, to realize potential
Esteem Needs	→ Recognition, achievement, status
Social Needs	→ Belonging, love from family and friends
Safety Needs	→ Security, protection, comfort
Physiological Needs	→ Hunger, thirst, sex, shelter

Source: Maslow, A., Frager, R., Fadiman, J., Motivation and Personality, 3/E, © 1987. Adapted by permission of Pearson Education, Inc., Upper Saddle River NJ.

---

applied. For example, safety needs are used to motivate people to buy life insurance and retirement plans. A tagline such as "Like a good neighbour, State Farm is there," captures the message of protection and security.

Beauty and personal care products are famous for appealing to social and esteem needs of women, but now they have a new target: teenagers and young males in their 20s. Apparently, these groups are as self-conscious about their looks as females. How their face and body look has an impact on social acceptance. Apparently these males are influenced by the images of the perfect-looking men in men's magazines—men such as David Beckham (the English soccer star) and other celebrities like actor Brad Pitt. One research study found that 95 percent of teenage boys think that good grooming improves their prospects with girls.[10] That fact alone has presented exciting opportunities for brands like Gillette, Nivea, and Biotherm Homme to appeal to the social and esteem needs of men. Refer to the illustration in Figure 1.7.

PERSONALITY AND SELF-CONCEPT

personality
A person's distinguishing psychological characteristics that lead to relatively consistent and enduring responses to the environment in which that person lives.

Personality refers to the individual's distinguishing psychological characteristics that lead to relatively consistent and enduring responses to the environment in which that person lives. Personality is influenced by self-perceptions, which in turn are influenced by family, reference groups, and culture. An understanding of that self-concept provides clues as to how to communicate with consumers. The self-concept goes beyond needs and focuses on our desires.

According to self-concept theory, the self has four components: real self, self-image, looking-glass self, and ideal self.[11]

Source: Courtesy of Biotherm Canada.

FIGURE
1.7

**Biotherm Homme Makes
Men Feel More Confident by
Appealing to Social and
Esteem Needs**

1. **Real Self:** An objective evaluation of one's self. You as you really are.
2. **Self-Image:** How you see yourself. It may not be your real self, but a role you play with yourself.
3. **Looking-Glass Self:** How you think others see you. This can be quite different from how they actually see you.
4. **Ideal Self:** How you would like to be. It is what you aspire to.

   Based on these descriptions, the real self and self-image are less significant. In contrast, the looking-glass self and ideal self seem dynamic—they focus more on desires, the way we would like to be perceived. Consequently, many communications campaigns revolve around the looking-glass self and the ideal self. Marketing communicators know that consumers buy on emotion, so they present messages for goods and services that make consumers feel and look better, for they know the next level of fulfillment is attractive.

As explained in the previous section, young males are buying grooming products to satisfy social and esteem needs. Such behaviour is being influenced by the desire to achieve their ideal self—how they would like to be! It seems that physical imperfection can be a crippling disability! Brands such as Old Spice, Gillette, and L'Oreal have responded with a complete range of face scrubs, moisturizers, and cleansing products for men. Yes guys...it's all about image!

ATTITUDES AND PERCEPTIONS

attitudes
An individual's feelings, favourable or unfavourable, toward an idea or object.

Attitudes are an individual's feelings, favourable or unfavourable, toward an idea or object. People form attitudes based on what they hear, read, and see about a product as well as from the opinions of others they have faith in. Friends, for example, certainly have a dramatic impact on the attitudes held by youth. Trendsetters and opinion leaders who embrace new products quickly also influence how consumer attitudes are shaped.

As a rule, organizations present their product in accordance to attitudes held strongly by their target audience. It makes little sense to go against the grain—many an organization has discovered it is very expensive to try to change an attitude. For example, if teens see themselves on the edge of what the rest of the world considers normal, they will be attracted to products where the advertising message pushes the boundaries. Apple understands youth, and that is why the iPod was an overwhelming success. The iPod offered a sexy design and strong features, and was positioned to be relevant to youth lifestyles (see the image in Figure 1.8). The brand acted out in true rebel style, and ads featured the music of Eminem and other musicians popular with youth. It's no coincidence that Apple is the dominant leader in the music player market.

perception
The manner in which individuals receive and interpret messages.

Perception refers to the manner in which individuals receive and interpret messages. Given the prevailing model of human behaviour, it is safe to say that consumers

FIGURE 1.8   The iPod's sexy design and strong features made it an overwhelming success

Source: Imago/ZUMAPRESS.com/Keystone Press

accept messages that are in line with their needs, personality, self-concept, and attitudes, and ignore or reject messages that are not. Theory states that we are selective about the messages we receive and that there are three levels of selectivity:

1. **Selective Exposure:** Our eyes and minds notice only information that interests us.
2. **Selective Perception:** We screen out messages that conflict with our attitudes.
3. **Selective Retention:** We remember only what we want to remember.

To demonstrate how perception works, consider a common perception held by consumers about the automobile industry. Domestic manufacturers like General Motors, Ford, and Chrysler have been losing market share to Japanese competitors. Why? There is a perception that the domestic models do not offer the same quality and reliability as do foreign models. Consequently, consumers may tune out messages for cars made by GM, Ford, and Chrysler (selective exposure). Even though domestic manufacturers have improved the quality of their products, they still suffer from poor reputations.[12] Consumers may not believe the advertising messages about the quality of their automobiles (selective perception). A common phrase applies here: "Perception is reality." And it is the perceptions held by consumers that advertisers must deal with.

In contrast, consumers will quickly tune in to messages for products and brands they trust and that trust is based on a good reputation—say for performance, dependability, and so on. A pending purchase of a cell phone represents a situation where consumers will be receptive to information—ads for trusted brands like Apple iPhone and Blackberry Bold suddenly become relevant and get noticed.

REFERENCE GROUPS

A **reference group**, or **peer group**, is a group of people with a common interest that influences the attitudes and behaviour of its members. Reference groups include schoolmates, sports teams, fraternities and sororities, and hobby clubs. There is considerable pressure on members to conform to the standards of the group—a desire to "fit in." Take, for example, the mild hazing that occurs among rookies of a college or university sports team, or the rituals associated with joining a fraternity. In the case of a fraternity, if a certain brand of clothing such as Polo or Ralph Lauren is popular with key members, then new members or members with less seniority will likely wear that brand.

In terms of marketing and marketing communications, it is common for brands to associate with a particular situation or lifestyle the target consumer could become interested in. For example, many young executives play golf and join golf clubs. To fit in properly with other club members, an assessment of clothing styles and what equipment to use becomes a priority. These people see Tiger Woods wearing Nike clothing and try to imitate Tiger by wearing the same brand and style.

Advertisers have to be very careful when approaching the youth market. Too much advertising and the target sees the practice for what it is: a disingenuous attempt to attract youth consumers without having a clue about their actual tastes.[13] Apparently, reaching youth only works if the message is authentic. Therefore, if a brand "goes underground" (the place where most pop culture originates), or uses some kind of viral marketing technique such as a video on YouTube it has a better chance of connecting with the target. The Levi's 501 anniversary campaign discussed earlier in the chapter on page 14 (see IMC Highlight: **Multiple Channels Deliver Levi's Message**) effectively employed a series of viral videos by Cutwater. A video titled "Jeans Jump" was YouTube Canada's "most-viewed video" for nearly a week.[14]

reference group (peer group)
A group of people who share common interests that influence the attitudes and behaviour of its members.

FAMILY INFLUENCES

Each member of a family has some influence on the behaviour of other family members and thus an influence on buying decisions. Perhaps the biggest influence on behaviour within families today relates to the *changing roles* and *responsibilities* of family members. Traditional attitudes, roles, and responsibilities are out—nothing is what it seems anymore.

Households are also different. There are same-sex households, lone-parent households, and dual-income (two-worker) households. In the dual-income household, much of the decision making is shared between partners. No longer can the maker of a household product assume the woman is the primary buyer, and a financial advisor cannot assume that the man makes all of the investment decisions. In fact, men are handling grocery shopping more than ever before, either on their own or shared with a spouse. In households with couples or multiple adults, 15 percent have a male who holds the primary responsibility for grocery shopping, and 41 percent share the responsibility equally.[15]

Companies that are in tune with these types of changes are **double targeting**—they are devising marketing strategies that reach both genders effectively. Financial companies, automobile manufacturers, and retailers recognize the role and influence of women in major buying decisions and are devising new campaigns that take advantage of such knowledge. Retailers like Canadian Tire, Home Depot, and Best Buy are very active in this area. Each retailer has redesigned its store layout, created a better shopping environment, and implemented a new marketing communications strategy aimed directly at women. See the illustration in Figure 1.9.

Today's children (commonly referred to as Generation Y or the iPod generation) have considerable influence on family buying decisions. They don't necessarily make requests, but parents actively seek their input on anything from clothing to cars to family vacations. "Their influence on family spending is that they essentially are co-purchasers," says Kelly Mooney, president of Resources Interactive.[16] Children are technologically savvy and are helping their parents research products and make online buying decisions—a real shift in power! Through sites such as MySpace and Facebook they access the opinions of their network of friends that they communicate with regularly.

Inputs for Marketing Communications Planning: Business and Organizational Buyer Behaviour

The buying process of organizations is very different from consumer buying. In a nutshell, organizations exhibit more rational behaviour than consumers—consumers do a lot of buying based on emotion. The **business-to-business (B2B) market** is managed by individuals in an organization responsible for purchasing goods and services needed to produce a product or service or promote an idea. This market includes business and industry, governments, institutions, wholesalers and retailers, and professionals.

The business market has several characteristics that distinguish it from consumer markets. Business markets have fewer buyers, and those buyers tend to be concentrated in industrial areas in and near large cities. The buying criteria are very practical, with decisions based on the best buy according to predetermined requirements, and there is usually a formal buying process for evaluating product and service alternatives. Business buying processes have changed dramatically because of advancing technology and the benefits derived from buying goods online.

The key issues that a business organization must address when marketing to other businesses are the criteria established by the buying organization. In most situations, those requirements are established in advance and companies can compete with each

double targeting
Marketing strategies that reach both genders effectively.

business-to-business (B2B) market
A market of goods and services needed to produce a product or service, promote an idea, or operate a business.

FIGURE
1.9

Double targeting by retailers is a reaction to changing gender roles and responsibilities

The invisible technology that makes a visible difference.   CURVETECH™

A real built-in bra controls and supports while the padded, moulded underwire cups deliver shape-enhancing support.

Source: Courtesy of Mark's Work Wearhouse.

other by submitting bids. The buyer customarily chooses the bid with the lowest price, assuming the criteria have been met. So, what are those requirements?

- **Quality:** Buyers want consistent quality on every order. What they buy could have a direct impact on the quality of goods they in turn produce and market.

- **Service:** Buyers want reputable suppliers who provide prompt service and believe that the initial order is simply the start of a business relationship.

- **Continuity of Supply:** Buyers want suppliers that can provide goods over the long term. A steady source of supply ensures consistent production scheduling.

- **Price:** Buyers evaluate price in conjunction with the other criteria. The lowest price is not always accepted. Potential long-term savings could outweigh an initial low price.

To ensure that the right buying decision is made, organizations employ a formal or informal approach. A formal approach involves a **buying committee**. The committee is made up of key representatives from various functional areas of the company, such as finance, marketing, manufacturing, purchasing, and so on. A committee takes a very rational approach when evaluating alternatives, and participants need to know that costly decisions are shared decisions.

buying committee
A formal buying structure in an organization that brings together expertise from the various functional areas to share in the buying decision process.

buying centre
An informal purchasing process in which individuals in an organization perform particular roles but may not have direct responsibility for the actual decision.

A **buying centre** is an informal purchasing process with individuals in an organization involved in the purchasing process, but not necessarily having direct responsibility for the actual decision. These roles are summarized in Figure 1.10.

In terms of marketing or marketing communications, the seller must know who on the committee or within the buying centre has the most influence. It could be one person or several people. Once that is known, the best means of communicating can be determined. Based on the nature of business buying, it becomes clear that personal selling and direct forms of communications are vital components when trying to influence the decisions of business buyers.

INTEGRATION AND PARTNERING INFLUENCES B2B COMMUNICATIONS STRATEGIES

Business markets have embraced customer relationship management in an attempt to establish efficient business systems. CRM promotes the seamless transfer of information throughout the channels to ensure the efficient and continuous flow of goods. Forming partnerships with suppliers implies a long-term relationship. Therefore, to be part of a CRM system, the marketer must be more familiar than ever with the role the product plays in the customer's operations. Collecting information about the customer and operations is crucial.

e-procurement
An online, business-to-business marketplace through which participants can purchase goods and services from one another.

The Internet has created buying opportunities through **e-procurement**. This is an Internet-based, business-to-business buying marketplace through which participants can purchase supplies and services from one another. It is an all-inclusive system that allows buyers to solicit multiple bids, issue purchase orders, and make payments. The combining of CRM practices with e-procurement systems fosters long-term relationships between buyers and sellers and presents a situation where participants are directly influenced by the decisions of other participants. This clearly is the future of business-to-business buying and marketing. Companies will either be part of the system or they will watch it unfold from the sidelines.

The strategies employed to reach business customers are also evolving. Yet, in spite of all the technological advances and the direct nature of the buying and selling process, customers must still be made aware of the product alternatives that are available. Creating awareness is always the first step. Therefore, the need for print advertising directed at

FIGURE 1.10
The Buying Centre

Role	Description	Example
Users	Those in the organization who use the product directly.	If the product is a personal computer, any end-user in the organization.
Influencers	Those who define the product specifications.	An engineer.
Buyers	Those with the authority to buy.	A purchasing manager.
Deciders	Those with the power to finalize the purchase.	Where high-cost decisions are involved, the CEO may be the decider.
Gatekeepers	Those who control the flow of information to the members of the buying centre.	A purchasing manager may also fulfill the role of gatekeeper.

business customers will continue, along with the need for strong personal sales contacts. The inclusion of sales promotion programs to assist salespeople is also important. Event marketing in the form of trade show participation will help keep marketing organizations on a buyer's radar screen, and direct marketing techniques such as direct mail and Internet-based communications will become more of a priority. A website containing essential product information is indispensable in B2B marketing situations. The same tools are employed in consumer marketing; they are just given different priority.

A recent survey published by the Center for Media Research provides interesting insights into business buying behaviour and the media that influence buyers. It suggests that simultaneous media usage presents a challenge for business-to-business marketers. Nearly half the respondents said traditional communications methods such as print, direct mail, and outdoor advertising are "not important" to them. In contrast, 44 percent said the Internet was "somewhat important," 81 percent said word of mouth was "very important" or "important," and 88 percent said they "sought the advice of others" before making a decision.[17] This clearly indicates that products must live up to the promise made by any form of marketing communications.

Ethical Issues in Marketing Communications Practice

The way an organization communicates is always under review by the public and critics of the marketing communications industry. Rightly or wrongly, planned or unplanned, advertisers sometimes deliver messages that spark controversy. Many organizations tolerate the controversy as long as the campaign is delivering sales, while others bow to public pressure and remove offending messages. Some of the key issues that make the headlines include the use of sex in advertising, presenting dangerous situations in commercials, and misleading the public with confusing messages.

SEX IN ADVERTISING

A common complaint about advertising revolves around the use of sex to sell something. As an old saying goes: "Sex sells!" So what's the beef among members of contemporary Canadian society? Using sex appeal in an appropriate manner and for appropriate products seems natural, but gratuitous sex is something consumers shouldn't have to tolerate.

An ad for the Kia Spectra (2007) was banished from the airwaves because it raised the hackles of the Montreal Police. In the commercial a lustful policewoman is passionately kissing a young male she has just pulled over, in the front seat of his automobile. The police cruiser is stationed behind the Kia with its lights flashing. Hearing a call from the cruiser the policewoman fixes her hair, dons her police cap, and drives away in the cruiser. The tagline for the ad was "Life's better in a Spectra." Advertising Standards Canada agreed with the complaint and judged the ad too racy for Canadian viewing.

Is it pornography or simply provocative advertising? An American Apparel ad in downtown Toronto featuring a woman leaning forward in a provocative pose is the kind that can spark controversy. The behaviour of passersby showed the impact of the advertisement. It did get noticed and it did draw a reaction. The ad has raised the ire of feminists, who suggest it objectifies women. The company's reaction is quite different. "It is a bit disconcerting to see what feminism has evolved into," says Marsha Brady, a creative director at American Apparel. "When there's a group of people attempting to shame female creativity, female beauty, female pride under the auspices of protecting women, it's really, really scary."[18] Consider the ad for Diesel that appears in Figure 1.11.

FIGURE
1.11

**A Diesel advertisement
sparks controversy**

A sexual appeal technique certainly draws attention to the ad and the brand name. Diesel markets jeans, footwear, bags, and shades.

EXTREME ADVERTISING

The strategy of depicting dangerous or disturbing situations in advertising has come under much scrutiny in recent years. Automakers are under the gun for showing unsafe driving practices in ads. In some cases dangerous driving practices are glamorized. A Corvette spot depicted clearly an enraged driver racing wildly in the sports car, under the title, "A Boy's Dream." Many critics believe an ad like this helps encourage young people to get involved in risky activities such as street racing.

When Nike launched a basketball shoe called the Hyperdunk, a shoe that Kobe Bryant (Los Angeles Lakers star) endorses, it got an unexpected boost from a viral video placed on YouTube. Actual commercial footage was doctored to show Kobe jumping over a speeding sports car. The video sparked plenty of questions about safety and the role of authenticity in brand positioning. The video garnered 2.5 million views and sparked an online debate as to whether it was real or not. On the basis of word-of-mouth alone, buzz was building for the new shoe. On the issue of safety, the real video opens with the obligatory legalese with Kobe saying "Don't try this at home." But who knows, a bored kid who suddenly wants to be brave and cool could try it, hence, the controversy.

MISLEADING ADVERTISING

Sometimes ads can mislead the public or simply misrepresent the brand. Sometimes the public misinterprets the advertiser's message and the campaign backfires. The control of misleading advertising is the responsibility of Advertising Standards Canada. (More information about its role in the advertising industry appears later in this chapter.) Some of the more interesting examples involve green marketing claims, targeting children, and cultural diversity.

EXAGGERATED GREEN CLAIMS

Given the rate at which organizations are making claims about how green they are and what they are doing to protect the environment, this category of misleading advertising is worthy of special attention. Manufacturers of bottled water, for example, claim they are offering a better product than the water that municipalities offer, forgetting that a large portion of the plastic bottles wind up in landfill sites, which ultimately harms the environment.

Evian North America recently launched Evian Les Petits, a new water product geared to children. The smaller bottles featured brightly coloured fish characters on the labels. In defending the product, Jeff Carswell, VP marketing, says, "Our consumers are looking for ways to support their kids' healthy lifestyles and are looking for alternatives to high-calorie sugar beverages." Sounds like a great idea, but what about the packaging and the environment?

A recent survey about environmental claims shows that 75 percent of Canadians take into account the environmental impact of their actions when they buy a product. As well, 75 percent of respondents firmly believe that most environmental claims are just marketing ploys. At present, phrases such as "green," "organic," or "low emissions" suggest all is good, but where's the proof?[19] Consumers want to ensure that companies are not getting away with "green murder," a term associated with the exploitation of environmental ideas to make a company look good. Even the best of companies can get caught. Lexus (a division of Toyota) faced consumer backlash for a headline in a British ad that read: "High Performance. Low Emissions. Zero Guilt." The ad was banned because the headline gave the misleading impression that the car caused little or no harm to the environment.[20]

TARGETING CHILDREN   Advertising messages directed at children often bypass parents. As a result, parents are concerned about the content of these messages, which have a powerful influence on the child's behaviour. Children may start demanding higher-priced "in" goods when parents prefer to buy less expensive alternatives. In other words, at what age do children become "brand conscious"?

Companies such as McDonald's, Kellogg's, PepsiCo, and Nestle, among many others, are frequently the target of critics who suggest the consumption of their products and the ads that encourage the consumption have contributed to the rise in childhood obesity. In fact, a panel appointed by the Chronic Disease Prevention Alliance of Canada called for a ban on all junk food advertising that targets children—a move the federal government has promised to consider. In the wake of the criticism, many food companies have committed to an industry-sponsored Children's Food and Beverage Advertising Initiative that encourages responsible marketing to children. Some companies are eliminating ads altogether, while others are promising healthier products for children.[21]

Should advertising directed at children be allowed at all or should the messages that are delivered be subject to stiffer regulations? The debate goes on. In Quebec, advertising to children under the age of 13 has been banned since 1980.

CULTURAL DIVERSITY Data from the 2006 census reveal that the visible minority population in Canada surpassed 5 million and now represents 16.2 percent of the population. The largest visible minorities are South Asians, Chinese, and black. These people tend to live in large cities. In Toronto, visible minorities comprise 43 percent of the population.[22]

Given this data, advertisers are often criticized for not reflecting the diversity of Canada's population in commercial messages. A study by the Canadian Advertising Foundation found that 70 percent of Canadians believe advertising is targeted too much at white consumers. As well, 36 percent of respondents said they think negatively about companies that exclude visible minorities in their advertising.[23] That could mean a lot of lost dollars if these negative feelings influence consumer buying decisions.

Many advertisers are adopting multicultural marketing communications strategies and are including ethnic populations in their ads. Some of the leaders in ethnic-oriented advertising include Walmart, McDonald's, Coca-Cola, and RBC Financial, among many others. Companies like these recognize the importance of appealing to the widest possible audience. It's only a matter of time before other organizations get on board.

Laws and Regulations Governing Marketing Communications

The marketing communications industry in Canada is highly regulated. Regulation and control come from Advertising Standards Canada (ASC), which administers regulations based on codes of practice that are voluntarily established; and the Competition Bureau (a federal agency) through the *Competition Act*, which established laws and regulations for all marketing activity in Canada.

ADVERTISING STANDARDS CANADA

Advertising Standards Canada is the industry body committed to creating and maintaining community confidence in advertising. Its mission is to ensure the integrity and viability of advertising through industry self-regulation. ASC members include advertisers, agencies, media organizations, and suppliers to the advertising sector.

ASC operates two divisions. The Standards Division administers the industry's self-regulating code, the *Canadian Code of Advertising Standards*; handles complaints from consumers regarding advertising; and administers the industry's *Trade Dispute Procedure*. The Advertising Clearance Division previews advertisements in five categories, helping advertisers to adhere to applicable legislation, regulatory codes, and industry standards.[24]

The *Canadian Code of Advertising Standards* (Code) is the principal instrument of self-regulation. The Code was developed to promote the professional practice of advertising and forms the basis upon which advertising is evaluated in response to consumer complaints. The Code is supplemented by other codes and guidelines, including gender portrayal guidelines, which are intended to help advertising practitioners develop positive images of women and men in their commercial messages. The Code also addresses the following concerns about advertising that include the accuracy and clarity of messages, disguised advertising techniques, price claims, bait and switch tactics, comparative advertising claims, unacceptable depictions, scientific claims, and advertising to children. Visit the ASC website at www.adstandards.com for more details.

In the previous section of this chapter, it was noted that Advertising Standards Canada rules against advertisers when necessary and makes suggestions for changes in message delivery. Copywriters and art directors are frustrated by such responses from the public or regulating bodies. It's no wonder there's so much dull advertising that simply blends together. Being cautioned to stay away from the creative edge is not good for the future of advertising. In the unregulated online world, user-generated content of a risky nature is quite common. The playing field doesn't seem as level as it once was.

Advertising Standards Canada
www.adstandards.com

COMPETITION BUREAU

The Competition Bureau is responsible for the administration and enforcement of the *Competition Act*, a law that governs business conduct and marketing practices in Canada. The *Competition Act* contains criminal and civil provisions to address false, misleading, and deceptive marketing practices. Among the practices that come under scrutiny are deceptive telemarketing, deceptive notices of winning prizes, and pyramid selling schemes. Other provisions prohibit representations not based on adequate and proper tests, misleading warranties and guarantees, false or misleading price representation, and untrue testimonials.

Organizations that violate these laws and regulations are subject to financial penalties and other actions. To demonstrate, the Competition Bureau determined that Premier Fitness Clubs did not disclose additional fees that consumers would be obligated to pay in some of its advertising and membership offers on the radio, billboards, storefront signs, and in newspapers and flyers. As a result, the actual fees were considerably higher than what advertisements led consumers to believe. Among the sanctions imposed by the Bureau were a monetary penalty of $200,000; an order to publish a corrective notice in daily newspapers, club facilities, and the company website; and an order not to make false or misleading representations in future promotional materials.[25] For more insight into the Competition Bureau visit its website at www.competitionbureau.gc.ca.

Competition Bureau
www.competitionbureau.gc.ca

≫ SUMMARY

The rapid pace of change in business today has forced organizations to re-examine and change the way they communicate with customers. More than ever before, organizations are demanding integrated marketing strategies to help resolve marketing problems and to take advantage of new opportunities.

The integrated marketing communications mix is composed of seven unique yet complementary components: advertising, direct response communications, interactive communications, sales promotion, personal selling, public relations, and experiential marketing. The organiza-tion evaluates marketing situations and employs the components of the mix that will effectively and efficiently reach its target market.

Several key issues and trends have led to the emergence of integrated marketing communications. Among the key issues are consumers' changing media habits, the strategic focus on customer relationship management (CRM), the expanding role of database marketing, the dramatic impact of digital communications technologies, and greater demand by senior managers for efficiency and accountability for the resources that are invested in marketing communications.

In the process of developing marketing communications strategies, an organization must understand and apply various consumer behaviour concepts. Among these concepts are needs and motives, personality and self-concept, attitudes and perceptions, reference groups, and family. Research into these factors provides clues about what forms of marketing communications to employ to deliver a more effective message.

Business buying behaviour is different from consumer buying behaviour. While consumers tend to be swayed by emotion, business buyers maintain a rational approach when making buying decisions. Business buying is based on predetermined criteria such as quality, service, continuity of supply, and price. Decisions are made formally by a buying committee or informally by a buying centre. Technology and relationship marketing practices have taken hold in business-to-business (B2B) marketing. Companies must adapt to this way of doing business or perish. Tools such as personal selling, direct response communications, and interactive communications will play a prominent role in the future.

Marketing communications practitioners must contend with ethical issues when devising message strategies. Some of the more contentious issues today include the use of sex in advertising, showing very risky and dangerous behaviour in advertising, and exaggerated green marketing claims.

Regulation and control of the marketing communications industry is the jurisdiction of the federal government and Advertising Standards Canada. Laws and regulations are enforced by the Competition Bureau and voluntary regulations are administered by Advertising Standards Canada.

KEY TERMS

advertising   4
attitude   18
business-to-business (B2B) market   20
buying centre   22
buying committee   22
consumer behaviour   5
customer relationship management (CRM)   7
database management system   11

digital (interactive) communications   6
direct response communications   6
double targeting   20
e-procurement   23
event marketing   9
experiential marketing   8
integrated marketing communications   3
motive   5

need   5
peer group   19
perception   18
personal selling   9
personality   16
product advertising   5
promotional advertising   6
public relations   8
reference group   19
sales promotion   7
sponsorship   9

REVIEW QUESTIONS

1. Identify and briefly explain the components of the integrated marketing communications mix.
2. Explain the difference between product advertising and promotional advertising.
3. Briefly describe the key issues and trends that have led to the emergence of integrated marketing communications.
4. "An understanding of Maslow's hierarchy of needs and theory of motivation has a direct influence on advertising strategy." Explain.
5. According to the self-concept theory, the self has four components. Identify and briefly describe each component.
6. How important is assessing customer attitudes when developing an advertising campaign? Explain.
7. What role and influence do reference groups have when a consumer is deciding what products to buy?
8. Explain the term "double targeting" and provide a new example of a company or brand that is applying this concept.
9. What essential criteria do organizational buyers consider when making buying decisions?
10. What is the difference between a buying committee and a buying centre?
11. What roles do the Competition Bureau and Advertising Standards Canada play in the marketing communications industry?

DISCUSSION AND APPLICATION QUESTIONS

1. How significant will digital communications be in future marketing communications strategies? Will advertisers continue to shift their dollars to digital communications? Conduct some secondary research to offer new information that will justify your opinion.

2. Experiential marketing is growing in popularity. Will this trend continue and will this form of communications play a more dominant role in future marketing communications strategies? Conduct some research on this topic and present an opinion on it.

3. "Relationship marketing practices will dramatically alter marketing communications strategies in the future." Is this statement true or false? Conduct some online secondary research and form an opinion on this statement.

4. Cite some examples and provide actual illustrations of companies or brands that use the following consumer behaviour theories when developing communications strategies. Provide a description that relates the theory to the practice.

   a) hierarchy of needs and theory of motivation
   b) personality and self-concept
   c) reference groups
   d) family influences

5. From the following list of goods and services, identify what you think is the most important marketing communications tool for building and sustaining the brand. Provide some justification for your choices.

   a) Labatt Blue
   b) BMW automobiles
   c) Michelin tires
   d) RBC Financial Group

6. How have integration and partnerships influenced marketing communications strategies in business-to-business markets? Explain.

7. Are advertising laws and regulations in Canada too conservative? Should riskier or more controversial advertising messages be allowed? Refer to the ethical issues section of the chapter for some background information before responding to this question.

ENDNOTES

1. Paula Gignac, "2007 Canadian Online Revenue Climbs to $1.2 Billion," press release, IAB Canada, July 3, 2008, www.iabcanada.com/newsletters/080703.sthml.

2. "Maple Leaf Brand Should Rebound in Months," *Marketing*, August 27, 2008, www.marketingmag.ca.

3. Eve Lazarus, "The new PR," Public Relations Report in *Marketing*, June 1, 2009, p. 4.

4. Aiden Tracey, "The Mosaic Experience," *Marketing*, June 1, 2009, p. 12.

5. Hollie Shaw, "Sponsors' Easy Score," *Financial Post*, May 30, 2008, p. FP14.

6. "2008 Canadian Online Advertising Revenue Grows to $1.6 Billion and Surpasses Radio," IAB press release, July 28, 2009, www.iabcanada.com.

7. Jean Halliday, "GM Roars Forward into Digital Ad Channels," *Advertising Age*, March 17, 2008, www.adage.com/abstract.php?article_id=125748.

8. "The Expansion of Cell Phone Services," Industry Canada, retrieved August 28, 2008, www.ic.gc.ca/epic/site/oca-bc.nsf/en/ ca02267e.html.

9. Richard Rotman, "When worlds combine," *Marketing*, September 29, 2003, p. 8.

10. Sarah Womack, "Boys anguish over their looks," *National Post*, May 24, 2005, p. A2.

11. John Douglas, George Field, and Lawrence Tarpay, *Human Behaviour in Marketing*, (Columbus, OH: Charles E. Merrill Publishing, 1987), p. 5.

12. Greg Keenan, "It's okay for people to loathe your car; just don't bore them," *The Globe and Mail*, October 10, 2003, pp. B1, B6.

13. Sam Grewal, "Manufactured cool," *Toronto Star*, February 22, 2005, p. C4.

14. Kristin Laird, "Levi opens up for 501s," *Marketing*, July 22, 2008, www.marketingmag.ca.

15. "Men doing more grocery shopping, survey shows," *Marketing*, August 27, 2008, www.marketingmag.ca.

16. Jennifer Waters, "Young, with tons of purchasing power," *Market Watch*, October 11, 2006, www.marketwatch.com.

17. Media Post, www.mediapost.com, June 19, 2003.

18. Dakshana Bascaramurty, "American Apparel is at it again," *The Globe and Mail*, August 23, 2008, p. M3.

19. Richard Blackwell, "Eco-friendly? Canadians want to see the proof," *The Globe and Mail*, July 28, 2008, pp. B1, B3.

20. "Green Murder," *Marketing*, October 29, 2007, p. 11.

21. Megan Harman, "Sprouts with that?" *Canadian Business*, April 14, 2008, p. 23.

22. "Near half in GTA minorities," *Toronto Star*, April 2, 2008, www.thestar.com.

23. Scott Feschuk, "Survey shows ads need racial diversity," *The Globe and Mail*, January 7, 1993, p. B7.

24. Advertising Standards Canada, www.adstandards.com.

25. Industry Canada, press release, "Competition Bureau Reaches Settlement with Ontario Fitness Club Chain," Novem-ber 27, 2007.

Strategic Planning Principles

Learning Objectives

After studying this chapter, you will be able to

1. Identify essential external trends and conditions that influence organizational planning

2. Describe the steps in the strategic planning process

3. Identify the distinctions and relationships among the various types of plans

4. Characterize the essential elements of a corporate plan

5. Outline the structure and content of a marketing plan

6. Outline the structure and content of a marketing communications plan

7. Show how integrated marketing planning provides solutions to marketing problems

All business planning is an integrated process that involves planning at three levels of an organization: corporate planning (planning conducted by senior executives), marketing planning (planning conducted by brand and marketing managers), and marketing communications planning (plans designed by communications specialists based on guidelines provided by brand and marketing managers). When a planning system works properly, each level of planning is linked to the other levels. Corporate plans provide guidance and direction for marketing plans, and marketing plans provide direction for marketing communications plans.

How plans are struck varies considerably from company to company. There is no perfect model to follow. Some organizations produce very detailed plans, while others take a more action-oriented approach. The common factor among all companies should be integration, meaning integrating one plan with another and integrating all the pieces of a plan together so that a consistent strategic direction is followed when the plans are implemented. What this chapter presents is a potential model for preparing strategic plans. Students should recognize that it can be altered to fit the specific needs of an organization.

Factors Influencing Strategic Planning

Strategic planning, or the **corporate strategy**, is the process of determining objectives (setting goals) and identifying strategies (ways to achieve the goals) and tactics (specific action plans) to help achieve objectives. Based on this definition, a strategic plan includes three common variables:

- **Objectives:** Statements of what is to be accomplished in terms of sales, profit, market share, or other measures.
- **Strategies:** Statements that outline how the objectives will be achieved, such as the direction to be taken and the allocation of resources needed to proceed.
- **Tactics:** Action-oriented details, including precise details about the cost and timing of specific activities.

Strategic planning is a cyclical process in most organizations. It is an annual "ccurring so fast that it is absolutely essential that a company keep abreast of change. A company's strategic plan is influenced by changes in the economy, among consumers, in technology, in laws and regulations governing business practices, in competitor activities, and in environmental issues. Occurrences and trends in each of these areas have an

strategic planning (corporate strategy)
The process of determining objectives (setting goals) and identifying strategies (ways to achieve the goals) and tactics (specific action plans) to help achieve objectives.

objectives
Statements of what is to be accomplished in terms of sales, profit, market share, or other measures.

strategies
Statements that outline how the objectives will be achieved, such as the direction to be taken and the allocation of resources needed to proceed.

tactics
Action-oriented details that outline how a strategic plan will be implemented.

tactics (execution)
Action-oriented details that outline how a strategic plan will be implemented.

impact on the nature and direction of corporate plans, marketing plans, and marketing communications plans. This section discusses briefly the nature and implications of these influences (see Figure 2.1).

ECONOMIC INFLUENCES

The general state of the economy has a direct impact on how aggressive or conservative a company is with its business plans. Should it be investing in marketing and marketing communications to expand its business, or should it conserve funds to protect profit margins? The general state of the economy is determined by growth rates in the gross domestic product, inflation rates, levels of employment, the value of the Canadian dollar in relation to foreign currencies, and income distribution among consumers. The relationship among these variables is dynamic. For example, and in very general terms, if the value of the gross domestic product has dropped for a few consecutive years, if levels of employment have been dropping, and if real income has been dropping marginally from year to year, the economy could be in recession. If consumers aren't spending, marketing organizations might adopt a conservative approach and control investment in marketing and marketing communications.

Based on all kinds of factors, a country's economy goes through cycles. Those cycles are recession, depression, recovery, and prosperity. In contrast to the scenario described above, an economy where gross domestic product is expanding, where real incomes are expanding, and where employment is plentiful would indicate recovery or prosperity. Such an economy would call for aggressive investment in marketing and marketing communications to take advantage of the increases in consumer spending.

To demonstrate the connection between various economic variables and how they influence marketing, consider the situation that occurred in 2008. Oil prices increased to record levels and the immediate impact was felt at the pumps. Higher gas prices had an impact on the demand for automobiles. Essentially, the demand for trucks and sports utility vehicles (gas guzzlers) dried up. Domestic automakers like GM, Ford, and Chrysler all announced layoffs and plant closings, which caused even more layoffs in the auto parts manufacturing industry. GM, Ford, and Chrysler were not producing the small economical cars consumers were demanding. To attract customers and liquidate inventories, huge cash-back offers and discounted financing became the norm. All three companies suffered financial losses. The faltering economy continued in 2009, and General Motors ultimately filed for bankruptcy protection.

COMPETITOR INFLUENCE

Assessing the activities of competitors is probably the most thoroughly analyzed aspect of marketing planning. Such analysis provides input into how one brand can differentiate

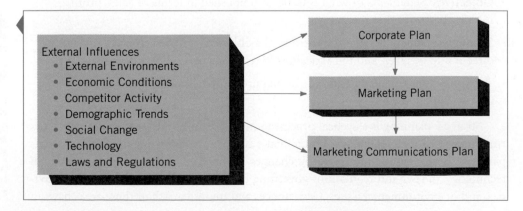

FIGURE 2.1

External influences affect all levels of planning in an organization

itself from the others and perhaps stand out more in the eyes of consumers. Most Canadian markets are very competitive and described as being an **oligopoly** (a market with a few major brands) or as being **monopolistically competitive** (a market with all kinds of brands). In either case, the consumer has a choice of what brand to buy, and the effectiveness of the marketing and marketing communications strategies will influence the decision.

Competition comes in two forms: direct competition and indirect competition. **Direct competition** is competition from alternative products and services that satisfy the needs of a target market. **Indirect competition** is competition from substitute products that offer customers the same benefit. In today's hypercompetitive marketplace, the lines between direct and indirect competition are becoming blurred. Coca-Cola's competitors used to be Pepsi-Cola, 7Up, and a few other popular soft drinks (direct competition). Now consumers have a much broader choice and in the age of healthier living are looking seriously at beverage alternatives such as bottled waters, fruit juices, iced teas, sports drinks, and energy drinks as substitutes for carbonated soft drinks (indirect competition).

Even though the beverage market has changed, both Coca-Cola and Pepsi-Cola made good product decisions to protect their position. Both companies offer popular brands in each segment mentioned above. The Coca-Cola portfolio includes Coca-Cola, Dasani water, Minute Maid juices, Powerade sports drinks, and Full Throttle energy drinks. PepsiCo markets Pepsi-Cola, Aquafina water, Tropicana juices, Gatorade sports drinks, and Mountain Dew Amp energy drinks. The competition between the two rivals is intense!

For more insight into the battles that rage on between Pepsi and Coke read the IMC Highlight: **Pepsi Leads in Quebec.**

DEMOGRAPHIC INFLUENCES

For the purpose of devising a profile of potential customers commonly referred to as a target market profile (see the discussion on this topic that appears later in this chapter), an organization must stay abreast of demographic and lifestyle trends occurring in Canada. This section highlights several of these trends.

THE POPULATION IS AGING At the end of 2006 Canada's population was 32.7 million, and the annual growth rate is about +1% a year. Two-thirds of Canada's population growth between 2001 and 2006 was attributed to immigration.[1] Within this framework, the population of Canada is aging. As Figure 2.2 shows, middle-aged Canadians (a group commonly called baby boomers) comprise the largest portion of the population. The baby boom generation (born between 1946 and 1964) were followed by a "baby bust" in the late 1960s and the 1970s; a mini-boom then occurred in the late 70s and early 80s. The latter group is commonly called Generation Y or Millennials (the computer/video generation). Generation Y is a primary target for marketers now and in the future.

Baby boomers will also be a primary target. By 2021 it is estimated that baby boomers will comprise 40% of the population. Brands that focus on this target now will have to adjust their marketing strategies to stay in tune with changing needs of older consumers. At the same time they must attract younger consumers if they are to experience growth in sales. This poses a challenge for many existing and popular brands.

To demonstrate, a brand like Nike is popular with older customers, but Generation Y is more interested in trendier brand names. Nike's sneaker sales are tumbling. Boomers and Generation Y are miles apart in age and attitude. Given the size of the Generation Y market and the impact it will have in the future, it is imperative that Nike find a marketing communications strategy that will deliver cachet to the brand once again.

oligopoly
A market situation in which only a few brands control the market.

monopolistic competition
A market in which there are many competitors, each offering a unique marketing mix; consumers can assess these choices prior to making a buying decision.

direct competition
Competition from alternative products and services that satisfy the needs of a target market.

indirect competition
Competition from substitute products that offer the same benefit as another type of product.

Pepsi Leads in Quebec

Coca-Cola is the market leader everywhere in North America except Quebec. Pepsi takes great pride in being the leader in Quebec for the brand has done all it can to implement marketing communications strategies that are in tune with French Quebec lifestyles. Other brands in other markets could learn from Pepsi-Cola and how it approaches Quebecers.

Most of Pepsi's success in Quebec is directly attributed to its unique style of advertising. While Coke typically translates its national and international campaigns in the province, Pepsi customizes the message to meet distinctly Québécois tastes. Pepsi has taken the time to learn and understand Québécois culture.

Here's the scenario of a recent television commercial: A Scandinavian-sounding tourist resembling a Mr. Bean type of character walks into a snack stop somewhere in Quebec's hinterland and orders a Coke. The snack bar falls silent, wildlife stops in the forest, and traffic grinds to a halt in Old Quebec. When the waiter finally pops open a can of the blue-and-red in front of him, the tourist clues in: "Ah! Ici, c'est Pepsi." The "Ici" theme has been used for the past few years.

A 2006 television commercial involved a runaway Pepsi coin machine that had fallen from a Pepsi truck. The machine rolled by a series of Quebec landmarks, hesitated, and then turned back when it reached the Quebec border—great humour!

What started Pepsi rolling (literally) was a 1980s campaign that featured then up-and-coming French comedian Claude Meunier. His humour was so in tune with French Quebec lifestyle and culture that the sales impact was immediate. From being 15 percentage points behind in Quebec, two years later Pepsi was 12 percentage points ahead of Coca-Cola. The lead grew to 20 percent in the 1990s.

If there is a moral to this story, it's go local, not national or global. It is important to understand the tastes and lifestyles of the target market you are pursuing. Tailored messages, if affordable, yield the desired results!

Adapted from Konrad Yakabuski, "How Pepsi Won Quebec," *The Globe and Mail*, August 28, 2008, pp. B1, B2.

URBAN POPULATION   The trend toward urbanization continues in Canada. According to the 2006 Census, 80 percent of the population lives in urban areas. Further, six metropolitan areas account for 45 percent of Canada's population: Toronto, Montreal, Vancouver, Ottawa-Gatineau, Calgary, and Edmonton. The population of Edmonton and Calgary has grown by 13.4 percent and 10.4 percent, respectively, over a five-year period (2001–2006). Much of the growth is attributed to flourishing oil and oil-based industries, which have attracted workers from other provinces.[2]

Keeping track of where Canadians live is an important consideration when developing marketing strategies and marketing communications strategies. With the population so clustered, companies now devise plans that are regional in nature or dwell specifically on key urban areas. A brand may be available nationally in terms of geography, but the way it is presented (nature of message) could be very different from one area to another. Such a trend also helps explain the popularity of regional brands. In Atlantic Canada, for example, Alexander Keith's beer is a leading brand of beer. A national brand like Molson Canadian or Labatt Blue must adapt its national strategy to suit the needs of Atlantic beer drinkers if it is to make headway in that region.

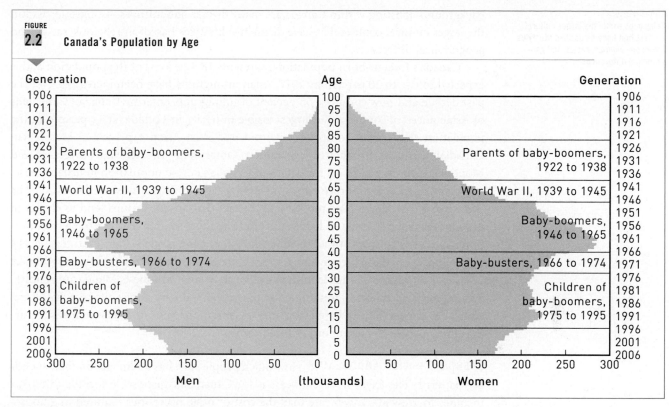

FIGURE 2.2   Canada's Population by Age

Source: "Canada's Population by Age", adapted from Statistics Canada publication Age and sex, 2006 Census, Catalogue 97-551-XWE2006001, http://www12.statcan.ca/census-recensement/2006/as-sa/97-551/figures/c7-eng.cfm.

CHANGING HOUSEHOLD FORMATIONS There was a time when the traditional family was described as a married couple with children. The father worked full time and the mother stayed at home to raise the children (a family structure reflected in the popular TV drama about advertising called Mad Men). Trends such as the postponement of marriage, the pursuit of careers by women, increases in divorce rates, and same-sex partnerships are producing new households in Canada. Now, married couples comprise only 69 percent of households.[3]

Today, modern households are described as lone-parent families (either from divorce or absence of a partner), same-sex families (openness and acceptance of gay and lesbian lifestyles), and blended families (families that bring together children of previous marriages).

Canadian households are also shrinking in size. Presently, the average size is 2.6, a reflection of the trends described above. Among the various types of households, the traditional household is showing the slowest rates of growth, so the trend to smaller households will continue. Products and services must explore unique opportunities these trends present. For example, companies in the packaged foods business or household goods business must offer a variety of sizes to meet the needs of such household variation. As described in Chapter 1 (consumer behaviour section) they must also be aware of who is making the buying decision or influencing the decision. To present a brand improperly or in an old-fashioned manner could be harmful to the brand's development.

ETHNIC DIVERSITY Canada is a culturally diverse country, a situation that presents unique challenges and opportunities for marketing organizations. The population is quickly changing from one of a predominantly European background to an Asian

subcultures
Subgroups within the larger cultural context that have distinctive lifestyles based on religious, racial, and geographical differences.

background. Existing within Canada are many diverse **subcultures**—subgroups within the larger cultural context that have distinctive lifestyles based on religious, racial, and geographical differences.

Canada's foreign-born population represents 18.4 percent of the population and is expected to rise to 20 percent by 2017. Asian immigrants have been increasing over the past decade and now comprise 58 percent of immigrants entering Canada.[4] Canadians of Asian ancestry comprise the largest visible minority in Canada, at 11 percent of the population (East Asian comprise 7 percent and West Asian 4 percent).[5] Most Asian Canadians reside in urban areas of southern Ontario, the Greater Vancouver area, and Montreal. Refer to Figure 2.3 for details of Canada's ethnic population in urban areas.

Companies that embrace ethnic marketing will profit the most in the future. The sheer size of this developing market and the fact that unique groups tend to cluster in urban areas make them a reachable target for Canadian brands. The key to an organization's success is to spend time learning more about the target—their customs, beliefs, mores and so on—and then formulate appropriate communications strategies. Walmart is a leader in this area. It has identified the South Asian, Cantonese, Mandarin, Spanish, Portuguese, and Italian communities as priorities. Walmart adjusts its merchandising strategies to meet culture-based local market conditions and runs television ads featuring ethnic people in the minorities listed above.

SPENDING POWER AND WEALTH How much people earn has an impact on their spending patterns. The trend in recent years is for Canadians' disposable income (after-tax income) to grow at a lower rate than the cost of basic necessities required in a household (food, shelter, car, clothing, household supplies, and so on). Canadians are working harder than ever, but there is less available for optional purchases such as vacations, sports, and recreational activities. Lower- and middle-income Canadians (the masses) are more cautious about how and on what they spend their money.

Another income trend in Canada is the concentration of wealth among upper-income groups. The old expression "the rich are getting richer and the poor are getting poorer" applies here. Census data from Statistics Canada verify a polarization of incomes at the upper and lower ends of the spectrum. The top one-fifth of Canadian families had an average after-tax income of $128 200 in 2005, while the lower fifth earned $22 800, a gap of $105 400.[6]

Earlier in the chapter the impact of gasoline prices on the automobile market was presented. Ironically, the sales of luxury vehicles such as Mercedes Benz, BMW, and Lexus were not negatively affected as people who can afford these cars continued to buy

FIGURE 2.3

Canada's Ethnic Population: Key Urban Areas

Source: "Canada's Ethnic Population: as Percentage of Each Market's Overall Population," adapted from Statistics Canada publication Ethnic Origin and Visible Minorities, 2006 Census, Catalogue 97-562-XWE2006001, http://www.statcan.gc.ca/bsolc/olc-cel/olc-cel?lang=eng&catno=97-562-X2006001.

Market	2006 (%)
Toronto	42.9
Montreal	16.5
Vancouver	41.7
Ottawa-Gatineau	16.0
Calgary	22.0
Edmonton	17.1
Winnipeg	15.0
Halifax	7.5

them—a reflection of their disposable income. Retailers such as Walmart also enjoyed increases in sales revenue as the masses, looking for better value, migrated away from traditional department stores like Sears and The Bay—a reflection of people wanting to stretch their disposable income as far as possible.

Given the income trends, it seems wise for organizations targeting lower- and middle-income groups to stress value in their marketing communications strategies. Walmart is an expert at this. In the midst of the 2009 recession, Walmart changed its slogan to "Save money. Live better." Walmart experienced monthly sales increases while other competitors were losing business. Walmart always emphasizes price and value in its marketing communications.

SOCIAL INFLUENCES

Marketers and marketing communicators must also stay in touch with social change. For a variety of reasons, the lifestyles of Canadians are always changing, and generally speaking, Canadians are very concerned about the natural environment and what companies are doing to preserve and protect it.

LIFESTYLES Two key issues prevail in terms of lifestyle: Canadians are living a very hectic lifestyle and they are trying to live a healthier lifestyle. Generally speaking, we are now a society that places greater emphasis on quality of life rather than work, but we need to work to sustain the type of life we desire. For many Canadians the mythical "40-hour" work week doesn't exist. People choose to work longer hours to get ahead.

Being pressed for time suggests a need for convenience. Many industries have reacted to this. For example, the home services industry has exploded as aging baby boomers that used to be "do-it-yourselfers" have become the "do-it-for-me" generation. They don't have the time for house-related chores and repairs. Drive-throughs at restaurants like McDonald's, Wendy's, and KFC now contribute as much as 50 percent of revenues as they directly appeal to the "on-the-go" consumer.

Canadians are also expressing more concern for health and welfare. Issues such as obesity and the aging process are causing consumers to make wiser choices. Marketers are responding to these demands by marketing healthier foods. Kraft Foods, one of the largest food companies, recently announced an "obesity initiative"—proposing healthful changes to its products and marketing strategies. They are putting a cap on portion size for single-serve packages and implementing new guidelines to improve the nutritional characteristics of all of its brands. In terms of marketing communications, Kraft plans to encourage appropriate eating habits and active lifestyles.

NATURAL ENVIRONMENT Today's consumers show serious concern for the natural environment and tend to favour companies that have a strong reputation for protecting our natural resources and for contributing to worthy causes. Essentially, companies with a strong social conscience stand to benefit now and in the future. Companies that are perceived to show only tokenism to such a serious issue can be quickly punished when consumers resist buying their products.

To demonstrate, Toyota and Honda are perceived by many to be leaders in automotive technology designed to protect the planet. Toyota's Prius model (a fuel-efficient hybrid) has been an overwhelming success in the marketplace with demand so high that dealers have to form waiting lists for the cars. Honda has developed low-emissions engines that will help preserve the planet. Both companies communicate their green initiatives to the public. Refer to the illustration in Figure 2.4.

FIGURE
2.4

Social issues have an impact on marketing strategies

yesterday's dream

today's dream

tomorrow's dream

From the world's first low-emission CVCC engine, to the 2010 Insight Hybrid, to the fuel cell-powered FC Sport concept, we're committed to doing our part to help lower emissions, preserve the environment and support our dream of a brighter tomorrow. Because at Honda, we believe in the Power of Dreams. Learn more at honda.ca.

HONDA
The Power of Dreams

TECHNOLOGY INFLUENCE

New products are coming to market so fast that consumers simply cannot grasp them all. Can anyone possibly keep up with the changes occurring in the telecommunications industry? How many electronic gadgets do we need simply to stay in touch? The technological environment consists of the discoveries, inventions, and innovations that provide for marketing opportunities. New products, new packaging, and new forms of communications are the direct result of technological advancement.

In a marketing communications context, how people communicate and conduct buying transactions is also affected by technology. The Internet has had an overwhelming impact on commerce and communications as websites and web-based communications seem imperative for reaching a tech-savvy public. Products like the iPod demonstrate why Apple Computer is a great company. With elegant hardware and friendly software, Apple's portable player made a profitable business out of digital music—a trick that eluded record labels and other companies, such as Sony and Microsoft.[7]

To demonstrate the influence of technology, examine your own behaviour when it comes to cell phones or a BlackBerry smart phone. Try not using this device for a few days—you will suffer slowly the pain of withdrawal! Research in Motion (RIM) is an example of a Canadian company growing exponentially based on the success of the BlackBerry. Blackberry is now the highest-ranking Canadian brand name in terms of dollar value, a value pegged at $5.6 billion.[8]

Advancing technologies are causing marketing organizations to re-examine their marketing communications mix. The digital media now play a more prominent role in the mix. In general terms Canadian consumers are spending less time with the traditional media (TV, radio, and print) as they increase their consumption of digital media. Consequently, media planners are moving away from mass reach and frequency campaigns toward strategies that stress selective reach and engagement with the target audience.

LEGAL AND REGULATORY INFLUENCE

Strategic plans are affected by new developments in the political and legal arenas. Most laws and regulations governing business practice are created by federal and provincial legislation. As well, many industries establish and abide by their own self-regulation policies and practices. In some cases, the self-regulation guidelines are more stringent. Industry Canada regulates Canadian businesses through the *Competition Act*. The act has three purposes: to maintain and encourage competition, to ensure small businesses have equal opportunity to participate in trade, and to provide consumers with product choice and competitive prices.

It cannot be assumed that all businesses follow the letter of the law. In terms of marketing communications, companies have to be careful about what they say to consumers. As discussed in Chapter 1 (Issues section), exaggerated product claims that mislead the public can cause ethical and financial problems for a company.

Advertisers should follow the *Canadian Code of Advertising Standards*. The Code contains regulations about gender portrayal, product claims, price claims, advertising involving product comparisons, and advertising to children. The Code is administered by Advertising Standards Canada, a group representing advertisers and advertising agencies.

Canadians are also protected by various privacy laws, the *Privacy Act*, and the *Personal Information Protection and Electronic Documents Act* (PIPEDA). The *Privacy Act* places limits on the collection, use, and disclosure of personal information and gives Canadians the right to access and correct any information about them held by government organizations. It also sets rules for how private organizations collect, use, and disclose personal information. The laws require organizations to obtain the consent of individual Canadian consumers when accessing and using information about them.

Self-regulation is an alternative to government regulation. The Canadian Marketing Association (CMA) has established policies and guidelines that all member organizations agree to follow. The CMA's *Code of Ethics and Standards of Practice* is a document cover-ing issues such as protection of personal privacy, protecting the environment, and media-specific standards of practice. The CMA also established a Privacy Policy that identifies policies regarding the protection of information collected by CMA members. For more insight into CMA regulations and policies visit its website at www.the-cma.org.

Canadian Marketing Association
www.the-cma.org

Strategic Planning Process

Organizations that develop strategic plans have their own unique ways of doing so. A fairly common approach to planning is to start the process at the top or senior level of the organization and work downward. In other words, the strategic plan, or corporate plan, devised by senior executives will influence the nature of the various brand mar-keting plans developed by middle managers, and the brand marketing plans will influ-ence the nature of the marketing communications plan.

In the corporate plan developed by senior executives, most objectives are financial in nature and become the goals that must be shared by all of the company's divisions or products. Typically, the **corporate plan** is not an exhaustive document. Once the cor-porate plan has been struck, the various functional areas, including marketing, start their planning process. Refer to Figure 2.5 for a visual illustration.

A **marketing plan** is developed for each one of a company's products and sets out the objectives for all brands. The plan determines how the various elements of the mar-keting mix will be employed so that they have the desired impact on the target market. The target market is identified through some combination of demographic, psycho-graphic, and geographic variables, and a positioning strategy statement guides the development of the plan.

Once the role of marketing communications has been determined, specific plans are then developed for the various components of the marketing communications mix. At this stage, the goal is to develop a synergistic communications plan that will improve the well-being of the product or service. As discussed in Chapter 1, advertising will achieve awareness and interest objectives and help build brand image over an extended period. Other variables, such as sales promotions, experiential marketing, public relations, and

corporate plan
A strategic plan formulated at the exec-utive level of an organization to guide the development of functional plans in the organization.

marketing plan
A short-term, specific plan of action that combines strategy and tactics.

FIGURE
2.5

Strategic Planning: Links among Various Organizational Plans

The corporate plan provides guidance for the marketing plan and the marketing plan provides guidance for the marketing communications plan. All plans are based on the same background information and any analysis stemming from that information. Corporate plans are strategic in nature. Marketing plans and market-ing communications plans are both strategic and tactical in nature.

personal selling, perform more immediate tasks and are designed to achieve desire and action—a purchase. The integration of all components in a strategic plan will help achieve short-term and long-term objectives. The saying, "A chain is only as strong as its weakest link" appropriately describes the relationships among various components of the marketing communications mix and the relationship between marketing and marketing communications. As in war, a unified attack has a better chance of success!

The corporate plan provides guidance for the marketing plan and the marketing plan provides guidance for the marketing communications plan. All plans are based on the same background information and any analysis stemming from that information. Corporate plans are strategic in nature. Marketing plans and marketing communications plans are both strategic and tactical in nature.

The Corporate Plan

The mission statement is the guiding light for all forms of strategic planning. A **mission statement** is a statement of an organization's purpose and an indicator of the operating philosophy the organization follows. A good mission statement is customer and marketing oriented, considers the competition, and looks to the long term. In other words, once a company establishes its mission, it must provide adequate time and resources to carry through with it. Figure 2.6 lists Mountain Equipment Co-op's purpose, vision, mission, and values—the components of its strategic plan.

mission statement
A statement of an organization's purpose and operating philosophy; provides guidance and direction for the operations of the company.

With the mission confirmed, executive attention turns to setting corporate objectives, determining strategic direction, and allocating resources. **Corporate objectives** are statements of a company's overall goals. These objectives are usually financial in nature and are used to evaluate the effectiveness or ineffectiveness of a company's strategic plan and the people who manage the organization. At the end of the year, actual financial results are compared to the objectives. The degree of success is there for all concerned to see. Corporate objectives can also be qualitative in nature, which are perhaps more difficult to measure immediately. Here are a few examples of corporate objectives, both quantitative and qualitative:

corporate objective
A statement of a company's overall goal; used to evaluate the effectiveness or ineffectiveness of a company's strategic plan.

• To increase company sales revenue from $50 000 000 to $60 000 000 in 20XX.

• To increase category market share (share in a market for all company brands) from 25 percent to 30 percent in 20XX.

• To increase return on investment from 10 percent to 15 percent in 20XX.

• To exhibit constructive social responsibility by investing in research and development to discover environmentally friendly new products.

The last objective on the list above is qualitative in nature. At the end of the year, however, the organization will evaluate in some way its investment in social responsibility programs. The first three objectives on the list are quantitative in nature. Objective statements like these have direct impact on the development of marketing objectives and strategies. All company brands must contribute to achieving the company's goals. It is the total of sales revenues for various brands, for example, that constitutes overall company sales revenue. The market share of several company brands, for example, Tide, Gain, Era, and Cheer, make up Procter & Gamble's total market share in the laundry detergent market.

When an organization determines its corporate strategy, it considers several factors: marketing strength, degree of competition in current or new markets under consideration, financial resources, research and development capabilities, and management commitment

FIGURE
2.6

Key Components of Mountain
Equipment Co-op's
Strategic Plan

Source: Courtesy of Mountain
Equipment Co-op.

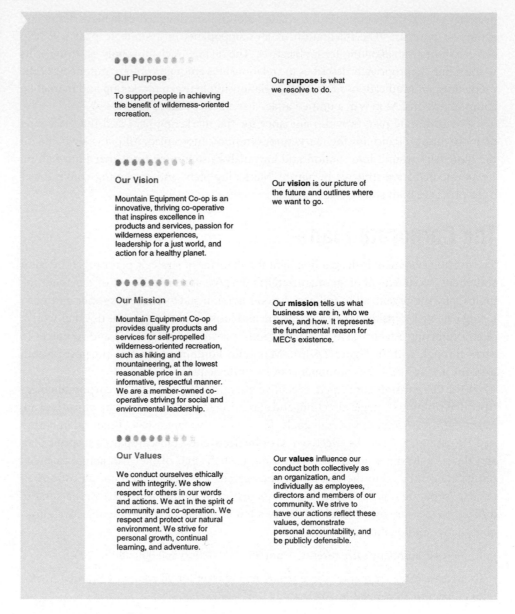

FIGURE 2.6 Key Components of Mountain Equipment Co-op's Strategic Plan

Source: Courtesy of Mountain Equipment Co-op.

to particular goals. It is common for a company to follow numerous strategic directions at the same time, largely due to the dynamic nature of the marketplace. To follow one direction and fail could have a negative long-term effect on the company.

A variety of strategic options are given due consideration. Among the options are a penetration strategy, an acquisition strategy, a new product development strategy, and a strategic alliance strategy. All these strategies imply a desire for growth. In some cases, a company may decide to get smaller. While that may seem odd, many companies find that too much expansion can have disastrous results on profits. Growing at the expense of profit doesn't make sense!

In such cases, a company may decide on a **divestment strategy** and sell off various divisions or products. In the aftermath of rising oil prices, waning interest in larger vehicles, and a recessionary economy (2009) General Motors decided to get smaller in order to survive. GM dropped the Pontiac brand, sold the Hummer and Saturn divisions, and eliminated 40 percent of its dealer network in North America.

divestment strategy
NEED DEFINITION

A **penetration strategy** involves aggressive marketing of a company's existing products. The goal is to build the business by taking customers from the competition or by expanding the entire market. Coca-Cola invests considerable sums of money into key brands such as Coca-Cola and Diet Coke to retain leadership in the soft drink category. Arch-rival PepsiCo invests considerable sums of money in Pepsi-Cola and Diet Pepsi to take market share away from Coca-Cola. It is a real marketing and marketing communications battle between the two companies!

New products, the result of a **new product development strategy**, offer another option for growth-minded companies. New products create new revenue streams at a much greater rate than simply trying to expand existing products. Apple Computer has enjoyed much success with new products—sales have never been stronger, earnings have never been better, and Apple's popularity as a company has never been as pervasive. This is all thanks to savvy marketing and engineering, which have made the iPod, iTunes, and iPhone very popular in the marketplace (see Figure 2.7). Apple is now a media company rather than a computer company.

Rather than invest in something new, some companies prefer to buy their way into a market by following an **acquisition strategy**. Google Inc., the most-used Internet search engine, acquired YouTube for $1.6 billion. With the acquisition, Google moves from seventh place to first place in terms of online video traffic.[9] Nike recently acquired Umbro PLC, the British marketer of soccer jerseys and shorts, for US$582 million. Umbro was a good fit to help raise Nike's profile in soccer-crazed European countries.[10]

penetration strategy
A plan of action for aggressive marketing of a company's existing products.

new product development strategy
A marketing strategy that calls for significant investment in research and development to develop innovative products.

acquisition strategy
A plan of action for acquiring companies that represent attractive financial opportunities.

FIGURE 2.7   Apple Launches New Products to Create New Revenue Streams

strategic alliance
The combination of separate companies' resources for the purpose of satisfying their shared customers; the companies have strengths in different areas.

Strategic alliances, when separate companies with complementary strengths join resources to satisfy their shared customers, are now very popular among companies searching for ways to reduce costs or improve operating efficiency. One wouldn't think that automotive competitors would work together to achieve common goals but that's exactly what's happening in a world of escalating research and development costs. Nissan Motor Co. and Chrysler recently formed an alliance that will see Nissan make a new small car for Chrysler while Chrysler will make a full-sized pickup truck designed by Nissan. Each company is capitalizing on the other's strength. Both products will be sold in North America.[11]

Senior executives also make decisions about the financial resources that are allocated to marketing and other functional divisions of the company. Prior to embarking on marketing plans for individual products, the vice-president of marketing usually knows how much money is available for marketing purposes. That person distributes the money among each of the company's brands. Competition among brand managers for such a scarce resource creates some very interesting marketing plans and presentations. Most companies have brands that are stars, and they are given budget priority. What's left is divided among the remaining brands.

Marketing Planning

marketing planning
The analysis, planning, implementing, and controlling of marketing initiatives to satisfy target market needs and achieve organizational objectives.

contingency plan
The identification of alternative courses of action that can be used to modify an original plan if and when new circumstances arise.

target market
The group of persons for whom a firm creates and markets a product.

With the details of the corporate plan determined, the marketing department starts the process of marketing planning. **Marketing planning** involves analyzing, planning, implementing, and controlling marketing initiatives to satisfy target market needs and achieve organizational objectives. Marketing plans are short term in nature (one year), specific in scope (they involve precise actions for one product), and combine both strategy and tactics (they are action oriented). The marketing plan should also include a **contingency plan** to provide alternative courses of action in the event that new circumstances arise.

The marketing plan revolves around the customer, specifically the knowledge an organization has of its customers. An essential ingredient in the development of a marketing plan is a precise description of the target market. The **target market** is the group of persons for whom a firm creates and markets a product that specifically meets the needs and preferences of that group.

A target market is typically described in terms of four different but related characteristics: demographics, psychographics, geographics, and behaviour responses. As described earlier in the chapter, an organization will keep track of demographic trends and develop profiles of potential customer groups based on those trends.

DEMOGRAPHIC CHARACTERISTICS Demographics describe a customer group in terms of age, gender, income, occupation, education, marital status, household formation, and ethnic background. Depending on the nature of the product, some characteristics may be more important than others. Some may not be important at all. Given the role changes among males and females in Canadian households, many brands and products that used to be gender-specific are rethinking their target market description.

PSYCHOGRAPHIC Characteristics Psychographics describe a customer group in terms of attitudes, interests, opinions, and activities. The focus is on the "lifestyle" of the members in the group. It is quite common in marketing and marketing communications to appeal to consumers based on their lifestyle or the lifestyle they would like to have. It's not so much what is said in a message but how it is said or portrayed visually. Psychographic knowledge can directly influence message and media strategy.

GEOGRAPHIC CHARACTERISTICS Geography does figure into market planning, as indicated earlier in the chapter. As many as 80 percent of Canadians live in areas defined as urban. More to the point, Canada's top three cities (and surrounding areas) comprise about one-third of the population. Marketers, therefore, have the option of marketing nationally, regionally, or in designated urban areas.

BEHAVIOUR RESPONSE The behaviour of group members rounds out a target market description. For example, many products (suntan products, skis, flowers, and toys) are seasonal in nature and consumers concentrate their purchases in short periods. Certain members may consume a product more quickly than others. Such users are described as "heavy users" and may have a slightly different profile than other users. And finally, some members may demonstrate more loyalty than others. Perhaps the profile of a truly loyal user is somewhat different from that of the average user. Can information about heavy users and loyal users be used to advantage? While usage and loyalty can never be taken for granted, it does give an opportunity for marketers to develop strategies aimed at the less loyal users who could switch to competitive brands if enticed the right way. As they say, "knowledge is power!"

There is no perfect format for a marketing plan, although Figure 2.8 offers an illustration. Marketing plans vary considerably from one organization to another in length, detail, and content. This section will examine the content of a marketing plan, but readers must realize that the content of a plan is modified to suit the needs of each specific organization. Essentially, a marketing plan is divided into two major sections. The first section is a compilation of background information about the market, target market, competition, and product. The second section is the plan itself; it contains the objectives, strategies, and tactics for the product for the year ahead and provides specific details about how the budget is allocated and the timing of all activities.

MARKET BACKGROUND

The direction a marketing plan takes is directly influenced by internal conditions (strengths and weaknesses) and external conditions (opportunities and threats). The first step in planning is analysis. In marketing terms, such an analysis is referred to as a **SWOT analysis**. The acronym SWOT stands for strengths, weaknesses, opportunities, and threats.

SWOT analysis
An analysis procedure that involves an assessment of an organization's strengths, weaknesses, opportunities, and threats; strengths and weaknesses are internal variables, whereas opportunities and threats are external variables.

STRENGTHS AND WEAKNESSES The internal capabilities and resources are reviewed to determine the relative condition of a brand and determine its capability to pursue new directions. The review considers a variety of controllable marketing factors and may extend to the areas of manufacturing, finance, human resources, and technology. Any limits on current strengths may justify developing new strengths.

OPPORTUNITIES AND THREATS The manager reviews relevant external data that may impact on the direction of the marketing plan. Such a review may include economic trends, demographic trends, social trends, legal and regulatory influences, competitive activity, and technology influences. Opportunities are prioritized, and threats are classified according to their seriousness and probability of occurrence. The absence of marketing action in either area could hinder the development of a brand.

A variety of information is collected and analyzed. The goals of a SWOT analysis are to capitalize on strengths while minimizing weaknesses and to take advantage of opportunities while fending off threats. Typically, a SWOT analysis should review the following information (refer to Figure 2.8 for an illustration of a marketing plan model).

FIGURE

2.8   An Illustration of a Marketing Plan Model

MARKETING BACKGROUND	MARKETING PLAN

External Influences
- Economic trends
- Social and demographic trends
- Technology trends
- Regulatory trends

Market Analysis
- Market size and growth
- Regional market size and growth
- Market segment analysis
- Seasonal analysis

Competitor Analysis
- Market share trends
- Marketing strategy assessment

Target Market Analysis
- Consumer data
- Consumer behaviour

Product (Brand) Analysis
- Sales volume trends
- Market share trends
- Distribution
- Marketing communications
- New product activity

SWOT Analysis*
- Strengths
- Weaknesses
- Opportunities
- Threats

Positioning Strategy
- Positioning strategy statement

Target Market Profile
- Demographic
- Psychographic
- Geographic

Marketing Objectives
- Sales volume
- Market share
- Profit
- Other

Marketing Strategies
- Product
- Price
- Marketing communications
- Distribution

Marketing Execution (Tactics)
- Product
- Price
- Marketing communications
- Distribution
- New products
- Marketing research
- Service
- Partnerships and alliances

Budget and Financial Summary
- Budget allocations (by activity, by time of year)
- Brand financial statement

Timeline or Calendar
- Activity schedule

Corporate Plan

Marketing Plan
- Marketing Background (SWOT Analysis)
- Marketing Plan

Marketing Communications Plan

*Note: Including a SWOT analysis is optional. Some planners believe that the SWOT analysis occurs when the information is compiled in the preceding sections of the plan. Other planners believe that such information must be analyzed further to determine priorities. The latter is the intention of a SWOT analysis.

EXTERNAL INFLUENCES

- **Economic Trends:** The current and predicted states of the economy are considered. Is the economy growing (recovery or prosperity) or is it sputtering (recession)? Appropriate statistical information is evaluated in this section of the plan.

- **Social and Demographic Trends:** Basic trends in age, income, household formation, immigration, migration, and lifestyles are evaluated to identify potential target markets. For example, the aging of Canada's population or concern for the environment will be a factor influencing marketing strategies in the future. There will be a new emphasis on older age groups.

- **Technology Trends:** Technological trends that affect buyer behaviour have to be determined. Technology quickens the speed with which new products come to market and the way companies deliver messages about products to customers.

- **Regulatory Trends:** A company should always stay abreast of changes to any laws and regulations affecting the marketing of its products. For example, new privacy laws have been introduced in Canada to protect consumers and regulate companies engaged in e-marketing practices and e-commerce.

Once plans are developed and implemented, evaluation and control procedures are applied during the plan period (e.g., quarterly reviews). At that stage there is an opportunity to revise marketing objectives and strategies according to current market conditions.

MARKET ANALYSIS

- **Market Size and Growth:** A review of trends over several years is considered for the purpose of making sales projections for the year ahead. Is the market growing or declining, and how fast?

- **Regional Markets:** Sales trends by region are analyzed to determine what areas need more or less attention in the year ahead. Some markets may be growing while others are not. A regional analysis helps determine priorities.

- **Market Segment Analysis:** There could be numerous product segments in a market. For example, in the hotel industry there are budget hotels, mid-priced hotels, and luxury hotels. Are all segments growing at the same rate, or are some segments doing better than others? Interpretive comments about the various segments should be included.

- **Seasonal Analysis:** Seasonal or cyclical trends over the course of a year are examined. For example, volume trends for beer and barbecue-related items would be much higher in the spring and summer seasons. The timing of proposed marketing activities needs to consider such trends.

TARGET MARKET ANALYSIS

- **Consumer Data:** The profile of primary users (and secondary users, if necessary) is reviewed for any changes during the past few years. The aging population and lifestyle changes could be affecting the profile of product users.

- **Consumer Behaviour:** The degree of customer loyalty to the market and products within a market is assessed. Are customers loyal to the brand or do they switch brands? Knowledge of such behaviour has a direct influence on advertising and promotion strategies. Should the plan attract new customers, prevent existing customers from departing, or do both?

PRODUCT (BRAND) ANALYSIS An assessment of a brand's past performance is included in this section of the plan. An attempt is made to link past marketing activities to the performance of the brand. Have previous strategies been successful, and will changes be needed in the year ahead?

- **Sales Volume Trends:** Historical volume trends are plotted to forecast sales for the year ahead.

- **Market Share Trends:** Market share is a clear indicator of brand performance. Market share trends are examined nationally, regionally, and by key markets to determine areas of strengths and weaknesses. Is the brand's market share growing faster or slower than competitors' shares? Where are the priorities for improving market share?

- **Distribution:** The availability of the product nationally and regionally is reviewed. Regional availability will affect how much marketing support a brand will receive. Should the new plan focus on areas where distribution is high or low?

- **Marketing Communications:** Current activities are assessed to determine if strategies need to be retained or changed. A review of expenditures by medium, sales promotions, and events and sponsorships is necessary to assess the impact of such spending on brand performance.

- **New Product Activity:** Sales performance of recently implemented initiatives is evaluated. For example, the performance of new product formats, sizes, flavours, and so on is scrutinized to determine the impact of those factors on sales and market share.

COMPETITOR ANALYSIS In order to plan effectively, a manager should know competitors' products as well as his or her own product. A review of marketing mix activities for key competitors provides essential input on how to revise marketing strategies. A brand must react to the actions of another brand or suffer the consequences of lack of action.

- **Market Share Trends:** It is common to plot and review the market share trends of all brands from year to year. Such analysis provides insight into what brands are moving forward and what brands are moving backward.

- **Marketing Strategy Assessment:** An attempt is made to link known marketing strategies to competitor brand performance. What is the nature of the competition's advertising, sales promotions, events and sponsorships, and interactive programs? How much are the competitors investing in these areas? Have they launched any new products or implemented any new distribution, pricing, or communications strategies? What changes are anticipated in the year ahead?

MARKETING PLAN

The SWOT analysis leads directly into the development of the action plan. The plan section clarifies the positioning strategy of the company's brands, establishes objectives for the year, determines how the various elements of the marketing mix will be employed, and outlines the investment and timing of all activities that are recommended.

POSITIONING STRATEGY **Positioning** refers to the selling concept that motivates purchase, or the image that marketers desire a brand to have in the minds of customers. The **positioning strategy statement** has a direct impact on the nature of the message that must be communicated to consumers. For example, Visa's positioning strategy statement might read as follows:

> Visa delivers innovative products and services that can be used anytime, anywhere, while offering customers the confidence to do anything.

The positioning statement clearly identifies where the company wants the product to be in the market and helps provide direction to the message that will ultimately be communicated to customers. Furthermore, it serves as the standard for considering what strategies to use and not use. For example, if a marketing communications agency presents a new creative strategy for the brand, the client will evaluate it against the positioning strategy statement to see whether the new creative plan fits with the strategy.

positioning
The selling concept that motivates purchase, or the image that marketers desire a brand to have in the minds of consumers.

positioning strategy statement
A summary of the character and personality of a brand and the benefits it offers customers.

In the case of Visa, the benefits of having and using a Visa card are portrayed in ads that say: "More people go with Visa." This slogan aptly reflects Visa's new global positioning strategy and brand platform. The slogan is used in ads everywhere. For an illustration of Visa's advertising see Figure 2.9.

TARGET MARKET PROFILE At this stage, the manager identifies or targets a group of customers that represents the greatest profit potential. As discussed earlier, a target market is defined in terms of similar needs and common characteristics based on the following:

- **Demographic Profile:** Characteristics such as age, gender, income, education, and ethnic background are considered. Depending on the nature of the product, some characteristics are more important than others. Some may not be important at all. For example, is the brand for males, females, or is it gender neutral? If the product is expensive, income will be an important factor.

FIGURE
2.9

A Print Ad Demonstrating Visa Canada's Positioning Strategy

Source: Courtesy of Visa Canada.

- **Psychographic Profile:** The lifestyle profile includes three essential characteristics: the target's activities, interests, and opinions. Knowledge about customer behaviour provides clues on how to best reach the customer with a compelling message. As discussed in Chapter 1, many advertising campaigns are designed in such a way that a brand associates itself with a lifestyle or desired lifestyle of the target. Information about media consumption is also relevant to the customer profile. Knowledge about what media customers refer to most frequently affects how funds are allocated across different media. For example, if the target market spends more time online and less time watching television than it used to, such knowledge could influence media strategy.

- **Geographic Profile:** The urban nature of Canada's population means geography has a significant influence on marketing strategy. Therefore, the profile considers the location of the target market in terms of region or key market. Geography is typically a key influence on how a budget is allocated across the country. Does a brand invest in regions of strength or regions that need shoring up?

To demonstrate target market profiling, consider the description of the primary customer for a Harley-Davidson motorcycle. Biker gangs do not keep Harley-Davidson in business! Its customer is described as follows:

Males, 40 to 55 years of age, earning $75 000 plus annually, living in major cities. They are "weekend warriors" who want to get away from the office. They are lawyers, doctors, or corporate executives looking for a way to alleviate stress. About 25 percent are new to biking and 45 percent have previously owned a Harley; 30 percent have come from a competing brand. Women account for 15 percent of purchasers.

This description aptly portrays a combination of demographic, psychographic, and geographic characteristics, at least the ones that are important to Harley-Davidson.[12] Figure 2.10 shows a sample of Harley-Davidson communications.

marketing objective
A statement that identifies what a product will accomplish in a one-year period, usually expressed in terms of sales, market share, and profit.

MARKETING OBJECTIVES **Marketing objectives** are statements that identify what a product will accomplish in a one-year period. Similar to corporate objectives, they tend to focus on financial measures, such as sales and profits or other quantitative yardsticks. Objectives may also be qualitative in nature and include new product introductions, product line extensions, launching of new packaging, and so on. Here, the objective may be to simply get the new activity into the market at the planned time. Objectives do not always have to be measured in terms of dollars or market share.

To illustrate how marketing objectives are written, let's assume you are the brand manager for Dasani bottled water (a brand marketed by Coca-Cola). You are developing your objectives for the next year based on your present market share of 7.3 percent. Dasani is a true challenger in the market following the brand leader, Aquafina (a Pepsi-Cola brand), which owns 7.5 percent market share.[13] The bottled water market is growing by about 3 percent a year and is presently estimated to be worth $700 million.

You might set out the marketing objectives for Dasani for the year ahead like this:

- To increase market share from 7.3 percent to 7.7 percent (reflecting a desire to be the new brand leader).

- To increase dollar sales from $51 100 000 to $55 517 000 (assumes a market growth of 3 percent and achievement of market share objective).

- To successfully introduce two new line extensions to extend Dasani's presence further in the bottled water market.

FIGURE 2.10   Harley-Davidson motorcycles targets middle-aged males by placing ads in magazines that segment reads

THE 2ND-CENTURY HARLEY-DAVIDSON® FOR THE 21ST-CENTURY MAN

TRUE FOR THE FIRST 100 YEARS. TRUE FOR THE NEXT 100 YEARS.

Shown above is a customized V-Rod. See retailer for details. With the purchase of any new model Harley-Davidson from an authorized Canadian Harley-Davidson retailer, you will receive a free, one year full membership in H.O.G.® We support the Canada Safety Council Rider Training Program. Always ride with a helmet. Ride defensively. Distributed exclusively in Canada by Fred Deeley Imports Ltd., Vancouver and Toronto. Fred Deeley Imports Ltd. is a proud sponsor of the Muscular Dystrophy Association of Canada.

It only took 100 years of Harley-Davidson® ingenuity to outstrip 2000 years of human evolution. Welcome to the 100th Anniversary Harley-Davidson V-Rod™ motorcycle. Revolutionary style and engineering for a whole new century of riding. www.harleycanada.com. 1-800-LUV2RIDE for a nearby retailer. **The Legend Rolls On.**

• To improve distribution levels in Quebec from 75 percent to 85 percent (in stores carrying bottled water).

Objectives are written so they can be measured to facilitate evaluation at the end of the plan period. Were the objectives achieved or not? Was the plan too aggressive or not aggressive enough? It will depend on the dynamics of the marketplace over the next 12 months.

marketing strategy
A plan of action that shows how the various elements of the marketing mix will be used to satisfy a target market's needs.

MARKETING STRATEGIES **Marketing strategies** are the master plans for achieving the objectives. The importance of having a good strategy must be emphasized. There is a saying that "Good strategy with weak execution can produce reasonable results." Likewise, there is another saying: "Poor strategy with good execution produces terrible results." The reason these have become such common sayings is that they are true. The goal should be to have the right strategy and then simply to work on better execution as time goes on. Most professional hockey or football coaches would agree with this principle.

In the development of the marketing strategy, the role and contribution of each component of the marketing mix are identified. Priority may be given to certain components depending on the nature of the market. For example, the success of a brand of beer depends largely on the impact of advertising on the target market. The nature of the message and the amount of money invested in advertising are critical decision areas for achieving differentiation.

In the transportation market, the product environment (a combination of product and additional services) is an important consideration among travellers. VIA Rail, for example, stresses the benefit of staying connected with Wi-Fi service on select rail cars and calls their railway "a more human way to travel." See the illustration in Figure 2.11.

The budget allocated to the product will be identified in the strategy section of the plan. There are various methods for arriving at a budget. Some methods estimate sales first and then base the marketing or marketing communications budget on sales. Other methods develop the budget first, a method based on the premise that investing in marketing communications creates sales, so the budget is not the outcome of sales. Regardless of the method used, the budget must be carefully calculated and defended when the plan is presented to the marketing managers. Figure 2.12 on page 54 shows further details about budget methodologies.

MARKETING EXECUTION (TACTICS) The tactics (execution) outlined in the plan are program details drawn directly from the strategy section of the plan. Such details will identify what programs are to be implemented, how much they will cost, what the timing will be, and who will be responsible for implementation. The unique action plan provides specific details regarding how the various elements of the marketing mix will be used to achieve the marketing objectives. This section of the plan may also include a description of activities in areas such as marketing research, service programs, and potential partnerships and alliances.

Typically, only the key elements of various marketing communications plans (advertising, sales promotion, Internet communications, public relations, direct response, and so on) are included in the marketing plan. The assumption is that specific communications plans are based on the same marketing objectives and marketing strategies described in the marketing plan. Specific and lengthier information about marketing communications strategies and tactics is presented in their respective plans or a marketing communications plan.

BUDGET AND FINANCIAL SUMMARY In order for a marketing plan to be improved, it is crucial to show the financial implications of the activities to be undertaken. Senior executives like to know how the company's money will be spent and how profitable the investment will be. Therefore, the budget section will itemize all activities and indicate the associated cost. Major areas such as media, consumer promotion, trade promotion, and marketing research are often subdivided into more specific activities.

In many companies, the brand managers and marketing managers are responsible for bottom-line profitability for their brands. If so, a financial statement for the brand

FIGURE
2.11

VIA Rail's Differential Advantage Is a Promise of Staying Connected when Travelling

Source: Courtesy of VIA Rail Canada.

is included. Such a statement should provide some financial history for the previous year, current year, and a forecast for the plan year. Senior executives are interested in seeing progress in marketing terms and financial terms. The financial statement will include such measures as sales, market share, cost of goods sold, gross profit, marketing expenses, and net profit before taxes.

EVALUATION AND CONTROL It is quite common for an organization to plan for semi-annual or quarterly reviews to assess its financial position. Marketing and marketing communications managers often fear such reviews because it is a time when budgets are frequently given the axe. Nonetheless, evaluation of activities is essential, because changes will likely be necessary while a plan is in midstream. **Marketing control** is

marketing control
The process of measuring and evaluating the results of marketing strategies and plans and of taking corrective action to ensure marketing objectives are achieved.

FIGURE
2.12

Methods for Determining
a Marketing Budget

Method	Procedure
Percentage of Sales	A predetermined percentage of forecasted sales is allocated to marketing or marketing communications.
Fixed Sum/Unit	A predetermined dollar amount per unit sold is allocated to marketing or marketing communications.
Industry Average	The average amount (current or forecasted) spent on marketing or marketing communications by all brands in a market is allocated to marketing.
Advertising Share/Market Share	Invest at a level to retain share (ad share equals market share); invest at a level to build marketshare share (ad is greater than market share).
Task (Objective)	Define the task, determine the activities to achieve the task, and associate a cost to the activities.

the process of measuring and evaluating the results of marketing strategies and plans and then taking corrective action to ensure the marketing objectives are attained.

The evaluation process also provides an opportunity to change marketing strategies if necessary. If financial obligations are not being achieved, then new strategies must be explored. Furthermore, it is an opportunity to review key financials, such as sales, costs, and profits, and reforecast the figures for the balance of the year. If the original objectives are not achievable, they should be modified, as should the marketing activities and expenditures that support the product.

Marketing Communications Planning

Since plans have to be struck well in advance of their implementation date, the marketing communications plan is developed simultaneously with the marketing plan so that its key components can be integrated into the marketing plan. The various components of marketing communications rely on the same input (background information, target market profiles, and positioning strategy statements) as do other components of the marketing mix. A marketing communications plan model is included in Figure 2.13. For a demonstration of how various types of plans are integrated and then implemented at the marketing communications level, read the IMC Highlight: **Differentiation Key to Audi's Canadian Success.**

marketing communications plan
A plan that identifies how the various elements of marketing communications will be integrated into a cohesive and coordinated plan.

A **marketing communications plan** is usually prepared by an outside organization. Depending on the nature of the plan, it could be an advertising agency, a public relations company, an experiential marketing agency, or any combination thereof. At some point, all the agencies working on the same plan must compare notes to ensure that their strategies are synchronized. Each aspect of the marketing communications plan has its own objectives, strategies, and tactical plans. In fact, it is crucial that the role and contribution of each component—advertising, sales promotion, public relations, direct response, interactive communications, experiential marketing, and personal selling—be identified.

The role of the marketing communications components will vary depending on the nature of the product and the market. As well, some components are suited for achieving long-term objectives while others are suited for short-term objectives. The key to success is the integration of the various components to produce a unified approach to building the brand (or company).

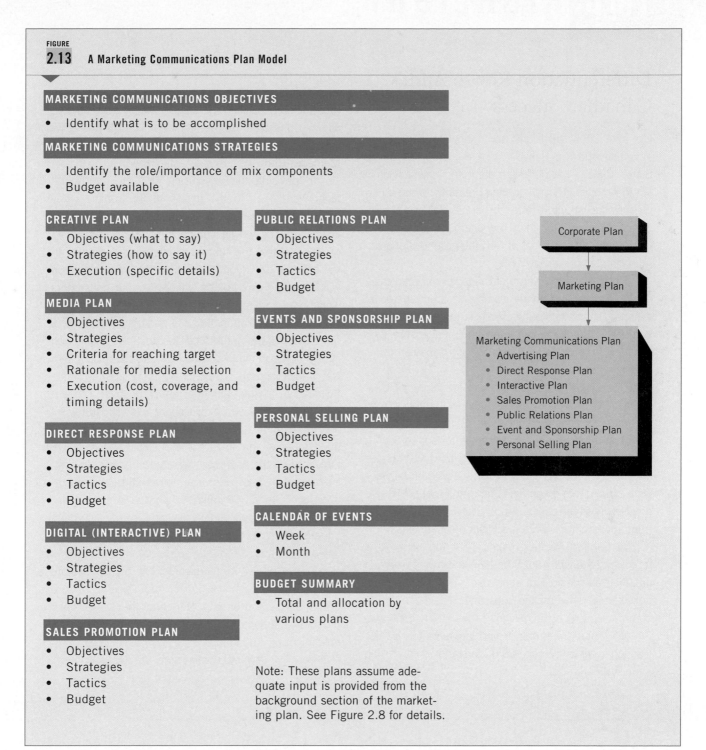

FIGURE 2.13   A Marketing Communications Plan Model

MARKETING COMMUNICATIONS OBJECTIVES

- Identify what is to be accomplished

MARKETING COMMUNICATIONS STRATEGIES

- Identify the role/importance of mix components
- Budget available

CREATIVE PLAN

- Objectives (what to say)
- Strategies (how to say it)
- Execution (specific details)

MEDIA PLAN

- Objectives
- Strategies
- Criteria for reaching target
- Rationale for media selection
- Execution (cost, coverage, and timing details)

DIRECT RESPONSE PLAN

- Objectives
- Strategies
- Tactics
- Budget

DIGITAL (INTERACTIVE) PLAN

- Objectives
- Strategies
- Tactics
- Budget

SALES PROMOTION PLAN

- Objectives
- Strategies
- Tactics
- Budget

PUBLIC RELATIONS PLAN

- Objectives
- Strategies
- Tactics
- Budget

EVENTS AND SPONSORSHIP PLAN

- Objectives
- Strategies
- Tactics
- Budget

PERSONAL SELLING PLAN

- Objectives
- Strategies
- Tactics
- Budget

CALENDAR OF EVENTS

- Week
- Month

BUDGET SUMMARY

- Total and allocation by various plans

Note: These plans assume adequate input is provided from the background section of the marketing plan. See Figure 2.8 for details.

Corporate Plan

Marketing Plan

Marketing Communications Plan
- Advertising Plan
- Direct Response Plan
- Interactive Plan
- Sales Promotion Plan
- Public Relations Plan
- Event and Sponsorship Plan
- Personal Selling Plan

MARKETING COMMUNICATIONS OBJECTIVES

In general terms, marketing communications objectives are very diverse and tend to involve

- Building awareness and interest in the product.
- Changing perceptions held by consumers about the product.
- Differentiating the product from others by presenting unique features and benefits.

Differentiation Key to Audi's Canadian Success

Up until 2005, decisions about how to market and advertise Audis in Canada were made in the United States. Canada was nothing more than a sales region in North America. That all changed recently, when a new organization structure and corporate plan were introduced. In late 2005, a key management group landed in Toronto to establish an on-the-ground Canadian management presence.

Under the former style of management marketing, the Audi brand in Canada was a classic lift-and-adapt exercise. Little attention was paid to market differentiation. Now, the Canadian managers make sure their products and marketing plans fit with Canadian tastes and lifestyles.

One of the first changes was the hiring of Lowe Roche, a Canadian advertising agency. At the time Audi was launching the TT sports car. Rather than recommending the traditional mass media to launch the TT, the agency went with stunt-like executions that created a lot of buzz for the car. Vast TTs—as in the letters— were mowed into green fields, and enormous TTs were erected in streetscapes. Traditional forms of targeted print advertising followed the initial buzz campaign.

As Geoffrey Roche explains, "The top job for us is to polish the entire Audi brand while drawing as much attention as possible to each car." The TT campaign delivered a differentiated message. The heart of the communications is the design of the cars. According to Roche, "There's a strong design language that carries through every single car. You understand you're looking at an Audi."

Just recently the Audi Q5, a crossover vehicle, was launched. The marketing communications objective was to clearly position the Q5 as a smart alternative to all other upscale crossover vehicles. The Q5 was arriving late to the party—Volvo, BMW, Range Rover, and Mercedes Benz were already established.

In devising the advertising strategy, the Roche team went back to the design of the vehicle—they would set the sleek and sexier lines of the Audi Q5 against the boxy-style competitors. The target would quickly see that the Q5 was a different automobile. In the creative execution, the entire class of competition was portrayed as a box on wheels. Curious consumers would read ad copy saying "don't buy another box."

The media plan included newspapers, magazines, out-of-home, and "stunt" cardboard SUVs placed on streets and parking lots. A very unique advertising idea was implemented on elevator doors in targeted office buildings in Toronto, Montreal, and Vancouver. The elevator doors displayed a cardboard car with the word "boxy" standing as the only piece of ad copy. When the doors opened, an image of the sleek and sexy Q5 appeared on the back wall bearing the powerfully contrasting word "foxy." Message delivered! Billboard executions used similar words: guzzle–sip; compensating–captivating; has corners–hugs corners. Various differentiating features were clearly communicated in the ads.

The results? Audi management is thrilled. Despite a rather messy economy (2009) Audi sales overall are up 11 percent over last year, and the Q5 is back ordered—the demand for the Q5 exceeds what Audi is able to supply to Canada.

Adapted from Jennifer Wells, "Thinking about the box," *The Globe and Mail*, June 12, 2009, p. B6.

- Attracting new target markets to the product.
- Engaging consumers with the brand or brand experience.
- Offering incentives to get people to buy the product.
- Creating goodwill and fostering a positive public image (usually for a company).
- Creating leads for follow-up at a later date.
- Motivating distributors to carry the product.

To demonstrate communications objectives, let's continue with the Dasani example initially presented in the "Marketing Objectives" section. Dasani is a firmly established and well-known brand, so awareness objectives are not relevant. However, here are some examples of other marketing communications objectives Dasani might identify:

- To achieve a brand preference score of 40 percent among primary buyers of bottled water products.

- To achieve a trial purchase rate of 20 percent among competitive brand users by offering incentives that encourage brand switching.

- To alter consumers' perceptions about the brand's image so that potential users perceive Dasani to be an innovative product and market leader.

These objectives imply that marketing communications will be an integrated effort including activities beyond advertising. For certain, sales promotions (both consumer and trade), public relations, and Internet communications will be employed. Advertising and sales promotions will satisfy the first two objectives, and public relations and Internet communications will satisfy the third objective. A brand such as Dasani uses many components of the marketing communications mix to retain its position in the marketplace relative to Aqauafina and other brands.

MARKETING COMMUNICATIONS STRATEGIES

The marketing communications strategy provides a basic outline of how the various components of the mix will be used. As indicated by the Dasani example, all components may not be used, but those that are used are often ranked in terms of priority and what they are able to achieve.

This section of the strategy also identifies the budget allocated to marketing communications and how funds will be allocated to the various activities. What percentage of the budget will be allocated to advertising, to sales promotions, to experiential marketing, and so on?

ADVERTISING PLAN The **advertising plan** is divided into two primary areas: creative (message) and media. The **creative plan** is concerned with what message will be communicated and how it will be communicated to the target market. The message usually stresses the most important attribute of the product—that which is most important to the customer. Where claims of performance are made, proper substantiation is provided. That hints at the "how" aspect of creative planning. Agencies draw on such techniques as humour, sex, emotions, and even facts to tempt us to buy something. To illustrate, consider the ad for JM that appears in Figure 2.14. A sexual appeal technique certainly draws attention to the ad and the brand name. JM markets underwear and swimwear. Complete details about creative planning are presented in Chapter 4.

The **media plan** involves strategic decisions about what media to use and how much money to invest in the media that are chosen. The overall goal of any media plan is efficiency: the plan must effectively reach the target audience at the lowest possible cost. Since a company invests considerable sums in media advertising, wise decisions about usage are critical. Other media decisions involve timing, what markets to advertise in, how much money to allocate to regional markets and to key markets (cities), how long the campaign should last, and so on. Developing a media plan is complicated and best left to media specialists. More details about media planning for mass media options are presented in Chapter 5.

advertising plan
A plan that includes creative and media components.

creative plan
A plan that outlines the nature of the message to be communicated to the target audience; involves the development of creative objectives, creative strategies, and creative execution.

media plan
A strategy that outlines the relevant details about how a client's budget will be spent; involves decisions about what media to use and how much money to invest in the media chosen to reach the target audience effectively and efficiently.

FIGURE 2.14   A sexual appeal technique grabs the reader's attention quickly

sport classic
www.jm.ca

DIRECT RESPONSE Plan Direct response communications have a significant advantage over traditional mass media advertising: the direct results of the investment can be determined. The fact that direct response techniques can be accurately measured for success or failure makes them attractive to companies that stress accountability in their operations. It has taken considerable time for large companies to adopt direct response techniques. The negative image of direct mail advertising, for example, formerly made such a technique unattractive. Advancing technology, database marketing practices, and customer relationship management programs have fostered interest in marketing and communicating directly to individuals. Now all forms of direct response are popular. More details about direct response communications are included in Chapter 6.

INTERACTIVE COMMUNICATIONS PLAN The Internet is a fast-growing medium for placing advertising messages or for placing important messages about a company or brand at a corporate website. What about a video on YouTube? If it goes viral, millions of views are a possibility, though that is the exception, not the rule! Many online consumers still perceive online advertising to be an intrusion, forgetting that the Internet is a medium much like television or newspapers. As consumers spend more time online, the commercial aspects of the Internet will become more acceptable. Certainly among youth, the Internet is becoming the medium of choice for personal communications.

Among the communications alternatives available to companies wanting to advertise online are banner ads in a variety of formats, sponsorships at websites where a target market congregates, and email correspondence. Other interactive options include text and video messaging through mobile telephones. Interactive communications strategies are discussed in more detail in Chapter 7.

SALES PROMOTION PLAN Sales promotions concentrate on reaching and influencing consumers, trade customers (distributors), and a company's sales force. Funds allocated to promotion strategies are traditionally divided between consumer promotions and trade promotions. Consumer promotions focus on objectives such as encouraging trial purchase, repeat purchase, or simply getting customers to buy a product in greater quantity. Refer to Figure 2.15 for an illustration of a promotion incentive designed to achieve trial and repeat purchases.

Trade promotions are designed to encourage merchandising and marketing support among distributors. Getting a product listed and on the store shelves of major

FIGURE 2.15   Manufacturers offer incentives to encourage trial and repeat purchases

Source: Photo by Keith J. Tuckwell.

supermarkets, for example, requires offering financial incentives to retailers such as Safeway, Sobeys, Loblaws, and others. In Canada, prominent retailers have significant clout with manufacturers, and as a result, considerable sums are spent on trade promotions each year. Sales promotion planning is discussed in detail in Chapter 8.

PUBLIC RELATIONS PLAN Public relations involve communicating with various groups beyond customers. For example, companies communicate with governments, prospective shareholders, the financial community, the media, and community groups. Typically, the goal of such communications is to enhance the company's public image. Public relations can be either corporate oriented or product oriented. At the corporate level, public relations are an important communications tool in times of crisis that show the public what the company is doing to resolve the crisis. PR can also be used to tell the public about the positive things a company is doing, for example, creating awareness of its environmental programs.

In a product sense, public relations play a role in generating interest in new products or spreading "news" about an existing product. Such communications are designed to secure media support for newsworthy information. The nature of public relations is such that written or broadcast news about a company or its products can be of more value. A third-party endorsement through public relations can have greater impact on consumers than advertising. Unlike advertising, public relations are an "unpaid" form of communications for the most part. For that reason alone, PR's usefulness must be exploited. The role and impact of public relations are presented in detail in Chapter 9.

EXPERIENTIAL MARKETING Engaging consumers in a brand experience is becoming a popular option for marketing and marketing communications managers. Participating in planned events hosted by others (say a sponsorship opportunity) or creating and implementing a unique branded event gets the target market more actively involved with a brand. Careful planning is needed if the organization is to achieve maximum value from the event. A variety of communications elements must be built into the plan to show how the event will be supported. All of this information is documented in the communications plan. Experiential marketing planning is presented in Chapter 10.

PERSONAL SELLING Plan Personal selling plays a key role in marketing, especially in business-to-business market situations. As indicated earlier, personal selling techniques create desire and action. The role of a sales representative is to present the benefits of products and show how they resolve a customer's problem. The sales representative is also responsible for presenting the marketing and merchandising support plans to distributors who resell the company's products. In this regard, there is a direct link to the media advertising, trade promotion, consumer promotion, event marketing, and sponsorship components of the marketing communications plan. Customers must be made aware of all activities that will potentially influence sales.

A sales manager directs the activities of the sales department and is responsible for setting sales objectives that are part of the marketing communications plan. The sales manager is also responsible for developing the sales strategies and tactics that will be employed by the sales representatives. Personal selling is discussed in more detail in Chapter 11.

MEASURING AND EVALUATING MARKETING COMMUNICATIONS

The final step in the marketing and marketing communications planning process involves measurement and evaluation. It is essential that an organization monitor all programs to distinguish effective activities from ineffective activities. There's a famous expression about marketing planning and budgeting: "50 percent of my budget works and 50 percent doesn't work. But I don't know which is which." Yes, a lot of marketing decisions are made on instinct, but many more are based on hard and fast measurements.

In marketing communications, some activities are difficult to measure and very often too much burden is placed on communications. It is such a visible aspect of marketing that it is convenient for senior managers to be critical of it. Each element of marketing communications should be accountable for what it can accomplish. If it is advertising, awareness scores can be measured; if it's public relations, brand mentions in the press may be a means of measuring success; if sales promotion, the number of entries in a contest may be a useful measure. Each component can be measured and evaluated in unique and different ways. This topic is discussed in detail in Chapter 12.

⟫ SUMMARY

Strategic planning is an integrated process that involves developing plans at three different levels of an organization. The planning process is cyclical and is subject to constant change based on conditions in the marketplace. To stay on top of things, an organization monitors the economy, competitive activity, social and demographic changes, technology, and laws and regulations.

A marketing communications plan (its direction and content) is influenced by a marketing plan and a corporate plan. When one plan is complete, it provides direction to the next plan. Planning usually starts with the corporate plan, a document prepared by senior executives. Corporate planning starts with the development of a mission statement followed by corporate objectives and strategies. When deciding upon a strategy, the organization evaluates its marketing strength, degree of competition, financial resources, research and development capabilities, and management expertise.

Marketing planning involves analyzing, planning, implementing, and controlling marketing initiatives. The plan revolves around the customer and includes a precise description of the target based on demographic, psychographic, and geographic characteristics; a sound positioning strategy statement; and clearly worded objectives, strategies, and tactics.

The marketing communications plan identifies the various communications objectives for the year and the strategies that will be employed to achieve them. The plan is subdivided into specific areas, depending on which components of the mix will be employed. The advertising plan focuses on creative and media decisions. In the creative plan, objectives and strategies (what to say and how to say it) are identified. The media plan states the media objectives by identifying the target market, how often its members should be reached, and when they should be reached. The media strategies rationalize the use of media alternatives and provide detailed information about how the budget is allocated.

If the plan is an integrated plan, other components of the mix are included. Depending on the situation a brand or company faces, the plan could include sales promotion, public relations, experiential marketing, direct response communications, interactive communications, and personal selling. Objectives, strategies, and tactics for each are included in the plan. The goal is to have a unified plan—all forms of marketing communications delivering a single message to a target market in a convincing manner.

KEY TERMS

acquisition strategy, 43
advertising plan, 57
contingency plan, 44
corporate objective, 41
corporate plan, 40
corporate strategy, 31
creative plan, 57
direct competition, 33
divestment strategy, 42
indirect competition, 33
marketing communications plan, 54

marketing control, 53
marketing objective, 50
marketing plan, 40
marketing planning, 44
marketing strategy, 52
media plan, 57
mission statement, 41
monopolistic competition, 33
new product development strategy, 43
objectives, 31

oligopoly, 33
penetration strategy, 43
positioning, 48
positioning strategy statement, 48
strategic alliance, 44
strategic planning, 31
strategies, 31
subculture, 36
SWOT analysis, 45
tactics (execution), 31
target market, 44

REVIEW QUESTIONS

1. What are the external trends and conditions that should be considered when commencing a new planning cycle?

2. What are the key components of a corporate plan? What guidelines does the corporate plan provide to operational plans such as marketing and marketing communications?

3. What is a mission statement and what role does it play in planning?

4. Identify and briefly explain the four variables or characteristics for describing a target market.

5. What role does a positioning strategy statement play in developing a marketing strategy?

6. "Marketing strategies are the master plans for achieving objectives." What does this statement mean?

7. What is the difference between marketing strategy and marketing execution?

8. What is meant by marketing control and how does it influence marketing planning?

9. What are the essential decision areas for a creative plan and a media plan?

10. What is the relationship between the various components of an integrated marketing communications plan?

DISCUSSION AND APPLICATION QUESTIONS

1. "Marketing communications objectives are diverse by nature, but a good campaign must have a specific focus." What does this mean?

2. Evaluate the marketing situation for the following companies. What makes them unique and what is their differential advantage(s) compared to their primary competitors? Develop a positioning strategy statement for each company based on your assessment of the situation.

   a) Canadian Tire
   b) Best Buy
   c) Roots

3. Using a variety of online sources, conduct a market analysis for a branded product of your choosing. The market analysis should include the following information:

   a) market size and growth
   b) importance of regional markets
   c) market segment analysis (which segments are growing, declining, etc.)
   d) seasonal analysis

   What conclusions can you draw from your analysis?

4. Compare and contrast the marketing communications strategies of two competing brands (a brand leader and a brand challenger). Do these brands use all elements of the marketing communications mix or do they selectively use only certain elements? What conclusions can you draw based on your analysis of each brand? Some brands to consider might be

a) Coca-Cola and Pepsi-Cola

b) Nike and Adidas

c) Dove soap and Olay soap

5. Analyze the marketing communications strategies for an automobile (car or truck) of your choosing. Based on the images portrayed in any and all forms of marketing communications, describe in detail the target market that the automobile is pursuing and the positioning strategy of the brand. Provide a profile based on demographic, psychographic, and geographic characteristics. The IMC Highlight: **Differentiation Key to Audi's Canadian Success** will give you some insight into automobile advertising.

ENDNOTES

1. "Portrait of the Canadian Population in 2006: Highlights," Statistics Canada, www.statcan.gc.ca.

2. Ibid.

3 "Married couples with children a shrinking group," *The Globe and Mail*, September 13, 2007, p. L1.

4. Eve Lazarus, "The Cultural Connection," *Marketing*, August 25, 2005, p. 15.

5 "List of Canadians of Asian Ancestry," Wikipedia, www.wikipedia.org/wiki/Asian_Canadian.

6 "Income of Canadians," The Daily, May 3, 2007, Statistics Canada, www.statcan.gc.ca/daily.

7. Bill Alpert, "Cell phones may bite off Apple," *Financial Post*, June 27, 2005, p. FP7.

8. Jennifer Wells, ""Brands on the run: RIM tops the lot," *The Globe and Mail*, June 16, 2008, pp. B1, B5.

9. Philip Kotler, *A Framework for Marketing Management*, 2nd ed. (Upper Saddle River, NJ: Prentice-Hall, 2003), p. 104.

10. Johnathan Thaw, "Google buys YouTube for $1.65 billion, grabs lead in web videos," *Bloomberg News*, October 10, 2006, www.bloomberg.com.

11. Barrie McKenna, "Nike shifts from the rink to the soccer pitch," *The Globe and Mail*, October 24, 2007, p. B3.

12. "Nissan, Chrysler to make vehicles for each other," *The Globe and Mail*, April 15, 2008, p. B12.

13. "Money Hog," an advertorial appearing in the *National Post*, Driver's Edge Section, January 3, 2002, p. D011.

14. "Top 10 Bottled Water Brands," *Advertising Age*, June 23, 2008, p. S-12.

CHAPTER

3

Branding Strategy

Yoshikazu Tsuno/AFP/Getty Images

Learning Objectives

After studying this chapter, you will be able to

1. Describe the concept of branding and the role it plays in marketing communications and other business-building programs

2. Identify the various components of a brand

3. Describe the benefits of branding for organizations and consumers

4. Characterize the various stages of brand loyalty

5. Describe the role and importance of brand positioning and its relationship to marketing communications plans

6. Explain various brand positioning strategies commonly used in marketing communications

7. Describe the role and influence of packaging and product design in the brand-building process

Think of marketing and marketing communications as a loop. The loop starts somewhere and ends somewhere, but exactly where? Well, it starts with the brand and ends with the brand. Marketing and marketing communications programs create awareness for the brand (the start of the loop). All kinds of messages are sent to consumers through a variety of touch-points such as packaging, personal selling, events, promotions, news articles, advertising, and even blogs published by everyday people. Collectively, these messages heighten the interest and desire for the brand. While all this is happening, competing brands are doing the same thing. The goal for all brands is to get the consumer to buy their brand. The consumer is now standing in front of a store shelf looking at all the different brands. Which one does he or she buy? The customer takes action and places one brand in the shopping cart. Which one? The loop just closed.

What this loop principle suggests is that every form of communication is going to have some kind of impact. The impact of the message and its ability to stimulate action are determined by what a brand has to offer (e.g., a compelling reason why someone should buy it) and the convincing way in which the message is delivered to potential customers. Essentially, the brand offering and the message communicated to consumers form the backbone of brand strategy and positioning strategy. This chapter provides insights into how brand strategy and positioning strategy are developed and shows the influence of marketing communications in developing a relationship between the customer and the brand. Communications is the glue that holds or binds the customer to the brand.[1]

Defining the Brand

Just what is a brand? A **brand** is a name, term, design, symbol, or any other feature that identifies one seller's good or service as distinct from those of other sellers. The legal term for brand is trademark. A brand may identify one item, a family of items, or all items of that seller.[2]

In today's hypercompetitive marketing environment, branding is a hot button. Marketing executives are busy trying to find or build their brand essence, brand architecture, or brand DNA. Maybe it's a little overdone! That said, brands and branding have been around for centuries; only recently has the concept worked its way into everyday conversation.

Marketing communications in any form have an impact on how customers perceive a brand. It seems that a brand is more than just a tangible product. It can embrace

brand
An identifying mark, symbol, word or words, or combination of mark and words that separates one product from another product; can also be defined as the sum of all tangible and intangible characteristics that make a unique offer to customers.

intangible characteristics as well. Customer perceptions of brands are largely based on the brand name and what it stands for. It is an image they hold of a brand over an extended period and that image is based on what they have learned about the brand. For example, a brand such as Rolex suggests a certain quality or status. A potential buyer does not have to question the quality of the watch; he or she is buying the image and reputation of the watch, created by marketing communications over a long period. Refer to the image in Figure 3.1. Consumers perceive Apple differently from the PCs it competes with. Apple is a contemporary, user-friendly seller of computers, portable music, and cell phones. Their comparison ads with the Mac guy and the PC guy aptly portray the "simple to use" image of the brand.

As indicated by the definition of a brand, there are elements beyond the name that contribute to a brand's image. These elements working together help differentiate one brand from the others that are available to customers. Let's take a closer look at the components of a brand.

The **brand name** is the part of the brand that can be spoken. It may consist of a word, letter, or group of words and letters. Nike, Rolex, Gatorade, WD-40, eBay, Tide, and Google are all brand names. Brand names are usually presented with their own unique font style. For example, Coca-Cola appears in a stylized font on all bottles, cans, and other forms of marketing communications. The presentation of the name is consistent at all times.

brand name
That part of a brand that can be spoken.

FIGURE 3.1

Messages for Rolex project a high-quality image; Rolex is often portrayed as a status symbol.

Source: Reprinted by permission of Rolex Canada Ltd.

Some kind of **symbol**, referred to as a **brand logo**, also plays a key role in branding and creating an image. When marketing communications work effectively, consumers can quickly identify a brand logo or associate a logo with a brand. With Apple, it's an apple with a bite taken out of it. With Nike it's a swoosh. A recent research study indicates that 97 percent of American citizens recognize Nike's swoosh logo. From a marketing perspective, you couldn't ask for anything more. However, so ubiquitous is the logo that it represents both positive and negative images. On the positive side Nike is known as an innovator offering high-performance products. On the negative side Nike represents two social ills: the commercialization of sports and the globalization of capitalism.[3] That's not good for business and gives meaning to the need for effective marketing communications.

> **brand logo (symbol)**
> A symbol that plays a key role in branding and creating an image.

The **design** of the product or package, along with a colour scheme, also plays a role in creating brand image. Coca-Cola has a unique bottle design and a red cap. Its canned beverage is red in color. In contrast, the dominant colour for Pepsi-Cola is blue. Brands protect their properties by trademark. A **trademark** is that part of a brand that is granted legal protection so that only the owner can use it. The symbol ™ designates trademark claims. The ® symbol is used when the trademark has not only been claimed, but registered with the government trademarks office. Trademarks can include the brand names and symbols described above. "Coke"®, "Coca-Cola"®, the unique style in which these names are printed, and the bottle design are registered trademarks of the Coca-Cola Company. For a selection of famous brand logos refer to Figure 3.2.

> **trademark**
> A brandmark or other brand element that is granted legal protection so that only the owner can use it.

What to name a brand is a critical decision. Consequently, companies spend considerable amounts of time and money developing and testing brand names. When you think of it, virtually every marketing activity undertaken revolves around the brand name. It has to be distinctive and meaningful. It has to be the right name. What to name a product involves a creative decision and a strategic decision.

Brand names come in many different forms. They can be based on people (Calvin Klein and Tommy Hilfiger), places (Air France and Air Canada), animals (Mustang and Dove), inherent product meaning (Ticketmaster and Lean Cuisine), product attributes (Bounty paper towels and DieHard batteries), or they can be completely made up to simply sound scientific or attractive. For example, Sony has family names like Bravia for HD-TVs, Cyber-shot for its cameras, Handycams for its camcorders, and PlayStation for its video console.

Brands are more than just a tangible product. A company adds other dimensions that differentiate it in some way from other products designed to meet the same need. These differences may be rational and tangible, or they may be emotional or intangible entities related to what the brand represents. Through marketing communications, the "personality" of a brand evolves, and the combination of brand attributes (tangibles) and brand personality (intangibles) is what influences brand choices by consumers. The

FIGURE 3.2

A Selection of Famous Brand Logos

key for any brand is to be perceived as offering something unique. You could probably name at least 10 different brands of deodorant. Why does one person buy Gillette, another Mennen, another Right Guard, another Axe, and so on?

When it comes to branding, you would think that a company with the heritage that the Hudson's Bay Company possesses would be an expert. Surprisingly, and for a variety of reasons, Hudson's Bay recently completed a branding exercise that saw its corporate identity change. In a market where stores like Walmart and Sears compete directly with each other, the stakes are high. Previously, Hudson's Bay referred to itself as HBC, but that acronym said little about the company. Was it a TV station? Was it a bank?

Moving forward, the company redesigned its corporate logo to reflect its heritage and quality. The new logo is a modernized version of the company's original crest and features stripes in the colours of the original Hudson's Bay blanket—green, red, yellow, and blue. The cleaner, modern look of the branded name and logo is an attempt to stay relevant in today's competitive shopping environment.[4]

Brand Image and Reputation

Brands are more than physical products and services. Whenever and wherever a consumer is choosing between alternatives, brands play a role in the decision-making process. While brands provide customers with an assurance of quality, they also express a set of values that customers can identify with. The Coca-Cola brand is more than just a sweet-tasting soft drink; it carries a set of American values that strike a chord with consumers all over the world. Similarly, a brand like Virgin represents a youthful, rebellious attitude, much like that of Virgin's maverick founder, Richard Branson.[5]

Marketing communications play a key role in building a brand's image and reputation. A good reputation just doesn't happen—it is the end result of a consistent approach to marketing and marketing communications over an extended period. According to a 2009 reputation survey, the brand with the best reputation among Canadians is Google (2009 *Marketing*/Leger Corporate Reputation Survey). Google is a brand that people recognize, trust, and appreciate. Google deserves special status among brands as its name has been turned into a verb. We don't do Internet searches anymore. We "Google" it. Google is the Kleenex of Internet search tools. What is the key to Google's brand status? Google spends an incredible amount of time, energy, and resources putting out products that ultimately make life easier for consumers.[6]

Canadian Tire is another brand with a solid reputation among Canadian consumers. Canadian Tire has withstood incredible competitive pressure from big American retailers like Home Depot and Walmart. It is an innovative company that experiments with new ways of providing value to its customers and as a result remains a leader in general merchandise and hardware retailing. For a list of the top brands in Canada by reputation, see Figure 3.3.

There are times and circumstances when an organization embarks on a rebranding strategy. Such was the case when Metro (a prominent Quebec-based grocery store chain) decided to rebrand all of its Dominion, A&P, The Barn, Loeb, and Ultra supermarkets in Ontario into Metro stores. For more insight into this branding challenge see the visual image in Figure 3.4 and read the IMC Highlight: **Five Brands Hop on to Metro Banner**.

brand loyalty
The degree of attachment to a particular brand expressed by a consumer. There are three stages of brand loyalty: brand recognition, brand preference, and brand insistence.

BRAND LOYALTY

Brand loyalty is defined as the degree of consumer attachment to a particular brand. Loyalty is influenced by such factors as marketing communications (what is said about

Rank 2009	Company	Survey Score	% Good Opinion	% Bad Opinion	Rank 2008
1	Google	91	92.6	1.7	—
2	Sony	83	87.3	4.3	3
3	Tim Hortons	83	89.9	7.4	2
4	President's Choice	83	87.5	5.0	—
5	Shoppers Drug Mart	79	85.8	4.5	6
6	Staples Business Depot	79	84.8	5.5	1
7	Panasonic	79	82.4	5.1	5
8	Kraft	78	86.0	7.8	8
9	Toyota	77	80.2	2.9	10
10	Canadian Tire	77	86.1	9.1	4

FIGURE 3.3

Canada's Brand Leaders by Reputation

Source: Courtesy of Rogers Publishing Limited and Leger Marketing. 2009 Corporate Reputation Survey published in *Marketing*, May 18, 2009, pp. 11-15. The rankings are based on a survey of 1500. Canadians and are representative of the Canadian population.

FIGURE 3.4 Metro undertakes a major rebranding strategy in Ontario

Source: Photo by Keith J. Tuckwell.

IMC HIGHLIGHT

Five Brands Hop on to Metro Banner

In September 2008, Metro Inc., the Quebec-based supermarket, launched a $200-million marketing and advertising campaign to rebrand its five Ontario grocery chains. Metro acquired the Ontario chains in 2005. By the end of 2009, Dominion, A&P, The Barn, Loeb, and Ultra Food & Drug stores would display the Metro name. Such a change is a huge undertaking for an organization.

According to VP Marketing Serge Boulanger, "extensive research preceded the branding switch so that any new branding effort would meet the needs of Ontario consumers." The research revealed that shoppers were well acquainted with the Dominion and A&P banners, but they didn't understand the difference between those stores and other grocers in Ontario. Boulanger saw this as an opportunity to introduce the new name and to clearly differentiate Metro from competitors.

Dumping well-known names like A&P and Dominion is risky; the other three are less prominent in the province. But in pure marketing terms the decision was an easy one, "There's synergy managing just one brand instead of five," says Boulanger. "It's cost effective on both the marketing and operations sides of the business."

One key piece of research solidified the decision to go with one banner. Apparently Ontario shoppers are more loyal to location than brand. If the nearest store is doing the job, why go elsewhere? With one banner Metro stores would have a strong presence in the province. As well, when it came to a name, "Metro" tested well with consumers. They saw it as fresh, modern, and urban—a desirable image to have and something the company could work with when devising new message strategies.

A key aspect of the rebranding was a new decor that would better facilitate a variety of changes to products and services, including five key differentiators—home meal replacements, bakery, meat, floral, and private brands. Other aspects of the rebranding involved internal and external marketing communications, new signage, training employees, and uniforms.

To more accurately evaluate consumer reaction to the planned changes, test stores were introduced in four locations—Whitby, Collingwood, Picton, and Gananoque. The test markets were successful and revealed Ontario consumers want the same things as Quebec consumers. They are looking for value and a good in-store experience.

From a communications perspective, the tagline "Food at its best" was developed by Cossette Communications, Metro's ad agency. According to Belanger, "It's clear, it's short, and it shows how the Metro banner wants to support the consumer." A second tagline, a play on words, "A store is born," illustrates that Metro wants to be the star of the industry.

The initial communications launch was in Toronto and involved an integrated media campaign that included television, print, out-of-home, direct mail, experiential marketing, and public relations. Among the executions were GO trains (commuter trains) wrapped with Metro banners, an out-of-home splash on bus shelters and billboards, street squads complete with shopping carts that gave out product samples, and direct mailings to homes in areas where stores were located. Full-page newspaper ads in the *Toronto Star* and *The Globe and Mail* announced store openings. Radio station CHFI did remotes at store level to encourage shoppers to visit.

What lies ahead? Boulanger is very satisfied with the transition in Ontario but his long-term vision is to make Metro a national banner. Through acquisition and rebranding, Metro will become a true national brand.

Adapted from Emily Wexler, "All Aboard!" *Strategy*, December 2008, pp. 15-17, and Jeromy Lloyd, "Metro begins to rebrand Ontario grocery stores," *Marketing Daily*, September 29, 2008, **www.marketingmag.ca**.

a brand), family or peer pressure, friendship with a salesperson, and ultimately how satisfied a person is with the product. For example, someone intending to buy a new car might return to the same dealer and person he or she has bought from before. Satisfaction based on experience with that individual and product helps build loyalty.

Brand loyalty is measured in three distinct stages: brand recognition, brand preference, and brand insistence (see Figure 3.5).[7]

In the early stage of a brand's life, the marketing objective is to create **brand recognition**. It is imperative to communicate the brand name, the unique selling point, and what the product looks like (e.g., the package if it is a consumer good, or the look and style if it is a shopping good such as an automobile or appliance). A marketing communications campaign plays a key role here.

brand recognition
Customer awareness of the brand name and package.

When a brand achieves the status of **brand preference**, it is on a short list of brand alternatives that the consumer will consider buying. Such a position is good because consumers only retain a select group of brand names in their minds for any product category. Furthermore, it is an indication that the message strategies and other marketing strategies are working; the customer knows something about the brand, has evaluated it in relation to his or her needs, and will purchase it if available when it is needed.

brand preference
The situation where a brand is perceived as an acceptable alternative by a customer and will be purchased if it is available.

At the **brand insistence** stage, a consumer will search the market extensively for a particular brand. No alternatives are acceptable, and if the brand is not available the consumer will likely postpone the purchase until it is. Such an enviable position shows the type of bond that can develop between a brand and a consumer.

brand insistence
A situation where the consumer searches the market for the specific brand.

As suggested earlier, consumers want consistent quality from their brands. The famous Coca-Cola marketing debacle of 1985 confirms how brand insistence works. Coca-Cola made the decision to replace Coca-Cola with a new formula. When the change was implemented, the backlash from customers was so swift and strong that the company had to bring back the original formula under the name Coca-Cola Classic. The Classic designation has just recently been removed from the brand name. Some critics insist that Coca-Cola is a brand that has gone beyond brand insistence. So strong is the bond with consumers, the product cannot be changed—ever.

Since one of the tasks of marketing is to keep customers loyal, smart companies plan and implement loyalty programs. Retailers such as Canadian Tire, Costco, and Choice Hotels, to name only a few, have their own rewards programs. More than 15.4 million people in Canada collect AIR MILES, a figure that represents more than 72 percent of Canadian households. AIR MILES has more than 100 sponsors across the country where consumers can earn points.[8] Loyalty-oriented marketing programs are presented in Chapter 8.

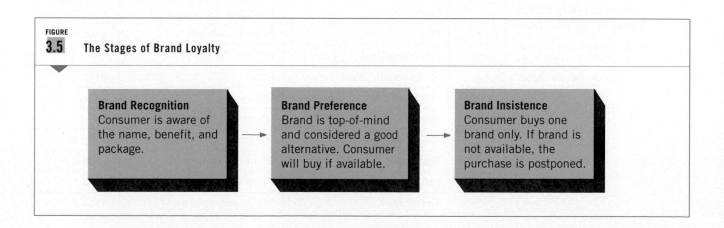

FIGURE 3.5   The Stages of Brand Loyalty

Brand Recognition
Consumer is aware of the name, benefit, and package.

→

Brand Preference
Brand is top-of-mind and considered a good alternative. Consumer will buy if available.

→

Brand Insistence
Consumer buys one brand only. If brand is not available, the purchase is postponed.

Brand-insistent consumers often become advocates for the brand—they like the brand so much they will openly recommend it to others. As discussed in Chapter 1, a word-of-mouth network is a powerful communications tool that influences buying decisions. To illustrate, many users of Apple computers are advocates. They often belong to Mac user groups (MUGs) and frequently end up in "religious wars" with PC users. The same can be said of owners of Harley-Davidson motorcycles, commonly known as HOGs. To Harley owners, there is no other kind of motorcycle. Over 1 million riders strong, HOG is the biggest strength of the brand.

BRAND EQUITY

brand equity
The value (monetary or otherwise) of a brand to its owners; influenced by brand name awareness, degree of customer loyalty, perceived quality, etc.

Brand equity is a confusing term that has been historically defined in different ways for different purposes. For our purposes, **brand equity** is defined as the value a consumer derives from a brand over and above the value derived from the physical attributes. Equity is influenced by several variables: brand name awareness, the degree of loyalty expressed by customers, perceived quality, and the brand's association with a certain attribute. When Canadian brands are ranked on these criteria, some familiar names pop up—Cirque du Soleil, Ski-Doo, CBC, Roots, and Toronto Maple Leafs (apologies to the fans of other Canadian hockey teams).

Brand equity can also be expressed in monetary terms, for a brand is an asset of an organization, and therefore has some tangible financial value. Brands such as Coca-Cola, Microsoft, Nokia, Toyota, and Google typically appear among the leaders when measured in financial terms. In fact, Coca-Cola is consistently ranked the world's leading brand with a value of US$66.7 billion.[9] When Canadian brands are ranked on this basis a different set of names emerge. Among the leaders are BlackBerry, RBC, TD Canada Trust, and Shoppers Drug Mart. For a list of Canada's top 10 brands by financial rank see Figure 3.6. BlackBerry, the portable digital communications device marketed by Research in Motion, is the North American leader in its product category.

Effective marketing and marketing communications strategies play a key role in building a brand's equity. To demonstrate, when the Royal Bank changed its name to RBC Financial Group in 2001 it did so for a good reason. One of the bank's objectives was to have a stronger brand outside Canada. With the change in name and a completely new marketing communications strategy, the bank transformed itself based on a message of trust—a concept that is the cornerstone of financial sector branding. The trust message is visible in its advertising where the interest of the customer is always the priority.[10]

FIGURE **3.6**	Rank 2008	Brand	Sector	Brand Value (C$Million)
Canada's Leading Brands Ranked by Financial Value	1	Blackberry	Consumer Electronics	5607.7
	2	RBC	Financial Services	4141.1
Source: Adapted from "Best Canadian Brands Ranking 2008," p. 10, www.interbrand.com/images/studies/BestCanadianBrands2008.pdf.	3	TD Canada Trust	Financial Services	3779.6
	4	Shoppers Drug Mart	Retail	3137.5
	5	Petro-Canada	Energy	3132.6
	6	Manulife	Insurance	2550.9
	7	Bell	Telecom	2537.0
	8	Scotiabank	Financial Services	1870.4
	9	Canadian Tire	Retail	1828.5
	10	Tim Hortons	Restaurant	1604.6

THE BENEFITS OF BRANDING

Based on the discussion of various branding issues in the preceding sections, it can be seen that consumers and organizations benefit from branding. Some of the benefits for consumers are as follows:

- Over time, the brand name suggests a certain level of quality. Consumers know what to expect; they trust and have confidence in the brand.

- There can be psychological rewards for possessing certain brands. For example, buying a brand-new BMW automobile might suggest achievement to the owner. The automobile says something about the driver; it expresses his or her self-image.

- Brands distinguish competitive offerings, allowing consumers to make informed decisions based on what a brand stands for. Such brand names as Cup-a-Soup (Lipton), Mr. Clean (Procter & Gamble), and Frosted Flakes (Kellogg) suggest clear messages or benefits about the product.

Over time, a relationship develops between a consumer and the brand; it's like a bond. Consumers offer their trust and loyalty in return for consistent product quality from the brand. A brand is a promise delivered. A brand protects its place in the consumer's mind by keeping its promise.[11]

The issue of trust is very important. Each year *Reader's Digest* commissions a research study conducted by Harris/Decima Research to determine the most trusted brands in various product categories. In the automotive category Toyota was ranked first in the passenger car and SUV categories, Visa led the credit card category, and Duracell was the leader in batteries. Toyota is proud of this accomplishment. Managing director of Toyota Canada Stephen Beatty states, "We're humbled to accept such an important endorsement from Canadians. We know that trust is something you have to earn—and keep. From proven environmental innovations to quality manufacturing that means fewer repair bills, to industry leading resale values, Canadians trust Toyota to deliver real value."[12] Clearly, the brand name Toyota is valued by Canadians, and their trust is the result of a dedicated effort by all operational functions of the company, including marketing and marketing communications. For a list of other trusted brands refer to Figure 3.7.

Brands play a key role and offer numerous benefits to an organization as well. At the operational level, they help staff to plan production runs, maintain inventory counts, and facilitate order processing and delivery. In a marketing context, the key benefits are as follows:

Product Category	Brand
Bank/Credit Union	TD Canada Trust
Cameras	Canon
Credit Card	Visa
Deodorant	Secret
Home Entertainment Equipment	Sony
Paint	Benjamin Moore
Passenger Car Manufacturer	Toyota
Razors	Gillette
Running Shoes	Nike
Shampoo	Head & Shoulders

FIGURE
3.7

Canada's Most Trusted Brands

Source:Canada's Most Trusted Brands, 2009. Survey commissioned by *Reader's Digest*; research conducted by Harris/Decima.

unique selling point (USP)
The primary benefit of a product or service that distinguishes it from its competitors.

- A good brand name communicates the point of difference, or **unique selling point (USP),** and highlights the distinctive value added. A name such as Lean Cuisine, for example, addresses two benefits: "lean" communicates low calories and "cuisine" implies it tastes good. The brand name is meaningful and pleasant sounding.

- Branding allows for the creation and development of an image. For example, Nike suggests an independent spirit. Maytag stands for dependability. For these brands, extensive advertising campaigns have instilled such images in the customer's mind.

- Satisfied customers will make repeat purchases and hopefully remain loyal to the brand. Such loyalty stabilizes market share and provides for certain efficiencies in production and marketing. Reliable estimates of future sales facilitate internal brand planning.

In summary, branding decisions are important decisions. A brand name stands for much more than simply differentiating one brand from another. Decisions about brand name, benefits offered, package design, and the desired image form the foundation for marketing and marketing communications strategies.

Building the Brand

brand manager
An individual assigned responsibility for the development and implementation of marketing programs for a specific product or group of products.

Building a brand (building brand image and equity) is the responsibility of the brand manager (or category manager or marketing manager, depending on a company's organizational structure). A **brand manager** develops and implements the marketing plans for the brands he or she is responsible for. The process of building a brand involves four essential steps (see Figure 3.8 for a visual illustration):

1. Identify and establish brand values and positioning strategy.
2. Plan and implement brand marketing programs.

FIGURE 3.8   The Brand-Building Process

Identify Brand Values and Positioning Strategy	Identify key attributes and benefits. Clearly state what brand will do for customers.
Plan and Implement the Marketing Program	Develop an integrated plan that draws upon key elements of the marketing mix and design and execute the marketing communications mix.
Measure and Evaluate Brand Performance	Evaluate the results against planned objectives, including loyalty, market share, and sales.
Build Brand Loyalty and Brand Equity	Alter, expand, and rejuvenate brands to retain their position in the marketplace.

3. Measure and interpret brand performance.
4. Grow and sustain brand equity (managing a brand through its life cycle).

Since the concept of brand equity has already been discussed, the remaining discussion in this chapter will focus on brand values and positioning, and the development of marketing programs.

ESTABLISHING CORE VALUES AND BRAND POSITIONING

What does a brand stand for? The answer to that question will relate to the core values of a brand. **Core values** are the primary attributes and benefits a brand delivers to the customer. An **attribute** is a descriptive feature; a **benefit** is the value consumers attach to a brand attribute. Very often the core values can be expressed in a very short statement about the brand. Here are a few examples from various product categories:

- Dove tells women to focus on internal beauty and the health of their skin; everyone should be happy with who they are (a self-esteem message). Dove emphasizes an attitude more than the product itself.

- Jergens tells women to "take care of what you wear every day" (your skin). Product-specific attributes focus on moisture-retaining capabilities that leave the skin feeling soft.

The skin-care category is large and very competitive. Every brand has a different means of communicating essentially the same message. They all offer the same proprietary benefit. Some brands focus on psychological benefits, while others focus on product-specific attributes. Each brand takes a different angle on how to communicate the key benefit. That's brand differentiation. With reference to the ad that appears in Figure 3.9, Jergens Ultra Care Lotion communicates how the product helps retain moisture in a person's skin. The visual imagery, which is sensuous yet simple, aptly portrays the usefulness of the product.

At Volvo, the brand situation is quite different. Safety is a fundamental core value. "An automobile is driven by people. Safety is and must be the basic principle of all design work."[13] From a branding perspective, safety is embedded into the Volvo brand, and through ongoing and consistent marketing communications consumers understand what the brand stands for. For BMW, the situation is different again. BMW is a high-performance automobile—the brand's pricing must capture the customer's perception of high-performance value. To accomplish this, BMW makes a direct link between price and the benefit of sector-leading performance and can credibly justify the premium. The BMW brand champions "performance" and as a result the general public perceives differential value versus competing offers.[14] Refer to the advertisement in Figure 3.10 for an illustration.

Brand Positioning Concepts

As discussed in Chapter 2, **positioning** is the selling concept that motivates purchase, or the image that marketers desire a brand to have in the minds of customers. It is a strategy influenced by core brand values and the values offered by competing brands. Simply stated, each brand wants to differentiate itself from competitive offerings. Therefore, positioning involves designing and marketing a product to meet the needs of a target market and creating the appropriate appeals to make the product stand out from the competition in the minds of the target market.

---

core values
The primary attributes and benefits a brand delivers to the customer.

attribute
A descriptive feature of a product.

benefit
The value a customer attaches to a brand attribute.

positioning
The selling concept that motivates purchase, or the image that marketers desire a brand to have in the minds of consumers.

FIGURE
3.9

Brands differentiate by focusing on unique attributes

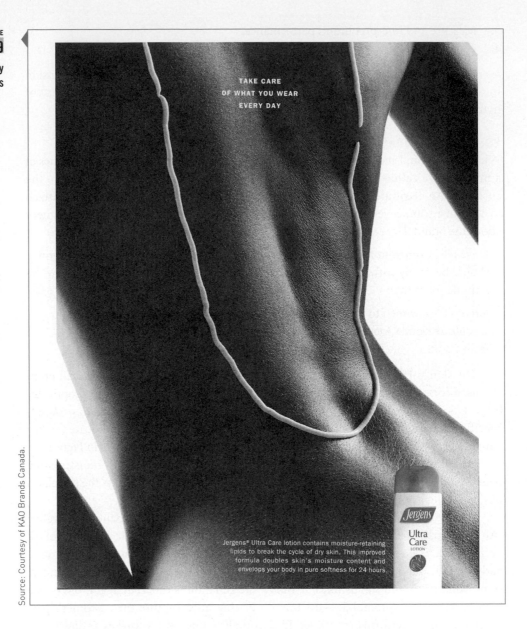

A clearly defined positioning strategy statement provides guidance for all marketing and marketing communications strategies. The strategy statement provides a compelling reason why potential customers should buy the brand. Figure 3.11 illustrates the importance of positioning.

Typically, a brand sticks to a single-benefit positioning strategy, but for many brands and companies the competition is so intense that additional benefits become the focus of marketing communications. For example, Ruffles, the leading brand of potato chips, offers great-tasting chips, but it constantly looks for new innovations to stay a step ahead of its competitors. With reference to Figure 3.12 (page 78), Ruffles launched a thicker ridged chip that will grip more dip in every scoop, an additional benefit since regular chips often break during the scoop. The image in the advertisement aptly portrays the benefit of the new product.

The positioning strategy statement should be clear, concise, and uncomplicated while addressing the target market's need and the primary benefit to be offered. Many experts adopt the 4D positioning rule when devising their strategy statement. A good positioning

FIGURE
3.10

Brand performance justifies a higher price and differentiates BMW from competing brands

FIGURE
3.11   The Importance of Positioning

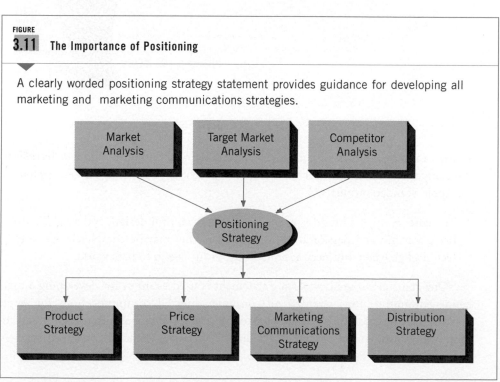

A clearly worded positioning strategy statement provides guidance for developing all marketing and marketing communications strategies.

FIGURE 3.12

An ad that communicates an additional benefit: a thicker chip makes it easier to scoop up chip dip

strategy must be *desirable* by consumers, *distinctive* from the competition, *deliverable* by the company, and *durable* over time. Here is a potential positioning strategy statement for Apple branded products.[15]

> The core of Apple's brand is great innovation, beautiful design, and an ability to bring warmth and passion to those customers who may be completely averse to technical gadgetry, but need it nonetheless to survive in today's world.

One can start to see how such a statement is used as input for developing a marketing communications strategy. All consumer-directed communications for Apple focus on how simple Apple products are to use yet they offer the absolute latest in technical innovation. For additional details on this strategy, see the discussion of head-on positioning which follows in this section.

There are all kinds of ways a product can be positioned in the minds of customers, but typically they relate back to some crucial element of the marketing mix such as product or product differentiation, price (low or high price), or the desired image a brand can create for itself through marketing communications. Let's discuss some of these positioning strategies.

PRODUCT DIFFERENTIATION

Here's what the product is! Here's what the product does! That's product differentiation—nothing could be more straightforward. When a **product differentiation strategy** is employed, the product will communicate meaningful and valued differences to distinguish itself from competitive offerings. Such differences focus specifically on what the product may offer, and refer to the form of the product (size, shape, or physical structure), performance quality (it lasts longer), durability (ability to withstand stress), reliability (it won't break down), or style (the look and appearance of the product or package). Glad food wrap products, for example, consistently differentiate on the basis of how a unique seal keeps things fresh.

No doubt you have tried to spread hard butter on soft bread—it doesn't leave much of a slice! To differentiate itself from other brands of butter, Gay Lea offers a spreadable butter with canola oil. With reference to the illustration in Figure 3.13 (page 80), Gay Lea stops toast brutality—the brand's differential advantage.

product differentiation strategy
A plan of action for communicating meaningful attributes and benefits of a product to a target market.

BRAND LEADERSHIP POSITIONING

As the name suggests, **leadership positioning** is a strategy often employed by brand leaders. Good marketing and marketing strategies from the past have helped such a product achieve an enviable position in the marketplace and in the minds of customers. These brands have high brand equity. The message such a brand delivers is designed to reinforce its lofty position. Probably the best example of leadership positioning is Coca-Cola (formerly Coca-Cola Classic). In most North American markets, Coca-Cola is the number-one brand, and in terms of brand equity, it is recognized as the most valuable brand name globally. In advertising, Coca-Cola struts its stuff. The brand has used phrases such as "Coke is it," "Can't beat the real thing," "Always Coca-Cola," "Life tastes good," and "All the world loves a Coke" to reinforce its position.

Brand leaders have characteristics in common that give them an advantage over competing brands: they have greater consumer awareness, are readily available, and have significant marketing budgets to protect their position. A brand like Tim Hortons, for example, whose positioning strategy is communicated by the phrase "Always fresh... Always Tim Hortons" shares these characteristics. Is any competitor capable of dethroning Tim Hortons? (See Figure 3.14.)

leadership positioning
A marketing strategy in which a product presents itself as a preferred choice among customers.

HEAD-ON POSITIONING (COMPARATIVE POSITIONING)

Head-on positioning involves a comparison of one brand with another. Typically, the brand doing the advertising presents itself as being better than another brand. The message focuses on an attribute that is important to the target market. To dramatize the claim of superiority or whatever the claim may be, it is common to demonstrate how both brands perform. For example, we often see popular brands of household products use head-on positioning strategies. Bounty towels, for example, shows how much water one of its towels can pick up, while a competing brand is shown to be incapable of picking up as much. The Bounty towel still looks partially dry; the competitor's looks saturated. Bounty is well positioned as "the quicker picker upper."

head-on positioning
A marketing strategy in which one product is presented as an equal or better alternative to a competing product.

Source: Gay Lea Foods Co-operative Ltd., 2009 Gay Lea Spreadables Advertising Campaign, www.gaylea.com.

FIGURE
3.13

Butter that is easy to spread is Gay Lea's differential advantage

Apple has built its computer business based on comparisons. The now famous "Get a Mac" campaign shows two male characters (Hello, I'm a Mac, and I'm a PC) sparring over various features of their respective products. Inevitably the PC guy is frustrated by the ease with which the Macintosh computers operate. Different features are compared in different ads, with the Mac always emerging as the winner. Apple's comparison ads are a deliberate attempt to appeal to the vast majority of computer users who have a Windows machine because they aren't aware of an alternative, or because they are nursing some erroneous perceptions about Macs.[16]

INNOVATION POSITIONING

An innovation is a product, service, or idea that is perceived by consumers as new. **Innovation positioning** is a marketing strategy that stresses that newness as a way to

innovation positioning
A marketing strategy that stresses newness (based on a commitment to research and development) as a means of differentiating a company or a brand from competing companies and brands.

Source: Photo by Keith J. Tuckwell.

FIGURE
3.14

Tim Hortons' "Always Fresh" positioning strategy is attractive to customers

differentiate its brand from the competition. Adding oat bran to a breakfast cereal is considered a *continuous innovation* since it only constitutes a small change in the nature of the product. A *discontinuous innovation* is something that has an impact on society and the way we do things. The iPod, for example, altered the way we listen to music. A company that employs innovative strategy uses continuous innovation to stay one step ahead of the competition. Periodically, it will also discover and launch that break-through product that will separate it from competitors. Innovation is a mindset of the company! At Apple, innovations like iPods and the iTunes online music store have liter-ally changed the way in which music is distributed.

In the razor and razor blade market, Gillette, Fusion, and Schick Quattro duel with each other for innovation supremacy. Which brand has the most blades and which brand actually delivers a better shave? The battle is waged in advertising messages show-ing how the various blades perform their function. Schick, for example, says "Clean up with the new Schick Quattro Titanium trimmer. It has four titanium-coated blades, an edging blade and a built-in trimmer in one simple tool." The tagline "Free Your Skin" summarizes the message.

PRICE (VALUE) POSITIONING

A **price positioning** strategy is based on the premise that consumers search for the best possible value given their economic circumstances. Some consumers search for low prices, others are willing to pay more for something perceived as offering good value, and still others don't even look at price. Some people shop for high-end goods and serv-ices and expect to pay a lot for the products they buy.

Walmart seems to have a lock on the low-price positioning strategy in the North American retail marketplace. The store's image is firmly entrenched in the consumer's

price positioning
A marketing strategy based on the premise that consumers search for the best possible value given their economic circumstances.

mind from ads showing prices always being slashed to save people money. Walmart launched a new slogan in 2007: "Save Money. Live Better." With the change, Walmart continued to stress low prices but now showed how people received better value and improvements to their lifestyle. New television ads had more of an emotional tone and showed how saving money on little things adds up and helps families live better.[17]

Another retailing example shows how high-price positioning is also an effective strategy. In men's fashion, Harry Rosen comes to mind. Harry Rosen has survived all kinds of economic and fashion trends over the years and has remained at the high end of the market. The Harry Rosen image has been carefully cultivated over time so that customers know exactly what to expect when they shop there—a quality suit that can cost anywhere from $1500 to $10 500.

Harry Rosen keeps its edge on the competition by carrying many exclusive products and by moving to customer relationship marketing and pitching wares directly to individual customers in mailings and through special events. According to retail consultant John Williams, Harry Rosen is "unique in North America and maybe the world. There's no other chain of high-quality menswear of any significance." Put a bit differently, Larry Rosen (president and son of the founder) states, "A man looks powerful, authoritative, confident and professional in a suit. To get the right suit that man knows where to shop—Harry Rosen.

FIGURE
3.15   A high-price, high-quality positioning strategy works for Harry Rosen

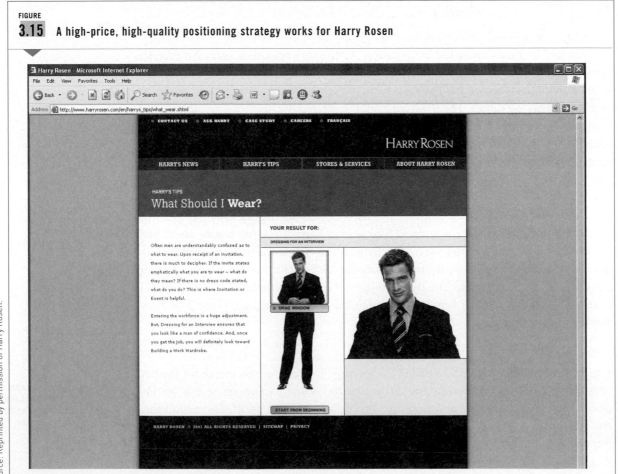

LIFESTYLE (IMAGE) POSITIONING

In very competitive markets where product attributes of so many brands are perceived to be equal by consumers, it is difficult to follow the positioning strategies outlined above. **Lifestyle** or **image positioning** involves moving away from the tangible characteristics of the product toward the intangible characteristics (things that aren't there, for example). Products in categories such as beer, alcohol, perfume, automobiles, and travel frequently use this strategy, as do brands that wish to attract a youthful customer.

The use of psychographic information allows companies to develop campaigns based on the lifestyle or desired lifestyle of the target market. Generally speaking, lifestyle positioning involves using emotional appeal techniques such as love, fear, adventure, sex, and humour to influence the target. The image must be communicated through every media vehicle and brand contact, including logos and special events. The automobile industry effectively uses lifestyle imagery to sell cars. It is common to see the rugged outdoors associated with SUVs and young urban professionals driving a luxury car. Volvo accomplishes both of these situations in the ad that appears in Figure 3.16.

lifestyle (image) positioning
A marketing strategy based on intangible characteristics associated with a lifestyle instead of tangible characteristics.

FIGURE
3.16

Lifestyle imagery positions competing brands in the customer's mind

Source: Courtesy of Volvo Cars of Canada Corp.

Various brands of sunglasses rely heavily on lifestyle imagery to appeal to their primary target. Sunglasses are a fashion item and how they "look" on the customer is an important aspect of one's lifestyle, as is the brand name itself.

PLANNING AND IMPLEMENTING MARKETING AND MARKETING COMMUNICATIONS PROGRAMS

To build brand loyalty and brand equity requires effective marketing programs: activities that produce a strong and favourable association to a brand in a consumer's memory. It is an information transfer process that considers two essential factors. First, decisions must be made about how to employ various brand elements. These decisions involve brand names, trademarks, and characters. Second, appropriate marketing strategies must be developed to communicate the brand values and brand positioning strategy.

The most common brand elements are brand names, logos, symbols, characters, packaging, and slogans. The content of most advertising in any medium, from television to print to websites, usually includes these elements. Characters sometimes become more famous than the brand itself. Some very popular brand characters include the A&W Root Bear, the Pillsbury Doughboy, Tony the Tiger, and Ronald McDonald, to name only a few. Slogans are commonly used in advertising to summarize the core value of the brand. Phrases such as "Because I'm worth it" (L'Oréal), "Think fresh. Eat fresh" (SUBWAY restaurants), and "Impossible is nothing" (Adidas) have an impact on people. Such slogans state the main benefit of the product or brand, imply a distinction between

FIGURE
3.17

Some Famous Advertising Slogans

Slogans are an effective means of drawing attention to a product. Typically, they make claims about a product or offer a significant benefit to the consumer. A good slogan reflects the positioning strategy of the brand and helps develop the personality of the brand. A good slogan is a memorable slogan.

Here are some famous slogans from the past:

From Canada

"I Am Canadian"	Molson Canadian
"Harvey's makes a hamburger a beautiful thing"	Harvey's
"The Champagne of Ginger Ales"	Canada Dry
"Only in Canada? Pity"	Red Rose Tea
"Always got time for Tim Hortons"	Tim Hortons

From the United States

"You're in good hands"	Allstate Insurance
"Just do it"	Nike
"The king of beers"	Budweiser
"Don't leave home without it"	American Express
"M'm, M'm good"	Campbell's Soup
"Finger-lickin' good"	KFC
"Pardon me, do you have any Grey Poupon?	Grey Poupon
"Melts in your mouth, not in your hands"	M&Ms Candy

it and other firms' products, and allow a brand to adopt a distinct personality of its own. For more insight into the role that advertising slogans perform, refer to Figure 3.17.

Based on the numerous examples already cited in this chapter, it should be abundantly clear that marketing communications are the "voice" of a brand's (or company's) positioning strategy. Regardless of the medium selected, that voice must deliver a message with clarity and continuity. If the communications strategies are executed effectively and with sufficient financial support, the desired message and image should be planted in the customer's mind.

In terms of how the various elements of the marketing communications mix are employed, advertising should be viewed as an aerial attack on the audience it reaches. It is the most visible form of communications—a form of communications that creates awareness and interest in a brand. Advertising gets people talking about a brand. It creates hype. The other forms of marketing communications play more specific roles and should be viewed as the ground attack. Communications in the form of sales promotions, street-level and buzz marketing, and event marketing, for example, help create desire and action. They provide the stimulus that gets the wallet out of the pocket or purse. The Internet has become a useful vehicle for providing detailed information and for creating buzz. The use of blogs, podcasts, and Twitter opens up new avenues for sanctioned and unsanctioned

IMC HIGHLIGHT

Vote Square or Vote Diamond

Hunter Somerville, an advertising intern at Ogilvy & Mather (a Toronto ad agency), had a simple idea about how to refresh a sleepy brand of cereal: turn a square Shreddie 45 degrees and you have a diamond-shaped Shreddie. His simple idea became the "big idea" the client, Kraft Canada, was looking for. A straight-faced marketing plan would be implemented around a tongue-in-cheek product launch.

Somerville wasn't even present when the idea was presented to senior executives at Ogilvy, but apparently the executives laughed out loud and embraced the idea. The next step was to sell it to the client. Would Kraft, a rather conservative-style advertiser, go for it? "We loved it," says Jennifer Hutchinson, Post Cereal Director of Marketing at Kraft.

The concept is unique in the world of advertising. By simply tilting a product on its side, literally, it succeeded

in tilting it afresh in consumers' imaginations. Advertising actually created a new product. No need to say "new and improved" here. In this case, the most significant change was no change at all.

An integrated campaign consisting of TV, print, outdoor, web, experiential marketing, and public relations launched diamond-shaped Shreddies. TV spots told the tale of a mishap in the Shreddies factory which resulted in the accidental creation of the "new" product. The spots drove consumers to diamondshreddies.com for recipes, a "win a diamond" contest, an interactive game, and the option to vote for diamond or square Shreddies. Videos of actual consumers testing the product were also shown online.

Consumers and critics alike reacted to the new idea. Many critics couldn't believe that Kraft bought the idea, but apparently Kraft loved it. Consumers couldn't get enough of Diamond Shreddies. The website generated over 100 000 visitors in the first four months and 28 000 people voted for their preferred shape. Limited-edition boxes sold out in two months. And of course there was a viral component. Bloggers debated the merits of the new shape, and videos of rants and parodies surfaced on YouTube. One die-hard fan put the "last" square Shreddie for sale on eBay, leading to a three-page article in *Maclean's* about the campaign.

John Bradley, of Yknot Strategic Solutions, says "the idea brings you back to the core product. It has all the benefits of noise and attention and pseudo 'new' news but it's the same old Shreddies. It definitely stands out." When all is said and done, that's exactly what a good ad campaign should do.

Did the idea work? Definitely! Shreddies has been revived in consumers' minds. And the media buzz surrounding the campaign has resulted in double-digit sales increases on a monthly basis. The campaign garnered 265 press stories and went on to win numerous advertising awards in Canada including the "Best of the Best" at the Canadian Marketing Association Awards 2008. And the guy behind the idea? Hunter Somerville is now a copywriter at the agency. Job well done!

Adapted from "Shreddies idea worth its weight in diamonds," Canadian Marketing Awards supplement to *Strategy*, November 2008, p. 6 and Anne Kingston, "Diamonds are a brand's best friend," *Maclean's*, May 19, 2008, pp. 41–44.

branded communications. Therefore, with all points of contact delivering the same message, a brand begins to build momentum—the brand-building process has begun.

For more insight into brand-building strategies and the role played by marketing communications, read the IMC Highlight: **Vote Square or Vote Diamond**.

Packaging and Brand Building

The package is what consumers look for when they are contemplating a purchase. For new products especially, the look of the package must be instilled in the customer's mind. For that reason, it is very common for the package to play a key role in introductory marketing communications programs. Over time, consumers start associating specific colours with a brand, and they know exactly what they are looking for when trying to spot a brand on a cluttered store shelf. Coca-Cola, for example, is strongly associated with the colour red, while arch-rival Pepsi-Cola is strongly associated with blue.

In today's competitive environment, packaging is playing a more significant role in differentiating one brand from another. Over the life cycle of a product, it may change several times to spruce up the image of a brand. As well, a common package design across all product lines that make up a brand (e.g., various sizes, shapes, and formats) helps maintain brand identity. As can be seen by the packages in Figure 3.18, Tide laundry detergent has a common look and colour scheme across various product formats.

A revolution is occurring in packaged-goods marketing, as marketers see packages having a growing influence on purchase decisions amid ongoing media fragmentation. In store is where a majority of decisions are made. It has been estimated that up to 70 percent of purchase decisions are made in store (40 percent in supermarkets) by people navigating aisles, scanning shelves, and making spur-of-the-moment decisions.[18] As well, changes in media consumer lifestyles are now forcing a dramatic shift, making the package itself an increasingly important selling medium.

Given the way in which consumers scan merchandise on store shelves, it is clear that colour plays a key role in attracting people's attention. Many brands actually own a colour, at least in marketing terms, a concept known as brand blocking. For example, the colour red demands attention and is a sign of power. In the soft drink market Coca-Cola owns the colour red, and it is no coincidence that Coca-Cola is a dominant market leader. In the hair-care aisle, Garnier Fructus owns a not-so-subtle bright green

Source: Photo by Dick Hemingway.

FIGURE
3.18

Consistent brand identification in packaging combined with an effective advertising message communicates the benefit of Tide laundry detergent

colour. Colours are an emotional trigger and consequently are powerful marketing tools. Dark colours project richness and are common in the coffee aisle on brands such as Maxwell House and Nabob. White denotes purity and is a popular colour in the soap aisle on brands like Ivory and Dove.

The package is a very important touch-point with consumers. Familiarity with a package helps build trust between the consumer and the brand, so ultimately the package is a factor that can influence consumer loyalty. A good package serves three functions: it protects the product, it markets the product, and it offers convenience to consumers.

PROTECTING THE PRODUCT

How much protection a product needs depends on how often it changes hands in the distribution process. For example, how long does it sit in a warehouse, how will it be transported, what kind of handling will it experience, and how much protection from exposure to heat, cold, light, and moisture will it need? Milk, for example, is traditionally packaged in bags and cartons, but the recent introduction of plastic containers in single-serving sizes has increased the shelf life of milk. In plastic containers, milk products are being positioned as "refreshing alternatives" to fruit juices, energy drinks, and soft drinks. Potato chips are packed in oversized bags to protect the chips while being transported or handled.

MARKETING THE PRODUCT

In its marketing role, the package does the same thing an advertisement in any medium would do. The design and colour scheme should be coordinated so that the overall look of the package creates a good impression. The package should be attractive and eye-catching to grab the attention of consumers. It should contain useful information and tell consumers what the product's benefits are so they will have a reason to buy it. Dole fruit juice, juice blends, and cocktails are refreshing beverages that are healthier than other alternatives. Dole's brand promise appears in its ads while colourful packaging expresses freshness at point of purchase.

Packages can also be used to communicate information about promotional offers such as coupons, contests, and giveaways. Since promotions of this nature are temporary, a package "flash" is usually added to the front panel of the package to draw attention to the offer. Details of the offer would appear on the side, back, or inside of the package (see Figure 3.19).

Beyond transferring essential information about a brand, marketers must be aware of legal and regulatory requirements associated with packaging. The universal product code (UPC) symbol (a series of black lines that identifies each item of a product line) is mandatory on all packaged goods. Other mandatory information includes the volume or weight designation and the company name and address. On pre-packaged food products, nutritional information is mandatory. Where appropriate and with substantiation from marketing research and approval from the appropriate government authority, a company can now make specific health claims about brands on the packages.

PROVIDING CONVENIENCE

A package should be easy to carry, open, handle, and reseal (if appropriate). Liquid detergents, for example, should be easy to pour without spills (on some brands the plastic lid is the measuring device for dispensing the product). No-drip spouts on products such as mustard and ketchup also offer convenience. If a product is heavy or bulky, handles should be built into the package design. Other examples of convenience include resealable plastic lids on margarine containers, twist-off caps on beer, wine, and soft drinks, straws on fruit juice containers, and canned goods with moulded metal bottoms that allow for stacking on store shelves.

FIGURE 3.19   A package face often communicates details of a promotional offer

Source: Photo by Dick Hemingway.

Branding by Design

Not all kinds of product are sold in a package. What attributes sell an appliance, an automobile, a computer, the services offered by a bank, and so on? For durable goods like cars and computers, the key influencer in the buying decision could be the design—the look and style of the product and the image it projects about itself. For products like mutual funds, trusts, and other financial offerings—products that are truly intangible—consumers are primarily influenced by the brand image as perpetuated by effective marketing communications programs.

Brand design integrates the brand experience into the product or service. It's about creatively designing innovative approaches in order to create a unique brand experience.[19] In the durable goods market, designers traditionally followed one basic premise: form follows function. This was a good premise because consumers wanted durable goods to perform specific functions dependably and reliably. Shopping for a stove or a dishwasher involved comparing the interior and exterior features of various brands. Since all brands offered the same benefits, the decision was based largely on the brand name and the perceptions the consumer held about the brand name. But consumers now want products that fit in with their lifestyle or the decor of their home furnishings. They are more style conscious and are purchasing durable goods like automobiles, appliances, and electronics products based more on emotion and style than function. Refer to the illustration in Figure 3.20.

Advancing technology has an impact on design. In the television market, sexy-looking flat screens have replaced the black boxes of yesterday. The television remains the focal point of the family room, but in a very different manner. Mounted on a display stand or right on the wall, the new televisions offer a feeling of contemporary stylishness that is very attractive to consumers who now spend more money and time on home entertainment.

To illustrate the importance of design and style, consider the initial success of Apple's iPhone (one million units sold the first day they were available). Apparently there was pent-up demand for a sexy cell phone—a phone that would also offer a variety of applications. In the automobile market, Volkswagen brought back a restyled Beetle and Chrysler returned to the 1930s gangster era when it launched the PT Cruiser. Both models flew out of the showrooms initially, but then sales weakened as a fickle public's attention turned elsewhere. The design of these cars captured the public's imagination initially but did not have staying power.

In contrast, the BMW Mini has achieved longer-term sales success. The original Mini Cooper was redesigned and launched by BMW in 2001. Unlike the Beetle and PT Cruiser, where sales dwindled as the novelty of the new design faded, the Mini experienced sales increases each year through 2007. According to BMW, the success of the Mini is due to its design and brand strategy. "The Mini was launched not as a car, but a brand. Right from the start BMW supplemented sales with a line of clothing, accessories and more. Minis were sold in separate showrooms beside existing BMW dealers."[20] Is there a brand design lesson here? Yes. A combination of marketing variables that included the design of the car, a solid branding strategy that extended beyond the car, and the manner in which the car was sold created a unique brand experience for customers.

On the services side of things, consider the problem that the Bank of Montreal was facing. The bank had dropped significantly in ranking despite major expansion into wealth-management products. People were not aware that they could get anything from mutual funds to complex financial planning assistance from the bank. It embarked

FIGURE 3.20

The design of a product plays a key role in building a brand's image in the minds of consumers

upon a rebranding program that had to communicate the perception that what they were offering was above banking and better than banking.

FutureBrand, a company specializing in developing brand strategies, worked on the Bank of Montreal's branding program. "The critical element of any rebranding is to understand what the current narrative about the brand is, as well as the business strategy to date. Then you clarify what's going to change and distill it into a narrative explaining why the changes are a good thing."[21]

Distilling a complex rebranding into an instantly recognizable message is crucial. The result was a new persona for the bank, which is now known as BMO. The new BMO positioned all of the bank's product lines under one consistent brand. The new identity system introduced the name "BMO Financial Group," but linked it back to the Bank of Montreal. The bank's new identity appears in Figure 3.21. An extensive marketing communications program was implemented to communicate the new name to the Canadian public. All touch-points with consumers—from stationery to ATMs to websites to bank signage—carry the BMO name. Such a change represents a huge internal and external undertaking.

FIGURE 3.21   BMO Bank of Montreal Logo

BMO
BMO Bank of Montreal
BMO Nesbitt Burns
BMO Harris Private Banking

Source: Photo by Keith J. Tuckwell.

SUMMARY

Developing a sound brand strategy and positioning strategy is the first step in the brand-building process. Having the right strategy is important since consumers form their impressions about a brand based on what they hear and see about it. Therefore, marketing organizations use branding as a means of identifying products and building an image.

Over time, consumers come to trust what a brand stands for and express their satisfaction in varying degrees of brand loyalty. Loyalty is expressed in terms of brand recognition, brand preference, and brand insistence. Brand equity is the value a consumer derives from a brand beyond its physical attributes. Such equity is based on how aware consumers are of a brand, their degree of loyalty, and perceptions held about quality. Brand equity may also be described in monetary terms as brands are a valuable asset of a company.

Branding offers several benefits for consumers. It suggests a consistent degree of quality, provides psychological rewards (e.g., a better self-image) for possessing certain brands, and it distinguishes competing brands from one another. Good brands are personal and they often become integral parts of people's lives. For manufacturers, the brand name communicates a point of difference, allows for the creation of an image, and helps build brand loyalty.

The brand-building process involves four essential steps: identifying brand values and positioning strategy, planning and implementing a brand marketing program, measuring and interpreting brand performance, and growing and sustaining brand equity. Brand values are the primary attributes (descriptive features) and benefits (the values consumers attach to a brand). Positioning refers to the image a marketer wants the brand to have in the customers' minds. A positioning strategy is based on an important element of the marketing mix. Some of the common positioning strategies include product differentiation, brand leadership, head-on (comparative), innovation, price and value, channel efficiency, and lifestyle.

When implementing a brand strategy, all elements of the marketing mix and the marketing communications mix come into play. The marketing communications mix is the voice of a brand's positioning strategy. A good strategy that is executed efficiently should instill the desired image about a brand in the customer's mind. In this regard, all elements of the communications mix work together to deliver a consistent message.

Packaging and product design play key roles in differentiating brands and help determine consumer perceptions. Therefore, it is important that a brand, in all of its different sizes, formats, and variations, have a consistent and distinctive package design. The ability of a package to stand out in a cluttered point-of-purchase environment is a key factor influencing buying decisions.

A good package design will protect the product, market the product, and provide consumers convenience in handling and using the product. Package designs should be unique and attractive to grab the attention of consumers as they pass by. Expensive durable goods rely on the design of the product to create images in the consumer's mind. The design must be functional yet attractive to the eye. Style and appearance are important influences on buying decisions for cars, appliances, computers, and other consumer electronic goods. Goods such as these are often an expression of one's self-image.

KEY TERMS

attribute, 75
benefit, 75
brand, 65
brand equity, 72
brand insistence, 71
brand logo, 67
brand loyalty, 68

brand manager, 74
brand name, 66
brand preference, 71
brand recognition, 71
core values, 75
head-on positioning, 79
image positioning, 83
innovation positioning, 80

leadership positioning, 79
lifestyle positioning, 83
positioning, 76
price positioning, 82
product differentiation strategy, 79
trademark, 67
unique selling point (USP), 74

REVIEW QUESTIONS

1. Identify and briefly explain the key components of a brand.
2. Identify two benefits of branding for consumers and two benefits of branding for organizations.
3. Identify and briefly explain the three stages of brand loyalty.
4. What is brand equity and how does a brand build it?
5. "A brand is a set of core values." What does this statement mean?
6. Define what positioning is and state the importance of having a clearly worded positioning strategy statement.
7. What is the difference between head-on positioning and brand leadership positioning? Provide an example of each not mentioned in the chapter.

8. If a brand is using a product differentiation positioning strategy, what will the advertising message focus on? Provide an example of this strategy not mentioned in the chapter.
9. If a brand is using a lifestyle positioning strategy, what will the advertising message focus on? Provide two examples of this strategy not mentioned in the chapter.
10. What essential roles does a package perform in the marketing of a brand? Briefly explain.
11. Explain the role and influence that the design of a product can have on prospective buyers.

DISCUSSION AND APPLICATION QUESTIONS

1. "A brand is more than the physical product." Explain.

2. "Selecting the name for a new product is a critical decision." What are the essential issues in naming a brand? Conduct some online secondary research to get to the bottom of this issue.

3. Select a lifestyle advertising campaign that you think is particularly effective. Write a brief report or make a brief presentation on why you think it is effective.

4. Explain the relationship between brand positioning and the development of an effective marketing communications strategy.

5. Evaluate the marketing situation for one of the following companies or brands. What makes this company (brand) unique and what is its differential advantage(s) compared to the primary competitors? Based on what you know of this company (brand) and what you see or hear in terms of marketing communications, develop a positioning strategy statement for the company (brand).

    a) Apple
    b) Walmart
    c) H&M
    d) Listerine
    e) Gatorade

6. Using a company or brand of your choosing, examine the relationship between its name, logo, and advertising slogan (e.g., "GE brings good things to life"). Are these brand and communications elements permanently entwined or can any of the elements be changed to build the brand's image? What are the benefits and risks associated with any kind of change?

7. Assess the role that package design plays in building a brand's image. To justify your position, provide an example of a package design that you perceive to be good and a design that you perceive to be less than good. What is the relationship between the package design and other forms of marketing communications?

ENDNOTES

1. Jo Marney, "Bringing customers back for more," *Marketing*, September 10, 2001, p. 33.

2. Definition of a brand, About.com, www.marketing.about.com/od/marketingglossary.

3. Kevin Keller, *Strategic Brand Management* (Upper Saddle River, NY: Pearson Education, 2003), p. 106.

4. Kristin Laird, "Hudson's Bay gets new logo," *Marketing Daily*, March 9, 2009, www.marketingmag.ca.

5. David Dunne and Julia Moulden, "Personal Branding: Applying the Lessons of Successful Brands to Yourself," *The Globe and Mail*, October 21, 2002, p. B9.

6. Matt Semansky, "Google's it," *Marketing*, May 18, 2009, p. 11.

7. Dale Beckman, David Kurtz, and Louis Boone, *Foundations of Marketing* (Toronto: Holt Rinehart and Winston, 1988), pp. 316–317.

8. Canadaloyalty.com, www.canadaloyalty.com/programs/airmiles.html.

9. "Best Global Brands," *Interbrand*, 2008, www.interbrand.com/best_global_brands.aspx.

10. Keith MacArthur, "Canada's top brands," *The Globe and Mail*, July 24, 2006, www.theglobeandmail.com.

11. Allan P. Adamson, "What's your brand job?" *Advertising Age*, September 16, 2002, p. 18.

12. "Toyota voted most trusted brand by Canadians in Reader's Digest survey," press release, *World Auto News & Reviews*, May 20, 2009, www.allworldcars.com.

13. Michael Hogan, "What do core values have to do with a brand? Everything." Brandology.com, www.brandology.com.au/thinking/article5.html.

14. Jeff Swystun, "Seven habits of highly effective brands," *Marketing*, October 9/16, 2007, p. 37.

15. Al Kreuger and Sara Meaney, "Become the Apple of Your Industry," Cometbrandingblog, October 6, 2008, www.cometbranding.com/blog/become-the-apple-of-your-industry/.

16. Dan Moren, "Analysis: The many faces of Apple advertising," *Macworld*, December 13, 2007, www.macworld.com.

17. "Wal-mart's ad slogan changes after 19 years," theStar.com, September 13, 2007, www.thestar.com.

18. "Retail Therapy," The Australian Centre for Retail Studies, Monash University, April 2009, p. 3.

19. Larry Light, "Brand design takes more than style," *Advertising Age*, November 6, 2006, p. 74.

20. Jeremy Cato, "It's all about building the brand at Mini," *The Globe and Mail*, June 28, 2007, p. G14.

21. Terry Poulton, "Communicating the new you," *Strategy*, October 7, 2002, p. 23.

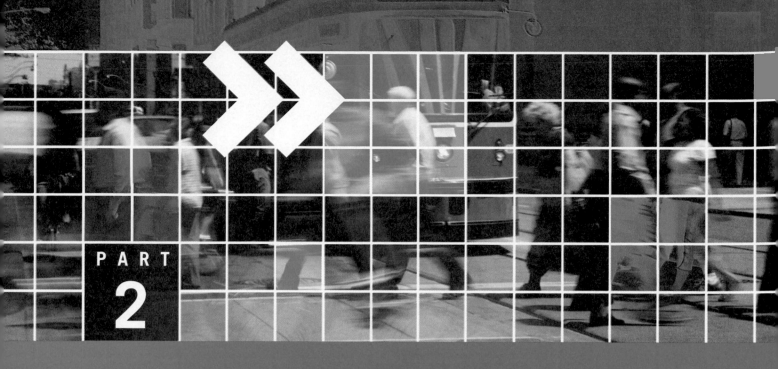

Planning for Integrated Media

Part 2 examines the steps, considerations, and procedures for developing message strategies and media strategies for television, radio, newspapers, magazines, various forms of out-of-home advertising, direct response media, and interactive media.

In Chapter 4, the basic elements of the communications process are introduced along with the various stages of creative (message) planning. Because creative plans are based on clearly defined objectives, strategies, and executions, the chapter draws clear distinctions among these three planning concepts. It finishes with a discussion of various creative appeal techniques and execution techniques that are employed by advertisers to present compelling messages to customers.

Chapter 5 describes the media planning side of advertising. Media planning involves identifying media objectives, creating media strategies, and executing those plans. The development of a sound media strategy is crucial, so considerable time is devoted to discussing primary issues that influence the strategy. Strategic decisions are largely influenced by the budget available and the strengths and weaknesses of each medium in the context of the problem the advertiser is attempting to resolve.

Chapter 6 examines the growing field of direct response communications. Direct response plans rely on database management techniques, and the chapter devotes considerable time to how organizations use information sources. Various direct response media options are introduced and the strengths and weaknesses of each option are examined.

In Chapter 7, the focus is on digital communications. The various strategies for delivering effective online messages are discussed and perspectives are offered regarding how to effectively integrate online messages with offline messages and related communications strategies. The emerging area of mobile communications is also examined in this chapter.

Advertising Planning: Creative

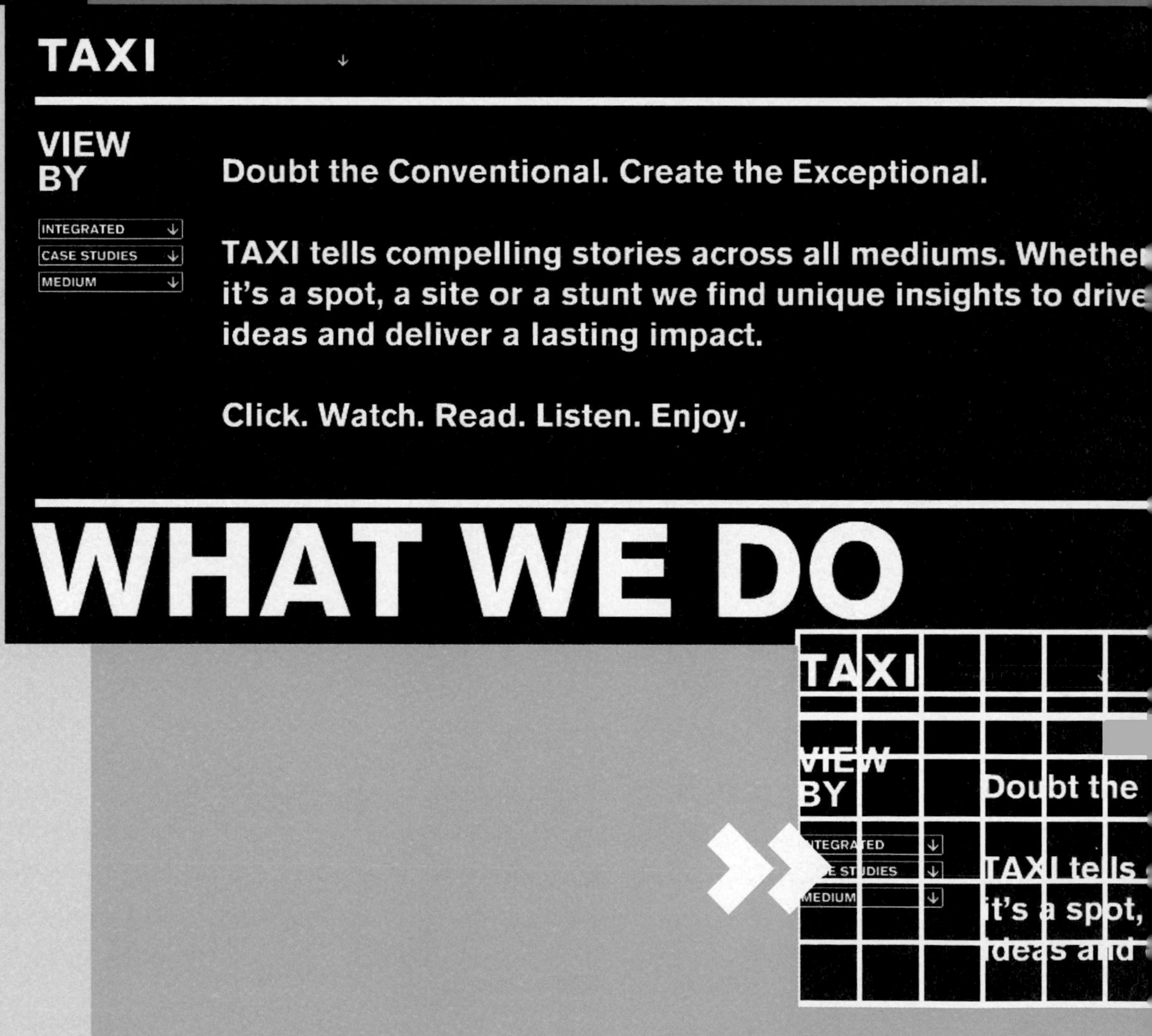

TAXI

VIEW BY

INTEGRATED
CASE STUDIES
MEDIUM

Doubt the Conventional. Create the Exceptional.

TAXI tells compelling stories across all mediums. Whether it's a spot, a site or a stunt we find unique insights to drive ideas and deliver a lasting impact.

Click. Watch. Read. Listen. Enjoy.

WHAT WE DO

TAXI

VIEW BY

INTEGRATED
E STUDIES
MEDIUM

Doubt the

TAXI tells
it's a spot,
ideas and

After studying this chapter, you will be able to

1. Identify the basic elements of the communications process

2. Explain the various stages of creative planning

3. Explain the role of a creative brief and describe the content of such a document

4. Distinguish between creative objectives, creative strategies, and creative execution

5. Describe the role of creative objective statements

6. Appreciate the variety of appeal techniques for developing creative strategies

7. Identify various execution techniques for best presenting creative strategies

From the previous chapter you have learned about the strategic planning process and seen how various elements of the marketing and marketing communications mix converge in a master plan of some kind. The role and nature of the individual plans—the plans for advertising, direct response, interactive, sales promotion, public relations, experiential marketing, and personal selling—are the focus of the remainder of the book. Separate external organizations may be responsible for developing these plans. Therefore, in the planning and development stages there is much communication between a company and its external suppliers.

This chapter will focus specifically on one aspect of advertising: the development and implementation of the message. The initial section discusses some fundamental communication concepts that are common to all of the components of the marketing communications mix. It is followed by a discussion of the creative planning process. Creative planning relies upon essential input from the marketing plan and involves the development of a separate plan that outlines the creative objectives, creative strategies, and creative execution (tactics).

Communications Essentials

The marketplace is dynamic and consumers are exposed to hundreds of messages each day from all kinds of sources. What do consumers recognize and recall at the end of the day? Can they say with certainty they saw a television commercial for Stride gum that shows production workers in a factory fooling around instead of working because the gum's flavour lasts so long? Do they remember that Ford automobiles are "powered by you"? Do they recall the brand of cough syrup that says of itself, "It tastes awful but it works"? The answer is not likely. In very simple terms, there is so much commercial clutter out there that consumers remember very little. The challenge, therefore, is to develop a message that will break through the clutter and leave a lasting impression on the audience. Easier said than done!

An understanding of the communications process and how consumers receive and interpret messages is essential. In Chapter 1, various consumer behaviour concepts were introduced—concepts such as needs and motives, attitudes and perceptions, and reference groups and family influences. Knowledge and application of these concepts influence the nature and content of a commercial message and the degree to which it is accepted and retained by consumers.

Communication is defined as transmitting, receiving, and processing information. Communication occurs when the message that was sent reaches its destination in a form

communication
The transmission, receipt, and processing of information between a sender and a receiver.

encoding
The transformation of a message into a meaningful format, such as an advertisement, a mailing piece, or an article in a newspaper.

transmission
The sending of a message through a medium such as television, radio, newspapers, magazines, outdoor advertising, Internet, and so on, or through personal selling.

that is understood by the intended audience. Commercial communications do not have to be a complex science. Simply stated, an organization develops a message, selects the right media to deliver it, and, if all things are planned effectively, it will reach the consumers and have an impact on them. Developing the message is referred to as **encoding**; that is, the message is transformed into some attention-getting form, such as a print advertisement, a direct response mailing piece, an article about the product in a newspaper, and so on. The message is then **transmitted**, usually by the media (television, radio, newspapers, magazines, outdoor advertising, Internet, and so on) or through personal selling. Refer to Figure 4.1 for an illustration.

In the delivery of the message, however, certain complications arise along the way. For example,

- The message was not in line with customer attitudes.
- The message did not reach the intended target with the desired frequency.
- The message delivered by the competition was more convincing.
- The competition spent more on advertising and had higher share of mind.
- New competitors entered the market and invested heavily in advertising.

noise
Any potential form of disruption in the transmission of a message that could distort the impact of the message; competitive advertising or the clutter of advertising messages in a medium are forms of noise.

Circumstances such as these are referred to as **noise** and dilute the impact of an advertiser's message. Whether or not a message breaks through the clutter is usually determined by the relationships among three separate factors: the quality of planning when developing message strategy, the execution of the plan being on target with the right timing and frequency, and the impact of competitive messages. The advertiser has control over the first two factors, but no control over the third.

Competing products are sending very similar messages to the same target market, creating noise. The objective, therefore, is to break through the noise. To do so, the message must be relevant to the consumer. For instance, the product's benefits must satisfy a need or suit the lifestyle of the target and be presented in such a manner that the brand becomes a preferred alternative.

If the message does not break through (if it is perceived as dull, uses the wrong types of appeals, or is simply confusing to the target), then no action will occur. Lack of action indicates a need to revisit the creative strategy and execution and make changes where necessary. For example, many soap and skin-care brands make similar claims and usually include good-looking females in their ads. Dove, in an effort to stand out, launched a "real beauty" campaign that encouraged women to celebrate themselves as they are. It was a bold and compelling message that regular women of all ages and sizes identified with—it broke through the clutter. The love-your-beauty attitude expressed by Dove led to the launch of several new Dove skin-care products.[1]

A consumer passes through a series of stages on the way to taking action. Advertising can influence the consumer at each stage. One such model is referred to as

FIGURE 4.1

The Communications Process

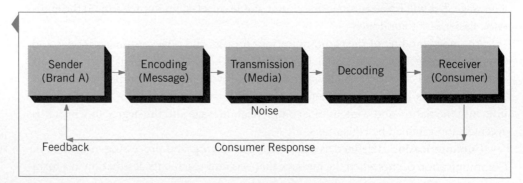

ACCA—awareness, comprehension, conviction, and action. This model is part of a theory called DAGMAR, which stands for Defining Advertising Goals for Measured Advertising Response. An advertising goal is a specific communication task to be accomplished among a defined audience in a given period. The task should be measurable, with benchmarks in existence to assess achievements.

The effectiveness of an advertising campaign is usually linked back to this model. For example, an advertiser wants to know (in percentage terms) the level of awareness of its product among the target market, and whether or not it is perceived as being a preferred brand. Furthermore, the advertiser may want to know what percentage of the target market has tried the product (in the case of a new product campaign). Post-campaign marketing research studies measure the achievement of the objectives.

An advertisement (or campaign) that achieves good scores with respect to awareness, comprehension, and conviction is likely to succeed. The desired action in the form of someone buying the product will likely occur. To protect its investment in advertising, an organization may also conduct marketing research while the message strategy is in the development stage. The message is tested for likeability, persuasiveness, and likelihood of purchase. Research measures that exceed the norms of other products in the category would suggest the advertiser is on to something. The various marketing research techniques used to evaluate advertising effectiveness are discussed in Chapter 12. The following is a description of each behaviour stage:

- **Awareness:** In this stage, the customer learns something for the first time. In an advertising context, a message tries to plant the brand name and the primary benefit offered in the customer's mind. Awareness can be measured by aided and unaided recall tests.

- **Comprehension:** At this stage, the consumer is expressing interest. The message is perceived as relevant. The brand is evaluated on the basis of need satisfaction. It is in the consumer's cognitive realm and becomes a candidate for potential purchase. A like or dislike for a brand can be measured using attitude scales.

- **Conviction:** At this stage, the consumer expresses stronger feelings toward the brand based on the perceived benefits it offers. The brand has moved higher in the consumer's frame of reference and become a preferred brand in his or her mind. In other words, a new attitude or a change in attitude about something has occurred. There may be sufficient motivation to take action and buy the product.

- **Action:** At this stage, the desired action occurs. The consumer buys the brand for the first time, visits the dealer showroom, or calls that 1-800 number!

This is the beginning of a customer relationship. An organization will invest a considerable amount of money in advertising and other forms of marketing communications to achieve one basic goal: to get the target customers to buy the product. The message delivered by marketing communications is nothing more than a promise—a promise that motivates someone to buy. The product must then live up to the expectations created by the marketing communications. As we say, no amount of advertising can make up for a lousy product.

A second theory of communications revolves around the degree of involvement the consumer has with a product in the purchase decision-making process. The extent of involvement, described as either high involvement or low involvement, has implications for the development of marketing communications strategy. Referred to as the FCB Grid, the grid was developed by Richard Vaughn, a senior vice-president of Foote, Cone, and Belding Advertising (see Figure 4.2).[2]

FIGURE
4.2

An Illustration of the FCB Grid
Source: Adapted from
www.public.iastate.edu/~geske/FCB.html.
Reproduced with permission.

HIGH INVOLVEMENT	
Quadrant 1 High Importance (expensive) Rational Decision **Example:** Automobile or computer	**Quadrant 2** High Importance (expensive) Emotional Decision **Example:** Designer clothing
Quadrant 3 Low Importance (less expensive) Rational Decision **Example:** Detergent	**Quadrant 4** Low Importance (less expensive) Emotional Decision **Example:** Soft drink, beer
LOW INVOLVEMENT	

Products that are included in Quadrant One are expensive and require a rational decision-making process during which alternatives are evaluated. Since the consumer will probably spend an extended period of time assessing alternatives, the message strategy should have an informative tone and style, and the media selected to deliver the message should be conducive to a long copy format (e.g., newspapers and magazines, and websites). Products in Quadrant Two are also high involvement, but consumers evaluate alternatives more on emotion. For example, designer clothing is bought to make the consumer feel good, feel sexy, or show status. Marketing communications must generate emotional responses and create an image that people will buy. The message will appeal to higher-level needs, the looking-glass self, and the ideal self. Television ads, glossy and visual magazine ads, and special inserts are effective media for such products.

Products that are included in Quadrant Three are low-involvement products that require rational decisions. Products such as household cleaning products, paper products, and other everyday items are in this category. Marketing communications should give the consumer a compelling reason to buy (e.g., it lasts longer, as in a battery; it acts quickly, as in a headache remedy; or it is convenient to use, as in a household product). The focus of the message is on the key benefit, so the message must be short. A catchy slogan might act as a reminder. The illustration in Figure 4.3 offers a good example. Here, Vim clearly focuses on a new benefit that consumers wanted—a spray top. The new format of the product and method of dispensing it (spray) offers more convenience to users.

Television, magazine ads with strong visuals, and point-of-purchase material are effective media choices for these kinds of products.

Products that are included in Quadrant Four are low-involvement products purchased on emotional decisions. The products are not expensive, but they make the consumer feel good. Examples of such products include snack foods, beer and alcohol, and soft drinks. There are not many rational reasons for buying these types of products, so it is common for messages to adopt a "feel good" strategy. For example, there is an abundance of lifestyle-oriented messages among popular Canadian beer brands such as Coors Light and Bud Light. It is the image or lifestyle association that the consumer buys into. Television, outdoor advertising, and point-of-purchase play a role in delivering messages for these products.

MARKETING COMMUNICATIONS PLANNING PROCESS

The various elements of the strategic planning process were presented in Chapter 2. This chapter concentrates on the advertising planning process, but will recognize the

FIGURE
4.3

Vim communicates a clear message about a key product benefit

relationships between advertising and the other forms of communication. Once the relationships are established, the chapter will then focus on creative planning. Media planning concepts for traditional media alternatives are presented in Chapter 5.

All aspects of a marketing communications plan are based on the same set of information. The current situation a brand or company faces is analyzed, a problem or opportunity is identified, and a plan of action is developed and implemented. As part of the planning process, the role and contribution of the various elements in the marketing communications mix are identified and those that are most appropriate are included in the plan. Separate plans, designed to achieve specific objectives, are developed for each element of the mix. Once completed, the key elements of these plans are integrated into the master plan—the marketing plan (see Figure 4.4).

With reference to Chapter 2 again, marketing communications plans are devised to meet a variety of challenges and are usually documented as communications objectives

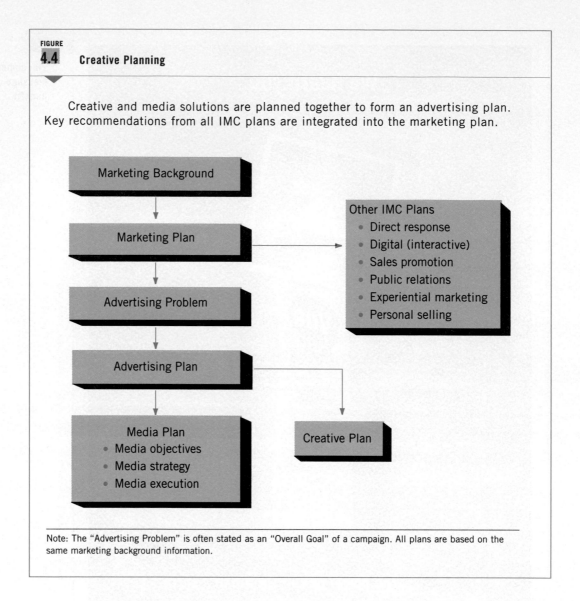

FIGURE 4.4   Creative Planning

Creative and media solutions are planned together to form an advertising plan. Key recommendations from all IMC plans are integrated into the marketing plan.

Marketing Background

Marketing Plan

Advertising Problem

Advertising Plan

Media Plan
- Media objectives
- Media strategy
- Media execution

Other IMC Plans
- Direct response
- Digital (interactive)
- Sales promotion
- Public relations
- Experiential marketing
- Personal selling

Creative Plan

Note: The "Advertising Problem" is often stated as an "Overall Goal" of a campaign. All plans are based on the same marketing background information.

in the marketing communications plan. As you will see in this chapter and subsequent chapters, certain elements of the marketing communications mix are better suited to achieving certain objectives. Marketing communications objectives can be diverse and tend to involve challenges, such as

- Building awareness and interest for a product.
- Encouraging trial purchase.
- Attracting new target markets.
- Encouraging brand preference.
- Altering perceptions held by consumers.
- Creating goodwill and fostering a positive public image.
- Motivating distributors to carry a product.

As indicated above, certain components of the marketing communications mix are more appropriate than others for achieving specific communications objectives. In this chapter you will see how advertising helps achieve some of these objectives.

ADVERTISING PLANNING—CREATIVE

Advertising is defined as the placement of announcements and persuasive messages in time or space purchased in any of the mass media by business firms, not-for-profit organizations, government agencies, and individuals who seek to inform and/or persuade members of a particular target market about their products, services, organizations, and ideas.[3]

The advertising plan is usually developed by an advertising agency, an external partner that works closely with the client. The agency is responsible for developing and managing the client's advertising. Historically, agencies focused their energy on creative and media planning, but in today's environment they have expanded into other areas, such as direct response, marketing research, digital communications, and public relations.

The starting point for any new advertising project is the creative brief. A **creative brief** is a business document developed by the company that contains vital information about the advertising task at hand. The information is discussed with advertising agency personnel so that copywriters, art directors, and creative directors fully understand the nature of the assignment. The brief is a discussion document and the content can change based on the nature of discussion between the client and agency. In some cases, certain sections are actually left blank, awaiting discussion between the two parties. For example, the agency's key responsibility is to develop the creative strategy. Clients that provide too much strategic direction are "stepping on toes." The content of a creative brief is contained in Figure 4.5.

Information that is provided by the client includes essential market background information, a statement that identifies the problem to be resolved or the overall goal to be achieved, and a list of communications objectives. The client also provides a positioning strategy statement to guide the development of the creative plan. The positioning strategy statement directly influences the creative objectives. For our discussions here, creative objectives deal with the content of the message to be delivered (e.g., what is the primary attribute and benefit to be communicated to the target market?). The remaining elements of the creative brief—the creative strategy and creative execution—are the responsibility of the agency. That's what they get paid to do!

Once the creative brief is finalized, the spotlight shines upon the copywriter and art director, a team charged with developing the **creative concept** or the "**big idea**," as it is often referred to, that will be the cornerstone of the campaign. At this point, the agency's creative team immerses itself in details about the brand, target market, and competition so that it can fully appreciate the current situation.

Let's examine the content of the creative brief in more detail. Since the market background information is drawn from the marketing plan, that section will not be discussed in this chapter. Simply refer back to Chapter 2 if you need more details. The market background section includes information about the market, brand, key competitors, a profile of the primary target market, and budget. Knowing a brand's market position and how consumers perceive it is important to developing message strategies. Knowing how competitors advertise their products is also important. The agency wants to ensure it recommends new and innovative ideas to its clients. An example of a creative brief is contained in Figure 4.6.

PROBLEM IDENTIFICATION   Advertising plans are usually designed to resolve a particular problem or pursue an opportunity. For example, an established brand will review its marketing strategy each year and make changes in strategic direction when necessary. Factors such as the stage at which a brand finds itself in the product life cycle, the intensity

advertising
A form of marketing communications designed to stimulate a positive response from a defined target market.

creative brief
A document developed by a client organization that contains vital information about the advertising task at hand; it is a useful tool for discussions between the client and its advertising agency.

FIGURE
4.5   **Content of a Creative Brief**

Market Information (information from marketing plan)

- Market profile
- Brand profile
- Competitor profile
- Target market profile
- Budget

Problem and Overall Objective

- Identification of the problem that advertising will resolve
- Statement of the overall goal for advertising to achieve

Advertising Objectives (based on problem or goal)

- Awareness
- Interest
- Preference
- Action
- New image
- New targets

Positioning Strategy Statement

- A statement of brand benefits, brand personality, or desired image

Creative Objectives

- Key benefit statement
- Support claims statement

Creative Strategy

- Central theme ("big idea")
- Tone and style
- Appeal techniques

Creative Execution

- Tactical considerations
- Production decisions

Note: The nature and content of a creative brief varies from company to company. A working model is presented here to show the typical content of a creative brief. Some companies include a problem statement or an overall goal, while others include both. Advertising objectives usually concentrate on one or two issues so the campaign remains focused on the problem at hand.

---

of competition, and changing preferences among target consumers are evaluated in the review process. Changes in these areas have an impact on marketing communications strategies.

Based on this creative brief model, the situation is encapsulated in a **problem statement**. Other models may require a statement that describes the **overall goal** of the campaign. Regardless of which option is used, advertising can only accomplish one thing at a time. A campaign must have a central focus. Simply stated, it's "Here's what we want to achieve!" To illustrate, consider the following examples:

problem statement
A brief statement that summarizes a particular problem to resolve or an opportunity to pursue and serves as the focus of a marketing strategy.

overall goal
The objective of an advertising campaign.

- To create or increase brand awareness.

- To alter perceptions currently held by consumers about a brand.

- To present a completely new image for a brand.

- To launch a new product into the marketplace.

- To attract a new target market to a brand.

- To create awareness and trial purchase for a brand line extension.

These examples suggest focus. To demonstrate, Wendy's has experimented with several different campaign ideas since the death of Dave Thomas, company founder and famous spokesperson in TV ads. One of its more recent campaigns revolved around a young man wearing a red wig with braided pigtails. According to Bob Holtcamp, Wendy's VP brand marketing, "It was a love it or hate it kind of campaign." The red wig idea did not enhance Wendy's image and had no impact on sales—it had to go. To restore Wendy's image with its key target audience of 18- to 34-year-olds (the problem), Wendy's launched a new campaign using the slogan "It's waaaay better than fast food. It's Wendy's."[4] The jury is still out on the effectiveness of this idea.

A campaign that tries to resolve too many problems at one time will only confuse consumers who see and hear the message.

ADVERTISING OBJECTIVES   Once the overall goal is determined, specific **advertising objectives** are identified. Wherever possible, advertising objectives should be quantitative in nature so that they can be measured for success or failure at a later date. Advertising objectives may be behavioural in nature or they may focus on issues related to the overall problem. For example, an objective may focus on creating a new image or on attracting a new target market.

advertising objectives
Quantitative measures related to behaviour or issues.

Advertising objectives should only deal with issues that advertising (the creative plan and media plan) can resolve. For example, a new product campaign will focus on awareness objectives. The objective is to build awareness gradually by presenting a message that informs consumers about what the product is and what it will do for them. If the market is very competitive and several brands are strong, the advertising objectives will focus on building preference. The message will focus squarely on unique attributes that show how the advertised brand performs better than other brands.

To demonstrate how advertising objectives are written, consider the following examples:

- To achieve an awareness level of 60 percent for Brand X in the defined target market within 12 months of product launch.

- To achieve a trial purchase rate of 25 percent for Brand Y in the defined target market within 12 months of product launch.

- To reposition (or re-image) Brand Z in the customer's mind by presenting images that will attract a younger target market.

The first two examples are quantitative in nature and can be easily measured for achievement at the end of the plan period. If the objectives are achieved, it indicates that current advertising strategies are working. If they are not achieved, the client and agency can re-evaluate the situation and make appropriate changes. The third example is not quantitative in nature, but it can be measured. Assuming the current image of the brand is known, a marketing research study near the end of the plan period can be conducted to determine if the brand has caught on with younger customers.

FIGURE
4.6

An Example of a
Creative Brief

Harley-Davidson

Market Information

- Market volume has been affected by the economic downturn and an aging rider population; unit sales for the industry dropped 20% versus one year ago (2008 versus 2007).

- Market divided into two segments: the heavyweight segment, which Harley dominates, caters to older buyers wanting style, quality, and status; the lightweight segment appeals to younger buyers seeking speed, agility, and affordability in a motorcycle.

- Harley generates 70% of its sales in the United States and 30% internationally.

- Canada accounts for 15% of Harley's international sales.

Market Shares

Harley-Davidson dominates the heavyweight segment. Current market shares are:

Brand	2007 Share %	2006 Share %
Harley-Davidson	49.4	50.0
Honda	14.2	15.1
Suzuki	12.5	12.9
Yamaha	9.2	8.6
Kawasaki	7.2	6.8

Brand Profile

Harley competes on design and quality (intentionally unique-sounding engines).

Harley's past growth and continued success is closely tied to its brand loyalty (Harley owners have been known to tattoo the brand's trademark on their bodies and are members of HOG—Harley Owner's Group).

Harley has distinguished itself from other brands based on its heritage, image, and reputation—a "rebellious" image the company doesn't have control over.

Harley does not promote functional benefits like power and performance; advertising messages portray the emotional connection between brand and rider.

Brand Insight from Loyal Customers

"I love everything about a Harley. From the bike and clothing to the people you meet when riding, and the instant friends everywhere you go."

"When you ride a Harley you feel a Harley. When you ride a [Honda] Gold Wing, you don't feel anything. The Harley engine has a soul. And a lot of Japanese bikes don't have soul."

Competitor Profile

Japanese competitors offer heavyweight models that appeal to price-conscious buyers more interested in the motorcycle's technology.

Features such as fuel injection and ABS brakes make Japanese bikes a sensible buy, but they lack the outlaw image of a Harley.

Target Market Profile (Current)

- Demographics: 45–59 years old; 88% male and 12% female; $75 000 plus annually; reside in urban markets
- Psychographics: adventurous; like to travel; break away from routine on weekends; enjoy the freedom of the open road
- Behaviour: current customers are extremely brand loyal and emotionally connected to brand. "Weekend Warrior" is a nickname describing the customer.

Problem

The current customer is aging and younger potential customers see a Harley as a bike that looks like their father's or grandfather's bike—it is the motorcycle of choice for aging baby boomers. Future growth depends upon Harley's ability to attract new, younger customers. How does Harley-Davidson attract a younger customer?

Communications Objectives

- Attract a younger customer in the 30–45 year age range.
- Alter perceptions held by younger customers about the brand.
- Present an image more in line with the lifestyles of the younger target.

Positioning Statement

Harley-Davidson represents a sense of freedom, independence, a chance to live on your own terms for a while, even rebelliousness. For individuals wanting to be a kindred spirit with others of like mind, Harley-Davidson is the brand for you.

Creative Objectives

- To communicate an image or set of images more in line with younger lifestyles.
- To portray the feeling of freedom and independence a younger rider will enjoy when riding a Harley.
- To communicate an emotional connection between Harley-Davidson and the rider (younger rider).

Creative Strategy

Strategy is left to the discretion of the agency but it must be in line with the brand's overall positioning strategy. Emotional and lifestyle appeals that focus on freedom and independence have been successful in the past but Harley-Davidson is open to new ideas. The recommended strategy must be suitable for print, broadcast, and digital media.

Creative Execution

- 4-colour print ads (magazine and outdoor executions).
- 30-second television spots.

Online video ads.

All images must portray the core positioning strategy of the brand while appealing to the younger target audience.

This brief was prepared by the author for illustration purposes. Adapted from Nathan Vanderklippe and Richard Blackwell, "Passionate riders, Few Buyers," *The Globe and Mail*, July 28, 2009, pp. B1, B4, Martin Patriquin, "Booting the outlaw off the chopper," *Maclean's*, August 24, 2009, p. 53 and Joseph, Tirella, "Is Harley-Davidson over the hill," *MSN Money*, www.moneycentral.com.

Let's examine a few of these challenges in more detail and determine how they influence the direction of creative planning and the message strategy that is ultimately employed.

CREATING OR INCREASING BRAND AWARENESS Creating awareness is always the first challenge for advertising. The higher the level of awareness, the stronger the likelihood consumers will buy the product. Achieving high levels of awareness depends on how memorable the message is and perhaps how frequently the message is delivered. The medium used to deliver the message will also influence awareness levels. The right plan will use the right medium, but the size of the budget often dictates media selection. Nonetheless, the use of a medium such as television may create higher levels of awareness than magazines or outdoor advertising, and so on. An example of an awareness-raising ad appears in Figure 4.7.

ENCOURAGING TRIAL PURCHASE Creating awareness and interest in a brand is one thing, but getting the wallets out is another. Sometimes incentives have to be offered to give consumers an extra nudge. If the timing of the incentive is right, positive action will be

FIGURE 4.7   **An Advertisement that Raises Awareness of a New Product**

taken. Therefore, many advertisements are designed specifically to include special offers, anything from cents-off coupons to manufacturers' rebates to low-cost financing. These incentives serve a specific purpose. They help reduce the risk associated with purchasing something for the first time. For expensive goods such as cars and computers, where the risk is very high, incentives help encourage consumers to buy in a time frame that is desirable for the manufacturer.

Considering how the consumer's mind works, people want to know they are making the right decision. If the product lives up to the promise presented in the advertising, subsequent purchases will be made without incentives. Consumers today are looking for better value in the products and services they buy and, as a result, incentive-oriented advertising is now more prominent than in the past.

ATTRACTING NEW TARGET MARKETS In order to attract a new target market, say a younger age group than the audience the brand currently appeals to, a new message strategy is needed. The tone and style of advertising may have to change. To illustrate, consider some recent communications from Ford automobiles in Canada. Typically, younger consumers include brands such as Toyota, Mazda, and Honda on their "to consider" list. The Ford Focus wasn't on their mind. To attract a younger (20-something) customer, Ford developed music-themed creative for television and the Internet. The new ads complemented the sportier look of the redesigned Focus model. The message promoted Ford's Sync sound system technology as much as the car.[5]

ENCOURAGING PREFERENCE

For an established brand in growth or mature markets, the objective is to stand out from competing brands. Therefore, the thrust of marketing activities is product differentiation. Advertising messages focus on the attributes the brand offers. Where continuous improvement programs are in place, it is possible for a brand to become better with age, so there may be new things to communicate. Such is the case in the potato chip market where myriad brands are available. Ruffles encourages consumers to "grip more dip" with their thicker chip. See the illustration in Figure 4.8.

The unique attributes that are important to consumers play a key role in differentiating one brand from another and in creating preference for one brand over another. But changes such as these must be communicated to consumers. Having advertising messages focus on something new about the brand may be just enough to position the brand in a better light with consumers.

ALTERING PERCEPTIONS HELD BY CONSUMERS Building a brand sometimes requires consumers to adopt a different view of the brand. The quickest way to alter an image is to launch a completely new advertising campaign with an entirely different message. The style and personality of the message will be different to create a new image in the customer's mind.

Such was the case when Subaru launched its 2009 Subaru Forester. The car had a dependable workmanlike image, but to attract new buyers something new that would build on its Japanese heritage was needed. A new creative campaign (a parody of a car being washed by some sexy girls) featured "sexy" sumo wrestlers. A 60-second spot titled "Car Wash" showed a Forester entering a car wash to the song "Fire in a Disco," by Electric Six. In slow motion a group of sumo wrestlers enter with a hose and buckets of water. They wash the car but soon end up in a hilarious water fight. "Japanese SUVs just got a little bit sexier," says a voice-over. The image change had immediate impact. In a span of two months, sales of the Forester were double that of the same period a year earlier.[6]

Source: Courtesy of Frito Lay Canada.

FIGURE
4.8

Messages and images
that focus on unique
selling points help encourage
brand preference

Positioning Strategy Statement

Positioning strategy has been discussed in the previous two chapters. Therefore, comments here will simply reinforce the necessity of having a clearly worded positioning strategy statement and discuss how to apply it in developing an ad campaign. The positioning strategy statement identifies the key benefit a brand offers, states what the brand stands for, and is a reflection of a brand's personality. These are the essential inputs assessed by the creative team when it develops the message strategy. It can be the trigger that leads to discovery of the "big idea."

To illustrate how the positioning strategy influences creative planning, consider the success a brand like Secret deodorant has experienced. You are probably very familiar with Secret's advertising tagline: "Strong enough for a man, but made for a woman." The tagline captures the positioning strategy of the brand—it is dependable, long lasting, and offers confidence to do what one must do. Secret deodorant appeals to females on an emotional level. It doesn't work any better than other brands and it doesn't have a magical ingredient, but the slogan reaffirms femininity and a woman's ability to do anything a man can. A clever and compelling message distinguishes Secret from the other brands.

In the mouthwash market, Listerine was losing market share to Scope. Consumers saw little difference between the two brands but Listerine was perceived as somewhat old-fashioned. Listerine needed a new image. Since consumers were becoming more interested in health benefits beyond fresh breath, Listerine adopted a new positioning strategy:

> Listerine will be positioned as the only mouthwash offering multiple benefits for a healthy mouth, particularly healthy gums.

A new, humorous ad campaign featuring two action heroes would draw the consumers' attention to the importance of brushing teeth and then rinsing with Listerine. The new positioning strategy and the action hero campaign lifted market share from 39 percent to 52 percent in a two-year period. This campaign demonstrates the relationship among positioning strategy, effective advertising, and business results.[7] See the illustration in Figure 4.9.

CREATIVE OBJECTIVES

Creative objectives are statements that clearly indicate the information to be communicated to the target audience. What to say about a brand in general terms is usually included in the creative brief. While formats may vary, objective statements tend to involve a key benefit statement and a support claims statement, because the content of an ad or an ad campaign needs focus.

creative objective
A statement that clearly indicates the information to be communicated to the target audience; usually involves a key benefit statement and a support claims statement.

FIGURE 4.9   Listerine's action hero effectively positioned the brand as a leader in the oral health care category

Source: Courtesy of Johnson & Johnson Inc.

When determining what to say about a brand and how to say it, the copywriter and art director refer to the advertising objective for context. As discussed earlier in the chapter, the advertising objective may be to achieve brand awareness, encourage trial purchase, attract a new target, encourage preference, or alter a perception. Somehow, the objective and the primary reason for buying the brand must be related together so that a cohesive message is presented to the consumer.

key benefit statement
A statement of the basic selling idea, service, or benefit promised to the consumer by the advertiser; appears in the creative plan section of an advertising plan.

- **Key Benefit Statement:** The **key benefit statement** expresses the basic selling idea, service, or benefit that the advertiser promises the consumer. This benefit should be the primary reason for buying a particular brand instead of competitive brands. The benefit can be something tangible, such as better performance, better quality, lower price, longer lasting, and so on, or it can be something intangible or psychological, such as the status and prestige that come with ownership. It is a promise to the consumer. For example, the Vitality toothbrush from Oral-B promises consumers to reduce plaque. People may need Oral-B to improve their dental health.

support claims statement
A substantiation of the promise made in the key benefit statement; appears in the creative plan.

- **Support Claims Statement:** A **support claims statement** describes the characteristics that will substantiate the promise. It provides proof of the promise based on criteria such as technical performance data, comparative product testing, and any other data generated from marketing research. Good support claims give customers a real reason why they should buy the product. In the case of the Vitality toothbrush mentioned above, a strong visual illustration and supporting advertisng copy provides proof. The image in Figure 4.10 aptly illustrates the point.

Support claims statements are less important for brands touting intangible benefits. Lifestyle imagery, for example, relies on the image presented and the connection between the image and the consumer who sees it to substantiate the promise.

To further demonstrate the application of and relationships between advertising objectives, key benefits, and support claims statements, consider the situation that Pine-Sol was facing. Pine-Sol ranks second in market share behind Mr. Clean and ahead of Lysol. Research showed Pine-Sol was thought to be old-fashioned and too strong for everyday use, with an overpowering smell. It suffered from back-of-the-cupboard syndrome. The advertising objective was to alter these perceptions. The solution was found in consumer research. Younger women wanted strength, but not the strength Pine-Sol stood for. In exploratory research, the women talked about different types of clean: the clean for when friends dropped by and the clean for when the mother-in-law dropped by. Out of this came the idea for a new level of clean: the thorough clean. Therefore, the key benefit statement for Pine-Sol might read as follows:

> For mothers in search of a cleaner that will thoroughly clean their floors and counters, Pine-Sol works best (the promise).

The support claims statement might read like this:

> While other leading brands get your floors and counters clean, Pine-Sol cleans and disinfects more thoroughly. It even cleans the dirt you don't know about, such as accidents and spills that go undetected (the proof).

Pine-Sol's message was communicated in a unique manner. The ads charmingly dramatized real life and included situations mothers could readily identify with (see Figure 4.11). One commercial showed a small boy whose "aim" is off in the bathroom. Another showed a dog resting on the kitchen table instead of his basket. In research, women said "That's my life." In short, the ads make them think of Pine-Sol differently than before.[8]

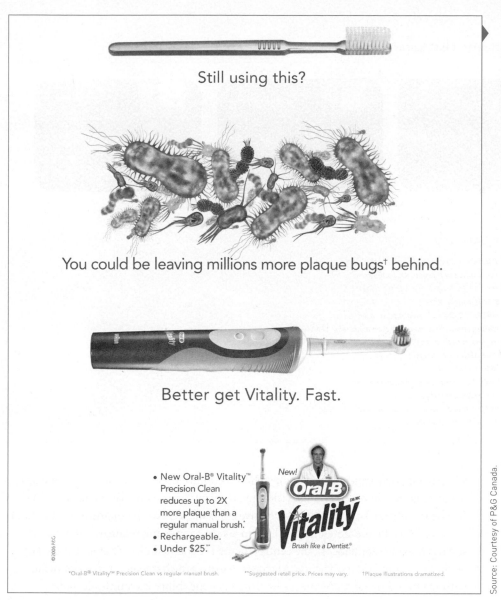

Still using this?

You could be leaving millions more plaque bugs† behind.

Better get Vitality. Fast.

- New Oral-B® Vitality™ Precision Clean reduces up to 2X more plaque than a regular manual brush.*
- Rechargeable.
- Under $25.**

New!
Oral·B
Vitality
Brush like a Dentist.®

©2006 P&G

*Oral-B® Vitality™ Precision Clean vs regular manual brush.   **Suggested retail price. Prices may vary.   †Plaque illustrations dramatized.

FIGURE 4.10

A Good Visual Illustration Demonstrates the Key Benefit of the Oral-B Toothbrush

CREATIVE STRATEGY

With the decisions about what to say in advertising determined, the creative team turns its attention to creative strategy. This is where the advertising agency starts to earn its keep. What the team searches for is the "big idea," or the central concept or theme that an entire campaign can be built around. All kinds of discussion and experimentation take place. It is an exercise in brainstorming. The guiding light is the positioning strategy. When the ad agency pitches its ideas to the client, the client evaluates the idea based on how it fits with the positioning strategy. Simply put: Is the big idea on strategy or off strategy?

The **creative strategy** is a statement of how the message will be communicated to the target audience. It deals with issues such as the theme, the tone and style of message that will be adopted, and the appeal techniques that will be employed. It is a statement about the personality a brand will project to consumers.

- **Central Theme:** The **central theme** or "big idea" is the glue that binds the various creative elements of the campaign together. As such, the theme must be transferable from one medium to another. For example, when someone sees an ad in print form

creative strategy
A plan of action for how the message will be communicated to the target audience, covering the tone and style of message, the central theme, and the appeal techniques.

central theme ("big idea")
The glue that binds various creative elements of a campaign together; transferable from one medium to another.

> FIGURE
> **4.7**   **An Advertisement that Raises Awareness of a New Product**

"BAD AIM"

VIDEO: *Open on a shot of an empty bathroom.*
Now a little boy runs into the bathroom.
The little boy begins to pee in the toilet.
SFX: *Tinkling in toilet.*
SUPER: *Pine-Sol cleans the dirt you know about.*
VIDEO: *Suddenly, his mom calls from downstairs. The boy turns to*
respond to her call, and in doing so pees on the floor.
MOM: *Max! We're going!*
SFX: *Tinkling on floor.*
VIDEO: *He turns back and casually finishes up.*
SUPER: *And the dirt you don't.*
VIDEO: *Cut to a mid-shot of Pine-Sol Original bottle.*
SUPER: *The thorough clean.*

(newspaper, magazine, or outdoor), it should conjure up images and meaning from something they have seen on television (a 30-second commercial). What the theme will be is truly the key decision the creative team makes. For the theme to see the light of day, it must be presented to the client in a very convincing manner. For a brand such as Maytag (appliances), the central theme is dependability. That is also the key benefit the brand offers. The idle Maytag repairman, a character strongly associated with the brand name, is the means by which dependability is communicated.

- **Tone and Style:** In an attempt to break through the clutter of competitive advertising, copywriters and art directors agonize over decisions about tone and style. Such a fundamental decision has a direct impact on how a campaign evolves over time and how the brand's personality gets ingrained in the customer's mind. Single words often describe the tone and style that is recommended. For example, the message will be presented in a persuasive manner, an informative manner, a conservative manner, a friendly manner, a contemporary manner, a straightforward manner, an upbeat manner, and so on and so on. What approach will have the most impact on the target audience? Knowledge about the target audience plays a key role in this decision.

A recent advertising campaign for Diet Pepsi aptly demonstrates how good decisions about theme, tone, and style have a positive impact on consumers. Diet Pepsi was losing ground to Diet Coke, and Diet Pepsi was being ruled by the image of regular Pepsi. Diet Pepsi's primary target market is young adults (people in their 20s and early 30s). Marketing research revealed they didn't want to lose their spontaneity and spirit even though they were getting older. Therefore, the big idea had to consider the youthful feelings of a maturing audience. Too much youth and Diet Pepsi would wind up back in regular Pepsi territory. Too little, and the brand would be just plain dull.

The creative team recommended a "Forever Young" theme (see Figure 4.12). The tone and style of ads, particularly on television, were "kind of wacky." They portrayed characters on a temporary break from maturity, not a breakdown in their entire way of life, just a longing for some crazy moments of their past. In one ad, a young couple start making out in their child's classroom on a parent-teacher night—the teacher glances over in dismay. Another commercial titled "Comb-Over" taps into the nostalgia of a balding man (see the illustration in Figure 4.12). The "Forever Young" tagline appears at the end of each commercial.

For more insight into how advertising resolves specific business problems and where the big idea comes from to do so, read the IMC Highlight: **Toyota Tundra Gets Guys on Board**.

APPEAL TECHNIQUES

How to make an advertisement appealing to the customer is another key decision. What techniques will be employed to bring the product benefit claims and theme to life? What can we do creatively to break through the perceptual barriers in the consumer's mind? There isn't a single, definitive formula for success, but there is a tendency to classify appeal techniques into certain areas. For example, when you see an ad, does it make you

Agency:	BBDO Canada	Title:	"Comb-Over"
Client:	Pepsi-Cola Canada Ltd.	Length:	30-second English Television
Product:	Diet Pepsi	Date:	01.02

PEPSI

We open on a balding man standing on a sidewalk somewhere. He is looking away, but turns towards camera as the camera approaches him
ANNCR VO: I see you're drinking Diet Pepsi. Is there anything else youthful you'd like to experience?

MAN: (thinking for a moment and then pointing at his bald head) Yeah...I'd like to have back all the hair I had in high school.

MUSIC: (The song "I Ran" from the Flock of Seagulls starts to play.)
Panning up we follow our hero walking towards camera - indeed he has his high school hair back - it's unfortunately the same 1980s Flock of Seagulls hairstyle he wore as teenager.

We see our hero in the middle of a serious business meeting.

His hair is casting an unusual shadow on the projection screen - disrupting the meeting.

Then we see our hero waiting for a serve.

His new hair is blocking 90% of his vision. His opponent winds up and serves. Just as our hero takes the ball in the head.

We match-dissolve back to our original scene - our hero looks back towards camera.
MAN: (thinking) Oh second thought, I'll stick to the Diet Pepsi.

FOREVER YOUNG
ANNCR VO: Taste the one that's forever young. Diet Pepsi.

FIGURE 4.12

An Illustration of Diet Pepsi's Central Theme or "Big Idea"

Toyota Tundra Gets Guys on Board

Toyota had been marketing the Tundra truck unsuccessfully since 1998. In a market dominated by Ford, GM, and Dodge where a macho image prevailed, Toyota Tundra was perceived as a lightweight. The product was overhauled and now offered the size, heft, and power that guys were looking for. The advertising challenge or problem was to find a way to alter the perception that guys had about the truck.

Prior to devising new creative, Toyota and its agency, Dentsu Canada, reviewed research information. True to form, the lightweight truck image prevailed and young guys didn't see a Japanese truck as part of their driving equation. Buried in the research, however, were some subtle shifts. Apparently younger, more educated drivers, new to the truck market, were open to change—change for the good. In their minds, "a hammer is great but if a nail gun works faster, why not embrace it?" The agency had to capture that attitude in any new message about the Tundra.

The strategy or big idea that was ultimately recommended to Toyota was "The Book of Truck," a leather-bound tome of philosophical wisdom that tapped into age-old pickup truck truths. A rough-looking spokesperson clad in jeans, long leather coat, and cowboy hat talked about the values of independence, loyalty, trustworthiness, and working smart. Folksy Zen-like sayings such as "A good truck will never quit" and "Revere tradition but keep an open mind" tapped into the new buyers' attitudes and were key elements of print ads. Dealer posters employed the same strategy and execution.

The campaign worked and Toyota exceeded its goals. Based on sales results, Toyota definitely altered perceptions of the Tundra held by young truck drivers. The 2007 sales objective was to sell 9000 units. By the end of the year 12 145 Tundras were sold. Is there a moral to the story? Yes. An improved product supported with the right message, a message in tune with buyer attitudes, works every time.

Adapted from "Toyota Tundra Re-Launch," The Cassies 2009, HYPERLINK "http://www.cassies.ca/winners/2009Winners" www.cassies.ca/winners/2009Winners.

snicker? Does it draw a tear? Does it make you think? How consumers respond to an ad is usually related to the effectiveness of the appeal. The following is a discussion of some of the more common appeal techniques.

POSITIVE APPEALS Presenting the message in a positive manner is always a safe approach, but it is also a very common approach. If combined effectively with the right theme, positive appeals will work. However, if the creative execution lacks impact, it will wind up being just another ad. The positive appeal stresses the positive benefits of the product and how a person can gain by purchasing the product. McDonald's is one of the country's biggest advertisers and dominates its market. The company is proud of its accomplishments so its ads reflect its position. The theme of McDonald's advertising does change from time to time, but the ads remain consistent in how they appeal to their target. McDonald's current campaign uses the theme and tagline "I'm lovin' it" to appeal to people in a positive manner. Typically, McDonald's ads include music and positive interactions among family members.

Kraft Canada launched a campaign for Kraft peanut butter that shows a variety of symbols drawn into the peanut butter spread on toast. A heart, happy face, and peace symbol are among 10 symbols used in the campaign. Kraft is reminding people of all the good feelings you get when eating peanut butter and that they should "spread the feeling." Refer to the illustration in Figure 4.13.

FIGURE 4.13   Kraft Uses Positive Appeal to Remind People How Good They'll Feel from Eating Kraft Peanut Butter

Source: Photo by Scott Anderson.

NEGATIVE APPEALS Unless you are Buckley's cough mixture, you don't say bad things about your product. "Tastes awful, but it works" is now a famous slogan coined by Buckley's. Following a philosophy of "do what your momma says and you will get better," Buckley's has experienced new popularity and a positive increase in market share based solely on its negative style of advertising.

For other products, though, negative appeals usually present a situation the consumer would like to avoid. Nobody wants to be in a car collision, but to dramatize the safety features of the Jetta, Volkswagen created a TV spot in which two young men suddenly collide with a truck backing out of a driveway. In a split second the front of the car implodes and the men's heads snap forward, making contact with the exploding airbags. The dramatic demonstration makes its point: in another car they would be dead.

HUMOROUS APPEALS Taking a light-hearted approach to communicating benefits can work effectively. In fact, many critics believe that for advertising to be successful it must entertain the audience. If true, then an advertisement that causes the audience to break into a smile or giggle should break through the clutter. A recent television campaign for NAPA Autopro, a chain of vehicle maintenance centres, shows how humour can be used effectively. In a series of commercials, various customers try to describe their car problems by sounding out the noises to the service manager. They are unsuccessful, so the service manager begins his rendition of what the problem may be. He sounds out one problem but that isn't it; he sounds out another and the customer says that's it. The service manager then says: "We can take care of that." You may have to see the commercials to laugh, but they are funny, even after many viewings.

Mr. Sub developed a humorous campaign around the tagline "so delicious, they make good people do bad things." In one of the spots an elderly woman sidles up to a young man waiting at a bus stop and steals his sub sandwich. She drops to the sidewalk and begins eating. When the young man reaches down to stop her, she yells out, "Help, help. He's hurting me." It's a creative way to amplify the key benefits (fresh bread, fresh toppings, and so on) that drive people to a sub-style restaurant.[9]

A major weakness of using humour is that it can wear out prematurely. After a few exposures, the audience may not find the message funny. Advertisers must also be wary of sarcastic humour that could insult cultural groups. Humour can backfire and bring on unwanted negative publicity. Since the use of humour allows for creative latitude, the creative team must ensure that the humour does not get more attention than the product. To keep the message fresh, a pool of commercials is needed so that individual spots can be rotated in and out of a media schedule.

SEXUAL APPEALS Sex in advertising! It will spark some controversy, some good, some not so good. When sexual appeals are used in advertising, certain values and attitudes toward sex are being sold to consumers along with the products. Consider, for example, a recent campaign for Reversa, a product designed to reverse the effects of skin's photo-aging. Reversa was well-known in cosmetician and dermatologist circles but was an unknown brand among the public. With little money to spend on advertising and lots of competition, the brand launched a print ad showing a cougar (a sexy-looking woman in her 40s) sitting serenely on a high-end sofa, with a naked Adonis alongside. The print ad suggested the reader visit a micro-site (seemoresideeffects.ca), which extolled the virtues of Reversa. The site features 12 video clips of rippling young men teasing the viewer. The sexual innuendo is quite clear.

The strategic direction for the campaign stems from the fact that women in their 40s start to worry about aging, but it is also a time when cougars are in their prime (yes, advertisers do think of these things). The cougar wants to be beautiful and seductive. She is financially independent, sexual, and looking for a fun, young sexual partner. According to Robert Lavoie, company president, "The ad campaign is sexy and addresses women in a bold, consumer-focused manner. The ads focus on the real benefits of Reversa—sex appeal!"[10] The campaign worked. Sales increased 31 percent over the previous year, compared to 2 percent historical growth. The Reversa campaign was a silver award winner for best integrated campaign in Canada at CASSIES 2007.[11] An award-winning campaign for Jergens effectively uses the female body in a sexy, smart, and simple way. The sensuous images and minimal copy portray the usefulness of the product. In a variety of executions, lines of lotion suggest clothing on an otherwise nude woman, which sparks consideration of that universal undergarment—your skin. Refer to Figure 4.14 for an illustration.

Sex is a strong physiological need, just behind self-preservation, so why not use it in advertising? The only real issue is the way in which it is used. Clearly, explicit sex increases the risks for the advertiser, since it may alienate consumers at large. But if core customers do not find it offensive, the advertiser may truly be on to something.

EMOTIONAL APPEALS Emotional appeals presented effectively will arouse the feelings of an audience. To demonstrate, consider the style of advertising used to promote social causes: anything from drinking and driving to spousal abuse to quitting smoking. In one TV ad that encourages people to stop smoking, a mature woman talks of the perils of second-hand smoke. Her husband, a smoker, is dead and she suffers from emphysema due to second-hand smoke. Such a message leaves the viewer with a disturbing feeling.

FIGURE
4.14 **Sexual imagery in advertising can be an effective appeal technique**

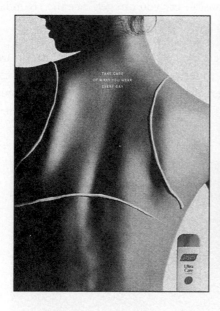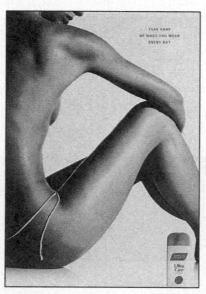

Source: Courtesy of KAO Brands Canada

Tapping into people's emotions also works in a positive setting. There is no disputing the popularity and dominance of Tim Hortons in Canada. Part of Tim Hortons's success is attributed to effective and sometimes emotional advertising that resonates with consumers. Its "True Stories" series of commercials connects with Canadians everywhere by depicting the emotional bonding that actually exists between customers and the company.

One such commercial titled "Proud Fathers" featured a grandfather and his middle-aged son watching the third-generation son play hockey. In the spot we see a coffee-toting grandfather headed to the rink to watch his grandson. Through flashbacks, we see how years before he would constantly nag at his own son to study more and play hockey less. But we learn, in a bittersweet twist, that despite his objections, he would also secretly watch his son play hockey.[12] Emotional advertising can have impact!

LIFESTYLE APPEALS Advertisers using lifestyle appeal techniques try to associate their brand with the lifestyle or desired lifestyle of the audience they are trying to reach. Some of the appeals already discussed, such as sexual appeals and emotional appeals, are frequently included as elements of a lifestyle campaign. Other elements may include action, adventure, and excitement to stimulate desire. Lifestyle appeals are popular among advertisers owing to the greater availability of psychographic information about Canadian consumers. Many beer brands use lifestyle appeals to establish an image firmly in the minds of drinkers 19 to 29 years of age. If you are what you drink, then there is a brand of beer for you.

The automobile industry uses lifestyle messages heavily, particularly in the sport utility and luxury segments of the market. The need to experience adventure, for example, is effectively portrayed simply by placing a vehicle in an exciting situation. Launch ads for the Hyundai Genesis Coupe provide an example. The sporty vehicle is shown in an exhilarating driving situation the target market would like to participate in. Hyundai presents an additional benefit: the thrill of the ride at a reasonable price. The headline says it all: "The most sensible, irresponsible car you can get." See the Hyundai Genesis Coupe ad in Figure 4.15.

COMPARATIVE APPEALS In comparative advertisements, the promise and proof are shown by comparing the attributes of a given product with those of competing products—attributes that are important to the target market. The comparison should focus on the primary reason for buying the product. Comparisons can be direct, such as when

Source: Courtesy of Audi of America.

FIGURE 4.15

Audi Uses Lifestyle Appeals to Attract Potential Buyers

the other brand is mentioned and shown, or they can be indirect, with only a reference to another leading brand or brands.

McCain Foods recently employed comparative advertising to get an edge on arch-rival Delissio (a Kraft brand). Both brands compete for leadership in the frozen pizza category. The commercial features a woman participating in a taste test with McCain's rising crust pizza and another leading brand. "Any thoughts," a man asks from behind a two-way mirror. "I like the McCain pizza," the woman says. "The crust and cheese are perfect, and there's lots of pepperoni." The man asks what she thinks of the other brand. She pauses, looks at it, and repeats her glowing praise of the McCain pizza. A voiceover at the end of the spot says: "Looks like people love McCain rising crust."

The associate creative director for the ad, Irfan Khan, says the ad offers a new approach to side-by-side taste tests. "Insight gained from research suggested Canadians are so polite that the woman in the ad had difficulty saying anything bad about the other pizza."[13]

Comparative campaigns are usually undertaken by a "challenger" brand, a brand that ranks behind the category leader in terms of market share. Showing comparisons where the challenger performs better than the market leader is a convincing presentation. It will make consumers think more about the brand they currently use. Such a strategy presents several risks. For one thing, the brand leader could fight back. If so, the brand that made the comparison may need adequate financial resources to fight an advertising war. As well, any claims must not mislead the public. If they do, the market leader could instigate legal proceedings to get the offending brand to offer proof of its claims. Critics of comparative appeals firmly believe a brand should stand on its own merits. Why cloud the issue by bringing in competing brands?

FACTUAL APPEALS Certain product categories lend themselves to a straightforward style of advertising. The ads simply state what the product will do and back it up with information that is easy for the customer to understand. Over-the-counter pharmaceuticals use this technique frequently. Brands in this category rely on technical information or scientific data to validate claims. Advil says it's for "today's kind of pain." Advil offers fast relief for the things that slow you down. Phrases such as "safe, reliable, and doctor recommended" verify the claim. Category leader Tylenol says, "Doctors recommend Tylenol more than all other brands combined to reduce fever and temporarily relieve minor aches and pains." The third-party endorsement by doctors has a definite impact. These competitive examples aptly depict the intent of factual appeals.

Factual appeals are also appropriate for products that are expensive or complex, such as expensive LED televisions or space-age kitchen appliances. Yes, these types of products have to look good, but they must also be dependable. Consumers want some hard and fast facts! In these cases, there is usually a high degree of involvement by consumers in the decision-making process, so ads in print and broadcast media often refer consumers to a website for detailed information.

For more insight into the nature of creative strategy, how creative concepts develop, and creative execution (the next section in this chapter), read the IMC Highlight: **New Creative Helps Build SpongeTowel's Business**.

CREATIVE EXECUTION

In the **creative execution** stage of creative planning, specific decisions are made regarding how to best present the message. If product comparisons are used, what kind of demonstration technique will be employed? Will sexual appeals be subtle or blatant? If lifestyle appeals are used, what kind of backdrops and settings will be needed? If music is called for, what kind of music will it be? If it is a print campaign, will the ads be copy

creative execution
The stage of creative planning at which specific decisions are made regarding how to best present the message.

IMC HIGHLIGHT »

New Creative Helps Build SpongeTowel's Business

What does a brand do when the market leader dominates market share? In the paper towel market, Bounty towels are the undisputed king of the hill. Bounty's market share is 24 percent while SpongeTowel's market share was a distant 13 percent.

Kruger Products turned to its ad agency, john st., to come up with a new creative campaign that would take some market share away from Bounty. Prior to thinking about anything new, Kruger and john st. evaluated some market research information. Bounty was firmly established as "the quicker picker-upper" and its strength and absorbency benefits could not be disputed. That presented a challenge since SpongeTowels offered similar absorbency benefits.

A nugget of research information was the key for a new creative campaign. In side-by-side branded product tests, consumers always preferred Bounty (probably from their perceptions of the brand based on all the advertising

they had been exposed to). However, in unbranded tests SpongeTowels achieved better preference scores. The research also indicated that women weren't that enthralled with Bounty's "it does everything" message. That caught the attention of the john st. creative team.

The theme or big idea that was ultimately recommended originated from the brand name and a key product feature—"sponge pocket embossing"—that helped with absorbency. A humorous strategy that dramatized the sponge pockets was the foundation of the new creative. In one commercial called "Jug," a little girl struggles carrying a pitcher of juice from the fridge to the kitchen counter. As it crashes to the floor, the sponge pocket characters (men dressed in sponge-like costumes) pounce on the mess and save the day.

The new creative campaign worked. In a market where unit volume was flat, unit sales of SpongeTowels increased by 17 percent. Such an increase strongly suggests an improvement in quality perceptions for SpongeTowels compared to Bounty.

Adapted from "SpongeTowels," The Cassies, 2009, www.cassies.ca/winners/2009Winners.

dominated or image dominated? Will artwork or photography be the key visual element? How big will the ads be? There are a host of decisions to be made.

The agency creative team evaluates specific ideas that it thinks have the potential to convert its vision of an ad into reality. In doing so, the team must answer two basic questions:

1. What is the best or most convincing way to present the brand's benefits to motivate the consumer to take action?
2. Is there a specific technique that will effectively convince consumers that this is the right brand for them?

For example, if a decision is made to use a celebrity as a spokesperson, who will the celebrity be? Will it be a famous rock star, movie star, or sports personality? A lot of behind-the-scenes discussion goes on for decisions of this magnitude. The following are some of the more commonly used presentation tactics.

PRODUCT DEMONSTRATIONS For products that want to make claims regarding performance (e.g., dependability, reliability, speed), demonstrations work well. As mentioned above, the simplest appeal is to say or show the product and what it will do. In print advertising, "a picture says a thousand words."

On television, showing the product in use is often the simplest and most direct way to make a claim. The BMW Mini is a small automobile with a "cute" reputation, not exactly the image BMW wanted for its high-performing vehicle. A series of commercials was developed to highlight safety, speed, and spaciousness. To demonstrate how much space there is in a Mini, a commercial showed a male and female suddenly popping up in the front seat while putting their clothes back on. If that wasn't enough to make the point, a second female pops up from the back seat, also putting her clothes back on. Message delivered!

TESTIMONIALS Advertisers that follow a traditional approach to advertising frequently use testimonials. In a **testimonial**, a typical user of the product presents the message. Real people in ads are often perceived to be more credible than models and celebrities who are paid handsomely to sell a certain brand. Walmart, for example, has developed a series of ads using people of various ethnic backgrounds to make the point that Walmart offers the value that their respective families are looking for. Such a tactic broadens the reach of Walmart in cosmopolitan markets. The Tim Hortons "True Stories" commercials referred to earlier in the chapter effectively use testimonials to advantage. Canadians identify with the individual or family situations presented in the commercials. In each commercial the customers tell a story about why Tim Hortons plays such an important and enjoyable role in their lives.

ENDORSEMENTS Star power is the heart of an **endorsement** execution. Stars from stage, screen, music, and sports form the nucleus of celebrity endorsers. Among the biggest and most expensive celebrities are Tiger Woods (Nike, American Express, and Tag Heuer) and Sidney Crosby (Reebok and Gatorade).

When a celebrity is used, the advertiser capitalizes on the popularity of the star. Gatorade was quick to sign Sidney Crosby as a spokesperson. According to Jeff Jacket, marketing manager at Gatorade, "The teenagers that Gatorade targets will more easily relate to a young up-and-coming star than a grizzled superstar."[14] And the relationship between Sidney Crosby and Reebok is a natural fit. Crosby's presence as a primary spokesperson immediately makes Reebok a viable competitor in the hockey equipment market. He is a significant addition to Reebok's "I Am What I Am" advertising campaign that includes famous athletes from other sports and that celebrates authenticity and individuality.[15] One television spot traces Crosby's most poignant moments growing up as a young hockey player in Cole Harbour, Nova Scotia—a story that Canadians can readily identify with.

Do celebrities work? That's a tough question to answer, but one asked frequently by clients. There isn't a definitive answer, but let's look at a situation and try to pass judgment. Where would Nike be in the golf business without Tiger Woods? Nike has invested millions in Woods, and in return, he alone has put Nike on the golf map. Star power like that does attract advertisers, and an audience.

TAGLINES AND SLOGANS Despite all of the time, energy, and money that go into developing an ad campaign, consumers only remember bits and pieces of the message. The most important thing for them to remember is the brand name and the primary benefit. To reinforce the primary benefit and the central theme of a campaign, and to reflect the positioning strategy of the brand, the creative team develops a **tagline** for individual ads, or a **slogan** that will appear in all forms of advertising. The slogan provides continuity within an advertising campaign. As described above, the slogan for Reebok's advertising campaign is "I Am What I Am." This tagline aptly summarizes the intentions of Reebok's message. Other slogans appearing on ads in this chapter include "Spread the feeling" for Kraft peanut butter and "The Best a Man Can Get" for Gillette.

Of the things that consumers remember about a brand, the slogan is something they have a tendency to recall. The repetition of messages consumers receive over an extended period helps ingrain the slogan in the customer's mind. From time to time the slogan will change, especially when a brand or company wants to change its image. However, it is more common for the slogan to remain in place even if the creative strategy and creative execution are completely new.

testimonial
An ad in which a typical user of the product presents the message.

endorsement
A situation where a celebrity speaks highly of an advertised product.

tagline
A short phrase that captures the essence of an advertised message.

slogan
A short phrase that captures the essence of an entire advertising campaign; it reflects the positioning strategy of the brand and is shown in all ads in all media.

The best slogans are short, powerful summations that companies use alongside their logos to drive the brand message home to consumers. Some of the more popular and longstanding slogans appear in Figure 4.16.

FIGURE
4.16   **Some Popular Brands and Slogans**

- Visa "All you need."

- Bounty "The quicker picker-upper."

- Burger King "Have it your way."

- Nike "Just do it."

- L'Oreal "Because I'm worth it."

- M&Ms "Melts in your mouth, not in your hands."

- Maxwell House "Good to the last drop."

A slogan is a key element of brand identification. Many of these slogans have stood the test of time. They are strongly associated with the brand name and appear in all forms of advertising.

SUMMARY

The marketing communications process begins with a sender (the advertiser) developing a message to be sent by the media to the receiver (the consumer or business customer). The goal of marketing communications is to break through consumers' perceptual barriers while recognizing that competitors' messages are trying to do the same. When messages are developed, consideration is given to how consumers receive and interpret messages. The consumer's mind goes through a series of stages: awareness, comprehension, conviction, and action.

Creative planning is a sequential process that involves analyzing market and customer information, identifying problems and opportunities, setting goals and objectives, and developing creative strategies and tactics. The planning cycle starts with a creative brief, a document prepared by the client for discussion with the advertising agency. The brief includes relevant background information, and identifies problems, goals, and advertising objectives. The document acts as a guideline for the creative team when it is brainstorming for new ideas.

Once the advertising objectives are identified, the creative team begins work on creative objectives, strategies, and execution. Advertising objectives provide focus to the creative

challenge (e.g., the objective is to create awareness, build preference, alter perceptions, encourage trial purchase, and so on). Creative objectives are statements that clearly identify the information to be communicated to the target market. They include a key benefit statement (a promise) and a support claims statement (proof of promise). Usually the client and agency collaborate when finalizing these statements.

Creative strategy is concerned with the theme, tone, style, and appeal techniques that are used to influence consumers to take action. Among the more commonly used strategies are positive and negative approaches using humorous, sexual, emotional, and lifestyle appeals; offering factual information; and comparisons with other products.

At the creative execution stage, specific decisions are made on how to implement the strategy. Some of the specific techniques that are commonly used include product demonstrations, testimonials from everyday users of the product, and celebrity endorsements. A good campaign will include a slogan. The slogan serves two essential roles. First, it communicates the essential idea the advertiser wants associated with the product; and second, it maintains continuity within an advertising campaign. In combination with the brand name, a good slogan helps build brand equity.

KEY TERMS

advertising, 103

advertising objectives, 107

"big idea", 114

central theme, 114

communication, 97

creative brief, 103

creative concept, 103

creative execution, 121

creative objective, 111

creative strategy, 114

encoding, 98

endorsement, 123

key benefit statement, 112

noise, 98

overall goal, 104

problem statement, 104

slogan, 123

support claims statement, 112

tagline, 123

testimonial, 123

transmission, 98

REVIEW QUESTIONS

1. Briefly explain the behavioural stages a consumer passes through prior to making the decision to buy a particular product.

2. What is a creative brief and what role does it play in the development of an advertising campaign?

3. In the context of creative planning, what is meant by the "big idea"?

4. Ad campaigns should have focus and aim toward an overall goal. Identify and briefly explain three specific goals a campaign may try to achieve.

5. How important is a positioning strategy statement and what role does it play in creative planning?

6. What is the difference between a key benefit statement and a support claims statement?

7. Briefly describe the various appeal techniques commonly used in advertising.

8. Briefly explain the following creative execution terms:
   a) testimonial and endorsement
   b) tagline and slogan

DISCUSSION AND APPLICATION QUESTIONS

1. Are humorous advertising campaigns effective? Conduct some online secondary research on humour in advertising and present a case for or against the use of humour.

2. "Lifestyle advertising strategies are ineffective because they communicate little about the product." Is this statement true or false? Conduct some online secondary research about lifestyle advertising and present a position on this issue.

3. "Good execution of a poor creative strategy will create positive results for the brand (company)." Is this statement true or false? Assemble some data that either support or refute this statement.

4. Clip an ad that catches your attention from a magazine in your household. After assessing the ad, try to determine the advertising objective, the creative objective (key benefit statement), and the creative strategy (appeal technique). Can you figure out what the advertiser intended when the ad was in the development stages?

5. Assess a series of advertisements for one brand (pick a popular brand that uses several different media). Based on everything you know about that brand and the marketing communications you are exposed to, write a positioning strategy statement that reflects the intentions of the brand. What message or image does the company want to instill in the customer's mind?

6. Select two brands that compete directly against one another. Assess the creative strategies and creative executions used by each brand. Since both brands are trying to reach and influence the same target market using advertising, which brand has more impact on consumers? Which style of advertising is more effective? Justify your position.

7. Find separate products or services that use the following creative appeal techniques:
   a) negative appeals
   b) humorous appeals
   c) comparative appeals

d) emotional appeals

e) lifestyle appeals

8. What is your assessment of each of the above strategies in terms of potential impact on the target market? Justify your position.

9. Assess a brand advertising campaign that features a celebrity spokesperson. Will that spokesperson have an influence on the intended target? What are the benefits and drawbacks of using a celebrity spokesperson?

ENDNOTES

1 Theresa Howard, "Ad campaign tells women to celebrate who they are," *USA Today*, September 7, 2005, www.usatoday.com.

2 "Ad Education," Iowa State University, www.public.iastate.edu/~geske/FCB.html.

3 American Marketing Association, "Marketing Definitions," www.marketingpower.com.

4 "Wendy's throws red wigs out," *Marketing Daily*, January 29, 2008, www.marketingmag.ca.

5 Karl Greenberg, "Ford Strategy to Market Focus to Younger Set is Paying Off," *Media Post*, May 12, 2008, www.publications.mediapost.com.

6 "Do you think I'm sexy?" *The Globe and Mail*, July 18, 2008, p. B5.

7 CASSIES, Canadian Advertising Success Stories, 2006, Listerine, www.cassies.ca/winners.

8 "Packaged Goods Other," CASSIES insert in *Marketing*, November 18, 2002, p. 5.

9 Matt Semansky, "Mr. Sub's good sandwiches inspire bad behavior," *Marketing Daily*, August 27, 2007, www.marketingmag.ca/daily.

10 "Reversa Side Effects," *The Inspiration Room Daily*, www.theinspirationroom.com/daily/2007/see-more-side-effects.

11 CASSIES, Canadian Advertising Success Stories, 2007, www.cassies.ca/winners/2007.

12 Keith McArthur, "The hard sell goes to the Olympics," *The Globe and Mail*, February 21, 2006, p. B7.

13 Kristin Laird, "If you can't say anything nice," *Marketing Daily*, June 10, 2008, www.marketingmag.ca.

14 Keith McArthur, "Crosby follows in Gretzky's footsteps," *The Globe and Mail*, April 17, 2006, p. B3.

15 "Reebok launches hard hitting 'I Am What I Am' TV ad starring Sidney Crosby," *The Globe and Mail*, November 10, 2005, www.globeandmail.com.

Advertising Planning: Traditional Media

Learning Objectives

After studying this chapter, you will be able to

1. Describe the steps involved in media planning

2. Distinguish among media objectives, media strategies, and media execution

3. Describe the various factors that influence media strategy decisions

4. Outline the characteristics, strengths, and weaknesses of mass media advertising alternatives

As mentioned in Chapter 4, the creative plan and media plan are developed at the same time and depend on the same information from the marketing plan. This chapter will focus specifically on the development and implementation of the media plan. Developing a media plan is a complex process. The primary goal of the agency media planners is to reach a target market efficiently. In doing so, they consider all kinds of strategic issues, along with conditions in the marketplace and what competitors are doing.

Efficiency in media planning can be loosely defined as gaining maximum exposure at minimum cost. In following this mantra, the agency planners must develop and execute a plan that achieves the client's objectives within certain financial constraints. As in the case of the creative plan, the media plan is part of a broader marketing communications plan and marketing plan. Therefore, the direction a media plan takes must fit in with and be coordinated (timed) with activities recommended in other marketing communications areas. Coordinating various communications activities creates synergy and maximizes the impact the plan will have on the target market.

Media planning is a complex task, and with consumers' media habits changing, mainly due to technology, it is more difficult than ever to reach people with advertising messages. In general terms, people are spending less time with traditional media and more time with digital media (online and mobile communications). A recent research report indicated that 20 percent of people are passing up the television to watch episodes of their favourite prime time shows online and that the largest portion are affluent, well-educated working women aged 25 to 44, a desirable target.[1] Planners must also adapt their thinking due to technologies such as satellite radio, digital video recorders, and video games.

It seems clear that consumers aren't going to be as receptive to the 30-second spot as they once were, and with the emergence of TiVo and digital video recorders (PVRs), many consumers zap right by the commercials that advertisers are paying top dollar to run. From a media planning perspective, new strategies have to be devised to reach an increasingly mobile and elusive consumer.

Media Planning

media planning
Developing a plan of action for communicating messages to the right people (the target market), at the right time, and with the right frequency.

Media planning involves developing a plan of action for communicating messages to the right people (the target market), at the right time, and with the right frequency. Both the client and the agency play a role in media planning (see Figure 5.1). The client's role focuses on providing necessary background information and then evaluating the recommendations that the agency makes. The agency assesses the information provided by the client and then prepares a strategic plan that will meet the client's objectives. Because there is a considerable amount of money involved, the client scrutinizes media plans carefully.

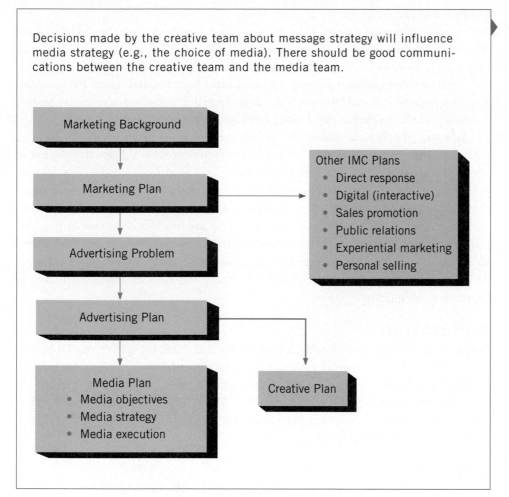

FIGURE
5.1

Media Planning Model

Decisions made by the creative team about message strategy will influence media strategy (e.g., the choice of media). There should be good communications between the creative team and the media team.

Marketing Background

Marketing Plan

Advertising Problem

Advertising Plan

Other IMC Plans
- Direct response
- Digital (interactive)
- Sales promotion
- Public relations
- Experiential marketing
- Personal selling

Media Plan
- Media objectives
- Media strategy
- Media execution

Creative Plan

Information provided by the client is contained in a **media brief** (much like the creative brief discussed in Chapter 4). The media brief is a document that contains essential information for developing the media plan and is used as a starting point in the discussion between a client and the agency. It includes some or all of the following information.

media brief
A document that contains essential information for developing a media plan; used to stimulate discussion between a client and agency.

MARKET PROFILE
Any relevant information about the current state of affairs in the market is useful to media planners. Such information includes historical sales data for leading brands, market share trends of leading brands, and rates of growth in the market. Is the market growing, flat, or declining?

COMPETITOR MEDIA STRATEGY
In general terms, what media do major competitors use, and how much money do they invest in media advertising? What the competitors are doing has some influence on the strategic directions that will be recommended. For example, if key competitors dominate a particular medium, it may be prudent to select another medium to reach the same target. Whatever competitive information is available should be in the hands of the media planners.

TARGET MARKET PROFILE

Perhaps the most important ingredient for a media plan is a thorough understanding of the target market. As discussed earlier, targets are described on the basis of demographic, psychographic, geographic, and behaviour response variables. The target profile must be clearly defined and key variables must be expanded upon. For example, knowing the activities and interests of the target (psychographic considerations) enables a media planner to select the best times and best places to advertise.

In terms of behaviour, knowledge of how the target interacts with the media (e.g., what media the target refers to most frequently) is important as it helps the planner to allocate funds across the recommended media. As indicated above, media consumption habits are changing. A research report from TVB Canada, for example, clearly shows that people aged 18 years and older continue to spend most of their weekly media time with television, but the number of hours spent on the Internet continues to rise. The report also indicates that people spend much more time with TV, radio, and the Internet than they do with daily newspapers and magazines. See Figure 5.2 for details.[2] This kind of information suggests that traditional advertisers will have to change their way of thinking—and quickly!

MEDIA OBJECTIVES

Based on marketing priorities, the client usually identifies key objectives. Objectives tend to focus on target market priorities by identifying primary targets and secondary targets, the nature of the message and its influence on media selection, the best time to advertise, and the geographic market priorities. Depending on the problem at hand or the overall goal of the campaign, the client may also identify priorities for reach, frequency, continuity, and engagement.

MEDIA BUDGET

Since media advertising is but one media expenditure, the funds available come from the marketing plan budget. In most cases, the client has already identified the amount that will be allocated to media advertising. Knowing the size of the budget is essential, because it provides the framework for the media planner's strategic thinking. Is there enough for television? Will this be strictly a print campaign? Is this a national campaign or will it be restricted to regional markets? Will this campaign rely on a few media or will it be a multimedia effort? The budget points the planners in a certain direction.

Once the media planners have been briefed on the assignment, they begin discussing potential alternatives. Their goal is to devise a media strategy and tactical plan (execution) that will achieve the stated objectives. Once the media plan has been

FIGURE 5.2

Time Spent with Media in Canada

Medium	Total Canada	Quebec
Television	25.0	25.1
Radio	19.6	19.8
Internet	13.7	10.0
Newspaper—Daily	3.2	3.4
Community Newspaper	0.4	0.5

All figures are hours per week for adults 18+ years. Canadians spend more time with television than any other medium.

Source: Courtesy of BBM Canada.

presented to the client and approved, agency media buyers negotiate with the media to buy the time and space. The media buyer's task is to deliver the maximum impact (on a target audience) at a minimum cost (client's budget).

Media planning is quantitative by nature. Agency personnel are experts in media trends and have all kinds of statistical information available to figure out which media are best suited to the client's needs. Furthermore, media software enhances the ability of media planners to generate efficient media plans. Once a plan has been implemented, the agency evaluates the plan in a post-buy analysis. A **post-buy analysis** is an evaluation of actual audience deliveries calculated after a specific spot or schedule of advertising has been run. The actual audience may be different from the estimated audience that was identified in the plan. The question to be answered is whether the plan delivered the audience it was supposed to.

post-buy analysis
An evaluation of actual audience deliveries calculated after a specific spot or schedule of advertising has run.

The Media Plan

The **media plan** is a document that outlines the relevant details about how a client's budget will be spent. Objectives are clearly identified, strategies are carefully rationalized, and execution details are precisely documented. The costs associated with every recommendation are put under the microscope when the agency presents the plan to the client. Because of the money involved, media plans often go through numerous revisions before being approved by the client. The structure and content of a media plan are the focus of this section of the chapter. Figure 5.3 summarizes the content of a media plan, although the content of a media plan varies from one agency to another. This model is strictly a guideline.

media plan
A strategy that outlines the relevant details about how a client's budget will be spent; involves decisions about what media to use and how much money to invest in the media chosen to reach the target audience effectively and efficiently.

MEDIA OBJECTIVES

Media objectives are clearly worded statements that outline what the plan is to accomplish. They provide guidance and direction for developing media strategies. If worded correctly, priorities will emerge. For example, there could be customer priorities, regional market priorities, and timing priorities. These priorities are based on historical information, the current situation a brand finds itself in, and the problem that the advertising plan must resolve. Such issues are part of the background information included in the media brief. For example, a plan may have a national or regional focus, or it may simply run in a few urban markets that are given priority.

media objective
A statement that outlines what a media plan is to accomplish (who, what, when, where, or how).

Media objectives typically deal with the following issues:

- **Who:** Who is the target market? The target market profile is defined in terms of demographic, psychographic, and geographic characteristics. Media planners use this profile to match the target with a compatible media profile. For example, magazines know their readership profile, radio stations know their listener profile, and television networks know who watches specific shows. If there is a means to reach the target directly (as an individual), that too is considered. Refer to the media strategy section of this chapter for a detailed discussion about target market matching strategies.

- **What:** What is the nature of the message to be communicated? Media planners must be informed about the message strategy. For example, is the message strategy information intensive (lots of copy) or image intensive (lots of visuals)? Does the budget permit television, and if so, is the creative team giving television due consideration? Issues such as these strongly suggest that basic creative and media decisions be made at the same time. Clients should provide guidance in this area. If certain media are mandatory, the client should say so.

FIGURE
5.3

**The Structure and
Content of a Media Plan**

Media Budget

- Total budget available (from client's marketing plan)

Media Objectives

- Who (is the target market)
- What (is the message)
- When (is the best time to advertise)
- Where (are the priority markets)
- How (important is reach, frequency, and continuity)

Note: Media objectives are usually clear, concise statements.

Media Strategy

- Target market matching strategy (shotgun, profile match, rifle)
- Market coverage
- Timing
- Reach considerations
- Frequency considerations
- Continuity considerations
- Engagement considerations
- Media selection rationale
- Media rejection rationale

Note: Media strategies expand upon the objectives and provide details about how the objectives will be achieved.

Media Execution

- Blocking chart (calendar showing timing, weight, and market coverage)
- Budget summary (allocations by media, time, and region)

- **Where:** Where are the market priorities geographically? The budget plays a key role in this decision. Typically, a brand has regions of strength and weakness. A media plan could be devised to correct a situation in a problem region. In such cases, a decision could be made to reduce media spending in a strong region and allocate more to a weaker region. In other situations, regions may be treated equally with media funds allocated based on population patterns. If this is to be a key market plan only, what key markets are given priority? The number of markets that must be reached and the level of intensity (media investment) are factors largely based on the budget.

- **When:** When is the best time to reach the target market? For example, is the product a seasonal product, such as suntan lotion or ski boots? If so, the media strategy will consider a heavier schedule of advertising in the pre-season, a time when consumers are starting to think about summer or winter activities. Knowledge of the target's daily schedule also plays a role in timing decisions. For instance, a busy executive who rises early and arrives home late may not have much time to spend with the media. How and when is the best time to reach this person? When is the best time to reach a student? Knowledge of media consumption patterns by the primary target is essential.

- **How:** The question of how conjures up all kinds of media issues. How many people to reach, how often to reach them, and for what length of time? These are strategic issues that are best left to the media planners at the ad agency. However, some basic guidance from the client is provided. For example, if the plan is for a new product, the absolute number of people reached and how often they are reached may be given priority. If a product is firmly established and the goal of the plan is to simply remind the target, then length of time may be given priority. Refer to the discussion about reach, frequency, and continuity in the next section for more details.

MEDIA STRATEGY

Media strategy focuses on how media objectives will be achieved while outlining how to reach the target market as effectively and efficiently as possible. Given the scarcity of clients' financial resources and their demands for accountability, having the right media strategy is crucial. Clients want to see a reasonable return for their investment. A media strategy addresses how often to advertise, how long to advertise, where to advertise, and what media to use, and it rationalizes why only certain media are recommended and others rejected. Strategic decisions are linked directly to the media objectives. The various factors that influence media strategy are discussed below.

media strategy
A plan for achieving the media objectives stated in the media plan; typically justifies the use of certain media.

TARGET MARKET PROFILE For some products and companies, the target description may be broad in scope. For example, a newspaper's primary readers include adults of all ages and income groups. In contrast, the primary buyer for a Lexus automobile may be described as a male business executive, 35 to 49 years of age, earning $75 000 annually, living in an urban market of 1 million plus. The extent of the target's description directly influences media strategy decisions.

The task of the media planner is to match the profile of the target market as closely as possible with the profile of the medium (e.g., the readership profile of a magazine or the listener profile of a radio station). The more compatible the match, the more efficient the strategy will be. For example, to reach that Lexus buyer, executive-oriented business magazines such as *Financial Post Business, Canadian Business,* and *Report on Business* are good matches. Figure 5.4 illustrates a readership profile. The same executive may watch television, but to place an ad in prime-time hours would reach people well beyond the target description. This would not be efficient. There are three basic target market matching strategies: shotgun, profile matching, and rifle.

- If a **shotgun strategy** is used, the target market's profile has a broad scope. The message is placed in media that reach a broad cross-section of the population. For example, television reaches all ages, although viewing by certain age groups varies by time of day. To reach teenagers and adults, prime-time television does the job. In the United States, the cost of placing one 30-second spot on *CSI: Crime Scene Investigation*, one of CBS's most popular drama shows, is US$347 000.[3] The same spot simulcast on the CTV Network in Canada would cost approximately C$35 000. Television is an expensive medium, especially if frequency is an important aspect of the media strategy.

    For advertisers on a tighter budget but with a diverse target market, options such as daily newspapers and out-of-home advertising are attractive. Out-of-home options include billboards, transit shelters, and subway stations. They reach a diverse population in key markets and generally cost less than television.

shotgun strategy
A tactic involving the use of mass media to reach a loosely defined target audience.

- If a **profile-matching strategy** is used, the target market profile is carefully defined by demographic, psychographic, and geographic variables. For example, assume a target profile described as follows: female head of household, working or stay-at-home mother, college or higher education, $50 000 household income, suburban

profile-matching strategy
A media tactic that involves matching the demographic profile of a product's target market with a specific medium that has a similar target profile.

FIGURE
5.4 **Readership Profile of *Canadian Business* Magazine**

Characteristic	Audience	
Circulation	98 000	
Readers per Copy	9.8	
Total Readership	964 000	
Male Readers	640 000	
Female Readers	324 000	
Demographics	**Readers**	**Index**
HHI $75 000+	583 000	136
HHI $150 000+	190 000	188
Senior Managers/Owners	107 000	318
Other Managers	206 000	158
Professionals	76 000	135
MOPES	388 000	176
Business Purchase Involvement		
Decisions $100 000+	57 000	252
Computer Decisions	180 000	220
Financial		
Savings/Securities $500 000	48 000	280
Own RRSPs, Mutual Funds, Stocks	569 000	115
Own Mutual Funds	334 000	115
Travel		
Taken 7+ Vacation Trips (year)	174 000	149
5+ Nights at Hotel Business Travel	139 000	173

Notes

1. Circulation multiplied by readers per copy equals total readership.

2. MOPEs are managers, owners, professionals, and executives.

3. The index in the right column shows how *Canadian Business* readers compare to the Canadian average. The index is calculated by dividing the percentage of *Canadian Business* readers by the percentage of Canadian adults in various categories being measured. *Canadian Business* readers are well above average in all categories.

Interpretation

Based on the above readership statistics, *Canadian Business* magazine is a good profile match for advertisers wanting to reach individuals with above-average incomes, including senior managers, professionals, and business owners. These individuals are decision makers in their places of employment.

Source: Adapted from *Canadian Business* Media Kit February 2010 and PMB 2009 Fall 2-Year Readership and Product Database.

lifestyle, with interests that include home decorating, entertaining, and travel. Several magazines are good possibilities for reaching such a woman: *Chatelaine, Canadian Living, Canadian Home & Country*, and *Homemakers*. The primary reader of each magazine is reasonably close to the description of the target. In contrast, Canadian Business magazine appeals to upper-income males and females commonly referred to as MOPEs (managers, owners, professionals, and entrepreneurs).

Profile matching can extend to television as well. Conventional networks such as CTV and Global have been losing viewers to specialty networks like TSN (sports), YTV (youth), and the Outdoor Life Network (OLN), among others. Specialty networks offer programming that is tailored to specific demographics. OLN caters to 20-something males and females with programs that have an action and adventure orientation. YTV reaches children and tweens (kids 11 to 14 years of age) with appropriate program content.

- In the **rifle strategy**, a common characteristic such as an activity or interest binds a target market together. For example, golfers are golfers, whether they play at a public club, an exclusive private club, or anywhere in between. All golfers look for similar equipment. They cross both genders and most income groups. Therefore, a publication such as *Score Golf* or *Golf Canada* offers a means of reaching the target directly. Enthusiasts look to these kinds of publications for information about golf products, golf vacation destinations, and anything golf related. Business publications target specific industries; therefore, to target decision makers within a particular industry, its trade publications are attractive. To reach people employed in the hospitality industry, for instance, a publication such as *Hotel & Restaurant* is an option.

rifle strategy
A strategy that involves using a specific medium that effectively reaches a target market defined by a common characteristic.

In Chapter 1, the concepts of database marketing and customer relationship management were discussed. A rifle strategy is ideally suited for organizations that practise these concepts. Non-traditional media such as the Internet, direct mail, and cell phones can reach customers on an individual basis. These media are discussed in more detail in appropriate chapters of this textbook.

NATURE OF THE MESSAGE Creative strategy and media strategy should be developed simultaneously to generate a synergistic effect in the marketplace. Planners should cooperate to ensure that the right message is delivered by the right medium. If a rational appeal technique is used with factual information to be communicated, then print media options take precedence. If emotional appeals are used and if action and adventure are prominent in the message, television is good. If engagement with the audience is a concern, then the Internet presents opportunities for delivering the message. If sales promotion incentives are part of the message, a combination of media may be called for. Television may be used to generate awareness of a contest, for example, while print media, the Internet, and in-store communications provide more details.

GEOGRAPHIC MARKET PRIORITIES With regard to where to advertise, strategic decisions must be made on how to divide a budget among the areas where advertising will be scheduled. A company or brand rarely advertises nationally on a continuous basis. It is common for some national advertising to occur during the course of a plan, but it is supplemented by additional advertising in markets where specific problems need to be resolved. In other instances, a brand might decide just to advertise in key urban markets. The top five Canadian urban markets reach about 40 percent of the total population— and much of the success (or failure) in Canada is governed by how successful the brand is in those five markets. Usually, the budget determines the extent of market coverage. Some of the coverage options include the following.

National Coverage Such a strategy assumes widespread availability of the product, with all geographic areas figuring equitably in the success of the product. For example, if product sales as expressed as a percentage of total sales by region are close to population splits by region, a national strategy is an option. Funds can be allocated across media that reach the national market. Network television shows in prime time (*CSI: Crime Scene Investigation, Survivor, Amazing Race, Without a Trace*, etc.) and national magazines such as *Maclean's* are good alternatives. Of course, the precise description of the target audience and the budget also influence this kind of strategy. Prime-time television and general-interest magazines reach a broad cross-section of the population, and the cost in absolute terms (the actual cost per ad) is high.

Regional Coverage A regional strategy involves an evaluation of each region's contribution to a brand's (or company's) success. Funds are allocated so that no particular region has an advantage or disadvantage—at least, that's the theory. The reality is different. Some regions will over-contribute to sales while others will under-contribute. An organization might assess the value of a region by analyzing two different indexes. The first index is called a **market development index** or **category development index (CDI)** and is a percentage of category sales (e.g., a category like women's deodorant) in an area in relation to the population of that area compared to the sales throughout the entire country in relation to the total population. For example, if the sale of women's deodorant in British Columbia represents 10 percent of total sales and BC represents 12 percent of the female population, the CDI is 83.3 (10 divided by 12). BC would be considered an underdeveloped region. Conversely, if Ontario represents 42 percent of women's deodorant sales and Ontario represents 38 percent of the female population, the CDI would be 110.5 (42 divided by 38). Ontario would be described as an overdeveloped women's deodorant market.

A **brand development index (BDI)** works the same way. It is a percentage of a brand's sales in an area in relation to the population in that area compared to the sales throughout the entire country in relation to the total population. For example, if Secret deodorant has 15 percent of its Canadian sales in BC and only 12 percent of the female population lives there, the BDI for BC would be 125 (15 divided by 12). This would indicate that BC is an important area for the brand; the brand is very popular there. Refer to Figure 5.5 for some additional calculations of the brand development index, which help explain why certain regions get disproportionate funds. There is only so much money to be allocated. For example, in a market where a brand is underdeveloped but potential for growth is present, that brand may temporarily receive additional funds that will be taken away from a region where the brand is doing well. The BDI is commonly used when determining regional media budgets.

In terms of media selection, a planner will focus on regional media opportunities to reach the target market. Television networks offer regional packages (e.g., all stations within a region) and national magazines such as *Chatelaine, Canadian Living*, and *Reader's Digest* offer numerous regional editions.

Key Market Coverage A third alternative is to give priority to those members of the target market residing in key urban markets. Usually there are predetermined criteria to establish what markets will receive media support. If population is the criterion, a planner will consider other strategic factors first and then go down the market list until the media budget is exhausted. Canada's top six cities (Toronto, Montreal, Vancouver, Ottawa-Hull, Calgary, and Edmonton) account for 43.9 percent of the population, while the top 10 cities account for 53.0 percent.[4] Given that the population is migrating steadily toward cities in Canada, a key market plan is a good option.

---

category development index (CDI) or market development index
The percentage of category sales in a geographic area in relation to the total population of that area; determines if a category is underdeveloped or overdeveloped in a particular region.

brand development index (BDI)
The percentage of a brand's sales in an area in relation to the population in that area; determines if the brand is underdeveloped or overdeveloped in each area.

FIGURE

5.5   Considerations for Allocating Budgets by Region

One method of determining the importance of a region for a brand (company) is to compare actual sales volume (as a percentage of total sales) to the region's population (as a percentage of Canada's population). Such an analysis is called a **brand development index (BDI)**. The BDI is determined by dividing the sales volume percentage by the regional population percentage.

Region	Sales Volume %	Population %	BDI
Atlantic Region	7.6	7.6	100.0
Quebec	21.5	23.9	89.9
Ontario	42.5	38.5	110.4
Prairie Region	13.4	16.8	79.8
British Columbia	15.0	13.2	113.6
Total	**100.0**	**100.0**	—

Example: The BDI in Ontario is 110.4. The BDI was determined by dividing 42.5 by 38.5

Analysis: Based on the BDI in each region, Ontario and BC over-contribute to sales while Quebec and the Prairies under-contribute. The media planner can concentrate advertising dollars in areas where the brand enjoys most usage. Another option is to transfer some funds from Ontario and BC to Quebec and the Prairies to help improve sales in those regions. Other factors can influence such a decision.

While this strategic approach seems equitable, smaller cities may never receive media support. For example, no city in the Atlantic region is among the top 10. If the Atlantic region doesn't receive media support, expectations for the brand should be lowered appropriately. In terms of media selection, key market plans offer the most flexibility and choice. Local market television stations, daily newspapers, outdoor and transit advertising, and radio are attractive alternatives. The combination of media to recommend depends on the media preferences of the target market and the budget available in the plan.

TIMING OF ADVERTISING Information about the target market and cyclical patterns in sales influence decisions about when to schedule advertising. The best time could refer to the time of day, day of week, or time of year. For products with a cyclical sales pattern, the media schedule may follow the ebb and flow of sales. If the media plan is for a new product, the planners may decide to hit the market heavily and frequently in a short period. Lower levels of advertising are scheduled later in the plan cycle. Typically, a media schedule is planned in flights. A **flight** is a period of time in which advertising is scheduled. Rarely is advertising scheduled continuously—creative scheduling just makes it seem like it is. There are many options available for planning the timing of a media schedule, all based on unique situations a brand (company) faces. Refer to Figure 5.6 for an illustration of the media schedules discussed below.

flight
A period of time in which advertising is scheduled.

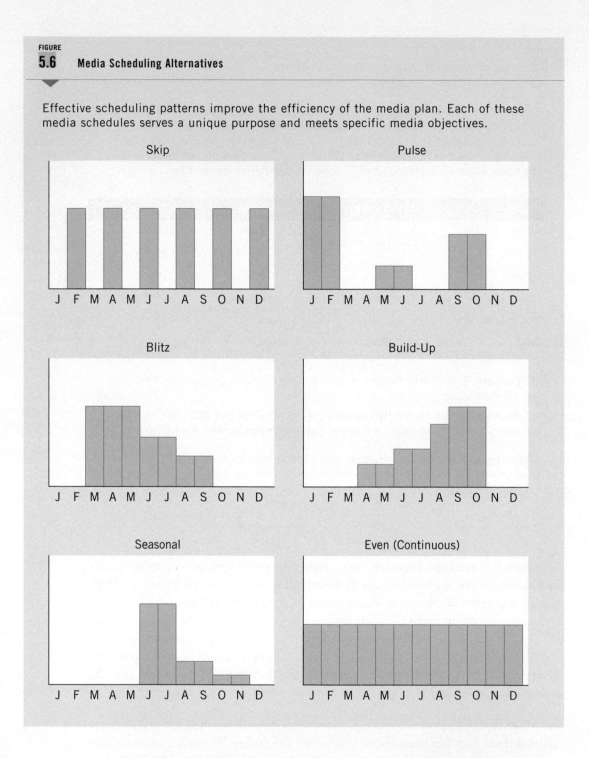

FIGURE 5.6   Media Scheduling Alternatives

Effective scheduling patterns improve the efficiency of the media plan. Each of these media schedules serves a unique purpose and meets specific media objectives.

skip schedule
The scheduling of media advertising on an alternating basis, such as every other week or every other month.

pulse schedule
A scheduling of media advertising in flights of different weight and duration.

- A **skip schedule** calls for scheduling advertising on an alternating basis. For example, ads are scheduled one week and not the next, or one month and not the next. This cyclical pattern is maintained for the duration of the campaign. A skip schedule strategically stretches a budget over an extended period while maintaining the effect of the advertising in the marketplace.

- A **pulse schedule** involves scheduling advertising in flights but with different weights (the amount invested in media) and durations (the length of time). Such a schedule looks random, but the weight and frequency of the spending patterns are carefully rationalized. To demonstrate, assume a schedule has three flights. The first is four weeks long and heavy, the second is six weeks long at a low level, and the third flight is four weeks long and heavy. There is a period of four weeks with no advertising between each flight. The variation in flights creates a "pulsing" effect.

- Many products are seasonal in nature so media advertising follows a **seasonal schedule**, with most of the advertising in the pre-season to create awareness and interest prior to the beginning of the seasonal purchase cycle. Banks and financial institutions have a heavy schedule of RRSP advertising in January and February, for example, as the tax-deduction deadline for contributions is the end of February.

- A **blitz schedule** is best suited for new products that want to hit the market with a bang—a multimedia strategy at a heavyweight level. Lots of money is spent in a very short period. Once the blitz is over, media spending tapers off considerably, and some media are dropped from the schedule.

- Frequently referred to as a teaser strategy, in a **build-up schedule** media advertising is scheduled at low levels initially and gradually builds (as more weight is added) as time passes. Often a teaser campaign is launched well before the product is available on the market (hence the name). The advertising creates a pent-up demand for the product when it becomes available. Hollywood movie releases and manufacturers of video game hardware and software use this strategy frequently.

- Often referred to as a continuous schedule, the **even schedule** involves the purchase of advertising time and space in a uniform manner over a designated period. This schedule is best suited for large advertisers that need to sustain a certain level of advertising spending due to competitive pressures. Such a spending pattern is not very common. Even in markets like the quick-serve restaurant market, where various companies seem to be advertising all of the time, the level of advertising they actually schedule does vary from month to month.

REACH/FREQUENCY/CONTINUITY Media planners must decide on the reach, frequency, and continuity needed to achieve advertising objectives. Much like a riddle, these three factors interact and, if planned effectively, will have a synergistic effect on the target market. It is unrealistic to have maximum reach, frequency, and continuity at the same time. Priorities are based on the situation and the budget.

- **Reach** is the total unduplicated audience (individuals or households) exposed one or more times to an advertiser's schedule of messages during a specific period (usually a week). It is expressed as a percentage of the target population in a geographically defined area. For example, a television ad on Ottawa's CJOH-TV may reach 40 percent of the households in the Ottawa region.

- **Frequency** is the average number of times a target audience has been exposed to an advertising message over a period of time, usually a week. It is calculated by dividing the total possible audience by the audience that has been exposed at least once to the message. Frequency may also refer to the number of times a publication is issued or the number of times a commercial is aired. The media planner must decide what combination of reach and frequency is appropriate for achieving the advertising objectives. In the case of a new product where awareness objectives prevail, the emphasis is on reach (and frequency if there is enough budget). A mature product that is trying to defend its position may opt for more frequency and aim the message at a precisely defined target market.

seasonal schedule
Scheduling media advertising according to seasonal sales trends; usually concentrated in the pre-season or the period just prior to when the bulk of the buying occurs.

blitz schedule
The scheduling of media advertising so that most spending is front-loaded in the schedule; usually involves a lot of money spent in a short period.

build-up schedule
The scheduling of media advertising so that the weight of advertising starts out light and gradually builds over a period of time; also called a teaser campaign.

even schedule
The uniform scheduling of media advertising over an extended period; also referred to as a continuous schedule.

reach
The total unduplicated audience exposed one or more times to a commercial message during a specific period (usually a week).

frequency
The average number of times an audience has been exposed to a message over a period of time, usually a week.

gross rating points (GRPs)
An expression of the weight of advertising in a media schedule; calculated by multiplying reach by frequency.

- Media planners use gross rating points as a method of designing a media schedule. **Gross rating points (GRPs)** are calculated by multiplying the total reach (the unduplicated audience) of the proposed schedule by the frequency (the average amount of exposures) in the proposed schedule. It is an expression of the weight of advertising in a market. To illustrate, assume the weekly reach is 50 percent of targeted households in a particular city and the average number of exposures is 3.5. The GRP level would be 175 (50 x 3.5). Depending on how important particular markets are, an advertiser usually varies the weight level (the GRP level) from one market to another. For more detailed illustrations of GRPs, refer to Appendix 1, "Media Buying Principles and Media Information Resources," at the end of the book.

continuity
The length of time required in an advertising medium to generate the desired impact on the target audience.

- **Continuity** refers to the length of time required to ensure impact has been made on a target market through a particular medium. During that period, a consistent theme is communicated (e.g., "Well Made. Well Priced. Well Dressed," the theme for Moore's, a men's clothing chain). Since advertising is scheduled in flights, continuity decisions deal with how long a flight will be. Will the schedule be four weeks, six weeks, or eight weeks?

Media planners must juggle reach, frequency, and continuity throughout a campaign. An increase in any one of these variables will increase the cost of advertising, so there would have to be a corresponding decrease in another variable to stay within budget. In debating the issues related to reach, frequency, and continuity, many media agencies will embrace the media concept referred to as "recency." The idea behind recency is that a single ad impression is most effective as long as it is served to a consumer when they are in the market to buy a product.[5] It is the timing of the message that is important, not the frequency of the message. Figure 5.7 offers additional information regarding the relationships among reach, frequency, and continuity.

engagement
The degree of involvement a person has with the medium when using it.

ENGAGEMENT **Engagement** refers to the degree of involvement a person has with the medium when that person is using it. It is a response driven by emotion and whatever happens inside a person's mind. Both the message and the medium play a role in encouraging engagement.

In a fragmented media universe, planners struggle to find ways of engaging the audience. People are easily distracted, or they multi-task when using a medium. It is very common for male television watchers to avoid commercials by channel surfing during commercial breaks. In contrast, Internet users are often focused on what they are doing. They are involved and may notice advertising messages—they know the ads are there. A magazine reader may spend 30 minutes of uninterrupted time with a favourite magazine—that's engagement! Earlier in the chapter (see Figure 5.2), it was noted how much time people spend with the media. Time spent does not necessarily translate into engagement.

From a strategic point of view, creative planners and media planners have determined that online and mobile advertising messages must be entertaining. Otherwise, consumers will reject the message. As well, planners encourage engagement with the brand by using an ad in one medium (TV, radio, or print) to get consumers to go online. Perhaps an incentive is offered or a contest is advertised and all of the details are available at a website. Taking the time to go online suggests engagement.

Engagement is an important strategic factor to consider. By selecting the right media, the advertiser will start to develop a relationship with the consumer, a relationship that can thrive if planned properly. For this reason media planners now recommend more use of the Internet in the media mix—a reflection of the time consumers spend with the medium and how they interact with it.

FIGURE
5.7   **The Relationship among Reach, Frequency, and Continuity**

Reach is the number of people potentially exposed to a message in one week.
Frequency is the average number of times a person is exposed to a message in a week.
Continuity is the length of time required to generate impact on a target market.

The relationship among these three variables is dynamic. Since the media budget is usually a fixed amount of money, if one variable is given more priority, then another variable will be given less priority. Otherwise, you will spend beyond the budget. Examine the numbers in the chart. Each plan is different but they achieve the same number of gross impressions.

Gross impressions are calculated by multiplying reach x frequency x continuity.

Variable	Reach	Frequency	Continuity	Impressions
Plan 1	500 000	4	6 weeks	12 000 000
Plan 2	250 000	8	6 weeks	12 000 000
Plan 3	125 000	8	12 weeks	12 000 000

INTERPRETATION
Each plan is different. The first plan stresses reach, the second stresses frequency, and the third stresses continuity. The costs of each plan would be about the same. It's all in the numbers!

In combination with all of the strategic variables described above, the media planners must recommend what media to use. Their media plan will include reasons why certain media were accepted and certain media were rejected. Knowledge of the target market's media preferences and the budget available have a direct and powerful influence on media selection. The section of this chapter titled "Assessing Media Alternatives" discusses the various media in more detail.

For more insight into how media objectives and various strategic media variables influence the direction of a media plan read the IMC Highlight: **Targeted Media Work for BMW.**

MEDIA EXECUTION

The final stage of the media planning is media execution. **Media execution** is a process of fine tuning the media strategy and translating it into specific action plans. This involves comparing various options within a class of media for cost efficiencies, finalizing a schedule in the form of a calendar or blocking chart, and allocating the budget in detail by specific activity. Then the agency buys the media time and space.

media execution
The translation of media strategies into specific media action plans; involves recommending specific media to be used in the plan and negotiating the media buys.

MEDIA SELECTION Selecting the right media to resolve the problem at hand is a three-step decision process: selecting the general type of media, selecting the class of media within the type, and selecting the particular medium. Of the media discussed in this chapter, the first decision involves what mix of media to use. Among television, radio, newspapers, magazines, and out-of-home, any combination is possible (direct response and interactive media are discussed in separate chapters). For the second decision, let's assume that magazines and television are the media chosen and that the campaign is national in scope. Will general-interest magazines, men's or women's magazines, or special-interest magazines be chosen? What television networks will be chosen? The characteristics of the target market will influence these decisions.

Targeted Media Work for BMW

The BMW 525i is an expensive automobile with a starting price of about $60 000. The brand and model appeal to men who like to drive. The goal of the campaign was two-fold: to highlight the xDrive (all-wheel drive) capability of the new model and to increase sales from the previous year.

The target market is described as an "urban-dwelling middle manager or professional with relatively high income." Age is not a factor, because owning a BMW is more of an income and "mind" thing—the status of owning the car! What media strategy would BMW and its agency, The Media Company, employ to reach this target?

The key to developing the media campaign was found in new consumer insights provided by BMW. "These guys love to drive, and because they love to drive, they are driving to work. So, we thought we could build a lot of frequency by placing messages on the routes that they take to work," says John Ware of The Media Company. The strategy also addressed the target's emotional needs in a rational manner so that the buying decision was easy to justify. The messages suggested there was no need to settle for anything less.

A key market media plan was implemented in Toronto, Montreal, and Vancouver. The media mix included print ads in *The Globe and Mail*; online communications (banner ads and a brand website); outdoor boards on busy traffic arteries to and from work and near the airports; print ads in downtown office elevators; a print ad in *enRoute*, Air Canada's in-flight magazine, along with 15-second spots on Air Canada's in-flight television programs; and radio spots on business-oriented stations. The execution literally hit the customer where the customer lived and worked.

Where possible the message was tied to the medium. For example, ads in elevators would read: "A better way to elevate yourself" or "You'll be tempted again tomorrow." If reading the online version of *The Globe and Mail*, the target would see advertising banners that directed consumers to the brand website for a video presentation. For those parking in a downtown garage, there was a beauty shot of the car placed on the wall.

The campaign worked! BMW exceeded its sales goals by 27 percent. This campaign offers good insight into how a media plan is strategically developed. Factors such as the target market profile, the message, reach and frequency, timing, and market coverage were all addressed when the plan was in the development stage. A combination of good strategy and good execution yielded great results!

Adapted from Natalie Williams, "It's All about the Insight," *Strategy*, April 2006, p. 41.

For the third decision, let's also assume the target market is men and women between 25 and 49, living in major cities across Canada. Magazines that reach both males and females would be selected: *Maclean's, Chatelaine*, and *Reader's Digest* are good candidates. Conventional television networks such as CTV, CBC, and Global are also good candidates.

When selecting specific media, the cost efficiencies of each alternative are analyzed. To demonstrate, magazines are compared on the basis of **CPM (cost per thousand).** CPM is the cost incurred in delivering a message to 1000 readers. It is calculated by dividing the cost of the ad by the circulation of the publication in thousands. Therefore, if an ad cost $20 000 and the circulation was 500 000, the CPM would be $40 ($20 000 divided by 500). When comparing publications that reach the same target market, the ones with the lowest cost per thousand are the most efficient at reaching the target.

Media planners also assess media alternatives qualitatively. In other words, do numbers tell the complete story? Factors such as editorial content, quality of reproduction, and demographic selectivity can lead the media planner to prefer one magazine over

cost per thousand (CPM)
The cost of delivering an advertising message to 1000 people; calculated by dividing the cost of the ad by the circulation in thousands.

142

another, even if the preferred magazine has a higher CPM. Perhaps there are more pass-along readers of one publication than another. If more people are exposed to the ad, then the real costs of reaching the target are lower than the CPM. Daily newspapers, television networks, and radio stations can be compared on a similar basis. The actual cost of advertising varies from one medium to another (see Figure 5.8). Appendix 1, "Media Buying Principles and Media Information Resources," has additional information about media selection and how various alternatives are compared when making decisions about what media to use.

MEDIA SCHEDULE AND BUDGET ALLOCATIONS The final stage for the media planners is developing the media calendar and assigning estimated costs to all activities. A **media calendar** or **blocking chart,** as it is also referred to, summarizes in a few pages all the details of the media execution (e.g., media usage, market coverage, weight levels, reach and frequency, and the timing of the campaign). Accompanying the calendar is a detailed budget. Typically, the media budget classifies spending by medium, region or key market, and time of year. Because plans change during the course of the planning cycle, clients and agencies must know how much money is committed at any point in time, in case there is a need to cancel activities. Taking the axe to the budget while the plan is in midstream is both common and frustrating for managers.

media calendar (blocking chart)
A document that shows allocation of a brand's media budget according to time of year and type of medium; shows coordination of various media recommendations.

MEDIA BUYING Once the client approves the media plan, media buyers execute the plan. Buyers work with media representatives to negotiate final prices for the various activities. If the required elements of the plan are unavailable, buyers are responsible for making

---

FIGURE
5.8   Comparing Media Alternatives for Efficiency

Magazine	Cost (1P, 4-color)	Circulation (000)	CPM
Report on Business	$24 350	335 515	$104.28
Financial Post Magazine	$20 500	207 143	$98.98
Canadian Business	$18 180	78 535	$231.59

Newspaper	Cost (1000 lines)	Circulation (000)	CPM
The Globe and Mail	$44 940	335 575	$133.94
National Post	$19 140	191 815	$99.79

Rates are from CARD, Spring/Summer 2009. Magazines ads are full colour; newspaper ads are black and white. *Report on Business* magazine is distributed free with *The Globe and Mail* and *Financial Post Business* is distributed free with the *National Post. Canadian Business* is a stand-alone subscriber-based magazine.
Analysis

Based on CPM, the cost of reaching 1000 readers, *Financial Post* magazine is the most efficient of the magazines. *The Globe and Mail* is not the most efficient newspaper but offers advertisers other advantages. It is an established and trusted newspaper that reaches an upscale reader. Advertisers will pay more for that kind of reach.

Source: CARDonline Print Directory, Spring/Summer 2009.

replacement buys that will achieve the same objectives. The demand for key time periods in television and preferred spaces in magazines and newspapers means that good timing and effective negotiations skills on the part of the buyer are critical elements of the media buy. In the role of negotiator, the media buyer seeks favourable positions and rates to maximize efficiency and achieve the objectives set out in the plan.

Appendix 2 includes an example of a media plan that shows applications of the various media strategy and execution principles discussed in this chapter.

Assessing Media Alternatives

Media planners choose between traditional media alternatives and non-traditional alternatives. The former category includes television, radio, newspapers, magazines, and out-of-home advertising. The latter includes the Internet, mobile communications through cell phones and personal digital assistants, and video games, all of which are interactive forms of media. Typically, a planner will include several media in the plan, as people refer to more than one medium for information. In the hectic world of today's consumers, the simultaneous use of media is popular. Teens, for example, are online or chatting on their cell phone while watching television. Adults frequently read the newspaper or a magazine while watching television. Knowing the right combinations for various age groups will influence media decisions.

Because consumers refer to so many different media, media planners usually recommend a **primary medium**, which will be allocated a higher percentage of the budget, and support it with **secondary media**, which complement the primary medium and receive less of the budget. As mentioned earlier, a medium such as television is ideal for creating awareness quickly, whereas print media are good for communicating detailed information over a longer period. The combination of the two media is usually effective. This section will analyze the major mass media alternatives and highlight the pros and cons of each. Chapters 6 and 7 will focus on direct response and interactive forms of advertising.

primary medium
A medium that receives the largest allocation of an advertiser's budget; the dominant medium in a media plan.

secondary media
Media alternatives used to complement the primary medium in an advertising campaign; typically less money is allocated to these media.

TELEVISION

For what seems like forever, television has been the preferred medium for advertisers, assuming sufficient funds are available. To create brand awareness across a wide cross-section of the population, no medium has traditionally done it better than television. But television as a medium for advertising is in a state of transition as consumers' eyeballs move from the "big screen" to the "small screen" (laptops and mobile devices). Consequently, media planners may include an online media recommendation in combination with a television recommendation.

Many advertisers are questioning the value of television advertising. Technology such as personal video recorders (PVRs) that allow automatic elimination of commercials when recording shows threatens the very economics of the television industry. Already, more than 80 percent of PVR users say they skip the commercials, so advertisers and broadcasters are understandably worried. Presently, only 13.5 percent of Canadian households own a PVR and only half of these households claim they skip through the commercials.[6] For now, mainstream television remains relevant and effective, but advancing technologies will negatively impact the medium's effectiveness in the future. It will be interesting to see what happens as television moves toward mobile medium status.

Generally, the number of hours a person spends viewing television each week has been drifting downward. The public's preoccupation with the Internet is one reason for this decline. There is a correlation between the two media, however, as people are multitasking—using both media at the same time. Data compiled by BBM Nielsen Media

Research show that Canadians remain avid TV watchers: men 18 and older spend 20 hours with TV each week, while women spend 25 hours with TV each week.[7] Figures like these suggest that television is not dead but in transition.

With the TV universe changing so rapidly, it is difficult to reach targets effectively. The biggest threat to television is audience fragmentation arising from the 300-channel universe that exists today. Conventional English-language television networks such as CBC, CTV, and Global, and French-language networks such as SRC and TVA, account for just 41 percent of the hours watched (2007), down from 79 percent in 1985.[8] Viewers have migrated to pay and specialty channels. Among the more popular specialty channels are TSN, YTV, Discovery Channel, Showcase, Rogers Sportsnet, and many more. Channels like these are tailored to special interests and attract a particular audience, which can be a benefit to advertisers.

More recently, new digital channels have been added to the mix. Channels such as ESPN Classic Canada, Leafs TV, Out TV, SexTV, and Showcase Diva attract very narrow audiences. Many of these channels are still searching for an audience.

Budget permitting, however, advertisers are still magically drawn to television. It is a multi-sense medium that is ideal for product demonstrations and appeals to consumers on an emotional level. As well, the reach potential is incredibly high. On an average day, 80 percent of Canadians view television at least once, and 40 percent of adults watch television at least once in prime time.[9] With television, media planners have four options: network advertising, selective-spot advertising, local-spot advertising, and sponsorships. Also added to the mix are product placement and branded content opportunities.

- **Network advertising** on networks such as CTV and Global is suitable for products and services that are widely distributed and have large media budgets. When a spot is placed on the network, the message is received in all network markets. The CTV network, for example, comprises 21 stations and reaches 99 percent of English-speaking Canadians. Popular prime-time shows such as *CSI: Crime Scene Investigation*, *CSI Miami*, *Flashpoint*, and *Two and a Half Men* attract big-budget advertisers.

network advertising
Advertising from one central source broadcast across an entire network of stations.

- At the regional or local level, stations fill the balance of their schedules with non-network programs and sell **selective spots** directly to interested advertisers. Local stations are also allocated a certain portion of a network program to sell directly to local advertisers. That's why you may see an ad for a local restaurant on *Hockey Night in Canada*.

  Strategically, selective spots benefit advertisers using a key market media strategy. For a large-budget advertiser, there is an opportunity to increase the level of advertising in local markets that are judged as priorities. Small-budget advertisers can simply choose the markets they wish to advertise in. Ads for national spots and selective spots are negotiated and scheduled by an advertising agency as part of the overall media buy.

selective spot
Commercial time during a network show that is allocated back to regional and local stations to sell; advertisers buy spots on a station-by-station basis.

- With **local spots**, local advertisers like independent retailers and restaurants buy time from local stations. Since local market advertisers don't usually work with an advertising agency, the stations usually provide assistance in the development and production of commercials for local clients.

local spot
Advertising bought from a local station by a local advertiser.

- **Sponsorship** allows an advertiser to take "ownership" of a property that is targeted at its consumer audience. If the fit is right, the advertiser can leverage the sponsorship by extending the relationship to include consumer and trade promotions, and alternate media exposure.

sponsorship
The act of financially supporting an event in return for certain advertising rights and privileges.

One of the most prominent sponsorship opportunities in Canada is *Hockey Night in Canada*, a Saturday night institution. Both major beer companies in Canada, Molson and Labatt, have taken turns as primary sponsor for the hockey broadcasts. At the end of a contract period, the rights for HNIC are up for renewal and various sponsors bid for the lead sponsorship position.

Within the game there are other sponsorship opportunities. For example, a Think Hockey segment brought to you by Home Depot is a between-period drill segment for coaches and young players featuring Ron MacLean and various professional players. Kraft Hockeyville has been another popular segment of HNIC for the past three years. In conjunction with the CBC, the NHL, and the NHLPA, Kraft pits communities across Canada against each other to be crowned Hockeyville. The winning community demonstrates how it embodies the spirit of hockey and hometown pride and wins cash for arena upgrades and improvements. Sponsors such as Home Depot and Kraft benefit from the brand mentions during the broadcast. They may also negotiate preferred positions for their commercials during the broadcast. Kraft sees the sponsorship and promotion as a way of giving back to the communities for being such great consumers of their brands—Kraft brands have a 99 percent household penetration in Canada.[10]

Television provides advertisers a means of reaching huge numbers of people in a short space of time with a compelling message. Companies that can afford to advertise in prime time on shows like *Survivor*, *Prison Break*, and *Law & Order* or on sports programming like *Hockey Night in Canada* or *NHL Playoffs* have high reach almost instantaneously. Television is an expensive medium, so to save money many advertisers are opting for 15-second commercials.

If reaching a well-defined target is a priority, television is not a good option. The audience in prime time, for example, spans all ages. You will reach your target, but you're also paying for everyone else who is watching. Furthermore, clutter is a problem on television: there are simply too many ads. Given that ads are scheduled in a cluster, does an advertiser want to be the third or fourth commercial in a cluster of six? Refer to the discussion about CPM in the "Media Execution" section for more details, and consult Figure 5.9 for a summary of the advantages and disadvantages of television advertising.

NEW STRATEGIES FOR REACHING A TELEVISION AUDIENCE Television and television advertising is not about to disappear, but new solutions for reaching viewers must be found to retain the economics of the system. Many advertisers have already found more compelling ways of delivering advertising messages on television. A few new alternatives include product placement, branded content, and shorter TV commercials.

product placement
The visible placement of brand name products in television shows, movies, radio, video games, and other programming.

Product placement refers to the visible placement of branded merchandise in television shows, films, or video games. Hollywood has been doing product placement in movies for years, but television is now catching on to the practice fast. For example, Coca-Cola glasses or containers are prominently displayed in front of the judges on *Canadian Idol*. Visa utilized product placement on the hit show *Corner Gas*. The Visa logo appears on the gas station's door and at the cashier stand. Exposure such as this has more credibility with the audience than regular advertising. Characters frequently interact with each other near the cash register so the Visa logo gets lots of exposure.

branded content (product integration)
The integration of brand name goods and services into the script (storyline) of a television show or movie. The brand name is clearly mentioned and sometimes discussed.

Branded content or **product integration** takes product placement a step further by integrating the brand into the script of the television show. Kia Canada has joined forces with the CBC's *Hockey Night in Canada* on numerous occasions to take advantage of sponsorship and branded content opportunities. The latest opportunity (2008–09 season) was the sponsorship of a Fantasy Pool presented by Kia Motors (fantasy pools are very popular with sports junkies). The event was mentioned several times by the

FIGURE
5.9

Advantages and Disadvantages
of Television Advertising

ADVANTAGES

Impact—sight, sound, motion; demonstration; emotion
Reach—high reach in short space of time
Some targeting—sports and specialty cable channels reach niche targets
Coverage flexibility—local, regional, and national options

DISADVANTAGES

High cost—desired frequency (message repetition) increases absolute cost
Clutter—too many spots in a cluster negates potential impact
Audience fragmentation—abundance of channels lowers audience size (reach potential)
Technology—electronic equipment records programs and edits out commercials

announcers during the broadcast and an update on pools standings was shown on the television screen between periods. An online component was integral to the pool entry process and entrants were encouraged to visit the contest site daily for updates on the standings. The prize: two Kia Sorento vehicles; one for the first-half winner and one for the second-half winner.

Programs that teach, demonstrate, or offer advice, such as the do-it-yourself home and decorating shows, are proving to be good opportunities for products to be integrated in a natural and positive way. Home Depot, for example, has formed partnerships with shows such as *Designer Guys*, *Home to Go*, and *Trading Spaces*. And don't forget about the brand name tools used in the popular show *Holmes on Homes!*

For additional insight into product placement and branded content opportunities, read the IMC Highlight: **Behind the Scenes Media Deals**.

Shorter commercials are another option for effectively delivering television ads. In fact, a double-edged strategy involving short commercials and websites offers great promise. The shorter TV ads are used primarily as a vehicle to drive viewers to a website, where a more thorough job of message delivery is accomplished. A recent Mott's Clamato campaign used a teaser TV ad claiming an intended ad was taken off the air (it was too hot!) and gave a website where viewers could get the full story. The "big idea" was a spicy campaign for a spicy drink—but not all of it could be shown on television. The website attracted 150 000 new visitors in its first week.[11] The short ad attracted attention and at a much lower cost than a standard 30-second commercial.

The changes occurring in the television industry have direct implications for advertisers. Essentially, advertisers have two basic options: they can reduce investment in television advertising, making it less important in the mix than previously, or they can shift their investment entirely. While the latter option seems radical, many large advertisers are doing a lot of soul searching about their TV budgets. Other advertisers firmly believe that television will remain the dominant medium and that it's mandatory if the goal is to build brand image.

RADIO

There are just over 1200 radio stations in Canada. Of the private commercial stations, 186 are AM and 441 are FM. Radio reaches 91 percent of Canadians 12 and older in the average week. FM stations are much more popular than AM. FM stations reach 80 percent of persons over 12 years of age, while AM reaches 32 percent. All radio stations are self-regulating, with no restrictions on the number of commercial minutes or on the placement of those minutes.[12]

Behind the Scenes Media Deals

Product placement and branded content: where did it begin and why is it now so popular? The roots of product placement can be traced to the 1982 hit movie *ET: The Extra-Terrestrial*. That movie made Reese's Pieces a household name in North America. Before that Reese's was relatively unknown.

More recently, the typical James Bond movie is nothing more than an extended infomercial for a variety of upscale brands. In *Die Another Day*, James Bond is seen using Samsonite luggage, Omega watches, a Phillips heart rate monitor, Sony security systems and laptops, and British Airways. Movie producers, and now television producers, find the link between brands and their media hard to resist.

According to research by PQ Media, advertisers spent $2.9 billion (worldwide) in 2007 on product placement in movies and TV shows, an increase of 37 percent over the previous year. Double-digit increases are expected for the next three years.

In television, many of the placement and branded content opportunities are on reality shows. In fact, product placements have gone from benign curiosity to the raison d'être for some shows. NBC's *The Restaurant*, for example, was fully funded by three brands: American Express, Coors, and Mitsubishi. It's not sure if product placements alienate an audience, but the question remains: how far can a TV show go with the placement idea?

Many critics of the practice believe the placement or discussion about a brand has to fit in a meaningful way. Overstating a brand name for no apparent reason will eventually grate on the viewers, and perhaps turn them against the brand. There is a risk! To demonstrate the concept of fit, consider a recent relationship between Sears Canada and the popular Canadian show *Corner Gas*.

With the Christmas season approaching, Sears needed exposure for its *Christmas Wish Book*. Ironically, some research findings indicated that viewers of *Corner Gas* were more likely to be catalogue shoppers. Sears pursued the opportunity and eventually had its catalogue successfully woven into the show's storyline. According to Brett Butt, the writer and star of the show, "Sears was the perfect match for the program." At the beginning of the episode, four of the show's main characters reminisced about using the catalogue to shop when they were kids. CTV included Sears in all pre-promotion for the episode—TV, newspaper, and radio spots promoted the show.

Was it worthwhile? The pre-Christmas exposure for Sears's *Christmas Wish Book* catalogue resulted in strong sales for the season. That episode of *Corner Gas* was the most watched episode of the season, attracting over 2 million viewers. The *Wish Book* definitely made an impression!

Adapted from "Case Study: Sears," *Strategy*, October 2006, p. 38.

Generally, Canadians are listening to the radio less today than they did 10 years ago. On average, people over 18 listen to the radio for 20 hours a week, about 1.5 hours less than a decade earlier. The drop-off is more pronounced among teens, since teens have more entertainment options available to them than before and more places to get music. Where people listen to the radio is a factor a media planner must consider. Presently, the proportion of time spent listening to the radio in the home is now 49 percent while listening to the radio in cars is 28 percent.[13]

One of the major advantages of radio is its ability to reach selective target markets. In fact, radio is a one-on-one medium more in tune with the lives of its listeners than television or newspapers, which appeal to the masses. Radio's ability to personally connect with listeners helps explain why it can be effective. For advertisers, this means that messages need to speak to listeners as individuals, not as a group.[14]

The audience reached depends on the format of the station. **Format** refers to the type and nature of the programming offered by a station. Basically, the content is designed to appeal to a particular target group, usually defined by age and interests. In radio, everything is based on demographics.

The most popular radio station formats among adults are adult contemporary, gold/oldies/rock, talk, country, and contemporary. Adult contemporary (AC) stations play popular and easy-listening music, current and past, and generally appeal to an audience in the 25- to 49-year-old range.[15]

The preference for FM is largely due to the better sound quality and the transfer of many stations from the AM band to the FM band. The news/talk format has been a renaissance for AM stations that moved in that direction. The news/talk format encourages interactivity with listeners and has attracted active rather than passive listeners. This format has been extended further to all-sports stations like THE FAN 590 in Toronto. THE FAN 590 is a niche station popular with sports-minded males who like to talk about sports news and rumours.

Because of its ability to reach precisely defined demographic targets in local markets, radio can be an ideal component of a "key market" media plan. As well, it is a relatively inexpensive medium. An advertiser can achieve high frequency on a weekly basis. In fact, radio is often referred to as the "frequency medium." If frequency is the strategic priority, then radio is a good fit.

While reach potential is high, a radio audience is fragmented in major urban markets. If several stations compete for the loyalty of the same demographic, an advertiser would have to buy spots on all the stations to reach the target. That would drive the cost of advertising up. Unlike TV, which is an evening medium, radio is a morning medium. In fact, breakfast time—between 8 am and 9 am—is the highest daily period for tuning in by all demographics. There is a downward drift in listening as the day progresses, with a slight blip upward in the afternoon drive-home period (4 pm to 6 pm). Refer to Figure 5.10 for details. Listening trends such as these can influence the placement (timing) of an advertiser's message.

format
The type and nature of the programming offered by a radio station.

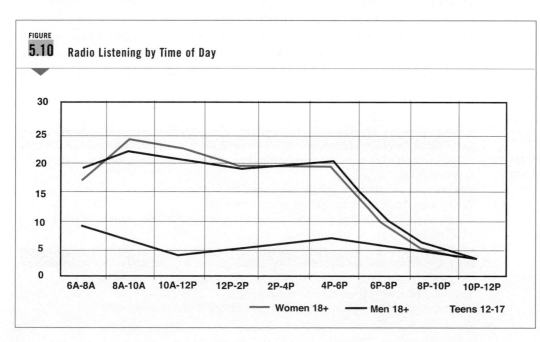

FIGURE 5.10   Radio Listening by Time of Day

Source: Courtesy of BBM Canada.

For additional information about the advantages and disadvantages of radio advertising, refer to Figure 5.11.

Several new technologies are having an influence on conventional radio broadcasting. Among these technologies are Internet radio, podcasting, and satellite radio. As the name suggests, **Internet radio** involves listening to audio broadcasts via the Internet. The broadcasts are streamed and played by a software media player in the computer. The broadcasts come from a myriad of different organizations as well as traditional radio stations. Since the signal is relayed over the Internet, it is possible to access stations from anywhere in the world.

The second and already popular technology is called podcasting. **Podcasting** describes audio programming that is downloadable to iPods and other portable digital media devices. It allows listeners to tune in when it is convenient for them to do so. Radio shows are recorded and posted as an MP3 file to a website where they can be downloaded to the player. Podcasting is unlikely to make conventional radio obsolete, but it does offer huge commercial potential for sponsors and specially packaged programming.[16]

The third technology is satellite radio. **Satellite radio** offers commercial-free programming and is available through two suppliers: XM Canada and Sirius Canada. Both services require a special radio and listeners must pay a monthly fee to obtain the music. Satellite radio is commercial free and is supported through subscriber fees. Since its launch, satellite radio has had only minimal impact on conventional radio and achieved only single-digit penetration. The question remains: are Canadians willing to pay for commercial-free radio?

NEWSPAPERS

Canada has 124 daily newspapers, with a total average daily circulation of 5.8 million copies. **Circulation** is defined as the average number of copies per issue of a publication that are sold by subscription, distributed free to predetermined recipients, carried within other publications, or made available through retail distributors.

Industry research indicates that 50 percent of Canada's adult population reads a daily newspaper on any given weekday. As well, 17 percent of adults read a daily newspaper online.[17] The trend to more online reading will continue for some time; therefore, from a publisher's perspective, advertising space must be sold both for hard copy and the online version of the newspaper if revenues are to be protected. Advertisers must also consider the movement to online reading as well. Newspapers are a popular

Internet radio
Listening to radio broadcasts via the Internet.

podcasting
Audio programming that is downloadable to iPods and other portable digital media devices; allows listeners to tune in when it is convenient for them to do so.

satellite radio
A radio service that offers commercial-free programming for a monthly fee.

circulation
The average number of copies per issue of a publication sold by subscription, distributed free to predetermined recipients, carried with other publications, or made available through retail distributors.

FIGURE
5.11

Advantages and Disadvantages of Radio Advertising

ADVANTAGES

Target selectivity—station format attracts a defined audience (profile matching possible)
Frequency—reach plans rotate messages through entire audience weekly
Cost—very favourable compared to other media
Flexibility—stations and markets selected according to priority (key market strategy)

DISADVANTAGES

Audience fragmentation—multiple stations competing for the same demographic reduces station's audience potential
Message retention—sound-only medium; clever creative required

medium among advertisers, particularly local market advertisers. Net advertising revenue generated by newspapers ranks second in Canada, behind only television.

Newspapers are produced in two formats: broadsheets and tabloids. A **broadsheet** is a large newspaper with a fold in the middle. Most Canadian dailies are published as broadsheets, including circulation leaders such as the *Toronto Star*, *The Globe and Mail*, and the *National Post*. A **tabloid** is a smaller newspaper in terms of surface area. It is sold flat and resembles an unbound magazine. The Sun newspaper chain (*Toronto Sun*, *Ottawa Sun*, *Calgary Sun*, and so on) publishes all of its newspapers in tabloid format.

Several "free" daily newspapers exist in Canada. *Metro* and *24 Hours* are targeted directly at commuters in Toronto, Vancouver, Calgary, and Edmonton. *Metro* and *24 heures* are distributed in Montreal. These newspapers are distributed at or near transit facilities. The free dailies continue to eat into the readership pie. In Toronto and Montreal they presently account for 14 percent of daily newspaper readers.[18]

Community newspapers are small-circulation newspapers usually published weekly. The community paper is the voice of the community. As such, it is well read. Among English Canadians, community papers are read by 68 percent of the population. Among French Canadians, readership is 77 percent. The readership of community newspapers parallels the demographics of the community. For that reason, they are an excellent advertising medium for local businesses.

Newspapers generate revenues from different types of advertising:

- **National Advertising:** National ads are sold to advertisers and ad agencies by a national sales department. Advertisers in this category include products and services marketed nationally or regionally. Brand name food and beverages, automobiles, airlines, banks and financial institutions, computers, and telecommunications products and services fall into this category.

- **Retail Advertising**: Retail advertisers include department stores, supermarkets, drug stores, restaurants, and a host of other independent retailers. These retailers usually advertise sales or re-advertise the nationally branded merchandise they sell. Retail advertising generates a majority of revenue for a newspaper. It truly is a local market medium.

- **Classified Advertising**: Classified ads provide an opportunity for readers and local businesses to buy, sell, lease, or rent all kinds of goods and services. Typically, the classified section is well read and in many large dailies is a separate section of the newspaper, a testament to its significance.

- **Preprinted Inserts:** The preprinted **insert** (often referred to as a free-standing insert) is a dedicated piece of advertising inserted into the fold of a newspaper. Large users of inserts include department stores (Sears, Walmart, and others), drugstore chains (Shoppers Drug Mart and others), large general merchandisers (Canadian Tire and Home Depot), and electronics retailers (Best Buy and Future Shop).

For advertisers, newspapers offer geographic selectivity and high reach in local markets. Furthermore, newspapers and readers have a relationship with each other. Readers have a tendency to read the entire newspaper in their own unique and sequential manner. For this reason, they are likely at least to see an ad in the paper. Newspapers are an effective choice for reaching broadly defined adult target markets. Unfortunately, the papers' life span is very short (one day for dailies). As the old saying goes, "There's nothing as stale as yesterday's news." Newspapers also suffer from a clutter problem. **Clutter** refers to the amount of advertising in a medium. About 60 percent of newspaper space is devoted to advertising, so standing out in the crowd is a design challenge for

broadsheet
A large newspaper with a fold in its middle.

tabloid
A smaller newspaper that is sold flat (not folded).

retail advertising
Advertising by a retail store; involves advertising the store name, image, location, and the re-advertising of branded merchandise carried by the store.

classified advertising
Print advertising in which similar goods and services are grouped together in categories under appropriate headings.

insert
A preprinted, free-standing advertisement (e.g., a leaflet, brochure, or flyer) specifically placed in a newspaper or magazine.

clutter
The amount of advertising in a particular medium.

the creative team. See Figure 5.12 for a summary of the advantages and disadvantages of newspaper advertising.

MAGAZINES

Currently, more than 880 consumer magazines and 950 business or trade magazines are published in Canada. Canadian consumer magazines are distributed on the basis of paid circulation or controlled circulation. **Paid circulation** refers to subscriptions and newsstand sales. Magazines such as *Maclean's, Chatelaine*, and *Canadian Business* are paid circulation magazines and rely on subscriptions, newsstand sales, and advertising space to generate revenues. Canada's most popular consumer magazines sold by subscription or at newsstands include *Reader's Digest* (922 300 circulation), *Chatelaine* (602 800), and *Canadian Living* (541 800).

Some magazines are distributed free to a predetermined target audience based on demographic, geographic, job function, or other characteristics. These are **controlled circulation** magazines. Typically, receivers of the magazines are in a unique position to influence sales, so they are attractive to advertisers wanting to reach them. City-oriented lifestyle magazines such as *Toronto Life, Ottawa Life*, and *Vancouver Magazine* are examples of controlled circulation magazines. Much of their circulation is based on distribution to selected households, hotels, and motels in their respective markets. Entertainment magazines distributed free in movie theatres also fall into this category. *Famous*, for example, is distributed monthly to 650 000 Cineplex Odeon patrons. *Famous Kids* has a distribution of 198 000 through the same theatres.

Business magazines are divided into various industry categories: food manufacturing and distribution, hardware trade, hotels and restaurants, telecommunications, engineering, construction, and so on. These magazines are very specialized, their content appealing to people employed in a certain industry or a particular job function. Some magazine titles include *Canadian Grocer, Hotel & Restaurant, Modern Purchasing*, and *Marketing Magazine*. The profile of readers is based on a common interest or function, so these magazines are an efficient means of reaching prospects with a business-to-business advertising message.

paid circulation
The circulation of a newspaper or magazine that is generated by subscription sales and newsstand sales.

controlled circulation
The circulation of a publication that is distributed free to individuals in a specific demographic segment or geographic area.

**FIGURE
5.12**

Advantages and Disadvantages of Newspaper Advertising

ADVANTAGES
Targeting capability—reaches a diverse adult audience in key geographic markets
Reach—ideal for reaching consumers in local markets frequently
Media environment—readers engage with paper based on editorial content; they are receptive to messages
Merchandising—national advertisers have cooperative advertising opportunities with local market retailers

DISADVANTAGES
Life span—daily; exposure to message reduced if paper not read on day of publication
Audience diversity—not suitable if target market profile is precisely defined (exception may be the *Globe and Mail*)
Clutter—lots of space devoted to advertising (many ads on one page)
Reproduction quality—primarily a black and white medium; speed of presses reduces colour quality

Magazines are ideal for advertising purposes. For advertisers using a profile-matching strategy or rifle strategy, they serve a useful role. Magazines are often referred to as a "class" medium rather than a "mass" medium. In other words, readership is well defined on the basis of demographic and psychographic variables (profile matching), and there are all kinds of magazines devoted to a particular interest or activity (rifle strategy). As well, many large-circulation consumer magazines offer regional editions, so if geography is a factor influencing the media strategy, magazines can be part of the solution. Magazines are read for their editorial content; therefore, advertisers' messages benefit from the prestige of being associated with the magazine and the quality it represents. Many studies have proven that readers are more engaged with magazines, and they consider advertising in magazines to be more acceptable and enjoyable than in other media.[19]

Clutter remains a problem in most consumer magazines. The clustering of ads at the beginning of a publication, for example, may mean that a reader skips over an entire section of ads on the way to reaching editorial content. Advertisers combat the problem by requesting specific locations in a magazine. Covers, for example, are preferred positions and command a higher price. If frequency is a key objective, magazines are not a viable option. Most are published monthly or every two months, so they are good for achieving reach among a defined target audience and delivering continuity of message from month to month. More information about the advantages and disadvantages of magazine advertising appears in Figure 5.13.

OUT-OF-HOME ADVERTISING

Out-of-home advertising represents a highly visible and effective alternative for advertisers. Think about it: if you drive a car, travel by transit, or stroll through shopping malls, you are constantly exposed to out-of-home advertising messages. Advertising investment in out-of-home advertising is increasing at a much greater rate than in other media. In 2007, outdoor advertising revenue in Canada totalled $422 million, a 14 percent increase over 2006.[20] Advertisers' concerns about the fragmentation of television audiences and the tuning out of broadcast messages have driven demand for out-of-home delivery.

If the goal of an advertising campaign is to reach as many people as possible, then out-of-home should be the medium of choice. Although considered by some to be

FIGURE

5.13

Advantages and Disadvantages of Magazine Advertising

ADVANTAGES

Targeting capability—good reach based on readers' demographic (profile-matching strategy) and psychographic (rifle strategy) characteristics
Coverage flexibility—city, regional, and national magazines available
Life span—magazines tend not to be discarded right away; opportunity for multiple exposures to message
Quality—excellent colour reproduction
Environment—message benefits from the prestige of association with the magazine's quality and image
Pass-along readership—actual readership goes beyond the subscriber (added reach)

DISADVANTAGES

Clutter—abundance of ads appearing in the initial section (advertising domination in some magazines)
Cost—colour is an added cost in production of ad
Frequency—distribution is usually monthly or bi-monthly

"pollution on a stick," outdoor boards are a proven way to reach an increasingly mobile population and to improve brand recognition. The major classifications of out-of-home media include outdoor advertising and transit advertising.

poster (billboard)
A common form of outdoor advertising; usually a picture-dominant advertisement with a minimum of copy.

OUTDOOR ADVERTISING **Posters** or **billboards**, as they are commonly referred to, are large sheets of poster paper mounted on a panel of some kind. To maximize reach potential, they are strategically located on major travel routes leading to or within a community's business and shopping districts. To maximize the frequency of message and to extend daily viewing by consumers, posters are often illuminated. A powerful light beams upward from the bottom of the poster.

Shreddies cereal used a combination of television and outdoor advertising to communicate its new, diamond-shaped Shreddies. A rather simple idea turned into the "big idea" when an advertising intern suggested that the square Shreddie be rotated 45 degrees to become the diamond-shaped Shreddie. Shreddies was a mature brand without any significant marketing support for years, but the new campaign, with the help of effective outdoor visuals, helped create a lot of buzz for the brand.

backlit (backlight) poster
A luminous outdoor sign printed on polyvinyl material.

A step up in quality is the **backlit poster**. On a backlit, the advertising message is printed on translucent polyvinyl material. When the posters are erected, lights shine through the material from behind the sign. The primary advantage is the image enhancement offered by this lighting; there is strong visual impact in the day and at night. Backlits are strategically located at major intersections and on high-volume traffic routes. For the advertiser, they cost more.

superboard (spectacular)
Outdoor advertising that is larger than a normal poster and much more expensive to produce; can include extensions beyond borders and electronic messaging.

A **superboard** or spectacular is an extremely large display unit positioned at the highest-volume traffic locations. It is created to the advertiser's specifications and can include space extensions, flashing lights, louvres, and electronic messaging. Since superboards are one-of-a-kind structures that are illuminated and frequently include moving objects, they require a long-term commitment from the advertiser due to the high expense of designing and constructing them. Spectaculars are beyond the budgets of most advertisers.

FIGURE
5.14

Mural advertisements are good attention grabbers

Source: mavrixphoto.com/Keystone Canada

Banners are large vinyl banners framed and mounted on the outside of a building. They can be moved and re-used. **Mural advertisements** are hand-painted outdoor extravaganzas placed on the sides of buildings. They are very large—often the entire height of the building. If size really matters, these kinds of ads are real attention grabbers. See Figure 5.14 on the previous page.

Technology is providing a means for outdoor advertising to be interactive. At one time all outdoor posters were static in nature, but now they can display multiple messages at the same time. **Electronic signs** display electronic messages on a rotating basis (typically 10 to 15 seconds in length). Electronic signs are proving to be a medium that helps build frequency of message on a weekly basis. Thus far, they are only available in major urban markets, usually in high-traffic downtown areas.

Street-level posters are rear-illuminated units consisting of two- or four-sided advertising faces. Street-level advertising includes transit shelters and blocks or columns with advertising faces. They are primarily available in urban centres. Transit shelters offer high levels of exposure to motorists, pedestrians, and transit riders. Transit shelter advertising offers the advertiser strong visual impact, as the colour reproduction is of superior quality. For an illustration see Figure 5.15.

Mall posters differ from the posters described above because they rely only on pedestrian traffic and aren't exposed to vehicle traffic. Located in shopping malls, they are directed at consumers who are actually shopping; therefore, they are a useful medium for the mall's retailers. Mall posters are good for supplementing other media and for reinforcing a brand's primary selling message.

The various forms of outdoor advertising are ideal for advertisers using a shotgun strategy. Posters reach a large cross-section of a market's population in a short period. Frequently, outdoor boards are included in a blitz or build-up schedule because they are good for launching new products where creating awareness for the brand name, brand logo, and package are important. Outdoor posters are also ideal for advertisers who want geographic flexibility; the advertiser selects only those urban areas that are given priority.

banner
In outdoor advertising, a large print ad that is framed and mounted on the exterior of a building. Online, an ad that stretches across a webpage; the user can click on the ad for more information.

mural advertisements
A hand-painted outdoor ad seen on the side of a building.

electronic signs
Advertisements that are displayed on electronic billboards that rotate about every 10 to 15 seconds so multiple messages can be displayed.

street-level posters
Rear-illuminated units consisting of two- or four-sided advertising faces such as transit shelters and blocks or columns with advertising faces.

mall poster
A form of advertising located inside shopping malls; relies on pedestrian traffic only.

FIGURE
5.15

Transit shelter advertising has a strong impact on motorists, pedestrians, and transit riders.

Source: Imago/ZUMApress.com/Keystone Press

There are a few drawbacks as well. The message must be brief, considering the circumstances in which people view outdoor boards. Since they reach a wide cross-section of the population, they are not a targeted medium. The message reaches people well beyond the target, which will increase the cost of reaching an actual target customer.

TRANSIT ADVERTISING People who use public transit are a captive audience for advertising messages. To relieve the boredom of travelling, ads offer a form of visual stimulation. I know from personal experience that passengers read the same ad over and over again while riding a subway car or bus.

Interior cards are print advertisements contained in racks above the windows of transit vehicles (buses, street cars, subway cars, and rapid transit cars). The average time spent travelling is approximately 30 minutes, offering the advertiser the flexibility of including longer messages—not an option in other forms of outdoor advertising. Refer to Figure 5.16 for an illustration.

Two different posters are available on the outside of buses. The **king poster** is a very large poster that stretches along the side of a bus. A **seventy poster** is smaller and located on the tail end of the vehicle. The unique characteristic of bus posters is their mobility. They move through the city and are seen by lots of motorists and pedestrians.

Superbus advertising involves painting the outside of a bus to carry one advertising message. Due to the costs, the advertiser must commit to a long-term contract (26 or 52 weeks) with the transit company. As part of the package, the advertiser gets all of the interior cards as well. Refer to Figure 5.16 for an illustration. **Bus murals** are also available and appear on the driver's side or the tail of the bus, or both. These are applied using vinyl products and are sold for commitments of 12 weeks or more.

Station posters are advertisements located on platforms and at the entrances and exits of subway and light rail transit systems. They are available in a variety of sizes and are either paper posters or backlit posters. Passengers waiting on platforms are exposed to the advertising message. A variety of new and innovative concepts have recently been introduced. Among them are *stair risers* (ads that appear on the sides of

Interior cards
A transit ad in the rack above the window or near the door of a bus or subway car.

king poster
An oversized poster attached to the side of a bus.

seventy poster
A small poster usually affixed to the back of a bus.

superbus advertising
An advertisement painted on the exterior of a bus; the advertiser also has exclusive use of interior cards.

bus murals
Advertisements that appear on the side or the tail of a bus, or both.

station poster
An advertisement located on the platform or at the entrance or exit of subways and light rail transit systems.

FIGURE
5.16

Interior cards have a captive audience

Source: *Toronto Star*/GetStock.com

FIGURE 5.

5.17   Advantages and Disadvantages of Out-of-Home Advertising

OUTDOOR POSTERS

Advantages

Reach and frequency—reach a large general audience daily
Coverage flexibility—markets selected geographically (key market plan)
Compatibility—a good complementary medium to reinforce a message
(name, logo, slogan)
Awareness—often included in teaser and blitz campaigns for new products due to
reach potential

Disadvantages

Creative limitations—message must be concise; good visuals mandatory
Targeting—not suitable for reaching precisely defined targets
Cost—absolute costs high compared to other media (minimum four-week cycles)
Image—often referred to as "urban clutter"

TRANSIT

Advantages

Reach and frequency—riders receive same message daily, weekly, and monthly
Continuous exposure—trapped riders view same ad many times
Coverage flexibility—markets selected geographically, based on priority
(key market strategy)

Disadvantages

Targeting—a diverse cross-section of population, therefore some circulation wasted
Environment—cluttered and crowded environment in peak periods makes message
less visible

steps that can be read from a distance), *ceiling decals* in vehicles, and *floor decals* on walk-ways and platforms. Another concept called *station domination* gives a single advertiser control of all advertising space in a subway station. These are good options for advertis-ers looking for new ways of standing out amid the clutter of out-of-home advertising.

From an advertising perspective, transit offers continuous exposure. That 30-minute commute provides ample opportunity to deliver an advertising message. In terms of advertising objectives, transit achieves both reach and frequency. Transit riders cut across all demographics, with the heaviest concentration being adults. Factors such as the increasing cost of operating a car and the increasing numbers of commuters travelling to and from a city each day have a positive effect on the reach potential of the medium. Like outdoor advertising, transit advertising is suited for media strategies designed to reach a diverse audience in key markets. Refer to Figure 5.17 for additional details about the ben-efits and drawbacks of the various forms of out-of-home advertising.

OTHER FORMS OF OUT-OF-HOME ADVERTISING   It's everywhere! It's everywhere! There are all kinds of unique opportunities to reach consumers when they least expect it. Among the more popular options with advertisers are washroom advertising, elevator advertising, and cinema advertising.

Washroom advertising involves the placement of mini-posters in public wash-rooms, usually above urinals in men's washrooms and on the backs of stall doors. They are located in colleges and universities, sporting facilities, hospitals, restaurants, and

washroom advertising
A mini-poster ad located in a public or institutional washroom; usually placed above the urinal or on the back of the stall door.

bars. Levi's and Budweiser are two brands that use this form of advertising. According to Gino Cantalini, marketing manager for Budweiser, "They are innovative and offer a certain degree of targeting."[21] Budweiser is reaching its audience in a location close to where purchase decisions are made.

elevator advertising
Advertising in display frames on elevator walls or on televisions mounted in the corner or above the door.

Elevator advertising is available in two forms: posters contained in display frames on the walls of elevators and slim-line televisions usually mounted in the top corner and tilted downward toward the passengers. The Elevator News Network (ENN) delivers up-to-date news and information along with ads on TV screens in office towers in major cities.

arena and stadium advertising
Advertising within arenas and stadiums, from the door to the court, rink, or playing field.

Arena and stadium advertising opportunities extend across North America and offer targeted reach for advertisers. In arenas that are home to professional hockey teams, advertising starts right above the front door, with companies paying megabucks to have an arena adorned with their name. GM Place in Vancouver, Air Canada Centre in Toronto, Scotiabank Place in Ottawa, and Bell Centre in Montreal are just some examples. See the illustration in Figure 5.18. In hockey arenas, there is also on-ice advertising, usually ads painted in the neutral zone between the blue lines. Signs can also be installed behind the players' benches and in the penalty box. At ballparks, rotating signs behind home plate are popular, and there are courtside signs on basketball courts. These signs receive additional exposure when a game is broadcast on television.

cinema advertising
Print advertising inside film theatres and broadcast advertising on screens; options include television-style ads on screen, slides, posters, and ads printed on tickets.

Cinema advertising offers a variety of options, everything from 30- and 60-second full-motion commercials, digital, pre-show commercials, lobby posters, theatre promotions, ads printed on movie tickets, and more. Cineplex Odeon, Canada's largest movie distributor, reaches 8 million moviegoers monthly. Cinema advertising is growing in popularity with Canadian advertisers. Cinema advertising is somewhat controversial as theatre patrons have paid to see the movie—many dislike the intrusion of advertising.

FIGURE 5.18

Advertising starts right above the front door.

Source: Phillip MacCallum/Getty Images.

Nonetheless, a captive audience and engaging content (a full-motion commercial that is entertaining and in Dolby sound) make the cinema a powerful advertising medium. Lifestyle products such as automobiles, telecommunications devices, and beverages find cinema advertising attractive.

SUMMARY

Media planning is the process of developing a plan of action for communicating messages to the right people at the right time. The end result is a media plan prepared by an advertising agency that covers all relevant media strategies and tactics. It is a document that is presented to the client for approval, and, once approved, is put into action.

The key elements of the plan are media objectives, media strategies, and media execution. Media objectives deal with five key issues: who to reach, what and how to present the message creatively, where to advertise, when to advertise, and how often to advertise. Media objectives establish priorities for the plan and provide guidance for developing media strategies.

Media strategy deals with the selection of appropriate media to accomplish the objectives. Strategies are influenced by variables such as the characteristics and behaviour of the target market; the nature of the message; the degree of market coverage desired; the best time to reach the target; competitive activity; reach, frequency and continuity; engagement; an assessment of the benefits and drawbacks of the various media options; and the available budget.

The advertising agency makes specific recommendations regarding the media a client should use. Depending on the assessment of the situation, and assuming the client wants to use traditional mass media, there are numerous alternatives: television, radio, newspapers, magazines, outdoor advertising in a variety of forms, and transit advertising. Some unique and newer options are also considered: washroom advertising, elevator advertising, advertising in arenas and stadiums, and advertising in cinemas. To meet the challenge, the advertising agency usually recommends a combination of media. Typically, there is one primary medium (a medium that receives a significant portion of the budget) supplemented with secondary media.

Media execution is the section of the media plan that outlines the specific tactics for achieving the media objectives. These include the specific media usage recommendations and summaries of how media funds will be allocated. Once the plan is approved, the agency's media buyers negotiate the best possible prices with media representatives. The plan is then put into action.

KEY TERMS

REVIEW QUESTIONS

1. What are the essential differences among media objectives, media strategies, and media execution?

2. Identify and briefly describe the key issues usually covered by media objective statements.

3. What is the difference among a profile-matching strategy, a shotgun strategy, and a rifle strategy? What media are best suited for each strategy?

4. What is the difference among the following market coverage strategies: national coverage, regional coverage, and key market coverage? What media are best suited for each strategy?

5. Briefly describe how the timing and amount of spending vary in the following media schedules: pulse, skip, blitz, and build-up.

6. Briefly describe the impact of reach, frequency, continuity, and engagement on strategic media planning.

7. What role does CPM play in media selection? How is it calculated?

8. Identify two key strengths and weaknesses for each of the following media: television, radio, magazines, newspapers, outdoor boards, and transit.

9. In television advertising, what is the difference between a network spot and a selective spot?

10. What is the difference between product placement and branded content?

11. Briefly describe the following media terms:
    a) format (of a radio station)
    b) broadsheet and tabloid
    c) paid circulation and controlled circulation
    d) clutter and cluster
    e) posters and backlit posters (outdoor)

DISCUSSION AND APPLICATION QUESTIONS

1. How will technological advances affect media strategy and media execution in the future?

2. Should the budget determine the media plan or should the media plan determine the budget? Briefly explain and establish an opinion on this issue.

3. Is it possible to implement a rifle media strategy by using television advertising? Justify your position by providing branded advertising campaigns that are scheduled effectively or ineffectively on television networks and channels.

4. Assuming you can't have both high reach and high frequency, under what circumstances should reach take precedence? Under what circumstances should frequency take precedence? Be specific and provide examples.

5. Given the nature of Canada's population and where the bulk of the population is located, when is it practical to implement a national media campaign? When do regional media campaigns or key market media campaigns make economic sense?

6. Using resources that are available in your library or online, compare the CPMs for three different magazines that compete with each other. They must be magazines that reach a similar target audience and attract similar advertisers. Which magazine is the most efficient at reaching the target audience?

7. Assume you are about to devise a media plan to launch a new luxury automobile (such as a BMW, Audi, Lexus, or Infiniti). The new model is a very sleek-looking sporty car. The target market is males aged 35 to 49 living in urban markets. What magazines and newspapers would you use to reach this target and why would you recommend them? What target-market media-matching strategy would you use? Is there any other medium you would recommend? Justify your position.

ENDNOTES

1. Jonathan Paul, "TV viewers are swapping remotes for mice," *Media in Canada*, July 7, 2008, www.mediaincanada.com.

2. "Major Media Comparison," TVB Canada, TV Basics, 2007–2008, p. 17.

3. "Network Pricing," *Advertising Age*, January 1, 2007, p. 22.

4. Canadian Media Directors' Council, *Media Digest*, 2008–09, p. 8.

5. Joe Mandese, "Commercial data zaps 'effective frequency,' supports recency," *Media Post*, June 29, 2004, www.mediapost.com.

6. "PVRs not yet impacting Canadian TV habits, says TVB," Friends of Canadian Broadcasting, September 4, 2008, www.friends.ca.

7. TV Basics, 2007–2008, p. 8.

8. Canadian Media Directors' Council, *Media Digest*, 2008–2009, p. 20.

9. Ibid., p. 17.

10. "Hockeyville growing in popularity," NHL.com, September 19, 2008, www.nhl.com.

11. Danny Kucharski, "The spots next shot," *Marketing*, August 15/22, 2005, pp. 19, 21.

12. Canadian Media Directors' Council, *Media Digest*, 2008–2009, p. 30.

13. Ibid., p. 30.

14. Patti Summerfield, "Radio connects with consumers," *Strategy*, September 2, 2004, www.mediaincanada.com.

15. "Radio listening," The Daily, June 26, 2007, www.statcan.gc.ca/daily.

16. Alexandra Gill, "Radio blogs get great reception," *The Globe and Mail*, March 23, 2005, p. R3.

17. "2007 Readership Highlights," NADbank, www.nadbank.com.

18. Canadian Media Directors' Council, *Media Digest*, 2008–2009, p. 39.

19. "10 top reasons to advertise in magazines," *Advertising Age*, September 26, 2005, p. M22.

20. Canadian Media Directors' Council, *Media Digest*, 2008–2009, p. 14.

21. David Carr, "Pinning down the young folk," *Marketing*, November 27, 2000, p. 25.

Planning for Direct Response Communications

Learning Objectives

After studying this chapter, you will be able to

1. Describe the direct response marketing communications planning process

2. Describe the various forms of direct response communications

3. Assess the role of database management techniques in the design and implementation of direct response strategies

4. Evaluate various external sources of list information and evaluate the role of these lists in building an effective direct response campaign

5. Explain the role and nature, and advantages and disadvantages, of the various forms of direct response communications

It was only a few decades ago that a mass marketing approach dominated the marketplace. Today, companies have the capability to deal with customers on an individual basis. In Chapter 1, the concepts of customer relationship management (CRM) and database marketing were introduced. Both concepts influence the development of programs that are designed to attract, cultivate, and maximize the return for each customer with whom the company does business. The end result is that companies are combining mass communications and marketing techniques with micro-marketing techniques. Database management and its influence on integrated marketing communications programs are discussed in more detail in this chapter. Information—that is, quality information—is the backbone of a direct response communications strategy.

Direct response communications involve direct mail, direct response communications in the mass media (mainly television, magazines, and newspapers), telemarketing, and catalogue marketing. Direct mail is the most common means of delivering messages directly to consumers, but advances in technology and database management techniques offer great potential for catalogues and the Internet to become more important in the mix. Internet communications are discussed in detail in Chapter 7. Using database management techniques, a company can look at a customer over an entire lifetime and plan appropriate strategies to encourage good customers to buy more often or in larger quantities. Communicating directly with customers makes the entire process much more personal.

Direct Response Communications and Direct Marketing

Just how important are direct response communications and other direct marketing practices in Canada? Recent statistics suggest direct response communications and direct marketing have a significant impact on advertising expenditures and sales revenues for goods and services. Direct mail advertising alone accounts for $1.7 billion, or 13 percent, of net advertising revenues in Canada. As an advertising medium, it ranks third, just behind television and daily newspapers, and ahead of the Internet, magazines, radio, and outdoor advertising.[1] If investments in direct response television, telemarketing, and catalogue marketing were included, the percentage of total media expenditures would be much higher.

Direct response communications are playing a more prominent role in the overall media mix of Canadian companies. Some of Canada's largest corporations have successfully integrated direct response communications with traditional forms of communications. These companies see the real value to be gained by managing customer relationships. Among these companies are Bell Canada, Rogers Communications, Shoppers Drug Mart, Mountain Equipment Co-op, and financial institutions such as RBC Financial Group and BMO Bank of Montreal.

Direct marketing and direct response communications will continue to grow for several reasons. First, companies want managers to be more accountable for the expenditures they oversee. Executives are looking for more immediate sales returns for the dollars they invest. Direct response advertising can be measured for success quickly. Second, the trend toward niche marketing and micro-marketing suggests the importance of forming good relationships with customers. Because direct response communications can be personalized, they constitute an ideal medium for nurturing relationships. Third, the availability of database management techniques provides the fuel that direct response communications run on. Specific message strategies for individual customers are now a possibility—if the organization can effectively analyze the information in its database. Advantages such as these clearly indicate why prudent marketing organizations include direct response as part of their communications mix.

It is important to remember that direct response communications is a subset of direct marketing. In other words, the communications program is a component of a much larger direct marketing program. What is the distinction between the two practices? In **direct marketing**, products are developed, messages about the products are sent directly to customers (business-to-consumer (B2C) and B2B) through a variety of media, orders are accepted, and then distributed directly to customers. In true direct marketing, all wholesale and retail intermediaries are eliminated.

In contrast, **direct response advertising** is advertising placed in any medium that generates an immediate and measurable response from the intended target. A direct response advertising plan involves the design and development of appropriate messages and the placement of messages in appropriate direct response media to encourage immediate action by the intended target. Alternatively, direct response advertising may be designed to build brand image, alter a perception, or attract a new target, much like other forms of advertising. Therefore, direct response advertising can be part of a fully integrated marketing communications campaign. Figure 6.1 illustrates the direct response planning process and its relationship with other components of marketing communications.

If traditional mass media are used (newspapers, magazines, radio, and television), the message includes a return mail address, 1-800 number, or website address where more information can be obtained or an order can be placed. Direct response advertising is capable of making a sale. Assuming adequate order taking and fulfillment strategies are in place, the entire transaction process from creating awareness to delivering the product is possible, and in a very short span of time.

Direct response communications can be divided between online communications and the more traditional forms. Online communications are presented in Chapter 7. The traditional forms of direct response communications are direct mail, direct response in the mass media (TV or print), telemarketing, and catalogue marketing:

- **Direct mail** is a printed form of communications distributed to prospective consumers by Canada Post or independent delivery agents (e.g., leaflets and flyers that may be dropped at a doorstep).

- **Direct response television (DRTV)** or **direct response print** refers to ads that appear in television commercials, extended commercials commonly referred to as infomercials, and print ads in newspapers and magazines. In each case, there is a direct call to action via a 1-800 number, return mail address, or website.

---

direct marketing
A marketing system for developing products, sending messages directly to customers, and accepting orders through a variety of media, and then distributing the purchase directly to customers.

direct response advertising
Advertising placed in a medium that generates an immediate and measurable response from the intended target.

direct mail
A printed form of direct response advertising distributed by Canada Post or independent delivery agents.

direct response television (DRTV)
Advertising that appears on television and encourages viewers to respond by telephoning a toll-free number, by mail, or online; often referred to as infomercials.

direct response print
An ad in print media that issues a direct call to action via a toll-free number, return mail address, or website.

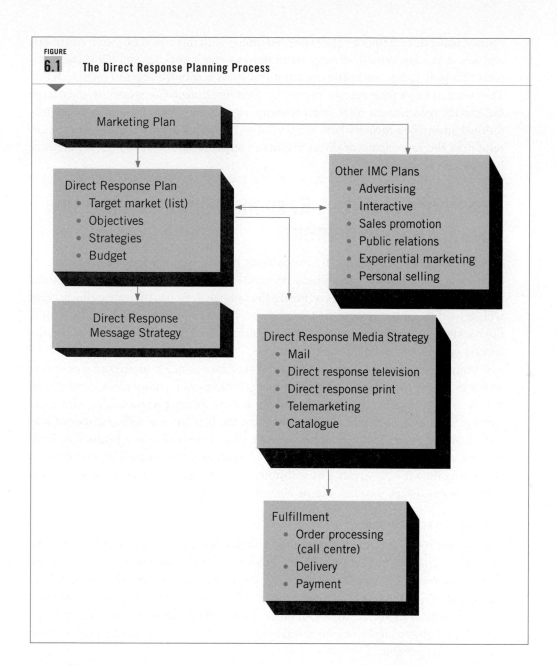

FIGURE 6.1   The Direct Response Planning Process

- **Telemarketing** refers to outbound sales calls (a company calls the customer) or inbound sales calls (the customer contacts the company) to secure an order. All calls are usually handled through a central call centre.

- **Catalogues** are important communications vehicles among retail organizations. Typically, they are mailed or hand delivered by independent agents to existing customers. New customers may request catalogues through some form of direct response communication. Catalogues promote the sale of goods the retailer carries and are now designed to move customers online for more information and to encourage sales. They are also useful tools for communicating information about goods in B2B situations.

It has taken considerable time for direct response communications to be accepted by blue-chip marketing organizations. For years, traditional advertising agencies

telemarketing
The use of telecommunications to promote the products and services of a business; involves outbound calls (company to customer) and inbound calls (customer to company).

catalogue
A reference publication, usually annual or seasonal, distributed by large retail chains and direct marketing companies.

resisted using direct response; they were unfamiliar with this aspect of communications and saw it as a last-minute strategy when things weren't working well. How the times have changed! Today, marketing organizations stress accountability and measurability. They want to know what they are getting for their investment. Consequently, most large full-service agencies now offer direct response expertise or have access to it. Many traditional advertising agencies have acquired direct response agencies. Such progression reinforces the importance of direct response communications in today's competitive business environment.

The Roots of Direct Response Communications: Database Management

Whether it's mail or telephone communications, there needs to be a convenient and efficient means of contacting customers. As experts in direct response communications often state, it's the list that makes or breaks the campaign. By list, they mean the list that will be used to contact current customers or prospective customers directly. That list is the backbone of the entire campaign; the quality of the list has a direct impact on the success or failure of the campaign.

house list
An internal customer list.

Companies recognize that it costs about six times as much to acquire a new customer as it does to keep an existing customer. Consequently, companies are compiling databases to keep track of existing customers and are forming relationships with them through mail and electronic means. Obviously, the best list is a well-maintained and well-managed internal list of customers. Such a list is referred to as a **house list**. Since the best customers are current customers, it is much easier to get them to buy more of something than it is to attract a new customer. If the goal is to generate new business from new customers, then lists can be obtained from external sources.

INTERNAL DATA SOURCES

A good database management system collects and maintains relevant information about customers. The information is stored in such a manner that managers have easy access to it when developing marketing strategies. For example, managers should be able to manipulate the data so that customer profiles will emerge, and future purchase patterns can be forecast from those profiles. In other words, a thorough understanding of a customer's past purchasing behaviour should provide ammunition for predicting his or her future buying patterns.

COLLECTING DATA

The names and addresses of customers are the most common forms of internal data, but simply knowing who the customers are offers little perspective when developing a strategic plan. Factor in technology, and all kinds of information about customers can be combined. Keeping track of purchasing behaviour and then linking it to a name and address is very meaningful. Therefore, the database should identify what a customer purchases, how often the customer purchases, how much the customer spends on average, what brands of goods the customer prefers, and so on.

Sophisticated retail organizations update this information automatically as goods are scanned through checkouts. Shoppers Drug Mart, for example, has an exhaustive database of customer information collected via its Optimum Card Rewards program. From this information, buying behaviour profiles of a customer can be developed. Once the behaviour information is linked to the name and address, and perhaps also other demographic information, it is then possible to develop specific offers for specific types of customers. Plus, the offer can be sent to each customer individually. Such profiles can also be used to search for new customers in external databases.

Adding external information to the database rounds out the profile of the customer. Information about customers using credit cards for purchases is readily available. Credit card companies such as Visa and MasterCard are sitting on nest eggs of information that marketing organizations can purchase. Statistics Canada makes census data available that are updated every five years. This information is available at reasonable cost to the marketing organization.

Demographic and psychographic information can also be obtained from commercial research companies like Millward Brown, or a company can hire an independent research company to conduct primary research to uncover such information. The combination of information dealing with age, gender, education, income, marital status, and household formation along with information about attitudes, lifestyles, interests, and hobbies forms an arsenal of information ready for use in strategic planning.

ACCESSING DATA

The second step in database management is devising a storage system that allows managers to access information easily when it is needed. In the realm of marketing communications, sales representatives and sales managers need instant access to customer sales records as they prepare for sales calls. Customer service personnel need access to historical information to handle complaints or simply serve customers better. Marketing managers and marketing communications managers need to clearly identify target customers and their behaviour to communicate directly with them and design special offers for them. To accomplish these kinds of tasks, relevant information must be convenient and accessible to all those who work with the database. Molson Canada, for example, has 1 million customers in its Molson Insider database. Molson uses the database to attract insiders to Molson-sponsored events and to inform customers about new products and promotional offers.[2]

The electronic era has resulted in an information explosion that allows for the storage and transfer of a great amount of business data in a short time. What has emerged is a new concept called data mining. **Data mining** is the analysis of information that establishes relationships among pieces of information so that more effective marketing strategies are identified and implemented. Rather than looking at an entire data set, data mining techniques attempt to locate informational patterns and nuggets within the database.[3]

data mining
The analysis of information to determine relationships among the data and enable more effective marketing strategies to be identified and implemented.

The goals of data mining are to produce lower marketing costs and to increase efficiency by identifying prospects most likely to buy in large volume. A firm's competitive advantage in the marketplace will depend increasingly on knowing the situation better than the competition and being able to take action rapidly, based on knowing what is going on. Look no further than your local Walmart to see data mining at work. Walmart is the acknowledged leader in data mining with the capability of tracking sales on a minute-by-minute basis. It can also quickly detect regional and local market trends. Such knowledge allows Walmart to customize each store's offerings while keeping suppliers abreast of how well their products are selling.[4]

Data mining offers an organization two essential benefits. First, it provides a means of profiling the "best" customers and the "worst" customers. Clearly, in these times, greater emphasis must be placed on customers who produce sales and high profit margins for an organization. As well, consideration can be given to dumping customers who are costing more than they generate in profit. Why keep customers if they are not profitable? Second, data mining techniques give an organization a means to predict future sales. Continuous compiling and analysis of data about current customers' sales histories should result in more accurate forecasts about what the future holds. As well, when a company wants to expand its business by attracting new customers, it can use the internal customer profile information as a guideline and then rent names from lists that have similar profiles.

For some insight into how a database system is used in a marketing communications program, read the IMC Highlight: **Mountain Equipment Co-op Believes in Direct Mail Marketing**.

IMC HIGHLIGHT

Mountain Equipment Co-op Believes in Direct Mail Marketing

The foundation of an effective direct marketing communications campaign is the quality of the customer list maintained by the organization. Not to exaggerate, but Mountain Equipment Co-op lives and breathes by its robust member (customer) list. The list, which comprises 2.5 million members across Canada, is constantly being updated to ensure MEC can gain the most benefit from it.

MEC operates retail stores and a direct marketing division (catalogue, web, and telephone) and has annual revenues in the area of $200 million. It is a member-based national cooperative—the largest retail consumer cooperative in Canada. MEC operates with a limited advertising budget, so rather than concentrate on attracting new customers, it works diligently to get current customers to buy more. That's where database marketing plays a key role.

The focus of MEC's database marketing is on data mining—the constant refining and analyzing of data in order to effectively serve the needs of its membership. When consumers sign up for a membership, they give the retailer permission to send relevant communications to their home or email address. According to Selena McLachlan, manager of marketing and

research, "When you demonstrate that you know your customer, through relevant messages that make them feel appreciated, you in turn create affection for the brand."

In terms of execution, the MEC catalogue is the key piece of communications. Members covet the catalogue, and there are two distributed to members—a spring edition and a winter edition. That catalogue goes well beyond product information. It is a reflection of the socially conscious yet hip brand, with profiles of adventurers and environmental and conservation crusaders. Members retain the catalogues for 6 to 12 months, and as soon as they are mailed there is a surge in retail sales.

Being environmentally conscious, MEC doesn't mail catalogues to all members. Instead, through data mining, catalogues are only sent to members who are most engaged with the brand—those customers who buy regularly! A variety of filters are used to determine who these members are. In the database, sales data are combined with attitudinal and behavioural information collected from primary research. Collectively, the data help MEC improve the retail shopping experience and allow it to target its most profitable members with new product information and special offers.

The net result is the distribution of about 500 000 catalogues for each issue, in addition to 250 000 postcards and 700 000 e-cards. MEC also produces specialty catalogues to serve members in niche sports such as canoeing and kayaking, among many others. "As much as possible, the specialty catalogues are targeted to ensure they reach members who are engaged and active in their sport," says McLachlan.

Given the nature of the business and the niche markets that MEC serves, McLachlan knows that effec-tive database marketing combined with catalogues will remain a key component of future success. With regard to catalogues, the organization is exploring magazine-quality paper that leaves less of an impact on the environment.

Adapted from "A Mountain of a Database," *Sorted*, Canada Post Publications, 2008, pp. 12–15.

EXTERNAL SOURCES

People who have a history of responding to mail offers tend to be attractive prospects for new offers. Buying by mail or from offers seen on television is part of their behaviour. Therefore, the challenge is to find prospects that have a similar demographic profile, and perhaps a psychographic profile that is close to the profile of current customers. A **list broker** can assist in finding these prospects. The buyer provides the broker with a profile of the target customer, and the broker supplies a list of potential prospects. Generally, a high-quality list is developed through a **merge/purge** process on a computer, whereby numerous lists are purchased, combined, and stripped of duplicate names. Names are purchased (actually rented) on a cost-per-thousand basis. List brokers charge a base rate for names and charge more if additional requests are made. Additional requests, called *selects*, are usually demographic variables, interest or lifestyle variables, or geographic variables.

> **list broker**
> A company specializing in finding or developing lists for direct response purposes; finds prospect lists based on target market criteria established by marketing organizations.
>
> **merge/purge**
> A process in which numerous mailing lists are combined and then stripped of duplicate names.

One of the biggest suppliers of external data about households is Canada Post. Working from postal codes that isolate a neighbourhood or a city block, prospective households are identified when census data is added. For example, relevant statistics regarding the ages and incomes of homeowners in the area and the presence of children in those households could be attractive information for marketing organizations. There are three types of lists available:

Response Lists A **response list** is a list of proven direct response buyers. It's a "hot" list so the price is high on a cost-per-thousand basis. Such lists include book-of-the-month buyers, CD music buyers, and people who routinely place orders with cooperative direct marketing firms. ICOM Information & Communications Inc., a large provider of response lists in North America, charges an additional $15/M (cost per thousand) for proven mail order buyers.[5] Cornerstone List Management is another provider of direct mail lists. For more insight into the lists and their costs see Figure 6.2.

> **response list**
> A list of direct mail buyers who have previously bought based on direct response offers.

Circulation Lists The word "circulation" indicates these lists are obtained from newspaper and magazine sources. **Circulation lists** can target consumers demographically, psychographically, and geographically. A publishing company, such as Rogers Communications, sells its list of subscribers to any other business that is interested in a similar target. A list management company is usually responsible for managing and renting all of the lists made available by the publisher.

> **circulation list**
> A publication's subscription list that targets potential customers based on specified demographic characteristics, interests, or activities.

FIGURE
6.2 The Costs Involved in Renting a Direct Response List

Requirement	*Chatelaine*	*Cottage Life*
List Size	202 145	29 394
Minimum Order	5 000	5 000
Base Cost	$125/M	$140/M
Selects		
Gender	$10/M	$10/M
FSA	$10/M	$10/M
Key Records	$5/M	$10/M
Province	$10/M	$10/M
Other Selects		
Age	$10/M	$20/M
Direct Mail Sold	$10/M	$15/M
Income	$10/M	$20/M

There are additional costs that depend on the data format required (e.g., peel-off label, tape, CD-ROM, email, etc.)

Chatelaine Reader Profile
- Average age 25 to 49.
- High female readership.
- Affluent households over $75 000 income.
- Households with children.
- Homeowners.

Cottage Life Reader Profile
- Household income $78 000 plus.
- Value of primary address $500 000 (affluent).
- Two-vehicle families.
- 50% are MOPEs (managers, owners, professionals, executives).

Source: Adapted from Cornerstone Group of Companies, www.cstonecanada.com/datacards.

For instance, *Chatelaine* magazine reaches women aged 25 to 49, with children, and busy with careers and family. The *Chatelaine* list has a base cost of $125/M, which rises as certain characteristics are added. There are also additional costs for requesting specific formats for the list, such as tape, disk, email, and so on.[6]

compiled list
A direct mail list prepared from government, census, telephone, warranty, or other publication information.

Compiled Lists **Compiled lists** are assembled from government, census, telephone, warranty, and other publication information. Less expensive than circulation lists and response lists, these lists are very common in B2B marketing. Names of prospects can be assembled from various print sources, such as *Fraser's Canadian Trade Index* and *Scott's Industrial Index*. Provincial and national associations like the Canadian Medical Association provide lists of their physicians, as do other associations: accountants, engineers, purchasing managers, teachers, and so on.

ONLINE DATABASES

Due to advancing technology, there has been a surge in developing online databases. Information from commercial sources can now be transferred to an organization almost instantly. An **online database** is an information database accessible to anyone with proper communications facilities. For example, census data from Statistics Canada are readily available online. Most of Statistics Canada data are based on census data collected every five years. The nature of the information and reporting of the information is very detailed, covering dozens of demographic and socioeconomic topics such as family and household structures, income, occupation, education, ethnic background, and marital status. For a marketing organization, knowledge about and understanding trend data are essential skills for planning effective marketing strategies.

online database
An information database accessible online to anyone with proper communications facilities.

From commercial sources like Dun & Bradstreet (D&B), marketing organizations can access information through directory databases. A **directory database** provides a quick picture of a company and its products (e.g., ownership, size in terms of sales revenue, company locations, number of employees, key management personnel, and profitability). Examples of business directories that are available electronically include the *Canadian Key Business Directory* and the *Canadian Trade Index*. The *Canadian Key Business Directory* provides more than 20 000 listings of the largest companies in Canada and over 60 000 key contact names.[7] For businesses marketing goods and services to other businesses, the information contained in these directories helps identify real prospects.

directory database
A commercial database that provides information about a company (e.g., size, sales, location, number of employees).

The Tools of Direct Response Communications

Essentially, five primary media compose the direct response tool kit: direct mail, direct response television, direct response print media, telemarketing, and catalogues. Among theses options direct mail still dominates, but other options are growing in importance. Let's examine each option in more detail.

DIRECT MAIL

The use of direct mail is widespread thanks to its ability to personalize the message by using names secured from internal databases or rented from external databases. As well, direct mail provides an opportunity to target customers demographically and geographically. For example, an organization might choose to do a mailing to a fairly general audience by distributing a magazine subscription leaflet to all households in Ontario, or by delivering a message to very selective upper-income households in a concentrated area of a city. Moreover, direct mail provides an opportunity to "tell a story." Since the average mailing includes several pieces, an expanded story can be told about the product or service. Unlike in the traditional mass media, the advertiser is not restricted by time (30-second commercials on TV or radio) or space (one page or less in a newspaper or magazine). Benefits such as these make direct mail an attractive option.

A typical direct mailing has several components, each designed to serve a specific purpose:

Envelope The envelope is a critical component of the mailing. Since direct mail is usually unsolicited, the envelope has to suggest strongly why the recipient should read the contents. There should be a sense of urgency to opening the envelope.

Letter The letter introduces the prospect to the product or service and encourages the receiver to read more about the offer in the other pieces included in the mailing. The letter may be unaddressed (delivered to the householder) or addressed (with the person's name and address). Addressed mail offers a certain degree of personalization and produces a higher response. Typically, the language used in the letter is persuasive, because the goal is to generate interest and desire and, ultimately, get the receiver to respond to the offer.

Leaflets and Folders These types of inserts can vary in size and structure. By definition, a **leaflet** is one page (though it may not be a full page), printed front and back, and contains vital information about the offer: here's what the product is and here's why you should buy it. Again the language is persuasive in nature. Visuals frequently support the copy. A **folder** can be larger in size and contain multiple pages. For example, a double page folded once results in a four-page layout. That amount of space gives the marketer ample room to sell. When an offer is put together, an **incentive** is often included to stimulate a more immediate response. An incentive might nudge a recipient interested in buying closer to taking action. The objective is to get that person to take the appropriate action, call a 1-800 number, go online, or fill in the order form. A selection of leaflets and folders is included in Figure 6.3.

Order Form A well-designed order form is essential. It must be easy to read, and it must communicate all details regarding price, additional costs such as shipping and handling

leaflet
A one-page flyer that offers relevant information about a direct mail offer.

folder
A direct response sales message printed on heavy stock that can be mailed with or without an envelope; may be several pages in length.

incentive
A free gift or offer included in a direct mail package.

FIGURE
6.3

A Selection of Leaflets and Folders in Various Sizes and Configurations

Source: Photo by Dick Hemingway.

charges, and means of payment (usually credit card information). The recipient must be able to place the order effortlessly.

Postage-Paid Return Envelope Eliminating the need for postage is another means of encouraging the recipient to take action. The combination of a clear and concise order form with a postage-paid return envelope makes it a no-hassle process from start to finish.

Statement Stuffers A **statement stuffer** or **bounce back** is an additional offer that rides along with the delivery of another offer or with the delivery of a monthly statement. Capitalizing on the ease of purchasing by credit or on the knowledge that the customer uses related products or services, such mailings make it convenient for the customer to take action. Bounce backs commonly arrive with Sears, The Bay, Visa, and MasterCard bills.

statement stuffer (bounce back)
An ad or offer distributed in monthly statements or with the delivery of goods purchased by some form of direct response advertising.

DIRECT MAIL STRATEGIES There are two basic options for delivering direct mail. The first is to deliver the mailing as a standalone piece. In this option, the organization bears all of the costs associated with developing the offer and distributing it to the target market. The second option is to deliver the offer as part of a package that includes offers from other companies. In this option, the distribution costs are shared equally among all participants. That is the difference between solo direct mail and cooperative direct mail.

solo direct mail (selective direct mail)
A unique advertising offer mailed directly to a target audience by a marketing organization.

Solo Direct Mail Also known as **selective direct mail**, with **solo direct mail** the organization prepares a unique offer and mails it directly to the target market. It is a standalone offer. As discussed earlier, today's technology makes it very convenient for organizations to assess buying information, devise unique offers for existing customers, and deliver offers directly to the customers. Such a plan of action sounds much more efficient than delivering a message blindly to all consumers on prime-time television, or through daily newspapers or national magazines. Furthermore, solo direct mail can play a key role in an organization's CRM program. It is an effective means of keeping the channel of communication open.

dimensional mail
Direct mail that can take any form other than the typical flat piece of mail.

Personalization is an important element of solo direct mail. According to Canada Post, 84 percent of Canadians open direct mail if their name is on it, and marketers experience an increase in response and conversion rates as a result of personalization. The illustration appearing in Figure 6.4 demonstrates solo direct mail and dimensional direct mail (discussed below) in one mailing piece.

Another type of direct mail that attracts more attention and gets higher response is dimension mail. **Dimensional mail** is a type of direct mail that can take any form other than the typical flat piece of mail. It could be something as simple as a pen or other object in an envelope or a unique box or package that contains the mail offer. Dimensional mail is meant to stand out—it is unique and often generates buzz for the product. For some interesting insight into how Canadians perceive and react to direct mail pieces see Figure 6.5.

The hotel industry now includes direct mail strategies as a key component of the marketing communications mix. For insight into how some hotels are maximizing the benefits of direct mail, read the IMC Highlight: **Hotels Bond with Customers via Direct Mail**.

FIGURE 6.4   A Direct Mail Piece that Combines the Elements of Solo Direct Mail and Dimensional Mail

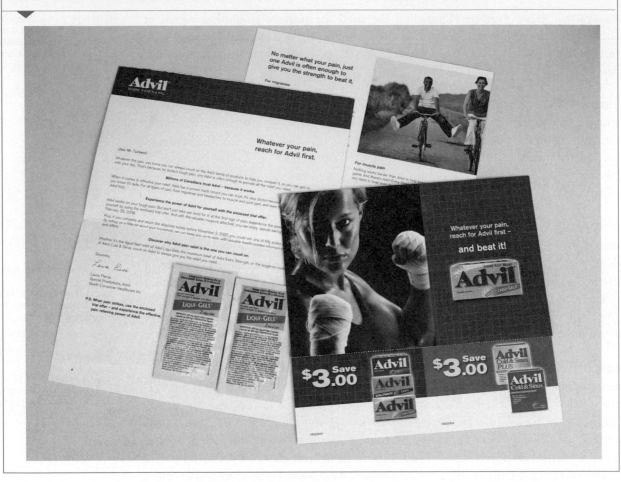

FIGURE 6.5   Consumers are responsive to personalized direct mail

According to Canada Post, 84% of Canadians open direct mail if it has their name on it, and marketers experience a significant increase in response and conversion rates as a result of personalization. Canada Post also reports that:

- 89% of Canadians open direct mail if it comes from a company they know.
- 86% open it if it looks intriguing or interesting.
- 79% open it if it has their address on it.
- 66% open it if it has a postage stamp.
- 52% open it if it mentions a free draw.

Marketers should have confidence in direct mail because consumers like receiving it. A survey conducted by Pitney Bowes reveals that:

- 73% of consumers prefer mail for receiving information about new products or offers from companies they do business with. Mail was also preferred by 70% of consumers for receiving unsolicited information on products from companies they are not currently doing business with.
- 86% of respondents prefer direct mail as their channel choice, as compared to 10% for e-mail.

Source: Canada Post Research as reported in "How to Get the Most Out of Your Direct Mail," Direct Marketing Resource Guide, *Marketing*, November 14, 2005, p. 4 and "Direct Mail More Likely to be Opened than Unsolicited Mail," Center for Media Research, June 21, 2007.

IMC HIGHLIGHT

Hotels Bond with Customers via Direct Mail

The hotel market in Canada is projected to be relatively flat over the next few years—a reflection of a faltering economy and consumers pulling back on their travel plans. The key then is to get travellers who are members of frequent stay programs to travel more. Some effective database marketing is needed!

The prestigious Hazelton Hotel, located in the trendy Yorkville area of downtown Toronto, has always relied on direct mail to bring in business. When the hotel first opened in 2007, it targeted 200 of Canada's top CEOs, inviting them to take advantage of an introductory offer. The allure of a VIP experience achieved a 20 percent response rate (40 CEO visits). The message delivered to the CEOs was variable and highly personal—Hazelton prides itself on its ability to know its clientele.

Just recently, the hotel used Canada Post's geo-targeting services to send a direct mail piece to 20 000 homes in Toronto's affluent neighbourhoods. The homeowners were invited to experience Hazelton's premier spa services as well as to become a member of the Spa at The Hazelton Hotel. According to Matthew Opferkuch, general manager of the hotel, "In the age of electronic communications, when you are trying to sell a luxury product, sending something personalized in the mail is almost a novelty."

The Hazelton Hotel is now implementing its own loyalty program unlike traditional rewards programs. Hazeltons' program is based on exclusivity, and membership will guarantee certan rates at various times of the year, have no blackout periods, and always offer last-room availability. To attract members, direct mail will again play a key role. "Sending a letter speaks volumes about personal attention; it leaves a lasting impression," says Opferkuch.

At Blue Mountain Resort, direct mail also plays a key role. The resort sends out 12 highly targeted mailings a year from its database of 250 000 names. According to Paul Pinchbeck, director of marketing, "The most effective mailings are those that go to niche markets." To demonstrate, a November 2008 season's renewal campaign targeted at lapsed guests of two years or more doubled the number of "win back" customers to 3000 from 1500 per annum. Three thousand pass holders at an average price of $200 generated $600 000 in revenue—very good ROI for a direct mailing!

Says Pinchbeck, "Being part of the hospitality industry, it's incumbent on us to communicate with our repeat guests and potential repeat guests in a manner that is more personal, and direct mail allows us to do that."

Adapted from "Check-In!" *Sorted*, Canada Post Publications, 2009, pp 17–18.

Cooperative Direct Mail **Cooperative direct mail** refers to packages containing offers from non-competing products and services. Consumer goods companies commonly use this method; they are attracted to it because the costs are shared among all participants. A typical mailing might include coupons for packaged goods items, magazine subscription forms, order forms for direct mail offers, and so on. For packaged goods marketers in the food and drug industries, cooperative direct mail has proven to be an effective means of generating trial purchase. Response rates to coupon offers in direct mail are significantly higher (5 percent) than for similar offers in newspapers (1 percent) and magazines (1 percent).[8] The illustration in Figure 6.6 is representative of a typical cooperative direct mailing.

In deciding how and when to use direct mail, a manager evaluates the benefits and drawbacks of the medium. Figure 6.7 on page 177 summarizes what direct mail has to offer.

cooperative direct mail
A mailing containing specific offers from non-competing products.

175

Contents of a Cooperative Direct Mailing Distributed by Open & Save

Source: Photo by Dick Hemingway.

DIRECT RESPONSE TELEVISION

Direct response television (DRTV) is gaining in popularity with advertisers. Essentially, there are three forms of direct response television: the 30- or 60-second commercial that typically runs on cable channels and sells gadgets and music products, the infomercial (a program-like commercial), and direct home shopping (as in The Shopping Channel).

The nature of direct response television advertising has changed over time. Once it was regarded as the "domain of schlock"; mainstream marketing organizations would not go near it. It was perceived as a last-resort tactic when all else failed. DRTV is now looked at in a more positive light due to the acceptance of infomercials and their improved level of quality. An **infomercial** is usually a 30-minute commercial that presents, in detail, the benefits of a product or service.

Infomercials today are presented in a more entertaining manner; there is less "hard sell." The transfer of information is less intrusive. Consumers can simply evaluate the message and take action if they so desire. Unlike general TV advertising, direct response TV ads, including infomercials, ask the consumer to take action immediately—to make the call, grab the credit card, and make the purchase. The effectiveness of the ad can be measured for impact on the spot. Did it work or not? These ads are measured quantitatively based on response. Typical measures include cost per order, cost per lead, cost per call, or some other criteria.

infomercial
A long commercial (e.g., 10 to 30 minutes) that presents in detail the benefits of a product or service; usually includes a call to action (e.g., a 1-800 number).

FIGURE
6.7

Direct Mail as an Advertising Medium

ADVANTAGES

Audience Selectivity—Targets can be precisely identified and reached based on demographic, psychographic, and geographic characteristics. It is possible to secure external lists that closely match internal lists.

Creative Flexibility—Unlike other media, the message can be copy oriented, visually oriented, or a combination of both. Because a mailing includes several components, there is ample time to expand on the benefits of the product.

Exclusivity—Mail does not compete with other media or other ads upon receipt. In contrast, magazines and newspapers include clusters of ads and create a cluttered environment to advertise in.

Measurability—Direct mail response is measured by the sales it generates. A sale can be directly linked to the mail offer (e.g., receipt of a phone call or order form in the mail). The success of a campaign is determined in a relatively short period.

DISADVANTAGES

Image—Direct mail is not a prestigious medium. Often perceived as junk mail, it can be easily discarded by the recipient.

Cost per Exposure—When all costs are included (e.g., printing, securing list, mail delivery, and fulfillment), total cost can be higher than an ad placed in another print medium, although selective targeting reduces waste circulation.

Lack of Editorial Support—As a standalone medium, compared to newspapers or magazines, it can't rely on editorial content to get people to read the message.

Well-produced and highly informative infomercials are now being run by serious mainstream marketing organizations. By industry, pharmaceutical marketers, automotive marketers, packaged goods marketers, and financial institution marketers are all on board. Companies within these industries that are using DRTV include Pfizer and GlaxoSmithKline, General Motors and Ford, Procter & Gamble and Unilever, and RBC Financial and TD Canada Trust.

These organizations evaluated the returns from their respective investments in mainstream advertising and decided that direct response communications would play a more vital role. For some companies the message could not be adequately conveyed in the usual 30-second television spot. Manulife Financial recently produced three 120-second commercials. According to Ian French, president and executive creative director at Northern Lights Direct Response, "We wanted to more clearly articulate the types of life circumstances that people would be in that lend themselves to insurance. For example, one commercial depicts a family facing child health care costs that are not covered by government insurance.[9]

Direct response commercials do not always have to sell something. In fact, a good infomercial can serve many different marketing communications objectives: it can establish leads, drive retail traffic, launch new products, create awareness, and protect and enhance brand image. Procter & Gamble, for example, is not selling direct to consumers, but uses infomercials to promote products sold by retailers. The infomercial gives consumers all of the information they need and raises interest in the product; when customers visit the store they feel assured that they know all about the product.

Some companies are even referring to the medium as "BRTV," or "brand response television." What this means is that advertisers are pursuing a dual benefit—they are combining a branding message with a DRTV technique. The ad builds the brand attributes and generates an immediate response through a 1-800 number and website. Its ability to do both is what excites the advertiser.

Getting into direct response television, however, is not cheap. Experts say it costs at least $150 000 to produce a 30-minute infomercial, with prices going as high as $500 000 depending on locations used and whether celebrity spokespersons are hired.[10] To keep media costs reasonable, shorter commercials (up to 60 seconds) usually use the run-of-schedule option rather than buying time on specific programs. They may also buy remnant time, which is unsold inventory available on short notice at a lower cost.

Direct home shopping is a service provided by cable television, for example, The Shopping Channel. Messages to prospects are presented in the form of close-up shots of the product or, in the case of clothing and accessories, by models wearing the goods. Items such as home gym equipment usually involve a full-scale demonstration. Details on how to place an order are broadcast frequently and a 1-800 number is usually shown continuously on the edge of the TV screen along with a description of the product.

Home shopping offers the shopper convenience. Without sounding too tacky, Joan Rivers sells a variety of jewellery and accessories through The Shopping Channel, and Tony Little is often seen there promoting his latest piece of exercise equipment, for example, Tony Little's Cheeks™ Exercise Sandals and the Gazelle Sprintmaster. Consumers have the option of buying these products by telephone or by visiting The Shopping Channel's website (theshoppingchannel.com).

Generally, the United States is well ahead of Canada in terms of direct response television and home shopping penetration. American companies embraced these techniques more quickly. The trend, however, suggests that the boom years for direct response television in Canada lie ahead.

DIRECT RESPONSE PRINT MEDIA

The print media—mainly newspapers and magazines—are good choices for communicating direct response offers or for fielding leads for future marketing programs. Given the local nature of daily newspapers, an organization can target prospects geographically. If the size of the budget restricts activity, then markets can be assigned priorities until the budget is exhausted. Local market retailers that want to take advantage of direct response techniques have a good option in newspapers.

A majority of magazines are targeted at specific audiences based on demographic and psychographic characteristics, so the direct response message can be sent to specific audiences based on criteria established by the advertiser. For example, a company marketing floating docks or cottage designs might want to reach cottage owners. A direct response ad placed in *Cottage Life* magazine will reach that target market. The basic point is that it is possible to identify magazines that closely match the profile of a company's best customers. If a direct response is the objective, the print ad should include a toll-free telephone number and a mailing address or website that facilitates the response. Viceroy, a designer and builder of modular homes, for example, uses direct response print ads to get potential customers to order a catalogue or to visit a dealer. The catalogue contains colourful pictures and the floor plans for all of the models. A DVD about the company and how it constructs the cottages is also sent to the prospective customer. This is a good example of an effective, integrated direct response campaign (see Figure 6.8).

Another option to consider is the insert, which was briefly discussed in Chapter 5 in the discussion of newspapers. An **insert** can be a single-page or multiple-page document that is inserted into the publication (see Figure 6.9). In some cases, the insert is

direct home shopping
A shopping service provided by cable television stations that offers products or services for sale by broadcast message (e.g., The Shopping Channel).

The Shopping Channel
theshoppingchannel.com

insert
A preprinted, free-standing advertisement (e.g., a leaflet, brochure, or flyer) specifically placed in a newspaper or magazine.

Source: Courtesy of Viceroy.

FIGURE
6.8

An Illustration of Direct Response Print Advertising

actually glued onto a page (rubber-like glue that is easily removed when the insert is removed from the page). This type of insert is referred to as a **tip-in**. Advertisers pay the publication insertion fees on a cost-per-thousand basis. A single-page insert in the *Toronto Star*, for example, costs $40.50/M, and a 16-page insert costs $56.50/M.[11] Preprinted inserts can be used for other communications purposes—they are good handouts at trade shows and other promotional events and can be used to draw attention to products at the point-of-purchase. They can also be mailed directly to customers in the company's database.

tip-in
An insert that is glued to a page in the publication using a removable adhesive.

TELEMARKETING

Telemarketers seem to call at the worst times, like suppertime, or just as you are sitting down to watch a favourite program. Can't telemarketers call at a more suitable time? Doesn't that sound like a common complaint? To a telemarketer, it's simply a fact of life. The best time to call is when the prospect is at home, and that's suppertime or shortly thereafter. Despite the negative feelings consumers have about telemarketing's practices, it is growing in popularity with marketers as a means of communicating with customers. Telemarketing communications are often directly linked to direct response television and direct mail campaigns. Working together, they are a potent combination for achieving all kinds of marketing objectives.

FIGURE
6.9

Inserts are flexible and can be used in print media, direct mail, and at point-of-purchase

call centre
A central operation from which a company operates its inbound and outbound telemarketing programs.

inbound telemarketing
The calls received by a company from consumers, whether to place an order, inquire about products or services, or in response to a toll-free telephone number promoted on a direct response television commercial.

outbound telemarketing
Calls made by a company to customers to develop new accounts, generate sales leads, and even close a sale.

Most telemarketing activities are conducted by call centres. A **call centre** is a central operation from which a company operates its inbound and outbound telemarketing programs. In Canada, the revenues generated by call centres climbed rapidly from just over $400 million in 1998 to $2.8 billion in 2006, an average annual increase of 27 percent. By comparison, the overall economy expanded at an average annual rate of 5.9 percent.[12]

There are two forms of telemarketing: inbound and outbound. **Inbound telemarketing** refers to the calls received by an order desk, customer inquiries, and calls generated from toll-free telephone numbers promoted on direct response television commercials. **Outbound telemarketing** refers to calls made by a company to customers to develop new accounts, generate sales leads, and even close a sale.

The call centre is a vital link in the database management system, because the telephone is a quick and convenient tool for capturing information about customers. Any information that is obtained can be added instantly to the database. Cost-effective software is available to manage this task.

In direct response communications, much emphasis is placed on message and media decisions. For example, how will the offer be communicated to entice the target market and what media will it be placed in? Managing the inbound sales calls generated by commercials has traditionally been a weak link. Therefore, an organization must effectively plan its activities to meet call volume, capture data, present selling opportunities, and handle closing calls. The better a company can do these things, the better the economics of the direct response campaign. To illustrate, consider that a national TV spot on a cable network for a direct response lead generation campaign can easily generate 500 or more inbound inquiries, 85 percent of which will occur within the first three minutes of airing.[13] The call centre has to be ready! If it has to dump the call, or if the consumer hears a busy signal and hangs up, the marketer's return on investment is undermined. The ability to manage an inbound call requires precision planning to maximize returns. It could be the start of a very fruitful customer relationship.

The primary advantage of telemarketing is cost. Compared to traditional forms of mass advertising and the cost of sending a salesperson into a business call, telemarketing offers considerable savings. In comparison to direct mail, the response rate for telemarketing is about 100 times higher, so even though direct mail may appear to be cheaper than telephone solicitation, it is actually more costly in the long run. To be effective, however, the telemarketing call must be carefully planned. There must be proper training and preparation for telemarketing representatives, just as there is for field sales representatives. Figure 6.10 summarizes the activities that can involve telemarketing.

FUNDRAISING

- Inbound (donations)
- Outbound (solicitations)

SALES SUPPORT

- Generating leads
- Qualifying prospects
- Securing appointments
- Marketing research

PERSONAL SELLING

- Opening new accounts
- Selling existing accounts
- Selling marginal accounts

FULFILLMENT

- Accepting orders
- Maintaining customer records
- Invoicing and payment processing

CUSTOMER SERVICE

- Handling inquiries and complaints
- Help lines

FIGURE
6.10

Telemarketing performs many marketing roles

Earlier in this section, the negative image of telemarketing was mentioned. Image is perhaps telemarketing's biggest drawback. A Canadian research study conducted by Ernst & Young found that 75 percent of Canadians consider marketing calls unwelcome and intrusive; they are ranked as one of the least-liked sales techniques.[14] People who react negatively to the calls simply hang up. In Canada, a "Do-Not-Call" registry was established in 2008 to protect consumers from unwanted telephone calls. By calling the registry number, consumers can have their telephone number included on the do-not-call list. The registry requires that telemarketers check the registry at regular intervals. Telemarketers that call individuals or households on the list are subject to fines should a complaint be filed.[15]

CATALOGUES

Catalogues are reference publications, often annual, distributed by large retail chains and other direct marketing organizations. Catalogue marketing involves the merchandising of products through catalogue sales. When someone thinks of catalogues, the Sears catalogue comes to mind immediately, and for good reason. The Sears catalogue is the largest in Canada and is distributed to more than 4 million households. Sears publishes two semi-annual catalogues (Fall & Winter and Spring & Summer) as well as numerous seasonal catalogues such as the *Christmas Wish Book* and sale catalogues. It is estimated that Sears distributes about 425 million catalogues in North America annually.[16]

Sears is now a fully integrated marketing communications organization that generates $6.3 billion in sales in Canada annually.[17] Much of its business is generated from catalogue sales. Sears also operates one of the busiest commercial websites in Canada. The company accepts orders by fax, email, and online. Its 1-800 number is the most frequently called toll-free number in Canada. Refer to Figure 6.11 for an illustration.

Other prominent catalogue retailers in Canada include Mountain Equipment Co-op and IKEA. Both retailers are merging their retail operations with online buying. The catalogues they distribute drive traffic to their respective websites or to their retail stores. When compared to the United States, the Canadian catalogue market is underdeveloped, yet it offers great potential in the future. One of the leading catalogue marketers in the United States is L.L. Bean. Based in Freeport, Connecticut, Bean is the nation's largest outdoor catalogue company, generating $1.2 billion in annual sales. Its inbound telemarketing operation is open 24 hours a day, 365 days a year. On average, Bean's telephone rings 50 000 times a day. Catalogue-based companies like Bean operate effective fulfillment programs. At Bean, logistics and order fulfillment are the heart of the operation. The Bean warehouse contains three-and-a-half miles of conveyor belts, stores 4 million items, has 25 shipping docks, and includes a built-in Federal Express shipping system.[18]

Retailers like Sears, Mountain Equipment Co-op, and IKEA see the value in catalogue and online marketing activities. Refer back to the IMC Highlight: **Mountain Equipment Co-op Believes in Direct Mail** for more information. Sales through catalogues definitely take away from store sales, but companies are responding to their customers' demand for convenience. Customers today are into multi-channel shopping. These companies effectively combine media advertising (television, print, and flyers) with nontraditional marketing communications (Internet, direct mail, e-mail, and catalogues).

Rather than distribute catalogues, some companies have taken the concept a step further and are publishing their own magazines for distribution to current customers. The purpose is to stay in touch with customers after the sale. Harry Rosen, a prominent,

FIGURE
6.11   **Sears effectively integrates retail, catalogue marketing, and web marketing**

Source: Courtesy of Sears Canada Inc. Photo by Dick Hemingway.

upscale men's wear store distributes *Harry* magazine in hard copy and online to customers and prospective customers. The magazine keeps customers informed about fashion, health and lifestyle trends, and stories of interest to them. The magazine provides a means of building a sound relationship with customers and is part of Harry Rosen's customer relationship management program. Refer to the image in Figure 6.12.

Source: Courtesy of Harry Rosen, Inc.

FIGURE
6.12

Harry Rosen builds a relationship with customers through *Harry* magazine

SUMMARY

Direct response advertising is the third-largest advertising medium in Canada and is growing at a pace faster than traditional mass media. Several factors are contributing to this growth: companies are looking for tangible returns for the money they invest in communications, direct response communications are a natural extension of database management programs, and direct response is a personalized medium that is ideal for enhancing customer relationships. The key components of direct response communications are direct mail, direct response television (DRTV), telemarketing, and catalogue marketing.

The foundation of direct response communications is the organization's database. An organization collects and analyzes data from internal and external sources. Customer or house lists record data about purchase transactions made by customers. This information is combined with demographic and psychographic information to form profiles of an organization's best customers. These customers are then targeted and reached through direct response communications. The analysis and manipulation of data constitute a process called data mining. The goal of data mining is to lower marketing costs and increase efficiency by identifying those customers most likely to buy in large volume.

The success of a direct response campaign depends on the quality of the list used by the advertiser. Lists are available from list brokers and other secondary sources such as directories and trade indexes. Lists provided by brokers are rented on a cost-per-thousand basis. Advertisers can choose between response lists (the most expensive), circulation lists, and compiled lists.

Direct mail is the most common form of direct response advertising. A direct mailing usually includes an envelope, letter, leaflet or folder, order form, and postage-paid return envelope. Each component performs a specific role in trying to get the recipient to take action. Advertisers choose between solo direct mail and cooperative direct mail. Solo distribution is more expensive but produces a higher response rate than cooperative distribution. An organization also has the option to use dimensional mail, which is mail of a different size and shape than traditional flat pieces. Dimensional mail draws attention to something inside the mailing piece and tends to break through the clutter of other mailings.

In recent years, direct response television has captured the attention of blue-chip marketing organizations. An advertiser can choose between 30- and 60-second direct response commercials and infomercials, which are much longer and are more like a program than a commercial. Direct response commercials are effective if an organization wants to establish leads, build image, and launch new products. Infomercials are effective in situations where there are lots of details to communicate or for explaining complex products. By definition, direct response ads are capable of completing a transaction with the recipient.

Direct response ads in the print media are another option. Advertisers frequently use the print media to encourage prospective customers to call 1-800 numbers or to visit websites to get more information. As well, print is a good medium for distributing inserts. By selecting the right newspaper or magazine, the advertiser can target its primary customer.

There are two types of telemarketing. Inbound telemarketing refers to calls made by customers to an order desk. Outbound telemarketing refers to calls made by a company to prospective customers to generate leads and even close a sale. Telemarketing programs are usually outsourced to a call centre. Companies are attracted to telemarketing because of its low costs. It is much less expensive than face-to-face personal selling and mass advertising. Its major drawback is the negative perception people hold about this form of communication. Recent government legislation and the establishment of a "do-not-call" list will adversely affect future growth of the telemarketing industry.

Catalogues are an underdeveloped alternative in direct response communications in Canada. However, companies such as Sears and Mountain Equipment Co-op see the value of producing catalogues. As well, there are all kinds of specialty companies that produce catalogues that include descriptions, pictures, and prices of the products they market. Time-pressed consumers appreciate the convenience of catalogue shopping, and catalogues help direct consumers toward offline purchases (at retail) and online purchases (at a website).

KEY TERMS

bounce back,   173

call centre,   180

catalogue,   165

circulation list,   169

compiled list,   170

cooperative direct mail,   175

data mining,   167

dimensional mail,   173

direct home shopping,   178

direct mail,   164

direct marketing,   164

direct response advertising,   164

direct response print,   164

direct response television (DRTV),
164

directory database,   171

folder,   172

house list,   166

inbound telemarketing,   180

incentive,   172

infomercial,   176

insert,   178

leaflet,   172

list broker,   169

merge/purge,   169

online database,   171

outbound telemarketing,   186

response list,   169

selective direct mail,   173

solo direct mail,   173

statement stuffer,   173

telemarketing,   165

tip-in,   179

REVIEW QUESTIONS

1. What is the difference between direct marketing and direct response advertising?
2. What are the major forms of direct response advertising?
3. Explain the concept of data mining. What impact does data mining have on marketing and marketing communications?
4. What is the role of the list broker in direct response advertising?
5. In the context of mailing lists, what does merge/purge refer to?
6. What are the differences among a response list, a circulation list, and a compiled list?
7. Briefly explain two advantages and two disadvantages of direct mail advertising.

8. Identify and briefly explain the components of a typical direct mail piece.
9. What is a statement stuffer?
10. What is the difference between a solo direct response campaign and a cooperative direct response campaign?
11. Identify and briefly explain how dimensional mail is different from other forms of direct mail.
12. Identify and briefly explain the various direct response television alternatives.
13. What is the difference between an insert and a tip-in?
14. What is the difference between inbound telemarketing and outbound telemarketing?

DISCUSSION AND APPLICATION QUESTIONS

1. Will direct response communications play a more significant role in the marketing communications mix in the future? Through secondary research, identify those factors that will encourage or discourage the use of direct response communications and formulate your position on the issue.

2. Direct mail advertising remains a popular medium for many profit-based and not-for-profit organizations. Why? What are the benefits and drawbacks of using direct mail? Identify some organizations that successfully use direct mail advertising to help achieve their marketing goals.

3. Collect two or three direct mail pieces that have been delivered to your household address. Did the mailing reach the appropriate target market? What components did the mailing include, and how effective were they in communicating the message? Is the message convincing enough to act upon?

4. Assume you are about to develop a direct response advertising campaign to launch a new and improved version of the George Foreman Grill. The target market is male and female heads of households, with a family income of $50 000 or more, living in markets of over 100 000. The campaign will be national in scope. What

direct response media would you use in the campaign? Assuming direct mail will be a component of the campaign, how would you find names for the mailing?

5. Conduct some research to find a company that has successfully used direct response advertising as part of an integrated marketing communications campaign (such as a major bank, financial services company, or not-for-profit fundraising campaign). What role did direct response communications play? Describe the successes that resulted from the direct response effort.

6. Is direct response advertising a viable option for Canadian packaged goods companies? Provide appropriate examples to illustrate your point of view.

ENDNOTES

1. Canadian Media Directors' Council, *Media Digest*, 2008–2009, p. 14.

2. Mary Dickie, "Change is brewing," *Strategy*, July 2007, www.strategymag.com.

3. Ross Waring, "The promise and reality of data mining," *Strategy*, June 7, 1999, p. D9.

4. Susan Pigg, "Diapers, drinking, and data," *Toronto Star*, August 16, 2002, pp. E1, E10.

5. ICOM Target Source Database, Spring/Summer 2004, p. 10.

6. Costs obtained from Cornerstone List Management.

7. *Canadian Key Business Directory*, www.dnb.ca/salesmarketing/keybusinessdir.html.

8 A Special Presentation on Consumer Promotion Fundamentals, NCH Promotional Services, 1998.

9. Matt Semansky, "Manulife Financial flexes DRTV muscle," *Marketing Daily*, January 9, 2008, www.marketingmag.ca/daily.

10. Chris Powell, "From Flowbees to Fords," *Marketing*, April 25, 2005, p. 17.

11. Toronto Star, http://mediakit.thestar.ca.

12. "Study: Trends in the telephone call centre industry," *The Daily*, February 27, 2008, www.statcan.gc.ca/daily.

13. Maria Eden, "One call, multiple sales opportunities," *Marketing Direct*, November 4, 2002, p. 16.

14. Mary Gooderham, "Level of antipathy a wake-up call for telemarketers," *The Globe and Mail*, May 7, 1997, p. C11.

15. "Do-not-call has strong Canadian support," *Marketing Daily*, November 1, 2007, www.marketingmag.ca/daily.

16. "Sears catalogue tagged naughty," Canada.com, retrieved October 13, 2008, www.canada.com/topics/lifestyle/holidayguide2007.

17. "The Top 1000," *Report on Business Magazine*, July/August 2008.

18. Kate Kane, "Bean delivers the goods," www.fastcompany.com/online/10/llbean.html.

Planning for Online and Interactive Communications

Scott Anderson

Learning Objectives

After studying this chapter, you will be able to

1. Assess strategies for delivering effective messages using online advertising

2. Describe the various roles played by online communications in a marketing and marketing communications environment

3. Evaluate the various advertising alternatives that are available online

4. Assess the potential of the Internet as an advertising medium

5. Assess the role of mobile media, video games, and social media networks as alternatives in integrated marketing communications campaigns

Online communications offer a high degree of personalization. Since personalization is one of the cornerstones of customer relationship management (CRM) programs, the Internet is becoming an attractive communications alternative for marketers. The medium is unique as it allows an organization to listen to customers, learn from them, and then deliver content and services tailored to their responses and actions. These benefits must be considered when devising an integrated marketing communications plan.

Technology is changing how marketing decision makers think about the media. Relatively new terms such as video-on-demand, rich media, broadband video, podcasting, blogs, and social networks, among many others, comprise the new environment in which marketing messages are communicated. Being new, the challenge for media planners revolves around how to best integrate this new individualized media environment with the traditional mass media environment.

A recent study prepared for the Interactive Advertising Bureau in Canada found that the Internet provides marketers with a "mirror image" of the age profile for users of other major media, particularly when comparing the Internet and television.[1] Thinking strategically, therefore, media planners see Internet communications as complementary to traditional media and expect that, when used together, they will more effectively and efficiently achieve desired communications objectives. Further, since all age groups are active online, media planners can balance media weight across all target audiences when shifting a portion of an advertising budget to the Internet.

Various Internet usage trends are cited in this chapter. The trends indicate that younger age groups who have grown up with technology are avid users of interactive communications devices. Therefore, advertisers trying to reach a 25- to 34-year-old target right now only have a short time to learn how to use online media channels since the high levels of Internet usage by 18- to 24-year-olds today will become high levels of usage for the entire 25- to 34-year-old group in eight years' time.

This chapter examines in detail a host of new interactive marketing communications opportunities that should be considered when planning an integrated marketing communications campaign.

Internet Penetration and Adoption

When compared to most other countries, Canada has one of the highest levels of Internet penetration and broadband access. Data from the Canadian Internet Project (2007) show Canadian Internet penetration levels have reached 78 percent.[2] Essentially, four of every five Canadians have Internet access by some means. Such high Internet penetration is having an impact on time spent with other media, but it seems that Canadians have seamlessly adopted new interactive media technologies while maintaining a strong appetite for traditional media.

The Internet is available to all Canadian consumers but inequalities do exist in specific demographic sectors. Internet adoption levels are lower among French-speaking households than English-speaking households (67 percent versus 82 percent). Canadians with higher income, education, and professional status are more likely to be online, although the divide between higher and lower socioeconomic groups is less smaller today than it was five years ago. Canadians online predominantly access the Internet from their homes (94 percent of all Internet users) compared to from work (43 percent) and public places (16 percent). While Internet access from wireless devices (cell phone or a BlackBerry) is relatively low, younger Canadians are increasingly making use of these devices to access the Internet from outside their homes. This behaviour will have an impact on future marketing communications planning.

Traditional media use by Canadians has declined from 50 hours a week to 45 hours. This drop in consumption embraces all age categories but is more pronounced in younger age categories. Such a drop is the result of more time being spent online. Internet users spend an average of 17 hours per week online, representing 28 percent of the Internet media users' media diet. By age, youth and younger Canadians (12 to 29 years old) use the Internet more while older Canadians use traditional media more.

Time spent with a medium is a factor that media planners must consider. The Internet now ranks third in terms of weekly time spent by all adults with all media. Among all Canadians, the Internet is just behind television and radio. Among the 18- to 24-year-old age group, the Internet is the number one medium in terms of weekly hours spent with a medium. Among 25- to 34-year-olds, the Internet is fast approaching the time levels of television and radio.

The trend data presented in this section strongly suggest the inclusion of online media in a marketing communications plan. The Internet is an ideal medium for reaching younger Canadians as well as middle- to upper-income households. Further, the Internet is taking on mass media status based on the amount of time Canadians spend with the medium. And just around the corner is the emerging wireless communications market. Mobile media such as iPods, BlackBerries, and cell phones represent the third screen that consumers are exposed to (television and computer screens are the first two). Soon, wireless communications will be the preferred method of connecting to the Internet and it will enable consumers to be exposed to advertising messages anywhere and any time. For additional insight into how and why Canadians refer to the Internet so often and what they do online, refer to Figure 7.1.

FIGURE
7.1

Internet Consumption by Canadians: The Facts and Figures

When asked, a majority of respondents to a media research survey agreed with the statement: "The Internet is an integral part of my lifestyle."

Here are some other highlights from the study:

The Internet now stands third—just behind television—in terms of total weekly time spent by all adults with all media.

The Internet is the number one medium in terms of percent share of weekly time spent for people aged 18–24 (40%) and 25–34 (33%).

The Internet now reaches more adults each week than either newspapers or magazines.

On average, people spend 17 hours a week online.

One in four Canadian Internet users visits social network sites once a week and more than 50% of Canadians under 30 use social network sites.

Source: Interactive Advertising Bureau of Canada, "IAB Canada Releases Annual Canadia n Media Usage Trends Study (CMUST)," February 3, 2009./Charles Zamaria and Fred Fletcher. *Canada Online! The Internet, media and emerging technologies: Uses, attitudes, trends and international comparisons 2007.* Toronto: Canadian Internet Project, 2008.

Online and Interactive Marketing Communications

Based on the data presented in the previous section, it is becoming clear that the Internet is a mass reach medium, much like television, radio, and print. As further evidence of the reach capabilities of the Internet, consider that 24 million Canadians are online and that the total audience reached by the most popular online sites far exceed the reach of popular television shows. For example, Google reaches over 21 million unique visitors and averages 11 million daily visits in Canada. A **unique visitor** is defined as an individual who has either accessed a site or been served unique content and/or advertising messages. It is the equivalent to a site's reach. In contrast, the most popular television shows such as *CSI*, *Grey's Anatomy*, and *Desperate Housewives* reach an average of 2.5 million per episode.

> **unique visitor**
> An individual who has either accessed a site or been served unique content and/or advertising messages.

In terms of targeting, the Internet is absolutely essential for reaching an audience under the age of 35 years. The Internet is now the number one medium among 18- to 24-year-olds and 25- to 34-year-olds in terms of time spent with media each week. Consequently, advertisers are investing considerable sums in online advertising; they are shifting funds out of conventional media and into online and mobile campaigns. The automobile industry is ahead of the curve when it comes to allocating funds to online campaigns. For 2009, Chrysler announced it would invest 30 percent of its media budget online and General Motors plans to invest 50 percent of its $3 billion North American media budget online within the next three years.[3] In Canada, net revenues for online advertising total $1.6 billion, placing the Internet in third place behind television and newspapers.[4] Refer to Figure 7.2 for a breakdown of advertising revenues by type of online advertising.

From a planning perspective, the Internet can no longer be classified as a new medium or an add-on to a marketing communications plan. It is now an imperative component of such a campaign. Advertisers such as Unilever, Molson's, RBC Financial, Canadian Tire, Colgate-Palmolive, Procter & Gamble, and McDonald's have participated in cross-media research programs that have convinced them that online advertising deserves an important place in the marketing communications mix.[5] Simply stated, if your target market is online you had better be there with your advertising message. The challenge facing marketers is two-fold: first, they must devise a plan that effectively integrates online advertising into the marketing communications mix; and second, they must determine how much to invest (share of budget) in online advertising.

FIGURE
7.2   Online Advertising Revenues by Types of Advertising

Type of Ad	2007 ($ in millions)	% of Total	% change (2006–2007)
Search	478	38	+38
Display	432	35	+39
Video	9	1	n/a
Classified/Directories	305	25	+37
Email	17	1	-15
Total	1241	100	+37

Note: 2008 total revenue was $1.6 billion (+33% over 2007). The breakdown by type of ad was not available at time of publishing.

Source: Interactive Advertising Bureau of Canada, "2007 Canadian online advertising climbs to $1.2 billion," July 3, 2008.

Unlike any of the traditional mass media, online advertising provides immediate feedback to advertisers regarding how effectively their message reached the target; it automatically gears ads to personal viewer's tastes, and it generally reaches receptive consumers—they want to see the ads they click on![6] Target marketing capabilities are discussed in more detail in the next section. Beyond targeting, the Internet delivers on the corporate mandate for marketers to be more accountable; since online advertising is measurable, it should be attractive to marketing organizations. Measurement and evaluation techniques for online media and all other media are presented in Chapter 12. Finally, the expansion of broadband capabilities and the growing penetration of cell phones and other small electronic devices will provide for video downloading, a very attractive option for advertisers who have relied on television advertising in the past.[7]

As consumers continue to embrace the Internet and other interactive media as an integral part of their everyday lives, marketers have little choice but to acknowledge that anything interactive is a critical medium to engage consumers and create deeper brand experiences. At the same time, online communications can go further than many other media because they can secure a purchase and make arrangements to have goods delivered. They are capable of closing the loop, from initial awareness to a buying decision, in a very short period, assuming a website has e-commerce capabilities. Figure 7.3 illustrates how Internet communications link with traditional advertising and e-commerce. For these reasons, the Internet is an exciting medium, and its potential must be exploited.

For more insight into the benefits of adding online advertising to the marketing communications mix, see the IMC Highlight: **Integrated Campaign Delivers Results for Canadian Tire**.

IMC HIGHLIGHT

Integrated Campaign Delivers Results for Canadian Tire

Canadian Tire is a very successful company. It is a company that prides itself on being a leader in the area of integrated media campaigns, for it saw the benefits of integration long before many of its competitors.

Terry Yakimchick, manager of media integration at Canadian Tire, says, "We strongly believe in the integration of consistent themes and branding through all of our communications as well as our in-store customer experience. We have increased our investment in online spending and believe that online plays an important role in our overall media mix."

The impact of Canadian Tire's investment in online communications has been proven through a research study conducted by the Interactive Advertising Bureau. The study, referred to as CMOST (Canadian Media Optimization Study), examines the impact of integrated campaigns on factors such as brand awareness, favourability, intent to purchase, and, ultimately, return on investment.

A two-week Father's Day campaign was tested at Canadian Tire. The campaign included 30-second radio spots, online banner ads, flyers (nationally delivered print flyers and e-flyers), along with the promotion of a contest and price promotional offers communicated at the Canadian Tire website.

The findings of the research study were as follows:

- The combination of online advertising and radio advertising increased awareness by an additional 6 percent.
- The combination of radio and online advertising increased scores for a variety of Canadian Tire brand attributes from 6 to 10 percentage points above those delivered by radio alone.
- The combination of online and radio had an impact on the female target, whose unaided brand awareness increased by 16 percent.

- The combination of online and radio produced the highest percentage of unique visitors to the Canadian Tire website in two years.

These results indicate the impact that online communications offer advertisers. Clearly, online communications have become an effective medium that must be given due consideration when planning an integrated campaign. A company must deliver its message where its customers are, and clearly they are online!

Adapted from "Fourth CMOST Study demonstrates online's ability to influence behavior in short period of time," *IAB News* Letter, www.iabcanada.com.

FIGURE
7.3 The Links among Online Communications, Traditional Communications, and E-commerce

Traditional forms of advertising drive customers online. Online communications provide detailed information. The information could lead to an online purchase (e-commerce) or an offline purchase. Online communications strategies must complement offline communications strategies.

Corporate Plan → Marketing Plan → E-commerce Plan

Marketing Plan → Advertising Plan (Traditional Media) → Online Communications Plan → Offline Purchase

Online Communications Plan → E-commerce Plan

THE INTERNET AND TARGETING

The reality of the Internet is that consumers voluntarily visit specific websites. To get what they want, they also give up valuable information about themselves. Smart companies use the Internet as a means of obtaining information for their databases. Once the information is analyzed, it can be translated into specific messages, and marketing offers can be tailored to specific customer needs.

The Internet is much like any other medium. Audiences can be targeted based on demographic and geographic variables, by time of day, and by behaviour. All websites accumulate data on who visits and how long they visit. Such information aids media planners when they are devising target audience reach and frequency scenarios. In terms of **demographics**, a popular website like TSN.ca attracts a male audience and is over-indexed for males in the 18- to 24-year age category. It's no wonder that Molson

House and Garden Television
www.HGTV.ca

Ontario Lottery Corporation
www.olg.ca

Toronto.com
www.toronto.com

Canadian is a heavy advertiser on this website—it reaches the company's primary demographic! A website like HGTV.ca has a strong female reach, particularly in the 35- to 49-year age category—an attractive target for any marketing organization in the home furnishing and decorating business.

Once targets are identified demographically, they can be qualified further by *geography*. Advertisers can zero in on users in specific regions, cities, or postal codes. For example, the Ontario Lottery Corporation (www.olg.ca) reaches Ontario. Toronto.com (www.toronto.com), a site that offers information about restaurants, entertainment, hotels, and shopping, reaches a Toronto audience.

Targeting by *daypart* is another planning decision. Unlike television, where prime time is night time, prime time online is during the day—when people are at work. Not only is the at-work online audience vast, it is comprised of a demographically attractive group of individuals who have higher-than-average incomes, education, and tendencies to shop and buy online. To demonstrate the impact of daypart targeting, Best Buy ran a three-week campaign on Yahoo! Its ads ran Monday to Friday between 5 am and 11 am in Ontario and Quebec. The campaign generated a 200 percent conversion lift (consumers who took action based on the advertising) over previous campaigns.[8]

Unlike other media, the Internet is a medium that allows marketers to target customers on the basis of their behaviour. In its simplest form, **behavioural targeting** means delivering ads based on a consumer's previous surfing patterns.[9] An individual's surfing behaviour is tracked by placing a **cookie**, which is a small text file uploaded to a consumer's web browser and sometimes stored on that person's hard drive. The cookie can be used to remember a user's preferences. By tracking preferences, an organization can directly tailor messages to reach specific consumers.

behavioural targeting
A means of delivering online ads based on a consumer's previous surfing patterns.

cookie
An electronic identification tag sent from a web server to a user's browser to track the user's browsing patterns.

When targeting based on behaviour, the reach component of an advertising campaign is less important. In mass media campaigns advertisers typically want to reach as many people as possible at a frequency that will motivate some kind of action. Such a practice is difficult to measure and evaluate. Behavioural targeting online allows an advertiser to reach fewer people, but the actual results can be measured and evaluated immediately.

To demonstrate the impact of behavioural targeting, an automotive insurance advertiser targeted consumers who recently visited automotive sites in order to generate leads. Two different plans were used: demographic targeting and behavioural targeting. The demographic targeting option resulted in 183 million impressions and generated 47 leads per 1 million impressions. An **impression** is defined as a measurement of responses from a web server to a page request from a user's browser. When behavioural targeting was employed only 6 million impressions were made (at much lower cost) but those impressions generated 116 leads per 1 million impressions. Behavioural targeting produced three times the number of leads that demographic targeting did.

impression
An ad request that was successfully sent to a visitor. This is the standard way of determining exposure for an ad on the web.

Behavioural targeting is ideal for reaching consumers when they are researching a purchase. The sheer amount of research done online by consumers is reason enough for a company to be actively engaged with consumers through online communications. A user who sees something of interest (that is, an advertising message that creates awareness) can obtain information immediately by clicking the ad and visiting the website. Therefore, well-designed, well-placed, and well-targeted messages are useful tools for consumers who engage in online product research. The potential of the Internet is huge—it will become the medium of choice for companies wanting to reach large numbers of people in a cost-efficient manner.

Beyond reaching people efficiently, an organization can complete a sale online. In terms of securing action, the Internet is very similar to direct response advertising (discussed in Chapter 6). Online storefronts such as those for Sears and Chapters/Indigo fall into this category. Finally, the Internet deals with the concept of mass customization. **Mass customization** refers to the capability of personalizing messages and, ultimately, products to a target audience of one—the ultimate form of targeting! The marketer has the potential to deal with each customer individually. For example, Dell Computer does not produce a computer until it hears directly from a customer. Once the exact specifications are determined through a process of interaction at the Dell website, a unique computer is produced and shipped directly to the consumer.

mass customization
The development, manufacture, and marketing of unique products to unique customers.

Online and Interactive Communications Planning

Interactive communications refers to the placement of an advertising message on a website, usually in the form of a banner, rich media ad, video ad, sponsorship at a website, or an ad delivered by email. Advertising messages may also be communicated through other electronic devices such as cell phones, personal digital assistants, MP3 players, and video games.

interactive communications
The placement of an advertising message on a website, or an ad delivered by email or through mobile communications devices.

When devising an interactive communications plan, decisions about which medium to use are largely based on the communications objectives and the budget available. Refer to Figure 7.4 for a visual review of the interactive planning process. The

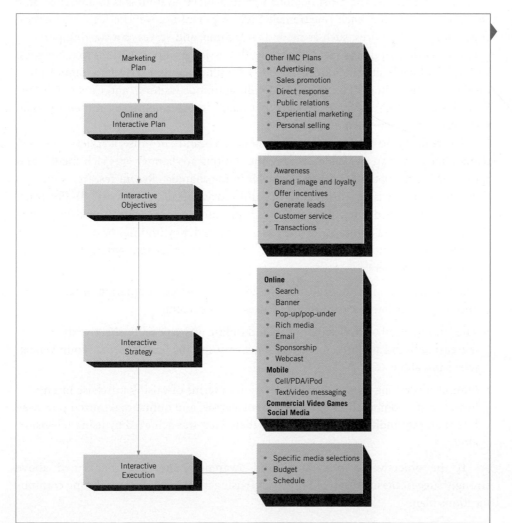

**FIGURE
7.4**

The Online and Interactive Communications Planning Process

first step in the process is to establish the objectives. The second step is to evaluate the various media options strategically. Will it be an online campaign, a mobile media campaign, a video game campaign, or any combination of alternatives? What interactive media are best suited for effectively delivering the message? Once the strategy is determined, the next step is execution. Here, decisions are made on specific media, how much to spend, and how to schedule media activities during the year.

Online and Interactive Communications Objectives

Online advertising performs the same or similar roles as traditional media advertising. It can help create brand awareness, build or enhance brand image, generate sales leads, provide a means to make a purchase, improve customer service and communications between customers and the company, and acquire meaningful data about potential customers (as in database management).

CREATING BRAND AWARENESS

portal
A website that serves as a gateway to a variety of services such as searching, news, directories, email, online shopping, and links to other sites.

Given the amount of time and the frequency with which consumers go online, there is ample opportunity for a company or brand to develop advertising that will generate brand awareness. The most obvious way to achieve awareness is to advertise on a web portal where the reach is extremely high. A **portal** is a website featuring several commonly used services, such as news or searching, and serves as a starting point or gateway to other services, such as shopping, discussion groups, and links to other sites. Examples of such sites include Google (21.9 million unique visitors), Yahoo! (16.3 million unique visitors), Facebook (16.3 million unique visitors), and Canoe (7.7 million unique visitors).[10] These are sites that people are automatically routed to when they launch their browser.

To create brand awareness and awareness of a brand's promise, a variety of advertising alternatives are available. Among the options are banner ads, rich media, and sponsorships (all options are discussed later in the chapter). Recent research indicates that Internet advertising works best when utilized as part of a media mix. To illustrate, when Dove launched a new line of skin-care products, a media mix of magazine, outdoor, television, and online advertising was employed. Key findings of the Dove study provided insight into how various media can work together in a synergistic manner. The key findings were:

• The addition of online and/or outdoor advertising to a combination of television and magazines improved awareness scores by 33 percent.

• The combination of television, print, and online was especially effective in increasing brand attribute scores among a very specific female target group versus television alone.

• Online advertising outperformed television in terms of raising purchase intent; however, the combination of television, magazine, and online maximized purchase intent an astounding 47 percent higher than what was achieved by using television alone.

If the objective is to create brand awareness, the data mentioned above strongly suggest the inclusion of online advertising in an integrated marketing communications plan.

BUILDING AND ENHANCING BRAND IMAGE

Brand building is the responsibility of marketing communications activities. The objective is to have the public perceive the brand in a positive manner. Therefore, online communications must present a message and image consistent with and comparable to any traditional form of communication. Consumers actively seek out product information on company websites, so it is important that the site project an image in keeping with overall company image.

It is common for consumers to be routed to sub-pages on a website (e.g., a brand page) as they search for the information they are after. Therefore, the brand page must comply with the brand's image and persona. Since it is common practice to include website addresses on traditional forms of advertising, it makes good sense to have an integrated message in terms of look, appearance, and style across all media. Such a practice helps produce a synergistic effect for the total communications effort.

Companies in the telecommunications, automotive, and financial services industries are masters at matching message strategies among traditional and non-traditional forms of media. Automotive sites in particular do an excellent job of creating and building an image for a new car model. When an interested consumer or tempted car buyer first sees a new car in a print ad or on television, he or she almost automatically migrates to the Internet for more information (see Figure 7.5).

OFFERING INCENTIVES

The Internet is a good medium for implementing a variety of sales promotion activities. To encourage consumers to make their initial online purchase, price discounts are commonplace. Canadian Tire, for instance, offers unique and special deals online as a means of getting people comfortable with online buying. Once they realize it is a safe and convenient way to buy, they go back for more. Companies that are active with customer relationship management programs are capable of delivering incentives to customers in their database by using email advertising. Incentives are designed to encourage current customers to try other products a company offers. Refer to the illustration in Figure 7.6.

Contests and sweepstakes are popular online promotions. Typically they encourage consumers to buy for the first time or they encourage brand loyalty (repeat purchases). Regardless, the true benefit to the company is the names and information that are collected through entry forms. For the chance of winning a prize, it is surprising how much personal information an individual will divulge to a marketing organization. This information can be used either to start or expand a database.

GENERATING LEADS

In a business-to-consumer or business-to-business marketing situation, the Internet is a useful medium for generating leads. As already indicated, consumers willingly disclose information when entering contests. Consumers and business people will also leave the same vital information when they are searching for information online. The stumbling block in retrieving the information they want is the transfer of personal or business information. However, online visitors are known to give out more details about themselves, or the business they are part of, so that they may retrieve the information they are searching for. Business sites often request information such as company size, number of employees, type of business, location, postal code, email address, and so on. It's a fact of life in doing business online. This type of information, once analyzed and mined (data mining), can be used to identify potential targets (one-to-one marketing) and to customize messages and products that are suited to that target. It's the start of CRM.

FIGURE 7.5   An integrated approach to message strategy across all media has greater impact

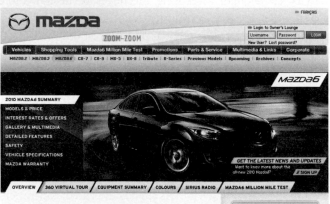

FIGURE 7.6

The Internet is a useful medium for delivering incentives to prospective customers

PROVIDING CUSTOMER SERVICE

In any form of marketing, offering good customer service is crucial. Satisfied customers hold positive attitudes about a company and are likely to return to buy more goods. Again, the Internet plays a pivotal role. It can be an efficient and cost-effective way of providing service, assuming a company's website is well organized. Service demands by customers tend to be high. Therefore, any frustration a customer experiences when searching for service on a website will only compound the problem. Speed of service is a primary benefit offered by the Internet. It goes without saying that customers should have quick and open access to service information. Carefully indexed FAQs (frequently asked questions) or key word searches are common ways to access online information quickly.

For specific questions and concerns, email is another good option. Of course, response time for handling email has unfortunately become a real issue. Making customers wait a few days for a response is not the type of service they expect. Successful online businesses don't forget that online activities must be backed up by a human component. They must pay close attention to inbound sales, order tracking, out-of-stock issues, deliveries and returns, and all the service issues associated with these tasks. All of these activities are part of a good CRM program.

CONDUCTING TRANSACTIONS

The business-to-business market is booming with online transactions, and the business-to-consumer market is growing steadily each year. Almost $12.8 billion worth of orders were placed by consumers online in 2007, an increase of 65 percent from 2005. More than 8.4 million Canadians made online purchases, with the busiest group of online shoppers being the 25- to 34-year-old age category—people with money, good credit ratings, and a high degree of comfort with online buying.[11] This rate of growth, combined with the knowledge that consumers use the Internet for researching purchases, makes it imperative that the messages delivered online be interesting and informative.

Having a website with e-business capabilities is important today. While shoppers remain concerned about security aspects of the Internet, they are using their credit cards online. Companies such as Canadian Tire, Sears, and Chapters-Indigo use the Internet to communicate effectively with shoppers, and they have combined e-marketing and e-business with their traditional methods of conducting business. More businesses will follow their lead. If they don't, they will be watching their competitors take business away from them.

Online and Interactive Communications Strategies

As indicated by the increase in advertising revenues from year to year and the amount of time consumers spend online each week, advertisers now embrace online communications from a more strategic perspective. Today's media planners are technologically savvy; they recognize the value of online communications and other forms of interactive communications and make appropriate recommendations when devising an integrated marketing communications strategy.

From a media strategy perspective, the Internet and other forms of interactive communications offer high reach and frequency, though advertisers have to be careful about budgets when the various cost models are evaluated (see later section of chapter for cost models). At portal sites such as Google and Yahoo! the number of unique visitors on a daily basis is incredibly high. In contrast, niche sites that focus on a particular interest, hobby, or activity reach smaller numbers of people, but they are more targeted. Both scenarios may be considered when devising an online media plan.

There are a variety of creative opportunities available to online advertisers: search advertising, banner advertising, rich media ads, sponsorships, websites, email advertising, webcasting, and websites. Beyond the Internet, an advertiser may consider text messaging and video messaging via cell phone and BlackBerry devices, placing messages in video games, and tapping the emerging potential of social networks. As with other media, the planner must evaluate the alternatives and devise a media selection and rejection rationale for the online and interactive components of a media plan.

Prior to examining the various online advertising alternatives, some basic terminology should be understood. All terms relate to how Internet ads are measured for strategic variables such as reach, frequency, and engagement:

- **Impressions** (**Ad Views**): An ad request that was successfully sent to a visitor. This is the standard way of determining exposure for an ad on the web.

- **Frequency**: The number of times an ad is delivered to the same browser in a single session or time period. A site can use cookies to manage frequency.

- **Ad Clicks** (**Clickthroughs**): This refers to the number of times that users click on a banner ad. Such a measurement allows an advertiser to judge the response to an ad. When viewers click the ad, they are transferred to the advertiser's website or to a special page where they are encouraged to respond in some way to the ad.

- **Clickthrough Rate** (**Ad Click Rate**): The ratio of ad clicks to ad impressions. For example, if during 1 million impressions, there are 20 000 clicks on the banner, the clickthrough rate is 2 percent. The formula is *clicks* divided by *ad views*. A high click rate indicates the banner ad was effective in its purpose.

- **Visitor** (**Unique Visitor**): Any individual who accesses a website or has been served unique content and/or ads. This is the equivalent of a site's reach. Visitors are identified by user registration or cookies.

- **Visit**: A sequence of page requests made by one user at one website. A visit is also referred to as a *session* or *browsing period*.

A site's activity is described in terms of the number of unique visitors, the time they spend visiting, and how often they return to the site. A site that can report, for example, that it had 8 million page views, 100 000 visitors, and 800 000 visits last month would be doing very well. It means that the average visitor returns to the site 8 times each month and views 10 pages on each visit. That's incredible "stickiness" (most sites don't do that well)! **Stickiness** (or sticky content) refers to the notion that the website has a compelling reason for users to stay for a longer visit or to come back frequently for more information.

SEARCH ADVERTISING

With **search advertising**, the advertiser's listing is placed within or alongside search results in exchange for paying a fee each time someone clicks on the listing. This is also known as **pay-per-click advertising**. Presently, search advertising ranks first in terms of revenue among the various online advertising options. Most search engines like AOL, Google, and Yahoo! set advertisers against one another in auction-style bidding for the highest positions on search results pages.

By far, Google is the leader in search advertising with its AdWords service. With AdWords, advertisers specify the words that should trigger their ads and the maximum amount they are willing to pay per click.[12] To illustrate, if a user types in the phrase "cell phones," those advertisers who bid the most will appear in order in the sponsored links column on the right side of the Google webpage. Advertisers that typically appear on the cell phone list include Telus Mobility, Koodo, Fido, BlackBerry, and Samsung. For these advertisers, AdWords provides a direct link to potential customers seeking cell phones or related services. When a consumer clicks on the sponsored link, that consumer is immediately directed to the advertiser's webpage where detailed information is provided.

ad views (impressions)
An ad request that was successfully sent to a visitor. This is the standard way of determining exposure for an ad on the web.

frequency (online)
The number of times an ad is delivered to the same browser in a single session or time period.

ad clicks (clickthroughs)
The number of times users click on a banner (clicking transfers the user to another website).

ad click rate (clickthrough rate)
The percentage of ad views that resulted in an ad click; determines the success of an ad in attracting visitors to click on it.

visit
A sequence of page requests made by a visitor to a website; also called a session or a browsing period.

stickiness
A website's ability to keep people at the site for an extended period or to have them return to the site frequently.

search advertising (pay-per-click advertising)
An advertiser's listing is placed within or alongside search results in exchange for paying a fee each time someone clicks on the listing.

BANNER ADVERTISING (DISPLAY ADVERTISING)

banner
Online, an ad that stretches across a webpage; the user can click on the ad for more information.

A **banner** refers to advertising on a website, usually placed by a third party. A standard banner ad resembles an ad on an outdoor board or an ad that stretches across the bottom of a newspaper. Not much copy can be included in a banner. The combination of brand name, short message, and visual must convince the user to click on the ad, which links to another website.

The industry, through the Interactive Advertising Bureau (IAB), has established standard ad sizes to reduce costs and inefficiencies associated with planning, buying, and creating online media. The size of an ad is based on Internet Measurement Units (IMU), an expression of the width and depth of an ad.

Four banner sizes were established in the initial standardization phase. Refer to Figure 7.7 for a visual illustration of the ad sizes.

FIGURE 7.7 Universal Ad Package Sizes for Internet Advertising

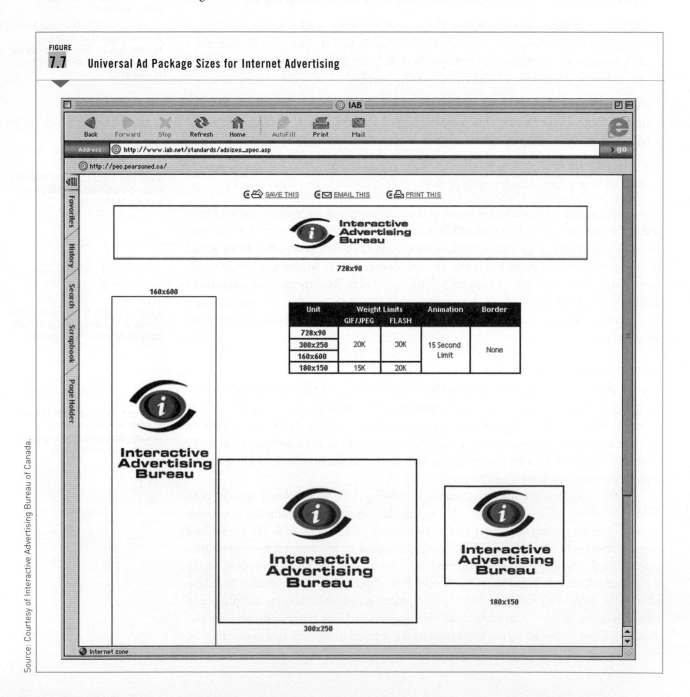

- **Rectangle:** A larger, box-style ad (180 x 150 IMU) that offers more depth than a standard-sized banner.

- **Big box:** A large rectangle (300 x 250 IMU) that offers greater width and depth to an ad.

- **Leaderboard** (Super Banner): An ad that stretches across the entire top of a webpage (728 x 90 IMU).

- **Skyscraper:** A tall, slim, oblong-shaped ad that appears at the side of a webpage (160 x 600 IMU).

Advertising research conducted by the IAB has concluded that larger formats that are naturally more visible and provide more creative freedom are significantly more effective than smaller, standard-sized banners across all campaigns. Larger ads make it more difficult for users to avoid them and provide an opportunity to deliver a more complete message, even if the user doesn't click on the ad. Because of their size and better performance, they command a higher price. Cost must be factored into the equation when an advertiser decides to use online advertising. For insight into the effects of ad size on brand awareness and message association, refer to Figure 7.8.

Given the interactive nature of the medium and the behaviour of Internet users who like to avoid ads if possible, the results achieved from banner ads have fallen short of expectations. Consequently, advertisers are experimenting with more animated forms of advertising, television-style online advertising, sponsorships, and email advertising.

RICH MEDIA

Rich media are a form of online communication that includes animation, sound, video, and interactivity. There are several inside-the-banner rich media options. An **expandable banner** employs multiple panels that are launched when the banner is clicked on. A **video strip** shows a strip of video in the banner space but, when clicked on, expands to reveal the video and audio in a full-sized panel. A **push down** banner slides advertising out of the way to reveal additional content rather than covering it up.

There are also some outside-the-banner options. A **floating ad** moves within a transparent layer over the page and plays within a specific area of the page. A **window ad** downloads itself immediately and plays instantly when a page is loading. A **wallpaper ad** is a large image that replaces the web background. Such a variety of styles can grab the viewer's attention in different ways.

rectangular ad
A large ad, slightly wider than it is tall, on a webpage.

big box
An online ad shaped like a large rectangle that offers greater width and depth to an ad.

leaderboard (super banner)
An ad that stretches across the entire top of a webpage.

skyscraper
A vertical, box-shaped ad that appears on a webpage.

rich media
A form of online communication that includes animation, sound, video, and interactivity.

expandable banner
An online ad that employs multiple panels that are launched when the banner is clicked on.

window ad
An online ad thatdownloads itself immediately and plays instantly when a page is loading.

wallpaper ad
An online ad thatis a large image that replaces the web background.

FIGURE 7.8   The Impact of Ad Size on Brand Awareness and Other Advertising Measures

Size of Ad	Brand Awareness	Message Association	Brand Favourability	Purchase Intent
Banner	1.8	2.4	0.3	0.2
Skyscraper	2.7	3.9	1.4	1.4
Large Rectangles	3.1	8.5	2.5	3.3

Large rectangles seem to offer the greatest benefit to advertisers. This information represents the point above the statistical baseline that helped increase the brand measure in absolute terms and is based on an aggregate of all online campaigns tested.

VIDEO ADVERTISING

Video advertising is presently a small component of online advertising, but it will grow in popularity due to its similarity to television advertising—a style of advertising that all advertisers are familiar with. The massive influx of video content available on the web (e.g., news, sports, and amateur video on sites such as YouTube and others) has spawned this new generation of online advertising. Video ads are delivered by a process called streaming. **Streaming** involves continuous delivery of small packets of compressed data that are interpreted by a software player and displayed as full-motion video. Through experimentation, advertisers have found that a 10-second ad is the maximum acceptable length for an online video ad, and if an ad is to be viewed in its entirety it must be entertaining.[13]

Television networks now stream their popular television shows from their websites. The CTV Network, for example, offers shows from its main network and many of its cable channels that include TSN, Comedy Network, MTV, Discovery, and Bravo, among others. Having shows available online is a reflection of the on-demand nature of the present television market. People want to watch shows when and where they like rather than abide by preplanned network schedules. Just like television, however, the online shows include video ads before, during, and after the show. **Pre-roll** ads refer to ads at the start of a video, **mid-roll** ads refer to ads placed during the video, and **post-roll** ads appear after the video. There can be several commercial breaks during the typical 44-minute prime time show being viewed online. When TV-style ads are embedded in programs or on news and sports highlight clips, it ensures an ad is viewed. To view the desired video content, viewers have no choice.

For an illustration of how various online advertising alternatives work together see Figure 7.9. The figure includes a banner ad and video ad for the Suzuki Vitara. When the banner ad is clicked, it links the viewer directly to a full-motion video commercial for the vehicle.

With online penetration continuing to increase and with high-speed broadband services expanding, advertisers will place more value in video advertising. Video ads grab the viewer's attention more quickly and can deliver the message on a more emotional level than any form of banner ad. The challenge for the advertiser is to effectively adapt offline creative strategies to the online environment. Shorter messages that are of less than perfect visual quality can be effective; duplicating the quality of television commercials is not the answer.

SPONSORSHIPS

An **online sponsorship** is a commitment to advertise on a third-party website for an extended period. Advertisers are attracted to sponsorships on the basis of web content. If the content of a site is particularly interesting to an advertiser's target market, visitors are apt to visit the site frequently. For example, investors in the stock market frequently visit BNN.ca, which broadcasts business news online. Business and recreational travellers visit theweathernetwork.com, and sports junkies frequently visit tsn.ca and other sports sites. Brands that are closely linked to the content of these networks pursue sponsorships.

Sports sites such as TSN and The Score run various sports contests throughout the year and seek appropriate sponsors. TSN, for example, celebrated its 25th anniversary by running a contest called the "Kraft Celebration Tour," sponsored by Kraft and some of the company's key brands. The public was invited to vote for the cities that would win a tour stop for a TSN sports broadcast (10 different cities in 10 days).

streaming
Audio or video delivered online in small, compressed packets of data that are interpreted by a software player as they are received.

online sponsorship
A commitment to advertise on a third-party website for an extended period.

Business News Network
www.BNN.ca

The Weather Network
www.theweathernetwork.com

FIGURE
7.9   A banner ad links a user to a full-motion ad

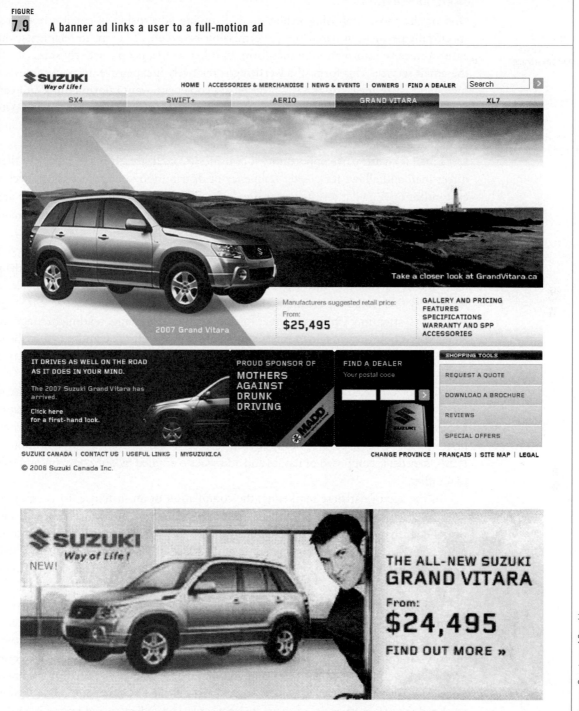

Source: Courtesy of Suzuki.

In sponsorship arrangements such as these, the sponsor benefits from the popularity of the website and the traffic it draws (high reach and frequency). TSN is one of the busiest websites in Canada and is a key site for reaching a young male audience that visits regularly. Consumers trust the sites that they visit frequently on the web, so a brand that is associated with the site could be perceived more positively through the sponsorship association.

EMAIL ADVERTISING

One of the most promising applications in online advertising is email advertising, specifically permission-based email. **Permission-based email** is sent to recipients who agree to receive information in that form. In other words, people actively subscribe to the email service. This form of advertising is relatively inexpensive, response rates are high and easy to measure, and it is targeted at people who want information about certain goods and services. An offshoot of email advertising is sponsored email. With **sponsored email**, the email includes a short message from a sponsor along with a link to the sponsor's website.

Email is an attractive opportunity for businesses of all sizes. It is less expensive than direct mail and allows for greater frequency of distribution and an incredible level of customization. Email is an efficient method of delivering new product information and information about promotional offers. Email campaigns cost $5 to $7 per thousand, compared with $500 to $700 per thousand for direct mail.[14]

Email advertising is similar to direct mail advertising, but at the same time it is very different. It does operate the same way insofar as it is based on a list contained in a database and it targets customers specifically interested in something. The difference, though, is that email advertising generates higher responses—and that is attracting advertisers' attention. Unlike any other form of online advertising, sending messages by email seems quite acceptable to Internet users. Users can subscribe and unsubscribe to email lists as they wish. The key for the advertiser is to keep the content of the email relevant to the receiver.

Similar to direct mail, the success of an email campaign depends on the quality of the list. The lists are called **opt-in lists**, an appropriate name because consumers agree to have their names included. There are two kinds of opt-in lists. A *first-party list* comprises people who have specifically agreed to receive email from an organization. A *third-party list* is composed of names and addresses compiled by one company and sold to another.

In the age of database marketing, the compilation of an in-house list is essential. Sending email to customers and prospects who specifically request it will almost always work better than using a rented list. Online promotions and contests sponsored by companies are another way of securing names and addresses. However, as indicated above, organizations should be careful how they distribute names to other organizations. There's a saying these days: "Permission rented is permission lost."

Although email advertising is attractive, that third-party list is what promotes spam. **Spam** is unsolicited email, even from reputable sources, and third-party lists can result in people receiving mail they do not expect. With a first-party list, subscribers agree to receive messages, but they might not have agreed to have their names sold for marketing purposes. The use of the Internet to send large volumes of email has infuriated many consumers, forced employees in organizations to waste precious time deleting junk email, overwhelmed the server capacities of many Internet service providers, spread viruses as well as the fear of viruses, and hurt the business of legitimate Internet marketers. This issue has to be addressed, for many of the efficiencies gained through the use of email are diminished as consumer suspicion rapidly grows with the flood of unsolicited commercial email.[15]

Email also opens up opportunities for a new communications technique called viral marketing. **Viral marketing** is a situation where the receiver of an online message is encouraged to pass it on to friends. A research study in the United States reports that 89 percent of adult Internet users share content with others via email. Only 5 percent of

permission-based email
Email sent to recipients who have agreed to accept email advertising messages.

sponsored email
Email that includes a short message from a sponsor along with a link to the sponsor's website.

opt-in list
A list of people who have agreed to receive messages via email.

spam
Unsolicited email.

viral marketing
Online marketing that encourages the receiver of a message to pass it along to others to generate additional exposure.

respondents in the study said they refuse to share content that contains a brand message.[16] Should an organization pursue a viral campaign, the goal is to create content that people feel compelled to pass around. Advertisers also have to be wary of the degree to which bad news about a company or brand can spread virally. As they often say, "bad news travels fast, even faster online."

One of the key objectives of email advertising is to establish and maintain a relationship with customers, and ultimately generate sales. Blue Mountain Resort, a winter and summer holiday destination, routinely sends email to its past customers. Its objective is to entice past customers to return to Blue Mountain instead of choosing another destination. In many cases, the email message includes special offers or other promotional incentives to spur action. An illustration of such a tactic is included in Figure 7.10.

WEBCASTING (WEBISODES)

Webcasting or **webisodes** involve the production of an extended commercial that includes entertainment value in the communications. While consumers are using digital video recorders to skip television ads they don't like, they are using the Internet to tune in to commercials they want to see—an interesting phenomenon!

webcasting (webisodes)
The production of an extended commercial presented on the web that includes entertainment value in the communications.

Many brands are experimenting with webisodes as a means of reaching younger target markets—they're online frequently so advertisers must take full advantage of the medium. Coca-Cola uses webisodes for its Nestea brand. Nestea's webisodes feature Tony Hale of *Arrested Development* fame as an office worker with the ability to change everyday reality by drinking Nestea. According to Annis Lyles, VP of media and interactive at Coca-Cola, "We saw a great opportunity to reach out and connect with younger consumers, specifically millennials. Our goal was to re-establish the brand and the millennials would be the perfect sweet spot for us to target."[17]

Webisodes are a form of online entertainment; used effectively, they present a great opportunity to develop a better relationship with consumers. Under the guise of entertainment people will watch as long as the content is enjoyable and engaging, and it isn't necessary to camouflage the brand—people expect the brand to play a key role. A series of webisodes can bring longer-lasting continuity to the brand experience.[18] From a media strategy perspective, the number of potential viewers of a webcast is much lower than for a conventional television ad, but the fact that viewers are there for a reason indicates the benefit of showing commercials online.

COMPANY WEBSITES

Traditional media communications and online communications encourage users to visit a company or brand website. Clicking on an ad automatically takes you to the website. The purpose of the ad is to attract attention; once the person is at the website, the purpose is to deliver more meaningful and detailed information in an entertaining manner. The website provides an opportunity to tell a story. A company cannot tell or show as much through traditional media as inexpensively as it can on the Internet. Advertising in the traditional media should always provide a website address and encourage potential customers to contact the site for additional information.

The nature of information communicated on a website varies from one organization to another. For example, news and information organizations such as the *The Globe and Mail* and Maclean's magazine provide copy-intensive information (they are online versions of their respective print editions). In contrast, sports sites such as TSN.ca and TheScore.com are loaded with video clips to entertain visitors.

TSN
TSN.ca

theScore
TheScore.com

FIGURE 7.10   A promotional email advertisement by Club Intrawest encourages past customers to visit Blue Mountain Resort again

----- Original Message -----
From: Blue Mountain
To: ktuckwell@cogeco.ca
Sent: Monday, June 29, 2009 11:36 AM
Subject: One Day Left to Get your Monterra & Raven 4 X FORE

If this email isn't displaying properly, please read it online. Click here.

Savings of up to $150 on regular green fees!

Don't miss the opportunity to experience two of the area's most captivating courses for one great price! Take advantage of the 4 X FORE golf pass - 2 rounds at Monterra Golf and 2 rounds at Raven Golf for only **$298 +GST** including cart. You can play your rounds from Monday - Thursday throughout the 2009 golf season.

It makes a great gift for the avid golfer, or a treat for yourself. The 4 X FORE golf pass is available for purchase until tomorrow, **June 30, 2009**.

» More Information & Buy Online...

www.bluemountain.ca/4xfore

BLUE MOUNTAIN RESORTS LIMITED I 108 JOZO WEIDER BLVD I COLLINGWOOD, ON I L9Y 3Z2

* Valid Monday-Thursday during the 2009 golf season. Includes golf cart rental. Available until June 30, 2009.

All Intrawest e-mail communications are sent from **memories@email.intrawest.com**. To ensure you keep hearing from us, add this address to your safe list or address book. How to add to contacts.

The information on a website must be presented in a manner that appeals to the primary target market. To demonstrate, consider a situation in the automobile industry. Automobile companies typically provide unique and vivid visual images of their latest makes and models along with technical specifications and related information. J.D. Power and Associates (an automotive consulting firm) ranked 25 Canadian automotive websites from the viewpoint of shoppers who intend to purchase a new vehicle in the next 12 months. The key factors in ranking the sites were information/content, ease of navigation, appearance, and speed of loading. The Subaru site topped the rankings based on its clean, simple, and inviting nature.[19]

Subaru's site was ranked highly because it was more in sync with its primary target audience—car buyers over the age of 50. To design a site for younger consumers in this market would be a mistake, since car buyers under the age of 30 only account for 12 percent of new car sales. The over-50 segment accounts for 50 percent of sales. It is important that a website meet the expectations of a target market. Sometimes it's the sizzle that wins, other times it's the substance!

Websites play a role in building brand awareness and preference and provide an opportunity for a brand to engage with its target audience. Axe (a line of male grooming products) effectively interacts with its 18- to 24-year-old male customers via its Axe U website. The brand hosts two events a year across Canada, allowing young men to interact with the fairer sex, including blonde Axe representatives. Users can also download Axe U "course materials," like playbooks and wallpaper, as well as chat. The message board seeds anticipation about events and captures feedback.[20] In a very short time, Axe has become a leading brand, and web communications have contributed to the brand's success. Refer to the illustration in Figure 7.11.

For a summary of the advantages and disadvantages of the various forms of online communications, refer to Figure 7.12. What is known is that younger target audiences—a desirable audience for many advertisers—spend considerable amounts of time online. Since this is a hard-to-reach target through any medium, the Internet represents an opportunity to get to them.

FIGURE 7.11   Axe encourages users to interact with the brand through an online experience

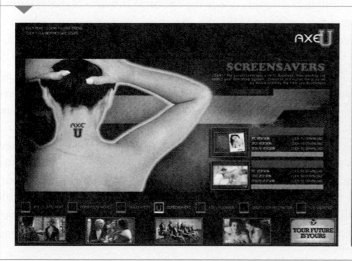

FIGURE
7.12

Advantages and Disadvantages of Online Marketing Communications

ADVANTAGES

- Targeting Capability—Advertiser reaches individuals based on browsing behaviour and preferences
- Broad and Flexible Reach—The online audience is growing rapidly; since ads are bought by the impression you can buy as much or as little of the audience as you desire
- Timing—Messages can be delivered 24 hours a day, 7 days a week
- Interactivity—Messages encourage consumers to interact with brands while online (perform a task, play a game, etc.)
- Tracking and Measurement—Detailed information on who saw an ad, in what context, and how many times, is available immediately
- Transaction—Assuming e-business capability at a website, an online purchase can occur

DISADVANTAGES

- Acceptance (Lack of)—Consumers continue to reject the notion of online advertising; it gets in the way of what they are doing
- Privacy—Concerns about transferring sensitive or personal information online along with misuse of information by marketing organizations
- Message Length—Ads can only communicate a short brand message initially (clickthrough is essential to communicate details)

Mobile Media

The screen is small, the audience's attention span is short, and the environment—a park bench or a busy subway station—is variable. Yet the possibilities of mobile marketing are capturing the attention of advertisers. Opportunities to communicate with consumers exist through text messaging, video messaging, and online games. Portable electronic devices such as a cell phone, BlackBerry, or iPod now allow advertisers to reach customers in a targeted manner.

TEXT MESSAGING

text messaging (short message messaging or SMS)
The transmission of short text-only messages using wireless devices such as cell phones and personal digital assistants.

It may be a generational thing, but people under the age of 35 are into **text messaging** (also called **short message messaging** or **SMS**), the transmission of short text-only messages on wireless devices. As of 2008, 20.1 million Canadians were cell phone subscribers, representing a penetration rate of 62 percent. In major metropolitan areas such as Toronto, Montreal, Vancouver, Calgary, and Edmonton penetration is in the 70 to 80 percent range. While voice communications remain the primary use of cell phones, text messaging has emerged as a popular alternative; in fact, Canadians send 45.3 million text messages a day.[21]

Cell phones are becoming multi-purpose devices as consumers use them to take and send pictures, browse the Internet, and play games. In 2008 only $5.2 million was spent on cell phone advertising in Canada, but the potential for growth is significant. Even though there is a threat of public backlash, should advertising take hold on cell phones, consumers will gradually adapt to the practice as they have done with the Internet. It will be the younger generations of consumers that make or break cell phone marketing communications.

Marketers interested in reaching the youth market are looking seriously at text messaging. It is one of the latest weapons in the arsenal of guerilla marketing tactics used to reach youth. Text messaging has proven to be a useful tactic for garnering consumer participation in contests and other promotional offers. Advertisers are asking consumers to take time to text message and interact with their brands. Marketers now add "call-to-action" short codes to their marketing material (outdoor posters, transit ads, bottle caps, and so on). Cell phone users can punch in the codes to participate in contests, download free music, and get ring tones or merchandise.

Scotiabank is one of the first Canadian banks to enter the cell phone advertising arena. Its initial effort was a contest in support of the bank's sponsorship of the Canadian Football League. Contest entrants earned the chance to win a VIP Grey Cup Experience and a selection of secondary prizes. Objectives of the promotion were to encourage participation, broaden reach beyond that of traditional media channels, and drive the brand's association with the sponsorship among consumers. The campaign was a multimedia effort with web, email, online media, TV, stadium Jumbotron, and mobile components. A full 20 percent of all entries were through the SMS short code "Scotia" (726842). The mobile component helped make the contest a success.[22]

All marketers must be careful how they use cell phones. If the messages are overly intrusive, their attempts could backfire and be perceived as negatively as a telemarketing call. It would also be dangerous for wireless carriers to open up their databases to commercial interests without having an *opt-in* from their customers. Opt-in means that customers agree to allow calls to be sent to them.

VIDEO MESSAGING

Video messaging, the next generation of cell phone communications, is in its experimental stages and only accounts for a small portion of mobile advertising revenue. Many cell phone users are already downloading short video clips such as news reports and sports highlights from major television networks, or they are playing games. Television program content can also be downloaded accompanied by five-second video ads that appear before and after the content.

Cell phones are referred to as the "small screen," and the popularity of small screen viewing is yet to be determined. The same consumers want the largest flat screen possible in their living room. Perhaps it will be nothing more than a convenient supplement to viewing content via a computer or conventional television.

The sweet spot for mobile users is the 15- to 29-year-old age category, but the industry is growing across all demographics. Teens and young adults have been attracted to text messaging because of its portability and low cost. Marketers are excited about video messaging due to its intimacy and immediacy. To demonstrate, the BlackBerry device offers a television service called bbTV in partnership with Rogers Wireless and CanWest MediaWorks. The service offers short audio and video clips from Global TV shows and Rogers Sportsnet highlights. All downloads are accompanied by commercials. Advertisers attracted to this service include RBC Financial, Labatt, and General Motors.

Hugh Dow, a prominent media planner, sees nothing but positives for the small screen. "We are living in a mobile generation now, where consumers are using a variety of methods to stay connected and receive information on the go. It is an important platform for reaching specific target markets."[23]

video messaging
The transfer of video messages and other content (e.g., television shows) via cell phones and other personal electronic devices.

VIDEO GAMES (ADVERGAMING)

advergaming
The integration of brands into video games, either games played online or games purchased directly by consumers.

Advertising in video games, or **advergaming**, refers to the placement of ads in commercially sold games or in games played online. The notion that video games are a male (young male)-dominated activity has somewhat restricted the level of interest in the medium by marketing organizations. However, recent research indicates that video games cross all demographics and the myth is about to explode. According to Packaged Facts, more than half of the North American game population is composed of moms, dads, and grandparents. "You essentially have a cultural phenomenon where video games are becoming a mainstream choice for family and adult entertainment."[24]

From a planning perspective, integrating a brand into games helps achieve several objectives: it can generate both positive brand awareness and higher brand preference ratings, and help stimulate purchases. The tactic is seen as being more effective than product placements in TV shows, mainly due to the intensity of the behaviour while gamers are playing—they see and recall the brand messages! For the record, Canadians spent a record $2 billion on video games in 2008, a sum that clearly indicates that games can play a key role as a medium for delivering advertising messages.

The changing demographic profile of gamers is one reason for advertisers to be attracted to the medium. Another reason is the time of day that consumers play games and the amount of time they spend playing. Much gaming activity overlaps with prime time television between the hours of 7 pm and 10 pm.[25] Further, if an advertiser wishes to reach 18- to 34-year-old males (heavy players of games), that audience spends as much as three hours per day with video games.[26]

Another benefit of video game advertising involves the attitude of consumers exposed to commercial messages. A study conducted by IGA Worldwide (a game vendor) found that 82 percent of respondents thought games were just as enjoyable if ads were present. Further, 70 percent of respondents said the ads made them feel better about the brands involved. Specifically, advertisers running in-game ads saw an average 44 percent increase in brand recall when compared to awareness prior to exposure in the game. These data indicate the medium's potential power as a branding vehicle.[27]

In terms of advertising in video games, an organization can go in two directions: create its own branded game or place ads in commercially produced games. Many brands have developed their own games for visitors to play at their website. American Express successfully included a video game concept in its "My Life, My Card" advertising campaign. A television ad featured tennis star Andy Roddick versus Pong. In the ad, Roddick's hardest serves were easily returned by Pong and Roddick only narrowly won the match by using a trick shot at the end of the commercial. The theme of the overall campaign was about meeting challenges in life, so the Roddick game was a good fit. At the website, visitors could take on Pong's challenge in an updated version of the classic Atari computer game. The ad and game concept were an ideal fit for American Express, which targets the 35-year-old-plus higher-income market. Pong is a game this group played when they were younger.[28]

If ads are placed in commercially produced games, a variety of options are available including interactive product placements, outdoor-style billboards, and 30-second video spots and audio clips. Gamers do not seem to mind the presence of ads. In fact, some research indicates that the fact that ads are included in a game adds some reality to it.[29]

Social Media Networks

A **social media network** connects people with different kinds of interests at a website. Social networking is a bit of a phenomenon—in a very short period it has become a fundamental aspect of the online experience. Social network sites such as Facebook, MySpace, YouTube, and Twitter are now the fourth-most popular online activities.

What started out as a means of communicating with friends by college students is now practised by all demographics. Early 2009 statistics show Facebook having 170 million users worldwide. The single biggest age demographic in North America on Facebook and MySpace is now between 35 and 44 and 50 percent of all users are over the age of 35.[30]

Messages delivered on social networks are mainly created by amateurs. **Consumer-generated content** refers to content created by consumers for consumers. It is done without provocation and in many cases presents the brand effectively. People who do this are often called brand evangelists and will do anything to promote their favourite brand—visit YouTube for video examples! For many people this type of content carries more weight than marketer-generated content. There is a shift in control (message control) occurring online. Some online experts refer to this phenomenon as **brand democratization**.

Coca-Cola experienced brand democratization first hand when two ardent fans (Dusty Sorg and Michael Jedrzeiewski) created a fan page (actually 253 fan pages) for the brand on Facebook. For a period of time, the Coke page was the second-most popular page on Facebook (Barack Obama's page ranked first). Rather than disrupt the momentum that was building on the fan page, Coca-Cola decided not to get directly involved. That's not the usual corporate reaction when the public starts tampering with a brand. Coca-Cola viewed the situation differently. The company actually flew the two fans to its Atlanta head office to talk openly about ideas and the future of the fan page.[31]

Marketers must take advantage of this shift in power. The fact that consumers create content on their behalf must be seen as a positive. There's an expression, "Any publicity is good publicity" that applies here. Consumer-generated content lets a consumer interact with a brand; it is experiential in nature—an experience that marketers pay for in other media. On social networks it happens voluntarily and with no cost to the company! For more insight into how brands and companies are experimenting with social network media, read the IMC Highlight: **Entering a New World**.

Since an increasing number of young people are spending time at these sites, marketers have to evaluate their potential for commercial purposes. Thus far, most advertising efforts have been experimental—some have opted for ads that are similar to those appearing on conventional websites; others have opted for branded content in order to take advantage of the viral effect of networking sites.

Finding a way of advertising on social networks has been difficult since the intimate environment of the network is not conducive to advertising; essentially ads are not welcome. Many companies have learned that simply posting commercial videos is not the answer—getting views is never guaranteed. However, the viral nature of social networks is real, and when something becomes popular word spreads fast.

Nissan took things a step further when it launched the Cube (a rather unique-looking vehicle) in Canada. Social media was the sole medium for launching the vehicle. The

social media network
A social website (e.g., Facebook and Twitter) that connects people with different interests together.

consumer-generated content
Content created by consumers for consumers.

brand democratization
A concept that states that consumers are now in charge of brand marketing (because of the amount of consumer-generated content produced and distributed online) instead of brand marketers being in control.

Entering a New World

Just as marketers were getting comfortable with various forms of online advertising, an explosion occurred with social media networks. No longer were marketers in control of their message. Consumers had taken control and were publishing videos about their favourite brands. Sometimes the message was good, sometimes not so good, but nonetheless, marketers had to live with the results.

Since consumers of all ages are spending a lot of time on social sites such as YouTube, Facebook, MySpace, and Twitter, marketers have to find ways to deliver their message on these networks. It is a challenge to implement a business application in such an environment but some marketers are having success.

Molson has been running a very successful summer promotion for the past six years. For its seventh edition (Summer 2009), social media played a key role. The promotion offered drinkers a chance to attend an event in BC in August where they could party with female caddies and play a version of golf that flouts the game's traditional rules and etiquette. Television, print, and in-store ads, and online banner ads, helped create awareness of the promotion.

For the 2009 promotion, the driving force was the "Become Part of the Legend" contest. The contest invited drinkers to win their way to the event by securing one of three honorary job titles—Honorary Maxim Caddy, Director of Mayhem, and Cold Beer Inspector. To earn a title, entrants had to create a profile at the contest site hosted at CoorsLight.ca and upload photographs, video, and text to make their case to online voters. Votes could be obtained by linking their profile to Facebook. The competitors were also encouraged to use social media tools such as Twitter, Digg, and MySpace to generate votes.

According to Coors Light senior brand manager Jo Bates "the 'Become Part of the Legend' contest improved participation levels and consumer engage-ment with the brand." The company received 3900 entries to the contest, nearly twice the amount generated the previous year. The number of votes cast doubled to 73 000. In addition, the Coors Light Facebook page added 5000 fans during the promotion period. Says Bates, "What I love about this promotion is that it gives consumers a chance to talk about their brand loyalty and affinity. They talk about the brand and engage with the brand on a much deeper level than with traditional media."

H&R Block, a tax preparation company, and not the hippest company going, has also enjoyed early success with social media. It sent tweets—short messages on Twitter—to customers and introduced an affable singing character called Truman Greene who serenaded and amused YouTube viewers as he extolled the brands' key benefits. In the popular Second City virtual world, the company offered a virtual tax preparation store. H&R found a way to educate and entertain prospective customers, fairly traditional tasks, but using new media to do so.

H.J. Heinz and Procter & Gamble sponsored video contests in which amateurs could produce brief commercials for their ketchup and Pepto-Bismol products, respectively. While some good videos were produced, some of the not-so-good ones, ones with uncomfortable parodies about their products, were posted on YouTube. The companies didn't like the results, but have to be given credit for being brave enough to experiment with social media.

These are but a few examples of what's going on in the brave new world of social media. Since consumers control social media, many marketers are reluctant to get involved. Those marketers unwilling to adapt their media strategies in a rapidly changing media environment face the wrath of consumers who use these tools. If you are not in a medium where your customers are, where are you and what are the consequences? Marketers will see the light very soon!

Adapted from "Molson puts social media at centre of legendary promotion," *Marketing*, June 4, 2009, www.marketingmag.ca and Harvey Schachter, "Businesses plunge into brave new world," *The Globe and Mail*, August 12, 2009, p. B15.

media budget focused on car prizing and an integrated social experiment targeted at "artsy" type individuals. Through Facebook, MySpace, and Twitter, artists of any kind could apply to audition for a creative assignment. Eager participants began to vie for an invite to the audition by attempting to rally support within their own communities while separating themselves from others via personal webpages, Twitter tweets, Facebook pages, and blogs that showcased their creative talents. "When you put something out there in the social community there's an incredible multiplier effect," says Tony Chapman, CEO of the agency behind the experiment. The challenge for successful applicants was to convey the message of what the Cube brand is about, leading up to the giveaways. Online voting for the creative efforts will determine the ultimate winners of the vehicles.[32]

From a media planning perspective, social media offer both macro- and micro-targeting opportunities. Popular sites such as Facebook, MySpace, and Twitter will reach a mass audience whereas niche sites will reach a more specific individual. Sports-related social networks are among the fastest-growing of these communities. Professional leagues such as the NBA (basketball), NHL (hockey), NASCAR (auto racing), and the PGA tour (golf) have opened up their sites, allowing fans to post comments on message boards, react to blogs, and create interest groups.[33] Users of niche sites tend to visit frequently, a behaviour that presents an "engagement" opportunity for brand advertisers.

Despite the potential benefits of communicating with consumers via social networks, the medium is not yet that popular with marketing executives. Executives are taking a cautious approach mainly due to their lack of knowledge of the medium combined with an absence of controls and standardization. Social media can build brand awareness, support product launches (as described above), and increase loyalty. However, since so many executives are new to social media, there is a large gap between attitudes and action that must be addressed.[34]

SUMMARY

As advertisers and agencies develop a stronger understanding of the role and importance of the Internet and other forms of interactive media in the daily lives of consumers, they will integrate more interactive communications into the media mix.

Internet penetration continues to rise, significant growth in wireless penetration is occurring, and consumers are spending much more time online than before. The combination of online and other forms of interactive communications represents significant opportunities for advertisers. The Internet has become a mass reach medium with the capability of reaching more people than traditional media. Therefore, the Internet must be considered an equal partner when a planner devises an integrated marketing communications strategy. The interactive nature of the medium allows a brand to engage consumers and create deeper brand experiences. The challenge for advertisers is to create useful and entertaining messages that will capture the imagination of Internet users who want to be entertained.

The Internet is a medium that allows marketers to target customers on the basis of demographics, geographics, and behaviour. Of particular interest to advertisers is the concept of behaviour targeting. By tracking preferences, unique messages are delivered to consumers on an individual basis. As well, there is the capability to design unique products for customers, a concept referred to as mass customization.

Advertising online plays a key role in achieving specific marketing objectives. Online advertising will help create brand awareness for the launch of new products and is an excellent medium for building brand image. The fact that so much information can be presented visually and in a tone and style comparable to television is a real asset.

Companies also find the Internet ideal for distributing buying incentives and for promoting contests. In both cases, information about consumers is collected and added to a database for use at a later date. In a business-to-business context, online advertising is a means of generating leads. It is also a good medium for implementing customer service programs. Furthermore, unlike other media (except direct response advertising), online advertising can complete a transaction.

There are a variety of advertising alternatives to choose from. Among the options are search advertising, banner ads in both static and rich media formats, video ads, sponsorships at other websites, email ads, and webcasting. Video ads are growing in popularity mainly due to their similarity to television ads. Permission-based email is also growing in popularity. Using lists generated from in-house databases or from other sources (rented lists), email represents a cost-efficient way to reach prospects and current customers.

As an advertising medium, the Internet provides targeting capability at a very reasonable cost and also offers tracking capabilities that measure effectiveness in a variety of ways (e.g., clicks, clickthrough rates, leads, and purchases). Because it is available at all hours of the day, seven days a week, there is ample opportunity for brand and company exposure online. Online advertising also presents an opportunity for a brand to engage consumers for an extended period, something not possible in other media. Some drawbacks of the Internet include selective reach (higher-educated and higher-income households are the main users) and the perception among users that advertisers are invading their privacy. Security issues involving the transfer of sensitive information can impede online purchases.

Mobile media represent new opportunities to deliver advertising messages. Electronic devices such as cell phones and personal digital assistants are part of the daily lives of many consumers. Text messaging and video messaging are relatively new media, but they allow consumers and brands to interact with each other, a definite step toward developing brand loyalty. Marketers are attracted to mobile media based on the immediacy and intimacy they offer.

Video games are proving to be an effective means of reaching all age groups. People are spending more time playing games (often in prime time) than they are watching television. Advertisers must capitalize on this trend and adjust their media budgets accordingly.

Finally, social media networks are increasing in popularity due to their social nature and intimate environment. Thus far, advertising efforts in this medium have been experimental in nature, but as people move around the web, advertisers must adapt and find new ways of reaching them.

KEY TERMS

ad click rate,   201

ad clicks,   201

ad views,   201

advergaming,   212

banner,   202

behavioural targeting,   194

big box,   203

brand democratization,   213

clickthrough rate,   201

clickthroughs,   201

consumer-generated content,   213

cookie,   194

expandable banner,   203

floating ad,   203

frequency (online),   201

impressions,   194

interactive communications,   195

leaderboard,   203

mass customization,   195

online sponsorship,   204

opt-in list,   206

pay-per-click advertising,   201

permission-based email,   206

portal,   196

rectangular ad,   203

rich media,   203

search advertising,   201

short message messaging
(SMS) 210

skyscraper,   203

social media network,   213

spam,   206

sponsored email,   206

stickiness,   201

streaming,   204

super banner,   203

text messaging,   210

unique visitor,   191

video messaging,   211

viral marketing,   206

visit,   xxx

wallpaper ad,   203

webcasting,   207

webisodes,   207

window ad,   203

REVIEW QUESTIONS

1. What is behavioural targeting and how is it applied in online marketing communications programs?
2. What is mass customization and how do online communications facilitate its practice?
3. What are the primary marketing and marketing communications roles that the Internet can provide marketing organizations? Identify and explain each role briefly.
4. In the context of online marketing communications, briefly explain what viral marketing is. Is it a worthwhile pursuit for marketing organizations?
5. Explain the following terms as they relate to online advertising:
   a) ad impressions
   b) clicks
   c) ad click rate
   d) visits
6. What is banner advertising and how does it work?
7. Identify and briefly describe the various types of banner ads.
8. What does rich media refer to and how does it work? What does streaming media refer to?
9. Briefly explain how an online advertising sponsorship works. What benefits does it provide? Illustrate the benefits with some examples.
10. Briefly explain the following email advertising terms:
    a) permission-based email
    b) sponsored email
    c) opt-in list
    d) spam
11. What is a cookie and what role does it perform in online communications and marketing?
12. What is a "webisode"? Briefly explain the difference between a webisode and other types of rich media advertising.

DISCUSSION AND APPLICATION QUESTIONS

1. Identify and briefly explain two advantages and two disadvantages of Internet-based advertising.
2. What future lies ahead for email advertising? Will it continue to grow or will consumers and businesses turn away from it? Conduct some online research on the issue and present a brief report on your findings.
3. "Persistent invasions of consumer privacy will be the undoing of online advertising." Is this statement true or false? Conduct some online secondary research on this issue. Report on your findings.
4. How important are websites to companies today? Examine their role in the marketing communications mix and present a position on what lies ahead for marketing organizations.
5. Visit some commercial websites of your choosing. Evaluate these websites in terms of their ability to achieve certain marketing and marketing communications objectives such as building brand image, offering incentives, generating leads, and providing customer service. Are communications on the websites coordinated with any other form of marketing communications?
6. Assess how consumer goods marketing organizations can use web-based communications to their advantage. Can it be an effective medium for building relationships with customers?
7. Will consumers accept or reject the notion of delivering advertising messages via cell phones and other portable devices? Examine the issues surrounding this emerging practice and formulate a position on the matter.
8. Assess the various online advertising alternatives such as banners and rich media. Which alternative is best at communicating with consumers?
9. Is it possible to launch a new product using online communications as the primary medium for creating awareness and interest? What strategies would be necessary to make such a plan work?

ENDNOTES

1. Garine Tcholakian, "Internet top media time grabber among Canadian youth, says new IAB study," *Media in Canada*, February 2, 2009, www.mediaincanada.com.

2. Marija Djukic, "Internet habits examined in new report," *Media in Canada*, September 24, 2008, www.mediaincanada.com.

3. Jean Halliday, "GM roars forward into digital ad channels," *Advertising Age*, March 17, 2008, p. 4.

4. "2008 Canadian Online Advertising Revenue Grows 29% to $1.6 Billion and Surpasses Radio," press release, IAB Canada, July 28, 2009.

5. "Interactive Marketing + Online Advertising," IAB Canada Conference, May 20, 2009, p. 50.

6. Kerry Munro, "Online: Be there or be square," *National Post*, March 10, 2006, p. FP9.

7. "What's driving growth?" Internet Advertising Bureau, www.iab.com.

8. "Interactive Advertising + Online Advertising," IAB Canada Conference, May 20, 2009, p. 145.

9. Andrea Zoe Aster, "Tactful targeting," *Essential Interactive*, Volume 2, pp. 29, 30.

10. "Interactive marketing + Online Advertising," IAB Canada Conference, May 20, 2009, p. 21.

11. "Online shopping becomes mainstream in Canada," *Canadian Press*, November 18, 2008, www.marketingmag.ca.

12. "AdWords," www.wikipedia.com.

13. Elinor Mills, "Ads 2.0: Beyond the repurposed TV spot," CNET News, November 22, 2005, www.news.com.

14. Kevin Marron, "E-mail gets the message across," *The Globe and Mail*, September 27, 2002, p. B11.

15. Tyler Hamilton, "Ottawa ponders junk e-mail," *Toronto Star*, January 23, 2003, p. C5.

16. Kris Orser, "Study finds consumers fans of e-mails," *Advertising Age*, February 13, 2006, p. 35.

17. Elaine Wong, "Coke's Nestea Takes Plunge into Webisodes," *Brandweek*, July 4, 2009, www.brandweek.com.

18. "Webisodes: Small but Mighty," July 10, 2008, www.advertisingforthedigitalage.com.

19. Kristin Laird, "Subaru on top of car website ranking," *Marketing Daily*, May 26, 2008, www.marketingmag.ca.

20. "Axe U educates marketing department, too," *Strategy*, January 2006, p. 9.

21. "Snapshot of the Canadian Mobile Market," Mobile Marketing Supplement to *Strategy*, 2008, p. S22.

22. "Take Possession," Mobile Marketing Supplement to *Strategy*, 2008, p.S32.

23. "New in mobile," *Mobile in Motion*, 2006, p. 15.

24. Aaron Barr, "Video Games Becoming Mainstream Alternative," *Media Post*, January 19, 2009, www.mediapost.com.

25. "Gaming Activity Overlaps with TV Prime Time," Interactive Advertising + Online Advertising Conference, Interactive Advertising Bureau, p. 270.

26. Grant Jenman and Stephanie Becker, "How disappearing demographics can be recovered through their video game consoles," Adweek.com, June 30, 2008, www.adweek.com.

27. Mike Shields, "IGA: Most Gamers Cool with In-Game Ads," MediaWeek.com, June 17, 2008, www.mediaweek.com.

28. "Classic video game bounces back for American Express," press release, American Express, August 18, 2006, www.home3.americanexpress.com.

29. Tamake Kee, "Study: In-game ads increase purchase consideration," *Media Post*, August 8, 2007, www.mediapost.com/publications.

30. Michael Learmonth, "Marketers Adapt as Social Networks Attract Older Users," *Advertising Age*, February 23, 2009, www.adage.com.

31. Abbey Klassen, "How two Coke fans brought the brand to Facebook fame," *Advertising Age*, March 16, 2009, www.adage.com.

32. Jonathan Paul, "Nissan starts new conversation," *Media in Canada*, March 18, 2009, www.mediaincanada.com.

33. Paula Lehman, "Social Networks that Break a Sweat," *Business Week*, January 24, 2008, www.businessweek.com.

34. Kristin Laird, "Marketers cautious about social media: study," *Marketing Daily*, January 3, 2008, www.marketingmag.ca.

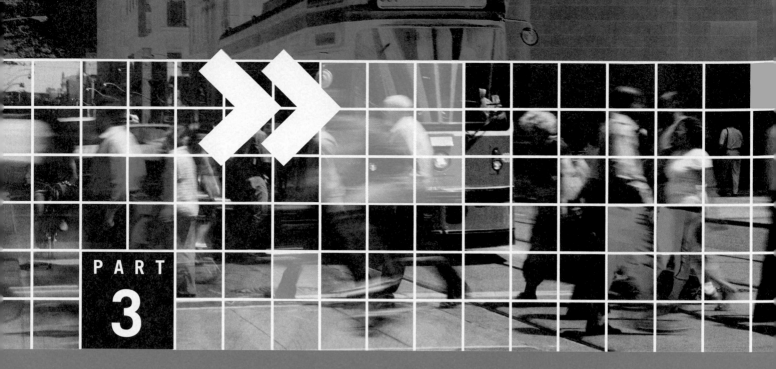

Planning for Integrated Marketing

Part 3 looks at non-traditional media choices and a variety of marketing and promotional choices that enhance the communications plan.

Chapter 8 introduces various sales promotion alternatives that are frequently used in integrated marketing communications plans. Discussion is divided between consumer promotions and trade promotions, with each area examined for its ability to achieve marketing and marketing communications objectives.

Chapter 9 describes the role of public relations communications in the marketing communications mix. Various public relations techniques are introduced. The process of planning public relations activities is examined in detail, along with various measurement techniques used to determine the effectiveness of public relations messages.

Chapter 10 discusses the role of experiential marketing techniques that embrace street marketing strategies along with event marketing and sponsorships. The criteria for participating in event marketing and the steps and procedures for planning an event are introduced, as are various evaluation techniques that determine the effectiveness of event marketing and sponsorship strategies.

In Chapter 11, the role of personal selling in a variety of business settings is examined. Personal selling adds a human component to the integrated marketing communications mix, and for this reason plays a very important role in an era where customer relationship management practices dominate.

Sales Promotion

Learning Objectives

After studying this chapter, you will be able to

1. Distinguish between consumer promotions and trade promotions

2. Describe the steps in the sales promotion planning process

3. Assess the role of consumer promotions in achieving specific marketing communications and marketing objectives

4. Assess the role of trade promotions in achieving specific marketing communications and marketing objectives

5. Outline the nature of various consumer promotion and trade promotion activities

6. Assess various criteria for integrating sales promotion strategies with other integrated marketing communications strategies

This chapter examines the role of sales promotions in the marketing communications mix. Promotions are activities that focus on making a sale, usually in a short period of time. When planning and implementing promotions, the marketing organization provides an offer to customers in return for something they must do. Because the offer is valid only for a certain period, the impact of the offer—and its success or failure—can be measured quickly.

A wide variety of promotion offers are presented here, all of which are suited to achieving specific marketing and marketing communications objectives. The right promotion must be offered at the right time if the offer is to bring true benefit to the brand or company. In order to create awareness and interest in the promotion, there must also be media advertising to support it, and possibly some publicity generated by a public relations campaign. A coordinated effort is usually required to make a sales promotion a success. This chapter focuses on two distinct yet related areas of sales promotion: consumer promotion and trade promotion. An organization must consider strategies for both if it is to grow and prosper.

Sales Promotion

Sales promotion is defined as activity that provides special incentives to bring about immediate response from customers, distributors, and an organization's sales force. It is a strategy that encourages action by the recipient. According to the definition, three distinct groups are considered when planning sales promotion strategies. First, the consumer or final user must be motivated to take advantage of the offer. Second, the distributor (reseller of goods) must be motivated to support the offer by providing merchandising support. Third, the company's sales force must be motivated to sell the promotion to its trade customers. Because the intent of a promotion is to provide some added excitement to the product, an organization's sales representatives must present it enthusiastically to the trade distributors.

Consumer promotions are designed to stimulate purchases or to encourage loyalty. Among the options readily available are coupons, free samples, contests, rebates, price incentives, and rewards programs. These types of promotions are planned to help **pull** the product through the channel of distribution. An organization creates demand for the product by directing its promotional efforts directly at the consumer. The combination of advertising and promotions, for example, creates demand and causes consumers to look for the product in stores or request a service; by asking for it specifically, they put

sales promotion
An activity that provides incentives to bring about immediate response from customers, distributors, and an organization's sales force.

consumer promotions
Incentives offered to consumers to stimulate purchases or encourage loyalty.

pull
Demand created by directing promotional activities at consumers or final users, who in turn pressure retailers to supply the product or service.

pressure on the retailer to provide it. Many companies now include experiential marketing activities, often referred to as buzz marketing, in their promotion strategies. These concepts are presented in detail in Chapter 9.

Consumers express a favourable opinion about the effectiveness of various consumer promotions so they should play a key role in an integrated marketing communications plan. A poll conducted by Delvinia Data Collection asked a sampling of Canadian consumers, "What would best convince you to try a new brand of beer?" Product sampling and tasting events garnered a 42.6 percent response; giveaways (clothing and hats) 20.6 percent; and contests 14.3 percent. In comparison, television advertising only garnered a 7.8 percent response.[1]

Trade promotions are less visible activities, given that they are offered to members of the channel of distribution. These promotions include options such as discounts and allowances, cooperative advertising funds, dealer premiums and incentives, and point-of-purchase materials. Offering financial incentives to distributors encourages them to support a manufacturer's promotion plans. Such promotions **push** the product through the channel of distribution. Refer to Figure 8.1 for a visual image of pull and push promotion strategies.

To be successful, an organization must determine what type of promotion will contribute the most to achieving its objectives. In most cases, it is a combination of both consumer and trade promotions. The real decision is to determine the extent to which each type of promotion is offered. Such a decision is based on the market analysis that precedes the development of any sales promotion plan. Sales promotion planning is discussed in the following section.

trade promotion
An incentive offered to channel members to encourage them to provide marketing and merchandising support for a particular product.

push
Demand created by directing promotional activities at intermediaries, who in turn promote the product or service among consumers.

Sales Promotion Planning

Like any other component of the marketing communications mix, a sales promotion plan is but one component of a much larger plan. It must directly fit into the marketing communications plan and play a role in achieving the specific objectives that are identified in that plan. Whereas advertising plans have a long-term perspective, and longer-term objectives, the sales promotion plan adopts a short-term view and achieves objectives of a more immediate nature. While advertising is building a brand's image, sales promotions are implemented to encourage a spike in sales.

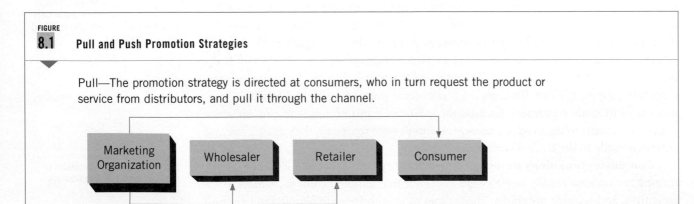

FIGURE 8.1   Pull and Push Promotion Strategies

Pull—The promotion strategy is directed at consumers, who in turn request the product or service from distributors, and pull it through the channel.

Marketing Organization → Wholesaler → Retailer → Consumer

Push—The promotion strategy is directed at distributors, who resell the product. Incentives help push the product from one distributor to another.

To demonstrate the difference between the roles of advertising and sales promotions, consider a recent campaign by Nestle Canada for its Aero chocolate bar. Aero developed a relationship with female consumers by using a "love" theme in its advertising (as in women love their chocolate). The campaign created a favourable image with women for the brand. To further engage females with the brand, Aero introduced the "Love Aero Contest," offering a chance to win $10 000 toward the prize of their choice.[2] The contest, combined with point-of-purchase ads and special packaging announcing the contest, helped boost sales in the promotion period.

Sales promotions are activities that complement advertising. When you consider the primary goals of advertising—awareness, comprehension, conviction, and action— the primary goal of sales promotion is to focus on one specific area—action. A well-timed promotional offer that coincides with an image-building advertising campaign, as described in the Aero chocolate example above, could be just the incentive needed to get the customer's money out of that wallet or purse. Such a relationship suggests that integration of advertising strategies and promotional strategies is essential and, on a larger scale, that their integration with online communications, events and sponsorships, and public relations is what promotes a brand or company with a sense of continuity.

Sales promotion planning involves developing a plan of action for communicating incentives to the appropriate target markets (consumers and trade customers) at the right time. Very often, an external company that specializes in sales promotion will assume responsibility for developing and implementing the consumer promotion plan. As with developing an advertising plan, the specialist must be briefed. The client's role is to provide the necessary background information and then evaluate the promotion concepts put forth by the agency. The promotion agency must assess the information provided by the client and then prepare a strategic plan that will meet the client's objectives (see Figure 8.2). A sales promotion brief typically includes some or all of the following information.

MARKET PROFILE

An overview of sales and market share trends provides market perspective to the promotion planners. Knowing if the brand is a leader, challenger, or follower has an impact on the nature of the promotion they will ultimately recommend. It is important to know if the market is growing and what brands are growing in the market.

COMPETITOR ACTIVITY PROFILE

In general terms, what marketing communications strategies do key competitors rely upon? The role of the various elements of the mix will vary from one brand to another. What brands dominate the market and what are their mixes? An evaluation of this kind of information may suggest that various combinations of activities have more or less impact on customers. A review of competitors' recent sales promotion activities is essential.

TARGET MARKET PROFILE

Perhaps the most important aspect of planning a promotion is a good understanding of the target customer. As discussed earlier in the text, customers are described according to demographic, psychographic, geographic, and behavioural characteristics. Additional information about shopping behaviour usually plays a role in developing a sales promotion plan. For example, many of today's consumers are time challenged and value conscious and are looking for good deals they can take advantage of quickly. When planning the promotion, the value must be immediately evident to the consumer.

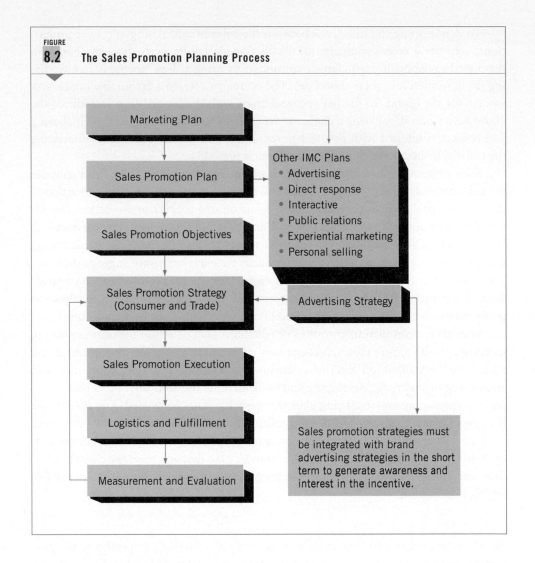

FIGURE 8.2   The Sales Promotion Planning Process

SALES PROMOTION OBJECTIVES

A variety of background factors will determine the objectives of the promotion campaign. Essentially, sales promotion plans focus on three distinct objectives: generating trial purchases, encouraging repeat or multiple purchases, and building long-term brand loyalty. Objectives for trade promotion plans concentrate on building sales and achieving merchandising support. These objectives are discussed in more detail in the "Consumer Promotion Execution" and "Trade Promotion Execution" sections of this chapter.

BUDGET

Funds for the sales promotion plan come from the overall marketing budget. In most cases, the client has already determined how much money is available for promotions. Knowing the size of the budget is crucial when the promotion agency is thinking about potential concepts. Will this be a large-scale national promotion, or will it be restricted to specific regions? Will it involve an expensive grand prize, or will there be a series of smaller prizes? How much media advertising support will be needed to create awareness for the promotion?

The Sales Promotion Plan

The **sales promotion plan** is a document that outlines the relevant details about how the client's budget will be spent. Objectives are clearly defined, strategies are justified, and tactical details are precisely documented. Similar to direct response communications plans, back-end considerations are very important. For example, if a fulfillment program is part of the package, details about how the offer will be handled from the time the consumer responds to the time the goods are delivered must be precisely planned. Promotions that include coupons, free samples, contests, rebates, and premiums might involve other companies that handle various aspects of the promotion. The structure and content of a sales promotion plan are the focus of this section. Figure 8.3 summarizes the content of a sales promotion plan, but because the content of a plan varies from one company to another, it is only a guideline.

sales promotion plan
An action plan for communicating incentives to appropriate target markets at the right time.

SALES PROMOTION OBJECTIVES

Sales promotion objectives are statements that clearly indicate what the promotion plan is to accomplish. Similar to other communications plans, objective statements should be realistically achievable, quantitative in nature to facilitate measurement, and directed at a carefully defined target market.

FIGURE
8.3   The Content of a Sales Promotion Plan

Situation Analysis

- Market profile
- Competitor activity profile
- Target market profile

Budget

- Funds available

Sales Promotion Objectives

A. Consumer Promotion

- Trial purchase
- Repeat purchases
- Multiple purchases
- Brand loyalty

B. Trade Promotion

- New listings
- Sales volume
- Merchandising support

Sales Promotion Strategy

- Incentive or offer (save, win, or reward)
- Merchandise, cash, or combination
- Balance between consumer and trade

Advertising Strategy

- Broadcast
- Print
- In-store
- Digital and interactive

Sales Promotion Execution

- Details of consumer offer (coupon, sample, contest, premium, rebate, loyalty promotion)
- Details of trade offer (trade allowance, performance allowance, cooperative advertising funds, dealer premiums, collateral materials, display materials, trade shows)

Logistics and Fulfillment

- Back-end plan to administer and implement the promotion

Budget and Timing

- Activity costs
- Calendar of events

The nature of the promotion plan (that is, consumer promotion versus trade promotion) determines the objectives. Although objectives for both are quite different, they complement each other when implemented. Let's start with consumer promotion objectives.

The most common objective of consumer promotion is to encourage consumers to make a *trial purchase*. When a product is new, for example, an organization wants to establish acceptance as quickly as possible. Therefore, trial-oriented promotions are common (see Figure 8.4). Even when a product is in the growth stage of development there is a need to distinguish one brand from another. At that stage, incentives that encourage purchase of a specific brand remain essential. Media-delivered coupons are an excellent promotion tool for encouraging trial purchase, as are product samples.

Welch's grape juice successfully offered a free sample via "Peel 'n Taste" edible strips placed with magazine ads. The ad showed a Welch's bottle with a glass of juice beside it. The line "For a tasty fact, remove & lick" appears above the glass, which doubled as a pouch holding a taste strip. Welsh's was using "flavour" as a means to differentiate the brand among consumers.[3]

The second objective is to stimulate *repeat purchases* by existing customers. An extension of this objective is to encourage consumers to make multiple purchases at one time. To illustrate, a well-conceived contest will encourage *multiple entries* by consumers. Persistent purchases of the brand in the contest tie the consumer to the brand for a period of time (see Figure 8.5). Those consumers won't be buying a competitor's brand!

The third objective deals with customer relationship management (CRM). Here, the objective is to encourage *brand loyalty* for an extended period. Traditionally, promotions encourage instant activity, but there are promotion alternatives that can meet both short-term and long-term brand objectives. Something as simple as the loyalty card offered by a local coffee shop helps keep a customer. Rewards bring customers back.

The overall goal of trade promotions is to give sales a jolt in the short run. But such an accomplishment is usually the result of promotion strategies combined with other marketing strategies to influence trade customers and consumers. Therefore, trade promotion objectives must be confined to what they can realistically achieve. Generally

FIGURE 8.4 Coupon and free sample offers are an effective means of achieving trial purchase

Source: Reprinted by permission of Yoplait.

FIGURE 8.5

A Consumer Promotion Designed to Encourage Multiple Purchases

speaking, trade promotion plans are designed to encourage distributors to carry a product and then sell it to retailers, and to increase the volume sold for products they already carry.

In the case of a new product, the first objective is to secure a listing with distributors. A listing is an agreement made by a wholesaler to distribute a manufacturer's product to the retailer it supplies. For example, when the head office of Canada Safeway or Sobeys agrees to list a product, it is then available to all of their retail outlets. Typically, trade promotions in the form of financial incentives are used to secure listings.

A second objective is to *build sales volume* on either a seasonal basis or a predetermined cyclical basis throughout the year. For example, baking products are promoted in the pre-Christmas season and there are usually displays of such products in retail stores. In other cases, it is common for a company to offer temporary discounts for its key brands on a quarterly basis because it recognizes that consistent activity keeps a popular brand in a preferred position with the trade and consumers. The nature of competition often dictates such a strategy.

A third trade objective is to *secure merchandising support* from distributors. Their support is crucial, because once the product leaves the manufacturer's warehouse the manufacturer is no longer in control of how it is sold. Consequently, funds are allocated to activities that get the product out of a distributor's warehouse and into displays on the retail sales floor. As well, the manufacturer will look for a sale price and perhaps a brand mention of the sale price in a retailer's advertising flyer. These activities constitute merchandising support.

Sales Promotion Strategy

Decisions about sales promotion strategy focus on the selection of the best promotion activity to meet the objectives. Decisions point the organization in a certain direction and, if agreed to, the tactical details are then developed. For example, on the consumer side of things, an organization can choose among coupons, free samples, contests, rebates, premiums, and loyalty programs. Other decisions may involve the selection of prizes. Should they be cash, merchandise, or a combination of both? The organization can use any one of these options or combine several to maximize the potential of the promotion.

Each of these options provides a different kind of incentive. For example, coupons and rebates save people money; contests give people a chance to win something; and samples, premiums, and loyalty programs offer something free with a purchase. As a result, the first decision relates directly to the incentive. Should the promotion program offer savings, a chance to win something, or a reward?

Key decisions about trade promotion strategy involve the allocation of funds among the different alternatives. Depending on the promotion objectives, preference may be given to listing allowances, trade and performance allowances, and cooperative advertising allowances. Alternatively, some combination of several of these allowances may be employed. The manager must also decide about the balance between consumer promotions (pull) and trade promotions (push). Successful promotions use both and are carefully integrated with other forms of marketing communications to maximize impact on the intended target audience.

The second component of the sales promotion strategy involves integration with the advertising strategy. You need to promote a promotion! In many cases, a brand will already be planning a brand-image campaign and several different media may be involved. Is special creative needed for the sales promotion? What media will be used to advertise the sales promotion?

With creative, the ideal situation is to have promotional creative blend effectively with existing brand creative. For example, in March each year, Tim Hortons implements its "Roll up the Rim to Win" promotion. Separate creative and a variety of media (television, outdoor boards, online communications, and in-store signage) are employed to announce details of the promotion. A promotion is an added incentive, so it temporarily becomes the brand's unique selling point. The combination of a strong ongoing sales message with the added bonus of a special offer will help achieve short-term and long-term objectives.

Marketing research by Resolve Corporation observes that consumers should be able to immediately see that a promotion offer provides significant real value. This means that the savings have to be meaningful in relation to the purchase price of the product and must also make sense in relation to the market strength and purchase frequency of the brand.[4] The lesson here is that the offer must be a good match for the product and the target market.

A sales promotion will only work if it receives the necessary media support, so another decision must be made about allocating funds specifically for promotion-related programs. Once that decision is made, the media strategy will focus on two objectives: creating awareness for the promotion and providing details about how the consumer can take advantage of the promotion (e.g., how to send in order forms for premium offers or entry forms for contests).

Typically, a variety of broadcast, print, and online media are selected. Television is an ideal medium for creating instant awareness of the promotion. High-impact television advertising in a short period (a blitz strategy) is common. In the case of a contest or sweepstakes promotion, television is ideal for creating excitement and for conveying a sense of urgency to consumers. It encourages them to take advantage of the offer right away. Television can also direct consumers to a website where all the details of the promotion are available.

In-store advertising can also assist in achieving awareness objectives while playing a key role in communicating details of the offer. Consumers are conditioned to look for details at point-of-purchase. In conjunction with trade promotion strategies, the ideal situation is to have brand displays in stores supported by posters and shelf cards at the product's regular shelf location to draw attention to the promotion. See the illustration in Figure 8.6.

Source: Photo by Keith J. Tuckwell.

FIGURE
8.6

In-store displays and signage draw attention to a Quaker/Gatorade promotion

Obviously, the nature and size of the promotion will dictate the degree of media support. It is common for brands such as Pepsi-Cola, Gillette, and Kellogg's cereals to invest in media advertising to promote contests that offer huge grand prizes. In contrast, a premium offer may simply be announced to the target market on the package itself and by shelf cards at point-of-purchase. The investment in media advertising in this case would be low.

Trade customers must be made aware of consumer promotion offers, a task that falls on the shoulders of the manufacturer's sales representatives. The manufacturer commonly prepares specific sales literature such as brochures, pamphlets, and display material for representatives to use to introduce the promotion. The sales representatives will integrate the consumer promotion offer with their trade promotion plans (a combination of pull and push) to maximize the impact of the dollars being invested in the promotion. A manufacturer will also consider direct mailings to trade customers to create awareness and interest in the promotion. The sales representatives must sell the promotion to the distributors and show how it will affect their business positively. Their objective may be to secure a listing for a new product or to ensure the distributor orders sufficient inventory of an existing product to cover the anticipated demand and to encourage adequate merchandising support in its stores. If the trade customers are on board, the promotion will be successful. Their support is crucial.

LOGISTICS AND FULFILLMENT

The final phase of planning a promotion campaign involves working out all of the details of the offer. Depending on the nature of the promotion, there will be a variety of dates and deadlines, there will be other companies involved in planning and implementing the offer, and there will need to be a system in place to deliver the goods to consumers, if the promotion so dictates. These are only a sampling of the potential decisions that are made.

To demonstrate the fulfillment process, let's assume that a major contest is the sales promotion offer. The grand prize is a trip to Disneyland with a series of smaller prizes to be awarded to runners-up. Answers to the following questions start to create a plan of action for implementing the awareness and fulfillment sides of the promotion:

- When will the promotion be announced to the trade and to consumers?

- Who are the contest prize suppliers and what are the costs?

- How will consumers enter the contest? Who will design the entry form?

- Where will the entry forms be sent?

- What is the deadline for receiving entries?

- Who will draw the prizes?

- How will the prizes be delivered to the winners?

- What costs are associated with contest administration by a third-party organization?

- Who will the third-party organization be?

- Who will prepare in-store promotional materials?

- Who will print the promotional literature and what will it cost?

- How will media advertising be coordinated with the sales promotion offer?

Such a list of questions reveals the logistical implications for running a sales promotion offer. Needless to say, the entire promotion must operate seamlessly from the front end (announcing the promotion) to the back end (delivering prizes to winners). Smart marketing organizations outsource the administration of the promotion to a specialist in this industry.

MEASUREMENT AND EVALUATION

Similar to any other marketing communications program, sales promotion activities must be evaluated for success or failure. As indicated earlier, a boost in sales is the immediate goal of most forms of promotion, but other factors beyond promotion also influence sales. Therefore, a promotion must be evaluated based on the objectives that were established for it. If the objective was to generate trial purchases, how many new users were attracted to the product? If the objective was loyalty, are current customers buying the product more frequently? To answer these questions, some pre- and post-promotion marketing research is necessary.

Specific promotions are also measured by response rates of consumers. For example, a coupon promotion could be assessed by the number of coupons returned. If the average return rate for coupons distributed by magazines is 1 percent and an offer draws a 2 percent response, the promotion could be judged a success. A contest is evaluated on the basis of the number of entries received. If the objective was 10 000 entries and only 7500 were received, the promotion could be judged a failure.

If there is a method of projecting revenues generated by a promotion, then it is possible to estimate some kind of financial payout from the promotion. The difference between revenues and costs would be the return on investment, because the costs of the promotion are known. Figure 8.7 illustrates how to evaluate the financial payout of a coupon offer.

A side benefit of consumer promotions is the collection of names. The names on entry forms from contests and order forms for premium offers and rebate offers can be

FIGURE 8.7   Evaluating the Financial Impact of a Sales Promotion Offer

This example shows the return on investment for a coupon offer distributed to households by cooperative direct mail. Costs and revenues are estimated to determine the return on investment.

Coupon Plan

Face value of coupon	$1.00
Handling charge for retailer	$0.15
Handling charge for clearing house	$0.05
Distribution cost	$18.00/M
Distribution	2 million households
Printing cost (digest-sized ad with perforated coupon at bottom)	$12.00/M
Redemption rate (estimated)	5.0%
Retail price of product	$3.89

(Manufacturer receives about 65% of retail price when distributors' mark-ups are deducted)

Costs	Cost Calculation	Total	Grand Total
Distribution	2 000 000 x $18/M	$36 000	
Printing	2 000 000 x $12/M	$24 000	
Coupon redemption	2 000 000 x 0.05 x $1.20	$120 000	
Total cost		**180 000**	**$180 000**
Cost per coupon redeemed	180 000/100 000	$1.80	

Revenues			
Per unit of revenue	$3.89 x.065	$2.53	
Total revenue*	2 000 000 x 0.05 x 0.80 x $2.53	**202 400**	**$202 400**
Return on investment			**$22 400**

*With any coupon offer, there is a risk of coupons being returned without a purchase being made. This is referred to as misredemption. In this example, the misredemption rate is 20%, hence the 0.80 factor in the revenue calculation equation.

added to the organization's database. Smart marketers seek additional information about consumers on promotion entry forms to develop more thorough customer profiles and determine who their primary target market is. Having more and better information about customers will assist in the development of customer relationship management programs.

When Boston Market restaurants entered Canada, consumer promotions played a key role in getting unfamiliar customers to visit. Figure 8.8 shows how Boston Market applied the sales promotion planning process. Its very unique offer generated extremely high response rates.

FIGURE 8.8 Summary Example of a Sales Promotion Plan for Boston Market

SITUATION ANALYSIS

- Canadian consumers totally unaware of Boston Market
- Boston Market is a subsidiary of McDonald's Restaurants
- 650 locations in 28 US states
- Food perceived as very good (home-cooked style); high incidence of repeat visits

SALES PROMOTION OBJECTIVES

- To show how Boston Market can benefit the everyday lives of consumers
- To generate traffic (trial usage)

TARGET MARKET

- Married households; two working adults; with or without children; suburban
- Time starved and searching for home replacement meals

SALES PROMOTION STRATEGY

- An incentive that ties into what the brand stands for: "Home-style meals made easy"
- Free sample offer to designated households in trading area

SALES PROMOTION EXECUTION

- Promotion theme: "Dinner on Us"
- Location: Mystery bag attached to front door knob of designated area households
- Message on bag: "Too much on your plate?" (a question to create curiosity)
- Incentive: Free meal for two (no strings attached)
- Action: Consumer must bring the dinner plate from the bag to the restaurant to get the free meals. Plate inferred a home-cooked meal away from home. The unique promotion would encourage positive word-of-mouth.
- Distribution: Different homes selected each Thursday

MEASUREMENT AND EVALUATION

- The Thursday rollouts created a high level of anticipation among households
- Very positive press coverage by local media (free advertising and endorsements)
- Redemption rate 70% (outstanding)

Adapted from Lisa McGillivray, "Bagging a tasty promo," *Marketing*, December 2, 2002, p. 15.

CONSUMER PROMOTION EXECUTION

As indicated earlier, an organization will combine various consumer promotion activities with trade promotion activities so that there is balance between the pull and push strategies. It is that combination of pull and push that creates a synergistic effect in the marketplace. This section will discuss the various forms of consumer promotions that are often included in sales promotion plans.

The major types of consumer promotions include coupons, free samples, contests, cash rebates and related incentives, premiums, and loyalty programs. The popularity of the various alternatives varies from one industry to another. In the packaged goods industry, all alternatives are used, but coupons and free samples tend to be very popular. In the automotive industry, rebates are the preferred tactic. Domestic manufacturers such as Ford, General Motors, and Chrysler frequently offer cash-back rebates and extremely low financing terms. Does anyone actually buy a car that doesn't have some kind of incentive offer attached to it? Let's analyze the various consumer promotions and determine the conditions for which each type of promotion is best suited.

COUPONS **Coupons** are price-saving incentives offered to consumers to stimulate quick purchase of a designated product. The motivation for distributing the coupons is the same across all industries, although the value of the coupons varies considerably. Grocery coupons, for example, may only be valued at $0.75, while a trial coupon for a restaurant may be valued at 50 percent of the cost of the meal. A common offer is "Buy one meal at regular price and save 50 percent off the price of the second meal."

coupon
A price-saving incentive offered to consumers to stimulate quick purchase of a specified product.

In packaged goods markets, coupons are the dominant form of sales promotion activity. According to the Promotion Marketing Association (U.S.), 76 percent of the adult population uses coupons.[5] The latest data available from Resolve Corporation, which keeps records on coupon distribution and redemption rates in Canada, reveal that more than 3.6 billion coupons are distributed annually. A total of 100 million are returned, for a total savings on goods of about $135 million. The average value of a redeemed coupon is $1.35.[6] For additional insight into coupon activity in Canada see Figure 8.9.

FIGURE
8.9   Coupon Facts and Figures

Coupon Activity	2006
Quantity Distributed	3.6 billion
Quantity Redeemed	100 million
Average Face Value of Coupons Distributed	$2.02
Average Face Value of Coupons Redeemed	$1.35
Average Valid Period	175 days
Consumer Savings	$135 million

Coupon usage in Canada has remained steady for the past 10 years.

83% of Canadian households have used a coupon in the past year; 60% have used a coupon in the last month (2006).

In more than half of Canadian households, coupons influence brand purchase decisions.

Free-standing inserts are the most significant method of distributing coupons (58% of all coupons distributed).

Source: Courtesy of Coupon Industry Association of Canada.

Coupons are an excellent medium for achieving several marketing objectives at various stages of the product life cycle. First, coupons can encourage *trial purchase* among new users (and encourage competitive brand users to switch brands), and they can encourage *repeat purchases* by current users. In the latter situation, the coupon is a means of building brand loyalty.

The method by which the coupons are distributed to consumers is based on the objectives of the coupon offer. When a product is new or relatively new, trial purchase is the marketer's primary objective, so **media-delivered coupons** are popular. Options for delivery include **free-standing inserts (FSI)** in newspapers, magazines, direct mail, in-store distribution, and the Internet. Websites such as Save.ca distribute coupons on behalf of manufacturers. Many companies distribute coupons to consumers who request them while visiting their website. Free-standing inserts are the most significant method of coupon distribution in Canada, accounting for 58 percent of all coupons distributed.[7] They are distributed via daily newspapers, usually on Saturday each week.

Once a product moves into the late growth and early mature stages of its life cycle, a marketer's attention shifts from trial purchase to *repeat purchase*. By now there are many competing brands, all of which have a certain degree of consumer loyalty. As a defensive measure, it is important to reward current customers in one form or another. The package itself becomes an important medium for distributing coupons. The insertion of a coupon in or on a package, for example, is an incentive for a customer to keep buying the product.

Coupons contained inside a package are called **in-pack self-coupons**, because they are redeemable on the next purchase. Usually the face panel of the package makes mention of the coupon contained inside. A coupon that appears on the side panel or back panel is called an **on-pack self-coupon**. Another option is the **instantly redeemable coupon**, which is attached to the package in some fashion and can be removed immediately and used on the purchase of the product. Sometimes two different products collaborate on a coupon offer. To illustrate, Tetley includes an in-pack coupon for Christie cookies, and Christie places a Tetley tea coupon in its package. The relationship between the two brands is obvious. Each brand capitalizes on the other's consumer franchise in its effort to attract new users. This type of coupon is called a **cross-ruff** or **cross-coupon**.

The success or failure of a coupon offer is often determined by the redemption rate that is achieved. The **redemption rate** refers to the number of coupons returned to the manufacturer expressed as a percentage of the total coupons in distribution. If, for example, 1 million coupons were distributed and 45 000 were returned, the redemption rate would be 4.5 percent (45 000 divided by 1 000 000).

For budgeting purposes, it is important to know the average redemption rates for the various methods of delivering coupons. For example, Resolve Corporation research shows the average redemption rate for addressed direct mail coupons to be 6.5 percent, while the range can be anywhere from 1.9 percent to 22.6 percent. Magazine coupons have a range of 0.1 percent to 7.0 percent with an average of only 0.8 percent. A key factor that influences the redemption rate and causes such variations in the rate is the perceived value of the offer in relation to the regular price of the product. If it is not a worthwhile incentive, it will not be acted upon.

PRODUCT SAMPLES

Product sampling is a powerful, yet expensive way to promote a product. It is an effective strategy for encouraging trial purchase, but due to the costs involved, many manufacturers do not select this option. Traditionally, **free sample** programs involved the

media-delivered coupon
Coupon packaged with another medium, such asnewspapers, magazines, direct mail, in-store distribution, and the Internet.

free-standing insert (FSI)
A booklet featuring coupons, refunds, contests, or other promotional advertising distributed by direct mail or with newspapers, magazines, or other delivery vehicles.

in-pack self-coupon
A coupon for the next purchase of a product that is packed inside the package or under a label.

on-pack self-coupon
A coupon that is printed on the outside of a package redeemable on the next purchase of the product.

instantly redeemable coupon
A removable coupon often located on the package or a store shelf that is redeemable on the current purchase of the product.

cross-ruff (cross-coupon)
A coupon packed in or with one product that is redeemable for another product. The product the coupon is packed with is the means of distributing the coupon.

redemption rate
The number of coupons returned expressed as a percentage of the number of coupons that were distributed.

free sample
Free distribution of a product to potential users.

distribution of trial-size packages (small replicas of the real package) or actual-size packages. The latter option is obviously an expensive proposition.

In order to implement a sampling program, the marketer must appreciate the true benefit of such an offer. In a nutshell, it is unlike any other form of promotion in that it is the only alternative that will convert a trial user to a regular user solely on the basis of product satisfaction. Essentially, the marketing organization has eliminated any perceived risk the consumer may have about buying the product. That's a compelling reason for using samples. When Harvey's launched its Angus Burger in 2008, free Angus Burger coupons were emailed to all present customers in the company's database. Refer to the illustration in Figure 8.10.

There are less expensive ways to implement sample programs, but they lack the impact of household distribution of free goods. A tried and true approach, particularly for food products, is in-store sampling. Costco uses this approach extensively by setting

Source: Courtesy of Cara Operations Limited.

FIGURE
8.10

Free samples encourage trial usage and initial purchase

up sample stations at the ends of food aisles. A smart shopper can practically have a free lunch while shopping at Costco on a Saturday! When packaged good grocery manufacturers do sample tasting in local supermarkets, they usually outsource the promotion to an independent company that specializes in this activity. Booths are strategically set up in stores to intercept customers as they shop.

Companies are discovering new ways of delivering samples while at the same time generating positive publicity for the brand involved in the promotion. Some refer to it as **on-site sampling**; others call it **experiential marketing**. The key objective of experiential marketing is to engage the consumer with the brand in some manner. Tetley iced tea engaged consumers when it targeted key urban markets and cottage country playgrounds with a summer sampling promotion. More than a half million samples were given away at community events in urban markets and by branded boats that travelled dock-to-dock in Ontario's Muskoka Lakes area.[8] True experiential marketing goes beyond distributing samples. A more thorough discussion of this topic is included in Chapter 10.

Larry Burns, co-chair of U.S.-based Promotion Marketing Association (PMA), says, "Targeted, well-thought-out sampling programs are the way to go in today's market." He cites research findings to back up his claim. From a survey conducted by the PMA, 94 percent of respondents view sampling as a way of increasing their comfort level when buying a product. A further 68 percent said they were "excited" about receiving the sample.[9]

When deciding whether to use a free sample program, a review of the benefits and drawbacks is essential. Samples are an expensive proposition due to product, package, and handling costs. In spite of these costs, samples rank second to coupons among marketers, so clearly the long-term benefit outweighs the short-term costs. The fact that samples eliminate the risk usually associated with new product purchases is a key benefit. On the downside, a sample is the fastest and surest way to kill an inferior product. In terms of timing, sample programs are best suited to the early stage of the product life cycle when the primary objective is to achieve trial purchase. For certain, the delivery of samples adds excitement to any new product launch.

CONTESTS **Contests** are designed and implemented to create temporary excitement about a brand. For example, offering a grand prize such as an automobile, vacation, or dream home can capture the consumer's imagination, even though the odds of winning are very low. Contests can be classified into two categories: sweepstakes and games. A **sweepstakes** is a chance promotion involving the giveaway of products and services such as cars, vacations, and sometimes cash. It's like a lottery: winners are randomly selected from the entries received. Typically, consumers enter a contest by filling in an entry form that is available at point-of-purchase, through print advertising, or at a website.

When companies are searching for the right sweepstakes idea, their objective is clear: it must light a fire under sales. In the world of promotional contests, experts generally agree that success hinges on three factors: cash, cars, and travel. As well, the prize must capture the imagination of the target for the promotion to be successful. To demonstrate, Pepsi and Pepsi Max offered Canadians a chance to win eight Mazda3 Sport GT vehicles and 1500 free fuel cards. Consumers engaged with the brand through an online entry system from which data could be collected about current consumers. According to Dale Hooper, VP marketing at Pepsi-QTG Canada, "this contest was an innovative way to reward our loyal customers, giving them a chance to enjoy the open road in a brand new Mazda."[10] It also established a base on which to form a stronger relationship with these customers in the future.

Games are also based on chance but can be more involving because they often require repeat visits for game pieces. This makes them a good device for encouraging

---

experiential marketing (on-site sampling)
A form of marketing that creates an emotional connection with the consumer in personally relevant and memorable ways.

contest
A promotion that involves awarding cash or merchandise prizes to consumers when they purchase a specified product.

sweepstakes
A chance promotion involving the giveaway of products or services of value to randomly selected participants.

game (instant-win promotion)
A promotional contest that includes a number of pre-seeded winning tickets; instant-win tickets can be redeemed immediately.

continuity of purchase by consumers. McDonald's is somewhat of an expert in this area. Its "Monopoly" game is a regular feature in annual marketing plans. As the saying goes, "You have to play to win," and the only way to play is to go to a McDonald's restaurant.

An offshoot of the game contest is the **instant-win promotion**, which involves predetermined, pre-seeded winning tickets in the overall fixed universe of tickets. For example, if the promotion is implemented nationally, prize tickets should be regionally dispersed based on population patterns. Pepsi-Cola ran an instant win promotion, "Win an iPod an hour," for several weeks. The contest was extremely popular with young people since gadgets like iPods are so important today. The connection between Pepsi-Cola and iPod was relevant. Pepsi benefited from the halo effect of being connected to such a hot brand.

Variations of instant-wins include *collect-and-wins* and small instant-wins combined with a grand prize contest. Tim Hortons's annual "Rrroll Up the Rim to Win" is an example of a contest combining instant-wins with a series of grand prizes. Most of the instant-win prizes involve food products available at the organization's restaurants, but it is the roster of bigger prizes that draws the consumer in. "Rrroll Up the Rim to Win" is another example of a longstanding successful promotion. It delivers a consistent theme and has a catchy and memorable slogan. According to Tim Hortons, the promotion is now less of a promotion and more like a brand unto itself: "Rrroll Up the Rim to Win" has become recognized as its own entity, much as a product would. Franchisees indicate that sales increase 10 to 15 percent during the promotion period.[11] This promotion is an integral part of the company's annual marketing plan.

Planning any kind of contest is a challenge. Most manufacturers rely on external suppliers to develop and implement a contest. In this regard, there is much upfront discussion with suppliers to ensure proper briefing on objectives and expectations. The success of a contest depends on the consumer's perception of the value and number of prizes being awarded and on the odds of winning. As well, the prizes must match the image of the product and the lifestyle of the target market. Successful contests tend to have a grand prize that captures the imagination of the target market, or have prizes of lesser value but awarded in large numbers to compensate for the disappointment factor associated with most contests. Contests that are combined with other purchase incentives provide added stimulus for consumers to take action. Refer to the illustration in Figure 8.11.

A cost–benefit analysis should be done prior to getting involved with a contest. In terms of benefit, a contest is a good device for achieving repeat purchase objectives. A well-designed contest encourages customers to come back or buy more frequently. By returning or buying more goods, consumers exhibit a certain degree of loyalty. As such, contests are ideal promotions for products in the mature stage of the product life cycle. They can boost brand sales in a time of need. According to Tony Chapman, president of Capital C Communications, "Contests have the ability to excite consumers, excite a sales force, sell incredible volume, and build brand equity, and that's a sweet spot every marketer dreams about."[12]

On the cost side of things, a contest requires a significant investment in media advertising to create awareness and interest. Contests such as "Rrroll Up the Rim to Win" are supported by multimedia advertising campaigns. A combination of media advertising and in-store promotional materials tends to be effective. When the cost of prizes and the cost of having an external organization implement the contest are factored in, the amount required for a contest promotion can be a sizeable portion of a marketing budget.

Legal issues are another concern for marketers when they get involved in contests. The manager must be familiar with some of the basic laws that govern contests in

Source: Photo by Keith J. Tuckwell.

FIGURE 8.11 An Example of a Promotion that Combines a Coupon and Contest Communicated by In-Store Shelf Pads

Canada. Section 189 of the *Criminal Code* and sections 52 and 59 of the *Competition Act* regulate most contests in Canada, and there are certain fairly standardized rules and regulations for what information must be communicated to participants. The following information must be clearly conveyed:

- The number of prizes and the value of each.
- The odds of winning, if known.
- Whether a skill-testing question will be administered.
- Whether facsimiles are acceptable in the case of a sweepstakes.
- How to enter, and what proof of purchase is required.
- The contest's closing date.

    For some tips on planning an effective contest, see Figure 8.12.

REBATES A **rebate** is a predetermined amount of money returned directly to the customer by the manufacturer after the purchase has been made. It is an incentive to get consumers to buy in greater volume during the promotion period. Initially, rebates were the promotion of choice among packaged goods marketers, but they are now an integral element of marketing programs for durable goods such as automobiles, major appliances, and consumer electronics.

rebate
A predetermined amount of money returned directly to customers by the manufacturer after the purchase has been made.

Effective contests do not happen by chance. They are carefully planned to spark interest and action and achieve specific marketing objectives. Here are some pointers from those in the business:

- Choose prizes that spark wish-fulfillment fantasies.
- Give consumers a decent chance of winning (low odds of winning create ill will).
- Plan an engaging media component to drive consumer awareness and generate publicity.
- Keep the company name in the contest moniker (again for positive press).
- Use strategic partnerships; co-brand the contest to leverage each other's equity.
- Make sure contest rules are clear and unambiguous.
- Ensure that fulfillment (awarding of prizes) occurs quickly.
- If it ain't broke, don't fix it! Stay with a successful contest if it's producing desired results.

Source: Adapted from "Tips for creating killer contests," *Special Report on Premiums and Incentives, Strategy*, August 26, 2002, p. 24.

FIGURE
8.12

Tips for Planning an Effective Contest

The most common type of rebate is the *single-purchase refund*, in which consumers receive a portion of their money back for the purchase of a specified product. Such an offer is one method of achieving trial purchases. Other variations of rebates include making an offer according to an escalating schedule. For example, an offer could be structured as follows: buy one and get $1.00 back, buy two and get $2.00 back, and buy three and get $5.00 back. The nature of the offer encourages consumers to buy three items at one time, thus helping achieve multiple purchase objectives.

Though many people buy a product because of the possibility of a rebate, many rebates go uncollected due to the hassle of filling out the form and mailing it in with the proof of purchase documentation a manufacturer requires. This phenomenon is referred to as **slippage**, when the consumer collects labels but fails to follow through and request the refund, even for a refund with a $100 value. Time-pressed consumers often forget about the rebate offer. In the retail environment, rebate promotions boost sales since retailers can feature items at lower prices than their manufacturer partners could otherwise afford. They attract more customers and provide opportunities for additional sales.

In recent years, incentives and rebates have become commonplace among automobile manufacturers. Offers such as zero percent (or an incredibly low percentage) financing and cash-back deals of between $1000 and $2500 entice consumers to buy now. These types of incentives were first instituted to help car companies reduce inventories, making way for the introduction of new models each year. But, in an uncertain economy, they have become more of an ongoing practice. In fact, so common are they now that many consumers have adopted an attitude that they won't buy a new car unless there is some kind of incentive provided.

Automobile incentives can boost sales in the short term, but in the long term they have increased the cost of an automobile and have affected the profitability of domestic manufacturers.

Rebate offers are best suited to products in the mature stage of the product life cycle. As indicated above, they are a good incentive for encouraging multiple purchases of inexpensive packaged goods products. Encouraging multiple purchases or building

slippage
The situation of a consumer collecting labels in a promotion offer but failing to follow through and request the refund.

frequency of purchases is a common objective for mature products. At this stage in the life cycle, maintaining customer loyalty is critical. Apart from the rebates offered by automobile companies, which tend to be very high, a rebate promotion is not that expensive to implement. Since it is current users who tend to take advantage of rebate offers, advertising support can be confined to the package and various in-store opportunities, such as shelf cards and product displays.

PREMIUM OFFERS A **premium** is an additional item given free, or greatly discounted, to induce purchase of the primary brand. The goal of a premium is to provide added value to tempt consumers to buy. McDonald's frequently uses premiums because they are effective with its primary target market of families with young children. A "Happy Meal," for example, becomes a "Nintendo Happy Meal."

Premiums are offered to consumers several ways: as a mail-in, by sending in proofs of purchase so the item can be delivered by mail; as an in-pack or on-pack promotion, where the item is placed inside or attached to a package; or by an order form that is usually available at point-of-purchase. Packaged goods companies frequently use their packages to distribute free premiums. Refer to the illustration in Figure 8.13. In this figure, existing Listerine flavours are used to offer a free sample of a new plaque-fighting Listerine product. Coupons on other company brands are also included in the offer.

Many marketers firmly believe that there is something to be said for offering a tangible, quality gift, which can surprise the consumer and build long-term equity through association. Others see the benefits of premiums as largely misleading, citing large increases in sales followed by an equally large tumble once the giveaway ends. Both Molson and Labatt experienced this feast-and-famine phenomenon when they packed everything from golf balls, to T-shirts, to ball caps in their beer cases. Both companies found the promotions expensive, and rather than create loyalty, they simply encouraged drinkers to switch brands constantly.[13]

An offshoot of a premium offer is the **bonus pack**. The traditional bonus pack offers the consumer more for less. For example, a brand offers a package size that gives the consumer 20 percent more product for the regular price. Another option is to bundle a product in pairs and offer a deal like "Buy One Get One Free." Offers like these, if implemented properly, will attract new users and reward current users. If done wrong, they can cheapen the image or value perception of the brand.

Marketing managers tend to rank premiums lower in terms of popularity, but they do offer some tangible benefits. They achieve several marketing objectives: they can increase the quantity of brand purchases made by consumers during the promotion period; they help to retain current customers, therefore building brand loyalty; and they provide a merchandising tool to encourage display activity in stores. A good premium offer will help differentiate one brand from another at a crucial point in time, the time when consumers decide which brand to buy.

LOYALTY PROGRAMS

Loyalty programs take the short-term premium offer a step further—they encourage long-term brand loyalty. How many loyalty cards do you have in your wallet? It seems that consumers are collecting points to obtain something for free years from now. In the meantime, we keep going back to the loyalty sponsor to earn more points. By definition, a **loyalty program** (**frequent buyer program**) offers consumers a small bonus, such as points or play money, each time they make a purchase. The bonus accumulates and can be redeemed for merchandise or some other benefit at a later date.

---

premium
An additional item given free, or greatly discounted, to induce purchase of the primary brand.

bonus pack
The temporary offering of a larger package size (e.g., 20 percent more) for the same price as the regular size.

loyalty program (frequent buyer program)
A program that offers consumers a small bonus, such as points or play money, each time they make a purchase; the bonus accumulates and can be redeemed for merchandise or some other benefit.

Source: Photo by Keith J. Tuckwell.

FIGURE
8.13

In-pack premiums encourage impulse purchases at point of sale

Shoppers Drug Mart has a frequent buyer program that is updated electronically. Member customers swipe their Optimum card each time they make a purchase. Shoppers can cross-reference transaction data electronically and tailor offers and services to specific customers. One such offer included free samples of a variety of brand-name grooming and personal care products. These samples were distributed by mail to a select group of Shoppers Drug Mart customers. As discussed elsewhere in this book, the true benefit of a loyalty program is the information it collects for database marketing. See the illustration in Figure 8.14.

The Intercontinental Group of Hotels, which operates in all price and quality segments of the lodging industry, has a program called "Priority Club Rewards." In this program the customer can redeem accumulated points on merchandise such as coffee makers, food processors, and small consumer electronic items; or the points can be used for hotel rooms and special travel packages sponsored by the hotel chain and its airline partners.

Perhaps the longest-running and most successful loyalty program in Canada is Canadian Tire 'Money.' For insight into its program, read the IMC Highlight: **Canadian Tire Keeps Customers Happy.** Canadian Tire rewards regular shoppers who pay by cash or Canadian Tire credit card with Canadian Tire 'Money' worth up to 5 percent of the value of the purchase. Now at an advanced stage, the program allows customers to collect virtual money at Canadian Tire's website. Canadian Tire 'Money' represents the true essence of a loyalty program: customers can actually receive something for free. In contrast, a program like AIR MILES takes considerable time before the consumer can get even the smallest of rewards.

Given that our wallets are bulging with loyalty cards, it is safe to say that loyalty programs are popular with consumers. In fact, a study conducted by Kubas Consultants revealed that 76 percent of adult Canadians participate in at least one loyalty program.[14] What consumers fail to realize is that while they are chasing a dream vacation or a

> **FIGURE 8.14** Database marketing techniques employed by Shoppers Drug Mart identify select customers to receive free samples of a variety of products

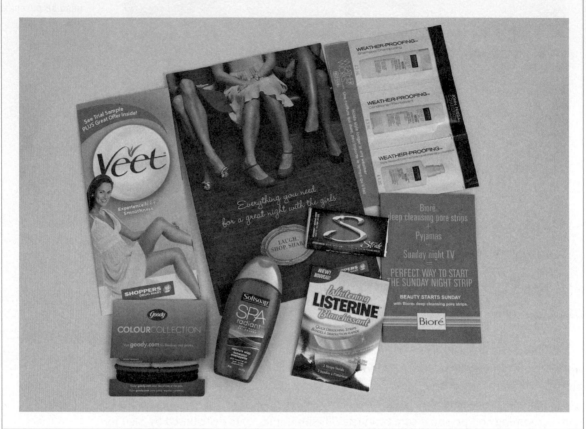

state-of-the-art, theatre-style television, the cost of the merchandise they are buying is going up. Loyalty programs add to the costs of a business in the form of additional employees, call centres, catalogues, and computers. As well, investment in media advertising is needed to draw attention to the loyalty program.

Plastic cards can function as both a loyalty card and a gift card. Gift cards are a booming market. In 2007, gift card sales in the United States reached US$97 billion—gift cards are extremely popular with consumers and retailers! The recipient of a gift card may be a completely new customer for a retailer. Temporarily shopping for free could lead to ongoing loyalty if the customer is satisfied with the purchases and the service provided.[15]

Marketing organizations must carefully consider the decision to use loyalty programs. In some cases, consumers perceive the "free" reward as a real incentive, but they don't realize they are paying for the privilege. Since loyalty programs add costs, customers may eventually tire of paying more for the goods they buy. The true benefit for the organization is the information it is collecting about customers. Members of loyalty programs voluntarily submit profiles with their age, gender, address, and consumer preferences. This information can be combined with transaction data, and when the data is mined at a later date it can be extremely useful as organizations move toward individualized marketing programs. Once an organization starts a loyalty program, it is an ongoing program.

Canadian Tire Money Keeps Customers Happy

Canadian Tire 'Money'... a simple concept. Yet it is the cornerstone of Canadian Tire's marketing mix. "Canadian Tire 'Money' is a most successful and popular customer reward program that has a 90 percent redemption and participation level. It is the very heart of what Canadian Tire stands for in today's competitive marketplace."

How and why did the Canadian Tire money program start? Apparently it was the brainchild of Muriel Billes, the wife of co-founder A.J. Billes. Apparently, Muriel was a marketing genius who had all kinds of ideas for getting customers into their stores. The program was launched in a period when there was fierce competition among gasoline retailers. Competitors were giving away premiums to entice customers, so Muriel came up with the money-back concept, offering gasoline purchasers 5 percent off on whatever they bought in the stores. It was a hit! Canadian Tire money helped associate the brand with value.

The program has evolved over the years but stays true to its original premise: reward good customers for their loyalty! To keep customers truly happy, the program lets customers determine what their reward will be. Unlike many other loyalty programs that are much more complex and only allow customers to select rewards from predetermined merchandise, Canadian Tire's program allows customers to claim their reward anytime and on anything the store sells. That formula still works today. Collecting Canadian Tire money represents a successful promotion that people have come to know, expect, and love. It encourages people to come back to the store.

Canadian Tire money can be used to pay part of a bill or used for an entire purchase; it can be redeemed immediately or hoarded so customers can save for a special purchase. Canadian Tire retains a focus on its loyalty program because the money is an important element of the customers' shopping experience. From a marketing perspective it allows the company to differentiate itself and provides immense competitive advantage. For the record, Canadian Tire is the most-shopped store in Canada: 90 percent of Canadians shop there. And the Canadian Tire brand is one of the top five most recognized brands in Canada.

Canadian Tire money actually feels like money, and it should because it is printed on paper with the same rag content as real money. It is also printed in a manner to foil counterfeiters. While that may seem ridiculous, consider that Canadian Tire distributes as much as $100 million in Canadian Tire money and the redemption rate is about 90 percent. There's room for fraud in those numbers!

As a loyalty program, Canadian Tire money remains successful because of its simplicity. It offers instant rewards, and customers are not required to enroll in a customer relationship management program.

Adapted from Sharon Adams, "Canadian Tire got the ball rolling," *Loyalty & Its Rewards*, supplement in the *National Post*, April 26, 2007, p. IS6, and Jeff Buckstein, "Benefits add up for consumers," *Loyalty & Its Rewards*, supplement in the *National Post*, April 27, 2005, p. JV4.

TRADE PROMOTION EXECUTION

Trade customers are the link between manufacturers and consumers, and in Canada they have incredible control in many markets. In the grocery industry, for example, the combination of two large wholesale/retail operations, Loblaw and Sobeys, controls more than half of all food store sales. In the hardware market, the combination of Canadian Tire and Home Hardware controls a significant portion of volume. Distributors make money by selling your products, but they are also in business to sell anyone's products. Consequently, their loyalty to any supplier can waver if they do not receive trade promotion offers they feel they deserve.

Simply stated, the trade looks for the best offers from suppliers and makes buying decisions accordingly. As with consumer promotions, trade promotions must be designed to deliver the highest possible value to the trade while costing as little as possible for the manufacturer. Manufacturers have a variety of trade promotion offers to choose from when developing a promotion plan. Typically, the offers work together to generate a high degree of impact during the promotion period. This section explores the various trade promotion options.

trade allowance
A temporary price reduction that encourages larger purchases by distributors.

TRADE ALLOWANCES A **trade allowance** is a temporary price reduction that encourages larger purchases by distributors. It can be offered several ways: a percentage reduction from the list price, a predetermined dollar amount off the list price, or free goods. A free goods offer may be something like "Buy 10 cases and get one free."

In addition to encouraging larger volume purchases, the manufacturer would like to see a portion of the allowance devoted to lowering the price of the product at retail for a short period. In the grocery industry, products are commonly offered on sale for one week. The manufacturer absorbs the discount offered to consumers. Trade allowances can be deducted from the invoice immediately, and in such cases are called *off-invoice allowances*. Or they can be offered on the basis of a *bill-back*, in which case the manufacturer keeps a record of all purchases shipped to the distributor and, when the deal period expires, reimburses the distributor for the allowances it earned.

performance allowance
A discount offered by a manufacturer that encourages a distributor to perform a merchandising function on behalf of a manufacturer.

PERFORMANCE ALLOWANCES A **performance allowance** is a discount that encourages the distributor to perform a merchandising function on behalf of the manufacturer. As indicated above, a trade allowance helps lower prices, but additional incentives are required to make the promotion a real success. It is common for the manufacturer to request automatic distribution of goods to retail stores, displays in stores, and a mention of the sale price in the retailer's weekly advertising flyer. The additional funds provided in the performance allowance help cover the distributor's costs of implementing these activities. The distributor may or may not comply with all of the requests of the manufacturer, but some kind of deal is negotiated and agreed to. Before paying the allowance, the manufacturer requires proof of performance by the distributor.

Given this information, you can now appreciate that many of the advertising flyers and in-store promotional activities that are undertaken by large retail chain stores are actually subsidized by the manufacturers' brands involved in the promotions. The costs of trade promotions are significant and take a considerable portion of a brand's marketing budget each year.

cooperative advertising allowance (co-op allowance)
The sharing of advertising costs by suppliers and retailers or by several retailers.

COOPERATIVE ADVERTISING ALLOWANCES A **cooperative advertising allowance**, or **co-op allowance** as it is commonly referred to, is a fund allocated to pay for a portion of a distributor's advertising. Marketing organizations often pay a percentage (often 50 percent or more) of the distributor's ad cost, provided the marketer's brand is featured prominently. An example of a co-op campaign that you see frequently is "Intel Inside." By featuring those two words and the logo, the computer manufacturer receives partial funding for its advertising from Intel.

To maximize the effectiveness of allowances offered to the trade, the above allowances are frequently combined to develop an integrated promotion plan. If a bigger plan is in place, the trade promotion plan will be integrated with consumer promotions and brand advertising. Combining the allowances is attractive to the retailers. The financial rewards will be much greater and the funds available are sufficient to support their own advertising and merchandising activities. Financial incentives are a great motivator among distributors.

dealer premium
An incentive offered to a distributor to encourage the special purchase of a product or to secure additional merchandising support from the distributor.

DEALER PREMIUMS A **dealer premium** is an incentive offered to a distributor by a manufacturer to encourage the special purchase of a product or to secure additional merchandising support from a retailer. Premiums are usually offered in the form of merchandise and distributed by sales representatives of the company offering the premium. Some common premiums include golfing equipment, cameras, audio equipment, and leisure clothing. The offering of premiums is a controversial issue. Some distributors absolutely forbid their buyers to accept them. They argue that the buyer is the only beneficiary and the buying organization might be purchasing more goods than it really needs. Many believe the practice of offering premiums, often referred to as "payola," to buyers is unethical. However, dealings between sellers and buyers sometimes occur under the table.

An offshoot of a premium offer is a **spiff**. Next time you're in a store, ask yourself why that retail sales representative recommended the Canon camera (or any other popular brand name) over the others. It could be that the manufacturer encouraged the sales representative to promote its brand by providing some kind of incentive. The retail sales representative stands to gain if more Canon products are sold. Such a practice is common in product categories where consumers have a tendency to ask for recommendations. In the camera illustration above, the buyer wants a certain type of camera, but choosing the brand to buy always presents risk—there are many good brands to choose from. The seller's job is to help eliminate such risk, but that may not always happen if spiffs are in play.

Clearly, the use of premiums and spiffs achieves certain marketing objectives. Many companies employ them when they are facing unusual circumstances, such as when trying to meet year-end sales objectives and it's a touch-and-go situation. Compared to other forms of sales promotion, though, they are not the kinds of activities that will be used regularly.

spiff
An incentive offered to retail salespeople to encourage them to promote a specified brand of goods to customers.

COLLATERAL MATERIAL The role of the sales representative cannot be underestimated, particularly in business-to-business selling situations. Companies invest significant sums in programs that tell consumers about their goods and services, but as indicated above, it is also important to invest in programs that help push the product through the channel. Sales representatives need selling resources, and that's where collateral material comes into play. **Collateral materials** are visual aids that are specific to special promotions or simply ongoing aids for the variety of products being sold. Collateral materials include price lists, catalogues, sales brochures, pamphlets, specification sheets, product manuals, and audiovisual sales aids.

collateral materials
Visual aids used by sales representatives in sales presentations, such as price lists, product manuals, sales brochures, and audiovisual materials.

In the age of electronics, it is now common for much of this material to be available in CD or DVD formats or on a company's website. Either medium is capable of communicating lengthy and complex information. From a buyer's point of view, sales information on a CD or DVD can be reviewed at a more leisurely pace and perhaps a more convenient time than during a sales call. Sometimes when a sales representative is selling the goods, the pace can be rapid and there isn't time to really digest the information. Therefore, the use of hard-copy and soft-copy collateral materials is a good combination.

DEALER DISPLAY MATERIAL As indicated earlier, one of the objectives of trade promotion is to encourage merchandising support from retail distributors. The manufacturer can assist in this area by providing **dealer display material** or **point-of-purchase material** as it is often called. Dealer display material includes posters, shelf talkers (mini-posters that hang or dangle from store shelves), channel strips (narrow bands that fit into the side of a store shelf), and advertising pads (tear-off sheets that hang from pads attached to shelves). Figure 8.15 provides an illustration of a shelf talker.

dealer display (point-of-purchase) material
Advertising or display material located in a retail environment to build traffic, advertise a product, and encourage impulse purchasing.

Material of a more permanent nature includes display shippers (shipping cases that convert to display stands when opened and erected properly) and permanent display racks. One of the problems with display material is that it frequently goes to waste. In

Source: Photo by Keith J. Tuckwell.

FIGURE
8.15

A shelf talker creates awareness and interest at a vital time: when a buying decision is about to be made

many retail outlets, permission to erect displays must be granted by the store manager and sometimes by the head office of the retailer. Some retailers do not allow manufacturer-supplied display material at all. To be effective, displays must be erected in a visible location. The retailer makes the location decision, and it may not be to the liking of the manufacturer. A poor location will diminish the intended impact of the display.

trade show
An event that allows a company to showcase its products to a captive audience and generate leads.

TRADE SHOWS **Trade shows** are an effective way for a company to introduce new products to the marketplace. There is no better opportunity to showcase something special than at a trade show. Where else will a manufacturer find as many customers, all in one place, actively and willingly seeking product information? All industries seem to have trade shows, and in many cases they move around the country to make it more convenient for prospective customers to visit. Depending on the nature of the show, it may attract consumers, trade distributors, or both.

The automobile industry and the recreation and leisure products industry are among the largest users of trade shows. Here, all manufacturers gather to show their latest models (see Figure 8.16). Auto shows are magnets for the media, so they generate all kinds of positive press for the participating companies. From a manufacturer's perspective, a trade show provides an opportunity to develop a prospect list that the sales force can follow up on. When visiting a trade show, customers leave a trail of valuable information about themselves, which can be added quickly to a database for analysis and use later. The very nature of a trade show, however, requires considerable planning by participants along with a considerable financial investment. There is a simple rule of thumb about participating in trade shows: "If you are going to do it, do it right." It's a great opportunity to outshine the competition.

FIGURE

8.16 Trade shows bring the customer to the marketer

Additional Considerations for Sales Promotion Planning

Sales promotions are not usually the focal point of a brand's marketing communications strategies but, as mentioned above, play a complementary role in achieving certain objectives. Therefore, sales promotions must be carefully planned so they effectively integrate with advertising, public relations, and any other marketing communications plans. Decisions must be made regarding how frequently promotions are offered, what types of promotions will have a positive effect on brand image, and how they will build brand value in the long term. Let's look at each situation briefly.

FREQUENCY OF PROMOTIONS

How frequently should a brand offer sales promotions? All kinds of influencing factors contribute to this decision: the type of product, the activities of the competition, the stage of the product life cycle the brand is in, and the receptiveness of customers toward promotions. A theme running throughout this chapter is that promotions are complementary in nature, so they should never disrupt the flow of regular and more dominant communications activities. There is a risk that too many promotions could cheapen the image of a brand—short-term gain for long-term pain! In general, coupon activity can be implemented more frequently than cash refunds, premium offers, and contests. It is less disruptive to the regular message expressed through media advertising.

BRAND IMAGE AND PROMOTIONS

Much of the discussion about promotion strategies in this chapter mentioned lowering prices so that consumers get a better deal. In the short run, such a strategy brings positive results. However, if this practice becomes frequent, consumers will perceive the sale price to be more of a regular price. In the long term, such a practice will hurt the brand's image and lower profit margins. Domestic automobile manufacturers are facing this dilemma right now. Advertising is so focused on rebates and low financing packages that much less time is devoted to building an image, the former priority of these companies.

Consumers who are continually exposed to low prices may begin to believe a brand is in trouble. They could desert it for another brand. When you consider the psychology of buying, brands are often a personal statement, and people like winning brands.

BUILDING BRAND EQUITY

The cumulative force of all marketing communications is a key factor in building brand equity. Marketers must be aware that sales promotions are a rather chaotic sequence of deals and events that create noise in the marketplace. They are not a sustaining message. It is preferable to adopt a view about promotions that will pay attention to long-term brand values and a consistent approach that will build good relationships with the trade and consumers. A few of the promotions mentioned in this chapter do just that. Among them are Tim Hortons's "Rrroll Up the Rim to Win" and Canadian Tire's reward money. Promotions like these become a positive part of the brand's heritage and reinforce relationships with customers.

SUMMARY

Sales promotions are incentives offered to consumers and the trade to encourage more immediate and larger purchases. Strategically, consumer promotions are designed to help pull a product through the channel of distribution, while trade promotions help push a product through the channel of distribution. A good sales promotion plan usually balances between pull and push.

Sales promotion planning involves a series of steps or decisions. After an assessment of the situation is made, specific objectives and strategies are established and the appropriate offers or incentives are determined. The plan must also consider fulfillment obligations at the back end, and a means of assessing the effectiveness of the plan must be in place.

A key to a successful sales promotion plan lies in how it is integrated with other marketing communications strategies. For certain, sales promotion strategies must be integrated with advertising strategies. Because sales promotions are short term in nature, they often become the focus of the advertising message while the promotion is in place. When the overall plan is implemented, advertising creates awareness for the promotion while in-store displays and websites provide additional details.

Some specific objectives of consumer promotions are to achieve trial purchase by new users and repeat and multiple purchases by current users. The types of activities commonly used to achieve these objectives include coupons, free samples, contests, rebates, premium offers, and loyalty programs.

Specific marketing objectives of trade promotions are to secure new listings and distribution, build volume on a preplanned cyclical basis, and encourage merchandising support at point-of-purchase. Trade promotion activities that help achieve these objectives include trade allowances, performance allowances, cooperative advertising funds, dealer premiums, point-of-purchase display materials, collateral materials, and trade shows.

The impact of sales promotions is short term in nature, and therefore promotions complement other integrated marketing communications strategies. As such, sales promotions should not disrupt regular brand advertising. They must be integrated into advertising strategies to enhance the overall impact on consumers and trade customers. When planning promotions, a manager should guard against running them too frequently so as to not harm the image of the brand. A good sales promotion concept will fit with the brand's image and help build brand equity.

KEY TERMS

bonus pack, 240

collateral materials, 245

consumer promotions, 221

contest, 236

cooperative advertising (co-op) allowance, 244

coupon, 233

cross-coupon, 234

cross-ruff, 234

dealer display material, 245

dealer premium, 244

experiential marketing, 236

free sample, 250

free-standing insert (FSI), 234

frequent buyer program, 240

game, 236

in-pack self-coupon, 234

instantly redeemable coupon, 234

instant-win promotion, 236

loyalty program, 240

media-delivered coupon, 234

on-pack self-coupon, 234

on-site sampling, 236

performance allowance, 244

point-of-purchase material, 245

premium, 240

pull, 221

push, 222

rebate, 238

redemption rate, 250

sales promotion, 221

sales promotion plan, 225

slippage, 239

spiff, 245

sweepstakes, 236

trade allowance, 244

trade promotion, 222

trade show, 246

REVIEW QUESTIONS

1. What is the difference between a pull strategy and a push strategy, and how do sales promotions complement both strategies?
2. What are the primary objectives of a consumer promotion plan?
3. What are the primary objectives of a trade promotion plan?
4. Briefly explain how sales promotion strategies are integrated with advertising strategies. Why is such integration essential?
5. In sales promotion planning, what is meant by logistics and fulfillment?
6. Briefly describe the following consumer promotion terms:
   a) redemption rate
   b) in-pack self-coupon
   c) cross-ruff
   d) on-site sampling
   e) instant-win promotions
   f) slippage

   g) bonus pack
7. What types of coupon distribution are appropriate for the early stages of the product life cycle? What distribution is appropriate for the later stages? Why?
8. What are the benefits and drawbacks of a free sample offer?
9. What elements contribute to the success of a contest offer?
10. What is the objective of a consumer premium offer and when is the best time to implement such an offer?
11. What are the benefits and drawbacks of loyalty promotions?
12. How do trade allowances, performance allowances, and cooperative advertising funds complement each other when implementing a trade promotion plan?
13. Briefly describe the following trade promotion terms:
    a) spiff
    b) dealer premium
    c) collateral material
    d) point-of-purchase material

DISCUSSION AND APPLICATION QUESTIONS

1. Assume you are a brand manager launching a new snack food or confectionary product. What balance would you recommend among consumer promotion, trade promotion, and media advertising? What specific sales promotion activities would you recommend? Justify your choices.

2. Conduct some secondary research on consumer and trade promotion budgets and spending patterns in various industries. Is there undue pressure placed on marketing organizations to spend more on trade promotions and less on other activities? Does the situation vary from one industry to another?

3. A common criticism of consumer premium offers is that they only encourage temporary brand switching. Once the offer is over, consumers switch back to their regular brand. Therefore, in the long run, the promotion will not contribute to sales objectives. Conduct some secondary research on this issue and determine if such a criticism is valid.

4. Consumers could be suffering from "loyalty promotion fatigue." Conduct some secondary research on loyalty promotions to find out how organizations view loyalty promotions. Do loyalty promotions provide real benefits to consumers and the sponsor? What are the elements that make a loyalty promotion a success?

5. What forms of sales promotion are best suited for the following brands? (Hint: you may want to consider the life cycle stage the brand is in). Justify your position.

   a) Secret deodorant

   b) Quaker Chewy Granola Bars

   c) Goodyear tires (replacement tires)

   d) Valvoline motor oil

   e) Hewlett-Packard laser printer

   f) New Balance running shoes

6. Evaluate the sales promotion strategies employed by Canadian Tire. What marketing and marketing communications objectives do they meet? How effective are the programs? How does Canadian Tire integrate sales promotions with other components of its marketing communications plan?

7. Evaluate the sales promotion strategies used by Tim Hortons. What marketing and marketing communications objectives do they meet? How does Tim Hortons integrate sales promotions with other components of the marketing communications mix?

8. Automobile manufacturers have used rebate programs for years to provide consumers with an incentive to buy (and buy now!). Is this an effective sales promotion strategy? Conduct some secondary research on rebate incentives and develop some kind of cost–benefit analysis for using this form of promotion.

ENDNOTES

1. "Asking Canadians," *Strategy*, March 2008, p. 12.

2. Kristin Laird, "Aero launches lovely contest," *Marketing Daily*, March 27, 2008.

3. Annette Boudreau, "Mmm, tasty ads," *Strategy*, April 2008, p. 25.

4. Wayne Mouland, "Coupon convenience," *Marketing*, May 9, 2005, p. 16.

5. Darrell Zahorsky, "Creating Powerful Promotional *Marketing*," About.com, www.about.com/cs/advertising/a/promos.

6. "Coupon Distribution Continued to Rise in 2006 to 3.6 billion," Resolve Corporation, February 2007.

7. Ibid.

8. Jesse Kohl, "Free iced tea . . . on Tetley," *Media in Canada*, July 18, 2008, www.mediaincanada.com.

9. Geoff Dennis, "Sampling growth spurs creativity," *Strategy*, May 20, 2002, pp. 1, 10.

10. Terry Poulton, "Pepsi, Mazda fuel up for contest," *Media in Canada*, May 23, 2008, www.mediaincanada.com.

11. Laura Pratt, "Roll up the Rim a major player for Tim Hortons," *Strategy*, May 22, 2000, p. 22.

12. Terry Poulton, "A winner every time," *Strategy*, August 26, 2002, p. 19.

13. John Heinzl, "Beer firms rethink giveaways," *The Globe and Mail*, March 3, 2003, p. B5.

14. John Heinzl, "You may be loyal, but it's costing you," *The Globe and Mail*, January 31, 2003, p. B8.

15. "Gift Card Facts," www.giftcardtraining.com.

Public Relations

Nathan Denette/CP Images

Learning Objectives

After studying this chapter, you will be able to

1. Identify and assess the various roles of public relations communications in achieving marketing and business objectives

2. Describe the various steps in public relations planning

3. Identify and evaluate various public relations execution techniques for potential application in public relations plans

4. Identify and assess the various evaluation and measurement techniques that determine the effectiveness of public relations strategies

Public relations are an often misunderstood form of marketing communications. The term often conjures up negative images of a company trying to cover something up or trying to put its own spin on a situation. Certainly, with all the news coverage that companies receive when they are in trouble, there is some truth to such perceptions, but public relations can have a very positive impact on a brand or company's performance, and are responsible for communicating all kinds of positive information.

The theme of this book deals with how messages from various disciplines in communications are integrated and how, whatever the discipline, all must work together to give the consumer a unified message. Today more than ever before, public relations have a rightful seat at the table. PR's place in the marketing mix and marketing communications mix is growing in importance, and marketing budgets are starting to reflect that.

Public relations is taking off as a profession! Perhaps the diversity of its role in an organization explains why. As you will read in this chapter, public relations specialists develop and implement communication, promotion, and information programs; publicize events; and maintain media relations for businesses, governments, not-for-profit organizations, and individuals.[1]

In the age of heightened competition and advancing electronic technology, marketers are looking for multiple solutions to brand building. This position further suggests the need for the integration of various forms of marketing communications. To rely on any one medium or channel of marketing communications could be harmful since consumers' media habits are constantly changing. An organization must embrace all communications channels in order to build better relationships with consumers and to achieve its business objectives.

Defining Public Relations

public relations
A form of communications designed to gain public understanding and acceptance.

Public relations are a form of communication that is primarily directed toward gaining public understanding and acceptance. Unlike advertising, which is a form of communication paid for by the company, public relations use publicity that does not necessarily involve payment. Public relations communications appear in the news media and, as such, offer a legitimacy that advertising does not have. Recently, companies have been using public relations to extol the merits of a product by assisting in new product launches or reporting eventful occurrences of the product. This form of communications is often referred to as marketing public relations or marketing PR.

internal publics
The publics with which an organization communicates regularly; can include employees, distributors, suppliers, shareholders, and customers.

The practice of public relations is used to build rapport with the various publics a company, individual, or organization may have. These publics are either internal or external. **Internal publics** involve those with whom the organization communicates regularly and include employers, distributors, suppliers, shareholders, and customers.

External publics are more distant and are communicated with less frequently. They include the media, governments, prospective shareholders, the financial community, and community organizations.

The goal of public relations is to conduct communications in such a way that an organization builds an open, honest, and constructive relationship with its various publics. In comparison to advertising, public relations communications are not controlled by the organization. Instead, the media determine what is said about the company regardless of what information the company provides. In other words, the media act as a "filter" for the information an organization releases.

external publics
Those publics that are distant from an organization and are communicated with less frequently.

The Role of Public Relations

The downturn in the economy in 2008 and 2009 resulted in many public relations communications by companies, unions, and governments. Specifically, the dire financial position of General Motors and Chrysler in the automobile sector resulted in countless news stories in the national and local media. The companies were threatening to reduce or eliminate Canadian production of automobiles unless financial concessions were offered by the unions and federal and provincial governments. Which side the public will support is largely determined by the quality of communications offered by the various parties. This situation demonstrates how important public relations can be!

Certainly public relations will play a more strategic role in the future and their role will vary from one organization to another. As a management function, public relations will help an organization anticipate and interpret public opinion that will impact on its actions. PR will also provide the means to plan and implement communications strategies that are in the best interest of the organization; for example, to devise communications intended to change public attitudes if necessary. From a marketing perspective, good PR will help launch new products and create awareness and excitement for them, just like advertising can, and at a much lower cost. In an era where marketing budgets are being squeezed, that's music to an executive's ears!

The role of public relations is varied, but generally falls into six key categories: corporate communications; reputation management; publicity generation; product placement, branded content, and product seeding; community relations and public affairs; and fundraising. The diversity of this list indicates how public relations can be company oriented or product oriented. Let's examine each category in more detail.

CORPORATE COMMUNICATIONS

An organization that believes in the benefits of public relations communications will take positive and constructive action to disseminate useful information about itself. This may involve communications that are paid for or not paid for. A good public relations plan strives to maximize communications in an unpaid manner, but there are times when paid communications are necessary. Such communications may be in the form of **corporate advertising**: advertising designed to convey a favourable image of a company among its various publics. It can do so by showing how the resources of the organization resolve customers' problems, by promoting goodwill, or by demonstrating a sense of social responsibility. For example, Shell Canada shows how it integrates economic progress with environmental issues, often a delicate challenge for a company in the oil exploration business (see Figure 9.1). This advertisement is an example of social responsibility marketing and reflects an attitude of corporate conscience that anticipates and responds to social problems. Corporate advertising is quite separate from brand-based integrated marketing communications strategies.

corporate advertising
Advertising designed to convey a favourable image of a company among its various publics.

FIGURE 9.1

An Illustration of Advocacy Advertising: Shell Canada Works Toward Finding Environmental Solutions

A company can also be active in the area of issue management. In such cases, the company delivers messages to the public to show where it stands on a particular issue, usually an issue that is important to its various publics. The Shell example shows a proactive stance on protecting the environment. Companies also engage in corporate advertising to generate goodwill in the communities they serve. With reference to the ad that appears in Figure 9.2, Shell is letting the public know how it financially supports educational programs and students in order to build a stronger company and country. Shell is investing today to build a better tomorrow.

REPUTATION MANAGEMENT

Chances are that a company in the headlines is there for all the wrong reasons. Something went wrong and key executives are being called upon to defend the company's position.

FIGURE
9.2

An Illustration of Corporate Responsibility: Shell Canada Is Investing to Build a Stronger Company with a Better Future

Source: J. W. Thompson, Toronto. Reprinted by permission of Shell Canada Limited.

Is a scholarship the only way for a company like Shell to help Canadian students?

McGill University grad Geneviève Savoie says no, and she has the experience to prove it.

Following a student work term at Shell, Geneviève graduated and started her engineering career at the company's Montréal East Refinery. It's a win-win relationship that demonstrates Shell's approach to building tomorrow's workforce. Over the years, Shell has invested millions of dollars in post-secondary institutions across Canada. But it's more than scholarships and recruitment; it's about finding innovative ways to support education, strengthening programs and engaging students in face-to-face dialogue. Because Shell knows that investing in students like Geneviève today will contribute to a stronger company - and country - tomorrow. For more information, visit **shell.ca**

Public relations play a vital role when a company finds itself in a crisis situation, because the final outcome often depends on how effectively an organization manages its communications during the crisis.

Menu Foods was involved in a much-publicized pet food scandal in 2007. The company manufactures dog food for many different national and private-label brands. An unknown ingredient in the food was killing cats and dogs throughout North America. The time lag between when the company knew about the problem and when it implemented a nationwide recall was too long—an unacceptable practice in the eyes of public relations experts. The source of the problem was ultimately traced to Chinese wheat that contained rat poison—a supply situation that Menu Foods had little control over.

When facing a crisis situation, acting quickly and decisively is the approach recommended by experts. The objective is to reassure the public that everything possible is being done to correct the situation. Menu Foods mismanaged its crisis and suffered in two different ways: with the company's public image in tatters many customers ended their contracts with Menu Foods, and there are class-action lawsuits to be dealt with over the longer term.

Another highly publicized case occurred in 2008 involving Maple Leaf Foods. Twenty people died from a strain of listeriosis linked to Maple Leaf's Toronto packaged-meat plant. For a food company that is a disaster! CEO Michael McCain estimates the outbreak and resulting recall of hundreds of Maple Leaf products cost the company $30 million, plus another $15 million in lost sales. That amount eliminated all third-quarter profits for the meat division and created an overall loss for the company.

From a PR perspective Maple Leaf handled the situation correctly. The company president immediately issued an apology via newspaper and television ads and promptly recalled all meat products produced at the Toronto plant. The health interests of the public were of paramount importance to the company.[2] For more insight into this crisis and how Maple Leaf handled it, read the IMC Highlight: **Maple Leaf Effectively Manages Crisis**.

IMC HIGHLIGHT

Maple Leaf Effectively Manages Crisis

When it comes to handling a crisis situation, the best strategy for an organization is to be open, honest, and forthcoming. That philosophy was adopted by Johnson & Johnson back in 1982 when some Tylenol capsules had been intentionally tainted with cyanide. The company recalled 30 million bottles, halted sales of the product, and reached out to hospital and medical practitioners to tell people not to use the product.

Driven by a simple principle—always put the public's interest first—Johnson & Johnson's response, which seems obvious, was revolutionary at the time. Even though market share dipped as low as 8 percent from a high of 30 percent, the brand was successfully relaunched with tamper-proof packaging and regained its leadership position.

Clearly, Maple Leaf Foods adopted a similar strategy in dealing with a listeriosis outbreak in 2008. Tainted meat from a Toronto processing plant was responsible for the

deaths of 20 people. Michael McCain, CEO of Maple Leaf, took quick and decisive action and did so in a manner much like Johnson & Johnson did for Tylenol.

McCain's first step was to apologize publicly. At a press conference McCain stated, "Tragically our products have been linked to illnesses and loss of life. To Canadians who are ill and who have lost loved ones, I offer my deepest sympathies. Words cannot begin to express our sadness for your pain. We have an unwavering commitment to keeping your food safe with standards well beyond regulatory requirements, but this week our best efforts failed and we are deeply sorry." His apology was heartfelt.

McCain went on to explain the actions the company would be taking to ensure the safety of the public. His plan included an immediate recall of all meat products produced at the plant—even those not linked to the listeriosis outbreak. McCain's announcement received national coverage and helped position the company positively in the eyes of the public. In fact, it invoked some sympathy at a time when lawyers were lining up class-action suits against Maple Leaf. To reassure the public and to inform the public of the actions the company was taking, Maple Leaf ran full-page newspaper ads in all major daily newspapers in Canada.

Much is at stake if a company is less than forthcoming. Michael Dunne, a marketing professor at U of T, commends Maple Leaf for its proactive approach. He says, "They were very proactive about it, unusually so, because most companies that go through crises of this nature tend to hide. Maple Leaf is protecting the brand, and it's the brand that matters in the long term for Maple Leaf. Without the brand they don't have anything. McCain's response showed a business savvy that recognized the danger of waiting too long to respond to the crisis."

Maple Leaf suffered a serious blow in this situation. Sales of Maple Leaf products declined by 35 percent following the recall, and the profits of the meat division were wiped out. The recall alone cost the company about $30 million. The company's stock price dropped to $6.15 from a high of $15.00. McCain also decided to quickly settle the class-action lawsuits by agreeing to pay $27 million. McCain said settling the lawsuit was part of understanding that "you can't accept accountability without accepting a consequence."

To summarize, hiding from the public doesn't work. The best approach for handling a crisis is to clearly and quickly communicate to the public an action plan that will reassure the public that all that can be done is being done. Having the CEO, who is the face of the organization, deliver the message is an effective strategy to employ.

Adapted from Kristine Owram, "A real example of how to do it right," *The Kingston Whig-Standard*, January 3, 2009, p. 24; Hollie Shaw, "On road to recovery," *National Post*, September 5, 2008, p. FP15; and "Maple Leaf brand should rebound in months: Experts," *Marketing Daily*, August 27, 2008, www.marketingmag.ca.

Situations like these clearly show how important it is for organizations to be prepared; having a plan in place to meet disaster head on makes more sense than simply reacting to an unforeseen circumstance. Senior executives must be ready to act instantly and demonstrate they are in control of the situation. All messages sent to the public must be credible and based on fact from the outset. Company executives must be ready to meet the demand of a more sophisticated and more demanding consumer audience, or suffer the consequences of its wrath. Some tips for handling a crisis situation appear in Figure 9.3.

An organization never knows when it will be caught off guard. Circumstances can arise quickly and get out of control if an organization is not prepared. Here are some tips for handling a crisis situation properly.

1. Take responsibility. If your name is on the problem you have to take responsibility for it. This is different from accepting blame. The public respects an organization that accepts responsibility.

2. Respond quickly and communicate directly and sincerely. Show the public you are going to resolve the problem.

3. Embrace the three fundamentals of good crisis communication:
   - Communicate very clearly what has gone wrong.
   - Communicate what you are doing about it.
   - Describe the steps you are taking to ensure it doesn't happen again.

4. Have access to a former journalist who knows how to deal with the media (their knowledge of what to expect when the media calls is essential).

5. Offer an apology if an apology is warranted. If the public is satisfied with your efforts in rectifying the problem, they will forgive and move on.

FIGURE
9.3

Tips for Handling a Crisis Situation

Adapted from David Menzies, "Silence ain't golden: Media crisis dos and don'ts," *Marketing*, August 1/8, 2005, p. 18.

PRODUCT PUBLICITY

publicity
News about an organization, product, service, or person that appears in the media.

Publicity is news about an organization, product, service, or person that appears in the media. There is often a tendency for people to confuse publicity and public relations, thinking they are one and the same. Publicity is but one aspect of many public relations activities. Essentially, publicity is something that a company and the media deem to be newsworthy.

Here's an example to demonstrate how publicity works. Perrier implemented a publicity campaign when it launched its new one-litre plastic bottle. Objectives of the campaign were awareness and trial of the new product in key markets. Perrier used a celebrity in the form of Ted Allen, star of *Queer Eye for the Straight Guy*, to promote the bottle. Recognizing that plastic isn't exactly good news to some people, the PR agency focused the message on new situations where the product could be consumed—in parks and at swimming pools. New recipes, summer entertaining tips, and a few planned events provided a timely news hook to emphasize the lightweight unbreakable bottle. The campaign garnered 35 broadcast interviews, more than 100 newspaper articles, and a 400 percent increase in website hits. Not bad for a plastic bottle![3]

One of the major opportunities for a product or company to generate positive publicity is during a new product launch. Nike, for example, benefited greatly from a seemingly impossible shot by Tiger Woods during the 2005 Masters. With an incredible chip shot, Tiger's ball rolled down the green toward the sixteenth hole only to pause at the lip for about two seconds—the Nike logo in clear view. As luck would have it, it was the new One Platinum ball that Nike was just about to launch on the market. Nike redesigned the launch campaign around this now very famous shot—one of the best ever in golf history! The live shot and subsequent replays on CBS and other stations were estimated to be worth $1 million in free advertising exposure at the time.[4]

The Perrier and Nike examples seem to indicate that a combination of public relations and other means of communications work more effectively than any one activity working exclusively on its own. When integrated, the impact on the customer is greater. Perhaps the current reality of advertising clutter enhances the opportunity for public relations to break through by placing effective messages in newspapers, on news broadcasts or shows, and on websites.

PRODUCT PLACEMENT, BRANDED CONTENT, AND PRODUCT SEEDING

product placement
The visible placement of brand name products in television shows, movies, radio, video games, and other programming.

Product placement refers to the visible placement of branded merchandise in television shows, video games, films, or other programming. With television viewers paying less attention to 30-second commercials, networks and advertisers are fighting back and are relying more on product placements to deliver brand messages.

Ironically, product placement was a popular strategy in the early days of television, as several cigarette companies had their brands included in shows. The theory behind placement is simple: a product featured in a TV show or movie, as opposed to a 30-second spot, will have more credibility with viewers and have a better chance of being noticed and remembered. To illustrate, an episode of *Law & Order Criminal Intent* (2008) could have been titled "Ode to a Range Rover." The plot, which involved a carjacking of a Rover, included seven mentions of the vehicle. In one scene detective Robert Goren (played by Vincent D'Onofrio) remarks, "Oh, nice car" as the camera pans the interior. It took 40 seconds for the detectives to search the vehicle—great exposure for the Land Rover![5]

An unplanned product placement benefited Bank of Montreal (BMO). The bank discovered that Toronto Football Club's Maurice Edu was named one of the three cover athletes and spokespersons for EA Sports' *FIFA Soccer 09* (a video game), one of the most popular soccer games in the world. A photograph on the cover of the video game shows Edu wearing his BMO-branded jersey. In the bank's words, "Having your logo on the box of one of the world's most popular soccer video games? Priceless."[6]

Product placement is a growing form of marketing communications. In the United States alone spending on product placement reached $2.4 billion (2007). About 70 percent or $1.7 billion was spent on television placements. A growth of 20 percent was forecast for 2008. This style of communications is driven by cross-promotional activities linking movie and television placements to ad spots, websites, point-of-purchase displays, and virtual embedding.[7] A box of Club Crackers was shown with some cheese on an episode of *Yes, Dear*, but the box did not really exist. Technology that uses computer graphics and digital editing can place products like soft drinks and potato chips right in the show.

Branded content takes product placement a step further by weaving the name of the brand right into the storyline of a show, movie, or video game. Volkswagen's Touareg 2 model was neatly integrated into Matt Damon's action movie *The Bourne Ultimatum*. What seemed like an indestructible Touareg was seen chasing Bourne in another vehicle. From Volkswagen's perspective, the alignment of the Touareg and the movie was a way to highlight the new vehicle's safety and performance features. According to Kurt Schneider, general manager of creative content at Volkswagen of America, "We wanted to find a way to connect Touareg with a highly visible property to communicate what's new. *Bourne Ultimatum* was a perfect opportunity and the producers wanted the car for the chase scene."[8]

Toyota Yaris launched a brand-supported video game free for downloading on the Xbox Live Arcade service. The game puts players behind the wheel of a customizable Toyota Yaris to complete an obstacle course and destroy enemies with an arsenal of weapons. It is the first Xbox game created by an advertiser to be distributed over Xbox Live. Like many other companies, Toyota is increasingly creating its own content, such as video games, rather than relying on advertising during commercial breaks.[9]

Product seeding is an activity that involves giving a product free to a group of trendsetters who in turn influence others to become aware of the product and, one hopes, purchase the product. The trendsetters or influencers are people that marketers use to pass on product information. These people use technology and their own social networks to spread their opinions about products. Marketers, therefore, can take advantage of their knowledge and their access to consumers—a concept referred to as **word-of-mouth marketing**.

The fact that the product is in the hands of a trendsetter helps create buzz for the brand. For this reason, product seeding is often referred to as **buzz marketing**, though buzz marketing can mean a host of other things as well. Imagine the buzz that was created for the new Audi R8 sports car when film stars such as George Clooney and Sean Penn used the vehicle exclusively when driving around Toronto during the Toronto International Film Festival (2007). "The timing of the event was perfect as it just preceded the advertising launch of the vehicle." Introducing the $140 000 vehicle with a star of Clooney's or Penn's magnitude inside was a way to show the world in which Audi travels.[10]

Product seeding offers several advantages. First, it is a low-cost strategy that is nowhere near the cost of an advertising campaign. Second, it can reach a narrowly defined target. There is a potential disadvantage as well. If the product does not meet expectations, influencers will inform other consumers of such a fact—word-of-mouth can backfire!

branded content (product integration)
The integration of brand name goods and services into the script (storyline) of a television show or movie. The brand name is clearly mentioned and sometimes discussed.

product seeding (buzz marketing)
Giving a product free to a group of trendsetters who promote the product to others by word-of-mouth.

word-of-mouth marketing
The transfer of a product message by people (often using technology) to other people.

Product placement, branded content, and product seeding have expanded opportunities for integration with other forms of marketing communications, particularly advertising campaigns and sales promotions.

COMMUNITY RELATIONS AND PUBLIC AFFAIRS

Companies today are operating in an environment where social responsibility is very important. Consequently, they place much higher value on programs that foster a good public image in the communities where they operate. Sponsoring community events, local groups, and sports teams is part of being a good corporate citizen. The effect of such an investment on sales is indirect and long term in nature. Very often, being part of the fabric of a community takes precedence over sales. Leaders of companies that place a high value on public relations will tell you that the public has to "like you before they will buy you." Tim Hortons is a good example of a community-minded company. It supplies sports jerseys to local hockey and soccer teams through its Timbits Sports program, offers free ice skating in local communities during the Christmas break, and sends thousands of needy children to camps each summer through the Tim Horton Children's Foundation.

public affairs
Strategies to deal with governments and to communicate with governments.

lobbying
Activities and practices designed to influence policy decisions that will affect an organization or all organizations in a particular industry.

Public affairs involve strategies to deal with governments and to communicate with governments. **Lobbying** involves activities and practices designed to influence policy decisions that will affect an organization or all organizations within a particular industry. Typically, a company or an organization wants government policy to conform to what's best for business.

Independently funded organizations like Greenpeace actively lobby governments to ensure industry maintains environmental standards. Recently, Greenpeace has been active in trying to ensure that Fortune 500 companies support the Kyoto Protocol (an issue dealing with the long-term effects of climate change largely caused by industry practices). Many leading companies, including oil exploration companies and automobile manufacturers, do not support the protocol and lobby the government from a different angle. The lobbying and counter-lobbying help shape national government policy on such issues. When making policy decisions, governments must balance economic well-being with social and environmental well-being, and that explains the conflict between government, business, and special interest groups.

FUNDRAISING

In the not-for-profit sector, public relations play a key role in fundraising. National organizations such as the Canadian Cancer Society, the Canadian Heart and Stroke Foundation, and the United Way face huge financial challenges each year. For these and similar organizations, public relations help educate the public about how funds are used. The message is designed to predispose people to give, to solicit commitment, and to make people feel good about giving. The overall goal of such campaigns is to create a positive image and secure support by sending a message that clearly states what the organization is all about. Such campaigns require an integrated communications plan and employ a variety of techniques to deliver the message. In addition to public relations communications, media strategies include direct mail, telemarketing, print advertising (outdoor, newspapers, and magazines), and websites (see Figure 9.4).

Public Relations Planning

As a component of the integrated marketing communications mix, public relations plans are designed to fit directly with the needs of the organization's marketing objectives. They

> **FIGURE 9.4**   A Public Relations Advertisement Encouraging the Public to Support an Important Social Cause

I believe
in possibility.

Please give to United Way's Community Fund

www.unitedwayhalifax.ca

United Way®

can be active (help support a brand or company positively) or reactive (help out in a crisis situation). Regardless of the situation, as already stated, a plan must be in place.

As with advertising, a good public relations plan can help build an image and assist in developing relationships with customers. Furthermore, a well-timed public relations plan can play a key role in the launch of a new product, especially in times when budget resources are scarce. Advertising is a very expensive endeavour; public relations are much more economical. In companies searching for greater effectiveness at lower cost, public relations look like a better option than advertising, or, at the very least, the two disciplines must work effectively together to achieve objectives efficiently.

Based on the discussion presented so far in this chapter, it is very apparent that the planning of public relations communications is best left to specialists. It is not an area of expertise in most organizations, though many have a senior-ranking officer assigned the responsibility. Typically, the in-house public relations specialist is a liaison with outside agencies that prepare and implement public relations plans. If there is an in-house public relations department, its responsibilities might focus on public affairs and community relations. For the preparation and implementation of corporate and product public relations plans, there is a tendency to hire an organization that specializes in these areas. Hill and Knowlton and NATIONAL Public Relations are examples of leading public relations agencies in Canada. The specialist is briefed by the organization on its needs and expectations. Then, the specialist assesses the information and prepares a strategic plan that will meet the client's objectives. Figure 9.5 illustrates the public relations planning process. Let's discuss each stage of the planning process in more detail.

FIGURE 9.5   The Public Relations Planning Process

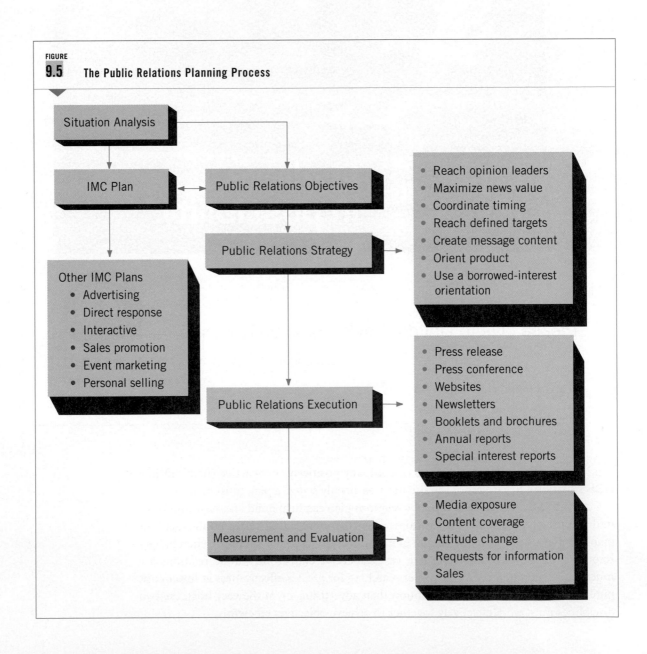

PUBLIC RELATIONS OBJECTIVES

Public relations objectives typically involve creating awareness, shaping attitudes, and altering behaviour. As marketing campaigns become more integrated and seamless, the ability both to quantify and to measure objectives becomes more difficult. On the surface, public relations objectives are very similar to advertising objectives. Therefore, to try to distinguish between the two is difficult. Increased awareness and predisposition to buy are influenced by numerous factors well beyond the scope of public relations, so trying to evaluate public relations in terms of sales and increased market share is next to impossible.

What can be measured, however, is the level of publicity generated by a public relations plan. Typically, the goal of public relations is to achieve media exposure, so quantifiable objectives can be established in this area. Publicity objectives should consider the media through which the message will be communicated and the target audience reached by the media. Surprisingly, even very targeted public relations plans can catch the attention of the national media, because good stories, no matter where they come from, are good stories on national news broadcasts, in national newspapers, and in general interest magazines.

Media exposure can be measured in terms of *gross impressions*, the number of times an item was potentially seen. If a news story appears in a large-circulation newspaper, what is the circulation or readership (circulation multiplied by the readers per copy) of that newspaper? An objective can be stated in terms of impressions. For example, the objective may be to achieve 10 million gross impressions nationally in Canadian daily newspapers.

Alternatively, publicity can be measured for its equivalent advertising value. For example, when a horse named Big Brown won the Kentucky Derby, UPS, the horse's sponsor, reaped an estimated $4 million in free publicity. Fortuitously for UPS, Big Brown was named after the shipping company by its original owner, a New York trucking agent. The sponsorship arrangement was struck just weeks before the Derby.[11]

Another objective could entail matching the message with the appropriate medium. To illustrate, assume you are doing a campaign for TaylorMade golf equipment (drivers, fairway woods, irons, golf balls, and shoes). The objective would be to reach golfers in a medium they refer to frequently to communicate to them the latest and greatest technology that has been built into your products. Some options include The Golf Channel and *Golf Digest* as well as a host of other golf-related publications and websites. Reaching your audience in highly targeted media offers several benefits: the message will be read or seen by influencers who will create a word-of-mouth network, and the message could influence the editorial agenda of the publication, station, or website. The media are constantly looking for new and innovative ideas to promote. If they don't find you, you have to find them. Figure 9.6 is an example of a press release announcing a new line of outerwear that offers different kinds of protection for golfers. Golf magazines and a variety of golf shows on The Golf Channel report on stories like this.

PUBLIC RELATIONS STRATEGY

Every form of marketing communications has its strengths and weaknesses. With public relations, the company cannot control the media or dictate the manner in which the message is communicated. Getting past the media gatekeepers is the first challenge; the second challenge is ensuring the message is communicated with reasonable accuracy. On the positive side, public relations messages provide enhanced credibility. When the consumer reads a story in a newspaper or hears and sees something positive on a news broadcast about a product or company, it is much more authentic than an advertisement.

Source: Courtesy of TaylorMade-adidas a Golf.

**FIGURE
9.6**

**A Press Release that
Presents a New Product
Favourably to the Media**

THE BEST PERFORMANCE GOLF BRAND IN THE WORLD

To download high-resolution visuals,
please go to http://www.tmag.com/media
(please use the password provided to you by the TMaG PR department.)

adidas Golf Announces New Outerwear Line

CARLSBAD, Calif. (January 13, 2006) - TaylorMade-adidas
Golf announces a new range of outerwear to be introduced
at the 2006 PGA Merchandise Show.

The range features garments that fall into five different
levels of protection categories. Categories include
ClimaProof® Wind in three levels, ClimaProof Rain,
ClimaProof Storm, ClimaWarm®, and ClimaCompression,
available in a lightweight and thermal version. Just as
ClimaCool® is designed to keep a player comfortable in
the heat, adidas outerwear is designed to protect the
golfer from the elements, whether it is a light wind or
driving rain, keeping the golfer dry and warm.

Integrating leading technologies in fabrications, laminates,
and constructions allows adidas to produce outerwear
garments that are comfortable, lightweight, and extremely
quiet. In ClimaProof Wind, ClimaWarm, and ClimaProof
Storm, adidas introduces both two and four way stretch
applications for additional comfort.

The new outerwear range can be seen at adidas Golf's
display at booth location #14037 within the apparel section
of the Orange County Convention Center during the PGA
Merchandise Show January 26-29, 2006. Also on display
will be the full-line of adidas footwear and apparel. Daily
fashion shows will also present the opportunity to explore
the new range of outerwear.

The full line of outerwear by adidas will be available at retail starting May 15, 2006.

About Taylor Made Golf Company, Inc. dba TaylorMade-adidas Golf Company
TaylorMade Golf has led the golf industry's technological evolution since being founded in 1979. adidas
Golf footwear and apparel is the choice of hundreds of professional golfers around the world. Consumers
can find more information on TaylorMade-adidas Golf at (800) 888-CLUB or www.tmag.com,
www.taylormadegolf.com, www.adidasgolf.com, www.maxfli.com or www.rossaputters.com.

For more information contact:
TaylorMade-adidas Golf
John Steinbach
Tel: 760.918.6330
eMail: john.steinbach@tmag.com

5545 fermi court   carlsbad   california   92008
www.taylormadegolf.com

phone 760.918.6000   fax 760.918.6014
www.adidasgolf.com

---

blog
A frequent, chronological publication of
personal thoughts at a website.

blogging
The act of posting new information and
thoughts on a blog.

Corporate blogging has put some message control back into the hands of the organization. A **blog** is a website where journal entries are posted on a regular basis and displayed in reverse chronological order. Adding information to a blog is called **blogging**. Consumers and consumer groups have developed blogs that often defame an organization—a situation an organization has little control over. Consequently, organizations are developing their own blogs to distribute favourable information. In this role it is becoming an important communications tool. Read the discussion about social media in the "Public Relations Execution" section of this chapter for more information about blogs.

The role of public relations is determined in advance and is outlined in the marketing communications plan. Typically, that role is to reach influential individuals such as industry analysts, key media representatives, and early adopters of products (refer back to the discussion about product seeding).

The strategic role of public relations should be examined based on how best to

- Reach the opinion leaders, including professionals, industry analysts, trade audiences, and media, well in advance of the public.

- Maximize the news value of new product introductions, new advertising campaigns, and event sponsorships. Messages must be written creatively and visuals must grab attention.

- Time public relations events to reinforce advertising and promotion campaigns and to maintain visibility between campaigns.

- Reach markets that are defined by demographics, psychographics, or geographic locations that might not be targeted by advertising.[12]

A public relations strategy allows an organization to tell a longer story about itself and its products. Strategy deals more with informing and educating rather than motivating someone to buy something. Therefore, when claims are made about a product, proper substantiation should be provided. Unlike advertising, where time and space are often restricted, public relations communications can spend additional time expanding on something of importance. News editors might edit the length of the story, but they will strive to maintain the credibility of the message.

A company may employ a **borrowed-interest strategy** to generate publicity. A borrowed-interest strategy will typically promote a newsworthy marketing activity that is related to the product. For example, participation in and sponsorship of a community event or national event is news, as is the launch of a national sales promotion offer designed to stimulate sales. An Olympic sponsorship involving significant sums of money is certainly a newsworthy item for a company like McDonald's. It wants Canadians to be aware of its involvement as a lead sponsor of the Vancouver 2010 Olympics. As stated in a McDonald's press release, "'Nothing unites this country in a more profound way than seeing our best and brightest shine on the world stage,' said John Betts, President, McDonald's Restaurants of Canada. 'McDonald's embodies many of the same values as the Olympic Games with our dedication to excellence and passion for bringing people together.'"[13]

McDonald's is very active in sales promotion activities as well. In 2009 the company announced by press release a two-week free coffee promotion to get Canadians acquainted with the quality of its premium coffee. Figure 9.7 is the press release that announced the McDonald's promotion and Figure 9.8 includes an example of a story that ran in The Globe and Mail as a result of the release.

PUBLIC RELATIONS EXECUTION

The tools available to execute public relations programs are diverse. Some are used routinely to communicate newsworthy information and some are brought out periodically or only on special occasions. This section examines some of the more routinely used media tools.

PRESS RELEASE   A **press release** is a document containing all the essential elements of the story (who, what, when, where, and why). Editors make very quick decisions on what to use and what to discard, so the release must grab their attention quickly. Copies of the release are delivered to a list of preferred editors, for example those with whom an organization has a good relationship. Alternatively, the release could be distributed to a national wire service as well as posted on the company's website. Note that contact information is provided should the media require any additional information. Refer to Figures 9.6 and 9.7 for examples of a press release.

borrowed-interest strategy
A plan to promote a marketing activity that is related to a product.

press release
A document prepared by an organization containing public relations information that is sent to the media for publication or broadcast.

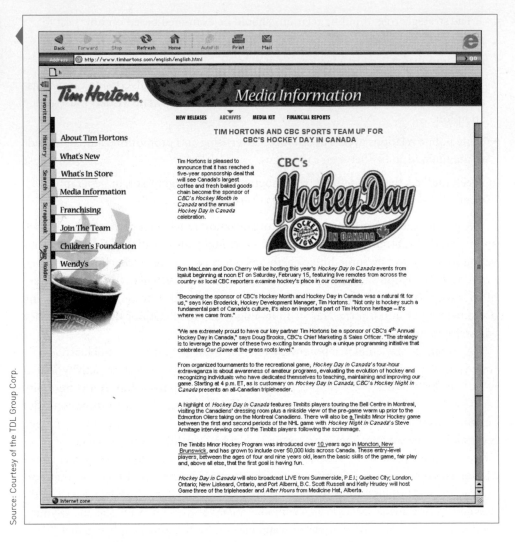

Source: Courtesy of the TDL Group Corp.

FIGURE 9.7

A Press Release Using a Borrowed-Interest Strategy to Promote a Company

press conference
A meeting called by an organization to present information to representatives of the media.

PRESS CONFERENCE A **press conference** is a meeting of news reporters invited to witness the release of important information about a company or product. Because a conference is time consuming for the media representatives, it is usually reserved for only the most important announcements. A crisis, for example, is usually handled by an initial press conference (see the IMC Highlight about Maple Leaf Foods that appeared earlier in the chapter). When a professional sports team is about to announce a new star player entering the fold, a press conference is very common. A conference allows the media to interact by asking questions, which results in the transfer of additional and perhaps more meaningful information for the story they will publish or broadcast.

media kit
A package of relevant information associated with a product or organization that is distributed at a press conference.

A media kit is usually distributed at a press conference. A **media kit** can include a schedule of conference events, a list of company participants including biographical information, a press release, historical fact sheets if applicable to the situation, a backgrounder that tells something about the character of the organization and the nature of what it does, a page of stand-alone facts about the company, sample products, photographs, copies of speeches, DVD material, contact information, and any other relevant information. Depending on need, any combination of these materials can be included. The key to developing a good media kit is to evaluate who will use it and what that person is likely to need. For example, a media kit for a special event or new sales

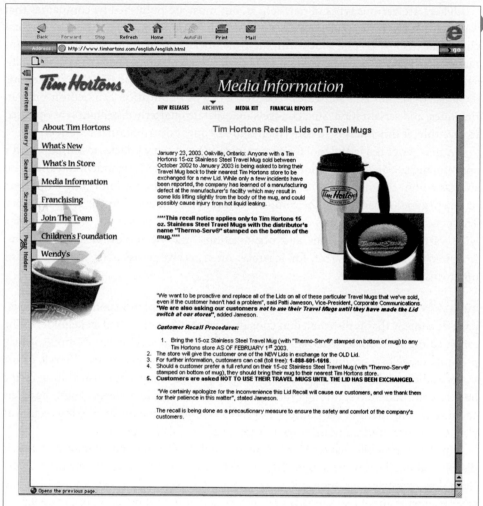

Source: Courtesy of the TDL Group Corp.

FIGURE
9.8

The Essential Elements of a Good Press Release: Who, What, When, and Where

promotion activity would be very different in tone, style, and content from one needed for a crisis situation.

WEBSITES Since the primary purpose of a website is to communicate information about a company or brand, it can be a very useful public relations tool. Visitors to a website quickly form an impression about the company based on the experience they have at the site. Therefore, the site must download quickly and be easy to navigate. Providing some kind of entertainment or interactive activity also enhances the visit. Unlike other media, the website can be updated easily and quickly, so the very latest news about a company and its products can be made available for public consumption. In large companies it is now common to have dedicated pages for specific brands. All press releases about the company and its brands are also posted at the company website.

NEWSLETTERS The **newsletter** is a very common public relations tool. By nature, it is a concise reporting of the news related to the organization and is very clear and to the point. A successful newsletter conveys information in a unique way so that the people who receive it pay attention to it. Newsletters are distributed regularly to their intended audience, so they are an efficient method of conveying information.

newsletter
A document sent to a predetermined audience that contains news about an organization (e.g., a newsletter sent to alumni of a school or to all employees of an organization).

There are various types of newsletters, but most are published by companies that want to communicate regularly with employees and customers, by recreation and sports clubs that wish to keep in touch with their members, and by professional associations that regularly convey information to members who are geographically dispersed. Typically, a newsletter is distributed by internal or external mail or email, and relies on an accurate database of names and addresses. The frequency of publication is based on budget, timelines, and serialization. Small budgets may dictate quarterly distribution as opposed to monthly; if timeliness is an issue, then more frequent distribution is required.

A newsletter is a useful tool for communicating company policies to employees, for announcing social and recreational events, and for acknowledging individual and team success within the organization. As well, a newsletter is useful for informing employees of news (good or bad) about the company before it is announced to the general public. The newsletter often assumes this role. *Special interest newsletters* are distributed by a wide variety of lifestyle clubs and organizations, and by professional associations. Investors in the stock market, for instance, often receive newsletters from a bank or other financial institution.

booklet (brochure)
A multiple-page document distributed to consumers and other interested stakeholders.

BOOKLETS AND BROCHURES A **booklet** or **brochure** is a brand-sponsored, multiple-page document that is distributed to consumers and other interested stakeholders. The information in a booklet is usually related to a product or service. For example, it may promote usage of a product in a variety of ways, or it may appeal to the lifestyle of the target audience it is intended for. Campbell's Soup is well-known for distributing recipe booklets in food stores, through direct mail, and through its website. These booklets encourage consumers to use Campbell's products more frequently in cooking recipes as well as in other nontraditional ways. Greater usage equals greater sales.

In the automobile market Mazda Canada publishes a semi-annual magazine that is distributed to all car owners in its database. The publication, appropriately titled *Zoom Zoom*, has a lifestyle orientation and includes general interest articles along with articles and advertisements about the company's newest models. See the illustration in Figure 9.9.

annual report
A document published annually by an organization primarily to provide current and prospective investors and stakeholders with financial data and a description of the company's operations.

ANNUAL REPORTS AND SPECIAL INTEREST REPORTS The primary purpose of an **annual report** is to provide current and prospective investors and stakeholders with financial data and a description of an organization's operations. But it can do much more to promote the company. In terms of public relations, it is a good opportunity for the organization to tell the public where it stands on social and environmental issues, for example. In fact, the annual report is often seen by audiences beyond the primary target—such as the media, community leaders, and employees. Word can spread fast about what a company stands for.

Special interest reports can be integrated into an annual report or can be stand-alone documents. For companies that want to portray to the public that there is more to business than a healthy bottom line, a special interest report is an ideal vehicle to get a different message out. Special interest reports are designed to appeal to a very selective audience—usually opinion leaders—and focus on issues that affect the organization and the target audience. To illustrate, RBC Financial Group issues a Corporate Responsibility Report each year. The report documents the social responsibility practices of the company and goes a long way in building trust with employees, customers, and clients. The report focuses on issues such as integrity in business, commitment to clients and employees, commitment to diversity, commitment to the environment, and policies regarding governance, compliance, and ethics (see Figure 9.10). How RBC supports local communities all across Canada is also profiled in the publication. The latest report shows RBC contributing

Source: Courtesy of the Marketing Department at Mazda Canada Inc.

FIGURE 9.9

Mazda distributes a magazine to current customers to keep them informed about new car models

$99 million to community causes worldwide through donations and sponsorship of community events and national organizations.[14]

SOCIAL MEDIA If you have read a blog, joined an online discussion group, sent a tweet via Twitter, or uploaded a photo to Flickr, you have participated in social media. **Social media** describes the online tools that people use to share content, insights, experiences, perspectives, and various media, thus facilitating conversations and interaction online between groups of people. These tools include blogs, podcasts, bookmarks, wikis, and vlogs (video blogs).[15] The emergence of social media has shifted control of the message from the organization to the consumer—the consumer can read the message, formulate an opinion on it, and communicate that opinion to others. Social media have changed communication from monologue (one to many) to dialogue (many to many).

social media
Online tools that people use to share content, insights, experiences, and various media, thus facilitating conversations and interaction online between groups of people.

Source: Courtesy of Royal Bank of Canada.

FIGURE 9.10

RBC Financial Group publishes a corporate responsibility report to document its contribution to communities

Social media have had a significant impact on the way many industries do business, and the impact on PR practitioners has been nothing short of extreme. Furthering the evolution is a shift in the way people relate to news. They don't just read it. They want to interact with it and influence opinions. That explains why many of the top websites are social media sites such as YouTube, Facebook, and Twitter.

As stated earlier, a blog is a frequent, chronological publication of personal thoughts at a website. Blogs are the property and works of everyday people who like to rant about things they don't like, and very often they will challenge the integrity of an organization in their blog. While an organization cannot control this situation, it must live with the reality that negative things are being said about it.

The growing popularity of blogs must be viewed positively from both a public relations and corporate communications perspective. A corporate blog can be an effective tool to fight back or be a proactive way to present information about a company and its brands. The popularity of blogs has changed the nature of public relations. Today, consumer-generated content contained in a blog has just as much weight as information presented by corporations and traditional media outlets. "Consumers are in control, and consumers are the media. It's a paradigm shift that's going to change PR forever."[16]

Blogs written by private individuals can harm an organization. To demonstrate, Engadget, a well-respected tech blog, published reports that Apple's launch of the iPhone and Leopard operating system in 2007 would be delayed. Apple's stock price took an immediate dive, dropping some $4 billion before it was discovered that the information came from a fake leaked memo. Apple was not amused, even though its stock value recovered by the end of the day.[17] This incident clearly demonstrates the immediacy and influence of online communications! It also demonstrates that bloggers may not check their sources as thoroughly as do writers and editors in traditional media outlets.

Blogs enable companies to speak directly to consumers, and as a result are pushing the news media out of their central role in public relations. Richard Edelman, president and CEO of Edelman Public Relations Worldwide, believes, "PR practitioners must become more like journalists and rely less on the media to get the message out. If we are putting information online and people are reading it and accepting it as truth, then we should have a journalist-level quality as our objective."[18] Instead of persuading the media to report a story, practitioners must speak directly to the public, or try to influence bloggers to post messages on their behalf. See Figure 9.11 for an illustration of how General Motors uses blogs.

Online video sharing sites are one of the fastest-growing media sectors, with sites such as YouTube attracting millions of visitors daily. Therefore, an organization must evaluate the benefits of including web-style videos in the communications mix. A web video is an enticing proposition since production and distribution costs are much lower than the costs of creating traditional broadcast material. For smaller businesses that compete with larger businesses, online video helps level the playing field.

Press releases for traditional media were discussed earlier. Social media provide an opportunity to communicate more detailed information. A social media news release can include a variety of social media elements such as photos and video, links to blogs, digital tags, and RSS feeds. These opportunities were discussed in Chapter 7, Planning for Online and Interactive Communications.

In summary, social media offer new and innovative ways to help a business achieve its marketing communications objectives. The techniques described above are much less expensive than traditional advertising. When using social media, an organization must consider that some control of the message may be lost. That loss can be weighed against additional exposure and engagement opportunities with potential customers.

TIMELINE AND BUDGET

A timeline is essential so that all activities are carefully coordinated with other marketing communications activities. In the case of a new product launch, for example, public relations programs can be put in place well before the product is actually available. One strategy is to start the public relations communications in a small way, slowly building credibility, and proceed with a slow rollout. This strategy creates demand in such a manner that the public is eager to buy the product once it is launched.

Public relations programs cost much less than advertising programs, but they are nonetheless costs that must be accounted for. If a company employs corporate

Source: Courtesy of General Motors.

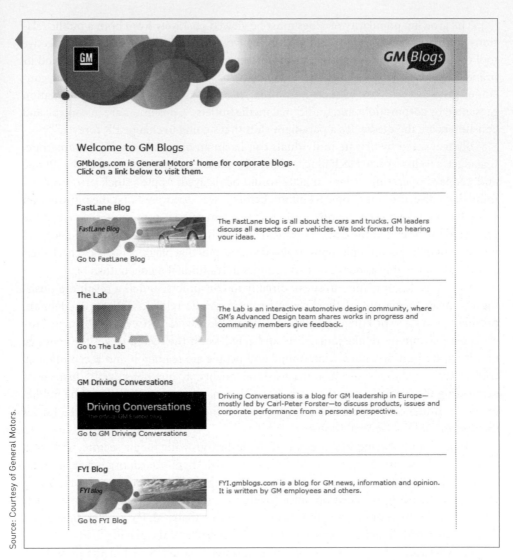

FIGURE 9.11

Companies are employing corporate blogs to communicate relevant information about their brands

advertising, the costs are similar to brand advertising programs. There are costs associated with producing print and broadcast materials and with buying time in the broadcast media, space in the print media, and in developing and maintaining websites and blogs. A company might also employ newsletters, brochures, annual reports, and media kits, and the costs of producing these materials must also be included in the public relations budget.

MEASUREMENT AND EVALUATION

To justify a financial investment in any form of marketing communications, certain expectations and results must be delivered. There must be some kind of financial return, increase in awareness, or change in behaviour. Walter K. Lindenmann, senior vice-president and director of research at Ketchum Public Relations, has identified levels for measuring public relations effectiveness: outputs, outgrowths, and outcomes.

- *Outputs* measure the transmission, that is, the amount of exposure in the media, the number of placements and audience impressions, and the likelihood of reaching the target audience.

- *Outgrowths* measure message reception by the target audience. Did the target pay attention to, understand, and retain the message?

- *Outcomes* measure attitude and behavioural change. Was there a change in attitude and did the recipient do something as a result of the message?[19]

Output measures are the most common means of evaluating public relations effectiveness. There are companies that specialize in tracking everything that is written and broadcast about a company and its brands. For example, if an article appears in the front section of the *Toronto Star*, a newspaper with a weekday circulation of more than 400 000, how many impressions will be made? If there are 2.5 readers for every newspaper, the potential number of impressions is 1 million (400 000 x 2.5). If a similar story appears in other newspapers, the total impressions accumulate.

It is also possible to attach an *equivalent advertising value* to such an article. The tracking firm examines the size of the article, the location in the publication, the number of brand mentions, and so on, and through the magic of mathematical calculations, determines the value in terms of advertising. While this may not be exact science, it does appease senior executives who are looking for some kind of return on their investment. While there is no real agreement on such matters, public relations experts believe that a good article about a product is worth anywhere from three times to ten times as much as an equivalent sized ad in the same publication.

Measuring for outgrowths involves determining if the target audience received and understood the message. Collecting this information involves a combination of qualitative and quantitative research methodologies, so it is much more costly. Since creating awareness is the primary objective of most public relations campaigns, many firms do not proceed with research in this area.

Marketing research is required to measure for outcomes such as a shift in behaviour. As with research conducted for any other marketing activity, this form of evaluation involves pre-campaign and post-campaign research. The initial research firmly establishes a benchmark. For example, the research identifies how consumers perceive and use a product or company before being exposed to the public relations message. The initial research group is then divided into a test group and a control group. The test group receives the public relations message and the control group does not. Post-campaign research determines the differences between the two groups in terms of what they know and if their attitudes have changed.

More detailed information about specific procedures for measuring and evaluating public relations activities is included in Chapter 12, Evaluating Marketing Communications Programs.

Public Relations as a Communications Medium

Senior executives today have a much better understanding of the role played by public relations in achieving their organization's marketing objectives. As a communications discipline, the status of public relations has been considerably elevated. The examples in this chapter show how public relations can play a key role in specific situations, and they will certainly continue to grow in terms of their contribution to marketing communications strategies and the achievement of an organization's objectives. Those responsible for corporate and brand communications should be aware of the basic benefits and drawbacks of public relations communications.

For some insight into some successful PR campaigns using some of the newer PR techniques, see the IMC Highlight: **Word-of-Mouth, Special Events, and Social Media Create Buzz for Brands.**

ADVANTAGES OF PUBLIC RELATIONS

If public relations are done properly, they can be a *credible source* of information. Unlike advertising, public relations messages are delivered by third parties who have no particular interest in the company or product. They are communicating information that they deem useful to their readers, listeners, viewers, and so on. Consumers reading or viewing such messages perceive those messages to be more objective than they do advertisements. If a company can win favourable press coverage, its message is more likely to be absorbed and believed.[20]

IMC HIGHLIGHT

Word-of-Mouth, Special Events, and Social Media Create Buzz for Brands

Senior marketing executives want results. They look for tangible benefits gained from their investment in any form of marketing communications. Public relations are no different. In planning a PR program, specific objectives are established; the campaign is implemented and then evaluated. Here are a few campaigns that really clicked using some of the newer PR techniques.

Procter & Gamble is one of North America's largest advertisers. When P&G launched Dawn Direct Foam, a new product that tackles the war on grease, there was lots of advertising support. Behind the scenes, however, the company experimented with something new—it employed an army of 450 000 mom "connectors" or "brand evangelists" who incited discussions with others about the brand. In test markets the moms did well as sales increased 50 percent, making it one of the most successful efforts in a quickly evolving sector of the communications industry: word-of-mouth advertising. Word-of-mouth is sometimes called buzz marketing or viral marketing.

How effective is word-of-mouth? "It totally outweighs all other forms of advertising and marketing in terms of trust," said Leo Kivijarv, VP of Research for PQ Media. A recent survey by Nielsen Media Research found that 78 percent of respondents viewed recommendations

from other consumers as trustworthy. That compares with 63 percent for newspaper ads and 4 percent for celebrity endorsements.

Toyota opted for an invitation-only special event to launch its 2010 Prius model. A select group of "green" motorists who had participated in some activities at the Prius microsite were invited to the Canadian International Auto Show in Toronto at 7:30 am on a Saturday to spend some up close and personal time with the new model—they were the first in Canada to explore the next-generation car. A complimentary breakfast was included. The participants mingled with Toyota engineers and hybrid experts, who answered questions about the technology. The invitation-only event was the first of its kind for Toyota Canada, and part of a new grassroots-style strategy led by online word-of-mouth buzz-generating efforts.

A&W jumped into social media with a campaign for its new sirloin Uncle Burger. The restaurant's "Ultimate Uncle Contest" invited customers to tell A&W why they have the best uncle at UncleBurger.ca. The site included a number of coupons for free Uncle Burgers and visitors could send their uncle an electronic "Uncle's Day" greeting card and print a coupon for a free Uncle Burger.

The objective of the promotion was to get people talking about the Uncle Burger, drive people to the website, and generate some excitement for the product. Soon after the launch, details and discussion of the offer were all over Twitter, Facebook, and other message boards. The site attracted 10 000 visitors in 48 hours and 2000 free burgers were claimed. By the end of the contest there were 41 000 entries.

Why social media when A&W targets baby boomers? According to David Waterfall, director of marketing, "We were looking at research showing increasing numbers of baby boomers involved with social media. It's not just teens that are texting and using Twitter." Tom Shepansky, the creator of the promotion said, "You want to be where people young or old will be going, either to get a deal or join a discussion. Put the deal out there and people will talk. Is it a good deal or not? Is it something worth eating? People will talk about the strangest things."

Adapted from Eve Lazarus, "A&W puts social media on marketing menu," *Marketing Daily*, April 13, 2009, www.marketingmag.ca, Garine Tcholakian, "Toyota Canada engineers WOM," *Media in Canada*, February 19, 2009, www.mediaincanada.com, Sinclair Stewart, "Hey did you hear about that great new toothpaste?" *The Globe and Mail*, November 20, 2007, p. B3.

Third-party endorsements by trusted media personalities can have a *positive impact on sales*. To illustrate, consider what happened when the CBS news program *60 Minutes* announced that drinking a moderate amount of wine each day could prevent heart attacks by lowering cholesterol. The effect was astonishing: red wine sales in the United States jumped 50 percent after the broadcast. Figure 9.12 illustrates how good public relations can increase sales.

Indirectly, public relations also play a role in developing sound *customer relationships*. Public relations campaigns offer a means to build rapport through ongoing dialogue with consumers and other stakeholders. Such a benefit is important, considering the rising costs of media advertising, the fragmentation of the media, and the clutter of commercial messages. A good public relations campaign can cut through the clutter faster and may encourage the desired attitude or behaviour change to occur more immediately.

DISADVANTAGES OF PUBLIC RELATIONS

One of the biggest drawbacks of public relations is the *absence of control* experienced by the sponsoring organization. Through press releases and press conferences, the company does its best to ensure that factual information is available and presented accurately to the public. In the process of communicating the information, however, the media might add their own opinions, which detract from the intent of the original message. Companies facing crisis situations often see stories in the media that misrepresent the company or mislead the public. In the case of blogs and other social media options, consumers act as publishers and control what is said about the product or company, be it good, bad, or indifferent.

A second disadvantage deals with the sheer *waste* of time, energy, and materials that go into a public relations campaign. This is not to say that the effort isn't worthwhile, but the challenge of catching the attention of editors (the media gatekeepers) is an onerous one. Enormous amounts of material flow into media newsrooms daily, so standing out in the crowd is part of the public relations challenge. Senior management must recognize the waste factor and be prepared to absorb the costs that go along with it. Finally, what is important to management may not be perceived as important by the media. End of story!

FIGURE
9.12

Successful public relations
campaigns have a positive
impact on sales

This public relations plan for Dunlop Tires demonstrates how a carefully planned public relations campaign can increase brand sales.

CLIENT

Goodyear Canada and its Dunlop Tire brand

AGENCY

Environics Communications, Toronto

PUBLIC RELATIONS OBJECTIVE

To increase consumer awareness for the Dunlop Tire brand and drive sales.

PUBLIC RELATIONS CAMPAIGN

The campaign theme revolved around the Dunlop name. Dunlop challenged people whose last name was Dunlop to change their name to Dunlop-Tire for a cash reward. It was promoted as the "Tired of Your Name Challenge."

The story received prominent coverage across Canada and the United States, including front-page stories, television features, and radio interviews.

MEASUREMENT AND EVALUATION

- 100% of media stories mentioned the name Dunlop Tire.
- Many stories were front-page or top stories reported on television news.
- The tone of all news coverage was positive and/or humorous.
- Forty-nine people named Dunlop inquired about changing their name.
- Four people legally changed their name to Dunlop-Tire.
- Sales increased 59 percent over two years in a market only growing by 3 percent.
- Canadian Tire (the largest distributor of tires) agreed to sell Dunlop tires, a decision attributed to the public relations support received by the brand.

Source: Adapted from Sara Minogue, "Proving value," *Strategy*, November 18, 2002, p. 18.

>> SUMMARY

Public relations are a form of communications directed at gaining public understanding and acceptance. They are used by organizations to change or influence attitudes and behaviour. Unlike advertising, which is a very costly means of communications, public relations go largely unpaid for. The organization presents information to the media in the hopes they will publish or broadcast it in a news story.

The primary roles of public relations are diverse. They constitute a useful channel for communicating corporate-oriented messages designed to build the organization's image. Public relations are also the most important form of communications when an organization finds itself in a crisis situation. In such times, an organization must be honest and forthright with the public. Public relations specialists help prepare organizations to handle crisis situations.

At the product level, public relations help generate positive publicity by distributing news releases and holding press conferences when there is newsworthy information to announce. As well, relatively new communications alternatives, such as product placement, branded content, product seeding, and social media opportunities, fall under the umbrella of public relations. Product placement and branded content are proving to be an effective alternative to regular television advertising, and product seeding offers a means of getting the product in the hands of trendsetters who influence the public's attitudes and behaviour through word-of-mouth marketing. Social media that include tools such as blogs, podcasts, wikis, and vlogs provide an opportunity for the public to engage and interact with an organization's message.

Public relations planning begins with a situation analysis. Usually, the client organization provides a brief containing all relevant background information to a public relations agency. Public relations are a form of communications that does require external expertise. The public relations firm establishes the goals and objectives, develops the communications strategy, selects the best execution techniques, and after receiving the client's approval, implements the plan.

The primary objectives of public relations programs tend to dwell on creating awareness, altering attitudes, and motivating a change in behaviour. The public relations strategy focuses on reaching opinion leaders, maximizing the news value of the story, and reinforcing other communications campaigns such as advertising, sales promotions, and event marketing activities. There are several techniques for getting a story into distribution. The most commonly used options include the press release, press conferences, websites, newsletters, booklets and brochures, and social media. Social media options include the use of blogs, postings on Facebook and Twitter, and video sharing websites such as YouTube.

Once the public relations plan is implemented, research is necessary to determine the effectiveness of the campaign. Output measurements are the most common evaluation technique. They measure message transmission—that is, the amount of exposure in the media, the number of placements and audience impressions, and the likelihood of the message reaching the intended target audience. If pre-campaign and post-campaign research is conducted (budget permitting), an organization can measure the impact of public relations messages in terms of influencing attitudes and altering behaviour.

Public relations communications offer several benefits: they help build credibility for a product or company with its various publics, and they help build brand awareness and interest and indirectly have an impact on brand sales. There are some drawbacks to public relations communications. For one, the organization has little control over the message that is delivered by the media. Also, a company often views the effort as wasteful as so little is actually reported by the media in comparison to the amount of information distributed to the media.

KEY TERMS

REVIEW QUESTIONS

1. What are the essential differences between media advertising and public relations communications?
2. Identify and briefly explain the role of public relations in the following areas:
   a) corporate communications
   b) reputation management
   c) product publicity
   d) product seeding
   e) community relations
3. What is the difference between product placement, branded content, and product seeding?
4. What is lobbying and why is it necessary for an organization to conduct such a practice?
5. What are the key elements of a public relations strategy?
6. What is a borrowed-interest public relations strategy? Provide an example of this strategy that isn't in the text.
7. What is a media kit and what role does it serve?
8. What are the roles of special interest newsletters and special interest reports that are distributed by companies, organizations, and associations?
9. Public relations effectiveness is measured based on outputs, outgrowths, and outcomes. Briefly explain each form of measurement.
10. What are the advantages and disadvantages of using public relations as a marketing communications medium? Briefly explain.

DISCUSSION AND APPLICATION QUESTIONS

1. Considering the nature of the business environment today, do you think that public relations will play a more significant role or less significant role in future marketing communications strategies? State your position and justify it based on your vision of the future business environment.

2. What is your opinion of the newer PR techniques such as product placement, product seeding, and social media communications? Will these techniques continue to grow in importance as PR tools? Review the IMC Highlight: **Word-of-Mouth, Special Events, and Social Media Create Buzz for Brands** for essential insights into a few of these techniques.

3. What role will social media play in future public relations practice? Will it change the very nature of the way an organization communicates with its publics? Conduct some secondary research on this issue and formulate an opinion on it.

4. Conduct some secondary research that involves an organization facing a crisis situation. How did it handle the situation from a public relations perspective? Were its strategies effective?

5. Conduct some secondary research that involves an organization using public relations strategies to launch a new product. How important was public relations in the marketing communications mix? What were the objectives of the public relations effort? Was the plan effective in achieving its goals?

6. Identify two different companies that compete with each other in the same industry or markets. Analyze the information they provide on their websites in terms of public relations value. Are these companies maximizing the potential of the web for communicating vital information to customers? Sample sites to visit may include Nike and Adidas, Coca-Cola and Pepsi-Cola, and Bell and Telus. Select other competitors if you wish.

7. Visit a company website of your choosing. Usually, there is a link to the press release section of the site. Review that company's five latest press releases. What subject matter did they deal with? Try to determine how the company uses public relations to its advantage.

ENDNOTES

1. "PR professionals gaining respect and big paycheques," *National Post*, March 28, 2007, p. WK7.

2. "Maple Leaf Expects Full Recovery in 12 Months," Canadian Press, *Marketing Daily*, October 30, 2008.

3. Public Relations Success Stories, "Delivering the message from a new bottle," Cone Public Relations, www.coneinc.com.

4. "Nike, Tiger on the ball," *Advertising Age*, April 18, 2005, p. 3.

5. "It's the future of television," *The Globe and Mail*, July 18, 2008, p. B5.

6. Patricia Best, "Unplanned publicity has BMO smiling," *The Globe and Mail*, August 14, 2008, p. B2.

7. Amy Johannes, "Global product placement to reach $7.6 billion by 2010: Report," *Promo Magazine*, www.promomagazine.com/paidplacementreport.

8. Karl Greenberg, "VW Touts Touareg via *Bourne Ultimatum*, Rally Racing," Media Post Publications, July 27, 2007, www.mediapost.com.

9. Jesse Kohl, "Toyota launches branded Yaris game on Xbox Live," *Media in Canada*, October 15, 2007, www.mediaincanada.com.

10. Terry Poulton, "If it's good enough for George Clooney . . . ," *Media in Canada*, September 7, 2007, www.mediaincanada.com.

11. Michael Bush, "Win or lose, UPS sees big payoff at Belmont," *Advertising Age*, May 26, 2008, p. 8.

12. Thomas L. Harris, *Value-Added Public Relations* (Chicago: NTP Publications, 1998), p. 243.

13. "McDonald's Canada Unveils Multifaceted Programs in Support of Vancouver 2010 Olympic Winter Games," press release, February 12, 2009, www.mcdonalds.ca/news.

14. "Create a Better Future," Royal Bank of Canada, 2008 Corporate Responsibility Review, p. 9.

15. Brian Solis, "The definition of social media," *WebProNews*, June 29, 2007, www.webpronews.com/blogtalk.

16. Kevin Newcomb, "MVW debuts blog marketing practice," www.clickz.com/news/print.php/3454471.

17. Beth Snyder Bulik, "Who blogs?" *Advertising Age*, June 4, 2007, p. 20.

18. Keith McArthur, "Online era leaves media out of the loop: PR expert," *The Globe and Mail*, March 21, 2005, p. B5.

19. Walter K. Lindenmann, Ketchum Public Relations, "It's the hottest thing these days in PR," a presentation at PRSA Counselors Academy, Key West, Florida, April 25, 1995.

20. Kevin Goldman, "Winemakers look for more publicity," *Wall Street Journal*, September 29, 1994, p. 53.

Experiential Marketing, Events, and Sponsorships

1. Explain the role of experiential marketing as a vehicle for building relationships with customers

2. Explain the importance of event marketing and sponsorships in contemporary marketing

3. Differentiate among the various forms of event sponsorships

4. Evaluate the role of event marketing and sponsorships in the marketing communications mix

5. Assess the criteria that a marketing executive considers before participating in event marketing and sponsorships

6. Identify and assess the various evaluation techniques that determine the effectiveness of event marketing and sponsorship activities

7. Describe the steps in event marketing planning

8. Evaluate various marketing strategies for making an event successful

9. Identify and explain the key elements of event marketing execution

Traditional forms of marketing communications tend to bombard consumers with messages; they emphasize reach and frequency, and the brand that barks the loudest gets the consumer's attention. In that scenario there isn't a true connection between the brand and the consumer. In contrast, experiential marketing focuses on giving a target audience a brand-relevant customer experience that adds value to their lives. It involves effective two-way communications between the brand and consumer.

Experiential marketing embraces several tried and true concepts such as event marketing, sponsorships, and product sampling, but it is the event itself rather than the product that becomes the key component of an integrated marketing campaign. The ultimate goal of experiential marketing is to get consumers actively engaged with the brand and, based on the experience, talk about the brand to others. A well-planned and implemented experiential marketing campaign can be the fuel for effective word-of-mouth marketing. This chapter explores the emerging world of experiential marketing, events, and sponsorships and shows how a variety of companies reap the benefits of these forms of marketing communications.

An Introduction to Experiential Marketing

experiential marketing (on-site sampling)
A form of marketing that creates an emotional connection with the consumer in personally relevant and memorable ways.

Experiential marketing is a form of marketing that creates an emotional connection with the consumer in personally relevant and memorable ways. Using one or more senses such as touch, taste, smell, sight, and hearing it establishes a touch-point or connection with consumers in the form of experiences that are personal, memorable, and interactive.[1] The touch-point may be something as simple as a free sample distributed at an event or a planned event where the brand is the centrepiece of the event.

The term experiential marketing is relatively new but the fundamental concepts behind it are not. Brands have always employed product sampling, special product promotions, public relations stunts, product seeding, and special events in their marketing arsenal, but it is just recently that the concept of consumer engagement with a brand has taken hold. To engage consumers requires a carefully designed and emotive experience that often integrates various forms of marketing communications. In an era where traditional media such as television and print are losing their ability to connect with consumers, alternatives such as experiential marketing become more important in the communications mix.

As discussed in Chapter 7, Internet communications are increasingly popular, especially through social networks. In an online environment consumers are more open and responsive to communications and in many cases take control of communications from the brand. Consumers willingly allow brands into their world! Leading social network sites such as Facebook and MySpace have fan pages devoted to Coca-Cola, Starbucks, and Red Bull, among many other brands. When a brand is committed to its fans there are positive spin-off benefits. To demonstrate, the existence of the Coke page on Facebook originated from two fans who simply loved Coca-Cola. Coca-Cola found the page and, rather than trying to buy it and take control or create another "official" page, rewarded the two fans and worked with them to continue building the page and representing the brand. By empowering its fans, Coca-Cola was able to build on the connections that were already established on Facebook.[2]

Stated earlier was the idea that the event itself may be the centrepiece of an experiential marketing campaign. And, in a non-traditional way, a well-conceived event can even launch a new product. Such was the case when Absolut, a global marketer of vodka, launched a new spirits brand named Cut in Australia. Rather than use the traditional mass advertising approach, Absolut leased two bars in Sydney and Melbourne. They put on DJ sets, band concerts, and photo exhibitions in these venues. Visitors were given a chance to contribute their photos to the exhibits, generating what Absolut hoped would be a viral component to the campaign. The marketing communications strategy was to target a few through experiential marketing to eventually reach the masses.[3]

Another component of experiential marketing is shopper marketing. **Shopper marketing** involves understanding how consumers behave as shoppers in all channels (retail, catalogue, and web) and then targeting these channels with appropriate marketing communications to enhance the sales of a brand. Shopper marketing is essential since 70 percent of brand selections are made in stores and 68 percent of buying decisions are unplanned.[4]

shopper marketing
Understanding how consumers behave as shoppers in all channels (retail, catalogue, and web) and then targeting these channels with appropriate marketing communications to enhance the sales of a brand.

With so many decisions made in store, shopper marketing is getting more attention from marketing decision makers. Samsung Canada has benefited from shopper marketing in a number of ways. According to marketing director Robert Gumiela, "The consumer is of critical importance and needs a positive buying experience. Essentially, customer experience is a new medium. We do more training in store and spend more money with retailers than all of our competitors and our sales results have made this investment worthwhile."[5] To illustrate, Samsung televisions are displayed on Samsung walls in all Future Shop and Best Buy stores. How Samsung televisions perform can be seen in an environment similar to the home environment.

Coca-Cola found a unique way to interact with its consumers when it launched a promotional tour experience called "Diet Coke Lounges" in major markets in the summer of 2007. The lounges were set up in malls and featured memorabilia, including old product packages and television spots, celebrating the 25th anniversary of Diet Coke in Canada. Visitors enjoyed a Diet Coke while perusing the artifacts. It was Diet Coke's way of expressing its appreciation to its customers—the customers would be part of the celebration![6] For some additional examples of experiential marketing refer to Figure 10.1.

Organizations are investing more money in experiential marketing and that investment is justified based on changing market conditions. In the past, an organization was concerned about making impressions on people (a staple means for measuring the effectiveness of advertising and public relations communications). Presently, emphasis has shifted so that the objective is to make quality impressions (fewer but better impressions) while engaging the consumer with the brand. Having the consumer interact with the brand helps to establish a stronger reason to buy the product and to build a relationship over an extended period.

One of the greatest challenges facing a company is where to invest its marketing dollars at a time when there are more choices than ever.

Experiential marketing is growing in popularity and companies are investing in it because consumers respond to it. Nine out of 10 consumers say they would purchase a good or service if they experienced it and were satisfied.

Here are a few unique examples of experiential marketing:

Tylenol PM
The over-the-counter drug product that makes a person sleep better reached 1 million target consumers by having packaged samples of the product placed on beds in resorts throughout the United States, with a note that said, "We know how long you've waited for this vacation, and we know how much you want to catch up on your sleep. Enjoy."

Lipton Brisk Green Tea with Apple
The Lipton tea beverage got some street marketing exposure by serving samples of "forbidden fruits" to "Adams and Eves" in the streets of key Canadian markets. Street teams, adorned in fig-leaf uniforms and accompanied by apple carts and trees, invited passersby to pick fruit and win prizes.

Stride Gum
Stride is a "ridiculously long-lasting" gum. To engage consumers, two "Stride Guys" visited 28 cities in a Volkswagen van, enticing people to play ping-pong with them wherever they stopped. Free gum was distributed at all stops to those who watched, and participants were given headbands and wristbands. The fun series of events engaged Canadians according to Cadbury Adams, the maker of the gum.

For more insight into the nature of experiential marketing campaigns read the IMC Highlight: **Experiential Marketing Pays Off**.

IMC HIGHLIGHT

Experiential Marketing Pays Off

True experiential marketing is a lot more than just distributing samples to prospective customers. According to Aidan Tracy, president of Mosaic Experiential Marketing, the key to experiential marketing is engaging with your consumers in a manner that leaves them with an impression that changes their perception of the brand. "It's about immersing the consumer in an experience circle—where the consumer learns about the product and tries the product."

Procter & Gamble provides a good example of how an experiential marketing program works. P&G uses the term "shopper marketing" to describe how it engages consumers with its brands. Shopper marketing is based on two key concepts, the first being the distinction between consumers who receive brand messages from various media while not shopping, and shoppers, who are described as consumers in action. Since 70 percent of purchasing decisions are made in store, the second concept of shopper marketing becomes clear—retail space must be viewed as a media platform, and used to advantage to get customers interested in your brand.

The marketing challenge is to devise content that is needed to change consumers' behaviour while they are on the retail floor. How can the stores serve as an effective communications channel?

Procter & Gamble worked with Walmart on a shopper marketing program to boost the profile of its Olay brand of beauty products. The program was based on the insight that the typical Walmart shopper buys for the family and neglects herself in the shopping process—not a good situation for a brand like Olay. That knowledge spawned a program theme: "Everything for the family, something for you." A series of health and wellness fairs were implemented in selected Walmart locations across Canada. Women entering the store were issued a passport-style card and were encouraged to visit the health and beauty aisles during their trip. Shoppers who picked up Olay items earned passport stamps, and those reaching the checkout with a fully stamped passport were entered in a grand prize draw. The passports forced the women to think about themselves for a moment.

Walmart was very satisfied with the sales the program generated and decided to bring it back for a second spin. This program demonstrates how marketers must think beyond traditional channels of communications and find new ways of motivating consumers to buy their brands. The sales floor as a communications channel opens up a new realm of possibilities at a critical time in the buying decision process.

Further to the point, four retailers—Walmart, Shoppers Drug Mart, Loblaw, and Costco—account for 65 percent of Procter & Gamble's Canadian business. With such buying concentration and the opportunity it represents to reach a huge number of consumers, there is little doubt that experiential marketing, or shopper marketing, as P&G calls it, will play a more dominant role in its marketing communications mix.

Adapted from Matt Semansky, "All Hail the Shopper," *Marketing*, May 12, 2008, p. 31, and Matt Semansky, "First-Hand Experience," *Marketing*, May 12, 2008, p. 34.

Event Marketing and Sponsorships

Event marketing and sponsorships are important components of many experiential marketing programs. Over the past five years investment in these areas has outpaced spending in traditional advertising. In 2008 alone, investment in sponsorships grew by 12.6 percent in North America while investment in traditional advertising grew by only 2 percent.

Event marketing is the design and development of a "live" themed activity, occasion, display, or exhibit (such as a sporting event, music festival, fair, or concert) to promote a product, cause, or organization.[7] For example, Nike plans and executes road races in large urban markets and supports the events with advertising, public relations, and sales promotion activities to achieve runner participation and buzz for each event. To maximize the true benefit of event marketing, a significant investment must be made in other forms of marketing communications. Such investments are necessary to generate awareness of the event, sell tickets to it, and generate publicity for it.

event marketing
The process, planned by a sponsoring organization, of integrating a variety of communications elements with a single event theme.

Event sponsorship is the financial support of an event, say a sports event, theatre production, or cause marketing effort, in return for advertising privileges associated with the event. Bell Canada, for example, is a premier national sponsor for the Vancouver 2010 Winter Olympics. Bell is giving the organizing committee $200 million: $90 million in cash; $60 million in communications equipment; and $50 million in games-related marketing. Will Bell Canada benefit from such a significant investment in a single event? According to then-CEO of Bell, Michael Sabia, "Just a 1 percent increase in market share will generate $300 million worth of improved shareholder value. Further, there is no better brand than the Olympic Games with which to associate our company. It is the perfect platform to enhance Bell's brand as the leading national provider of communications services."[8]

event sponsorship
The financial support of an event in exchange for advertising privileges associated with that event.

Usually, an event marketer offers sponsorships on a tiered basis. For instance, a lead sponsor or sponsors would pay a maximum amount and receive maximum privileges. Bell is one of six lead national sponsors of the 2010 Olympics in Vancouver and will maximize the benefits of that association. Other companies in this category include Hudson's Bay Company, RBC Financial, GM Canada, Petro-Canada, and Rona. Other sponsors, classified as official supporters, will pay less and receive fewer privileges. Some companies in this group include Air Canada, Canadian Pacific, and British Columbia Lottery Corporation.

Event marketing is big business! According to IEG, LLC, a Chicago-based sponsorship measurement firm, the North American sponsorship market is estimated to be valued at $16.5 billion (2008).[9] The sponsorship market in Canada is estimated to be worth $1.2 billion.[10] Growth in event marketing is being fuelled by deals with traditional broadcast properties that include a sponsorship element. As well, marketers today are reluctant to rely on traditional forms of marketing communications. With television viewership waning and newspaper and magazine readership declining each year, marketers are shifting their dollars to alternatives. With event marketing and sponsorships there is an opportunity for a brand or company to directly engage with its target market at a sponsored event.

A recent survey among North American marketing executives indicates that events deliver the greatest return on investment over other customary tools, including advertising. As indicated in the Bell example above, Bell expects considerable financial return for its Olympic investment. There are a few other reasons why sponsorships offer value to an organization. First, the company or brand can form an emotional connection with the fans, simply by being there and participating (fans expect sponsors to be at events), and second, an event can reach or target a certain demographic more effectively than advertising. Billabong, for example, derives these benefits by sponsoring Wakestock, an annual wakeboarding competition in Toronto. The event attracts 15- to 25-years-old interested in action sports—Billabong's primary target market.[11] Wakestop happens over several days and its festive-type atmosphere creates a strong interaction between advertisers like Billabong and the audience.

Investment in event marketing and sponsorships is mainly divided among five areas: sports, entertainment, festivals and fairs, causes, and the arts. A list of the leading event marketing and sponsorship companies in North America appears in Figure 10.2. Among the leaders are PepsiCo, General Motors, and the Coca-Cola Company. In Canada, GM sponsors the Canadian national ski team as well as numerous national and

FIGURE 10.2

Leading Sponsorship Investors in North America

Source: Courtesy of IEG, LLC. IEG Sponsorship Report, Chicago 2007.

Rank	Company	Amount ($ million)
1	Anheuser-Busch	$330M–$335M
2	PepsiCo Inc.	$305M–$310M
3	General Motors Corp.	$230M–$235M
4	The Coca-Cola Co.	$225M–$230M
5	Nike Inc.	$225M–$230M
6	Miller Brewing Co.	$175M–$180M
7	DaimlerChrysler Corp.	$150M–$155M
8	Ford Motor Company	$140M–$145M
9	Sprint Nextel	$ 135M–$140M
10	Visa	$ 120M–$125M

international ski and snowboarding events held here each year. Among GM's entertainment sponsorships are the annual Juno Awards and the Montreal Jazz Festival. GM also has a philanthropic side, making annual contributions to educational, civic, social, and environmental causes.

SPORTS MARKETING SPONSORSHIP

Sports sponsorship occurs at amateur and professional levels and can be subdivided into classifications from local events to global events (see Figure 10.3). Among the various categories of sponsorships, sports sponsorship is by far the largest in terms of dollars invested by marketing organizations. It presently accounts for about 66 percent of all sponsorship investments in North America, or approximately $10.9 billion.[12]

Sports sponsorships tend to be dominated by certain industries and manufacturers. In Canada, for example, the automobile industry is well represented by General Motors and Ford, the brewing industry by Molson and Labatt, and the financial industry by RBC Financial Group, BMO Financial Group, Scotiabank, Visa, and MasterCard.

Sponsorships are a key component of BMO's marketing mix. BMO partners with organizations that help create brand exposure nationally while also building regional visibility. BMO is a proud sponsor of major figure skating events in Canada, acting as lead sponsor of the National Figure Skating Championships and the Skate Canada Junior Nationals. The bank also sponsors the BMO Bank of Montreal Vancouver marathon and the BMO Financial Group Nations' Cup at Spruce Meadows (an equestrian event held each year in Calgary). BMO is also active in professional sports via sponsor partnerships with the Toronto Maple Leafs and Calgary Flames (NHL), the Toronto Raptors (NBA), and Toronto FC (soccer).[13]

The investment in sports sponsorship increases at each level moving upward on the chart. Organizations choose between spending locally to support community events at relatively low cost to investing in national and international sponsorships at significantly higher cost. Such decisions are based on how sponsorships fit with other marketing communications strategies and the overall marketing strategy of the organization.

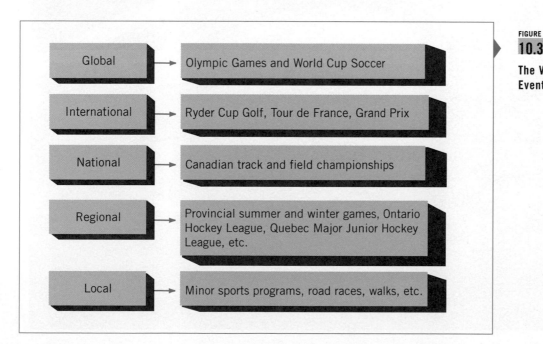

FIGURE
10.3

The Various Levels of Sports Event Marketing

An organization's involvement in sports sponsorship does not have to be extravagant; involvement and commitment depend upon the organization's marketing objectives and its overall strategy. To illustrate, Visa associates with national and international events, a reflection of the card's status around the world, while Tim Hortons prefers to sponsor local sports programs all across Canada. The company's Timbits Minor Sports Program provides team jerseys for community-based youth soccer and hockey leagues. The local sponsorship program fits nicely with the target audience the company is trying to reach.

A recent phenomenon associated with event sponsorship is the practice of ambush marketing. **Ambush marketing** is a strategy used by non-sponsors to capitalize on the prestige and popularity of an event by giving the false impression they are sponsors. The ambush of all ambushes was a Nike effort at the 1996 Atlanta Olympics. Saving the US$50 million that an official sponsorship would have cost, Nike plastered the city with billboards, handed out Swoosh banners to wave at the competitions, and erected an enormous Nike Centre overlooking the stadium. The tactics devastated the International Olympic Committee's credibility. Such tactics have lead to more assertive anti-ambushing strategies by subsequent Olympic organizing committees.[14]

Venue marketing or **venue sponsorship** is another form of event sponsorship. Here, a company or brand is linked to a physical site such as a stadium, arena, or theatre. In Canada, there is the Air Canada Centre (home of the Toronto Maple Leafs and Raptors), GM Place (home of the Vancouver Canucks), and Rexall Place (home of the Edmonton Oilers). Pre-eminent title positions like these break through the clutter of other forms of advertising, but they do come at a cost. Air Canada spent $20 million for a 20-year agreement for the naming rights to the Leaf's home rink. Sony, the Japanese

ambush marketing
A strategy used by non-sponsors of an event to capitalize on the prestige and popularity of the event by giving the false impression they are sponsors.

venue marketing (venue sponsorship)
Linking a brand name or company name to a physical site, such as a stadium, arena, or theatre.

FIGURE
10.4   The branding of sports venues helps improve brand awareness

Source: Photo by Dick Hemingway.

electronics giant, paid $10 million to have its name on a performing arts centre in downtown Toronto (formerly the O'Keefe Centre, then Hummingbird Centre). As part of the deal, the centre will be fitted with the most technically advanced audio and video equipment made by Sony.[15]

Besides their name on the building, most naming rights partners receive a luxury box plus a selection of regular seat tickets, rights to use the team's trademark in advertising, and coach or player appearances. Companies may also receive in-arena display areas for their products.[16] It's all a matter of negotiating the right deal. Venue marketing is illustrated in Figure 10.4.

At the Air Canada Centre, an arena owned by Maple Leaf Sports and Entertainment, there are also sponsors within the building—platinum, gold, and silver—depending on the desired scope of the association. Platinum members pay $2 million a contract for the best advertising inventory and title rights to special time-out segments during the games. Among the platinum sponsors are Air Canada, Ford Motor Company, Molson Canada, and IBM Canada. These companies can entertain clients in the Hot Stove Lounge, have access to special rooms for business presentations, and then attend a Raptors or Leafs game. Schmoozing like that can help move a potential sale further down the pipeline.[17]

Many prominent Canadian companies have invested in venue sponsorships in Canada and the United States. For a list of some of these companies and the costs involved, see Figure 10.5.

What's thriving in sports marketing is the concept of **value-added sponsorships**, where hefty doses of public relations and media exposure accompany a marketer's sponsorship agreement. The key in this strategy is a lucrative player endorsement. Reebok International was quick to strike an endorsement deal with young hockey sensation Sidney Crosby—a five-year deal worth $2.5 million, more money than any hockey company has ever paid established stars. Crosby is included in Reebok's global advertising campaign that uses the slogan, "I am what I am." Reebok is investing heavily in Crosby's ability to help build its hockey business, and for marketing purposes Reebok sees him as "the total package." When interviewed by the media Crosby is always seen wearing

---

Air Canada Centre ($20 million, 20-year deal)

Sponsor: Air Canada
Toronto Maple Leafs (hockey), Toronto Raptors (basketball), Toronto Rock (lacrosse)

Bell Centre ($60 million, 20-year deal)

Sponsor: Bell Canada
Montreal Canadiens (hockey)

General Motors Place ($25 million, 20-year deal)

Vancouver Canucks (hockey)
John Labatt Centre ($2.9 million, 10-year deal)

London Knights (Ontario Hockey League)

RBC Centre ($80 million, 20-year deal)
Carolina Hurricanes (hockey)

TD Banknorth Garden ($120 million, 20-year deal)

Boston Bruins (hockey) and Boston Celtics (basketball)

FIGURE
10.5

Venue Marketing Is Popular Among Canadian Corporations

*Source:*Courtesy of Revenues From Sports Venues, 2009.

Reebok clothing and equipment. As part of the deal, Crosby will participate in a variety of company business-building functions throughout the life of the deal.[18]

For different reasons, Energizer Canada signed on with Alexander Ovechkin (Crosby's arch rival). Energizer saw Ovechkin as a perfect fit for its Energizer brand battery and the core essence of its "Keeps on going" brand promise. "He plays the game with great determination . . . he just exudes such a positive energy that's right for our brand.[19]

Why do corporations invest in sports marketing and how effective is the investment? The true benefits of event marketing are discussed later in the chapter. For now, simply consider that key indicators of success are brand awareness and brand association with the event or, in some cases, celebrity. For example, which credit card sponsors the Olympics? Which company sponsors the men's national curling championships each year, an event called the Brier? What brands do you associate with Tiger Woods? If you can or can't answer these questions, it helps a company justify the benefits and drawbacks of investing in sports sponsorships.

ENTERTAINMENT SPONSORSHIPS

Canadian corporations invest huge amounts of money to sponsor concerts and secure endorsements from high-profile entertainment personalities in the hopes that the celebrity-company relationship will pay off in the long run. Companies like Molson and PepsiCo, which are interested in targeting youth and young adult segments, use entertainment sponsorship as a vehicle for developing pop-music and youth-lifestyle marketing strategies.

Pepsi-Cola recently decided to end its sponsorship of the *Academy Awards* because it is not a distinct enough platform for reaching younger people. Typically, shows such as the *Academy Awards* present opportunities to launch a big-event commercial or a new campaign. Coca-Cola replaced Pepsi on the broadcast, citing the "continuing marketing power" of the show and the "diverse audience" it reaches as reasons to get involved.[20] Coca-Cola is also a lead sponsor of the hit show *American Idol*; branded product placements for Coca-Cola are common on *American Idol*. Other companies sponsoring the *Academy Awards* include American Express, L'Oréal, and McDonald's. For these companies the benefit is clear: the Oscars show reaches a large number of affluent women. Advertising insiders refer to the show as the "Super Bowl for women."[21]

FILM FESTIVAL SPONSORSHIPS Film festivals are enticing because they reach a cross-section of adult target audiences. At a top film festival, a corporate sponsor hitches a ride on the most glamorous coattails of all—movie stars! For two prominent film festivals, the Toronto International Film Festival and the Festival des Films du Monde in Montreal, there are waiting lists for platinum sponsorships. These events showcase branded products not only to filmgoers, but also to the thousands of deep-pocketed domestic and international wheeler-dealers who do business at festivals. Key clients get to hobnob with the movie stars.

Sponsorship revenue for the Toronto International Film Festival averages $4 million annually, with top sponsor spots occupied by Bell Canada and RBC Financial. Other sponsors include Visa, Motorola, and FedEx. Through its sponsorship of the Toronto and Vancouver International Film Festivals, Visa provides its cardholders with exclusive benefits. Visa cardholders can purchase tickets and special ticket packages in advance of the general public, get access to exclusive ticket passes, enjoy priority access to the Visa Screening Room—Visa-branded theaters during the film festivals. Visa Premium cardholders (Visa Gold, Visa Platinum, and Visa Infinite cardholders) also have exclusive access to the Visa Premier Lounge in Toronto, where they can enjoy refreshments and access to the Visa Premier Lounge in Toronto, where they can enjoy refreshments and complimentary snacks one hour before evening screenings at the Visa Screening Room (see Figure 10.6).

Film and other types of theatre festivals are now popular with marketing decision makers as organizers are offering customized packages better suited to sponsor's unique needs. The Toronto International Film Festival approaches sponsorships as true partnerships. It offers a broad spectrum of associations, from corporate entertaining to marketing exposure and product sampling opportunities.[22] As the saying goes, these types of sponsorships reach a "class" audience rather than a "mass" audience. To illustrate, the Toronto International Film Festival reaches a young, urban, and affluent audience: 47 percent are 18 to 34 years old; 92 percent have a university education; 73 percent have a household income of $50 000+, 33 percent in excess of $100 000; and all are culture and experience seekers who spend money on entertainment.[23]

FIGURE

10.6   Visa capitalizes on entertainment sponsorships to reach a more exclusive audience

VISA   Film Festival Sponsorships

The hottest ticket in town, the Toronto International Film Festival† has grown to be one of the most popular and important film festivals in the world. Stars, stargazers and cinephiles alike will mix and mingle every September, taking in the best the international film industry has to offer. And with your Visa® card you can be part of the excitement.

Pull out your Visa card for V.I.P treatment

As the Visa card is the exclusive credit card of the Toronto International Film Festival, Visa cardholders are entitled to purchase ticket packages in advance of the general public. This year Visa cardholders will have new Visa Screening Room packages to choose from.

For more information about the festival go to www.tiff.net/thefestival

Call (416) 968-FILM (3456), or visit www.tiff.net/thefestival starting on July 6 to purchase ticket packages, or to receive more information.

Visa Screening Room

Enjoy a unique opportunity to see some of the festival's biggest films at the Visa Screening Room.

Special Access with Visa Gold, Visa Platinum® and Visa Infinite® cards

As a Visa Gold, Visa Platinum or Visa Infinite cardholder you can enjoy refreshments and complimentary snacks in the Visa Premiere Lounge at the Visa Screening Room.

† Toronto International Film Festival is a registered trademark of Toronto International Film Festival Inc.

About Visa | About Visa Canada | Disclaimer | Privacy Policy | Global Visa Sites   more people go with Visa.® | **VISA**

Source: Courtesy of Visa Canada.

TELEVISION SPONSORSHIPS Due to the waning impact of the 30-second TV commercial, the television industry and programs are offering branded sponsorship opportunities. One of the hottest sponsorship properties in Canada is on hockey broadcasts on networks like the CBC and TSN. In 2008, TSN and Molson got together on a sponsorship package under the newly branded *Molson Canadian Wednesday Night Hockey* broadcast. According to Pamela Oulette, brand manager for Molson Canadian, "*Molson Canadian Wednesday Night Hockey* puts the middle of the week right in the middle of the action." *Molson Canadian Wednesday Night Hockey* is the flagship program of TSN's program lineup.[24]

Largely due to television exposure, branded products are capitalizing on the poker trend. Degree deodorant's sponsorship association with TSN and the Degree Poker Championship, a nationally broadcast show, has helped revitalize the brand. For Degree, poker was a perfect fit—it was seen as a metaphor to help position Degree as "the thinking man's deodorant" and for the man who takes "calculated risks." The Degree name and logo are prominent in the broadcast, and there is the "Degree All-in Moment" that is mentioned and flashed on the screen at the critical moment in a high-risk hand. The tournament broadcast successfully reached the 25- to 40-year-old demographic Degree was after.[25]

CULTURE AND THE ARTS SPONSORSHIPS

Arts and cultural event opportunities embrace such areas as dance, film, literature, music, painting, sculpture, and theatre. What separates cultural events from sports and entertainment events is the audience size. Depending on the sponsor, this is an advantage or a disadvantage. A company such as Molson might prefer the mass audience reach of a sports event, whereas Mercedes-Benz and BMW might prefer to reach a more selective and upscale audience through an arts event. Perhaps only 2500 people attend the arts event, but those people can be powerful. Typically, their education level would be above average, as would their income. Such an audience profile would be a good match for promoting a new luxury car. A financial services company such as RBC Financial Group or MasterCard may sponsor both large-audience and small-audience events given the diversity of age and income of its customers.

The primary benefit these companies gain by sponsoring the arts is goodwill from the public. Most firms view this type of investment as part of their corporate citizenship objectives; that is, they are perceived as good, contributing members of society. Bell Canada has always invested in the communities it serves and has a varied sponsorship portfolio that includes major cultural and sporting events that enable it to be present in the community throughout the year. Some of the cultural events sponsored by Bell include the Stratford Festival, the Shaw Festival, and the *Just for Laughs* Festival in Montreal.

CAUSE MARKETING SPONSORSHIPS

Cause-related marketing is relevant in the minds of consumers, corporations, and not-for-profit organizations that mean something to consumers. This feeling, when associated with a brand or company, can have a positive effect on the consumer's perception of the brand. Such is the benefit that the CIBC derives from its ongoing title sponsorship of the Canadian Breast Cancer Foundation CIBC "Run for the Cure," where the overall goal is to raise funds to help find a cure for breast cancer. Other sponsors of this cause include Kimberly-Clark Worldwide, M&M's, Sears, 3M, and the Ford Motor Company of Canada, among many other companies (see Figure 10.7).

FIGURE
10.7

Kimberly-Clark Is an Ongoing Sponsor of the Canadian Breast Cancer Foundation

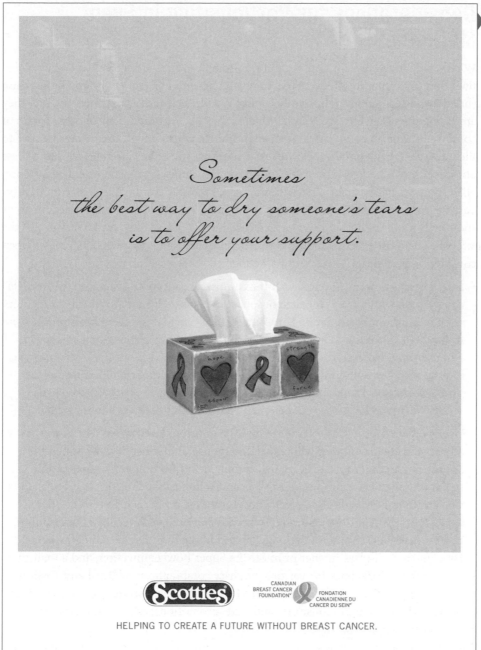

Source: Courtesy of john st. advertising.

In today's competitive business world brands drive marketing, but as brand loyalty diminishes, marketing executives are searching for new ways to connect with consumers emotionally. Not-for-profit organizations are proving to be good business partners for achieving this goal. The right combination produces a win-win situation for both parties. BMO Financial Group, for example, makes a significant investment in civic and community causes to help build vibrant, safe, and tolerant communities. BMO sponsors the United Way, a Take Our Kids to Work program, and Fashion Cares, a program to help fight against AIDS and HIV. BMO also makes financial contributions to countless hospitals and various foundations. In 2007, BMO's total corporate donations were $50.4 million, of which $20 million was in charitable donations.[26]

Considerations for Participating in Event Marketing

When companies enter into events and sponsorships, there are typically two key objectives they are trying to achieve. First, they are trying to create a favourable impression (build awareness and/or enhance their image) with their target audience. Second, they are trying to engage the target audience directly with the brand. Unlike other forms of communication, an event provides an environment where people are more receptive to the message—they expect to hear from the sponsors when they attend. To achieve these objectives the fit between the event and the sponsor must be a good one. For instance, Nike sponsors national and international track and field events as well as community-based events, such as fun runs. Much of the company's success has been based on event sponsorship and the distribution of merchandise that bears Nike's trademark logo—the swoosh. The most effective sponsors generally adhere to the following principles when considering participation in event marketing:

- **Select Events Offering Exclusivity:** If a company needs to be differentiated from its competition within the events it sponsors, it calls for exclusivity so direct competitors are blocked from sponsorship. For example, Bell Canada's sponsorship commitment to the 2010 Vancouver Winter Olympics shuts out all other communications companies from the event. Also, sponsors are often concerned about the clutter of lower-level sponsors in non-competing categories that reduce the overall impact of the primary sponsor. There is a lot of clutter, for example, in sports events such as NASCAR (brand logos seem to be everywhere, as can be seen in Figure 10.8).

- **Use Sponsorships to Complement Other Promotional Activities:** The roles that advertising and promotion will play in the sponsorship must be determined first. Sponsoring the appropriate event will complement the company's other promotional activities. For example, Pepsi-Cola and Frito Lay (both PepsiCo brands) sponsor the Super Bowl and place several ads during the broadcast. To leverage the association with the Super Bowl, both brands combine to advertise a Super Bowl contest (game tickets and other major prizes) in the months preceding the game. Huge in-store displays further promote the Super Bowl connection, and a mail-in rebate offer ($10.00 back for various purchase combinations of Pepsi and Tostitos products) encourages consumers to buy. Pepsi's integrated strategy embraces advertising, sales promotion (consumer and trade promotion), and event marketing across key company brands.

- **Choose the Target Carefully:** Events reach specific targets. For example, while rock concerts attract youth, symphonies tend to reach audiences that are older, urban, and upscale. As suggested earlier, it is the fit—or matching—of targets that is crucial, not the size of the audience.

- **Select an Event with an Image That Sells:** The sponsor must capitalize on the image of the event and perhaps the prestige or status associated with it. For example, several brands of automobiles place a high value on associating with professional golf and sponsor various tour events: Mercedes-Benz Championship, Buick Open, and Honda Classic are examples. The prestigious image and status of such events have an impact on the sale of products that project a comparable image: the image and status that come with ownership of a Mercedes-Benz automobile, for example.

Source: Christa L. Thomas/ZUMApress.com/Keystone Press.

FIGURE
10.8

Brand logos seem to be everywhere at NASCAR races

- **Establish Selection Criteria:** In addition to using the criteria cited here, companies should consider the long-term benefit that sponsorship offers compared with the costs in the short term. For example, being associated with an event that is ongoing, popular, and successful is wise because there is less risk for the sponsor. Before committing financial resources to an event, a company should also consider whether it is likely to receive communications exposure through unpaid media sources and whether the event organizers will be able to administer the event efficiently. The company must establish objectives in terms of awareness and association scores, image improvement, sales, and return on investment so it can properly evaluate its participation in the activity.

For insight into why BMO Financial Group chooses to sponsor figure skating events in Canada see Figure 10.9. Figure skating attracts an audience that BMO is interested in.

BMO believes figure skating enjoys a special cultural significance to Canadians. More than 6 million Canadians are involved in the sport. Today, interest in figure skating is at an all-time high largely based on the international success of our nationally ranked skaters. Canada has won more than 500 medals at competitions that include world championships, junior world championships, and the Olympic Winter Games.

A recent survey at the Canadian Championships provided BMO with additional information to support its investment in figure skating:

- 85% of the audience hold a positive image of companies that sponsor such events, and 68% are more likely to choose their products.

- The audience is 75% female and 25% male.

- 50% of the audience are between 20 and 54 years old.

- Nearly 60% of the audience have a household income of $60 000 and half of these have household income over $100 000.

- Students compose 30% of the audience.

- 50% of the audience have post-secondary education.

These demographics are attractive to a financial institution in search of new customers.

Source: Adapted from information available at the BMO Financial Group website, www.bmo.com.

Measuring the Benefits of Event Marketing and Sponsorship

One reason many companies are reluctant to enter into sponsorship programs is that results are difficult to measure. Large sums of money are spent at one time for a benefit that may be short-lived. Will the investment produce a reasonable ROI (return on investment)? The basic appeal of event marketing is that it provides an opportunity to communicate with consumers in an environment in which they are already emotionally involved. Beyond this, companies conduct marketing research to determine the impact of the sponsorship association. The following indicators, many of which are obtained from research, are used to measure the benefits of sponsorship.

- **Awareness:** How much awareness of the event is there within each target group? How well do people recall the brand or product name that sponsored the event?

- **Image:** What change in image and what increase in consumer perception of leadership or credibility result from the sponsorship?

- **New Clients:** How many new clients were generated as a result of the company's sponsoring an event? Entertaining prospective clients in a luxury box at an event goes a considerable way in building a relationship.

- **Sales:** Do increases in sales or market share occur in the period following the event? Be aware that the real sales benefit may take years. It takes time for a sponsor to become closely associated with an event.

- **Specific Target Reach:** Do the events deliver constituency? Carefully selected events reach specific targets that are difficult to reach by conventional communications. For example, pre-teens and teens are difficult to reach through conventional media but can be reached effectively through sponsorship of concerts and music tours. As discussed earlier, events need not be big in terms of attendance to attract constituency.

- **Media Coverage:** What value was derived from editorial coverage? Did the sponsorship result in free publicity for the sponsor? The industry benchmark for sports sponsorship is currently four to one, meaning $4 in exposure (e.g., free air time) for every $1 spent on sponsorship and its marketing support.

From the above benefits it can be determined that companies sponsor events for different reasons. Bell Canada's commitment to the 2010 Vancouver Olympic Games (discussed near the start of the event marketing section) will achieve awareness and image objectives that the company has established. Bell also sees the Games as a critical element of its customer experience. Consumers will be able to watch the games live on their cell phones. "It showcases in a very hands-on, face-to-face way how Bell products and services actually make these events and the customer experience better."[27]

For sponsorships to be successful they must be seamlessly integrated into corporate marketing and marketing communications plans. All forms of communications must be complementary. The organization must leverage the use of its website and incorporate the sponsorship into public relations campaigns as well as run thematic promotions to get all customer groups (trade and consumers) involved. Above all, it has to make a financial commitment above and beyond the rights fees. A general ratio for spending should be three to one: $3 should be spent to promote the relationship to the event for every dollar spent on securing the rights.[28]

For smaller events, success or failure is determined by the financial outcome of the event. Key indicators of success would be the profit the event generated. The event planner and perhaps a financial executive would scrutinize all the revenues and costs associated with planning and operating the event to determine if a profit or loss was ultimately generated. In the pre-planning stage, the budget statement and profit-and-loss statement are based on anticipated revenues and cost estimates, but after the event it is time to compare plan figures to actual figures.

An organization must choose between event marketing (planning and implementing its own event) and event sponsorships (providing financial support in return for advertising privileges). Either option presents challenges and opportunities. For more insight on how and why companies participate in event marketing and sponsorships and the benefits they derive read the IMC Highlight: **Niche Events Ideal for Billabong.**

Niche Events Ideal for Billabong

Billabong is a leader in board sports clothing and equipment, and much of its success is the result of a solid grassroots connection to surf, skate, snow, and wakeboard youth. That connection is largely based on successful event marketing sponsorships in each market. Billabong, now a $1 billion company, is a classic tale of rags to riches.

The company was started by Gordon Merchant, an ardent surfer, who spent 15 years following waves and wearing out countless pairs of swim trunks. In 1973 he developed a heavy-duty triple stitch, designed his own pair of board shorts, and started selling them on Australian beaches out of the back of his station wagon. He called his company, "Billabong." From there Merchant and Billabong rode the wave of other board sports, designing clothing for all of them. Surf culture is a year-round business—big business that embraces wet suits, a full line of casual wear, and jackets and pants hardy enough for the coldest winter weather.

Canada is a key contributor to Billabong sales, especially in Quebec. According to Risto Scott, marketing manager for Canada, "Quebec is the place to be since events are always well attended there. The kids are consumed with riding boards and the lifestyle." The culture thing is something Billabong figured out very early. From the beginning, Gordon Merchant focused his marketing on the "core board sports channels," a philosophy that remains in place today.

In Canada, for example, Wakestock is a big wakeboard event in Toronto. Billabong has been a sponsor since Wakestock's inception 10 years ago. In 2008, Wakestock attracted 40 000 spectators. Snowboarding has the Billabong World Junior Pro Contest, an event in Europe that gives amateur riders much-needed exposure. Skateboarding has many grassroots events in towns and cities across North America. Surfing and surfing events remain the heart and soul of the company. For the Association of Surfing Professionals world tour, Billabong is the title sponsor of four men's events and two women's events.

Billabong's primary targets are typically 15 to 25 years old and either involved or interested in action sports. They are familiar with the events mentioned above and identify with the athletes who participate in them. According to Scott, "the key for the company is to be constantly seen giving back to the sport, encouraging development locally, and providing spectacle internationally. It's great for the brand, and it's great for the sport for us to be involved."

Another aspect of Billabong's sponsorship is forming relationships with key athletes. It's essential for rising stars as well as seasoned veterans to be seen wearing the Billabong brand. As marketing manager in Canada, Scott spends about 50 days a year searching out new talent to ensure Billabong always has a strong presence in the water or on the slopes. He works closely with these Canadian athletes to ensure they are doing the best things for the brand and themselves.

Scott sees a bright future for the company as mainstream consumers are becoming more interested in action sports. "It's no longer just surfers and snowboarders buying our product. The industry as a whole is seen as a fashion leader. Retailers like The Gap, Banana Republic, and American Outfitters are aligning with action sports events and imagery—that's new distribution for the Billabong brand!"

Adapted from Brad Holden, "Making Waves," *Marketing, Sports Marketing Supplement*, November 2007, pp. 3–4.

Planning the Event

Should an organization decide to develop its own event, it must be comfortable with an exhaustive planning process. Putting the plan into place is one thing—executing it is quite another! As in the case of many other forms of marketing communications, a more prudent approach may be to outsource the activity, allowing experts in this field to do the job.

An organization's marketing team carefully considers the role of an event or sponsorship to ensure it is an appropriate opportunity for achieving the company's business objectives. The organization's primary role is to identify the overall goal and marketing objectives, identify the target audience and timing, consider the financial implications (revenues, costs, and profit), and evaluate the results. Working with the client organization, the event planner develops the event theme, identifies the best venue, and establishes the marketing strategy and implementation plan. The event planner's role is tactical in nature at the implementation stage, as all kinds of concerns need to be addressed. Among these are staging the event, having adequate and trained staff, operations and logistics planning, and safety and security. Successful events run smoothly, moving like clockwork from one activity to another. To do so requires careful planning down to the minutest of details (see Figure 10.10).

FIGURE
10.10 The Experiential Marketing and Event Planning Process

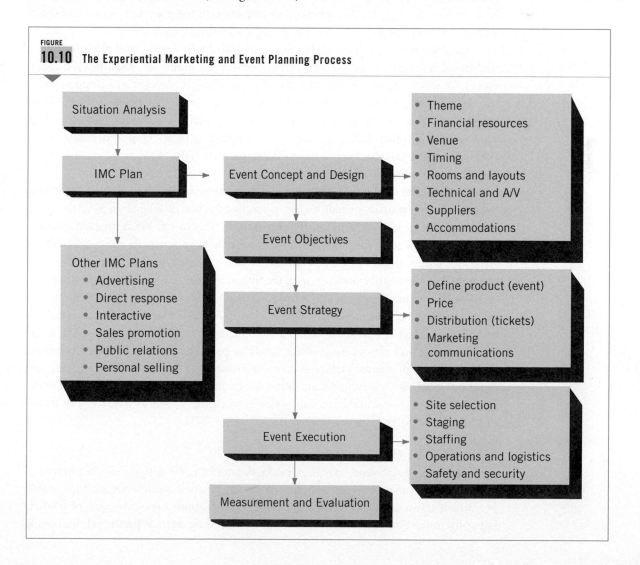

EVENT CONCEPT DEVELOPMENT

The initial stage of planning is developing the concept. In determining the nature of the event, the planner considers the event's *purpose*, the audience it will reach, available resources, potential venues, and timing. In terms of purpose, an event that is designed to transfer information to prospective clients would be much different from one intended to entertain an audience. The former might have a business tone and style, while the latter would be much more upbeat and participative. To illustrate, an event with a trade show orientation (e.g., some kind of business fair where new products are introduced to the market) is much different from the annual Calgary Stampede. The Calgary Stampede is a community event that is presented with all the enthusiasm and passion that the people of Calgary and all of Alberta can muster. The Stampede represents the historical and cultural fabric of the West.

The **theme** of the event should be linked to the purpose and consider the needs of the audience. Events tend to adopt a colour scheme and a tagline that tie various components of the event together. For example, tickets, programs, promotional literature, and signs are usually designed to look like they are all part of a package. Key influences on theme development are one's imagination and money. The latter always brings a sense of reality to one's imagination! Potential themes could involve history (the organization's history), geography and culture (the location of the organization or the event), sports (being part of a sports event that fits with the product), music and entertainment (offers significant appeal for younger audiences), and so on.

Once the theme is determined, the next decision is *venue*. Will the venue be a traditional setting such as a hotel, convention centre, arena, or stadium (see Figure 10.11)? Or will it be something unusual such as a parking lot or a site at a company facility? Or will it move from location to location, as in the case of product promotional tours? Regardless of the venue, the planner must carefully consider factors such as sound, lighting, other technical issues, and availability of parking and public transportation. And of course, there's always the unpredictability of the weather. Should the event be inside or outside?

The **financial resources** must be considered immediately. Much like an advertising budget, where a relatively small budget precludes the use of television advertising, an event's budget quickly determines the degree of extravagance. What an event planner would like to do and what the planner can actually do are usually quite different—a good idea is only a good idea if it is financially viable. Therefore, the event planner must carefully balance creative instincts with the financial resources of the organization.

The timing of an event is often linked to the season or weather. For example, the Canadian Home Show, an annual show held at Exhibition Place in Toronto, is held in early April each year. The show is timed to coincide with the public's interest in home improvements and renovations, which tends to peak in the early spring. Essentially, there are four time-related factors to consider: season, day of the week, time of day, and duration of the event. Business trade shows, for example, are usually scheduled on weekdays. In contrast, home and leisure shows cover weekends as well as weekdays, with traffic at the show peaking on the weekends.

DESIGNING THE EVENT

Once the concept decisions have been made, the next stage is design. For the purpose of illustration, let's assume we are planning a two-day business conference at which several prominent business speakers will make presentations about various aspects of marketing communications. Attendees will include advertising agency personnel, marketing

10.11 Hotel and conference centres actively market their facilities to conference planners

Source: Courtesy of The Old Mill Inn & Spa, oldmilltoronto.com.

executives, as well as managers employed in web-based communications, sales promotion, and public relations. The theme of the conference is "How to Communicate Effectively with Youth," a hot topic among marketing communications practitioners.

In designing this conference, key decision areas include venue, room layout, technical requirements, food and beverage requirements, material suppliers, and hotel room availability. Regarding **venue**, a downtown hotel location in a major city would likely be a logical choice because the target audience works in that environment. The hotel's banquet room facilities will be considered, because a room for 250 to 300 attendees is required, and an additional banquet room will be needed for some of the meals. For example, it is common for keynote speakers to make their presentations after a meal in the main banquet room. Meals without keynote speakers are often in an adjacent room where the atmosphere is less formal.

The **layout** of the banquet room has a bearing on how well the audience and speakers interact with each other. A common layout at this type of conference includes carefully spaced round tables with eight people seated at each. Attendees usually like this arrangement because a table can be reserved for a large group from one company. Such an arrangement encourages collegiality at the table even if the people did not know each other initially. The speakers usually address the audience from an elevated podium at the front of the room.

In today's technologically driven world, the use of proper and effective **technology** is crucial. Most speakers today use slides or video presentations as their primary visual aid to illustrate their key points. Therefore, an event planner must consider all possible audiovisual needs in advance. Typically, the audiovisual aspect of the conference is outsourced to an expert company in this field. This company brings in the equipment (sets it up and tears it down) and is responsible for coordinating the visual aspect of the presentation with the speaker. For extremely large conferences where attendees are distant from the speaker, it is common to have additional screens that display the speaker making the presentation.

Food and beverage requirements are another decision area. Since attendees are investing their time and money in the conference they expect *good-quality food* and *efficient service* by hotel staff. A poor experience in this area can negate any other positive experiences the attendee has at the conference. Buffet-style meals, for example, seem efficient, but only if there are enough serving stations so the lineups aren't too long. If the meal is served directly to tables, adequate staff must be on duty so that the meal is served within the time allocated. Conferences must stick to their schedule. Light snacks and beverages must be readily available in convenient locations during the break periods.

Dealing with **suppliers** behind the scenes is another key decision area. At our example of the marketing communications conference, print materials were prepared and copied by a printing company to be distributed at registration. It is quite common to have a booklet containing an event schedule, profiles of the various speakers, information about the host sponsor, and copies of the various presentations. As indicated earlier, audiovisual supply requirements must also be confirmed in advance. Food and beverage supplies are the responsibility of the hotel, but all meal requirements must be confirmed ahead of time between the event planner and catering manager.

The final decision area involves having adequate **hotel rooms** available for the anticipated number of attendees. Hotels usually block off rooms until a specified date before the conference. If there aren't enough rooms at the host hotel, additional rooms should be reserved nearby. All promotional materials should include hotel information and indicate the key dates and reservation procedures.

SETTING OBJECTIVES

As indicated earlier in the chapter, an organization must establish concrete objectives to justify any financial investment in event marketing. Therefore, quantitative objectives are identified—objectives that are realistic, achievable, and measurable. They must be within the realm of what event marketing is capable of achieving. A direct link to sales is not possible, but it may be possible to measure changes in awareness about a company's product as a result of event participation.

Other objectives might relate to the size of audience reached, the ability to reach a specific target audience (e.g., the quality of reach), sponsor recognition levels, sales of sponsor products, the economic impact of the event, and profit. In the example of the marketing communications conference, the event's objective may have been to attract 300 participants (perhaps any number above 200 participants would produce a profit for the event). Since the event will attract a quality target audience of marketing communications practitioners, it could attract additional sponsors who will help defray the costs of planning and executing the conference.

PLANNING TOOLS

The initial stage of planning is the preparation of an event proposal. The *proposal* should include the objectives of the event as well as details about organization, layout, venue, technical requirements, and any other key considerations such as those discussed above (see Figure 10.12). Certain planning tools are essential in the planning stages. Most important is a *timeline chart* that indicates when various planning activities start and finish. As well, a schedule of daily events, often called a **run sheet**, is essential to list the various dates, times, and locations of activities (see Figure 10.13). The importance of the

run sheet
A schedule of daily events that shows the various dates, times, and locations of activities at an event.

FIGURE
10.12

Key Elements of an Event Proposal

An event proposal is drafted in the preliminary stages of planning to highlight key elements. As planning progresses, the proposal becomes more detailed and execution oriented.

EVENT DESCRIPTION
- Type of event and event name
- Location
- Timing
- Event concept (including goals and objectives)

EVENT MANAGEMENT
- Management responsibilities
- External supplier requirements
- Facility requirements (venue, rooms, layout, etc.)
- Identification of target audience

MARKETING
- Assessment of audience needs
- Competitor analysis (similar events, timing, etc.)
- Product (event definition)
- Price strategy (price ranges, ticket availability, etc.)
- Marketing communications strategy (media advertising, web, public relations)
- Distribution strategy (registration procedures, methods, etc.)

FINANCIAL
- Budget (consideration of all associated costs)
- Profit and loss statement

STAGING
- Theme
- Decor
- Layout

- Sound and lighting
- Catering
- Services (parking, transportation, vehicle requirements, electricity, etc.)

STAFFING
- Recruitment of staff
- Staff training (roles and responsibilities)
- Recruitment of volunteers
- Volunteer training

SAFETY AND SECURITY
- Risk identification and management
- Safety strategy (audience, presenters, entertainers, etc.)
- Security strategy (premises, equipment, cash, etc.)
- Reporting procedures and communications
- First aid

OPERATIONS AND LOGISTICS
- Bump-in (setup)
- Room layout
- Technical execution (sound, lighting, computers, projectors, etc.)
- Attendee traffic flow (venue layout, room locations, meeting rooms, etc.)
- Contingencies (weather, technology failure, accidents, etc.)
- Bump-out (teardown)

EVALUATION
- Actual versus plan (based on objectives)
- Profitability

timeline chart will become clear in the discussion of execution issues later in this chapter. With so many logistical things to consider, it is important to identify a critical path for those elements of the plan that are essential for a successful outcome.

Marketing the Event

Marketing an event is no different from marketing a product; an integrated plan is needed. The key decisions involve carefully defining the product (event) and then positioning it in the minds of the target audience in a favourable way. Motivating people to attend the event depends on the quality and quantity of marketing communications activities. This section examines some of the essential strategic planning elements.

PRODUCT STRATEGY: DEFINING THE EVENT

In defining the event, the planner must identify the essential features and benefits of the event that can ultimately be used in messages directed at the target audience. For example, is the purpose to entertain, to provide a learning experience, or to simply have fun with friends? The marketing communications conference cited earlier in the chapter offers a learning experience for participants, who gain from the success and expertise of others.

FIGURE

10.13

A Sample Run Sheet

A run sheet is an indispensable planning tool that is updated as needed during planning. It is particularly useful for hotels and conference centres at the execution stage of an event. The schedule below was used at the Ambassador Resort Hotel and Conference Centre, Kingston, Ontario, when it hosted the Ontario Colleges' Marketing Competition in 2002.

THURSDAY, NOVEMBER 14, 2002	
2:00–4:00 p.m.	Registration and Team Photographs *(Atrium)*
5:30–7:00 p.m.	Complimentary Buffet Dinner *(Ballroom)*
7:00–7:15 p.m.	Opening Ceremonies *(Ballroom)*
7:15–9:30 p.m.	Marketing Quiz Bowl *(Ballroom)*
10:00–11:30 p.m.	Faculty Social *(Prime Minister's Suite)*

FRIDAY, NOVEMBER 15	
7:00–8:00 a.m.	Judges' Breakfast *(East Ballroom)*
7:00–8:00 a.m.	Continental Breakfast, Students and Faculty *(West Central Ballroom)*
8:00 a.m.	First Participants Enter Prep Rooms *(refer to event schedules)*
8:00 a.m.–12:00 p.m.	Judging Begins for Cases, Job Interview, and Sales Presentation
12:00–1:00 p.m.	Judges' Lunch and Faculty Lunch *(East Ballroom)*
1:00–4:00 p.m.	Competition Continues
6:30–7:30 p.m.	Reception *(Ballroom)*
7:30–10:00 p.m.	Awards Banquet *(Ballroom)*

All activities take place at the Ambassador Resort Hotel and Conference Centre.

In contrast, attending the Rogers Cup Tennis Championships brings tennis enthusiasts together to cheer and celebrate tennis at the highest level of performance. Clearly, the nature of communications to motivate attendance for these two events would be very different. Promotional information for the Rogers Cup stresses words such as intense competition, excitement, and emotion.

In contrast, promotional information for a business conference is quite different. A recent conference planned and implemented by *Strategy* magazine used the theme "Metro versus Retro: How well do you understand the male market?" The conference was officially titled: Understanding Men: Metro versus Retro. The following pitch was used to attract marketing and marketing communications practitioners to attend:

> This exploration of the evolving state of masculinity around the world will help marketers understand the opportunities and challenges in reaching men today. Advertisers will miss real men unless they tune in to the ways in which they are adapting to the changing environment. The conference provides pointers for getting it right. The secrets behind some recent and successful campaigns will be presented.[29]

In defining the product (event) and understanding the motivation of the target audience, the event planner discovers what buttons to press to motivate participation.

PRICING STRATEGY

Price also plays a role in motivating attendance. Literature promoting professional seminars and conferences is easily discarded if the price–value relationship is incongruent. Charge too much for a conference and the value is questioned. Charge too little and people may think they won't learn anything important by attending. All things considered, the pricing decision is a delicate one. To put things in perspective, the registration fee for the one-day "Understanding Men: Metro versus Retro" conference mentioned earlier was $600, not including hotel and travel costs. Such an event might attract 200 people and could prove to be profitable for the sponsoring organization. However, if the price were lowered to less than $500 (say $495), would it attract a larger audience? Pricing an event is much like pricing a product—a lot of psychology is involved.

In contrast, the RBC Canadian Open (a professional golf association tour event) offers tickets in a range of prices starting as low as $110 for a weekly grounds badge to $250 for an Executive Rooftop patio pass. An event like this attracts groups, so rates are also established for groups of four, eight, and ten. Some rates include daily parking, some do not. In other words, pricing for an event sometimes has to be flexible and meet a variety of customer needs.[30]

Canadian Open
www.thecanadianopen.ca

For the four days of the event (Thursday through Sunday), an average of 90 000 people along with 1600 volunteers will be on the grounds.

A second pricing consideration involves a plan for purchasing tickets. The sale and distribution of tickets for an event or the registration process for a business conference must be convenient for the participant. As well, the planning organization must decide if it will sell the tickets directly or outsource this task to a specialist, such as Ticketmaster. Consumers now find online ticket buying and event registration very convenient. Therefore, registration could be handled by an organization's website or by the website of a ticket intermediary. All details about pricing and how to buy tickets should be clearly stated on the organization's website (see the tickets page at HYPERLINK "http://www.thecanadianopen.ca" www.thecanadianopen.ca for an example).

MARKETING COMMUNICATIONS STRATEGY

The success of any event is often dictated by the effectiveness of the marketing communications strategy. What message will be delivered to the target audience to motivate participation, and what media will be used to efficiently reach that audience? A separate budget must be drawn up for marketing communications, because it may take a considerable portion of the event's overall budget.

The initial marketing communications decisions are basically **branding** decisions. Typically, an event will adopt a distinctive name, logo, colour scheme, and image. Every component of the communications mix, including tickets, will bear the same logo and colour scheme. Such consistency of presentation gives the event a branded look. For the CN Canadian Women's Open (a national golf championship), all forms of marketing communications have a common look. The CN logo appears in all communications materials related to the Open and the website for the event includes links to other golf partnerships that CN is involved with. CN is a strong supporter of golf development programs in Canada. Refer to the illustration in Figure 10.14.

Among the various elements of the marketing communications mix, advertising, public relations, and Internet communications frequently play key roles in promoting an event. The *advertising strategies* for the event are based on the target market profile and

Source: Courtesy of Royal Canadian Golf Association.

FIGURE 10.14

An event is a brand with a branded look

how best to reach the target given the financial resources available. The content of the message and the style of delivery must combine effectively to meet the motivational needs of the audience. Media alternatives include television and radio advertising, magazine and newspaper advertising, direct mail (letters, brochures, and pamphlets), and the Internet.

The size of the media budget obviously dictates media decisions. An event like the Rogers Cup Tennis Championships for both men and women, which attracts a broad cross-section of ages, will adopt a multimedia strategy to create awareness and will rely heavily on the Internet to communicate specific information and sell tickets. In contrast, an event like the "Understanding Men: Metro versus Retro" conference will use targeted media such as direct mail, email, and business-oriented print media to effectively reach business executives.

Public relations are also essential in generating positive publicity for an event. Organizers of large events frequently hold press conferences, timed appropriately, to build some pre-event publicity. Organizers may also issue press releases, as in the case of the Tim Hortons Brier, held in Calgary in 2009, to stimulate interest in the community where the event is taking place and among people who may wish to attend the event. Refer to Figure 10.15 for an illustration. Smaller and more local events send a press release to all local media and then hope for the best—and take care to invite the press to the actual event.

FIGURE 10.15 A Press Release Announcing Details of the Tim Hortons Brier

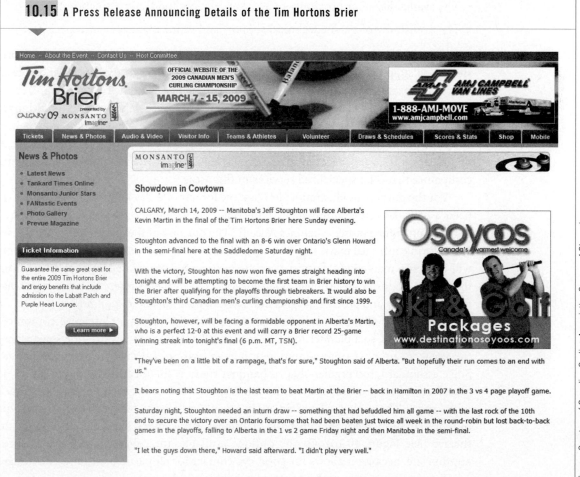

Source: Courtesy of Canadian Curling Association Season of Champions.

Event Marketing Execution

Execution involves dealing with specific details about an event. A planner usually works from a checklist to ensure that all details are taken care of in the planning stage and the execution stage of an event. For the purpose of illustrating event execution, this section assumes that a planner is planning a marketing conference. Discussion will focus on several key areas, including site selection and staging, staffing, operations and logistics, and safety and security. Event execution is complex and a full discussion of such a topic is beyond the scope of this textbook.

SITE SELECTION AND STAGING

In the theatre, the *stage* is the scene of action. The same is essentially true in event marketing. The scene of action for an event involves a site selected according to considerations such as theme development, sound and lighting, and availability of essential services. The venue chosen should be consistent with the event's purpose and theme, and it should provide all of the essential services that are required. Some of the key factors influencing site selection include

- The size of the event (e.g., the number of participants).
- The suitability of the site for planned activities (e.g., formal and informal activities).
- The primary field of play (e.g., the theatre or conference room where the main event will be held).
- The availability of or proximity to accommodation, food, and attractions.
- The availability of on-site technical support and venue management experience.

Theme development was discussed earlier in the chapter. At the event, the theme should be supported in every aspect, including sound and lighting, decor, and special effects. For example, the theme at a marketing conference could be very subtle and communicated only by signage and colour schemes. At much larger events of a longer duration, music and entertainment (e.g., specific acts revolving around the theme) could be included, along with special props appropriately placed around the venue. If the latter is the choice, an event planner is wise to seek advice from staging and rental companies that offer specialized services in this area.

For the purpose of illustration, let's assume for our one-day marketing conference we need a hall that can accommodate 150 people. The conference theme will be billed as "Marketing in the Future: What Lies Ahead?" The purpose of the conference is to educate and inform concerned marketing managers about what trends and external environments will influence marketing strategies over the next decade. Influential guest speakers from the ranks of industry, government, and the services sectors will present their views on what the future holds and provide insights into how they are already responding.

At this type of conference, most of the speakers' presentations involve computer-generated shows, so a planner must be concerned about room layout—the stage where the speakers are positioned, sound, lighting, and vision. Let's start with **room layout**. Since a standard, rectangular-shaped banquet room is the theatre, the speakers will be placed at one long side of the room, reducing the distance between the front and back of the room. The seating will be laid out in a way conducive to taking notes. For this type of a presentation, there are four basic seating layouts: cabaret, banquet, classroom, and theatre (see Figure 10.16). Of the options available, the cabaret layout seems most appropriate, because it allows for good eye contact for all participants and encourages communication among participants at each table.

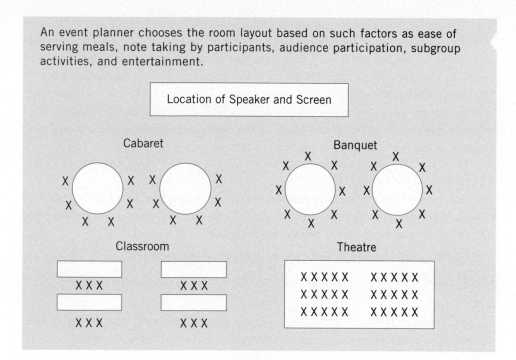

FIGURE
10.16

**An event planner can choose
from a variety of room layouts**

The guest speakers will be on an elevated platform at one side of the room. The height of the platform considers the sight lines of the audience. The audience must be able to see the speaker and the screen clearly. Appropriate backdrops should be on stage to isolate the presentation area and create a more intimate feeling. At such a conference, the speaker rarely controls the slide presentation—technical coordination is usually the responsibility of an audiovisual expert who is located at the side of the room.

Proper **sound** and **lighting** are essential to create mood and ambience. Professional advice from a sound and lighting expert is recommended. Such advice is usually readily available at conference centres. If audience communication is going to be important, microphones should be strategically situated throughout the conference room.

With all details addressed, the final aspect of staging is **rehearsal**. The rehearsal is an opportunity for everyone to integrate their efforts and to ensure that all technical glitches are remedied. Contingency plans should be established in case the unexpected occurs, which it often does! For example, there should be a plan in place in case a speaker falls ill at the last minute or the projector breaks down.

Additional staging considerations include making arrangements for catering and **accommodations**. Since the marketing conference is being held at a conference centre, food and beverages are readily available. Decisions involve the style of service (e.g., buffet or set menu with table service), the timing and availability of snacks and beverages (e.g., during planned breaks), and choosing the menu for each meal. Hotels and conference centres usually offer food and beverage packages that are available in a range of prices. Of course, the planner must negotiate room rates with the host hotel or conference centre. Typically a group rate is negotiated based on number of rooms that will be booked.

STAFFING

Planning and executing an event are complex undertakings and, depending on the size and scope of the event, the human resources required can vary considerably. Can you imagine the number of people that are required (paid and volunteers) when a city hosts the Olympic Games or a national sports championship? For large-scale events the roles and responsibilities of all individuals must be spelled out in detail. Therefore, organization charts are needed for various stages of event planning: pre-event, event, and post-event. In the pre-event stage, the focus is on planning, so anyone connected with marketing, financial, and human resource planning is involved. During the event itself, human resources capacity expands to its fullest, so it is essential that reporting relationships for all operations be delineated. After the event, only those people involved with evaluation and financial planning play a key role.

OPERATIONS AND LOGISTICS

To illustrate the importance of operations and logistics, consider the planning required to get a major golf championship such as the RBC Canadian Open up and running. For the participants alone, a plan is needed to ensure that

- All golfers, their entourage, and their equipment arrive on time.

- Golfers are settled in the correct accommodation and all equipment is safe and secure.

- The golf course is in immaculate condition (a process that starts months before the competition) and spectator stands, scoreboards, and crowd barriers are in place.

- Golfers arrive in time for their tee-off each day.

bump-in (setup)
The setting up of structures and other equipment at an event.

This set-up process is referred to as the bump-in. **Bump-in**, or **setup**, involves setting up structures and facilities required for an event. For an event such as our marketing conference example, tasks such as installing sound and lighting equipment, computers, projectors, and screens involve the services of a specialist. Regardless of how the bump-in occurs, it is essential that all facilities and equipment are in place and in good working condition prior to the official start of the event. Simply stated, logistics is about getting equipment and people into the right place at the right time so that things run smoothly, and then, once the event is complete, taking everything down. The process of dismantling is referred to as **bump-out**, or **teardown**.

bump-out (teardown)
The process of dismantling everything after an event.

SAFETY AND SECURITY

Imagine the potential safety and security concerns there would be for a Grand Prix racing car event where the race is conducted on city streets. For that matter, any sports event where large numbers of fans congregate requires a detailed plan outlining safety and security measures. The plan must consider potential crowd behaviour and methods for controlling crowds should the need arise.

At an event everyone must feel safe, including the audience, the staff, and the subcontractors (e.g., technical crews). At large events, accidents can occur, people might fall ill, or something completely unexpected may happen. Potential risks include fires, bomb threats, gas leaks, overzealous fans (even riots), and so on. A few years back some NBA basketball players and fans were involved in an ugly brawl, a situation that threatened the safety of both fans and players. Crowd management—the orderly flow of spectators in and out of the venue—is very important. Signage indicating direction and staff barking out commands where necessary play a key role in moving audience pedestrian traffic smoothly.

Proper security measures for property, equipment, and cash must also be planned for. As well, the planner must ensure that only certain people have access to specific areas and must act responsibly in case of emergency. Typically, people in positions of authority or special responsibility wear badges identifying their role at the event. Vehicles may be necessary to transport security personnel to areas where emergencies occur. Event planners have a choice of hiring private security firms or members of the local police force. Over the years there have been many incidents involving unruly crowds at soccer matches that have resulted in death. Since safety and security is such a critical issue, it is recommended that organizers of large events employ external organizations that are experts in this field to take care of all of the planning and implementation.

SUMMARY

Experiential marketing is a growing component of marketing communications campaigns. Organizations see greater value in activities that actively engage a target audience with a brand, and that is what experiential marketing does. Activities such as free product samples, product promotional tours, shopper marketing programs, and event marketing and sponsorships are potential components of an experiential marketing campaign. Typically, experiential marketing strategies reach fewer consumers than traditional advertising strategies, but the quality of the association a brand develops with consumers is stronger.

Event marketing and sponsorships are now an important element of a firm's marketing communications mix. Sponsorships tend to be concentrated in four areas: sports, entertainment and the arts, festivals and fairs, and causes. Events and sponsorships can be local in nature or they can be expanded to become regional, national, or international in scope. Sports sponsorships and events draw the majority of the sponsorship pie, but interest is now growing faster in the other areas.

Prior to getting involved with sponsorships, an organization should establish specific criteria for participation. Factors to consider include product category exclusivity, relationships with other marketing communications programs, the event's ability to reach the desired target market effectively, and the image-building potential offered by the event.

Once the event is over, attention turns to evaluation. In relation to objectives that were established for the event, measures are determined for criteria such as awareness, image enhancement, new business clients, product sales, target market reach, and media coverage. There will be an assessment of all revenues and costs to determine profitability, and to make recommendations for improvements should the event be planned for another occasion.

Should an organization decide to plan its own event, it must be comfortable with a rather exhaustive planning process. The first decision is to evaluate the role of the event or sponsorship to ensure it offers a good opportunity for achieving business objectives. The organization is responsible for establishing goals and objectives, identifying the target audience, determining the best time for the event, providing adequate financial resources, and evaluating the event for effectiveness. The event planner develops strategies for staging the event, making available properly trained staff to execute the event, planning operations and logistics to make sure everything runs smoothly, and preparing for safety and security issues that could arise during an event.

The first stage in developing an event is to determine the event's concept and design. This involves decisions about the type of event, the name, and the theme of the event. Once these decisions are made, attention focuses on issues such as venue alternatives, financial resources required, timing, room layouts, and technical requirements. To secure proper technical advice and support, a planner usually works with a specialist. Technical support is commonly outsourced.

As with other forms of marketing communications planning, qualitative and quantitative objectives are established. Typically, event marketing objectives focus on quality and quantity of target audience reach, potential new business and product sales, the economic impact of the event, and profit. Event marketing strategies involve carefully defining the product (the event) and then positioning it in the minds of the target audience. A good event title and theme become the foundation for building an effective communications strategy for motivating attendance at the event. An effective price strategy is also crucial, because prospective participants evaluate the potential benefits against the cost of attending. To promote the event, a combination of media advertising, online communications, and public relations is an effective mix. All communications must have a branded look and present a similar message to the target audience.

At the execution stage, concerns focus on specific details in the following areas: site selection and staging, staffing, operations and logistics, and safety and security. All details must be checked and rechecked to ensure a smooth flow of activities and people.

KEY TERMS

ambush marketing,   288
bump-in,   310
bump-out,   310
event marketing,   285
event sponsorship,   285

experiential marketing,   282
on-site sampling,   282
run sheet,   303
setup,   310

shopper marketing,   283
teardown,   310
venue marketing,   288
venue sponsorship,   288

REVIEW QUESTIONS

1. Briefly explain how experiential marketing is different from other forms of marketing communications activities. What benefits does it offer?
2. What is shopper marketing? Briefly explain and offer a new example of this concept.
3. What is the difference between event marketing and event sponsorship?
4. What is ambush marketing and what benefits does it offer?
5. Identify and briefly explain the main classifications of event marketing.
6. Briefly explain the criteria an executive considers before pursuing an event marketing opportunity.
7. What are the measures commonly used to evaluate the effectiveness of event marketing participation?
8. Identify the basic steps in the event marketing planning process.
9. Developing the event concept is the initial stage of planning an event. What are the key decision areas in this stage? Briefly explain each.
10. Designing the event is the second stage of event planning. What are some of the key decision areas in this stage? Briefly explain each.
11. Briefly explain the purpose of the following planning tools:
a) proposal
b) run sheet
12. A key element of event marketing strategy is defining the event. What decisions are associated with defining the event?
13. Briefly explain the following stages of event marketing execution:
a) site selection and staging
b) staffing
c) operations and logistics
d) safety and security

DISCUSSION AND APPLICATION QUESTIONS

1. Marketers seem to be growing wary of sports event marketing, particularly at the professional level. Can you suggest any reasons why this is so?
2. Why are companies becoming more actively involved in cause-related event sponsorships? Conduct some secondary research on this issue and formulate a position on the matter.
3. Do value-added sponsorships such as the one between Reebok and Sidney Crosby offer significant benefits to the sponsoring organization? If so, what are the benefits? Discuss.
4. What classification of event sponsorship is appropriate for the following companies or brands? (More than one can apply.) Justify your decision.
   a) Becel margarine
   b) Michelin tires
   c) Perrier water
   d) BMW automobiles
   e) McDonald's
5. Assume you are responsible for planning an event such as a marathon/half-marathon race to raise funds for the Alzheimer's Association of Canada or some similar not-for-profit organization. What are your objectives? Consider both qualitative and quantitative objectives. Provide examples of a few objective statements. What marketing strategies will you employ to create awareness and interest in the event? Provide details of the activities you recommend.
6. Provide some examples of companies and brands that are involved with "experiential marketing." Based on your observations of their activities, identify the strengths and weaknesses of this form of marketing communications.

ENDNOTES

1. Adapted from Levon Guiragossian, The Definition of Experiential Marketing, *Web 2.0 Marketing*, http://web2pointz weromarketing. blogspot.com.
2. Callan Green, "Killer Facebook Fan Pages: 5 Inspiring Case Studies," *Mashable.com*, June 16, 2009, www.mashable.com/2009/06/16.
3. "Experiential Marketing," Canadian Marketing Blog, Canadian Marketing Association, April 17, 2008, www.canadianmarketingblog. com.
4. www.gmaonline.org/publications/docs/2007/shoppermarketing. pdf. and www.mediabuyerplanner.com/2006/08/29/ nielsen_instore_ads_sway_68/
5. Robert Gumiela, comments from a presentation at the Experiential Marketing Conference, Toronto, June 2, 2009.
6. "Diet Coke takes lounge act across Canada," *Marketing Daily*, July 5, 2007, www.marketingmag.ca/daily.
7. www.businessdictionary.com/definition/event-marketing.html.
8. "Vancouver 2010 Selects Bell Canada as premier national partner," press release, Bell Canada Enterprises, November 18, 2004.
9. "Sponsorship Spending to Total $16.5 billion in 2008," press release, January 18, 2008, www.IEGsponsorship.com.
10. Data obtained from Sponsorship Workshop, Toronto, May 19, 2009, Partnership Group, www.sponsorshipcongress.ca.
11. Brad Holden, "Making Waves," sports marketing supplement in *Marketing*, November 2007, p. 4.
12. IEG Sponsorship Report, 2007.
13. BMO Financial Group, www.bmo.com.
14. Abran Sauer, "Ambush Marketing: Steals the show," *Brand Channel*, May 27, 2002, www.brandchannel.com.
15. "Sony takes over from Hummingbird," *Marketing Daily*, September 10, 2007, www.marketingmag.ca.
16. Rick Westhead, "What's in a name? $$$," *Toronto Star*, August 19, 2003, p. E3.
17. Paul-Mark Rendon, "Hot Properties," *Marketing*, June 27, 2005, p. 11, and Air Canada Centre *Event Promoter Guide* 2007, p. 44.
18. Robert Thompson, "The next one sets record off the ice," *National Post*, March 9, 2005, p. A3.
19. Kristin Laird, "Energizer gets going with Ovechkin," *Marketing Daily*, April 9, 2009, www.marketingmag.ca.
20. Kate McArthur, "Pepsi is out, Coke is in as 2006 Oscars sponsor," *Advertising Age*, June 2, 2005, www.adage.com/news.
21. Elizabeth Blackwell, "Oscar sponsors set example for small firms," *TheStreet.com*, February 20, 2009, www.thestreet.com.
22. Toronto International Film Festival, www.tiff.ca.
23. Toronto International Film Festival, www.tiff.ca/sponsorships.
24. Kristin Laird, "Molson signs up with TSN for Wednesday night hockey," *Marketing Daily*, October 17, 2008, www.marketingmag.ca.
25. "Trend: Degree taps into poker craze," *Strategy*, August 2005, p. 30.
26. BMO Financial Group, www.bmo.com/corporate.
27. Robin Roberts, "Game On," Marketing, February 9, 2009, p. 14.
28. Wendy Cuthbert, "Sponsors pump ROI with experimental approach," *Strategy*, March 12, 2001, p. B7.
29. "Metro versus Retro," Brunico Communications, Toronto.
30. RBC Canadian Open, www.thecanadianopen.ca.

Learning Objectives

After studying this chapter, you will be able to

1. Understand the role of personal selling in retail, business-to-business, and direct selling environments and its relationship to integrated marketing communications

2. Describe the evolution of personal selling strategies and evaluate the role that relationship selling plays in integrated marketing communications programs

3. Identify the human variables that contribute to the successful application of personal selling strategies

4. Learn how to apply this knowledge to a variety of personal selling situations

5. Identify the fundamental roles and responsibilities of a sales representative

6. Identify the essential steps in the selling process and the key elements required for preparing a successful sales presentation

7. Assess how selling strategies need to adapt to a changing business environment

Among the various components of the integrated marketing communications mix, personal selling differentiates itself due to its personal nature. Advertising and promotions rely on the media to spread the word, public relations use various tools to seek the media's support in spreading the word, and direct response communications rely on the mail, telemarketing, the Internet, and mobile communications. All these forms of communications are impersonal. In spite of all of the changes that have occurred in the marketplace, and in spite of the fact that industry has come to rely on technology as a means of communication, personal selling still remains a vital component. Organizations continue to sell—they just sell differently than they used to.

To demonstrate, customer relationship management (CRM) practices affect all forms of communication, but none more than personal selling. The human contact and the ability to negotiate form the foundation of CRM practices. Furthermore, all of the technical wizardry in the world can only go so far. Once the show is over, someone has to ask for the order. And that's the responsibility of the sales representative. This chapter examines the role of personal selling in the context of integrated marketing communications.

Personal Selling and Integrated Marketing Communications

Personal selling is a personalized form of communications that involves sellers presenting the features and benefits of a product or service to a buyer for the purpose of making a sale. It is an integral component of marketing communications, because it is the activity that in many cases clinches the deal. Advertising and promotions create awareness and interest for a product; personal selling creates desire and action. In creating desire and action, the interaction between the seller and buyer is crucial.

Personal selling can be divided into three main areas: retail selling, business-to-business (B2B) selling, and direct selling, either to consumers or other businesses (see Figure 11.1). In all these areas, personal selling is connected to other aspects of integrated marketing communications planning. For example, a sales representative for Kraft Foods who calls on the head office of a grocery chain such as Safeway or Sobeys does more than just communicate the benefits of various product lines. If the salesperson's presentation

personal selling
Face-to-face communication involving the presentation of features and benefits of a product or service to a buyer; the objective is to make a sale.

FIGURE
11.1

Classifications of
Personal Selling

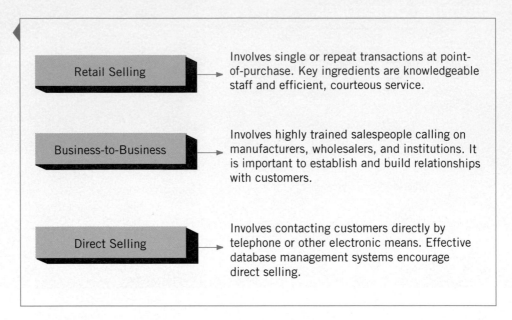

Retail Selling — Involves single or repeat transactions at point-of-purchase. Key ingredients are knowledgeable staff and efficient, courteous service.

Business-to-Business — Involves highly trained salespeople calling on manufacturers, wholesalers, and institutions. It is important to establish and build relationships with customers.

Direct Selling — Involves contacting customers directly by telephone or other electronic means. Effective database management systems encourage direct selling.

involves a new product launch, the objective is to get the product listed by the chain's head office so that retail stores in the chain can order it. Buyers want to know what kind of marketing support will be provided by Kraft. Therefore, at the very least, the salesperson must include information about advertising plans and sales promotion plans (both consumer and trade promotions) that will help create demand for the new product. Details about when advertising is scheduled, what markets it will run in, and what incentives will be offered to the consumer and the trade are all critical factors that influence the buying decision. Similar situations exist in other industries. Personal selling is directly linked to other communications strategies.

RETAIL SELLING

Transactions occur on the sales floor of a department store, in a checkout line of a grocery store, at an insurance agent's office, and at the service desk of an automobile maintenance shop, to name just a few examples of retail selling. In these situations, the nature of the sale is defined as a single transaction or a repeat transaction. The quality of service offered at the point of sale and the degree of satisfaction the customer receives usually influence repeat transactions. In fact, the retail salesperson is the face of the organization, and how that person deals with customers affects the buyer's experience.

A **single transaction** occurs when a salesperson spends time with a customer and eventually closes the sale on the spot. In many organizations, **order taking** is becoming popular. Stores such as Canadian Tire, Walmart, Home Depot, IKEA, and other large retailers have popularized the concept of self-serve. In these stores, floor personnel assist customers in locating the goods they need and provide useful information, but the customer simply passes through the checkout when purchasing the goods.

In situations where **repeat transactions** occur, there is an ongoing relationship between the buyer and seller. For example, a customer will return to the same automobile repair shop after getting to know the people who are working on his or her car. The customer wants to avoid the potential risk in dealing with different repair shops. The relationship between the buyer and seller is usually based on factors such as trust, respect, and satisfaction with the goods or services provided. These factors must be present if the retailer is to profit in the long run.

single transaction
A retail sales situation where a salesperson spends time with a customer and closes the sale on the spot.

order taking
In retail sales, a floor clerk provides product information and shows goods to the customer who then goes to the checkout counter to pay for purchases.

repeat transaction
A retail sales situation that involves a relationship between the buyer and the seller; the customer returns to the same store for similar goods and services.

Successful retailers continuously stress the importance of customer contact at point-of-purchase. How a retail salesperson interacts with the customer has a significant impact on how the customer perceives the retailer and helps determine if that individual will make a purchase. It is the seller's responsibility to clarify what the customer actually needs, usually by politely asking a few questions. The seller must then offer some product suggestions and demonstrate knowledge by presenting the essential benefits of the products to the customer.

When the purchase decision is made, the seller should look for opportunities for add-on sales or suggest service warranties to protect the customer's long-term interests. In retail stores where single transactions are the goal, high-pressure sales tactics are often applied. Although these kinds of tactics may work in the short term, many customers react negatively to them and simply leave the store feeling frustrated. Generally speaking, a low-key approach involving positive customer contact in a pleasant and courteous manner is the main ingredient for retail selling success. In retail, the salespeople are the most essential point of contact in the purchasing process—integral to a well-planned integrated marketing communications program.

BUSINESS-TO-BUSINESS SELLING

Business-to-business salespeople either sell products for use in the production and sale of other products, or sell finished products to channel members who in turn resell them. For example, a Xerox sales representative sells photocopiers to another business for use in its daily operations; a representative from Nike sells a line of running shoes to the head office of a specialty retailer such as the Forzani Group, which in turn distributes the running shoes through its retail locations (Sport Chek).

Thoroughly trained and adequately prepared sales representatives are crucial in all these examples. Investment in other forms of marketing communications could be all for naught if the personal selling execution is weak. B2B organizations usually have different types of sales personnel. A **field sales force** is composed of sales representatives who call on customers regularly. They make presentations to existing and new customers and provide ongoing customer contact to establish a good business relationship. A company may also operate with an **inside sales force**, often referred to as order takers, who seek out new customers and provide useful information to them. Working from the organization's premises, an order taker handles orders that are received by telephone, fax, or online.

field sales force
An organization's external sales representatives who regularly call on customers to pursue orders.

inside sales force
An internal group of sellers, often referred to as order takers, who accept orders from customers by telephone or other means.

DIRECT SELLING

Direct selling to customers either by telephone or the Internet can be accommodated in the retail selling and B2B selling situations described above. **Telemarketing** involves using the telephone as an interactive medium for a marketing response. It uses highly trained people and database marketing techniques to seek and serve new customers. Figure 11.2 summarizes the role that telemarketing can play in the selling process. Telemarketing improves productivity by reducing direct-selling costs, specifically the costs associated with keeping sales representatives on the road (automobiles, accommodations, and related travel expenses). It is also useful in screening and **qualifying** incoming leads, generating leads from various database directories and mailing lists, calling on current customers to secure additional orders, and determining the level of customer satisfaction.

Online selling refers to the use of websites to conduct sales transactions. Consumers who are looking for convenience now include the web as part of their shopping experience.

telemarketing
The use of telecommunications to promote the products and services of a business; involves outbound calls (company to customer) and inbound calls (customer to company).

qualifying (a customer)
Assessing if a prospect needs a product, has the authority to buy it, and has the ability to pay for it.

online selling
Using the Internet to conduct sales transactions.

Source: Grocery Gateway, Mississauga, Ontario.

FIGURE
11.2

Some of the Roles Played by Telemarketing in Personal Selling

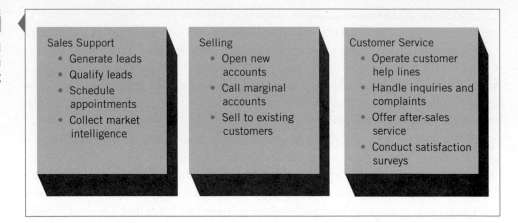

Sales Support
- Generate leads
- Qualify leads
- Schedule appointments
- Collect market intelligence

Selling
- Open new accounts
- Call marginal accounts
- Sell to existing customers

Customer Service
- Operate customer help lines
- Handle inquiries and complaints
- Offer after-sales service
- Conduct satisfaction surveys

Figure 11.3 shows how Grocery Gateway, an online supermarket, provides its consumers convenience. Websites like Grocery Gateway's are capable of accepting and processing orders, receiving payment, and arranging for the delivery of goods and services directly to consumers and businesses. Indigo Books & Music, operator of Chapters and Indigo stores, sells goods in a similar fashion. Since all transactions are electronically recorded, companies accumulate huge databases of information that can be used for marketing purposes in the longer term.

FIGURE
11.3   **Online selling offers convenience to consumers**

The Evolution of Selling

Over the years, the nature of selling has changed. Since the 1970s, personal selling has passed through three distinct stages: consultative selling, strategic selling, and relationship selling.[1] Relationship selling has been extended a step further as companies adopt electronic data interchange practices. For these companies, partnership selling is now the name of the game (see the next section for details).

Consultative selling stresses open, two-way communication between sellers and buyers. The initial task of the seller is to discover a need or set of needs by asking questions and listening carefully. The seller then uses that information to formulate appropriate product recommendations—acting as a consultant. Once the sale is complete, the seller gets involved with after-sales service and customer care programs. A satisfied customer remains a customer!

Changes in the marketplace have dictated changes in selling strategies. Products are now more sophisticated and complex, competition is more intense and occurs on a broader (global) scale, and *customer* expectations of quality, price, service, and individualized solutions have increased considerably. Similar to other components of the marketing communications mix, strategic selling strategies are influenced by an organization's strategic marketing plan. The marketing plan acts as a guide for the strategic selling plan. Refer to Figure 11.4 for an illustration of the planning model.

Strategic selling takes consultative selling to the next level. It considers the most recent yet continuously changing conditions in the marketplace, adds technology to enhance the methods of presenting products to buyers, and focuses on serving customers one customer at a time. The goal is to remain flexible while providing solutions that are unique to each customer. There are three key factors to be considered when formulating a strategic sales strategy. First, the seller must do what is necessary to form a good relationship with the customer. Second, the seller must effectively match products and position them so that they meet customer needs. And third, the seller must develop a compelling presentation that will clearly portray the usefulness of a product in resolving a customer's problem.

In **relationship selling**, the goal is to develop a plan of action to establish, build, and maintain customers. In involves taking a long-term perspective on selling and considers the fact that good relationships don't necessarily form very quickly. Instead, a seller must take the necessary steps to form a relationship, such as establishing rapport and building trust and respect, over a long period of time. Having a positive attitude, projecting a good image, and being able to get along with all kinds of different people and personalities are key factors that contribute to a sales representative's ability to build a solid relationship with customers.

Establishing a good relationship depends on how well the seller positions products in the minds of customers, how effectively (persuasively) the product's benefits are presented, and how well the seller guards the relationship in the long run. The latter requires ongoing customer contact and the implementation of customer care programs. Figure 11.5 reviews the key aspects of relationship selling.

With relationship selling, it is the seller's responsibility to match the right product to the customer and then develop the communications strategy that will position it appropriately in the customer's mind. A sales representative for Apple Computer, for example, will capitalize on the user-friendly positioning strategy that Apple uses in other forms of marketing communications to sell computers. The representative differentiates Apple from other brands based on benefits such as uniqueness, degree of innovation,

consultative selling
A form of selling that stresses open, two-way communication between a buyer and seller.

strategic selling
A form of consultative selling that involves dealing with each customer as an individual, stressing that in the transfer of product information.

relationship selling
A form of selling with the goal of developing a plan of action that establishes, builds, and maintains a long-term relationship with customers.

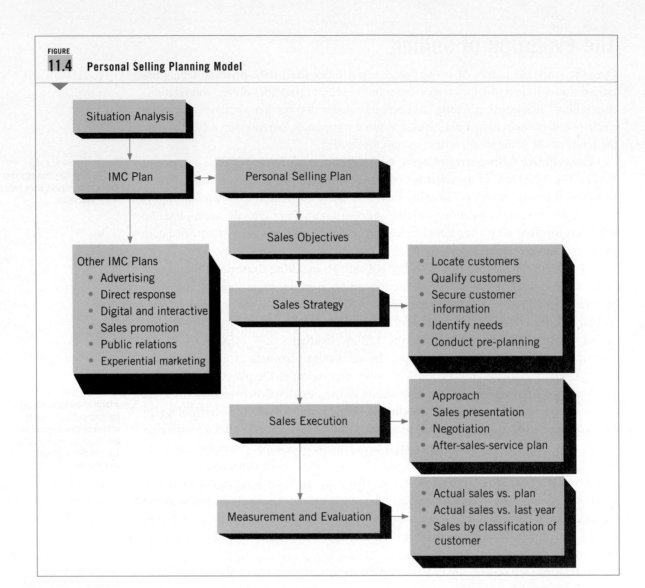

FIGURE 11.4   Personal Selling Planning Model

performance capabilities (speed of performing functions), and reliability. A wise representative will also build in the lifestyle imagery associated with the brand—for example, it is perceived as a sleek and sexy brand, a lifestyle brand compared to PCs.

The formation of the right positioning strategy depends largely on the seller's know-ledge of the customer. The more knowledge the seller has going into the presentation, the easier it is to structure the presentation. A good salesperson continuously updates his or her files with customer information. In the age of technology, such a practice is easy to do and vital to success. People in organizations move around, so it is very important to be constantly on top of who is responsible for what.

A good salesperson formulates a **presentation strategy** that focuses on what to say to customers when presenting the product. A good plan is based on the seller's knowledge of the customer and his or her immediate needs; it summarizes potential benefits that will be stressed (often prioritized from most important to least important) and considers potential objections that the buyer might raise. As with most marketing communications strategies, a sales strategy must remain flexible. The seller, for example, must be able to adapt the presentation based on new information that surfaces during a presentation, or to rephrase relevant benefits if the buyer introduces the benefits of a

presentation strategy
A plan of what to say to a customer in a sales presentation to identify customer needs, summarize benefits, and prepare for potential objections.

Overall Goal	To establish, build, and maintain customers.
Personal Strategy	The seller must initiate steps that will build rapport with customers. The seller must earn the trust and respect of the customer. The salesperson must have a strong and positive self-image and be flexible when dealing with many different people and personalities.
Selling Strategy	The salesperson must effectively position the product (a solution) in the customer's mind by relating the right benefits to a unique problem or situation that the customer presents. The benefits should be related to the rational needs of the buying organization and the emotional needs of the buyer. A salesperson must make a convincing presentation and be flexible enough to adapt to the unexpected while the presentation is in progress. A persuasive presentation should lead the buyer to the right decision.
Building Relationships	Customers not only want good products, but also want good relationships. Selling today is not about selling products—it's about selling solutions!

FIGURE
11.5

The Key Elements of Relationship Selling

competitor's product. The importance of knowledge in a variety of areas and the key elements of a presentation are discussed in more detail later in this chapter.

PARTNERSHIP SELLING

Partnership selling is an extension of relationship selling. It involves a strategically developed, long-term relationship to sell products, provides comprehensive after-sales service, and encourages effective two-way communications to ensure complete customer satisfaction. The goal is to form partnerships with customers in a manner that fosters prosperity among partners.

Changing conditions in the marketplace have fostered the concept of partnership selling. There was a time when companies could rely on the strength of their company, product, and service components to secure stability and growth. Now, however, the intensity of competition, the availability of copycat products, the need to constantly reduce costs, and the speed with which innovative products are introduced necessitates strong buyer–seller partnerships. Therefore, sellers are transforming their selling procedures and methods to build formal relationships with other organizations in the channel of distribution.[2] It is all part of the CRM philosophy discussed earlier in this book.

Selling organizations today must be willing to invest time and money into finding good solutions. It's not about selling products any more—it's about selling solutions! To illustrate, consider that UPS has moved from being a courier service to become a supply chain management company with the goal of assisting customers with their long-range growth needs (see Figure 11.6). The company has evolved with changes in the marketplace and with the changing needs of its customers.

In a marketing communications context, smart managers know that customers rely on different pieces of information as they proceed through the buying process. Various components of the mix may take priority. For example, an event may be more important than advertising depending on the target audience. An event combined with effective personal selling strategies may be just the right mix to motivate a potential buyer. For more insight into how various components of the communications mix may be combined, read the IMC Highlight: **Personal Connections Work for Jaguar and Jeep.**

partnership selling
A strategically developed long-term relationship that involves selling products and providing comprehensive after-sales service and effective two-way communications to ensure complete customer satisfaction.

Source: Courtesy of UPS and The Martin Agency.

Personal Selling: The Human Communications Element

If establishing and building effective relationships are the keys to modern-day success, what strategies must the salesperson use to form a good working relationship with his or her customers? To be successful, a salesperson must focus on three primary areas: personal characteristics, verbal communications, and non-verbal communications. A well-prepared and energetic salesperson knows how to communicate effectively both verbally and non-verbally, and as a result, will be successful. Let's examine each area briefly.

PERSONAL CHARACTERISTICS

To survive in selling, certain personal characteristics are required. Typically, successful salespeople are self-confident, motivated, flexible, optimistic, and project a good image when confronted with social and business situations. These characteristics can be

IMC HIGHLIGHT >>

Personal Connections Work for Jaguar and Jeep

With the help of some good database marketing, Jaguar Canada was able to identify prospective customers it would invite to an invitation-only test-drive event. Imagine driving a 400-horsepower Jaguar around a track, sampling gourmet pasta, and relaxing over drinks. Jaguar's mission: get owners of competitors' vehicles inside a Jaguar—kind of a "try it and you will like it" marketing strategy.

Jaguar is a small brand that doesn't advertise all that much. Given the upscale nature of the vehicle and the selective audience that has the means to buy the car, Jaguar prefers relationship marketing events. Jaguar president Gary Moyer says, "Someone buying a $100 000 car doesn't watch TV ads or read magazine ads. But this kind of thing makes their hair stand up on the back of their neck."

Test-drive events are growing in importance, and for some companies they now take centre stage in the overall marketing strategy. These events are costly to plan and implement but there is a payoff. People who test drive a vehicle are more likely to consider that brand when they buy. In fact, some research indicates they are three times more likely to buy the test-drive vehicle.

At Chrysler the Jeep brand runs a three-day event called Camp Jeep and invites brand loyalists and prospective customers to it. Lou Bitonti, a marketing executive at Chrysler, says, "You have to keep that human connection and passion point. We show them the Jeep in real conditions and have specialists there to answer all of their questions." He adds that events help dispel false impressions about Jeep while creating positive new ones.

To promote the Toyota Tundra truck, Toyota participates in farm, fishing, and outdoor shows. At these events Toyota shows how the truck complements the lifestyle of the target audience, as in showing one packed and ready to go on a fishing trip. That gets the prospect excited!

From a strategic perspective, auto marketers like these kinds of events for three reasons: first, there is a personal connection with the customer; second, they can convey the vehicle's character; and third, events break through the cluttered media landscape and can target hard-to-reach targets such as young trendsetters. More to the point, the automaker has the complete attention of the buyer, who can actually touch and feel the car, interact with the brand at his or her own pace, and test the vehicle to discover in a very personal way what it has to offer. Marketing today is about reaching people wherever they are. Test-drive events do just that but in a very personal and creative manner.

Adapted from Jeremy Cato, "Automakers finding new ways to move metal," *The Globe and Mail*, August 16, 2007, www.globeauto.com.

---

learned and practised, and given time and proper training, poorly performing salespeople can be transformed into prosperous salespeople. All that is required are dedication and a desire to confront the challenges of selling.

Self-image is a psychological term referring to one's attitude and feelings about oneself and one's roles in relation to others. It certainly plays a key role in selling. Perhaps the most important aspect of self-image is one's confidence. For example, an individual who approaches a challenge with enthusiasm, or possesses that "I'm going to win" attitude, is likely to succeed. In contrast, an individual who tends to forecast failure, or has a "doom and gloom" attitude, will almost certainly get disappointing results. To succeed, therefore, you have to think you can succeed.

self-image
One's own idea about oneself and one's relationship with others.

Among all the theories about building self-confidence that exist, three essential strategies stand out. First, a positive self-image will exist if a person does not dwell on past mistakes. Instead, people must learn from those mistakes and move forward. Second, a salesperson should develop some expertise in a certain area because there is special status in being an expert. Others will call upon you for advice. Third, a salesperson should develop a positive outlook. For example, taking courses that reinforce the principles of success and simply associating with other positive and successful people are both good practices to follow.

VERBAL AND NON-VERBAL COMMUNICATIONS

verbal skills
Comfort and ability with speaking and listening.

Typically, good salespeople have good **verbal skills**. They are generally comfortable when addressing a buyer, buying committee, or even a larger audience. When one thinks of a salesperson the stereotype of the fast talker often comes to mind, but the reality is that listening skills are just as important. A salesperson who listens carefully to what the buyer says can respond better. Communications in a selling situation is a two-way street.

non-verbal communication (body language)
The expression of thoughts, opinions, or information using non-verbal cues such as body movement, facial expressions, and eye contact.

Non-verbal communication or **body language** is another essential aspect of self-confidence. Non-verbal communication refers to the imparting of thoughts, opinions, or information without using spoken words. An observer (in this case the buyer) will notice non-verbal cues such as body movement, facial expressions, and eye contact.[3] A buyer's perceptions of a salesperson are often determined by body language. For example, does the seller squirm in the chair while conversing or does the seller fidget with a small object while speaking? Such body language could be perceived as a lack of confidence. Alternatively, does the seller make direct eye contact? Was that handshake firm and friendly? Such body language suggests positive self-confidence. For a summary of some essential characteristics and traits for successful selling, refer to Figure 11.7.

Other non-verbal characteristics that influence buyers' perceptions include facial expressions, personal appearance, and manners. The old expression that "the lips say one thing, but the eyes say another" applies to selling situations. Facial gestures can communicate confidence, as does a smile; boredom, as does a grin; or evaluation or judgment, as in a frown or perplexed expression. Given that the goal in selling is to express confidence, successful salespeople always wear a sincere and winning smile when they approach customers and when they present information to them.

FIGURE
11.7

Personal characteristics and planning lead to selling success

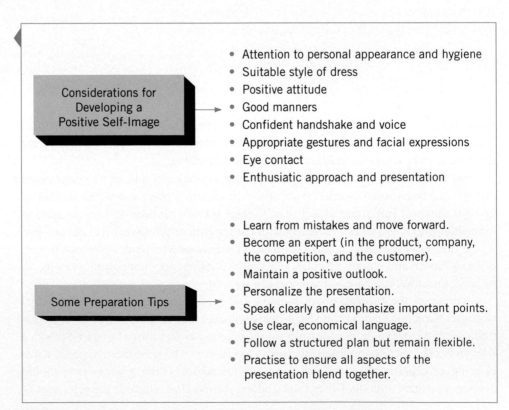

Considerations for Developing a Positive Self-Image

- Attention to personal appearance and hygiene
- Suitable style of dress
- Positive attitude
- Good manners
- Confident handshake and voice
- Appropriate gestures and facial expressions
- Eye contact
- Enthusiatic approach and presentation

Some Preparation Tips

- Learn from mistakes and move forward.
- Become an expert (in the product, company, the competition, and the customer).
- Maintain a positive outlook.
- Personalize the presentation.
- Speak clearly and emphasize important points.
- Use clear, economical language.
- Follow a structured plan but remain flexible.
- Practise to ensure all aspects of the presentation blend together.

Dress codes have changed drastically in recent years. The business world moved away from formal attire (business suits) and toward informal attire (business casual) for a period of time. The "Casual Friday" concept spread to the entire week. Recently, however, there has been a return to more formal dress. Wardrobe experts believe clothing makes a significant difference in building one's credibility and likeability with customers. Experts offer different opinions on how to dress, but generally there is one common theme: the situation (or appropriateness) dictates the style of dress. For example, if you are meeting your customer in a business office or boardroom setting, formal dress is appropriate. If the meeting is in a factory or at a construction site, less formal attire is suitable. Other traditional guidelines for wardrobe focus on simplicity, quality, and the selective use of accessories. Accessories such as earrings, necklaces, and facial jewellery could be a distraction for the buyer and anything causing a distraction should be avoided.

There is a relationship between verbal communication and non-verbal communication in a selling situation. Successful salespeople effectively blend together verbal and non-verbal communications. They communicate the message in a positive and enthusiastic manner and reinforce it with body language that is consistent with what they say. Such a combination builds confidence in the buyer and gives the buyer the impression you can be trusted. Such perceptions certainly go a long way in building and maintaining a business relationship.

Beyond these personal characteristics, good salespeople possess other intangible characteristics that have an impact on their performance. For some insight into these characteristics, see the IMC Highlight: **What Separates Successful Salespeople from Everyone Else?**

PREPARATION AND THE IMPORTANCE OF KNOWLEDGE

In a nutshell, the primary task of a salesperson is to provide a customer with a solution to a problem by matching the right product or service at a price that is agreeable to the customer. It sounds so simple! But it requires much advance preparation, and that preparation is divided into three primary areas: product knowledge, company knowledge, and competitor knowledge. With regard to product knowledge, the salesperson must become an expert and know exactly what benefits to stress with any particular customer. For example, two different customers might require the same product, but one customer is motivated by quality, the other by service. The salesperson would have to adapt the presentation to offer different perspectives based on each buyer's unique needs and priorities. In complex situations, such as when various products must be combined to form a solution, the salesperson must be capable of bringing the right products and services together. This process is called **product configuration**.

product configuration
The bringing together of various products and services to form a solution for the customer.

PRODUCT KNOWLEDGE

Essentially, product knowledge can be classified into four key areas: product development and quality improvement processes, performance data and specifications, maintenance and service, and price and delivery. Te various combinations of this information make up the essential elements of a planned sales presentation. To grow, companies develop new products to solve new needs. It is important for a salesperson to know how a product was developed, how much it cost to develop, and why it was developed. This sort of information strongly suggests to a customer that the company takes research and development seriously and strives to build better products for its customers. In terms of performance and quality, a salesperson should be familiar with quality control standards so that information regarding product claims can be substantiated and compared with

What Separates Successful Salespeople from Everyone Else?

Successful salespeople possess intangible skills that go beyond product, company, and competitor knowledge. These salespeople know it is the "little things" that separate successful salespeople from the rest of the pack. So, what are some of these intangibles? Here are a few of them.

They Are Persistent

Successful salespeople don't let obstacles stand in their way. They are tenacious and are constantly looking for new solutions.

They Set Goals

Successful salespeople establish specific goals, then visualize their target, determine how they will achieve their goals, and take action daily.

They Listen

Effective salespeople know the customer will tell them what they need to know; therefore, they listen and learn.

They Are Passionate

When you love what you do you put more passion into it. Effective salespeople are passionate about their company and products.

They Are Enthusiastic

Effective salespeople remain positive even in tough times. When faced with negative and challenging situations they always focus on the positives.

They Keep in Touch

Effective salespeople go well beyond routine follow-up. They keep track of key dates such as birthdays and anniversaries and deliver communications on a more personal level in order to enhance the relationship

They Work Hard

Successful salespeople start early, make more calls, and stay late when necessary. They know that making more presentations will produce more sales.

Adapted from Kelley Robertson, "Characteristics of Successful Salespeople," *SOHO*, Summer 2006, pp. 14, 15.

claims made by competitors. Knowing that a product meets or exceeds certain standards often provides a competitive advantage in a sales presentation.

A buyer usually poses questions or raises objections about performance data and specifications in the middle of a sales presentation. To illustrate, assume you are planning a business conference and considering various conference centres. What kinds of questions would you ask the sales manager of a potential conference centre? Here are a few examples:

• Does the conference centre offer technical support if we need it?

• Is there an Internet connection available to delegates and at what cost?

• s there sufficient accommodation available for 200 delegates?

• How efficient is the catering department in serving a buffet dinner to 200 people?

Certainly the list could be longer and much more diverse. And that is the key point. A good salesperson must be ready to respond to the expected and the unexpected.

If the competing products are similar, it could be that information about maintenance and service provide product differentiation. If service is provided as part of a package deal, all specifications regarding additional services must be part of the sales presentation. Specifications must be agreed upon about who is responsible for what service, when it will happen, how often it will happen, and so on. It is very common for selling companies to draw up official service contracts based on specific requirements provided by the buying organization. Such contracts play a vital role in the relationship-building process.

Other knowledge that helps differentiate one product from another is knowledge about price and delivery. The easiest and most common objection that buyers raise is price: "Your price is too high!" Knowing how to respond appropriately is crucial to closing the sale. If your price is higher than the competition, that fact must be acknowledged, and additional and tangible product benefits must be presented to justify the higher price. In such situations, the buyer simply wants more information; the salesperson must show good product knowledge.

COMPANY KNOWLEDGE

Since the salesperson is the customer's primary source of contact, the salesperson is the company. The perceptions formed by a customer or prospective customer about a company depend largely on the attitude, style, behaviour, and communications ability of the salesperson. If perceptions are positive there is a stronger likelihood of making the sale and developing a long-term business relationship. A salesperson, therefore, should integrate essential information about the company into a sales presentation.

Business organizations exist to serve their customers, and all employees must recognize that they contribute to this effort. This attitude, often referred to as **corporate culture**, is defined as the values, norms, and practices shared by all employees of an organization. A good corporate culture always puts the customer first. A successful and diversified organization such as 3M thinks "customer" all the time. All employees are part of a marketing team and consider themselves to be in the customer care business. In fact, 3M uses the phrase "From need to... 3M Innovation" as its advertising slogan. At the 3M website there are other phrases such as "From Imagination to Innovation" and "Leading through Innovation." 3M identifies customer needs and develops innovative products to satisfy those needs. Such information should be passed on to prospective customers by sales representatives, because it sends out a clear signal about the type of company 3M is: a company willing to develop new products and to respond to new challenges in an ever-changing marketplace. Figure 11.8 provides some insight into the innovations of 3M in the consumer marketplace and the B2B marketplace.

What services a company provides after the sale is also crucial information to provide to customers. As many experts say, "The relationship begins once the sale is made." Therefore, after-sales service, which is a function that is usually implemented by other departments of a company, must be integrated into a sales presentation. It is important for a company to track the level of satisfaction that customers are experiencing, so it is quite common for organizations to contact customers directly by telephone or mail. The results of surveys, for example, can be passed on to sales representatives for follow-up.

COMPETITOR KNOWLEDGE

A good salesperson knows the competitor's products almost as well as his or her own. In a sales presentation, comparisons inevitably crop up, making it essential to know the benefits and weaknesses of competing products and adapt the selling strategy accordingly. If a seller cannot respond to the challenges posed by a buyer, the chances of making a sale are lost.

Talking about competing products is usually awkward. Obviously, a salesperson does not want to acknowledge a competitor's strengths, but at the same time a seller cannot be too critical of competitors' products. The customer may already be doing business with the competition. Here are a few basic guidelines for dealing with competing products:[4]

corporate culture
The values, beliefs, norms, and practices shared by all employees of an organization.

FIGURE
11.8 **3M responds to the challenge of developing new and innovative products for a changing marketplace**

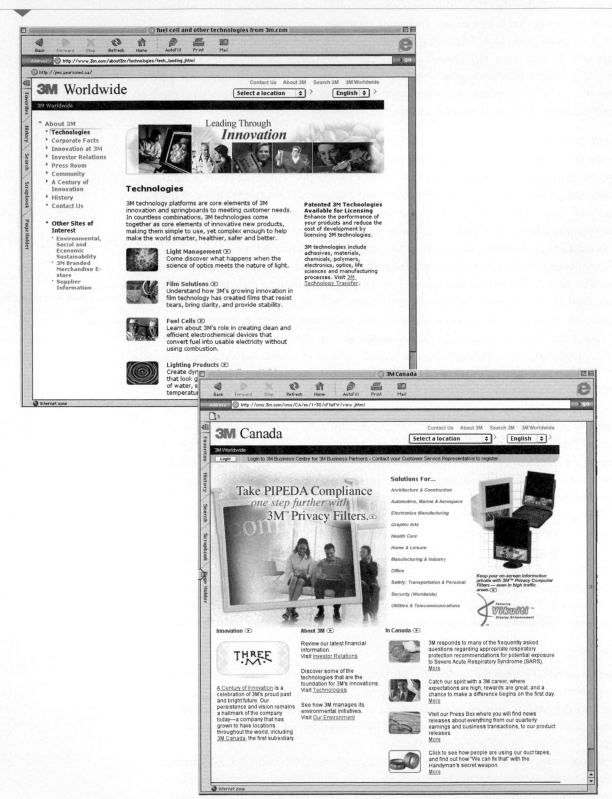

- Do not deliberately include reference to competitors in your presentation as it shifts the focus off your own product. Do, however, respond to questions about the competition.

- Do not make statements about the competitor if you are uncertain of the facts. Your credibility will suffer if you make inaccurate statements.

- Do not criticize the competition. State the facts as you know them and avoid emotional comments if you have to make a comparison.

Remember, prospective customers are forming perceptions of you and your company when you are making the sales presentation. How you handle competing products goes a long way in creating a favourable or unfavourable impression.

Roles and Responsibilities of Salespeople

The primary tasks of a salesperson, particularly in a business-to-business environment, are to gather market intelligence, solve customers' problems, locate and maintain customers, and provide follow-up service. This section examines each key responsibility.

GATHERING MARKET INTELLIGENCE

In a competitive marketplace, salespeople must be attuned to the trends in their industry. They must be alert to what the competitor is doing, to its new product projects, and to its advertising and promotion plans, and they must listen to feedback from customers regarding their own products' performance. As indicated earlier, competitive knowledge is important when the salesperson faces questions involving product comparisons. Data collected by a salesperson can be reported electronically to the company's head office. Managers can retrieve the information and use it appropriately at a later date.

PROBLEM SOLVING

The only way a salesperson can make a sale is to listen to what a customer wants and ask questions to determine his or her real needs. Asking, listening, and providing information and advice that is in the best interests of the customer are what relationship selling is all about. The seller must demonstrate a sincere concern for the customer's needs.

LOCATING AND MAINTAINING CUSTOMERS

Salespeople who locate new customers play a key role in a company's growth. A company cannot be satisfied with its current list of customers, because aggressive competitors are always attempting to lure them away. To prevent shrinkage and to increase sales, salespeople actively pursue new accounts. Their time is divided between finding new accounts and selling and servicing current accounts.

FOLLOW-UP SERVICE

The salesperson is the first point of contact should anything go wrong or should more information be required. Maintenance of customers is crucial and, very often, it is the quality of the follow-up service that determines if a customer will remain a customer. Since the salespeople are the company's direct link to the customer, it cannot be stressed enough how important it is that they handle customer service well. The sale is never over! Once the deal has closed, numerous tasks arise: arranging for delivery, providing technical assistance, offering customer training, and being readily available to handle any problems that might emerge during and after delivery. The personalized role of the sales representative is instrumental in building relationships.

Personal Selling Strategies

Before discussing the various steps involved in successful personal selling, let's first explore the difference between features and benefits. A product **feature** is anything that can be felt, seen, or measured. Features include such things as durability, design, and economy of operation. They provide a customer with information, but do not motivate a customer to buy. A **benefit** provides the customer with advantage or gain, and shows how a product will help resolve a specific problem. Benefits provide motivation! To demonstrate, consider all of the technical features usually associated with a laptop or desktop computer. The list seems endless and includes much technical jargon. Assuming the customer wants quick access to information when using the computer (information the seller would seek out by asking a few questions), the seller can quickly zoom in on the appropriate features and translate them into benefits that are appropriate for and meaningful to the customer.

Regardless of the sales situation—whether retail selling, business-to-business selling, or direct selling—the steps in the selling process are similar. They are simply adapted to each situation. This section covers the seven essential steps in the selling process (see Figure 11.9).

PROSPECTING

The first step is **prospecting**, which is a procedure for systematically developing sales leads. If salespeople do not allocate enough time to finding new customers, they risk causing a decline in sales for their company. If their income is geared to the value of the business they produce, they risk the loss of personal compensation as well. Prospecting is also important because of attrition. Attrition refers to the loss of customers over a period of time. Even with extensive CRM programs in place as a means of retaining customers, buyers switch suppliers when better products and services become available.

Potential customers, or prospects, are identified by means of published lists and directories, such as Scott's Industrial Directories, the *Frasers Trade Index*, and the *Canadian Key Business Directory*. Another strategy for seeking new customers is the referral. A **referral** is a prospect that is recommended by a current customer. The salesperson also seeks new customers by **cold canvass**, the process of calling on people or organizations without appointments or advance knowledge of them. Other sources of leads include names obtained from trade shows, advertising, direct response communications, telemarketing and online communications, sales promotion entry forms, and channel members.

PRE-APPROACH

The **pre-approach** involves gathering information about potential customers before actually making sales contact. During the pre-approach stage, customers are qualified, which is the procedure for determining if a prospect needs the product, has the authority to buy it, and has the ability to pay for it. There is little sense in pursuing customers who lack the financial resources or have no need to make the business relationship successful. In the process of qualifying customers, the seller also gains insights that can be used in the sales presentation: information such as the buyer's likes and dislikes, personal interests and hobbies, buying procedures, and special needs and problems.

APPROACH

The **approach** is the initial contact with the prospect, often in a face-to-face selling situation. Since buyers are usually busy, little time should be wasted in the approach. In the

---

feature
Tangible aspect of a product, such as durability, design, and economy of operation.

benefit
The value a customer attaches to a brand attribute.

prospecting
A procedure for systematically developing sales leads.

referral
A recommendation by a current customer of a potential new customer to a sales representative.

cold canvass
The process of calling on people or organizations without appointments or advance knowledge of them.

pre-approach
The gathering of information about customers before actually making sales contact.

approach
The initial contact with a customer.

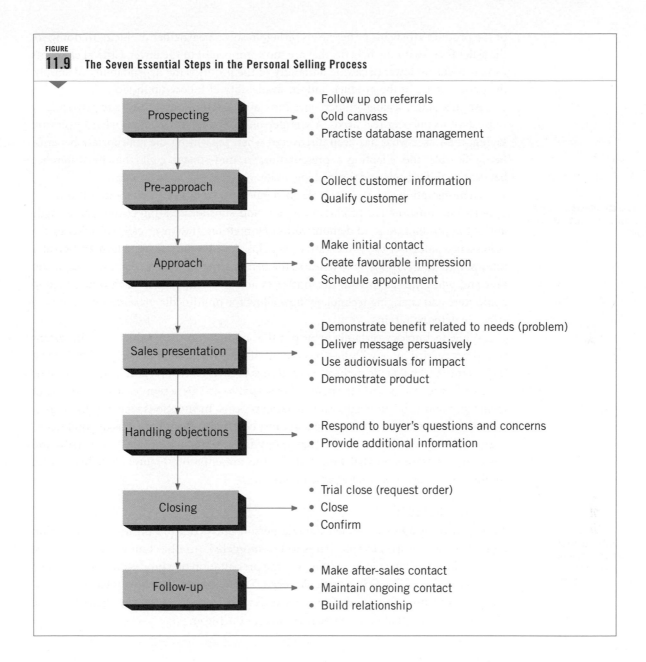

FIGURE 11.9   The Seven Essential Steps in the Personal Selling Process

Prospecting
- Follow up on referrals
- Cold canvass
- Practise database management

Pre-approach
- Collect customer information
- Qualify customer

Approach
- Make initial contact
- Create favourable impression
- Schedule appointment

Sales presentation
- Demonstrate benefit related to needs (problem)
- Deliver message persuasively
- Use audiovisuals for impact
- Demonstrate product

Handling objections
- Respond to buyer's questions and concerns
- Provide additional information

Closing
- Trial close (request order)
- Close
- Confirm

Follow-up
- Make after-sales contact
- Maintain ongoing contact
- Build relationship

first few minutes of a sales interview, the salesperson must capture the attention and interest of the buyer and create a favourable first impression so that there is an effective environment for the presentation of the product's benefits.

SALES PRESENTATION

It is common for a salesperson to make presentations to individuals (one-on-one selling) or to buying teams (one-on-group selling). Buying teams are classified as buying centres (an informal grouping of people in the buying group) or buying committees (a formal group with a structured buying procedure in place). In dealing with buying committees, the salesperson must listen attentively and observe body language to determine which members of the group are the real influencers and decision makers.

The actual **sales presentation** consists of a persuasive delivery and demonstration of a product's benefits. An effective sales presentation shows the buyer how the benefits

sales presentation
A persuasive delivery and demonstration of a product's benefits; shows buyers how the product's benefits will satisfy their needs.

of the product satisfy his or her needs or help resolve a particular problem. In doing so, the seller focuses on the benefits that are most important to the buyer. Critical elements usually focus on lower price, the durability of the product, the dependability of supply, the performance of the product, and the availability of follow-up service.

At this stage, asking proper questions and listening attentively are particularly important to uncover real needs. A salesperson listens to and analyzes what buyers are saying, then uses what has been discovered when presenting the appropriate benefits. Being flexible and adapting a presentation in mid-stream could be the difference between making a sale and not making a sale.

Demonstrations play a key role in a sales presentation. A **demonstration** is an opportunity to show the product in action and substantiates the claims being made about the product. A good demonstration (something the buyer can see) adds to the convincing nature of the presentation. It helps hold the buyer's attention and creates interest and desire. It is wise to rehearse the demonstration so that what the salesperson says and what the salesperson demonstrates are in harmony with each other. Laptop computers and changing technology now allow for multimedia presentations and very effective demonstrations.

While technology certainly helps put the spotlight on the product, it is important not to get carried away with it—the content of the presentation is always what is most important. A useful tactic in the presentation is to involve the prospect by letting him or her handle the product and the materials relevant to it. This action results in a feeling of ownership and helps in the decision-making process. In situations where technology is part of the presentation, the salesperson must be certain all equipment is in good working condition. A failure with the technology is embarrassing for the salesperson and costly in terms of potential time lost for the presentation. Figure 11.10 lists useful reminders for planning a sales presentation.

HANDLING OBJECTIONS

An **objection** is an obstacle that the salesperson must confront during a presentation and resolve if the sales transaction is to be completed. An objection is a cue for more information. The buyer is suggesting that the presentation of a product has not revealed how the product will satisfy a particular need. The objection, therefore, is feedback to be analyzed and used. It may enable the salesperson to discover another benefit in the product, a benefit that can then be presented to the buyer.

demonstration
A sales technique that involves showing the product in action to portray its benefits to a buyer.

objection
An obstacle that a salesperson must confront during a sales presentation.

FIGURE 11.10

Useful Reminders for Planning a Sales Presentation

- Ask the buyer questions and listen attentively to the responses.
- Include useful information about the company.
- Watch for cues by observing body language.
- Include a product demonstration (rehearse to make sure it works).
- Involve the buyer in the presentation.
- Remain flexible throughout the presentation and adapt it based on feedback.
- Add technology where appropriate to enhance the presentation.
- Respond to objections pleasantly (be prepared for the expected and unexpected).
- Ask for the order (always be closing).

Typical objections involve issues related to the following: product quality and the level of service and technical assistance; the price or the level of discounts suggested, for example the price may be too high, discount too low, or credit terms unacceptable; and sourcing issues such as how the buyer feels about the company in comparison to other potential suppliers. Objections are a normal response from buyers, so salespeople should not take them personally. Instead, the salesperson should ask questions of the buyer to confirm his or her understanding of the situation, answer the objection, and then move on to the next benefit or attempt to close the sale. A good salesperson develops effective strategies for handling objections; being prepared for the expected and unexpected is essential. When responding to objections, the salesperson can call upon the product itself, testimonials and case histories of success, test results shown in a variety of formats (e.g., graphs and charts), and other forms of audiovisual support.

CLOSING

Does the buyer voluntarily say, "Yes, I'll buy it"? The answer is "rarely"! Getting the buyer to say "yes" is the entire purpose of the sales interview, but this task is only accomplished if the salesperson asks for the order. **Closing** consists of asking for the order, and it is the most difficult step in the process of selling. Salespeople are reluctant to ask the big question, even though it is the logical sequel to a good presentation and demonstration. In fact, a good salesperson attempts a close whenever a point of agreement is made with the buyer. If the buyer says "no," the close is referred to as a **trial close,** or an attempt to close that failed. The salesperson simply moves on to the next point in the presentation.

The close can occur at any point in a sales presentation. Knowing when to close is essential. Therefore, as the sales presentation progresses, the salesperson must be alert to closing cues. A **closing cue** is an indication that the buyer is ready to buy. The cue may be verbal or non-verbal. If a cue is detected, a close should be attempted. Verbal cues include statements such as "What type of warranty do you provide?" Such a statement shows that the buyer is thinking ahead. Another cue is "The delivery and installation schedule fits well with our factory conversion schedule." Such a statement suggests confirmation of a key benefit. Or another: "We need the product in one week." In other words, if you can supply it, we'll buy it! Statements such as these are closing cues that must be acted upon.

Positive non-verbal communications include changing facial expressions, a change in the buyer's mood (e.g., the buyer becomes more jovial), or the buyer nods in agreement or reads the sales information intently. Good salespeople do not miss such opportunities, even if they are not finished their presentation. The buyer is telling you it is time to close—do it!

Timing a close is a matter of judgment. Good salespeople know when to close—it is often referred to as the "sixth sense" of selling. The salesperson assesses the buyer's verbal and non-verbal responses in an effort to judge when that person has become receptive, and at the right moment, asks the big question with a high degree of self-confidence. A list of commonly used closing techniques appears in Figure 11.11.

Once the sale has been closed, it is time to reassure the customer that a good decision has been taken and to confirm that you will provide all the essential services that were promised in the presentation. Parting on a positive note is crucial, because buyers very often experience cognitive dissonance. **Cognitive dissonance** refers to a feeling of doubt or regret once the buying decision has been made. The buyer wants to be reassured that the best choice has been made. This is the start of the relationship-building process.

closing
Asking for the order at the appropriate time in a sales presentation.

trial close
A failed attempt at closing a sale; the buyer said "no."

closing cue
An indication that the buyer is ready to buy; can be expressed verbally or non-verbally.

cognitive dissonance
A feeling of doubt or regret in a consumer's mind once a buying decision has been made.

FIGURE
11.11

Successful Closing Techniques

The objective of the sales presentation is to get the order. To do so, the seller must close the sale by asking for the order. Asking for the order can be accomplished in a variety of ways.

Assumptive Close
The seller assumes the buyer has already decided to buy. The seller says, "I'll have it delivered by Friday," or "What is the best day for delivery?" An agreement or answer confirms the seller's assumption.

Alternative-Choice Close
The seller assumes the sale is made but asks for clarification on another point. He or she may say, "Would you prefer metallic blue or cherry red?"

Summary-of-Benefits Close
At the end of the presentation the seller calmly reviews the key points the buyer has already agreed to (price, service, quality, reliability, etc.). Once the summary is complete the seller says, "When would you like it delivered?"

Direct Close
No beating around the bush here. The seller confidently says, "Can I deliver it on Friday?" then stops talking and awaits the response.

Take-Away Close
It is human nature to want what one can't have. The seller says, "This product isn't for everyone. It's a certain kind of person who can appreciate the finer qualities of this product."

FOLLOW-UP

There is an old saying: "The sale never ends." There is truth to this statement, because a new sale is nothing more than the start of a new relationship. Keeping current customers satisfied is the key to success. Effective salespeople make a point of providing **follow-up;** that is, they keep in touch with customers to ensure that the delivery and installation of the goods were satisfactory, that promises were kept, and that the expectations of the buyer were met. When problems do occur, the salesperson is ready to take action to resolve the situation.

In the current competitive business environment, good follow-up strategies help reduce customer attrition. Companies realize that a satisfied customer is a long-term customer. As discussed elsewhere in this textbook, customer relationship management programs now act as a foundation for long-term business success. Keeping track of customer transactions and customer preferences provides an opportunity for incremental sales. Larry Rosen, president of upscale clothier Harry Rosen, firmly understands this concept. Harry Rosen has implemented programs that ensure the utmost in customer service and care. "We don't look at a person in terms of an immediate sale. We look at him in terms of potential lifetime value."[5]

Success in selling requires dedication, determination, and discipline. What separates the successful salesperson from the unsuccessful one usually boils down to how well an individual follows an established set of principles. While the wording of these principles might vary from one source to another, the intent behind them is consistent. See Figure 11.12 for some pointers on what separates the professionals from the average salespeople.

Effective salespeople should possess knowledge in three key areas: customers and the industries they operate in, their own company and products, and the competition. They should follow the essential steps in the selling process if they are to be successful. Unfortunately, it is not that easy. Personal motivation also plays a key role in one's success.

follow-up
Maintaining contact with customers to ensure that service has been satisfactory.

FIGURE
11.12

Tips for Successful Selling

1. SELLING SKILLS ARE LEARNED SKILLS

Successful salespeople take the time to develop their skills. They ask meaningful questions, listen attentively, and observe buyer behaviour. Through learning, they can relate appropriate product benefits to the customer's needs. Knowledge of the product, company, customer, and competition is essential.

2. THE SALESPERSON IS THE MOST IMPORTANT PRODUCT

Successful salespeople sell themselves. They project a positive image about themselves and their company. If the customer isn't sold on you, he or she won't buy your product.

3. EMOTIONS, FEELINGS, AND RELATIONSHIPS ARE IMPORTANT

Successful salespeople present more than just facts. They create positive emotions about themselves, their products and services, and their company. Through effective communications, they bring the buyers into the relationship, showing how their problems will be resolved.

4. PREPARATION IS CRUCIAL

Be prepared! A sales presentation is like a stage performance. You may not get a second chance. Command the buyer's attention immediately and encourage participation throughout the presentation. Through participation, the buyer will discover the product's benefits. Ensure that all components of the presentation are coordinated and all electronic aids are in working condition.

5. NEGOTIATION SKILLS ARE IMPORTANT

A successful salesperson can deal with any and all concerns raised by the buyer. Be prepared to meet challenges by offering additional information and package together all points of agreement in order to close the sale.

6. ALWAYS BE CLOSING

Closing begins at the start of a presentation. The challenge is to build agreement and help the prospect decide how to buy, not whether to buy. When the prospect agrees, ask for the order. If the buyer refuses, continue with the presentation and ask for the order again when the prospect agrees. Persistence pays off!

Selling in a Changing Business Environment

The nature of selling is changing rapidly. To be successful in the future, a salesperson and his or her company must consider the importance of teamwork in communicating with customers (another aspect of integration), the importance of building long-term relationships, and the importance of adapting to technologies that directly influence the selling process.

SELLING IS A TEAM EFFORT

Traditionally, selling has been thought of as an individual effort (e.g., the salesperson calling on the customer and presenting a product to an individual or to a committee of buyers). Today, selling is a team effort involving everyone in an organization, spearheaded by the salesperson. For example, selling sophisticated technical equipment in a B2B environment requires a team of experts, including research and design specialists, engineers, and other marketing personnel in addition to the salesperson. They all bring different expertise to the presentation and make the customer feel more at ease with the decision-making process.

Buyers also form teams to better evaluate the product offerings of sellers. From a buying perspective, the team approach helps eliminate financial risks and other risks that are associated with large and complex buying decisions. As well, the personalities of people on both sides of the relationship are put to a test. If the chemistry is good, it is a good sign that the business relationship will grow and prosper.

COMPANIES SELL RELATIONSHIPS, NOT PRODUCTS

Organizations abiding by contemporary corporate culture—that is, those that believe in relationship marketing—actively pursue relationships in the selling process. Making a sale or getting the order is simply one step in the sales continuum. It symbolizes the start of a new relationship or the solidification of an existing one.

The key for the seller is to determine how the company's resources can give the customer an edge. It is a consultative process in which the seller proves to the buyer that there is an advantage in doing business together. The search for a good fit between sellers (suppliers) and buyers stems from customers' relentless search for value in everything they purchase.

TECHNOLOGY IS CHANGING SELLING

The nature of selling is changing in many industries due to the advances in communications technology. Members of a channel of distribution that includes raw material suppliers, manufacturers, wholesalers, retailers, and end users are working cooperatively on supply chain management programs. By electronically transferring information among the participants in the supply chain—a cornerstone of true CRM programs—basic buying decisions are automated. Therefore, the challenge facing creative sellers is how to get their products into such a system. The practice of online marketing is a threat to the traditional ways of selling. Companies that do not pursue relationship and partnership selling strategies risk losing sales.

Technology-based CRM programs and a company's ability to sell goods online also have consequences for salespeople and the way they communicate with customers. Technology makes it possible to use fewer people in personal selling, and these sellers find themselves spending less time in personal contact with customers and more time in electronic contact with them. Companies using technology to help market goods and services are finding that geographical boundaries are being eliminated as buyers search for the best value in what they require. Because customers contact companies in a variety of ways, such as by telephone, in person, by email, or through websites, it is important to send out a consistent and integrated marketing communications message.

SUMMARY

Personal selling refers to personal communications between sellers and buyers. Typically, personal selling is divided into three main areas: retail selling, business-to-business selling, and direct selling. In all forms, the immediate goal is to complete a sales transaction, and then adopt appropriate strategies to encourage repeat transactions, thus building a relationship with the customer that will last for an extended period.

The nature of selling has evolved with the changing marketplace. Since the 1970s, selling has moved from consultative selling to strategic selling to relationship selling. Relationship selling involves strategies to establish, build, and maintain customers. It approaches selling from the perspective of the lifetime value of a customer and the concept that retaining satisfied customers is much more profitable than constantly finding new ones. In many cases, relationship selling has extended into partnerships between sellers and buyers. Partnership selling is but one aspect of customer relationship management programs and is strategically developed to encourage a profitable long-term relationship.

There are several essential attributes for successful selling today. A good salesperson possesses the right combination of personal characteristics (characteristics that can be learned and practised) and communication skills (both speaking and listening). A good self-image and positive approach to selling are essential—a successful outlook breeds success! The ability to read a customer is also necessary. Observing and interpreting verbal and non-verbal cues from the customer allow the salesperson to adapt a presentation while in progress and to close the sale at the appropriate time.

Adequate advance preparation is another key to successful selling. A good salesperson possesses sound knowledge in four key areas: product, company, competition, and customer. The task of the salesperson is to match the right product or combination of products and services with the customer's needs. In doing so, the salesperson plans a presentation strategy that shows how the products meet customer needs better than the competition's products. Other essential roles of the salesperson include gathering market intelligence, solving problems, locating and maintaining customers, and providing follow-up service.

The selling process involves seven distinct steps: prospecting, pre-approach, approach, sales presentation, handling objections, closing, and follow-up. Contemporary selling strategies involve the presentation of appropriate product benefits to meet customer needs. A benefit provides the customer with a gain or advantage and shows how the product will resolve a specific problem. Product benefits that are identified as important for a particular buyer are built into a pre-planned presentation designed to resolve a unique problem. During the presentation, a seller's negotiation skills are called upon to respond to the buyer's objections and concerns. Once those are answered, the seller closes the sale by asking for the order. Assuming a satisfactory response, the sale is confirmed and follow-up strategies are implemented. This is the start of the CRM process that, if nurtured carefully, will be profitable for both parties.

Advances in technology are changing the nature of personal selling. Less time is now spent in personal contact while more time is devoted to electronic contact and activities designed to service and retain customers. As in other forms of marketing communications, the challenge is to develop effective strategies to solidify relationships.

KEY TERMS

REVIEW QUESTIONS

1. What are the distinctions between single transactions and repeat transactions?
2. What are the fundamental differences among consultative selling, strategic selling, and relationship selling?
3. In relationship selling, what is meant by the phrase "positioning the product in the customer's mind"?
4. Briefly define partnership selling and explain its importance.
5. What personal and non-personal characteristics are essential for successful selling?
6. Advance preparation is crucial to successful selling. Briefly describe the importance of knowledge in the following areas: product, company, and competition.
7. Briefly explain the roles and responsibilities of a salesperson.
8. List and briefly describe the seven steps in the selling strategy process.

DISCUSSION AND APPLICATION QUESTIONS

1. "Advances in communications technology will dramatically change the role and nature of selling in the future." Discuss this statement and provide examples of changes that are already influencing selling strategies or will have an influence on them in the future.
2. Conduct some secondary research on the concept of partnership selling. How prevalent is partnership selling in business today? Provide some examples of organizations that have adopted this strategy.
3. Conduct an interview with a salesperson involved in business-to-business selling. Ask if he or she has a relationship strategy for working with customers. How are the relationship strategies adapted to the changing conditions in the marketplace? Present a brief outline of what those strategies are and if they are effective.
4. Assess the role of follow-up in the context of customer relationship management practices. How important is it, and how much emphasis do sales representatives place on this aspect of selling?
5. Evaluate the personal selling strategies of the following retail businesses: Future Shop, Best Buy, and Canadian Tire. Do the style and nature of personal selling vary from one business to the other? Which approach is more effective at selling goods at retail? Justify your opinion.
6. Conduct a brief interview with a business-to-business sales representative for a company in your area. Inquire about his or her role in the context of integrated marketing communications. Are there links to other aspects of marketing communications that offer assistance in selling goods and services? Explain the various links as best you can.

7. Conduct some secondary research on telemarketing practices in Canada. Is telemarketing an effective form of personal selling? What are the strengths and weaknesses of this type of selling? Will new privacy laws hamper the development of telemarketing programs?

8. Pre-planning is an essential step in making a sales presentation. Assume you are working for Apple Computer (or any other marketer of desktop and laptop computers) and plan to make a sales presentation to your school. The school is going to purchase or lease desktop computers for a new 50-station lab and is in the process of securing information from various computer suppliers. What questions would you ask to determine your prospect's specific needs? What benefits would you stress when planning the sales presentation and why? What objections do you foresee being raised by the buyer? You may wish to discuss this question with the individual responsible for information technology at your school.

ENDNOTES

1 Gerald Manning, Barry Reece, and H.F. MacKenzie, *Selling Today*, 3rd Edition (Toronto: Prentice Hall, 2004), pp. 7–14.

2 Terrance Belford, "Re-arm your sales force," *National Post*, May 5, 2003, p. BE1.

3 *Dictionary of Marketing Terms* (Barron's Educational Series Inc., 1994), p. 367.

4 Gerald Manning, Barry Reece, and H.F. MacKenzie, *Selling Today*, 3rd Edition (Toronto: Prentice Hall, 2004), p. 137.

5 "Relationship Marketing," Venture (Canadian Broadcasting Corporation), broadcast on April 7, 1998.

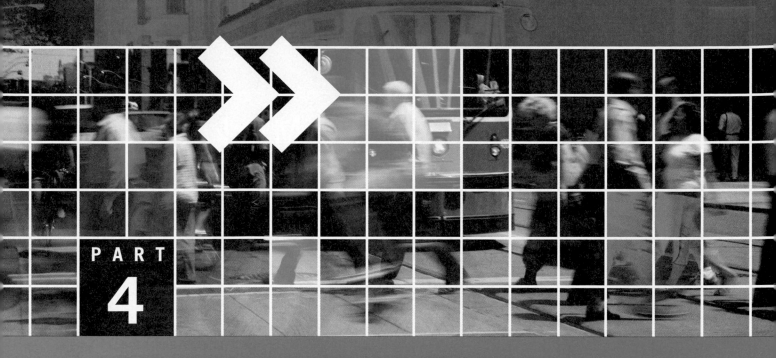

PART 4

Measuring Performance

Part 4 takes a look at the role of marketing research in evaluating the effectiveness of marketing communications programs. Because so much of the evaluation process relies on the collection of qualitative and quantitative data, it is essential to develop an appreciation of the various research techniques and procedures available.

Chapter 12 introduces some fundamental methodologies for collecting primary research data and distinguishes between qualitative and quantitative data. It discusses the relationship between data analysis and interpretation, and their impact on the development and evaluation of marketing communications strategies and executions.

Evaluating Marketing Communications Programs

After studying this chapter, you will be able to

1. Define the role and scope of marketing research in contemporary marketing organizations

2. Describe the methodologies for collecting primary research data

3. Distinguish between qualitative data and quantitative data

4. Determine the influence of primary data and information on the development of marketing communications plans

5. Assess a variety of marketing research procedures and methodologies that measure and evaluate behavioural responses to communications messages

6. Identify the unique methods that measure the effectiveness of individual components of marketing communications.

Because a considerable amount of money is invested in marketing communications activities, a marketing organization is very concerned about protecting its investment. In addition, its desire to remain competitive and be knowledgeable about consumers' changing needs makes it necessary to collect appropriate information before and after critical decisions are made. Certainly, a firm understanding of relevant and contemporary consumer behaviour will play a major role in the development of a marketing communications campaign (refer to Chapter 1 for details). Carefully planned and well-timed marketing research is the tool that provides organizations with the insight necessary to take advantage of new opportunities. This chapter will discuss some fundamental concepts about the marketing research process and present various specific research techniques that are used to measure and evaluate the effectiveness of marketing communications programs.

The Role and Scope of Marketing Research

Research provides an organization with data. The data do not guarantee that proper decisions and actions by the firm will be taken, because data are always open to interpretation. The old saying that "some information is better than no information" puts the role of marketing research into perspective. A vital marketing tool, it is used to help reduce or eliminate the uncertainty and risk associated with making business decisions. Of course, this principle applies to marketing communications decisions as well.

In many ways, marketing research is a form of insurance. It ensures that the action a company might take is the right action. For a multi-million-dollar advertising decision, a manager would want to have good information (a foundation, so to speak) available to make sure the right decision is made. To demonstrate, consider a problem once faced by Toyota and its Corolla model. The company wanted to make the car more appealing to a young "achiever-oriented" target market (24 to 35 years old). Many in this age group consider expensive cars such as a BMW. From research the company learned that these people work hard and want a vehicle that reflects the fact that they are on their way up. Therefore, a decision was made to avoid the usual approach of pitching entry-level cars as party and personalization accessories. A conscious effort was made to attract the person who gets up and works hard every day. The creative combined humour with sophistication and used the tagline "Live the dream for less coin" to summarize the message.[1]

marketing research
A marketing function that links the consumer/customer/public to the marketer through information; the information is used to define marketing opportunities and problems, generate marketing strategies, evaluate marketing actions, and monitor performance.

Marketing research links the consumer/customer/public to the marketer through information—information used to define marketing opportunities and problems, to generate, refine, and evaluate marketing actions, to monitor marketing performance, and to improve the understanding of marketing as a process. It designs the method for collecting information, manages and implements the information collection process, analyzes the results, and communicates the findings and their implications.[2]

The scope of marketing research seems endless. In a marketing communications setting, research is useful for identifying consumer insights that can be considered when developing message strategies, for measuring the impact and effectiveness of message and media strategies, for tracking brand awareness during the life of a campaign, for pre-testing and post-testing advertising strategies, and for measuring changes in behaviour based on the effects of all forms of marketing communications. Regardless of the nature of the research study, the information obtained will assist managers in their decision making.

The very nature of marketing research, however, requires a significant investment by a marketing organization. Due to the diversity of marketing communications and the complementary ways in which the various components blend together, it is difficult to isolate one communications component and state definitively that it determined success or failure. Wise marketing managers also rely on their own experience and intuitiveness when making decisions. When the situation so dictates, marketing research should be undertaken.

How do managers go about collecting information? Prudent marketing decision makers combine their intuition and judgment with all other information sources available. They use the scientific method, which implies that the data generated are reliable and valid. **Reliability** refers to the degree of similar results being achieved if another study were undertaken under similar conditions. **Validity** refers to the research procedure's ability to measure what it was intended to measure.

reliability (of data)
Degree of similarity of results achieved if another research study were undertaken under similar circumstances.

validity (of data)
A research procedure's ability to measure what it is intended to measure.

Research Techniques for Marketing Communications

When an organization attempts to measure the potential impact of its advertising messages on consumers, it implements a variety of primary research techniques. Students should be aware of the basic steps involved in planning various research procedures to appreciate the value of the data. Essentially, the evaluation of advertising messages or any other form of marketing communications involves the collection of primary data.

PRIMARY RESEARCH

Once the organization decides it requires input from customers and potential customers before making a decision, the research process moves to the stage of collecting primary data. **Primary research** refers to the process of collecting and recording new data, called **primary data**, to resolve a specific problem, usually at a high cost to the sponsoring organization. Primary research is custom designed and focuses on resolving a particular question or obtaining specified information. A procedure is developed and a research instrument designed to perform the specific task. Figure 12.1 summarizes the steps involved in collecting primary data.

In directing the primary research, the marketing organization identifies the precise nature of the problem, the objectives of the study, and the hypotheses associated with it. **Research objectives** are statements that outline what the research is to accomplish, while **hypotheses**, which are statements of predicted outcomes, are confirmed or refuted by the

primary research
The collection and recording of primary data.

primary data
Data collected to resolve a problem and recorded for the first time.

research objective
A statement that outlines what the marketing research is to accomplish.

hypothesis
A statement of outcomes predicted in a marketing research investigation.

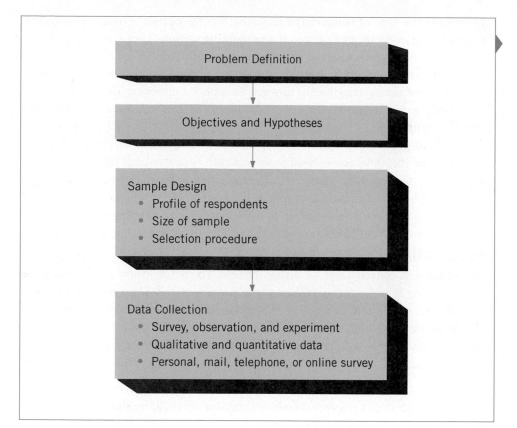

FIGURE
12.1

**The Steps Involved in Primary
Research**

data collected. The outcome of the research often leads to certain actions being taken by the marketing organization. Refer to Figure 12.2 on page 347 for an illustration of research objectives, hypotheses, and action standards. Conducting a marketing research study is beyond the scope and expertise of most marketing organizations in Canada. Consequently, independent market research firms are hired to perform this task.

SAMPLE DESIGN

Prior to implementing a research study, the researchers identify the characteristics of the people they would like to participate in the study. This process is referred to as sample design. A **sample** is defined as a portion of an entire population used to obtain information about that population and must form an accurate representation of the population if the information gathered is to be considered reliable. Some basic steps must be taken to develop a representative sample:

- **Define the Population (Universe):** A **population (universe)** is a group of people with specific age, gender, or other demographic characteristics. It is usually the description of the target market or audience under study. For the purposes of primary research, a description of a population might be "single or married females between the ages of 21 and 34 years living in cities with more than 500 000 residents." A proper research procedure will screen potential respondents for these characteristics.

- **Identify the Sampling Frame:** The **sampling frame** refers to a list that can be used for reaching a population. The telephone directory could be used as a sampling frame for the population described above. If Sears wanted to conduct research among its current customers about the style of advertising it uses, it could use its credit card account holder list as a means of access.

sample
A representative portion of an entire population that is used to obtain information about that population.

population (universe)
In marketing research, a group of people with certain age, gender, or other demographic characteristics.

sampling frame
A list used to access a representative sample of a population; it is a means of accessing people for a research study.

- **Determine the Type of Sample:** The researcher has the option of using a probability sample or a non-probability sample. If a **probability sample** is used, the respondents have a known or equal chance of selection and are randomly selected from across the population. For example, the researcher may use a predetermined and systematic procedure for picking respondents through a telephone directory. The known chance of selection enables statistical procedures to be used in the results to estimate sampling errors.

  In a **non-probability sample**, the respondents have an unknown chance of selection, and their selection is based on factors such as convenience for the researcher or the researcher's judgment. The researcher relies on experience to determine who would be most appropriate. For example, Sears could randomly stop shoppers inside its stores to seek their input on a variety of marketing concerns. Factors such as cost and timing are other reasons for using non-probability samples.

- **Determine the Sample Size:** Generally, the larger the sample, the greater the accuracy of the data collected and the higher the cost. The nature of the research study is a determining factor in the number of participants required. Some researchers use a 1 percent rule (1 percent of the defined population or universe), while others state absolute minimums of 200 respondents. The accuracy of the sample is usually calculated statistically and stated in the research report. Therefore, a researcher considers the margin of error that is acceptable and the degree of certainty required.

  Figure 12.2 contains a sample design. It should be noted that errors in the design and implementation of a research sample could distort the validity and reliability of the data collected.

DATA COLLECTION METHODS

There are three primary methods a researcher can use to collect data: surveys, observation, and experiments (see Figure 12.3). The data collected can be qualitative or quantitative in nature.

  For **survey research**, data are collected systematically through some form of communication with a representative sample by means of a questionnaire that records responses. Most surveys include predetermined questions and a selection of responses that are easily filled in by the respondent or the interviewer. This technique is referred to as **fixed-response (closed-ended) questioning**. Surveys will also include **open-response (open-ended) questions**, a situation where space is available at the end of a question where verbatim comments by the respondent are recorded. Survey research can be conducted by personal interview, telephone, mail, or online.

  Most surveys are designed with a high degree of structure. The questionnaire follows a planned format: screening questions at the beginning, central issue questions (dealing with the nature of the research) in the middle, and classification (demographic) questions at the end. In survey research, closed-ended or fixed-response questions (questions that include predetermined answers that a person simply checks off) are most popular. They permit the data to be easily transferred to a computer for tabulation and subsequent analysis.

  In **observation research**, the behaviour of the respondent is observed and recorded. In this form of research, participants do not have to be recruited; they can participate in a study without knowing it. In other situations, respondents are usually aware of being observed, perhaps through a two-way mirror, by a hidden camera while being interviewed, or by electronic measurement of impulses. All of these techniques can be used when consumers are asked to evaluate advertising messages.

FIGURE
12.2

A Sample of Research
Objectives, Hypotheses, and
Sample Design for a Marketing
Communications Study

PRODUCT

Labatt Blue

PROBLEM

Labatt Blue has been using a humorous appeal technique in its "Cheers to Friends" advertising campaign. The brand manager is less than satisfied with the impact of this campaign on current customers and would like to evaluate alternative appeal techniques.

OBJECTIVES

1. To determine the potential impact of a lifestyle appeal technique on current Labatt Blue drinkers.
2. To determine the potential impact of a sexual appeal technique on current Labatt Blue drinkers.

HYPOTHESES

1. The communication of lifestyle appeals may have impact initially but over the long term will not be viewed as unique and distinctive because so many competing brands use lifestyle imagery.
2. The communication of sexual appeal will break through the clutter of competitive beer advertising and separate Blue from other leading brands.

ACTION STANDARD

Given the assumption that research results indicate a preference for either the lifestyle appeal technique or the sexual appeal technique, and preference can be sustained for an extended period, then a new creative campaign will be devised for Labatt Blue. The implementation date for a new campaign will be May 2005.

SAMPLE DESIGN

Population

Input will be sought from Blue's primary target market, described as males, 19 to 29 years old, living in urban markets.

Sampling Frame

Current Blue drinkers will be recruited by telephone and by using telephone directories in three cities: Toronto, Edmonton, and Vancouver. A series of qualifying questions will be asked of potential respondents to determine their degree of brand loyalty.

Type of Sample

A probability sample is essential to ensure accurate and reliable data. A systematic procedure will be devised to recruit respondents in each city.

Sample Size

It is anticipated that a mixture of qualitative research and quantitative research will be employed. A focus group will be conducted in each city to derive qualitative information. Survey research will require a minimum of 200 respondents in each city to secure accurate quantitative data.

The above is a hypothetical example and is intended for illustration purposes only.

SURVEYS

- Data are collected systematically by communicating with a representative sample, usually using a questionnaire.
- Questionnaires can be disguised (purpose hidden) or undisguised (purpose known), and structured (fixed responses provided) or unstructured (open-ended question format).

OBSERVATION

- The behaviour of the respondent is observed by personal, mechanical, or electronic means.

EXPERIMENTS

- Variables are manipulated under controlled conditions to observe respondents' reactions.
- Experiments are used to test marketing influences such as product changes, package changes, and advertising copy tests.

The Ford Motor Company found that observing online chatter provided insights for developing better marketing communications strategies. From its observations Ford learned that information presented on blogs (information that is either positive or negative) quickly becomes the subject of much online discussion. Ford was so impressed with the discussion about the Ford Edge (a crossover vehicle), it decided to add consumer-generated content to its professionally produced creative executions.[3]

In **experimental research**, one or more factors are manipulated under controlled conditions, while other elements remain constant so that respondents' reactions can be evaluated. Test marketing is a form of experimental research. In a marketing communications context, **test marketing** involves placing a commercial or set of commercials in a campaign (could be print ads as well) in one or more limited markets, representative of the whole, to observe the potential impact of the ads on consumers. Do the ads generate the desired level of awareness and preference? Do they provide sufficient motivation so that consumers take the desired action? Good test marketing provides valuable experience prior to an expensive regional or national launch of the campaign. If the test market proves the campaign to be less than effective, a pending disaster can be avoided.

For more insight into how observational research influences creative strategies, read the IMC Highlight: **Scott Paper and P&G Dig Deep for Clues.**

QUALITATIVE DATA VERSUS QUANTITATIVE DATA

According to the nature of the information sought, research data are classified as either qualitative or quantitative. There are significant differences between these two classifications.

Qualitative data are usually collected from small samples in a controlled environment. They result from questions concerned with "why" and from in-depth probing of the participants. Typically, such data are gathered from focus group interviews. A **focus group** is a small group of people (usually eight to ten) with common characteristics (e.g., a target market profile), brought together to discuss issues related to the marketing of a product or service. A typical qualitative project consists of four to six groups representing various regions or urban areas of Canada.

experimental research
Research in which one or more factors are manipulated under controlled conditions while other elements remain constant so that the respondent's actions can be evaluated.

test marketing
Placing a commercial, set of commercials, or print ad campaign in one or more limited markets that are representative of the whole to observe the impact of the ads on consumers.

qualitative data
Data collected from small samples in a controlled environment; they describe feelings and opinions on issues.

focus group
A small group of people with common characteristics brought together to discuss issues related to the marketing of a product or service.

Scott Paper and P&G Dig Deep for Clues

"Seek and ye shall find." Perhaps that's the mantra of marketing research practices today. Many companies now hire anthropologists to gather deeper consumer insights. What they discover can enhance positioning strategies and offer guidance for the development of effective message strategies. They will go shopping with people, follow them around, and watch how they interact with others.

Scott Paper placed an anthropologist in selected homes to observe its primary target, women 25 to 54 years old. The objective was to discover a central brand idea by finding out what goes on in the bathroom. Scott discovered that women view the bathroom as a place of solitude and privacy. For many women it is a shrine. An idea was born! Cashmere toilet paper (formerly known as Cottonelle) would be positioned as a "luxury" brand, a step up from all others. It was aligned with the idea that solitude can be a luxury in a hectic life. One of Cashmere's print ads showed a roll of toilet paper unfurling into a cashmere scarf.

Procter & Gamble designed a completely new campaign for Tide based on what it learned from spending a week with consumers in two American cities. The visitors from P&G and its advertising agency literally tagged along with the family. The objective was to learn more about the role of laundry in people's lives. While that may sound ridiculous, Tide is a global brand that contributes significantly to P&G's sales and profits.

Instead of asking questions related directly to laundry, the executive visitors asked questions about their lives, what their needs were, and how they felt as women. In doing so, they discovered how unimportant laundry was in people's lives today and that Tide wasn't the most important thing on a woman's mind. The executives quickly determined that Tide needed to be repositioned in the minds of women. Tide had always been about cleaning power; simply stated, the brand performs better than competing brands. In repositioning the brand, the new emphasis would be on fabric protection.

After the new insights were assessed, the agency developed a new advertising campaign with the theme "Tide knows fabric best." The ads rely on music, rich visual imagery, and emotional benefits—quite a departure from the traditional demonstration and side-by-side comparisons with other brands that Tide had been using for years. In one commercial for Tide with Febreze, Tide's laundry-odour removal benefit gets an emotional heft, billed as "the difference between smelling like a mom and smelling like a woman" amid shots of mom with baby and then mom with husband cuddling, all to the tune of "Be My Baby."

P&G is pleased with the results. Tide is once again building its market share in a very competitive product category. Tide holds a 43 percent share and has been climbing gradually since the new campaign was launched. Any new products that come on stream will undoubtedly adopt a similar style of advertising.

Adapted from Jack Neff, "Five years in the making, Tide gets a new ad campaign," *Advertising Age*, February 8, 2006, www.adage.com/news, and Andrea Zoe Aster, "Digging deeper," *Marketing*, November 22, 2004, p. 31.

The word "focus" implies that the discussion concentrates on one topic or concept. A trained moderator usually conducts the interview over a period of a few hours. The role of the moderator is to get the participants to interact fairly freely to uncover the reasons and motivations underlying their remarks. Probing uncovers the hidden interplay of psychological factors that drive a consumer to buy one brand rather than another.

With regard to advertising evaluations, it provides a multitude of favourable and opposing views on how effective a message might be. Consumers' reactions to the message, the characters that present the message, the campaign theme and slogan, and their general likes and dislikes of the ad can be discussed at length.

The major drawback of using focus groups concerns the reliability of the data. The sample size is too small to be representative of the entire population, and most people in a focus group do not like to show disagreement with a prevailing opinion. For that reason, interviews are usually held in several locations.

Marketing decisions involving considerable sums of money are very risky if based on such limited research. One of the most spectacular focus group failures, the launch of new Coke in the 1980s, came about because the soft drink maker was not asking the right questions. Worried that archrival PepsiCo had a better-tasting product, Coca-Cola asked consumers if they liked its new formulation without ever asking if they wanted its tried-and-true beverage changed.[4] The new version of Coke failed miserably when it was launched, and the public backlash was so significant that Coca-Cola had to reintroduce the original Coke as Coca-Cola Classic.

The Coca-Cola example shows the potential weakness of focus groups—they are exploratory in nature. A follow-up quantitative survey is often required to establish numbers, which costs organizations additional money and time. On the positive side, attitudes that are revealed in a focus group can be used as a foundation for forming questions and questionnaires if and when quantitative research is required. The attitudes uncovered can be expressed as answers for closed-ended questions in a questionnaire.

Quantitative data provide answers to questions concerned with "what," "when," "who," "how many," and "how often." This research attempts to put feelings, attitudes, and opinions into numbers and percentages. The data are gathered from structured questionnaires and a large sample to ensure accuracy and reliability. The interpretation of the results is based on the numbers compiled, not on the judgment of the researcher. Quantitative research will statistically confirm the attitudes and feelings that arose in qualitative research. Therefore, a manager will have more confidence in the decisions that are based on the research. Figure 12.4 briefly compares qualitative and quantitative research.

With so much risk involved in major decisions about marketing communications, the wise organization should use both forms of data collection. Molson, for example, has a vice-president accountable for marketing research. Molson does focus groups and

quantitative data
Measurable data collected from large samples using a structured research procedure.

FIGURE
12.4

A Comparison of Qualitative
and Quantitative Data

QUALITATIVE DATA

- Collected from a small sample, usually in a focus-group environment.
- Unstructured questions.
- Questions seek attitudes, feelings, and opinions.
- Data not always reliable because of small sample.

QUANTITATIVE DATA

- Collected from a large, representative sample of target market.
- Structured questions with predetermined responses.
- Deals with who, what, when, how many, and how often.
- Statistically reliable, with calculated degree of error.

qualitative research, but it also does quantitative research on all television ads before production of the ad takes place. Each ad must hit a specific persuasion level. "We do not shoot ads until we know they will persuade beer drinkers to drink that brand," says Michael Downey, Molson's senior vice-president of global marketing.[5]

SURVEY METHODOLOGY

There are four primary means of contacting consumers when conducting surveys to collect quantitative data: telephone, personal interview, mail, and the Internet. **Personal interviews** involve face-to-face communication with groups (e.g., focus groups) or individuals and are usually done through quantitative questionnaires. Popular locations for interviews are busy street corners, shopping malls, and the homes of respondents.

personal interview
The collection of information in a face-of-face interview.

Telephone interviews involve communication with individuals over the phone. Usually, the interviews are conducted from central locations (i.e., one location that can reach all Canadian markets), and, consequently, there is supervised control over the interview process. Telephone technology is now so advanced that research data can be transferred from the telephone directly to a computer. However, there is a very high refusal rate for telephone surveys. A recent study by the Professional Marketing Research Society observed that 78 percent of people contacted refuse to participate.[6]

telephone interview
In marketing research, the collection of information from a respondent by telephone.

Mail interviews are a silent process of collecting information. Using the mail to distribute a survey means that a highly dispersed sample is reached in a cost-efficient manner. The main drawbacks are the lack of control and the amount of time required to implement and retrieve the surveys.

mail interview
In marketing research, the collection of information from a respondent by mail.

Online surveys allow an organization to be much less invasive in collecting information. Some companies have found that consumers seem more willing to divulge information over the Internet compared with the more traditional means of surveying. Furthermore, compared to traditional data collection methods, online research offers results quickly and at much lower cost. In a paper environment, a company like P&G would spend $25 000 and get results in two months. Online, the same test costs $2500 and results are available in two weeks.[7] On the downside, recruiting participation can be a lot like fishing—participation is left up to the fish. Therefore, the validity of the information is questionable.

online survey
In marketing research, using an online questionnaire to collect data from people.

Figure 12.5 summarizes the advantages and disadvantages of each survey method.

DATA TRANSFER AND PROCESSING

Once the data have been collected, then editing, data transfer, and tabulation take place. In the **editing stage**, completed questionnaires are reviewed for consistency and completeness. Whether to include questionnaires with incomplete or seemingly contradictory answers is left to the researcher to decide. In the **data transfer** stage, answers from questions are transferred to a computer. Answers are pre-coded to facilitate the transfer. In the case of telephone surveys, it is now common to enter the responses directly into the computer as the questions are being asked.

editing stage
In marketing research, the review of questionnaires for consistency and completeness.
data transfer
In marketing research, the transfer of answers from the questionnaire to the computer.

Once the survey results have been entered into a computer, the results are tabulated. **Tabulation** is the process of counting the various responses for each question and arriving at a frequency distribution. A **frequency distribution** shows the number of times each answer was chosen for a question. Numerous cross-tabulations are also made. **Cross-tabulation** is the comparison and contrasting of the answers of various subgroups or of particular subgroups and the total response group. For example, a question dealing with brand awareness could be analyzed by the age, gender, or income of respondents.

tabulation
The process of counting various responses for each question in a survey.
frequency distribution
The number of times each answer in a survey was chosen for a question.
cross-tabulation
The comparison of answers to questions by various subgroups with the total number of responses.

FIGURE
12.5

The Advantages and
Disadvantages of Various
Survey Methods

ADVANTAGES	DISADVANTAGES
Personal Interview	
• High rate of participation	• Higher cost due to time needed
• Visual observations possible	• Respondents reluctant to respond to certain questions
• Flexible (can include visuals)	• Interviewer bias possible
Telephone Interview	
• Convenient and allows control	• Observation not possible
• Costs less	• Short questions and questionnaires
• Timely responses	• Privacy concerns (bad time of day)
Mail Surveys	
• Cost efficient	• Lack of control
• Large sample obtainable	• Potential for misinterpretation by respondent
• Relaxed environment	• Time lag between distribution and return
• Impersonal nature produces	• Low response rates accurate responses
Online Surveys	
• Efficient and inexpensive	• Immature medium compared to alternatives
• Less intrusive (respondent driven)	• Limited sample frame (Internet users only)
• Convenient for respondent	• Image concerns associated with spam
• Fast response time (days)	• Reliability of information suspect

DATA ANALYSIS AND INTERPRETATION

data analysis
The evaluation of responses question by question; gives meaning to the data.

Data analysis refers to the evaluation of responses question by question, a process that gives meaning to the data. At this point, the statistical data for each question are reviewed, and the researcher makes observations. Typically, a researcher makes comparisons between responses of subgroups on a percentage or ratio basis.

data interpretation
The relating of accumulated data to the problem under review and to the objectives and hypotheses of the research study.

   Data interpretation, on the other hand, involves relating the accumulated data to the problem under review and to the objectives and hypotheses of the research study. The process of interpretation uncovers solutions to the problem. The researcher draws conclusions that state the implications of the data for managers.

RECOMMENDATIONS AND IMPLEMENTATION

The recommendations outline suggested courses of action that the sponsoring organization should take in view of the data collected. Once a research project is complete, the research company will present its findings in a written report and highlight the key findings in a visual presentation. These days, thanks to changing technology and fast turnaround times, market research is more streamlined, with clients expecting solid decision-making results—yesterday.

Measuring and Evaluating Advertising Messages

One of the first steps in measuring advertising messages is an evaluation of agency creative ideas by the client. It seems that a creative idea is just that—an idea—until it is sold to the client for approval. Very often, these kinds of evaluations are subjective in nature because they rely on opinions put forth by brand managers, marketing directors, and presidents of companies. The chain of command for approving advertising creative and media expenditures can go very high in an organization.

CLIENT EVALUATION

Creative can be tested at several stages of the development process. The first step is usually a qualitative assessment by the client to determine if the message conforms to the strategic direction that was provided to the agency. This evaluation is conducted by means of a managerial approach. In this evaluation, a client needs to resist the impulse to assess the creative on personal, subjective bases. However, if a "to proceed or not to proceed" decision must be made, the client reserves the right to conduct consumer research prior to making the decision.

Clients using the **managerial approach** for evaluating creative may apply some or all of the criteria listed below:

1. **In terms of content, does the advertisement communicate the creative objectives and reflect the positioning strategy of the brand (company)?** The client reviews the creative for its ability to communicate the key benefit and support claims that substantiate the benefit. All creative objectives would have been outlined in the creative brief. As well, the client would determine if the message strategy and execution conform to the overall positioning strategy of the brand. If it is off strategy, the ad will be rejected.

2. **In terms of how the ad is presented (strategy and execution), does it mislead or misrepresent the intent of the message? Is it presented in good taste?** The client must be concerned about the actual message and any implied message since it is responsible for the truthfulness of the message. Legal counsel often has the final say regarding message content. Consumers frequently lodge complaints about ads they find offensive or that encourage risky behaviour. Molson-Coors Canada received complaints about a Coors Light billboard ad it ran in Vancouver. The copy read: "Colder than most people from Toronto." Molson's intent was to simply poke fun at East-West rivalries in Canada, but the ad drew so much negative attention the company was forced to remove it.

3. **Is the ad memorable?** Breaking through the clutter of competitive advertising is always a challenge, and a lot of advertising that is approved doesn't quite cut it. Is there something that stands out that customers will remember—what will they take away from the ad? For instance, characters in ads often build momentum for a brand and become strongly associated with the brand itself. For example, the computer-generated beavers, Frank and Gordon, did a great job for Bell Canada during their advertising run. So memorable are some characters that the public misses them when they are not included. The loveable A&W Root Bear is one of those characters.

4. **Is the brand recognition effective?** There must be sufficient brand registration in the ad. Some companies go as far as to stipulate how many times the package should be shown in a television commercial or how many times the brand name should be mentioned. The creativity of the commercial or print ad should not outweigh the product—it should complement the product. For example, people often recall

funny ads and they can talk at length about the humorous situations that were presented. Sometimes, however, they are unable to recall the name of the product that appeared in the ad. So much for the laughs!

5. **Should the advertisement be researched?** When it comes to assessing the impact and effectiveness of the advertisement, subjective judgments by the client have the disadvantage of not being quantifiable. Prior to spending money on production, the client may decide to conduct consumer research to seek quantifiable data that will help the decision-making process. Better safe than sorry!

The evaluation process can occur at any stage of the creative development process. A television commercial, for example, could be evaluated by consumers at the storyboard, rough-cut, or finished commercial stage. Although it is not practical to test commercials at all stages, if the quality or effectiveness of the commercial is ever in question, the client should conduct research to avoid costly and embarrassing errors in judgment.

It is difficult to isolate any particular form of marketing communications and state categorically that it had an impact on sales. There are simply too many factors that influence buying decisions by consumers and business customers. The source of motivation to take action could be any combination of product quality, services offered, price, availability, advertising, public relations, sales promotions, and so on. As this book reiterates time and time again, it is the integrated effort of all forms of marketing communications that ultimately influences the customer's buying decision. It is very difficult to measure the direct effect of any single communications element on sales.

EXTERNAL RESEARCH TECHNIQUES AND PROCEDURES

Creative evaluation involves a variety of research techniques. The objective of most creative research is to measure the impact of a message on a target audience. Creative research is conducted based on the stage of creative development. It is either a pre-test or a post-test situation. **Pre-testing** is the evaluation of an advertisement, commercial, or campaign before it goes into final production or media placement to determine the strengths and weaknesses of a strategy and execution. By getting input from the target market at an early stage, a company will have more confidence in the creative once it is placed in the media. **Post-testing** is the process of evaluating and measuring the effectiveness of an advertisement, commercial, or campaign during or after it has run. Post-testing provides information that can be used in future advertising planning.

Common techniques used to measure the effectiveness of creative are *recognition* and *recall testing*, *opinion-measure testing*, and *physiological-response testing*. Procedures such as inquiry tests and controlled experiments used in post-testing also measure the effectiveness of the message.

RECOGNITION AND RECALL TESTING

In **recognition tests**, respondents are tested for awareness. They are asked if they can recall an advertisement for a specific brand or any of the points made in the advertisement. For example, consumers who have read a publication in which an ad has appeared are asked if they remember what brand was advertised and what the basic message being communicated was. Typically, an individual is asked a series of questions to determine what they know about an ad.

Several factors affect the level of recognition of an ad. For example, a large print ad occupying a full page usually has a higher level of recognition than an ad occupying only a portion of a page. The inclusion of a celebrity might draw more attention to an ad

pre-testing
The evaluation of commercial messages prior to final production to determine the strengths and weaknesses of the communications.

post-testing
The evaluation and measurement of a message's effectiveness during or after the message has run.

recognition test
A test that measures a target audience's awareness of a brand, copy, or of the advertisement itself after the audience has been exposed to the message.

simply because consumers like the celebrity. The amount of text in the ad may also be a factor. Ads with lots of copy might get lower recognition simply because consumers don't read all of the copy.

In **recall tests**, respondents are tested for comprehension to measure the impact of advertising. The test can be an *aided* situation (some information is provided the respondent to stimulate thinking) or an *unaided* situation (no information is provided). In either situation, respondents are asked to name or recall ads and asked to recall specific elements of an advertisement or commercial, such as its primary selling points, the characters in it as presenters, and its slogan. Test scores are usually higher when some form of aid is provided.

Recognition and recall both help develop a brand's image with consumers over a period of time. Therefore, once an advertiser finds an ad or advertising campaign that is performing well, it must resist the temptation to make changes. In the long run, effective advertising plays a role in building sales and market share.

Two of the most common methods for collecting recognition and recall information are Starch readership tests and day-after recall tests. A **Starch readership test** is a post-test recognition procedure applied to both newspaper and magazine advertisements. The objectives of the test are to measure how many readers saw an ad and how many actually read the ad.

In a Starch readership test, a consumer is given a magazine to read, after which an interviewer goes through it ad by ad with the respondent. For each advertisement in the magazine (the entire magazine is "starched"), responses are divided into three categories:

- **Noted:** the percentage of readers who remembered seeing the ad in this issue.
- **Associated:** the percentage of readers who saw any part of the ad that clearly indicated the brand or advertiser.
- **Read Most:** the percentage of readers who read half or more of the written material.

The Starch readership test offers several benefits. The client can measure the extent to which an ad is seen and read; by reviewing the results of other ads that were tested, the extent of clutter breakthrough can be determined; and by reviewing scores obtained by other products in previous tests, various layouts and design options can be evaluated for effectiveness.

In the broadcast media, particularly television, the use of **day-after recall (DAR) testing** is common. As the name implies, research is conducted the day after an audience has been exposed to a commercial message for the first time. By means of a telephone survey technique, a sampling of the client's target market is recruited and asked a series of questions to determine exposure to and recall of particular commercials. Respondents who saw the commercial are asked what the ad actually communicated. The test seeks specific information about the primary selling message, what the respondent likes and dislikes about the ad, areas of disbelief or confusion, and purchase motivation.

The actual quantified measures obtained in a DAR test are described as related recall levels. Related recall measures two dimensions of the test commercial: *intrusiveness* and *impact*. **Related recall** refers to the percentage of the test-commercial audience who claim to remember the test execution and who are also able to substantiate their claim by providing some description of the commercial.

For additional details about the research methodologies described above visit the websites for Gallup and Robinson (www.gallup-robinson.com) and Starch Research (www.starchresearch.com).

---

recall test
A test that measures an ad's impact by asking respondents to recall specific elements (e.g., the selling message) of the advertisement; can be aided (some information provided) or unaided.

Starch readership test
A post-test recognition procedure that measures readers' recall of an advertisement (noted), their ability to identify the sponsor (associated), and whether they read more than half of the written material (read most).

day-after recall (DAR) test
Research conducted the day following the respondent's exposure to a message to determine the degree of recognition and recall of the advertisement, the brand, and the selling message.

related recall
The percentage of a test-commercial audience who claim to remember the test commercial and can provide as verification some description of the commercial.

Gallup and Robinson
www.gallup-robinson.com

Starch Research
www.starchresearch.com

OPINION-MEASURE TESTING

opinion-measure testing
A form of research yielding information about the effect of a commercial message on respondents' brand name recall, interest in the brand, and purchase intentions.

Measuring attitudinal components is another means of evaluating advertising effectiveness. Attitudes and opinions can be gathered from surveys or focus groups. The intent of attitude surveys is to delve a bit deeper with consumers to determine their true feelings about an ad and the product.

With television commercials, **opinion-measure testing** exposes an audience to test-commercial messages in the context of special television programs. In a research setting, respondents view commercials on a large screen (theatre) or on television monitors. Once all of the ads are viewed, participants respond to a series of questions.

The test commercial is usually presented twice during the program, in cluster situations. Also included in the cluster is a set of control commercials against which the test commercial or commercials (sometimes more than one commercial is being tested) can be compared. The position of the test commercial is different in each cluster. The test measures three key attributes: the audience's awareness of the commercial based on brand name recall, the extent to which the main idea of the ad is communicated, and the effect the commercial could have on purchase motivation—that is, the likelihood of the respondent buying the brand. This final measure is based on a comparison of pre-exposure brand purchase information and post-exposure brand preference data.

This procedure is often referred to as a *forced exposure test*, a name that suggests its potential weakness: the artificial environment in which it occurs. However, the results for commercials are compared to results from previous tests, and since the procedure remains constant, the data should provide reasonable direction to advertisers. Millward Brown, a marketing research company, uses a procedure it calls TVLink™ to predict how well an ad will perform. Visit its website (www.millwardbrown.com) for additional details.

Millward Brown
www.millwardbrown.com

PHYSIOLOGICAL-RESPONSE TESTING

eye movement–camera test
A test that uses a hidden camera to track eye movement to gauge the point of immediate contact in an advertisement, how the reader scans the ad, and the amount of time spent reading.

pupilometer test
A device that measures pupil dilation (enlargement) of a person's eye when reading; it measures emotional responses to an advertisement.

voice-pitch analysis test
A test that uses a recording of a person's voice response to measure change in voice pitch caused by emotional responses to the communications.

Advertisers also have access to a variety of physiological testing methods that measure involuntary responses to a specific element of an advertisement. In an **eye movement–camera test**, consumers read an advertisement while a hidden camera tracks their eye movements. Such a test gauges the point of immediate contact, how a reader scans the various components of an ad, and the amount of time spent reading it. The **pupilometer test** measures the dilation of a person's pupil to see how it changes based on emotional arousal. For example, a person's pupils widen when frightened or excited and are smaller when the response is negative. In a **voice-pitch analysis test**, a person's voice response is recorded. The test measures changes in voice pitch caused by emotional responses. The change in pitch indicates how strongly a person is affected.

These types of tests are popular with researchers because emotions trigger physiological responses that can be measured. Physiological responses to something a person sees or hears are difficult to mask. In two of the tests mentioned above, reactions are monitored with no words being spoken. Sometimes respondents try to hide their true feelings by saying something that contradicts their physiological reaction. For example, a person might respond in the desired way physiologically to a print ad with sexual imagery but might state that the ad should not be shown in a magazine. In such a case, physiological reactions speak louder than words.

Testing procedures and the need for them are controversial issues in the industry, particularly among advertising agencies whose work is being tested. Many creative directors argue that too much testing defeats the creative process (because it stifles creativity) and that what people say in research and do in the real world can be completely different.

These same creative directors also realize it is the client's money at stake, so if the client is inclined toward research, the ad agency must deal with the situation as best it can.

For additional insight into how research influences the development of advertising messages, refer to the IMC Highlight: **Branding Oregon**.

IMC HIGHLIGHT

Branding Oregon

How consumers perceive a brand and how an organization would like consumers to perceive a brand can be two different things. The latter is the ideal situation, because it suggests that the marketing and marketing communications strategies actually had an effect on people. A primary role of marketing communications is to influence or alter perceptions. The state of Oregon and the Pacific Northwest are well-known as an outdoors region. The area has the beautiful Pacific coastline, majestic mountains, great camping, and scenic vistas. People instantly think of its natural beauty, but they generally know little else about the region.

Ten years ago, the Oregon Tourism Commission implemented a branding campaign to portray the state as having a special quality of life where nature and the built environment coexist, where "fresh" and "clean" permeate everything, where culture is alive and the heritage showcased. The slogan for the campaign was "Oregon. Things Look Different Here." Wieden+Kennedy, an ad agency renowned for its Nike advertising, created the campaign.

To determine how well the campaign was working, a three-tiered research program was devised and implemented by Longwoods International, a U.S. marketing research company. The research involved an overnight visitor profile, an advertising effectiveness study, and an image study. The primary goal was to determine how well Oregon compared to other regional and national norms for tourism communications.

The commission found that the campaign did encourage new visitors to the region, but that Oregon's image did not compare well to that of Washington, British Columbia, and California in terms of excitement, unique opportunities, and entertainment. Looking critically at its advertising, it determined that there was too much focus on the pristine environment. There was little emphasis on things to do.

The commission also discovered that visitors rated their experiences very highly, and that Oregon's actual tourism product is rated much higher than its image. In other words, Oregon's image did not live up to the product! Oregon recognized that a good communications solution would correct this problem. New advertising was developed to build Oregon's image in specific areas such as being exciting, showing cultural amenities, and being a real adventure. The new campaign focused on "capturing the moment" and "people having fun."

To supplement media advertising, the commission also formed partnerships with cultural organizations and destinations to launch a cultural tourism campaign, with public relations and other marketing communications elements. High-end resorts, world-class golf courses, regional cuisine, and historic trails serve as backdrops for advertising. It's culture packed with beauty!

The commission's investment in research demonstrates the importance of crafting a message that communicates what life in Oregon is really like. The research helped to identify information that really helped develop an effective marketing communications campaign.

Adapted from Julie Curtis, "How research shapes a message," *Longwoods International*, www.longwoods-intl.com/case-study-Oregon.htm (accessed November 2003).

Measuring and Evaluating Sales Promotions

The overall goal of sales promotions is to produce an increase in sales in the short term and to build brand loyalty in the long term. As discussed in Chapter 8, promotions are classified as consumer promotions and trade promotions. Consumer promotions embrace activities such as coupons, contests, free samples, cash rebates, premium offers, and loyalty card programs. These activities are designed to encourage trial purchase by new customers, repeat purchases by existing customers, and, generally, brand loyalty. Therefore, consumer promotions are measured against these objectives.

Trade promotions include activities such as trade allowances, performance allowances, cooperative advertising allowances, dealer premiums, and dealer display materials. These activities are designed to secure listings of new products with distributors, build sales volume in the promotion period, and secure merchandising support from distributors. Trade promotions are measured against these objectives.

Specific sales promotion measures include response rates to coupon offers, the number of entries received for a contest, and the number of cash rebate forms returned to the company. A marketing manager typically compares response rates for current promotions to response rates received for past and similar promotions. For example, some brands may run a major contest each year in the peak season. Brands like Pepsi-Cola and Coca-Cola and Coors Light and Bud Light usually run a summer contest. If a particular contest generates significantly more entries than usual, the manager will attempt to isolate the elements of the promotion that led to the higher degree of interest.

redemption rate
The number of coupons returned expressed as a percentage of the number of coupons that were distributed.

Coupon offers are usually evaluated based on the **redemption rate**, which is defined as the number of coupons returned, expressed as a percentage of the number of coupons distributed. The higher the redemption rate, the more successful the coupon promotion. For example, if a magazine coupon draws a 2 percent return rate and the norm for magazine coupons is only 1 percent, the offer is an overwhelming success.

Historical redemption rates for coupon offers are used to develop budgets for new coupon offers. Again, should response to a particular coupon offer be significantly higher than past offers, the manager would try to identify the elements of the offer that contributed to the increase in redemptions. Was it the face value of the offer? Was it the timing of the offer? Are consumers generally more price sensitive than they previously were? For an illustration of such a calculation, refer to Figure 12.6.

The absolute number of entry forms received from contests and rebate offers is a means of measuring the effectiveness of these types of offers. The names collected provide an additional marketing benefit, as they can be added to the company's database. Smart marketers seek additional information about consumers on the contest or rebate entry form such as demographic and psychographic information that can be used to plan direct response communications programs.

The use of dealer display materials affects the success of sales promotions. Point-of-purchase advertising helps create awareness of promotion offers and reminds consumers about a product at precisely the right time—the purchase decision time. This medium provides a good finishing touch to a well-integrated advertising and promotion program.

Figure 12.7 shows that a significantly higher purchase response is achieved if various combinations of in-store merchandising activities are implemented. The importance of these activities is highlighted by the fact that 70 percent of brand purchase decisions are made in store.[8]

FIGURE
12.6

**Measuring the Effectiveness
of a Coupon Promotion**

ASSUMPTION

A manufacturer offers a $1.00 coupon on a branded box of cereal that has a regular retail price of $4.09. The coupon is distributed through a cooperative direct mail package. For the purposes of budgeting, an average coupon redemption rate for cooperative direct mail will be used. A misredemption rate of 20% is considered, because on average only 80% of coupons redeemed are on valid purchases. The manufacturer receives about 65% of the retail price when wholesale and retail profit margins are considered.

COUPON INFORMATION

Face value:	$1.00
Handling charge (retailer)	$0.10
Handling charge (clearing house)	$0.03
Distribution cost	$15.00/M
Printing cost	$10.00/M
Total coupons in distribution	2.5 million
Redemption rate	5.0%

COSTS

Distribution	2 500 000 x $15.00/M	$37 500
Printing	2 500 000 x $10.00/M	$25 000
Redemption	2 500 000 x 0.05 x $1.13	$141 250
Total cost		**$203 750**

REVENUES

Revenue from each purchase	$4.59 x 0.65	$2.98
Total revenue	2 500 000 x 0.05 x 0.80 x $2.66	**$266 000**

PAYOUT

Total revenue minus total cost	$266 000 – $203 750	**$62 250**

From the total revenue line, it can be determined that the coupon offer generated 100 000 purchases (2 500 000 x 0.05 x 0.80).

Measuring and Evaluating Direct Response and Internet Communications

One method of measuring direct mail and direct response television messages is to include a toll-free telephone number or website address. The number of inquiries received or the actual sales that result from a particular offer can be compared to those of offers in the past. From this, an observation can be made about the effectiveness of a new offer. As well, a great deal of information can be collected about consumers responding to phone calls. Sales data can be recorded and demographic information gathered. Sales data can be tied to demographic information to determine who is actually buying

FIGURE
12.7

Measuring the Effectiveness
of Point-of-Purchase
Communications

FORM OF COMMUNICATION	INCREMENTAL RESPONSE RATE
Brand signage	+2%
Sign plus base wrap	+12%
Display stand and sign	+27%
Display stand, sign, and mobile	+40%
Display stand plus sign about sports tie-in	+65%

On average, point-of-purchase communication generates incremental sales ranging from +2% to +65%, independent of any price reductions. The above figures were based on research in 250 stores in 22 cities, and 94 brands in eight different product categories (beer, salty snacks, cold and allergy products, dog food, soft drinks, laundry detergent, shampoo, and conditioner).

Adapted from "Initial results from supermarket phase of POPAI/ARF study reveal linsights into POP advertising," *Point-of-Purchase Advertising International*, March 27, 2000.

response card
A card filled in, usually at the time of purchase, that collects information about customers that can be added to the organization's database.

cookie
An electronic identification tag sent from a web server to a user's browser to track the user's browsing patterns.

ad clicks (clickthroughs)
The number of times users click on a banner (clicking transfers the user to another website).

ad views (impressions)
An ad request that was successfully sent to a visitor. This is the standard way of determining exposure for an ad on the web.

hit
Each time a server sends a file to a browser.

visitor
A unique user of a website.

visit
A sequence of page requests made by a visitor to a website; also called a session or a browsing period.

stickiness (sticky)
A website's ability to keep people at the site for an extended period or to have them return to the site frequently.

the product. Knowing who is responding to each offer helps a firm better understand its customers and provides insight into how to develop better marketing communications strategies to reach particular targets.

Response cards are another means of assessing impact and collecting information about customers. Typically, these cards are filled in at the time of purchase. Any information that is collected can be added to the organization's database and be combined with other information that may be available on a particular customer.

In an online environment, a **cookie** (an electronic identification tag sent from a web server to a user's browser to track the user's browsing patterns) enables an organization to track online responses. The Internet is a unique communications medium that has built-in technology unlike any other medium. That technology allows for all communications to be measured for effectiveness. In fact, Internet communications are much easier to measure in terms of hard numbers than any other form of media advertising.

Online observation is a common form of recording and analyzing usage patterns. Banner advertising, for example, is measured in terms of **ad clicks** (the number of times users click on a banner) and **ad views** (the number of times a banner ad is downloaded). Every time a server sends a file to a browser, it is recorded in that organization's server log. This statistical information, frequently referred to as **hits**, is readily available for analysis and interpretation. A high number of hits can be attributed to the effectiveness of the message.

The number of visitors to a website and the number of visits that each visitor makes over a period of time are factors that measure a website's ability to communicate. A **visitor** is a unique user who comes to a website. A **visit** is a sequence of page requests made by a visitor at a website. Websites are evaluated based on their **stickiness**—how long visitors stayed at the site. Sticky sites are ones that people are interested in, as shown by their tendency to revisit favourite sites frequently. A plethora of factors influence visits: site design, navigation speed and ability to move from page to page conveniently, site content, and more. If all of these factors work together effectively a consumer can be engaged with a brand for an extended period—a situation that could impact brand loyalty.

Measuring the effectiveness of search ads is relatively easy since advertisers only pay for the ads' placement when people click on them, and they can also track when clicks translate into purchases. The impact of video and display ads on the web is as difficult to measure as the impact of television spots.[9]

Measuring and Evaluating Public Relations Communications

There are several ways to evaluate public relations communications: counting clippings, calculating the number of impressions based on the numbers of clippings, and employing a mathematical model that equates public relations to an advertising value. The latter is referred to as an *advertising equivalency*.

Many organizations that are active in public relations subscribe to a **clipping service**, which scans the print and broadcast media in search of a company's name. Each time the name is found it is recorded and compared to the number of press releases that were issued. For example, if 500 press releases were issued and there were 50 clippings, the return rate would be 10 percent. The success of the campaign would be based on historical comparisons of return rates.

The number of *impressions* generated is based on the circulation of the medium in which the organization's name is mentioned. For example, if an article appears in the *Toronto Star* on a Tuesday and the circulation that day is 450 000, the total number of impressions is 450 000. A company may also "gross up" the number of impressions by considering the actual readership of the paper. If the average number of readers is 2.5 per copy, the gross impressions would be 1 125 000 (450 000 x 2.5).

There is a problem associated with counting clippings and impressions. Such a procedure ignores the nature of the article written or broadcast about the organization. Was it positive or negative? There is a presumption that an article that is critical of a company is of equal value to one that praises a company. It could be argued that positive articles and negative articles should be separated. For certain, companies receive a lot of negative publicity when they face a crisis situation, and such publicity negates much of the positive publicity that is generated by planned public relations communications. On the other hand, there are also those who believe that any publicity is good publicity.

Trying to equate public relations to a corresponding advertising value is an attempt to eliminate the problems associated with clippings and impressions. A technique called **advertising equivalency** involves an evaluation of the space occupied by a public relations message and relating it to a similar amount of advertising space. To demonstrate, assume that a one-page article about a company appeared in *Canadian Business* magazine. If a one-page ad costs $25 000, then that is the value of the public relations to the organization. Similar calculations can be made for the broadcast media. Based on this type of calculation, the sum total of a public relations campaign can be considerable. Specialist companies exist to provide this service.

Ideally, some form of evaluation in relation to specific public relations objectives would be preferable, but rarely does a company have sufficient funds to perform pre-campaign and post-campaign research—the techniques required for such an evaluation. For instance, if the objective of public relations were to increase awareness of a company's name, the pre-campaign research would establish a benchmark figure. Once the campaign was over, a second research study would determine how the level of awareness increased. Justifying such an investment for so many different types of communications programs is often difficult. Again, it is the combination of marketing communications activities that determines true success or failure.

clipping service
An organization that scans the print and broadcast media in search of a company's or brand's name.

advertising equivalency
A mathematical model that equates public relations to an advertising value by evaluating the space occupied by a public relations message in relation to advertising space.

Measuring Experiential Marketing, Events, and Sponsorships

Among all of the integrated marketing communications components, event marketing and sponsorships are the most difficult to evaluate, particularly on a quantitative basis. At their best, sponsorships are a high-profile way to increase sales and improve brand recognition. At their worst, they're a haphazard form of promotion.[10]

Event marketing is attracting a bigger piece of the marketing communications pie each year, but it doesn't get the respect it deserves because there aren't any widely accepted, standardized methods of measuring its results. Examples of proposed event measurement systems include adopting accepted methods of measuring attendance, total number of consumer contacts, and the level of consumer immersion in an event. Despite measurement flaws, event marketing and sponsorship programs continue to be a valued element in many marketing plans.

The most common measures of an event's success are **how well the event reaches the target audience** and **how well the brand or company is associated with the event**. If some form of return on investment can be added to the evaluation mix, so much the better. But, unless you are establishing leads or selling something at the event, the true impact of the sponsorship won't be felt immediately. Nowhere are sponsorships more visible than in the world of sports. In professional football, basketball, and hockey leagues, there is no shortage of sponsors willing to jump in. The Olympics are also a hot ticket, resulting in a sponsorship battle among bidding advertisers. McDonald's was very pleased with the results of its sponsorship of the Beijing Olympics (2008). McDonald's garnered the highest unaided recall among Olympic sponsors in a post-Olympics survey. In a survey of 1000 Canadians 12 years and older, 33 percent recalled McDonald's as a major Olympic advertiser (ahead of Coca-Cola, Visa, Bell, and RBC).[11]

Most managers rely on less concrete evidence to justify investing in event marketing and sponsorships. Having Tiger Woods walking around a golf course wearing a Nike hat, for example, has a positive impact for all kinds of Nike products that extends well beyond golf products. Seeing Tiger Woods driving a Buick Rendezvous adds an element of prestige to the automobile; it also has a halo effect on the image of General Motors. Ironically, the presence of Tiger Woods did not help Buick sales, and he was dropped after an eight-year relationship with the brand.

How beneficial are naming rights on a building? Scotiabank has the name rights to the building where the Ottawa Senators play, which is called Scotiabank Place. Will it enhance Scotiabank's brand image? Industry experts believe Scotiabank will get lots of media exposure for its $20-million investment at Ottawa's Scotiabank Place. Media exposure is a true benefit of event marketing, since hockey games are broadcast and covered by newspapers, radio, and TV stations.

As discussed in Chapter 10, certain indicators are commonly used to measure the benefits of sponsorship. As described above in the McDonald's example, an organization might look at **awareness** and **association** measures as well as changes in **image perceptions** among its customers. However, to measure for changes in awareness and image, pre-event and post-event marketing research is necessary. Is the organization willing to invest further to get some measure of how well an event is contributing to achieving certain marketing objectives? Many managers presume that if an event effectively reaches the desired target audience, then measures for awareness, event association, and image will be positively affected and no investment in research is necessary.

Another common measure is the impact on **brand sales**. Is it immediate, during the event period, or will it happen after the event? The sales of Roots Olympic clothing rose considerably during the Olympic period and the few months that followed the Olympics. The clothes were so popular that they remained a staple item commanding their own section in stores for extended periods, a clear indication that the association with Canada's Olympic team paid dividends. For a variety of reasons, however, Roots is no longer associated with the Olympics. Perhaps the costs started to outweigh the benefits.

Measuring the Integrated Marketing Communications Effort

Because integrated marketing communications is a coordinated and collaborative effort among many different individuals and organizations and many different communications disciplines, perhaps the best form of measurement and evaluation is to look at the big picture. In other words, how healthy is a particular brand or the company as a whole based on all of the marketing and marketing communications strategies that have been implemented over the past year (a typical planning cycle)?

Some typical indicators of success or failure include market share, productivity, sales and profitability, customer satisfaction levels, and social responsibility. As in most evaluation systems already discussed in this chapter, the organization should look back at the corporate objectives it established in these areas to see how well it performed.

An increase in **market share** would indicate greater acceptance by more customers, a higher degree of brand loyalty among current customers, and a strong competitive position. A well-planned integrated marketing communications program would have contributed to such an outcome. **Productivity** measures are more difficult to come by, but where tangible results can be attributed to a specific communications activity, it should be noted. Did the integrated marketing communications program generate new customers? Was brand awareness higher than it was previously? Was the company's or brand's image altered in a positive way? These kinds of measures indicate whether or not a plan is working.

Marketing managers are responsible for producing sales while keeping marketing and marketing communications investments at reasonable levels. *Sales* must generate an adequate level of **profit** for the company to thrive and survive in the long term. Most brands in an organization have their own profit and loss statement, which is reviewed continually to ensure that sales, costs, and profit targets are always within sight. Alterations and adjustments to a marketing plan or marketing communications plan will occur during the year when necessary.

As discussed elsewhere in the text, every employee of an organization plays a role in providing **customer satisfaction**; all employees must adopt a marketing attitude. Therefore, it is very important for all employees to be aware of the marketing and marketing communications strategies. Informed employees play a key role in implementing the strategies; they thus directly influence how customers perceive the organization.

With regard to **social responsibility** objectives, planned public relations programs play a key role. An organization must promote its positive contributions while eliminating, as best it can, the negative outcomes. Brand equity and company image are directly influenced by the quality of social programs and ethical behaviour that a company and its employees demonstrate to the public.

In summary, the real challenge for an organization is to develop an integrated marketing communications strategy that will communicate clearly and effectively with the organization's various publics. The company that does so stands a very good chance of achieving both short-term and long-term success.

market share
The sales volume of one product or company expressed as a percentage of total sales volume in the market the company or brand is competing in.

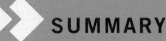

SUMMARY

Marketing research must be viewed as a tool that assists the manager in the decision-making process. It is a systematic procedure that, if used properly, will produce reliable and valid data.

The research process begins with a firm becoming aware of a problem situation. Problems associated with evaluating marketing communications typically involve primary research. Primary research is the gathering of new data from a representative sample. Primary data are collected from surveys, observation, and experiments. Survey data are either qualitative or quantitative in nature. Qualitative data are collected by focus group or one-on-one interviews and answer the question "why." Quantitative data are obtained by questionnaires through personal interview, telephone, mail, or online surveys and involve translating thoughts and feelings into measurable numbers. Once the data are secured, they are processed for analysis and interpreted by the researcher.

Experimental research involves testing a marketing mix activity within a controlled situation to measure the effectiveness of the activity. Test marketing is an example of experimental research. In a test market involving marketing communications, an advertisement, a commercial, or set of ads in a campaign is placed in designated geographic markets to evaluate the potential impact on consumers. Knowledge gained from such tests allows an organization to make changes to a campaign before it is launched in additional markets.

In order to measure the effectiveness of marketing communications programs, various research procedures are implemented. In advertising, several pre-test and post-test techniques are available. If recognition and recall are a concern, a Starch readership test, a day-after recall test, and opinion-measure tests can be applied. These tests generate data on brand identification and message comprehension. If there is a desire to measure emotional responses, various physiological tests that evaluate eye movement, pupil dilation, and voice pitch are available.

Sales promotion measures include response rates to coupon offers and the number of entries received for contest and cash rebate offers. Response rates for current promotions are compared to response rates of previous promotions. The manager will evaluate the various elements of the promotion to determine what elements contributed to success or failure.

Direct response communications and online communications are easier to evaluate quantitatively. Direct response communications usually include a toll-free telephone number, a website address, or response cards. Inquiries can be tracked, and any sales that occur can be attributed to specific customers. With Internet communications, the use of cookies allows an organization to track responses. Other forms of Internet measures include ad clicks, impressions, hits, numbers of visitors to a website, and time spent while at a website.

The most common ways of measuring public relations communications include counting actual clippings that appear in the print and broadcast media, calculating the number of impressions that the press clippings generate, and converting the press coverage (the size of space or amount of time it occupies) to some kind of advertising equivalency. The latter places a monetary value on public relations and is a popular means of justifying investment in public relations.

Event marketing and sponsorships remain difficult to measure. Nonetheless, events and sponsorships are popular among marketing executives because they are perceived as a high-profile way to increase sales and improve brand recognition. The most common measure of an event's success is determined by how well the event reaches the target audience. Other commonly used measures include changes in brand awareness levels and image, both of which are based on how well a brand associates with an event.

When measuring the success of an integrated marketing communications campaign, an organization looks at the bigger picture. Typical indicators of success or failure include shifts in market share, productivity, sales and profitability, employee performance and attitude, and the public's perceptions of an organization's social responsibility. A carefully planned marketing communications program contributes to achieving objectives in all of these areas.

KEY TERMS

ad clicks,   360
ad views,   360
advertising equivalency,   361
clipping service,   361
closed-ended questioning,   346
cookie,   360
cross-tabulation,   351
data analysis,   352
data interpretation,   352
data transfer,   351
day-after recall (DAR) test,   355
editing stage,   351
experimental research,   348
eye movement–camera test,   356
fixed-response questioning,   346
focus group,   348
frequency distribution,   351
hit,   360
hypothesis,   344
mail interview,   351

market share,   363
marketing research,   344
non-probability sample,   346
observation research,   346
online survey,   351
open-ended questioning,   346
open-response questioning,   346
opinion-measure testing,   356
personal interview,   351
population,   345
post-testing,   354
pre-testing,   354
primary data,   344
primary research,   344
probability sample,   346
pupilometer test,   356
qualitative data,   348
quantitative data,   350
recall test,   355
recognition test,   354

redemption rate,   358
related recall,   355
reliability (of data), 344
research objective,   344
response card,   360
sample,   345
sampling frame,   345
Starch readership test,   355
stickiness,   360
survey research,   346
tabulation,   351
telephone interview,   351
test marketing,   348
universe,   345
validity (of data), 344
visit,   360
visitor,   360
voice-pitch analysis test,   356

REVIEW QUESTIONS

1. In the context of marketing research, what is the relationship between the following sets of terms?
   a) secondary data and primary data
   b) research objectives and hypotheses
   c) observational and experimental techniques
   d) population and sampling frame
   e) qualitative data and quantitative data
   f) probability sample and non-probability sample
   g) frequency distribution and cross-tabulation
   h) tabulation and cross-tabulation
   i) data analysis and data interpretation
2. What is the problem-awareness stage of the marketing research process?
3. Briefly explain the four steps in the sample design process.
4. What is a focus group? What are the benefits of focus group research?

5. Under what circumstances would you use the telephone for collecting survey data? When would you use the personal interview?
6. In terms of measuring the effectiveness of advertising, what is the difference between pre-testing and post-testing? What benefits does each form of research provide?
7. What is the difference between a recognition test and a recall test?
8. What are the three categories of measurement in a Starch readership test? Briefly explain each category.
9. What does opinion-measure testing refer to?
10. What are the three primary ways of measuring the effectiveness of public relations campaigns? Briefly discuss each form of measurement.
11. What are the primary ways of measuring the effectiveness of event marketing and sponsorship participation? Briefly discuss each form of measurement.

DISCUSSION AND APPLICATION QUESTIONS

1. Compare and contrast the nature of qualitative data and quantitative data. Is it essential to have both types of information prior to investing in a new advertising campaign? Prepare a position and provide appropriate justification for it.

2. You are about to devise a new advertising strategy (a message strategy) for the Porsche Boxster. You do not know how to present the automobile to potential customers and would like to find out more about them. What information would you like to obtain, and what procedure would you recommend to obtain it?

3. "Too much information obtained from marketing research ultimately stifles creative thinking and the production of innovative creative." Many creative directors have expressed this opinion. Conduct some secondary research and present an opinion on the issue. Justify your position with appropriate examples.

4. Companies are now using online surveys to learn more about their customers and how they feel about the company's products. What are the benefits and drawbacks of using online research? Is it as useful and effective as traditional survey methodologies? Briefly discuss the key issues.

5. If event marketing and sponsorships are so difficult to measure for tangible business results, why do so many large and prosperous companies pursue such associations? What are the advantages and disadvantages of being involved in this form of marketing communications? Is it a worthwhile investment? Present an opinion supported with appropriate justification.

ENDNOTES

1. Karl Greenberg, "Toyota Pitches Corolla to Dreamers with Little Coin," *Media Post Publications*, February 13, 2008, www.mediapost.com

2. "New definition of marketing research approved," *Marketing News*, January 22, 1987, p. 1.

3. Jean Halliday, "Car talk: Ford listens to consumer chatter," *Advertising Age*, February 5, 2007, p. 3.

4. "Managers should rethink the power and limitations of focus groups," *Financial Post*, December 14, 1999, p. C4.

5. Wendy Cuthbert, "Hold the numbers," *Strategy*, June 4, 2001, pp. B6, B7.

6. Colin Flint, "Marketing researchers facing a lot of hang-ups," *Financial Post*, March 26, 2004, p. FP4.

7. Jack Neff, "P&G weds data, sales," *Advertising Age*, October 23, 2000, pp. 76–80.

8. Sarah Mahoney, "Companies shifting more funds, brain cells to shopper marketing," *Media Post Publications*, October 16, 2007, www.mediapostpublications.com.

9. Aaron Patrick, "Yahoo to track impact of Web advertising," *The Globe and Mail*, December 16, 2005, p. B9.

10. Patrick Maloney, "Do sponsorships measure up?" *Marketing*, July 8, 2002, p. 13.

11. Chris Powell, "McDonald's wins Canadian Olympic recall," *Marketing*, September 11, 2008, www.marketingmag.ca.

Media Buying Principles and Media Information Resources

This appendix presents the essential aspects of media buying and acquaints the student with a variety of media rate cards and how to read them. The rate cards used in this section have been gathered from online sources and *Canadian Advertising Rates and Data (CARD)*. Rate cards are usually posted on a media company's website under a title like "Advertise with Us" or "Media Kit." Students can refer to *CARD*, a publication usually available in the reference section of college and university libraries. *CARD* contains summary rate cards for all print and out-of-home media in Canada.

In addition, this section exposes the student to a variety of media information sources often referred to by marketing organizations and communications agencies. In most cases, specialized software available by subscription is required to access specific data. However, students are encouraged to visit the various websites listed under "Media Information Resources" to gain exposure to basic information that is available for free.

A set of review questions dealing with various media calculations is included at the end of the appendix.

Media Buying Principles

NEWSPAPER ADVERTISING

Newspaper space is sold on the basis of agate lines or modular agate lines. An **agate line** is a non-standardized unit of space measurement, equal to one column wide and 1/14" deep. For **broadsheets**, a standard page is 11 1/2" wide with column widths of 1 1/16". The number of columns ranges from 7 to 10, so full-page lineage ranges from 1800 to 3150 agate lines. In **tabloids**, the number of columns ranges from 6 to 10, and full-page lineage ranges from 1134 to 2000 agate lines. Most broadsheets and tabloids use agate lines to determine the size of an advertisement.

A **modular agate line (MAL)** is a standardized unit of measurement equal to one column wide and 1/14" deep. Standard column widths are 2 1/16" in broadsheets. An MAL is wider than an agate line. For a broadsheet, the full-page lineage is usually about 1800 MALs. For a tabloid, the full-page lineage ranges from 890 to 1050 MALs.

Note that in this context "lines" and "columns" are not physical lines and columns. They are invisible lines and columns that the newspaper industry uses to measure the size of an ad.

The basic procedure for buying newspaper space is to determine the size of the ad either in agate lines or modular agate lines. In either case, the cost is calculated by multiplying the width of the ad (number of columns) by the depth of the ad (inches of depth). One column inch of depth equals 14 agate lines. Other factors that influence costs include the number of insertions, creative considerations such as the use of colour, and position charges, if applicable.

Some newspapers offer standard-size ads that are easier to understand in terms of size. With reference to *The Globe and Mail* (see Figure A1.1), some of the standard-size options include full page (1800 agate lines), 1/2 page (900 agate lines), magazine page (616 agate lines), and 1/4 page (453 agate lines).

agate line
A non-standardized unit of space measurement, equal to one column wide and 1/14" deep, used in newspaper advertising.

broadsheet
A large newspaper with a fold in its middle.

tabloid
A smaller newspaper that is sold flat (not folded).

modular agate line (MAL)
A standardized unit of measurement used in newspaper advertising equal to one column wide and 1/14" deep.

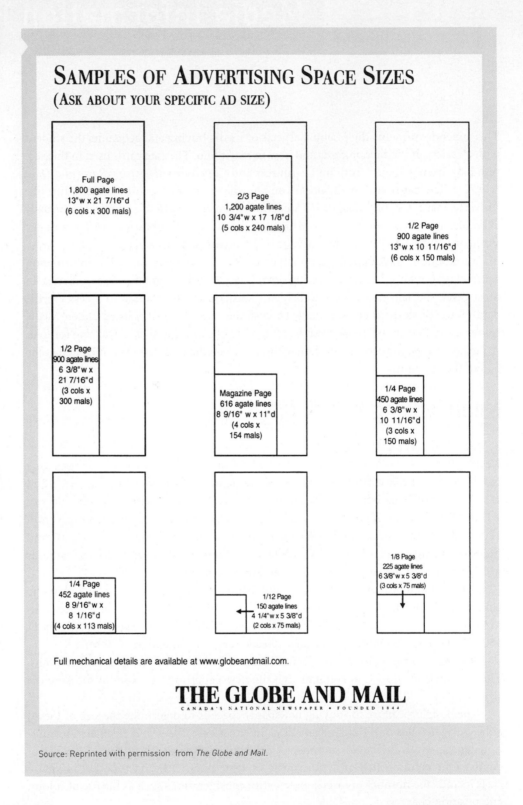

SAMPLES OF ADVERTISING SPACE SIZES
(ASK ABOUT YOUR SPECIFIC AD SIZE)

Full Page
1,800 agate lines
13"w x 21 7/16"d
(6 cols x 300 mals)

2/3 Page
1,200 agate lines
10 3/4"w x 17 1/8"d
(5 cols x 240 mals)

1/2 Page
900 agate lines
13"w x 10 11/16"d
(6 cols x 150 mals)

1/2 Page
900 agate lines
6 3/8"w x
21 7/16"d
(3 cols x
300 mals)

Magazine Page
616 agate lines
8 9/16" w x 11"d
(4 cols x
154 mals)

1/4 Page
450 agate lines
6 3/8"w x
10 11/16"d
(3 cols x
150 mals)

1/4 Page
452 agate lines
8 9/16"w x
8 1/16"d
(4 cols x 113 mals)

1/12 Page
150 agate lines
4 1/4"w x 5 3/8"d
(2 cols x 75 mals)

1/8 Page
225 agate lines
6 3/8"w x 5 3/8"d
(3 cols x 75 mals)

Full mechanical details are available at www.globeandmail.com.

THE GLOBE AND MAIL
CANADA'S NATIONAL NEWSPAPER • FOUNDED 1844

Source: Reprinted with permission from *The Globe and Mail.*

DETERMINING SPACE SIZE To illustrate the concept of agate lines, let's assume the size of the ad is 4 columns wide by 10 column inches deep. Considering that each column inch of depth equals 14 agate lines, the size of the ad would be calculated by the following formula:

$$\text{Number of columns wide} \times \text{Inches of depth} \times 14$$

$$4 \times 10 \times 14 = 560 \text{ agate lines}$$

If the size of the advertisement is 5 columns wide by 8 inches deep, the size of the ad in agate lines will be:

$$5 \times 8 \times 14 = 560 \text{ lines}$$

These two examples illustrate that different configurations of ads (combinations of width and depth) can produce the same size of ad in terms of space occupied and rates charged.

The calculations above would be the same for modular agate lines. The only difference is that the modular agate line is slightly wider than the agate line. Before calculating the costs of an ad, the planner must be aware of what system the newspaper is using: agate lines or modular agate lines.

Newspaper space can be sold on the basis of **modular agate units**, though only a few daily newspapers use this system. In this system, the size of the ad is expressed in terms of units of width and units of depth (e.g., 4 units wide by 6 units deep). In effect, the page is sectioned off into equal-sized units with each unit being 30 modular agate lines deep. Therefore, to calculate the actual size of an ad that is 4 units wide by 6 units deep, the calculation would be as follows:

modular agate unit
A standardized unit of measurement in which a newspaper page is divided into equal-sized units, each 30 modular agate lines deep.

$$\text{Number of columns wide} \times \text{Units deep} \times 30 = \text{Modular agate lines}$$

$$4 \times 6 \times 30 = 720 \text{ MAL}$$

RATE SCHEDULES **Line rate** is defined as the rate charged by newspapers for one agate line or one modular agate line. With regard to rate schedules, several factors must be noted. First, rates charged by line go down as the volume of the lineage increases over a specified period. Second, costs for the addition of colour or preferred positions are quoted separately. Third, the line rates may vary from one section of the paper to another. For example, the transient rate (the highest rate paid by an advertiser) for advertisers in *The Globe and Mail*'s News and Report on Business sections is higher than in other sections of the newspaper. Fourth, line rates may vary by day of the week. The *Toronto Star*, for example, charges more per line for its Saturday edition, since the circulation is significantly higher that day.

line rate
The rate charged by newspapers for one agate line or one modular agate line.

In the chart in Figure A1.2, the rates quoted start with a **transient rate**, which is defined as a one-time rate, or base rate, that applies to casual advertisers. *Discounts* are offered to advertisers as the number of lines purchased increases. Lines accumulate over a period of time, usually a year. The volume discount scale is clearly indicated in Figure A1.2.

transient rate
A one-time rate, or base rate, that applies to casual advertisers.

To illustrate how costs are calculated in newspapers, let's develop a hypothetical plan using the rate card for *The Globe and Mail*. For the illustration assume *The Globe and Mail* uses the agate line format.

Newspaper: *The Globe and Mail*—Wednesday Edition, News Section, National Edition

Size of ad: 4 columns wide x 10 column inches deep

Rate: Transient Rate

Frequency: Once

The first calculation determines the total number of modular agate lines:

$$4 \text{ columns wide} \times (10 \text{ column inches deep} \times 14) = 560 \text{ lines}$$

NEWSPAPER MAGAZINE DIGITAL EXPERIENTIAL

THE GLOBE AND MAIL

2010 ADVERTISING RATES

GENERALRATES

An Ideal Way to Reach Canada's Most Coveted Audience

In print for more than 166 years, The Globe and Mail has consistently delivered Canada's best and deepest coverage of national, international and business news.

The Globe's audience consists of Canada's most influential and affluent citizens – readers who depend on our timely, balanced reporting and analysis in order to form their own opinions and plan their lives, careers and investments accordingly.

When you advertise in The Globe and Mail, your message reaches Canada's thought-leaders – individuals who lead or intend to lead in politics, business, the workplace or the home.

More importantly, Globe and Mail readers have the purchasing power – whether personal or corporate – to follow up on the needs and desires advertisements in The Globe generate.

NEWS, REPORT ON BUSINESS, GLOBE T.O.

News appears daily, in all editions.
Report on Business appears daily in the National Edition.
Globe T.O. appears Saturday as a stand-alone in the Metro edition only.

Monday to Friday

	National	Ont/Que	Metro
Transient	$45.84	$39.42	$36.21
$25,000	38.96	33.52	30.78
$50,000	37.81	32.52	29.87
$100,000	36.67	31.53	28.97
$150,000	35.52	30.56	28.07
$250,000	34.38	29.56	27.16
$350,000	33.00	28.39	26.07
$500,000	31.62	27.21	24.98
$750,000	30.24	26.02	23.89
$1,000,000	28.88	24.84	22.82
$1,500,000	27.51	23.66	21.73
$2,000,000	26.13	22.46	20.66
$2,500,000	24.76	21.29	19.56

Saturday

	National	Ont/Que	Metro
Transient	$50.42	$43.37	$39.84
$25,000	42.86	36.86	33.86
$50,000	41.60	35.77	32.86
$100,000	40.34	34.69	31.86
$150,000	39.09	33.61	30.88
$250,000	37.81	32.52	29.87
$350,000	36.31	31.22	28.68
$500,000	34.78	29.92	27.50
$750,000	33.28	28.63	26.30
$1,000,000	31.77	27.32	25.09
$1,500,000	30.24	26.02	23.89
$2,000,000	28.73	24.71	22.71
$2,500,000	27.23	23.42	21.51

Advertising rates shown are per line, based on annual dollar volume contract commitment.

SPORTS, REVIEW/'7', GLOBE LIFE STYLE, GLOBE FOCUS & BOOKS, GLOBE LIFE

Sports appears daily in the Metro and National editions.
Review appears Monday through Thursday and Saturday in the Metro and National editions ('7' tabloid replaces Review on Friday in Metro).
Globe Life Style appears Saturday in the Metro and National editions.
Globe Focus & Books appears Saturday in the National edition.
Globe Life appears Monday through Friday in the Metro and National editions.

Monday to Friday

	National	Metro
Transient	$21.55	$17.02
$25,000	18.31	14.46
$50,000	17.78	14.04
$100,000	17.24	13.62
$150,000	16.70	13.19
$250,000	16.16	12.76
$350,000	15.51	12.25
$500,000	14.85	11.74
$750,000	14.22	11.24
$1,000,000	13.58	10.73
$1,500,000	12.93	10.21
$2,000,000	12.28	9.71
$2,500,000	11.64	9.19

Saturday

	National	Metro
Transient	$23.70	$18.73
$25,000	20.16	15.90
$50,000	19.56	15.44
$100,000	18.95	14.98
$150,000	18.36	14.50
$250,000	17.78	14.04
$350,000	17.06	13.46
$500,000	16.36	12.91
$750,000	15.64	12.34
$1,000,000	14.94	11.80
$1,500,000	14.22	11.24
$2,000,000	13.52	10.67
$2,500,000	12.80	10.12

All rates are gross. Prices in Canadian dollars.

Advertising Rates effective January 1, 2010

NEWSPAPER
MAGAZINE
DIGITAL
EXPERIENTIAL

TRAVEL

Travel appears Wednesday and Saturday in the Metro, Ontario/Quebec and National editions.

Monday to Friday

	National	Ont/Que	Metro
Transient	$28.42	$24.44	$22.45
$25,000	24.15	20.77	19.07
$50,000	23.45	20.18	18.52
$100,000	22.74	19.56	17.96
$150,000	22.03	18.94	17.40
$250,000	21.32	18.33	16.84
$350,000	20.46	17.60	16.17
$500,000	19.61	16.86	15.49
$750,000	18.77	16.14	14.81
$1,000,000	17.91	15.39	14.15
$1,500,000	17.05	14.68	13.46
$2,000,000	16.20	13.93	12.80
$2,500,000	15.35	13.20	12.13

Saturday

	National	Ont/Que	Metro
Transient	$31.25	$26.89	$24.69
$25,000	26.58	22.85	20.99
$50,000	25.80	22.17	20.38
$100,000	25.01	21.51	19.76
$150,000	24.23	20.83	19.14
$250,000	23.45	20.18	18.52
$350,000	22.50	19.36	17.79
$500,000	21.57	18.55	17.04
$750,000	20.64	17.75	16.30
$1,000,000	19.69	16.94	15.56
$1,500,000	18.77	16.14	14.81
$2,000,000	17.82	15.33	14.09
$2,500,000	16.88	14.51	13.34

COLOUR CHARGES

National	Ont/Que	Metro
$10,083	$9,169	$8,436

NOTICES

Appointment Notices	$74.65
Financial Notices/Tombstones	49.34

GLOBE CAREERS

| Includes 3 insertions –
Wednesday, Friday and
Saturday or Monday	48.51

RESERVATIONS AND DEADLINES

Issue Day	Camera Ready	Pub-set Material

News, Report on Business, Sports and Globe Life (Mon.-Fri.)*

Mon.	Thurs.	4:30pm	Wed.	4:30pm
Tues.	Fri.	4:30pm	Thurs.	4:30pm
Wed.	Mon.	4:30pm	Fri.	4:30pm
Thurs.	Tues.	4:30pm	Mon.	4:30pm
Fri.	Wed.	4:30pm	Tues.	4:30pm
Sat.	Thurs.	4:30pm	Wed.	4:30pm

CAREERS

Mon.	Thurs.	2:00pm	Wed.	2:00pm
Wed.	Mon.	2:00pm	Fri.	2:00pm
Fri.	Wed.	2:00pm	Tues.	2:00pm
Sat.	Thurs.	2:00pm	Wed.	2:00pm

TRAVEL

Wed.	Fri.	4:30pm	Thurs.	4:30pm
Sat.	Tues.	4:00pm	Mon.	4:30pm

GLOBE LIFE STYLE / FOCUS & BOOKS

Sat.	Tues.	4:00pm	Mon.	4:30pm

REVIEW

Mon.	Thurs.	4:00pm	Wed.	4:00pm
Tues.	Fri.	4:00pm	Thurs.	4:00pm
Wed.	Mon.	4:00pm	Fri.	4:00pm
Thurs.	Tues.	4:00pm	Mon.	4:00pm
Fri. (7)	Wed.	12:00pm	Tues.	4:30pm
Sat.	Thurs.	10:00am	Wed.	4:30pm

GLOBE T.O.

Saturday	Thurs.	10:00am	Wed.	4:30pm

All deadlines are based on Eastern Standard Time.

Complete deadlines listed on our Web site:
globelink.ca/newspaper/deadlines

Colour advertising
4 business days in advance for space booking and material.

Double truck
4 business days in advance for space booking and material.

Colour and double truck advertising is subject to availability.

* See Globe Life Style for Saturday deadlines.

COPY CHANGES

NEWS, REPORT ON BUSINESS, SPORTS, GLOBE LIFE
2:00pm business day prior to publication date.

Wednesday Travel:
Monday 2:00pm.

Globe Life Style/Focus & Books:
Thursday 12:00pm.

Review:
Monday - Thursday
12:00pm business day prior.

Saturday Travel/Review/Globe T.O.:
Thursday 2:00pm.

ADDITIONAL INFORMATION

- Deadlines and specifications available separately.
- There is a $79 production charge for ads under 50 MAL that are not camera-ready.
- Minimum display space in News, Style, and Report on Business is 30 MAL; unless specified, it is 15 MAL in other sections.
- Advertising columns 251 MAL or more in depth are charged full depth.
- Double Trucks: Gutter is charged as full column.
- Regional copy changes: $579 per plant. Not available in ROB, Books or Careers.
- Position charge: +25 per cent.
- Front News Banner: +50 per cent and must be colour.
- Page 3, News: +40 per cent.
- Front ROB banner: +25 per cent and must be colour.
- Pages 2 & 3, ROB: +40 per cent.
- Charge for Globe and Mail box number: $79.
- Charge for affidavits: $79.

- Cancellation charge: 50 per cent for ads cancelled after deadline. No cancellations for colour advertising two days prior to publication. No cancellations accepted the day prior to publication.
- The Publisher shall not be liable for errors in advertisements beyond the actual space paid. No liability for non-insertions of any advertisement.
- Not responsible for return of advertising material.

NEWSPAPER SPECIFICATIONS

Complete mechanical and digital specifications available at http://adforward.globeandmail.ca.

Number of columns: 6

Column depth: 300 modular agate lines for full page ads (1,800 lines per 6 column page).

The next step is to multiply the number of lines by the line rate by the frequency to determine the cost of the insertion. In this case, the *transient rate* applies because there is not enough lineage to earn a discount.

$$560 \times \$45.84 \times 1 = \$25\ 670.40$$

Advertisers earn discounted line rates based on annual dollar volume line commitment. To demonstrate, assume an advertiser commits to $100 000. At that level, the line rate drops to $35.95 if the ads are placed in the News section or Report on Business section. Therefore, if the dollar commitment is divided by the line rate ($100 000/$36.67), the advertiser can place ads in various sizes totalling approximately 2725 lines. From the previous example, the total line space was 560 lines for one ad, which means that this ad could run five times (560 lines × 5) for a total of 2800 lines. This lineage earns the discounted line rate and on a dollar basis is just over the $100 000 discount plateau:

$$560 \text{ lines} \times 5 \times 36.67 = \$102\ 676.00$$

If the advertiser only has $100 000 to spend, one option would be to marginally reduce the size of the ad so there are fewer total lines.

POSITION CHARGES Since one disadvantage of newspaper advertising is clutter, advertisers and agencies normally request positions in the newspaper that are deemed to be favourable. The request may be for a particular section, or it could be for the first few pages of the newspaper. With reference to Figure A1.2, *The Globe and Mail* charges more for preferred locations. A general request for a specific section will increase rates by 25 percent while a request for an ad to appear on page 3 (news section) will increase the rates by 40 percent.

position charge
The cost of requesting a preferred position in a newspaper.

The privilege of having a preferred position in a newspaper at a higher cost incurs a **position charge**. An advertiser usually justifies the additional expense of a position request by referring to the improved recognition and recall that will result from the better position.

COLOUR CHARGES Although newspapers are often referred to as the black-and-white medium, colour is available to advertisers willing to pay for it. With reference to *The Globe and Mail*'s rate schedule in Figure A1.2, a separate cost of $10 083 is added if the ad runs in colour. The colour charge applies each time the ad is run. Other newspapers quote cost increases for each additional colour that is added. The addition of a particular colour is often referred to as **spot colour**. A newspaper will also indicate if there is a minimum size requirement for ads running in colour. Make sure you read the fine print on the rate cards!

spot colour
The addition of one colour to an otherwise black-and-white newspaper or magazine ad.

Generally speaking, there is higher recognition and recall of ads that appear in colour, but given the constraints of most budgets, the use of colour in newspaper advertising is reserved for very large advertisers.

PREPRINTED INSERTS Preprinted inserts, such as advertising supplements for supermarkets, drug stores, and mass merchandisers, are inserted into most newspapers and distributed by them. Rates are usually quoted on CPM (cost per thousand). As the size of an insert increases (number of pages) or the delivery circulation increases, the rates on a cost per thousand basis also increase. For example, a 24-page catalogue insert would cost more than a four-page folded insert. Insert rates are quoted separately on newspaper rate cards. In many cases, there is only a reference to the rates on the rate card. Advertisers must contact the newspaper for details.

COMPARING NEWSPAPERS FOR EFFICIENCY In large metropolitan markets where several newspapers compete for advertising revenue, advertisers must decide which papers to place advertising with. For instance, the *Toronto Star* and *Toronto Sun* compete for ad dollars in Toronto as do the *Calgary Herald* and *Calgary Sun* in Calgary. If using a shotgun strategy, the advertiser may use all newspapers. Conversely, if the budget is limited and the target market is more precisely defined, the advertiser might be more selective.

Since the circulation and the cost of advertising (line rates) vary among newspapers, the advertiser must have a way of comparing the alternatives. To make this comparison, the advertiser may use a standard figure called the **cost per thousand (CPM)**. CPM is the actual cost of reaching 1000 readers in a market. The formula for calculating CPM is as follows:

cost per thousand (CPM)
The cost of delivering an advertising message to 1000 people; calculated by dividing the cost of the ad by the circulation in thousands.

$$\frac{\text{Cost}}{\text{Circulation (in thousands)}} = \text{CPM}$$

To illustrate the concept of CPM, assume an advertiser that wants to reach adults in the Calgary market is considering both the *Calgary Herald* and the *Calgary Sun*. Refer to Figure A1.3 for specific details on how the newspapers are compared.

As shown by Figure A1.3, the newspaper CPM is strictly a quantitative figure and the results vary considerably. If the advertiser bases the decision of which newspaper to use solely on this principle, the decision is an easy one—the *Calgary Herald* has a much lower CPM than the *Calgary Sun*. However, to reach the adult population of Calgary effectively, the advertiser will realize that the circulation of both newspapers will be needed. Even though the *Calgary Sun* costs more, it will help an advertiser expand its reach in that market.

MAGAZINE ADVERTISING

The procedure for buying magazine space begins with deciding on the size of the ad, which involves choosing from among the variety of page options sold by the magazines under consideration. The rates quoted are based on the size of page requested. Other factors that influence the cost of advertising in magazines include the frequency of insertions and appropriate discounts, the use of colour, guaranteed-position charges, and the use of regional editions.

FIGURE
A1.3
Comparing Newspapers for Efficiency

The CPM, or cost per thousand, is used to compare newspaper alternatives. It is calculated by dividing the cost of the advertisement by the circulation (in thousands) of the newspaper.

Specifications	Calgary Herald	Calgary Sun
Ad size	1000 lines	1000 lines
Cost per line	$6.68	$4.11
Ad cost (rate x lines)	$6680	$4110
Circulation	129 043	57 207
CPM	$51.78	$71.85

Interpretation: Both newspapers reach adult males and females in Calgary, but the *Calgary Herald* reaches the audience in a more cost-efficient manner. An advertiser would have to place ads in both newspapers to effectively reach an adult target in Calgary.

Source: Adapted from rate card information published in CARD, Winter 2009, pp. 7, 8

SIZE OF AN ADVERTISEMENT AND RATE SCHEDULES Magazines offer a variety of page options or page combinations. For example, *Canadian Geographic* sells space in the following formats: full page, double-page spread, 2/3 page, 1/2 page, and 1/3 page. See Figure A1.4 for illustrations of various magazine ad sizes. The size selected for the advertisement determines the rate to be charged. Magazine rates are typically quoted for all page combinations.

To illustrate how costs are calculated, let's consider a simple example. Assume an advertiser would like to purchase a one-page, four-colour ad in *Canadian Geographic* for January/February and March/April (see Figure A1.5 for rate card details). *Canadian Geographic* is issued six times a year. The column headings on the rate card: 1X, 3X, 6X, and so on, refer to frequency (1 time, 3 times, 6 times). In this example, the frequency is only two. Therefore, the rates in the 1X column are used to calculate the campaign. A discount does not apply until the advertiser commits to three advertisements. The cost calculation would be as follows:

$$\text{One-page rate} \times \text{Number of insertions} = \text{Total cost}$$

$$\$17\ 290 \times 2 = \$34\ 580$$

FIGURE
A1.4 **Various Sizes of Magazine Ads**

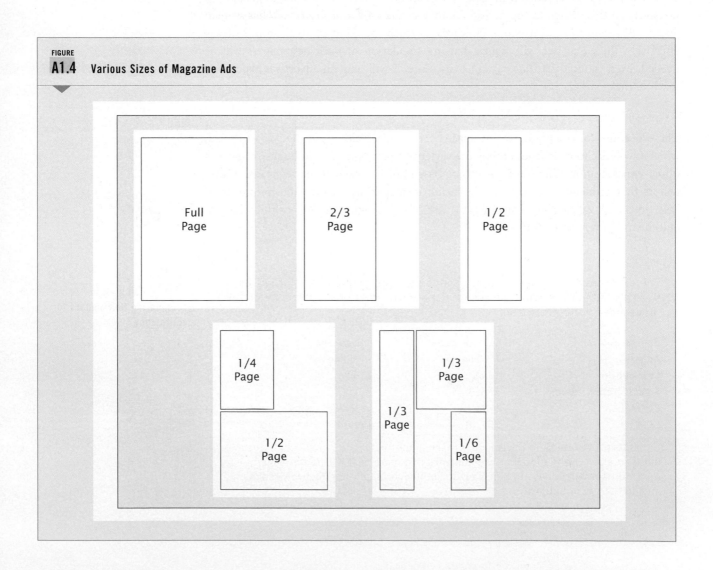

FIGURE
A1.5 *Canadian Geographic* Rate Card

www.canadiangeographic.ca

2010 NATIONAL RATES AND DATA

 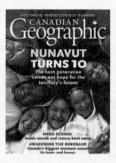   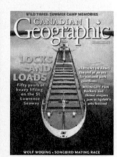

PUBLISHING SCHEDULE 2010-2011

6 ISSUES ANNUALLY	CANADIAN GEOGRAPHIC EDITORIAL FEATURES	CLOSING DATES (insertion orders & material)	ON NEWSSTAND (subs. arrive earlier)
Jan/Feb 2010	Annual Photo Contest Winners	December 9, 2009	January 7, 2010
April 2010	Sound and Nature Safari	February 24, 2010	March 25, 2010
June 2010	Annual Environmental Issue	April 28, 2010	May 27, 2010
July/Aug 2010	Special Report: The Canadian/American Border	June 9, 2010	July 8, 2010
October 2010	Regional Profile: Saskatchewan	August 25, 2010	September 23, 2010
December 2010	Wildlife Stories of the Year	October 27, 2010	November 25, 2010
Jan/Feb 2011	Annual Photo Contest Winners	December 8, 2010	January 6, 2011

NATIONAL ADVERTISING RATES 2010

NATIONAL	1X	3X	6X	9X	12X
Full page	$17,290	$16,770	$16,250	$15,730	$15,210
Double-page spread	$32,845	$31,855	$30,875	$29,885	$28,910
2/3 page	$13,830	$13,415	$12,995	$12,585	$12,170
1/2-page	$12,965	$12,575	$12,190	$11,790	$11,405
1/3 page	$8,640	$8,385	$8,120	$7,865	$7,595
IFC spread	$38,035	$36,895	$35,750	$34,610	$33,465
IBC	$22,470	$21,795	$21,125	$20,450	$19,780
OBC	$20,745	$20,015	$19,415	$18,840	$18,265

EAST/WEST SPLIT RUNS	1X	3X	6X	9X	12X
Double-page spread	$24,685	$23,950	$23,215	$22,530	$21,880
Full page	$12,995	$12,610	$12,220	$11,865	$11,515

*GROSS CANADIAN DOLLARS

Source: Courtesy of *Canadian Geographic*.

DISCOUNTS Advertisers that purchase space in specific magazines with greater frequency will qualify for a variety of discounts. The nature of these discounts varies from one publication to another. Some of the more common discounts include frequency, continuity, and corporate discounts. In magazines, a **frequency discount** refers to a discounted page rate, with the discount based on the number of times an advertisement is run. The more often the ad is run, the lower the unit cost for each ad. In the *Canadian Geographic* rate card, the unit rate is reduced when the ad is run three times, six times, nine times, and twelve times.

A **continuity discount** is an additional discount offered to advertisers that agree to purchase space in consecutive issues of a magazine (such as buying space in 12 issues of a monthly magazine). When continuity discounts are combined with frequency discounts, lower unit costs per page of advertising result.

Large advertisers that use the same magazine to advertise a variety of products (note that such an advertiser would likely be a multi-product firm with products that share similar target markets) may qualify for corporate discounts. A **corporate discount** involves consideration of the total number of pages purchased by the company (all product lines combined), and a lower page rate for each product. Companies such as Procter & Gamble or Unilever that advertise extensively in women's magazines such as *Chatelaine* and *Canadian Living* would earn preferred rates for the advertising pages they buy in those magazines.

COLOUR AND POSITION CHARGES Most magazines publish in colour. Therefore, rates for black and white ads or ads that only include spot colour are usually quoted separately. Additional costs for requesting a guaranteed position are also quoted separately on the rate card. For a guaranteed position, such as the outside back cover (OBC) or the inside front cover (IFC) and inside back cover (IBC), the additional costs are usually in the +20 percent range. With reference to the *Canadian Geographic* rate card, the rate for the outside back cover is $20 745, compared to a full-page ad inside the magazine at $17 290. The difference is about 20 percent.

To illustrate the cost calculations of buying magazine space, let's develop a couple of examples based on the *Canadian Geographic* rate card (see Figure A1.5) and the following information:

Example 1:

Magazine:	*Canadian Geographic*
Size of ad:	one-page, 4-colour ad
Number of insertions:	one-page ad to run in 6 consecutive issues

The calculation for this buying plan will be as follows:

Costs for one page, 4 colour:

Base rate	6X rate applies
$16 250 × 6	= $97 500

Example 2:

Magazine:	*Canadian Geographic*
Size of ad:	double-page spread, 4-colour ad
Number of insertions:	6 issues

The calculation for this buying plan will be as follows:

Costs for DPS, four colour:

Base rate	6X rate applies
$30 875 × 6	= $185 250

COMPARING MAGAZINES FOR EFFICIENCY Let's assume the advertiser has decided to use magazines because they usually have a well-defined target audience based on demographic variables. The advertiser still must choose particular magazines in which to advertise. Because costs and circulation figures vary, the advertiser needs a way to compare alternatives. As with newspapers, CPM is an effective quantitative means of comparing competing magazines.

In most magazine classifications, there is usually a group of publications competing for the same market. For example, *Chatelaine*, *Homemaker's*, and *Canadian Living*, among others, compete against each other in the women's classification. Although the editorial content varies from one magazine to another, each reaches a similar target, so advertisers must look at the efficiencies of each.

Figure A1.6 contains the comparative calculations for two of the magazines in the women's classification. In terms of a purely quantitative measure, both magazines are almost equal, which is why they attract the same types of advertisers. Advertisers wanting to reach the demographic profile of readers of these magazines have little choice but to allocate dollars to both. They reach different readers, but readers with the same profile. Therefore, to advertise in both increases the reach of the magazine campaign. The question to be answered is, how much weight does each magazine receive?

TELEVISION ADVERTISING

As indicated earlier, stations and networks tend not to publish a rate card. There are a variety of factors that influence the costs of television advertising: the supply of advertising time available and the demand for that time, the type of program, the time of day the ad will appear, and the length of the commercial.

Similar to newspapers, CPM (cost per thousand) comparisons are made between magazines that reach similar target markets. In this case, *Chatelaine* and *Canadian Living* compete head-to-head for advertisers.

FIGURE A1.6

Comparing Magazines for Efficiency

Specifications	Chatelaine	Canadian Living
1 time, 4-colour rate	$49 400	$40 315
Circulation	579 920	510 078
CPM	$85.19	$79.05

Both magazines charge different rates and have different circulations. In this comparison it appears that *Canadian Living* is more efficient at reaching female adults. If the objective were to maximize reach, an advertiser would have to include both magazines in the media mix. Similar CPM comparisons can be made on the basis of total readership for each magazine (circulation × the number of readers = total readership).

Source: Calculation based on data published in *CARD*, Winter 2009, Rogers Publishing Limited.

SUPPLY AND DEMAND For major networks such as CTV, CBC, and Global, fundamental economic principles rule the cost of advertising. Advertising space is restricted to 15 minutes per hour, so the network has to maximize advertising revenues on shows that are popular. Top-rated shows like *CSI* (CTV), *American Idol* (CTV), *House* (Global), *NCIS* (Global), and *Hockey Night in Canada* (CBC) attract advertisers willing to pay a premium price for being on a popular (highly watched) show. The low supply and high demand for the space drives the rates upward. Canada's top-rated shows are determined weekly by research organizations such as the BBM and Nielsen Media Research. A sample of their research appears in Figure A1.7.

The rates ultimately paid for popular shows depend largely on their advertising agency's ability to negotiate with the networks. To illustrate, the quoted 30-second spot on a popular show like *CSI* might be $50 000 or more, an indication of the show's popularity. The **negotiated rate**, typically given to larger year-round advertisers after negotiations, packaging strategies, and agency agreements will be much lower, possibly in the $35 000 to $40 000 range. Again, negotiation skills play a key role in the rates an advertiser actually pays.

negotiated rate
The rate ultimately paid by an advertiser as a result of negotiations between an ad agency and a particular medium.

TYPES OF PROGRAMS Special programs such as drama specials, sports events, and miniseries are usually distinguished from regular programming. They are designated as special buys and are sold separately from regular programs. In the case of sports programs, for example, hockey and baseball broadcasts tend to appeal to a particular demographic: males between 18 and 49. They are attractive shows for certain types of advertisers. For these shows, networks need sponsors that are willing to make a long-term commitment, and there are separate rates and discount schedules for those that make such a commitment. For instance, Scotiabank, Ford, and Kraft are regular sponsors of *Hockey Night in Canada*.

Rates for one-time annual sports programming are usually separate from rates for regular programming because these special events attract a particular audience. For example, advertising rates for commercials on major golf events such as the U.S. Open and the PGA Championship command high prices for day-time spots, often well beyond those of a prime-time spot on the same network.[1] These events appeal to advertisers wanting to reach males in the 25- to 49-year age group.

TIME OF DAY Television is divided into three time categories: *prime time, fringe time*, and *day time*. Prime time is usually between 7 pm and 11 pm, fringe time between 4 pm and 7 pm, and day time from sign-on to 4 pm. Because television viewing is highest in prime time, the advertising rates are higher for that time period. Rates vary from show to show and are based solely on the size of viewing audience each show reaches. As indicated above, shows like *CSI* and *American Idol* reach a very large audience, so their rates are among the highest. Other shows in prime time with a smaller audience have rates that are adjusted downward proportionately. The difference is based on the popularity of the show and the size of the audience.

Television viewing in fringe time and day time is much lower, so the advertising rates are adjusted downward. Program content is of a different nature: talk shows, children's shows, reruns of popular programs, and so on. CKCO-TV does publish a rate card, which illustrates how rates fluctuate based on time of day and the popularity of the show (see Figure A1.8).

FIGURE
A1.7 Canada's Top TV Shows

Measuring Audiences. Delivering Intelligence.

Auditoires mesurés. Décisions éclairées.

Top Programs – Total Canada (English)
January 11 - January 17, 2010
Based on confirmed program schedules and preliminary audience data, Demographic: All Persons 2+

Rank	Program	Broadcast Outlet	Weekday	Start	End	Total 2+ AMA(000)
1	AMERICAN IDOL 9 AP	CTV Total	.T.....	20:00	22:00	3167
2	GOLDEN GLOBE AWARDS	CTV Total	......S	20:00	23:01	2896
3	C.S.I. NEW YORK	CTV Total	..W....	22:00	23:00	2472
4	CRIMINAL MINDS	CTV Total	..W....	21:00	22:00	2347
5	TWO AND A HALF MEN	CTV Total	M......	21:00	21:31	2281
6	GREY'S ANATOMY	CTV Total	...T...	21:00	22:00	2267
7	HOUSE	Global Total	M......	20:00	21:00	2168
8	NCIS	Global Total	.T.....	20:00	21:00	2147
9	THE MENTALIST	CTV Total	...T...	22:00	23:00	2139
10	BIG BANG THEORY	CTV Total	M......	21:31	22:00	2099
11	AMERICAN IDOL 9 AR	CTV Total	..W....	19:30	21:00	2080
12	C.S.I. MIAMI	CTV Total	M......	22:00	23:00	1968
13	BONES	Global Total	...T...	20:00	21:00	1729
14	DRAGONS' DEN	CBC Total	..W....	20:00	21:00	1718
15	CTV EVENING NEWS	CTV Total	MTWTF..	18:00	19:00	1714
16	C.S.I.	CTV Total	...T...	20:00	21:00	1670
17	LAW AND ORDER:SVU	CTV Total	.T.....	22:00	23:00	1658
18	NFL PLAYOFFS	CTV Total	.....SS	16:27	19:40	1590
19	24	Global Total	......S	21:00	23:00	1421
20	NCIS: LOS ANGELES	Global Total	.T.....	21:00	22:00	1399
21	HUMAN TARGET	CTV Total	....F..	22:00	23:00	1262
22	CTV NATIONAL NEWS	CTV Total	MTWTFSS	23:00	23:30	1209
23	NFL PLAYOFFS	CTV Total	.....S.	20:10	23:14	1198
24	H.N.I.C. GAME #1	CBC Total	.....S.	19:06	21:54	1169
25	GHOST WHISPERER	CTV Total	....F..	20:00	21:00	1156
26	GLOBAL NATIONAL	Global Total	MTWTF..	17:30	18:00	1117
27	WHEEL OF FORTUNE	CBC Total	MTWTF..	19:00	19:30	1105
28	JEOPARDY	CBC Total	MTWTF..	19:30	20:00	1102
29	H.N.I.C. GAME #2	CBC Total	.....S.	21:54	0:55	1084
30	RICK MERCER REPORT	CBC Total	.T.....	20:00	20:30	1070

Understanding this report ...
This chart shows the Top 30 TV programs for all national networks and Canadian English specialty networks for the week indicated. Programs are ranked based on their AMA(000). AMA(000) is the average minute audience in thousands. The chart also indicates the broadcast outlet on which the program aired and the program's start and end time (shown in Eastern Time).

© 2010 BBM Canada

BBM Canada
1500 Don Mills Road, 3rd Floor
Toronto, ON M3B 3L7
416 445 9800 Tel
416 445 8644 Fax

Sondages BBM
2055, rue Peel, 11' étage
Montréal, QC H3A 1V4
514 878 9711 Tél.
514 878 4210 Téléc.

BBM Canada
10991 Shellbridge Way, Suite 208
Richmond, BC V6X 3C6
604 249 3500 Tel
604 214 9648 Fax

www.bbm.ca

Source: Courtesy of BBM Canada.

FIGURE A1.8 CKCO-TV Rate Card

2005-2006 RATE CARD

REVISED EFFECTIVE: June 6/05
30 SECOND - PUBLISHED RATE (GROSS)
FOR INTERNAL USE ONLY
RATES ARE PROTECTED FOR 5 WORKING DAYS

PRIME

DAY	TIME	PROGRAM		GROUP #	FALL SEP 12/05-DEC 11/05	WINTER DEC 12/05-FEB 19/06	SPRING FEB 20/06-JUN 4/06	SUMMER JUN 5/06-SEP 17/06	52 WEEK SEP 12/05 - SEP 17/06
M-F	557-7P	CTV NEWS AT 6PM	O	015	$1,140	$970	$1,140	$970	$1,010
SA-SU	558-7P	CTV NEWS AT 6PM	O	162	$690	$590	$690	$590	$610
M-F	7-730P	ETALK DAILY	O	153	$600	$510	$600	$510	$530
M-F	730-8P	JEOPARDY	SIM	001	$820	$690	$820	$690	$720
MO	8-830P	CORNER GAS	O	198	$930	$790	$930	$790	$820
MO	9-10P	MEDIUM	PRE	157	$1,600	$1,360	$1,600	$1,360	$1,420
MO	10-11P	CSI MIAMI	SIM	192	$3,400	$2,890	$3,400	$2,890	$3,020
TU	8-9P	AMERICAN IDOL	SIM	057		$3,150	$3,700		
TU	8-9P	CLOSE TO HOME	PRE	071	$1,140	$970	$1,140	$970	$1,010
TU	9-10P	THE AMAZING RACE	SIM	073	$4,010	$3,410	$4,010		
TU	10-11P	LAW & ORDER SVU	SIM	092	$1,880	$1,600	$1,880	$1,600	$1,670
WE	8-9P	LOST	PRE	096		$1,070	$1,260		
WE	8-9P	INVASION	PRE	075	$910	$770	$910	$770	$810
WE	9-10P	LOST	SIM	146	$1,890			$1,610	
WE	9-10P	AMERICAN IDOL	SIM	084		$2,690	$3,160		
WE	10-11P	CSI NEW YORK	SIM	052	$2,160	$1,840	$2,160	$1,840	$1,920
TH	8-9P	THE O.C.	SIM	167	$1,580	$1,340	$1,580	$1,340	$1,400
TH	9-10P	C.S.I.	SIM	068	$4,940	$4,200	$4,940	$4,200	$4,380
TH	10-11P	ER	SIM	049	$3,700	$3,150	$3,700	$3,150	$3,280
FR	8-9P	GHOST WHISPERER	SIM	185	$690	$590	$690	$590	$610
FR	9-10P	NIP/TUCK	O	137	$1,220	$1,030	$1,220	$1,030	$1,080
FR	10-11P	INCONCEIVABLE	SIM	061	$910	$770	$910	$770	$810
SA	7-8P	W-FIVE	O	039	$420	$350	$420	$350	$370
SA	8-9P	COLD CASE	PRE	128	$690	$590	$690	$590	$610
SA	9-10P	CRIME TIME SATURDAY	SIM	035	$690	$590	$690	$590	$610
SA	10-11P	SOPRANOS	O	104	$690				
SA	10-11P	SUE THOMAS F.B.EYE	O	172		$660	$780	$660	
SU	7-8P	LAW & ORDER CI	PRE	103	$1,010	$860	$1,010	$860	$900
SU	8-9P	THE WEST WING	SIM	042	$1,540	$1,310	$1,540	$1,310	$1,370
SU	9-10P	DESPERATE HOUSEWIVES	SIM	025	$4,010	$3,410	$4,010	$3,410	$3,560
SU	10-11P	GREYS ANATOMY	SIM	066	$2,240	$1,900	$2,240	$1,900	$1,990

Source: Courtesy of CKCO-TV.

LENGTH OF COMMERCIAL Most advertisers run 30-second commercials, so rates are normally quoted based on that length. Due to the rising costs of television advertising, however, advertisers are starting to use 15-second commercials more frequently. There is a slight premium for using 15-second commercials; rates are normally about 65 percent of the cost of a 30-second commercial on the same network or station. A 60-second commercial is normally twice the cost of a 30-second commercial. If an advertiser can accomplish creatively what it desires by using 15-second commercials, it will cost less to advertise in absolute dollars. This is an important budget consideration.

GROSS RATING POINTS The weight of advertising in a market is determined by a rating system referred to as gross rating points. **Gross rating points (GRPs)** are an aggregate of total ratings in a schedule, usually in a weekly period, against a predetermined target audience. GRPs are based on the following formula:

$$\text{GRPs} = \text{Reach} \times \text{Frequency}$$

gross rating points (GRPs)
An expression of the weight of advertising in a media schedule; calculated by multiplying reach by frequency.

To illustrate how GRPs work, assume a message reaches 40 percent of target households three times in one week. The GRP level would be 120 (40 x 3). If the message reaches 35 percent of households with an average frequency of 3.6 per week, the GRP level would be 126 (35 x 3.6). The reach of a television show is referred to as a rating. For example, if *CSI: Crime Scene Investigation* reaches 40 percent of households during its weekly time slot, the show has a 40 rating. Therefore, another way to calculate GRPs is to multiply a show's rating by the frequency of messages on that show. See Figure A1.9 for an illustration of this calculation.

Decisions about reach and frequency are difficult. Traditional wisdom suggests frequency is the more important variable because it is necessary to drive the message home before people take action. Traditional models are based on achieving awareness, attitude, and action. But there is a threshold at which an advertiser starts to turn the consumer off.[2] Consequently, many advertisers buy into a concept called recency. **Recency** is a model that suggests advertising works best by reminding consumers about a product when they are ready to buy; this model suggests the timing of an ad is the crucial decision.[3] The debate goes on!

recency
A model that suggests advertising works best by reminding consumers about a product when they are ready to buy.

Since reach, frequency, and GRPs are discussed in the negotiation process, along with a host of other factors, it is next to impossible to illustrate its application in this

---

The weight of advertising in a market or on a particular show is determined by a rating system. Media weight is expressed in terms of gross rating points (GRPs). GRPs consider two key variables: the size of the audience reached and frequency with which the ad is run against that audience. The chart shows some sample calculations to arrive at total GRPs.

FIGURE
A1.9

Calculating GRPs for Television

Audience Demographic	Rating	Number of Spots	GRPs
18–49	30	2	60
18–49	25	2	50
18–49	20	2	40
18–49	23	2	46
Total		**8**	**196**

If the eight spots were scheduled in a one-week period, the weight level for the advertising would be expressed as 196 GRPs for the week.

book. However, to illustrate the basic use of a television rate card, let's look at a few examples. The rate card for CKCO-TV included in Figure A1.8 will be used as reference for these illustrations.

Example 1:

CSI: Miami:	2 spots per week
The OC:	1 spot per week
eTalk Daily:	3 spots per week

All ads are scheduled over a 12-week period between September 19 and December 2.

Cost Calculations:

Based on the time period, the Fall rates would apply from Figure A1.8 (see the rate card for details).

CSI: Miami:

$3400 × 2 spots per week × 12 weeks = $81 600

The OC:

$1580 × 1 spot per week × 12 weeks = $18 960

eTalk Daily:

$600 × 3 spots per week × 12 weeks = $21 600

Total cost: $122 160

Example 2:

Grey's Anatomy:	2 spots per week (13 weeks from February 20 to May 19)
CSI:	1 spot per week (13 weeks from February 20 to May 19)
American Idol:	1 spot per week (8 weeks from Feb 20 to April 14)

Cost Calculations:

Based on the timing of this campaign, the Spring rates would apply from Figure A1.8 (see the rate card for details).

Grey's Anatomy:

$2240 × 2 spots per week × 13 weeks = $58 240

CSI:

$4940 × 1 spot per week × 13 weeks = $64 220

American Idol:

$3700 × 1 spot per week × 8 weeks = $29 600

Total cost: $152 060

volume discount
A discount linked to the dollar volume purchased over an extended period; the more volume purchased, the higher the discount.

A variety of discounts are usually available to television advertisers. A frequency discount is usually earned by purchasing a minimum number of spots over a specified period. A **volume discount** is linked to the dollar volume purchased over an extended period, usually 52 weeks. The greater the volume purchased, the greater the discount. A continuity discount is earned when advertisers purchase a minimum number of spots over an extended period (also usually 52 weeks). With reference to Figure A1.8, note the average rates for a spot are lower in the 52-week column. This reflects the continuity discount offered by the station. Generally, discounts are not published. Instead, they are part of the discussion when buyers and sellers are negotiating with each other.

RADIO ADVERTISING

The rates paid by radio advertisers are affected by several factors: the season or time of year in which commercials are placed, the time of day at which the commercials are scheduled, the use of reach plans, and the availability of discounts offered by individual stations.

SEASONAL RATE STRUCTURES

Radio stations use grid-rate schedules that reflect seasonal listening patterns and reach potential. Refer to Figure A1.10 for an illustration of specific grid-level rates. Generally, radio rates fluctuate with the seasons as follows:

Time Period	Rate
May–August (summer) and December	Higher
September–October	Mid-range
March–April	Mid-range
January–February	Lower

DAYPARTS Since the size and nature of the audience vary according to the **daypart** (a broadcast time period or segment), different rates are charged for each. Generally, the dayparts are classified as follows:

Classification	Time
Breakfast	6 to 10 am
Midday	10 am to 4 pm
Drive	4 to 7 pm
Evening	7 pm to midnight
Nighttime	Midnight to 6 am

Dayparts vary from one station to another, with some stations having more or fewer classifications than those listed above. In addition, weekend classifications are often different from weekday ones, as the listening patterns of the audience change on weekends.

REACH PLANS Radio advertisers can purchase specific time slots and schedule a particular rotation plan during the length of the media buy, or they can purchase a reach plan. For the first option, a **rotation plan**, the advertiser specifies the time slots and pays the rate associated with them. Two types of rotation plans are available:

- *Vertical Rotation:* the placement of commercials based on the time of day (within various dayparts).
- *Horizontal Rotation:* the placement of commercials based on the day of the week (same daypart on different days).

Radio stations sell reach plans so that advertisers can maximize reach. In a **reach plan**, commercials are rotated through the various dayparts according to a predetermined frequency to reach different people with the same message. As shown in Figure A1.10, the reach plan divides spots equally between breakfast, daytime, drive time, and evening/Sunday dayparts. For the advertiser, the benefit of the reach plan is twofold. First, the reach potential is extended; and second, the rates charged for the reach plan collectively are lower (because of the discounts) than those that would result from the individual purchase of similar time slots. Reach plans do require a minimum spot purchase on a weekly basis (16 spots per week is common).

daypart
A broadcast time period or segment on radio or television.

rotation plan
The placement of commercials in time slots purchased on radio; can be vertical according to the time of day or horizontal according to the day of the week.

vertical rotation
The placement of radio commercials based on the time of day (within various dayparts).

horizontal rotation
The placement of radio commercials based on the day of the week (same daypart on different days).

reach plan
Rotation of commercials in various dayparts on radio according to a predetermined frequency.

CJAZ-FM Radio
101.7 JAZ-FM
Jazz that Rocks!

30-sec spot rates Daypart/Grid	1	2	3	4	5
Breakfast 6:00 to 10:00 am	300	275	250	225	200
Daytime 10:00 am to 3:00 pm	245	225	205	185	165
Drive 3:00 to 7:00 pm	250	230	210	190	170
Evening and Sunday	220	200	180	160	140

Reach Plan - 30 sec spots

	1	2	3	4	5
Breakfast 25% Daytime 25% Drive 25% Evening and Sunday 25%	250	225	200	175	150

Discount Schedule

Contract Buy (Continuity)		*Volume (Spots)*	
14 to 26 weeks	Grid 3	250	Grid 3
27 to 39 weeks	Grid 4	450	Grid 4
40 to 52 weeks	Grid 5	700	Grid 5

DISCOUNTS OFFERED BY RADIO Advertisers that purchase frequently from specific stations qualify for a variety of discounts.

A **frequency discount** is a discounted rate earned through the purchase of a minimum number of spots over a specified period of time, usually a week. Having earned such a discount, advertisers are referred to a lower-rate grid schedule, or could be quoted a percentage discount, such as 5 percent for 15 to 20 spots per week, 8 percent for 21 to 30 spots per week, 10 percent for over 31 spots, and so forth. With a **volume discount**, the advertiser is charged a lower rate for buying a large number of spots; the discount might be 5 percent for 260 spots, for example, or 10 percent for 520 spots. A **continuity discount** applies when an advertiser agrees to place ads over an extended period such as intervals of 26, 39, and 52 weeks.

Advertisers can increase reach by buying a reach plan. The **reach plan** offers a minimum number of weekly spots across all dayparts in return for a packaged discount rate. Refer to Figure A1.10 for examples of discounts.

BUYING RADIO TIME A strategic plan guides the purchase of radio commercial time. To get the best possible rate from a station or network of stations, all details of the plan must be known by the radio station. Factors such as volume and frequency (the total number of spots in the buy), the timing of the schedule (in terms of time of day or season in which the plan is scheduled), and continuity (the length of the plan) collectively affect the spot rate that is charged the advertiser. It places an advertiser on a particular grid with the station. Refer to Figure A1.10 for a listing of grid rates and how an advertiser arrives at a certain grid. For advertisers that purchase large amounts of time, the discounts described above usually apply.

To illustrate some basic cost calculations used in buying radio time, let's develop some examples based on the CJAZ-FM rate card in Figure A1.10.

Example 1:

30-second spots

10 breakfast spots per week

15 drive spots per week

12-week schedule

Cost Calculations:

The advertiser does not qualify for a continuity discount. Therefore, the first calculation is to determine the total number of spots in the buy to see if a volume discount applies.

Total number of spots	= Spots per week × Number of weeks
Breakfast	= 10 per week × 12 weeks = 120
Drive	= 15 per week × 12 weeks = 180
Total spots	= 300

Based on the total number of spots (300), the rate charged will be from Grid 3. In this case, the 30-second rate is $250 for breakfast and $210 for drive time. The cost calculations are as follows:

Total cost = Number of spots × Earned rate	
Breakfast	= 120 spots × $250 = $30 000
Drive	= 180 spots × $210 = $37 800
Total cost	= $67 800

Example 2:

The advertiser would like to evaluate a reach plan (involving 16 commercials per week) against a specific buying plan. Details of each plan are as follows:

Plan A: Reach Plan (30-second spots)

16 spots per week (reach plan)

Rotated between breakfast, drive, day, and evening/Sunday

Schedule over 16 weeks, June through September

Plan B: Specific Plan (30-second spots)

8 breakfast spots per week

8 drive spots per week

16-week schedule

Cost Calculations for Plan A:

The advertiser qualifies for a continuity discount because of the 16-week schedule. The rate would be in Grid 3 in the reach plan. The earned rate is $200 per spot.

Total Cost	= Total number of spots × Earned rate
	= (16 spots per week × 16 weeks) × $200
	= $51 200

Cost Calculations for Plan B:

The total number of spots is as follows:

Breakfast	= 8 spots per week × 16 weeks = 128 spots
Drive	= 8 spots per week × 16 weeks = 128 spots
Total spots	= 256

Based on this calculation, the advertiser qualifies for either a volume or a continuity discount. The advertiser is charged the rate from Grid 3.

Breakfast	= 128 spots × $250 = $32 000
Drive	= 128 spots × $210 = $26 880
Total cost	= $58 880

In conducting a comparative evaluation of Plan A and Plan B, the advertiser must weigh the more selective reach potential of Plan B against the savings of Plan A. Perhaps the advertiser wants to reach business commuters in drive time to and from work. With Plan A, the advertiser can reach a somewhat different audience by means of a daypart rotation of spots. The net result is a cost difference of $7680 in favour of Plan A. Should the advertiser decide to go with the cost savings of Plan A, or with the more selective reach of Plan B at greater cost?

OUT-OF-HOME ADVERTISING

Out-of-home advertising offers a variety of outdoor poster options, street-level advertising, wall murals, and transit shelters, vehicles, and station advertising. Regardless of the alternative, the media buying procedure is similar. Out-of-home rates can be based on GRPs or on a per panel basis.

Referring to Figure A1.11, a rate card for CBS Outdoor transit shelters, let's assume an advertiser wants to buy 50 GRPs in Toronto. That means the advertiser will reach the equivalent of 50 percent of Toronto's population. The word "equivalent" is important because vehicle and pedestrian traffic in a city is partly habitual; that is, people tend to travel the same routes each day. Therefore, in the Toronto example, the advertiser might reach 25 percent of the population twice a day for a total of 50 daily GRPs.

All out-of-home advertising rates are quoted on a four-week basis and are sold on a market-by-market basis. Posters and transit shelters are typically sold on the basis of a four-week minimum purchase. To illustrate outdoor cost calculations, let's consider a couple of media buying examples. Rates and data from Figure A1.11 (transit shelter rates) and Figure A1.12 (outdoor poster rates) are used to calculate costs.

FIGURE A1.11 Outdoor Rate Card for Transit Shelters

2010 NATIONAL RATEBOOK

TRANSIT SHELTERS

Market	Outdoor Operator	2010 Est. Population	25 GRP Panel Range	25 GRP 4-Week Net Rate	50 GRP Panel Range	50 GRP 4-Week Net Rate	75 GRP Panel Range	75 GRP 4-Week Net Rate	100 GRP Panel Range	100 GRP 4-Week Net Rate
ATLANTIC										
005 St. John's CMA (Nfld.)	St. John's Trans.Com.	181,700	6	$3,180	11	$5,214	17	$8,058	23	$10,534
019 Halifax CMA	CBS Outdoor	375,403	10-11	$4,725	21-23	$9,000	31-35	$12,825	42-46	$16,200
025 Cape Breton CA (Sydney)	CBS Outdoor	102,700	3	$1,065	5	$2,025	6-7	$2,885	8-9	$3,645
023 Annapolis Valley & Region	Atcom	103,000	$562 per panel*							
048 Saint John CMA (NB)	CBS Outdoor	120,700	3-4	$1,300	6-7	$2,475	10-11	$3,530	13-14	$4,455
QUEBEC										
060 Quebec City CMA	CBS Outdoor	714,500	17-19	$10,170	34-38	$19,375	51-57	$27,610	69-75	$34,875
065 Saguenay (Chicoutimi-Jonquiere) CMA	CBS Outdoor	145,300	4-5	$1,560	8-9	$2,975	12-13	$4,240	16-18	$5,355
077 Trois-Rivieres CMA	CBS Outdoor	140,800	4-5	$1,560	9-10	$2,975	13-14	$4,240	18-20	$5,355
088 Sherbrooke CMA	CBS Outdoor	187,500	3-4	$1,445	6-7	$2,750	9-10	$3,920	12-13	$4,950
090 Montreal CMA	CBS Outdoor	3,635,600	61-67	$42,925	123-133	$81,760	187-197	$116,510	251-261	$147,170
107 Montreal Core	CBS Outdoor		$2,575 per panel							
Montreal CMA										
057 Blainville	Imagi	51,900	$495 per panel							
123 Boucherville	Imagi	39,500	$495 per panel							
118 Brossard	Imagi	71,200	$495 per panel							
070 La Prairie	Imagi	22,700	$355 per panel							
119 Longueuil	Imagi	224,200	$435 per panel							
081 St. Constant/Ste.Catherine/Delson	Imagi	46,600	$355 per panel - non standard format***							
085 St-Jérôme	Imagi	64,400	$355 per panel - non standard format***							
111 Terrebonne & Mascouche	Imagi	136,000	$495 per panel							
105 Varennes	Imagi	21,000	$355 per panel - non standard format***							
144 Ottawa-Gatineau CMA (Quebec)**	Imagi	287,600	9-11	$4,346	19-21	$8,301	27-31	$11,649	37-41	$15,304
108 Drummondville CA	Imagi	78,700	$435 per panel							
098 Joliette CA	Imagi	45,100	$355 per panel - non standard format***							
100 Shawinigan CA	Imagi	55,400	3	$1,490	5	$2,425	7	$3,304	9	$4,140

** Ottawa-Gatinea CMA - Quebec (144) includes Gatineau, Hull and Alymer
*** Non-standard format size 55 1/4"H x 48"W

2010 Ratebook 19/02/2010

Visit our web site at www.cbsoutdoor.ca

20

FIGURE A1.11 Outdoor Rate Card for Transit Shelters *(continued)*

2010 NATIONAL RATEBOOK

TRANSIT SHELTERS

Market	Outdoor Operator	2010 Est. Population	25 GRP Panel Range	25 GRP 4-Week Net Rate	50 GRP Panel Range	50 GRP 4-Week Net Rate	75 GRP Panel Range	75 GRP 4-Week Net Rate	100 GRP Panel Range	100 GRP 4-Week Net Rate
ONTARIO										
172 Toronto CMA/Hamilton CMA	CBS Outdoor	6,100,300	82-90	$82,250	167-177	$156,665	253-263	$223,245	339-349	$281,995
182 Toronto CMA	CBS Outdoor	5,391,000	65-71	$77,870	131-141	$148,325	199-209	$211,360	267-277	$266,980
199 Hamilton CMA	CBS Outdoor	709,400	18-20	$10,670	35-39	$20,320	52-58	$28,955	71-77	$36,575
224 London CMA	CBS Outdoor	470,400	9-10	$4,685	19-21	$8,925	28-30	$12,720	37-41	$16,065
243 Windsor CMA	CBS Outdoor	332,100	8-9	$4,325	16-18	$8,240	24-26	$11,740	32-36	$14,830
250 Sarnia CA	CBS Outdoor	90,000	3-4	$2,435	7-8	$4,640	11-12	$6,610	14-16	$8,350
284 Sault Ste. Marie CA	Superior 7	81,400	2	$970	4	$1,935	6	$2,905	8	$3,870
309 Timmins CA	BK Corporate Mktg.	42,600	2	$1,200	4	$2,200	6	$3,000	8	$3,600
311 Sudbury CMA	BK Corporate Mktg.	160,800	3	$2,100	6	$4,050	9	$5,850	12	$7,200
PRAIRIES/BRITISH COLUMBIA										
318 Winnipeg CMA	CBS Outdoor	695,100	9-10	$4,135	18-20	$7,880	27-29	$11,230	35-39	$14,185
362 Calgary CMA	CBS Outdoor	1,106,300	28-30	$18,770	55-61	$35,750	83-91	$50,945	111-121	$64,350
395 Edmonton CMA (mediacolumns/kiosks)	CBS Outdoor	1,047,900	19-21	$13,780	37-41	$26,250	55-61	$37,405	74-80	$47,250
430 Vancouver CMA	CBS Outdoor	2,219,000	29-33	$35,800	58-64	$68,190	87-95	$97,175	116-126	$122,745
431 Vancouver Core	CBS Outdoor		$2,625 per panel							

* GRPs not applicable
For single panel rates contact your CBS Outdoor account manager.

2010 Ratebook 19/02/2010

Visit our web site at www.cbsoutdoor.ca

21

A1.12 Rate Card for Outdoor Backlight Posters

2010 NATIONAL RATEBOOK

BACKLIGHTS

Market	Outdoor Operator	2010 Est. Population	Isolation Rate	50 Weekly GRPs Approx. Panels	4-Week Net Rate	75 Weekly GRPs Approx. Panels	4-Week Net Rate	100 Weekly GRPs Approx. Panels	4-Week Net Rate
QUEBEC									
060 **Quebec City CMA**	CBS Outdoor	714,500		$4,220 per panel*		n/a		n/a	
090 **Montreal CMA**	CBS Outdoor	3,635,600	$5,000	6	$18,000	9	$25,650	12	$32,400
ONTARIO									
182 **Toronto CMA**	CBS Outdoor	5,391,000	$5,000	17	$51,000	25	$71,250	33	$89,100
299 **Sudbury CMA**	Outdoor Exposure	160,800		1	$1,550	n/a		n/a	
PRAIRIES/BRITISH COLUMBIA									
362 **Calgary CMA**	CBS Outdoor	1,106,300	$2,500	4	$8,000	n/a		n/a	
395 **Edmonton CMA**	CBS Outdoor	1,047,900	$2,500	4	$8,000	6	$11,400	8	$14,400
425 **Vancouver CMA**	CBS Outdoor	2,219,000	$5,000	7	$21,000	10	$28,500	n/a	

* GRPs not applicable
For single panel rates contact your CBS Outdoor account manager.

Visit our web site at www.cbsoutdoor.ca

2010 Ratebook 19/02/2010

23

Example 1: Outdoor Buying Plan

Medium:	Transit shelters (CBS)
Markets:	Toronto/Hamilton (CMA), Montreal CMA, Calgary (CMA), and Edmonton (CMA)
Weight:	25 GRPs weekly in Toronto/Hamilton and Montreal; 50 GRPs weekly in Calgary and Edmonton
Contract length:	16 weeks in all markets

Cost Calculations:

The costs for a four-week period for each market would be as follows:

Toronto/Hamilton	$82 250
Montreal	$42 925
Calgary	$35 750
Edmonton	$26 250
Total	$187 175

Because the contract is for 16 weeks, the costs are multiplied by four (16 weeks divided by four-week rates). The gross cost would be as follows:

$$\$187\ 175 \times 4 = \$748\ 700$$

Although not shown in this particular illustration and rate card, outdoor media usually offer advertisers volume discounts (e.g., a reduced rate based on dollar volume purchased) and continuity discounts (e.g., a reduced rate for extended buys such as 12 weeks, 16 weeks, etc.).

Example 2: Outdoor Buying Plan

Medium:	Horizontal Backlights (CBS)
Markets:	Toronto (CMA), Montreal (CMA), and Vancouver (CMA)
Weight:	Toronto and Montreal at 50 GRPs and Vancouver at 75 GRPs
Contract length:	16 weeks in Toronto; 12 weeks in Montreal and Vancouver

Cost Calculations:

Using the data from Figure A1.12, the appropriate costs for each market over a four-week period would be as follows:

Toronto	$51 000 × 4	= $204 000
Montreal	$18 000 × 3	= $54 000
Vancouver	$28 500 × 3	= $85 500
Gross cost		**= $343 500**

Because the length of the contract in Toronto is 16 weeks, the costs are multiplied by four (16 weeks divided by the four-week rate). In Montreal and Vancouver, the contract is 12 weeks. Therefore, the costs are multiplied by a factor of three (12 weeks divided by the four-week rate). Should volume and continuity discounts apply, they would be deducted from the gross amount shown in this illustration.

DIRECT MAIL ADVERTISING

Three basic steps are involved in buying direct mail: obtaining a proper prospect list, conceiving and producing the mailing piece, and distributing the final version.

OBTAINING DIRECT MAIL LISTS The direct mail list is the backbone of the entire campaign. Both the accuracy and definition of the list can have a significant bearing on the success or failure of a campaign. Since it is much less expensive to keep a current customer than to find a new one, a company should compile accurate lists of customers in their database and form relationships with customers through mail and electronic means. Internal lists compiled from a database management system are referred to as **house lists.**

Prospective names are also gathered from external sources. People with a history of responding to mail offers tend to be attractive prospects for new offers. Buying by mail is part of their behaviour. Therefore, the challenge is to find prospects that have a demographic profile and, perhaps, a psychographic profile that mirror the profile of current customers. A **list broker** can assist in finding these prospects. The buyer provides the broker with the profile of the target customer, and the broker supplies a list of possible prospects on a cost-per-name basis. Generally, a high-quality list is developed through a **merge/purge** process on a computer, whereby numerous lists are purchased, combined, and stripped of duplicate names.

Cornerstone Group of Companies, a database management company, compiles lists for various consumer, business, and professional targets. A consumer list can be compiled based on predetermined criteria such as income, home ownership, marital status, and type of dwelling. Business lists can be developed based on the type or size of business (e.g., small, home-based businesses). Professional lists are available for medical, legal, and engineering practitioners, among many others.

Canada Post also supplies information vital to the accurate targeting of messages. For example, a postal code can isolate a small geographic area—say, a city block—and can then be combined with census data to provide relevant statistics regarding the ages and incomes of homeowners in the area and whether children are present in the households.

A few types of lists are available: *response lists*, *circulation lists*, and *compiled lists*. A **response list** is a list of proven mail-order buyers. Such lists include book-of-the-month-club buyers, CD music buyers, or people who order from cooperative direct mailing firms. Because these lists include proven mail-order buyers, they tend to cost more. A minimum rental of 5000 names is required in most cases.

Circulation lists are magazine subscription lists that target potential customers according to an interest or activity. A publishing company, for example, might sell its list of subscribers to another business interested in a similar target. Rogers Media offers a consumer database composed of unduplicated active subscribers to a host of its publications, including *Maclean's*, *Chatelaine*, and *Flare*.

Compiled lists are prepared from government, census, telephone, warranty, and other publication information. These are the least expensive of the lists and are not always personalized. Provincial and national associations, such as the Canadian Medical Association, commonly provide mailing lists of their members. A list broker, for example, could compile a list of a cross-section of professionals from various occupations, if required by a client.

PRODUCTION Direct mail packages are usually designed by a specialist agency. Once the mailing package is designed, it is ready for printing. Various factors that influence cost include size, shape, number of pieces, use of colour, and so on. Costs are usually quoted

house list
An internal customer list.

list broker
A company specializing in finding or developing lists for direct response purposes; finds prospect lists based on target market criteria established by marketing organizations.

merge/purge
A process in which numerous mailing lists are combined and then stripped of duplicate names.

response list
A list of direct mail buyers who have previously bought based on direct response offers.

circulation list
A publication's subscription list that targets potential customers based on specified demographic characteristics, interests, or activities.

compiled list
A direct mail list prepared from government, census, telephone, warranty, or other publication information.

CPM or on a cost per unit basis, with larger runs incurring lower unit costs. Once printed, the mailing pieces are turned over to a letter shop that specializes in stuffing and sealing envelopes, affixing labels, sorting, binding, and stacking the mailers. Once this task is complete, the mailing units are sent to the post office for distribution.

DISTRIBUTION Distribution costs of direct mail replace placement costs in traditional forms of media advertising. The most common means of delivery is Canada Post. Several options are available through the postal system: first-class mail, third-class mail, and business-reply mail. Obviously, the quicker the means of delivery the higher the costs will be. Most direct mail pieces—whether single pieces, bulk items, catalogues, or cooperative mailings—are delivered third class. The advantage over first class is the cost savings.

DIRECT MAIL BUYING ILLUSTRATION The procedures for estimating the cost of solo direct mail and cooperative direct mail are similar. However, with a solo direct mail campaign, the advertiser absorbs all the costs rather than sharing them with other advertisers. Taken into consideration are factors such as costs of renting a mailing list, distribution costs, printing costs, mailing costs, and costs associated with fulfillment. For this example, we will assume a cooperative direct mail program will be undertaken in the Open & Save Cooperative Mailing package (see Figure A1.13). The Open & Save mailer is distributed to a predetermined list of households across Canada and contains offers from non-competing brands in various product categories.

Buying Information:

Open & Save Cooperative Mailings (QPONZ Inc.)

The offer:	one-page folded ad on regular paper that includes a $1.50 coupon
Redemption rate:	3 percent
Distribution:	2 000 000 households

Cost Calculations:

Printing and distribution costs (cost for inclusion in Canada Post envelope)	$2\ 000\ 000 \times \$.023$	= $46 000
Redemption costs (based on a 3 percent redemption rate)	$2\ 000\ 000 \times 0.03 \times \$1.50$	= $90 000
Total cost		**= $136 000**

Depending on how the coupon offer is returned, there could be additional costs for the advertiser. For example, there is a handling fee provided to the retailer for conducting the coupon transaction. As well, coupons are usually sent from the retailer to a clearing house for processing. The clearing house pays the retailer and provides periodic reports to the advertiser about how many coupons are being redeemed. The advertiser pays a fee for this service.

INTERNET ADVERTISING

The most common model for quoting advertising rates on the Internet is CPM. An advertiser may pay each time its ad is downloaded to a browser, creating an ad view or impression. Or the advertiser may only pay when its ad is clicked on, a pay for performance model.

FIGURE
A1.13 Open & Save Cooperative Mail Rate Card

2010/2011 Rates
(in cents per flyer), including creative, print and delivery by Canada Post

Regular Stock: 4 colour front / 2 colour back

Print Quantity	3.5 x 8.5	5.5 x 8.5	8.5 x 11
50,000	2.7	3.1	4.3
100,000	2.6	3.0	4.2
150,000	2.5	2.9	4.1
200,000	2.4	2.8	4.0
300,000	2.3	2.7	3.9
400,000	2.2	2.6	3.8
600,000	2.1	2.5	3.7
800,000	2.0	2.4	3.6
1,000,000 +	1.9	2.3	3.5
Print Only	1.9	2.3	3.5

Hi bulk add 25% extra.

Glossy Stock: 4 colour front and back

Print Quantity	4.25 x 7.5	5.5 x 8.5	8.5 x 11	7.5 x 16.5	8.5 x 22
50,000			4.8	5.2	6.2
100,000	2.9	3.7	4.7	5.0	6.0
150,000	2.8	3.6	4.6	4.9	5.9
200,000	2.7	3.5	4.5	4.8	5.8
300,000	2.6	3.4	4.4	4.7	5.7
400,000	2.5	3.3	4.3	4.6	5.6
600,000	2.4	3.2	4.2	4.5	5.5
800,000	2.3	3.1	4.1	4.4	5.4
1,000,000 +	2.2	3.0	4.0	4.3	5.3
Print Only	2.2	3.0	4.0	4.3	5.3

*Rates subject to change without notice.

Source: Courtesy of Louise Montreuil, Sales Director for Open&Save, QPonz Inc. Scarborough ON.

CPM MODEL **CPM** is the price charged for displaying an ad one thousand times. The calculation for CPM is cost divided by impressions (number of impressions divided by 1000). For online advertising, an organization pays a rate for every 1000 impressions made.

CPM (online)
The price charged for displaying an ad 1000 times. The calculation for CPM is cost divided by impressions (number of impressions divided by 1000).

Therefore, if the total number of impressions desired is 500 000 and the CPM is $30, the total cost of the advertising campaign will be $15 000 (500 000 impressions/1000) × $30.

CPM rates vary according to the level of targeting desired by the advertiser. Typical options include *run of site, run of category, geographic targeting,* and *keyword targeting.* With reference to the rate card for globeandmail.com shown in Figure A1.14, if run of site or run of network is selected, the rates charged are those quoted for the various sizes and styles of advertising for ads that will appear anywhere on the website—see the column titled Net CPM rate on the rate card. For example, a big box ad is $37/M, a skyscraper is $35/M, and so on. The difference in rates is indicative of the effectiveness of the different sizes of ads—bigger ads are more effective.

If **targeting requests** are applied, a 15 percent premium is charged for each targeted request (see the geo-targeting column on the rate card). Volume discounts might be offered based on the total dollar value of the advertising space that is purchased (see the volume discount scale at the bottom of the rate card).

CPM rate cards vary from one site to another, but the high-traffic sites of course charge a higher CPM. Popular portal sites like MSN, Canoe, Sympatico.ca, Yahoo!, Google, and various sports and media sites (TSN and Rogers Sportsnet) attract significant traffic and price their CPMs accordingly.

Here are a few illustrations to show how online advertising costs are calculated. Rate information is obtained from Figure A1.14.

targeting request
An ad placed to reach a specific target audience of a website, for which a premium is usually paid.

Example 1:

Type of ad:	Leaderboard
Impressions desired:	3 000 000
CPM:	$37

Cost Calculation:

(3 000 000/1000) × $37 = $111 000

Since a volume discount of 20% applies in this situation (see volume discount section of the rate card) there is an additional calculation:

Volume Discount: 111 000 x.20 = 22 200

Therefore, the net cost is $88 800 ($111 000 – $22 200).

Once the ad achieves the desired number of impressions it will be removed from the website.

Example 2:

Type of ad:	Skyscraper
Impressions desired:	3 000 000
CPM:	$35
One geographic target request	+ 15%

Cost Calculation:

(3 000 000/1000) × $35 × 1.15 = $120 750

In this example, a volume discount of 20 percent applies (see the dollar volume discount scale in the rate card). Therefore, the additional calculation would be:

Volume Discount: $120 750 × 0.20 × $24 150

Therefore, the net cost would be $96 600 ($120 750 – $24 150).

FIGURE
A1.14 *The Globe and Mail* Online Advertising Rate Card

NEWSPAPER MAGAZINE DIGITAL EXPERIENTIAL

THE GLOBE AND MAIL
2010 ADVERTISING RATES

Globe and Mail.com

CREATIVE FORMAT	PIXEL SIZE	MAX FILE SIZE ANIMATIONS	NET CPM RATE**	EXPANDING CREATIVE +15%	GEO-TRACKING +15%	FREQUENCY CAPPING +15%
Big Box	300x250	40k - 5 rotations	$37	600 x 250*	yes	yes
Leaderboard	728 x 90	40k - 5 rotations	$37	728 x 360*	yes	yes
Superbanner	960 x 90	40k - 5 rotations	$43	960 x 360*	yes	yes
Skyscraper	160 x 600	40k - 5 rotations	$35	n/a	yes	yes
Half Page Skyscraper	300 x 600	40k - 5 rotations	$50	n/a	yes	yes
Earlug	310 x 56 static	15k - no rotation	$5	n/a	yes	yes
Tile	120 x 240	15k - 3 rotations	$13	n/a	yes	yes
Pre-Roll Video**	534 x 299	1.5 meg	$52	n/a	yes	yes
Top Layer (Volken)	500 x 500 max	40k - no rotations	$40	n/a	yes	included
Pop Up	250 x 250 max	40k - no rotations	$37	n/a	yes	included
Full Screen Transition	640 x 480	40k - no rotations	$70	n/a	yes	included
Text Link	95 characters	n/a	$2	n/a	yes	n/a
.mobi	300 x 48	7k - 3 rotations	$35	n/a	no	no

* For complete expanded ad specs go to: **www.globelink.ca/onlinespecs** ** Rich media +15% ***With companion Big Box (300 x 250)

■ NEWSLETTERS

NAME	SITE	SUBSCRIBERS	DEPLOYMENT RATE
Business Ticker	GAM	50,000	Daily
Weekly Tech Alert	GT	29,000	Thursday
News Update	GAM	64,000	Daily
Personal Finance Reader	GI	130,000	Friday
Advisor Focus	GA	12,000	2nd Friday
Style Counsel	GAM	13,000	Daily
Globe Investor Magazine	GI	120,000	Bi-monthly

■ ADVERTISING EXCLUSIVES

CATEGORY	SUBSCRIBERS
Arts & Entertainment	48,000
Auto	33,000
Consumer Electronics	30,000
Computer Hardware/Software	40,000
Fashion & Style	30,000
Food & Groceries	31,000
Health & Well-Being	53,000
Personal Finance & Investing	63,000
Sporting Goods & Events	30,000
Travel & Accommodations	54,000
Wine & Spirits	33,000
Real Estate	36,000
Rates: $7,500 NET	**25,000***
Rates: $11,000 NET	**50,000***
Rates: $13,500 NET	**75,000***
Rates: $15,000 NET	**100,000***

■ VOLUME DISCOUNTS

VOLUME DISCOUNT BUY	DISCOUNT	VOLUME DISCOUNT BUY	DISCOUNT
$0 – $4,999	0%	$200,000 – $249,999	30%
$5,000 – $9,999	5%	$250,000 – $349,999	35%
$10,000 – $49,999	10%	$350,000 – $499,999	40%
$50,000 – $99,999	15%	$500,000 – $749,999	45%
$100,000 – $149,999	20%	$750,000 – $999,999	50%
$150,000 – $199,999	25%		

FOR COMPLETE ADVERTISING INFORMATION: **GLOBELINK.CA** TO UPLOAD COMPLETED ADVERTISING: **GLOBELINK.CA/ADFORWARD**
FOR DETAILED PRODUCTION SPECIFICATIONS: **GLOBELINK.CA/DIGITAL/PRODUCTION CENTRE** TO DOWNLOAD GLOBE AND MAIL TEARSHEETS AND INVOICES: **GLOBEBILLING.CA**

TORONTO (ONTARIO & MANITOBA) **TEL**: 416.585.5111 | **TOLL-FREE**: 1.800.387.9012 | **FAX**: 416.585.5698 | advertising@globeandmail.com
EASTERN CANADA (OTTAWA REGION, QUEBEC & ATLANTIC CANADA) **TEL**: 514.982.3050 | **TOLL-FREE**: 1.800.363.7526 | **FAX**: 514.982.3074 | advertisingeasternca@globeandmail.com
BRITISH COLUMBIA, NORTHWEST TERRITORIES AND NUNAVUT TEL: 604.685.0308 | **TOLL-FREE**: 1.800.663.1311 | **FAX**: 604.685.7549 | advertisingwesternca@globeandmail.com
ALBERTA AND SASKATCHEWAN TEL: (CGY) 403.245.4987 | **FAX**: 403.244.9809 | **TOLL-FREE**: (EDM) 1.800.663.1311 ext. 6606 | **FAX**: 604.685.7549
TOLL-FREE: (SK) 1.800.663.1311 ext. 6639 | **FAX**: 604.685.7549 | advertisingwesternca@globeandmail.com
UNITED STATES, MEXICO & CARIBBEAN TEL: 858.366.4265 | **TOLL-FREE**: 1.866.744.9890 | **FAX**: 866.355.5990 | rlaplante@media-corps.com

YOU ALSO NEED TO KNOW: Any advertising published by The Globe and Mail in the newspaper or any of its other publications may, at our discretion, be published, displayed, retained and archived by us and anyone authorized (including any form of licence) by us, as many times as we and those authorized by us wish, in or on any product, media and archive (including print, electronic and otherwise).

All advertising must meet Globe and Mail terms and conditions – ask for a printed copy from your Globe and Mail advertising representative.

Source: Reprinted with permission from *The Globe and Mail*.

Although these are the quoted rates, the reality of the situation is similar to offline advertising. CPM rates are negotiable and depend on factors such as length of the campaign, season, and relationship between client and vendor. Effective negotiation skills in the media buying process could result in lower CPM rates.

PAY FOR PERFORMANCE MODEL Advertisers must remember that the purpose of online advertising is to create interest so that the viewer clicks the ad for more information. Once clicked, the viewer sees the ad in its entirety, or is linked to the advertiser's website. Since clicking is the desired action, many pricing models are based on a **cost-per-click (CPC)** basis instead of CPM. The benefit of such a system is clear: the degree of clicking achieved by an ad indicates the effectiveness of the ad.

If the success of an ad is based on the clickthrough rate, then many current campaigns are not doing very well. In fact, clickthrough rates have been declining for years and now average about 0.2 percent across all major web destinations. This reflects a surge in new ads on web pages, fuelled by the rise in social media.[4] As responsiveness declines, ad targeting is becoming more attractive to online advertisers. The ability to target based on location and behaviour does have a positive impact on click rates. Pricing models based on cost-per-click are becoming more popular, but they are plagued with all kinds of click fraud that is costing advertisers money unnecessarily. Tighter restrictions and controls are needed for this pricing model to be applied successfully.

FLAT-FEE MODEL Some websites charge a flat fee for advertising—typically, it is a set amount for the length of time the ad appears on the site. Sponsorships, for example, are usually sold on a flat-rate basis rather than on the number of impressions. For example, a site such as TSN.ca may offer a flat-fee sponsorship opportunity to an advertiser in combination with a CPM or CPC (cost-per-click) advertising package. Fee structures vary from one site to another.

Media Information Resources

Media planners rely on secondary research data provided by specialist media organizations. **Secondary research** refers to data compiled and published by others for purposes other than resolving a specific problem. In advertising, secondary sources are frequently used to gain access to media information that benefits media analysis and planning. This information is available through various media associations, specialized media research companies, and individual media outlets (e.g., a daily newspaper, national magazine, or a local television station).

Most organizations that provide media data also provide appropriate software that can be used to sift through the data (e.g., data can be cross-tabulated with product and service consumption data to determine the best way of reaching a specific target audience). Much of the information is made available through the media research companies and organizations mentioned above, or through specialist companies that develop software for use with database information provided by these organizations. Agencies pay for the data provided by the various media research organizations.

TELEVISION RESOURCES

The organizations that compile television media data on a continuous (year-to-year) basis include BBM Bureau of Measurement, Nielsen Media Research, and the Television Bureau of Canada.

---

cost-per-click (CPC)
An Internet advertising pricing strategy where advertisers pay based on the number of ad clicks received.

secondary research
Data compiled and published by others for purposes other than resolving a specific problem. In advertising, secondary sources are frequently used to gain access to media information that benefits media analysis and planning.

BBM CANADA BBM Canada is the leading supplier or television and radio audience ratings services to the Canadian broadcast advertising industry. The service is divided into two divisions for recording and analyzing data: BBM TV and BBM Radio. BBM TV collects audience data through a combination of electronic observation and diaries that are returned by mail. The BBM employs three commercially available methodologies: paper diaries, picture matching technology (PMT), and portable people meters (PPM).

When the **diary system** is used, participants complete a seven-day log by recording the television viewing for all television sets in the household for each quarter hour of the day from 6 am to 2 am. Information from returned diaries is keyed into computers for processing and verification.

In the case of the **portable people meter (PPM)**, a form of electronic observation is employed. BBM Canada and Nielsen Media Research launched a joint venture that measures television viewing nationally and in major markets such as Toronto, Vancouver, Edmonton, and Calgary. The meter registers what is being watched every minute of every day in every metered household. Because the households are a representative sample, extrapolations are made about how people view programs on local, regional, and national bases.

Picture matching technology (PMT) is relatively new. It determines what viewers are watching by periodically "sampling" the video image on their television screens, and then comparing this time-stamped video "fingerprint" with a library of all television sources that are available at that time. It measures minute-by-minute viewing behaviour in 5000 households across Canada. PMT meters help determine the Top 30 programs broadcast each week.[5]

BBM data focus on national and local markets. BBM conducts its surveys three times a year—fall, winter, and spring—in 40 television markets. Its reports contain current audience ratings and share data, as well as full coverage data for local market stations. The data are presented in four sections: time block, program, time period, and trend.

BBM also conducts a "sweep" survey in the fall and spring that covers the national market (television viewers two years of age and older). The data collected during the ratings period are used to estimate the audiences of programs on individual stations and networks. **Ratings** are audience estimates expressed as a percentage of a population in a defined geographic area. For example, if a show has a rating of 20, it reaches 20 percent of that market's population. For some examples of basic trend data available from BBM, visit www.bbm.ca.

NIELSEN MEDIA RESEARCH Nielsen Media Research provides advertising information services including advertising expenditures, GRP analysis, and creative monitoring services for advertising messages. Its advertising expenditure estimates are available for television (network and spot), radio, magazines, daily newspapers, and out-of-home media. These data allow an advertiser to compare its expenditures against those of its competitors.

Nielsen Media Research also offers a variety of competitive tracking services that provide the quantitative information necessary for strategic determination and tactical execution of communications plans. Advertisers and agencies use Nielsen Media's audience analyses and applications to estimate the future performance of television shows, to execute television buys, and to measure the performance of campaigns. Nielsen's software can be used to perform reach/frequency, duplication, and quintile delivery analyses.[6] For additional information about Nielsen Media Research, visit www.nielsenmedia.ca.

---

diary system
A system to collect audience data where participants complete a seven-day log by recording the television viewing for all television sets in the household for each quarter hour of the day from 6 am to 2 am.

portable people meter (PPM)
A form of electronic observation where electronic metering devices are carried by household members that register what is being watched on television every minute of every day.

picture matching technology (PMT)
A relatively new way to collect television audience data; determines what viewers are watching by periodically "sampling" the video image on their television screens, and then comparing this time-stamped video "fingerprint" with a library of all television sources that are available at that time.

BBM Canada
www.bbm.ca

rating
Television and radio audience estimates expressed as a percentage of a population in a defined geographic area.

Nielsen Media Research
www.nielsenmedia.ca

TELEVISION BUREAU OF CANADA The Television Bureau of Canada (TVB) is a sales and marketing resource centre for the commercial television industry. Its mandate is to promote television as an effective advertising medium. Each year, this organization publishes a booklet, "TV Basics," that contains the latest data on television trends. It covers viewing trends by demographic and geographic variables, programming preferences by demographic variables, and television-station circulation by gender and age for all station markets. The TVB provides such data as viewing by time of day, day of week, and time of year. For additional information about the data provided by the TVB, visit www.tvb.ca.

RADIO

The organizations that compile radio consumption data on a continuous basis are the BBM Bureau of Measurement and the Radio Marketing Bureau.

BBM CANADA The radio division of BBM Canada measures radio audiences in 115 Canadian markets up to four times a year, in eight-week periods, using seven-day personal diaries. In addition to collecting tuning data, the diary contains questions collecting product usage and lifestyle data.

Twice yearly, BBM Radio produces a *Reach Report*. The report contains reach, hours, and share data for each member station in each measured market for five standard demographics. This allows advertisers to plan their buys better since they will know the exact profile of each station's audience. Audience data is available based on hours tuned per week, listening by daypart, and listening by location (e.g., home, automobile, and other locations). For some samples of basic trend data published by the BBM, visit www.bbm.ca.

RADIO MARKETING BUREAU The Radio Marketing Bureau is the marketing, sales development, and resource centre for radio advertising in Canada. It provides statistical data while seeking to educate advertisers and agencies on the effective use of the medium. In conjunction with BBM, the Bureau conducts a Radio Product Measurement (RPM) study in selected major markets. This study is designed to generate information about product usage and media consumption of radio, television, magazines, and newspapers. For more information about the Radio Marketing Bureau, visit www.rmb.ca.

MAGAZINES

The companies and organizations involved in magazine research and data collection include the Audit Bureau of Circulations, PBA Worldwide, and the Print Measurement Bureau.

AUDIT BUREAU OF CIRCULATIONS The Audit Bureau of Circulations (ABC) issues standardized statements verifying circulation statistics for paid-circulation magazines (consumer and business publications) and most daily newspapers in Canada. All publications that are members of ABC receive an audited **publisher's statement**. This statement is the authority on which advertising rates are based (verified circulation is used to establish the advertising rate base as shown in the publication's rate card). The statement is issued twice each year. A publisher's statement includes the following information: average paid circulation for the past six months, paid circulation for each issue in the last six months, an analysis of new and renewal subscriptions, paid circulation by county size, and geographic analysis of total paid circulation. For a selection of sample data published by ABC, refer to www.accessabc.com.

Each year the ABC publishes the Canadian newspaper *Circulation Fact Book* that outlines circulation data for all daily newspapers by market, county, and province. Five-year circulation trend data are included in the report. ABC also publishes the magazine *Trend Report*, an annual report providing circulation and advertising rate trends for five years for all Canadian magazines.

BPA WORLDWIDE (FORMERLY CANADIAN CIRCULATIONS AUDIT BOARD—CCAB) The CCAB division of BPA Worldwide (a global provider of audited data) audits all paid, all controlled, or any combination of paid and controlled circulation for over 450 business and farm publications, consumer magazines, and community and daily newspapers throughout Canada.

BPA
www.bpaww.com

Statements include type of circulation (e.g., paid or controlled circulation), recipient qualification (e.g., distribution to a predetermined target based on demographic data), circulation for the past six months, average paid circulation per issue, and a geographical breakdown of the circulation. Additional information about the CCAB is available at www.bpaww.com.

PRINT MEASUREMENT BUREAU The Print Measurement Bureau (PMB) provides standardized readership information for members, a group that includes advertisers, agencies, publishers, and other related companies in the Canadian media industry. The PMB publishes Canada's leading single-source multimedia study.

The major data component of the annual PMB study is the detailed readership data for more than 125 magazines and newspapers and the linking of those data with information on readers' product usage patterns, their usage of brands, their retail shopping habits, extensive demographic data, and their lifestyles.

The study also provides general usage data on other media such as television, daily newspapers, outdoor, transit, and the Internet. Data provided by the PMB study benefit advertisers and agencies in the media planning process. Based on cross-tabulations of data concerning media, product, brand, and lifestyle, the information can be used to identify target markets more precisely, to assist in budget allocation, and to make better decisions regarding media selection and placement. PMB information is available to clients electronically and requires special software to access it. As of 2009 the PMB Study will be released biannually. For additional information about the PMB, visit www.pmb.ca.

NEWSPAPERS
As stated in the magazine section, newspaper circulation and readership data are available from the Audit Bureau of Circulations and BPA Worldwide. Readership information is also compiled by an industry-sponsored measurement organization known as NADbank.

NADBANK—NEWSPAPER AUDIENCE DATABANK NADbank provides advertisers, advertising agencies, and daily newspapers with accurate and credible information on newspaper readership, retail data, and consumer behaviour. NADbank is an annual survey among more than 30 000 adults 18 years and older that compiles relevant data about newspaper circulation and readership. NADbank members have access to readership data for 82 daily newspapers in 54 markets and 58 community newspapers in 33 markets.

NADbank
www.nadbank.com

The nature of information produced by NADbank includes weekday and weekend readership, demographic profiles of readers, product ownership and purchase intentions, media habits (e.g., other media referred to), and shopping habits (e.g., malls visited and frequency of visits). Additional information and some sample data published by NADbank are available at www.nadbank.com.

OUT-OF-HOME MEDIA

Canadian Out-of-Home Measurement Bureau
www.comb.org

CANADIAN OUT-OF-HOME MEASUREMENT BUREAU The Canadian Out-of-Home Measurement Bureau (COMB) audits the circulations of outdoor posters and backlight posters, outdoor digital, mural advertising, furniture advertising, and superboards. COMB also audits indoor media that include backlight boards, mini-boards, eBoards, digital screens, and mall posters.

Audience data are location specific, full coverage, and in-market in nature. Circulation data concerning all outdoor media are based on municipal and provincial traffic counts and converted to circulations according to an established traffic-variation factor. COMB currently uses an average occupancy factor of 1.75, which represents the average number of people in an automobile.[7] Mall counts are based on observation (head counts) in each location by an independent research firm.

COMB publishes the *Market Data Report* on a semi-annual basis. The report contains daily and weekly audience averages for each product in each market. Verification reports are also provided. These reports verify that suppliers are delivering what they are contracted to deliver and compare the percentage of audience delivered to what was contracted. For more information about COMB, visit www.comb.org.

INTERNET DATA SOURCES

Measuring the number of people who notice web-based advertising has been a difficult and controversial task, but a few organizations are constantly updating their technologies to provide more precise and accurate information. These organizations include the Interactive Advertising Bureau, comScore Media Metrix, and TNS Media Intelligence.

Interactive Advertising Bureau
www.iabcanada.com

INTERACTIVE ADVERTISING BUREAU (IAB) The Interactive Advertising Bureau (IAB) is a national organization of Internet publishers, advertisers, and agencies acting as the collective voice to represent companies engaged in selling advertising on Internet-based media. IAB promotes the value of Internet advertising to advertisers and agencies and serves as an educational resource through which advertisers can increase their knowledge and gain a competitive edge in the marketplace.

The IAB actively promotes advertising standards and guidelines that make it easier to plan, buy, execute, track, and evaluate online advertising plans. As well, it provides cross-media usage data via an annual research study and other interactive research.[8] The IAB reports that the Internet is the second-most popular medium in terms of time spent with the media by Canadians.

Research studies conducted by independent organizations for IAB show the effectiveness of online advertising. When online is added to the media mix, scores for various brand measurements increase. Tests among many leading brands in various product categories are the foundation of the research findings. Details of these studies are available at the IAB website. For more information about the IAB, visit www.iabcanada.com.

COMSCORE MEDIA METRIX comScore Media Metrix Canada is an Internet audience measurement service that reports details of website usage, visitor demographics, and online buying behaviour. The company collects data from a nationally representative panel of Internet users.

A variety of quantitative data is available to advertisers including measures for a website's unique visitors; reach; average usage days per user; average unique pages per user per month; average minutes spent per person per page per month; and age, gender, and other demographic characteristics of visitors.

Other services offered by comScore Media Metrix include online buying power metrics based on actual consumer purchases made online, local audience measurement for major Canadian markets, and detailed measurements of online search behaviour. With the Internet growing in importance as a medium, the research that supports it is becoming more sophisticated. For more information, go to www.comscore.com.

comScore Media Metrix Canada
www.comscore.com

TNS MEDIA INTELLIGENCE—EVALIANT SERVICES Evaliant Services provides online advertising data for brands and products sold in North America. The company provides data on the following issues: who is advertising on the web, where brands are advertising, when advertising is occurring and how much is being spent, what the media dollar value is (ad spending), what new ads are running, and what the ads actually look like. In Canada, over 450 sites are tracked daily. Trend data is compiled for advertising spending by product category and brands within categories, so it is a good source of competitive advertising information. For more information, visit www.tns-mi.com.

Evaliant Services
www.tns-mi.com

Research Data by Individual Media

The specific media vehicles often conduct their own marketing research, or use research data provided by independent sources such as those just described. These data provide advertisers and agencies with objective, reliable information showing the relative strengths of the given medium as an advertising vehicle. In local market situations, a daily newspaper or a local radio station provides advertisers and agencies with data to assist them in the decision-making process. Here, local media compete with each other for advertising revenue, so comparisons on criteria such as reach, readership, number of people listening and watching, and so on are inevitable. When assessing this type of data, the advertiser should ensure that it is audited data and that it has been verified by an independent organization. Much of this data is available at the website of the particular magazine, newspaper, radio station, and so on.

The same situation exists for magazines and newspapers. All magazines and newspapers have their circulation and readership data readily available for review by advertisers and agencies. The viewer of such information should ensure it is audited data, possibly audited by the various research organizations cited in this appendix.

agate line, 367
broadsheet, 367
circulation list, 391
compiled list, 391
continuity discount, 376
corporate discount, 376
cost-per-click (CPC), 396
cost per thousand (CPM), 373
CPM (online), 393
daypart, 383
diary system, 397
frequency discount, 376
gross rating points (GRPs), 381

horizontal rotation, 383
house list, 391
line rate, 369
list broker, 391
merge/purge, 391
modular agate line (MAL), 367
modular agate unit, 369
negotiated rate, 378
picture matching technology (PMT), 397
portable people meter (PPM), 397
position charge, 372
publisher's statement, 398

rating, 397
reach plan, 383
recency, 381
response list, 391
rotation plan, 383
secondary research, 396
spot colour, 372
tabloid, 367
targeting request, 394
transient rate,
vertical rotation, 383
volume discount, 382

REVIEW QUESTIONS

1. Calculate the cost of the following newspaper campaign. Refer to Figure A1.2 for rate card information.

   Newspaper: *The Globe and Mail*,
   National Edition,
   Sports Section
   Ad Size: 4 columns wide by
   6 column inches deep
   Colour: All ads are black and white
   Frequency: 2 ads per week (Wed. and Fri.)
   Continuity: 8 weeks
   Rate: Transient

2. Calculate the total cost of the following magazine campaign. Refer to Figure A1.5 for rate card information.

   Magazine: *Canadian Geographic*
   Ad Size: Double-page spread
   Frequency: 4 insertions

3. Calculate the total cost of the following magazine campaign. Refer to Figure A1.5 for rate card information.

   Magazine: *Canadian Geographic*
   Ad Size: 1/2 page
   Frequency: 8 insertions

4. Calculate the total cost of the following television campaign. Refer to Figure A1.8 for rate card information.

Station: CKCO-TV Kitchener
Type of Ad: Selective spot
Shows and Frequency:
Law & Order: SVU, 2 spots per week
The Amazing Race, 1 spot per week
Close to Home, 1 spot per week
Continuity: 15 weeks between February 20 and June 4

5. Calculate the total cost of the following radio campaign. Refer to Figure A1.10 for rate card information.

   Station: CJAZ-FM
   Nature of Plan: Specific times requested during breakfast and drive periods
   Breakfast: 8 spots per week
   Drive: 8 spots per week
   Continuity: 6 weeks

6. Calculate the total cost of a 16-spot weekly reach plan for the same period of time as in Question 5 on CJAZ-FM radio. Refer to Figure A1.10 for rate card information. When the total costs of the reach plan are compared to the total costs of the specific request plan in Question 5, how much does the advertiser save by using the reach plan?

7. Calculate the total cost of the following outdoor campaign. Refer to Figure A1.11 for rate card information.

   Medium: CBS Outdoor Transit Shelters
   Markets and GRPs:

Toronto CMA, 25 GRP

Calgary CMA, 50 GRP

Halifax CMA, 50 GRP

Vancouver CMA, 25 GRP

Continuity: 20 weeks in all markets

8. Calculate the total cost of the following outdoor campaign. Refer to Figure A1.12 for rate card information.

Medium: CBS Outdoor Backlight Posters

Markets and GRPs:

St. John's, 50 GRP

Montreal, 50 GRP

Toronto, 75 GRP

Edmonton, 50 GRP

Calgary, 50 GRP

Continuity: Montreal and Toronto 16 weeks; Edmonton, Calgary and St. John's 12 weeks.

9. Calculate the total cost of delivering a $2.00 coupon to 4 million Canadian households using the Open & Save direct mail envelope. The estimated redemption rate for the offer is 2.5 percent. Refer to Figure A1.14 for rate card information.

10. Calculate the total cost of the following online banner campaign. Refer to Figure A1.15 for rate card information.

Medium: globeandmail.com

Ad Type: Big box

Impressions: 10 million

ENDNOTES

1. Rick Westhead, "Ad rates par for the course," *Toronto Star*, April 8, 2004, p. D13.

2. Andrea Zoe Aster, "How much is way too much?" *Marketing*, August 16, 1999, p. 14.

3. Chris Daniels, "Media buying gets scientific," *Marketing*, July 31, 2000, pp. 11, 12.

4. "So many ads, so few clicks," *Business Week*, November 12, 2007, www.businessweek.com.

5. Canadian Media Directors' Council, *Media Digest*, 2008/09, p. 75.

6. Ibid, p. 75.

7. *Market Data Report*, Canadian Out-of-Home Measurement Bureau, 1986, p. 4.

8. www.iabcanada.com.

Integrated Marketing Communications Plan: Mr. Sub

Market Background

MARKET ANALYSIS

The quick-serve restaurant (QSR) market is a mature market. The degree of competition among the various banners is intensive and extensive.

- The restaurant industry is growing only marginally (+2% a year).
- Quick-serve segment sales totalled $11.2 billion in Canada (2004).
- The quick-serve segment is saturated and offers limited growth potential over the next five years.
- The casual dining segment, composed of mid-range establishments like Montana's and Kelsey's, is experiencing higher growth (+8% a year).
- The sandwich segment of the market is presently worth $1.3 billion and accounts for about 10 percent of the quick-serve restaurant market.
- The sandwich segment is growing at the rate of +2.5% a year.

EXTERNAL INFLUENCES ON THE MARKET

ECONOMIC TRENDS The cyclical nature of the economy influences the volume of business in the QSR market segment. Generally, the Canadian economy is growing at a moderate rate, as is the restaurant industry. There is a variation in trends within the various segments of the restaurant industry.

DEMOGRAPHIC TRENDS

- With the population aging, restaurants must reposition themselves to maintain customers.
- Youthful generations who are influenced less by traditional marketing methods are the next generation of customers.
- Ethnic Canadians are creating a demand for ethnic dishes in QSR establishments.

SOCIAL TRENDS

- The health boom associated with the late 1990s appears to be over, but in general terms, a healthier lifestyle is an ambition for many people.
- People are maintaining an active lifestyle, but are subject to indulgences.
- Youthful generations favour non-traditional methods for learning about products; peer influences are very important.
- Time-pressed consumers are constantly searching for products and services offering convenience.

TECHNOLOGY

- Non-traditional methods of communication are popular with younger generations of consumers.

- Multi-tasking consumers refer to several media at the same time, so reaching consumers is now more challenging for marketing organizations.

CONSUMER DATA

Consumers indicate that the following criteria are important when selecting a quick-serve restaurant:

- Value (in terms of food quality at competitive prices).

- Reduced wait times.

- Convenience (location in time of need is important).

- Food served "their" way.

COMPETITIVE ANALYSIS

Mr. Sub competes directly with SUBWAY and Quizno's in the fresh sandwich segment. Quizno's is somewhat different as it specializes in hot-served or toasted sandwiches.

SUBWAY dominates the sandwich segment. Much of its strength can be attributed to the number of restaurant locations it operates across Canada.

McDonald's and Tim Hortons compete in the sandwich segment, but sandwiches account for only a portion of their business. Both restaurants offer only a limited selection of fresh and toasted sandwiches, but are very popular destinations for quick meals.

Market shares for the national chains (in the sandwich segment only) are as follows:

Chain	Share	Locations
SUBWAY	25.0	2100
Tim Hortons	8.0	2000
Mr. Sub	6.5	500
McDonald's	3.5	1375
Quizno's	3.0	350

SUBWAY As the commercials say, "SUBWAY...Eat Fresh." SUBWAY is positioned as the premier destination for fresh sandwiches. SUBWAY's success in the QSR market is due to the following factors:

- The brand name is synonymous with fresh food.

- High-quality and healthy food products are available.

- It has an association with social responsibility causes such as childhood obesity.

- It has an ability to react quickly to consumer preferences (e.g., introducing healthier breads).

- Financial resources are available for marketing and marketing communications.

- The "Jared" ad campaign (weight-loss message) was a success.

- It has extensive distribution with over 2000 restaurants coast to coast.

- Its successful rewards program encourages loyalty.

QUIZNO'S The market share for Quizno's has tripled in the past two years. The company's success is based on the following factors:

- It claims to own the "toasted" and "grilled" segment (even though other brands offer similar items).

- An advertising campaign that included celebrities such as Don Cherry and Tie Domi helped establish the brand.

- A focus on quality justifies higher prices; consumers seem willing to pay more for a sandwich.

BRAND ANALYSIS (MR. SUB)

Mr. Sub was the original submarine sandwich retailer in Canada, but over the years it has not maintained marketing and marketing communications support at a sufficient level to build the brand. Mr. Sub has lost considerable market share to SUBWAY. Mr. Sub's present position in the marketplace is a result of the following factors:

- It is a popular destination for former generations of young people.

- Quality products are offered at competitive prices.

- Its product range includes popular items such as sandwiches, wraps, salads, and hot and cold beverages.

- Its present positioning fits with customer expectations and is based on "quality, freshness, and quantity."

- It has a loyal following among older age groups (40+ years).

- The brand is not well-known among younger age groups.

- Only 500 locations (1:4 ratio of stores compared to SUBWAY) exist coast to coast, with more than 60 percent of locations in Southern Ontario.

- Investment in advertising and marketing communications is much lower than that of its competitors.

SWOT ANALYSIS

BRAND STRENGTHS

- Products offered are as good as the leading brand.

- The brand is well-known with older consumers (a sense of loyalty exists).

- Its good reputation will enhance new marketing initiatives.

BRAND WEAKNESSE

- Young consumers are unfamiliar with the brand and its offerings.

- It has low visibility among primary targets due to lack of marketing communications activity.

- Lack of availability (convenience); its key competitor has a significant distribution advantage.

MARKETING OPPORTUNITIES

- Fit the brand into healthier and contemporary lifestyles.

- Take a fresh marketing approach to attract a younger target audience.

- Appeal to consumer demand for value (a combination of convenience and quality).

THREATS

- The marketing and financial resources of direct competitors are extensive.

- Taste preferences among consumers (less demand for fresh) shift.

- Further encroachment from other fast-food restaurants and casual dining establishments is possible.

Marketing Communications Plan

TARGET MARKET
To rebuild/rejuvenate Mr. Sub requires that greater attention be given to younger generations of consumers, for they are the primary consumers of QSR establishments.

PRIMARY TARGET

Demographic

- Males and females 15 to 29 years old.

- Secondary and post-secondary education level.

- Students and newly employed graduates.

- Income not important.

Psychographic

- Time-pressed and fast-paced daily routines.

- Socially active (peer groups are influencers).

- Technologically savvy (online and mobile communications generation).

- Active with a healthy outlook.

Geographic

- All across Canada, with emphasis on major urban markets.

SECONDARY TARGET

- Males and females 35+ years old.

- Young families.

- Active lifestyles.

- Located in major urban markets.

- More inclined to refer to traditional media for information.

MARKETING OBJECTIVES

1. To increase market share from 6.5 percent to 7.5 percent.
2. To position Mr. Sub as a restaurant offering healthy and hearty sandwiches at reasonable prices.

MARKETING COMMUNICATIONS GOAL (CHALLENGE)

- To create more top-of-mind awareness for Mr. Sub among younger generations of consumers and secure a place on their "consideration list."

- To associate Mr. Sub with a contemporary urban lifestyle that will appeal to the primary and secondary targets.

MARKETING COMMUNICATIONS OBJECTIVES

1. To achieve a 70 percent brand awareness level among the primary target market.
2. To achieve a trial purchase rate of 20 percent among the primary target market.
3. To communicate the quality, variety, and freshness of the various menu items offered by Mr. Sub.
4. To create an image for Mr. Sub that is in keeping with contemporary lifestyles.
5. To build buzz for Mr. Sub among a new generation of consumers currently unfamiliar with the brand.

MARKETING COMMUNICATIONS STRATEGY

BUDGET For the first year of the campaign, a budget of $3.0 million is available to cover all marketing communications expenditures. The budget will cover a multimedia campaign and will include various integrated marketing communications activities.

POSITIONING STRATEGY STATEMENT The current positioning strategy will be retained and is described as follows:

> "Mr. Sub is a restaurant that offers the best in terms of fresh, healthy food served quickly. Mr. Sub prides itself on giving the customer a little bit more for their money."

MARKETING COMMUNICATIONS MIX A mix of marketing communications elements will combine to create a synergistic impact on the primary and secondary target markets. The various elements of the mix will each contribute to achieving the marketing communications objectives. The marketing communications mix will include traditional media advertising, sales promotions, event marketing, and online and interactive communications. The rationale for this combination of media is as follows:

- **Advertising**—Traditional forms of media advertising are needed to make a "visual impression" in key urban markets and to achieve the awareness objective.

- **Sales Promotion**—A variety of "incentives" are needed to achieve the trial purchase objectives. Some street-level activities will help achieve the "brand buzz" objective.

- **Event Marketing**—A significant event will be staged in Toronto that will start an association between Mr. Sub and basketball (a popular and growing sport). Basketball appeals directly to the primary male target, and the street-level marketing event will create buzz for Mr. Sub.

- **Online Communications**—The primary target audience is the biggest user of online and mobile technologies; therefore, these media are both effective and efficient for delivering Mr. Sub's message.

ADVERTISING PLAN—CREATIVE

CREATIVE OBJECTIVES

1. To communicate that Mr. Sub offers quality sandwiches, wraps, and salads.
2. To portray Mr. Sub as an appealing restaurant destination suited to a contemporary urban lifestyle.

CREATIVE STRATEGY Mr. Sub does not have the physical presence of its primary competitor; therefore, the message will focus on the quality of the food (scrumptious shots of sandwiches and wraps) and people (teens and 20-somethings) enjoying the food. It's worth searching a little harder for!

Selected messages in various media will also include members of the secondary target enjoying the Mr. Sub experience.

Central Theme All messages, regardless of media, will show the sandwich being created or the finished product; a mouth-watering selection of sandwiches that will satisfy any type of hunger will be visually presented in advertisements.

Appeal Technique The message will combine a positive appeal (with an emphasis on the product and what it looks like) with a lifestyle appeal (the target will be shown enjoying the food).

Tone and Style A straightforward approach will be used. All messages will be clear, product focused, and easy to understand. Print media will stress visual imagery by showing the "scrumptious" aspect of the sandwiches.

Tagline Some options to summarize the message strategy include
"Mr. Sub. More than enough"
"Mr. Sub. Enough and then some"
"Mr. Sub. It's all about the sandwich."

CREATIVE EXECUTION The campaign will include 30-second television spots, 4-colour print advertising, 4-colour newspaper inserts, outdoor posters, online banner ads, and an interactive component. Selected messages will encourage consumers to visit the Mr. Sub website to participate in a selection of new video games.

Print and outdoor media will be product focused, while broadcast media will feature consumer enjoyment and the fun associated with the Mr. Sub experience.

Integrated aspects of the campaign will include trial incentives delivered by newspaper inserts, a contest, a street-level marketing program in Toronto, and a television and online sponsorship element. Creating awareness for the brand and tagline will be a priority throughout the campaign.

ADVERTISING PLAN—MEDIA

BUDGET A budget of approximately $2.0 million has been allocated for media advertising to cover a one-year period from January 2007 to December 2007.

MEDIA OBJECTIVES

Who As described earlier, the primary target is teens and 20-somethings residing in urban locations. The secondary target is adults 35+ years residing in urban markets.

What The message to be communicated will focus on the scrumptious quality of the food and people enjoying the Mr. Sub experience.

When The launch phase of the plan will be given heavier support to set the new campaign in motion. Spending will be slightly higher than normal in the summer when promotions are in progress. A steady spending pattern will be implemented at other times of the year.

Where The campaign will be national in scope with additional emphasis placed on key urban markets.

How Creating awareness and developing a new image for a brand takes time; therefore, reach and frequency will be a priority in the initial phase of the campaign (the first three months). Continuity will be more important as the campaign progresses.

MEDIA STRATEGY

Target Market Strategy In the initial phase of the campaign, a shotgun strategy is recommended to reach the primary and secondary target markets. A multimedia approach will be employed to achieve reach objectives. As the campaign progresses, there will be a shift to a profile-matching strategy to effectively reach the primary target.

Market Coverage Since this is a national campaign, media that reach the national market will be used. Supplementary media will be added in urban markets to increase reach and frequency against the primary and secondary targets. The budget available will determine the extent of key market coverage.

Timing Spending will be heavier in the initial phase (first three months), reflecting a blitz strategy. Spending will then taper off for a few months but rebound upward during the summer months when various integrated marketing activities are scheduled. For the remaining months of the campaign, spending will follow a moderate but steady pattern.

Reach/Frequency/Continuity The initial phase of the campaign is devoted to attracting a new target market to Mr. Sub. Therefore, reach and frequency are the priorities. Various media will be employed to reach the target market in different ways. As the campaign progresses, continuity of message will be more of a priority. Media advertising will be scheduled in flights to ensure maximum impact, regardless of the media employed.

MEDIA SELECTION RATIONALE

A multimedia campaign that embraces network television, specialty television stations, national (targeted) magazines, key market daily newspapers (for inserts), out-of-home advertising, and online media is recommended.

Television Television reaches the national target audience with a strong visual message (the message emphasis on food and friends is best delivered by television). Prime-time ad placements will ensure a high level of brand recognition. A television sponsorship opportunity will associate Mr. Sub with basketball, a popular and growing sport in Canada.

Print A combination of targeted lifestyle magazines, newspapers, and inserts in selected daily newspapers will assist in creating brand awareness and distributing trial incentives. Inserts will be used exclusively to announce discounted meal combinations and special coupon offers to encourage trial visits.

Out-of-Home In major markets, outdoor posters will deliver the message while people are "on the move." The decision about where to dine is often made when people are in transit, presenting an ideal opportunity to remind them about Mr. Sub.

Online Since the primary target market spends a lot of time online, there is an opportunity for consumers to interact directly with the brand. In conjunction with messages delivered by other media, the target will be encouraged to visit a new Mr. Sub website to play a selection of new sports games. Banner ads will also appear on two third-party sites that will move viewers to the Mr. Sub website.

MEDIA EXECUTION The CTV Network and TVA Quebec are recommended to reach a broad cross-section of the population. TSN and The Score are recommended to reach the primary target market.

Outdoor posters will complement television ads and reach a broad cross-section of the population in 12 major markets across Canada.

Both *Tribute* and *Inside Entertainment* magazines are recommended as they effectively reach males and females in the primary target. *Maclean's* is also recommended since it effectively reaches a cross-section of the adult population regardless of age.

For a summary of all media activity (timing and expenditures), refer to Figures A2.1 to A2.3.

FIGURE A2.1
Television Advertising

Network	# of Spots	Cost/Spot	Total Cost
CTV	40	$16 500	$660 000
TVA	30	$3 000	$90 000
TSN	50	$3 500	$175 000
The Score	65	$300	$19 500
Total	**185**		**$944 500**
The Score TV Sponsorship			$25 000
Total TV Costs			**$969 500**

Note: All ads are 30-second spots.

FIGURE
A2.2

Outdoor Advertising

Market	GRPs	Weeks	Total Cost
Toronto/Hamilton	25	12	$295 800
Vancouver	25	12	$223 500
Ottawa	25	12	$108 600
Calgary	25	12	$64 800
Edmonton	25	12	$57 600
Quebec City	25	8	$40 800
Winnipeg	25	8	$20 800
London	25	8	$19 600
Kitchener	25	8	$22 200
Halifax	25	8	$13 400
Regina	25	8	$7 200
St. John's	25	8	$8 600
Total Cost			**$882 900**

Note: All ads are horizontal outdoor posters.

FIGURE
A2.3

Magazine Advertising

Magazine	# Inserts	Cost/Insert	Total Cost
Maclean's	4	$25 400	$101 600
Tribute	4	$18 900	$75 600
Inside Entertainment	4	$15 000	$60 000
Total	**12**		**$237 200**

Note: All ads are 1-page, 4-colour

SALES PROMOTION PLAN
PROMOTION OBJECTIVES

1. To encourage trial purchase among primary and secondary targets.

2. To secure interactivity between the consumer and the brand by encouraging consumers to visit the Mr. Sub website.

PROMOTION STRATEGY Trial coupons offering a discounted price for any sandwich or wrap will be distributed by daily newspapers in major urban markets. In many cases, the daily newspapers offer reach well beyond their designated market area.

Consumers visiting a Mr. Sub restaurant during the first two months of the campaign will receive a coded entry form for a contest. Consumers must visit the Mr. Sub website to enter their contest code.

SALES PROMOTION EXECUTION

Trial Coupon A $1.50 coupon for the purchase of any sandwich or wrap (with a two-month expiry date) will be circulated. The initial coupon drop is timed for February/March.

Contest A grand prize and two secondary prizes will be awarded:

• Grand Prize: $25 000 cash.

• Second Prize: One of three all-expenses-paid ski trips for two to Whistler/ Blackcomb (value: $5000 each).

• Third Prize: One of five Sony HDTV flat-screen televisions (value: $2000 each).

The contest is open to all residents of Canada with winners randomly drawn from all entries received. Winners will be announced at the Mr. Sub website the day following the closing date of the contest. Complete contest details are available at the Mr. Sub website and all restaurant locations.

Trial Coupon A second wave of $1.50 coupons (with a two-month expiry date) will be distributed by national daily newspapers in the August/September period.

The coupon inserts will be distributed via daily newspapers in the following markets: Toronto, Hamilton, Vancouver, Ottawa, Calgary, Edmonton, Quebec City, Winnipeg, London, Kitchener, Halifax, Regina, Saskatoon, St. John's, and Windsor.

Coupon inserts will be distributed by community newspapers in the following markets: Oshawa/Whitby/Clarington, St. Catharines, Niagara Falls, Cambridge, Barrie, Kingston, Peterborough, and Sudbury.

Component	Circulation	Cost/M	Frequency	Total Cost
Distribution	2 785 000	$40	2	$222 800
Printing	2 785 000	$10	2	$55 700
Coupon Redemption*				$83 500
Total Cost				**$362 000**

* Circulation × Redemption Rate × Value of Coupon × Frequency = Coupon Cost
2 785 000 × .01 × $1.50 × 2 = $83 500

FIGURE A2.4

Sales Promotion Costs for Coupon Inserts

Prize	# Winners	Prize Cost	Total Cost
Cash Grand Prize	1	$25 000	$25 000
Ski Trip	3	$5 000	$15 000
Sony HDTV Flat Screens	5	$2 000	$10 000
Total Cost			**$50 000**

FIGURE A2.5

Sales Promotion Costs for Coupon

For cost details on these sales promotion activities see Figures A2.4 and A2.5.

ONLINE AND INTERACTIVE PLAN

OBJECTIVES

1. To increase brand awareness among teens and 20-something males.
2. To associate the Mr. Sub brand with a sporting activity popular with young urban males.

STRATEGY A combination that involves online banner advertising, a combination television and online sponsorship, and a brand new website will help build awareness among the primary target and help associate the brand with an urban lifestyle.

EXECUTION

BANNER ADS Banners will be scheduled on the TSN and The Score sports websites that are popular with a younger male audience.

Sponsorship In conjunction with The Score television channel, Mr. Sub will sponsor a highlight segment shown once a week. Each Wednesday night during the last four months of the basketball season, The Score broadcasts a show called NBA Court Surfing. During the show, Mr. Sub will sponsor a segment called "Dunks of the Week" that features all of the exciting dunks from the previous week's NBA action. The same video clip sponsored by Mr. Sub will be available on The Score's website, www.thescore.ca.

Mr. Sub Website An entirely new and exciting website will be constructed. The new site will offer essential product information and provide opportunities for consumers to engage in some entertaining activities. A selection of sports and action video games will be available for play at the site.

Refer to Figure A2.6 for online and interactive cost details.

EVENT MARKETING PLAN

To further develop the association between Mr. Sub and basketball, a street-level marketing event is planned in conjunction with the Toronto Raptors basketball team. This event fits with the Raptors objective of being "more visible in the community" and provides an opportunity to generate positive publicity for the Raptors in the off-season.

FIGURE A2.6

Online and Interactive Costs

Site	Impressions/Month	CPM	# Months	Total Cost
TSN.ca	500 000	$40	6	$120 000
thescore.ca	125 000	$20	6	$15 000
Mr. Sub website				$200 000
Total Cost				**$335 000**

Note: Mr. Sub website costs include development and maintenance costs of the site.

OBJECTIVES

1. To encourage members of the primary target market to participate in a "3-on-3" basketball tournament.
2. To create buzz for Mr. Sub in a key urban market.

STRATEGY To associate Mr. Sub with the growing sport of basketball (playground, high school, college, and university level) in a key urban market.

To associate Mr. Sub with the Toronto Raptors (an exciting team that is creating its own "buzz" in Toronto based on recent player acquisitions and performance).

EXECUTION

- The Mr. Sub Toronto Raptors 3-on-3 Tournament (straight elimination) will be held on half-size courts at Exhibition Place, Toronto, over one weekend in July.

- A predetermined number of teams (128 teams) will compete against each other in four age categories: 8 to 12 years; 13 to 16 years; 17 to 21 years; and 21 to 30 years. The youngest age category will attract the children of Mr. Sub's secondary target, while the older categories will attract the primary target. A total of 32 teams will be entered in each age category.

- Toronto Raptors players will participate in a skills competition to determine "the most skilled Raptor."

- Prizes will be awarded to each member of the winning team (five members on each team) in each category.

- Mr. Sub kiosks will be set up at the event to serve meals.

- The general public will be invited to the event, though all viewing of the games and Raptor skills competition will be on a "stand and watch" basis.

- A one-month outdoor ad campaign just prior to the event will create awareness and recruit teams for the event. A press release will also be issued to the media outlining all event-related details.

Cost details for this event marketing activity are included in Figure A2.7.

Item or Activity	Estimated Cost
Equipment Rental	$50 000
Site Rental	$25 000
Bump-in (Setup)	$10 000
Staffing	$10 000
Security	$8 000
Bump-out (Teardown)	$10 000
Administration Costs	$15 000
Prizes	$40 000
Miscellaneous Costs	$10 000
Total Cost	**$178 000**

FIGURE A2.7

Event Marketing Costs

For summary details of all marketing communications expenditures and the timing of all activities, refer to Figures A2.8 through A2.11.

Activity	Expenditure	% of Total
Television	$969 500	32.2
Outdoor	$882 900	29.3
Magazine	$237 200	7.8
Sales Promotions (Coupons and Contest)	$412 050	13.7
Online and Interactive	$335 000	11.1
Event Marketing	$178 000	5.9
Total	**$3 014 650**	**100.0**

Month	Expenditure	% of Total
January	$211 300	7.0
February	$708 900	23.5
March	$426 850	14.2
April	$169 150	5.6
May	$117 000	3.9
June	$398 700	13.2
July	$264 000	8.8
August	$261 050	8.7
September	$100 500	3.3
October	$144 300	4.8
November	$118 500	3.9
December	$94 400	3.1
Total	**$3 014 650**	**100.0**

Estimated Budget (Based on Activities)	$3 014 650
Plan Budget	$3 000 000
Expenditure Over Budget	$(14 650)

The marketing communications budget will be reviewed quarterly. Adjustments to the budget will be made when necessary.

FIGURE A2.11 Marketing Communications Calendar

Activity	Jan.	Feb.	Mar.	Apr.	May	June	July	Aug.	Sept.	Oct.	Nov.	Dec.
Television												
CTV	8	8	8	4	4				4	4		
TVA	5	5	5	5						5	5	
TSN	10	10					10				10	10
The Score	15	15	10	10					5	10		
The Score Sponsorship	←			→								
Outdoor												
Top 5 Markets		←	→			↔						
Remaining Markets		↔				↔						
Magazines												
Maclean's				1		1		1		1		
Tribute						1		1		1		1
Inside Entertainment					1		1		1		1	
Sales Promotions												
Coupon Insert	←	→						←	→			
Contest	←	→										
Online												
TSN.ca					←			→			←	→
thescore.ca	←			→							←	→
Mr. Sub Website	←											→
Event Marketing												
3-on-3 Basketball						↔						

Notes:

Television: Figures represent the number of spots on each network each month. All spots are 30-seconds long and run in prime time.

Outdoor: Top five markets include Toronto/Hamilton, Vancouver, Ottawa, Calgary, and Edmonton. Remaining markets include Quebec City, Winnipeg, London, Kitchener, Halifax, Regina, and St. John's. All ads are outdoor posters.

Magazines: Figures indicate one insertion in each month scheduled (*Maclean's* is a weekly magazine; others are monthly). All ads are 1P, 4-colour

Online: 500 000 impressions monthly on TSN.ca and 125 000 impressions monthly on the thescore.ca.

Coupon Insert: Coupons will be distributed in key market daily newspapers or community newspapers. Dailies include: *Toronto Star, Toronto Sun, Vancouver Sun, Vancouver Province, Ottawa Citizen, Ottawa Sun, Calgary Herald, Calgary Sun, Edmonton Journal, Edmonton Sun, Regina Leader Post, Saskatoon Star Phoenix, Winnipeg Free Press, Hamilton Spectator, Kitchener Record, London Free Press, Windsor Star, Halifax Chronicle Herald,* and *St. John's Telegram.* Community newspapers include: *Oshawa/Whitby/Clarington This Week, St. Catharines News, Niagara This Week, Cambridge Times, Barrie Examiner Complimentary, Kingston This Week, Peterborough This Week,* and *Sudbury Northern Life.*

Glossary

Acquisition strategy – A plan of action for acquiring companies that represent attractive financial opportunities.

Ad click rate (clickthrough rate) – The percentage of ad views that resulted in an ad click; determines the success of an ad in attracting visitors to click on it.

Ad clicks (clickthroughs) – The number of times users click on a banner (clicking transfers the user to another website).

Ad views (impressions) – An ad request that was successfully sent to a visitor. This is the standard way of determining exposure for an ad on the web.

Advergaming – The integration of brands into video games, either games played online or in games purchased directly by consumers.

Advertising – A form of marketing communications designed to stimulate a positive response from a defined target market.

Advertising equivalency – A mathematical model that equates public relations to an advertising value by evaluating the space occupied by a public relations message in relation to advertising space.

Advocacy advertising – A form of advertising paid for by a sponsor that promotes a particular view on a recognized, controversial issue.

Agate line – A non-standardized unit of space measurement, equal to one column wide and 1/14" deep, used in newspaper advertising.

Ambush marketing – A strategy used by non-sponsors of an event to capitalize on the prestige and popularity of the event by giving the false impression they are sponsors.

Annual report – A document published annually by an organization primarily to provide current and prospective investors and stakeholders with financial data and a description of the company's operations.

Approach – The initial contact with a customer.

Attitude – An individual's feelings, favourable or unfavourable, toward an idea or object.

Attribute – A descriptive feature of a product.

Backlit (backlight) poster – A luminous outdoor sign printed on polyvinyl material.

Banner – In outdoor advertising, a large-sized print ad that is framed and mounted on the exterior of a building. Online, an ad that stretches across a webpage; the user can click on the ad for more information.

Behavioural targeting – A means of delivering online ads based on a consumer's previous surfing patterns.

Benefit – The value a customer attaches to a brand attribute.

Big box ad – An online ad shaped like a large rectangle that offers greater width and depth to an ad.

"Big idea" – See **Central theme**.

Billboard – see **Poster**.

Blitz schedule – The scheduling of media advertising so that most spending is front-loaded in the schedule; usually involves a lot of money spent in a short period.

Blocking chart – See **Media calendar**.

Blog – A frequent, chronological publication of personal thoughts at a website.

Blogging – The act of posting new information and thoughts on a blog.

Body language – See **Non-verbal communication**.

Bonus pack– The temporary offering of a larger package size (e.g., 20 percent more) for the same price as the regular size.

Booklet (brochure) – A multiple-page document distributed to consumers and other interested stakeholders.

Borrowed-interest strategy – A plan to promote a marketing activity that is related to a product.

Bounce back – See **Statement stuffer**.

Brand – An identifying mark, symbol, word or words, or combination of mark and words that separates one product from another product; can also be defined as the sum of all tangible and intangible characteristics that make a unique offer to customers.

Brand democratization – a concept that states that consumers are now in charge of brand marketing (because of the amount of consumer-generated content produced and distributed online) instead of brand marketers being in control.

Brand development index (BDI) – The percentage of a brand's sales in an area in relation to the population in that area; determines if the brand is underdeveloped or overdeveloped in each area.

Brand equity – The value (monetary or otherwise) of a brand to its owners; determined by the success of marketing activities; influenced by brand name awareness, degree of customer loyalty, perceived quality, etc.

Brand insistence – A situation where the consumer searches the market for the specific brand.

Brand loyalty – The degree of attachment to a particular brand expressed by a consumer. There are three stages of brand loyalty: brand recognition, brand preference, and brand insistence.

Brand manager – An individual assigned responsibility for the development and implementation of marketing programs for a specific product or group of products.

Brand name – That part of a brand that can be spoken.

Brand preference – The situation where a brand is perceived as an acceptable alternative by a customer and will be purchased if it is available.

Brand recognition – Customer awareness of the brand name and package.

Branded content (product integration) – The integration of brand name goods and services into the script (storyline) of a television show or movie. The brand name is clearly mentioned and sometimes discussed.

Brandmark or logo – A unique design, symbol, or other special representation of a brand name or company name.

Broadsheet – A large newspaper with a fold in its middle.

Brochure – See **Booklet**.

Build-up schedule – The scheduling of media advertising so that the weight of advertising starts out light and gradually builds over a period of time; also called a teaser campaign.

Bump-in (setup) – The setting up of structures and other equipment at an event.

Bump-out (teardown) – The process of dismantling everything after an event.

Bus murals – Advertisements that appear on the side or the tail of a bus, or both.

Business-to-business (B2B) market – A market of goods and services needed to produce a product or service, promote an idea, or operate a business.

Buying centre – An informal purchasing process in which individuals in an organization perform particular roles but may not have direct responsibility for the actual decision.

Buying committee – A formal buying structure in an organization that brings together expertise from the various functional areas to share in the buying decision process.

Buzz marketing – See **Product seeding**.

Call centre – A central operation from which a company operates its inbound and outbound telemarketing programs.

Casual rate – A one-time rate, or base rate, that applies to casual advertisers.

Catalogue – A reference publication, usually annual or seasonal, distributed by large retail chains and direct marketing companies.

Category development index (CDI) or market development index – The percentage of category sales in a geographic area in relation to the total population of that area; determines if a category is underdeveloped or overdeveloped in a particular region.

Central theme ("big idea") – The glue that binds various creative elements of a campaign together; transferable from one medium to another.

Channel positioning – A marketing strategy based on an organization's position in its distribution channel and its market coverage.

Cinema advertising – Print advertising inside film theatres and broadcast advertising on screens; options include television-style ads on screen, slides, posters, and ads printed on tickets.

Circulation – The average number of copies per issue of a publication sold by subscription, distributed free to predetermined recipients, carried with other publications, or made available through retail distributors.

Circulation list – A publication's subscription list that targets potential customers based on specified demographic characteristics, interests, or activities.

Classified advertising – Print advertising in which similar goods and services are grouped together in categories under appropriate headings.

Clickthrough rate – See **Ad click rate**.

Clickthroughs – See **Ad clicks**.

Clipping service – An organization that scans the print and broadcast media in search of a company's or brand's name.

Closed-ended questioning – See **Fixed-response questioning**.

Closing – Asking for the order at the appropriate time in a sales presentation.

Closing cue – An indication that the buyer is ready to buy; can be expressed verbally or nonverbally.

Cluster – Ads grouped in a block of time during a break in a program or between programs, or in a section of a publication.

Cluster profiling – See **Geodemographic segmentation**.

Clutter – The amount of advertising in a particular medium.

Cognitive dissonance – A feeling of doubt or regret in a consumer's mind once a buying decision has been made.

Cold canvass – The process of calling on people or organizations without appointments or advance knowledge of them.

Collateral material – Visual aids used by sales representatives in sales presentations, such as price lists, product manuals, sales brochures, and audiovisual materials.

Communication – The transmission, receipt, and processing of information between a sender and a receiver.

Compiled list – A direct mail list prepared from government, census, telephone, warranty, or other publication information.

Consultative selling – A form of selling that stresses open two-way communication between a buyer and seller.

Consumer behaviour – The combined acts carried out by individuals choosing and using goods and services, including the decision-making processes that determine these acts.

Consumer promotion – Incentive(s) offered to consumers to stimulate purchases or encourage loyalty.

Contest – A promotion that involves awarding cash or merchandise prizes to consumers when they purchase a specified product.

Contingency plan – The identification of alternative courses of action that can be used to modify an original plan if and when new circumstances arise.

Continuity – The length of time required in an advertising medium to generate the desired impact on the target - audience.

Continuity discount – A discount offered to advertisers that purchase space in consecutive issues of a publication.

Controlled circulation – The circulation of a publication that is distributed free to individuals in a specific demographic segment or geographic area.

Cookie – An electronic identification tag sent from a web server to a user's browser to track the user's browsing patterns.

Co-op – See **Cooperative advertising allowance**.

Cooperative advertising allowance (co-op) – The sharing of advertising costs by suppliers and retailers or by several retailers.

Cooperative direct mail – A mailing containing specific offers from non-competing products.

Core values – The primary attributes and benefits a brand delivers to the customer.

Corporate advertising – Advertising designed to convey a favourable image of a company among its various publics.

Corporate culture – The values, beliefs, norms, and practices shared by all employees of an organization.

Corporate discount – A discount based on the total number of pages purchased by a single company (all product lines combined).

Corporate objective – A statement of a company's overall goal; used to evaluate the effectiveness or ineffectiveness of a company's strategic plan.

Corporate plan – A strategic plan formulated at the executive level of an organization to guide the development of functional plans in the organization.

Corporate strategy – see **Strategic planning**.

Cost-per-click – An Internet advertising pricing strategy where advertisers pay based on the number of ad clicks received.

Cost per thousand (CPM) – The cost of delivering an advertising message to 1000 people; calculated by dividing the cost of the ad by the circulation in thousands.

Coupon – A price-saving incentive offered to consumers to stimulate quick purchase of a specified product.

CPM (online) – The price charged for displaying an ad 1000 times. The calculation for CPM is cost divided by impressions (number of impressions divided by 1000).

Creative brief – A document developed by a client organization that contains vital information about the advertising task at hand; it is a useful tool for discussions between the client and its advertising agency.

Creative objective – A statement that clearly indicates the information to be communicated to the target audience; usually involves a key benefit statement and a support claims statement.

Creative plan – A plan that outlines the nature of the message to be communicated to the target audience; involves the development of creative objectives, creative strategies, and creative execution.

Creative strategy – A plan of action for how the message will be communicated to the target audience, covering the tone and style of message, the central theme, and the appeal techniques.

Cross-coupon – See **Cross-ruff**.

Cross-ruff (cross-coupon) – A coupon packed in or with one product that is redeemable for another product. The product the coupon is packed with is the means of distributing the coupon.

Cross-tabulation – The comparison of answers to questions by various subgroups with the total number of responses.

Customer relationship management (CRM) – A process that enables an organization to develop an ongoing relationship with valued customers; the organization captures and uses information about its customers to its advantage in developing the relationship.

Data analysis – The evaluation of responses question by question; gives meaning to the data.

Data interpretation – The relating of accumulated data to the problem under review and to the objectives and hypotheses of the research study.

Data mining – The analysis of information to determine relationships among the data and enable more effective marketing strategies to be identified and implemented.

Data transfer – In marketing research, the transfer of answers from the questionnaire to the computer.

Database management system – A system that collects information about customers for analysis by managers to facilitate sound business decisions.

Database marketing – The use and analysis of accumulated information on customer buying behaviour to develop more effective marketing strategies.

Day-after recall (DAR) test – Research conducted the day following the respondent's exposure to a message to determine the degree of recognition and recall of the advertisement, the brand, and the selling message.

Daypart – A broadcast time period or segment on radio or television.

Dealer display material (point-of-purchase material) – Advertising or display materials located in a retail environment to build traffic, advertise a product, and encourage impulse purchasing.

Dealer premium – An incentive offered to a distributor to encourage the special purchase of a product or to secure additional merchandising support from the distributor.

Demographic segmentation – The identification of target markets based on characteristics such as age, income, education, occupation, marital status, and household formation.

Demonstration – A sales technique that involves showing the product in action to portray its benefits to a buyer.

Diary system – A system to collect audience data where participants complete a seven-day log by recording the television viewing for all television sets in the household for each quarter hour of the day from 6 am to 2 am.

Direct competition – Competition from alternative products and services that satisfy the needs of a target market.

Direct (customized) segmentation – The identification of a target audience at the level of the individual; marketing programs designed for and communicated to individual customers.

Direct home shopping – A shopping service provided by cable television stations that offers products or services for sale by broadcast message (e.g., The Shopping Channel).

Direct mail – A printed form of direct response advertising distributed by Canada Post or independent delivery agents.

Direct marketing – A marketing system for developing products, sending messages directly to customers, and accepting orders through a variety of media, and then distributing the purchase directly to customers.

Direct response advertising – Advertising placed in a medium that generates an immediate and measurable response from the intended target.

Direct response communications – The delivery of a message to a target audience of one; the message can be distributed by direct mail, direct response television, or telemarketing.

Direct response print – An ad in print media that issues a direct call to action via a toll-free number, return mail address, or website.

Direct response television (DRTV) – Advertising that appears on television and encourages viewers to respond by telephoning a toll-free number, by mail, or online; often referred to as infomercials.

Directory database – A commercial database that provides information about a company (e.g., size, sales, location, number of employees).

Editing – In marketing research, the review of questionnaires for consistency and completeness.

Electronic signs – Advertisements that are displayed on electronic billboards that rotate about every 10 to 15 seconds so multiple messages can be displayed at the same time.

Elevator advertising – Advertising in display frames on elevator walls or on televisions mounted in the corner or above the door.

Encoding – The transformation of a message into a meaningful format, such as an advertisement, a mailing piece, or an article in a newspaper.

Endorsement – A situation where a celebrity speaks highly of an advertised product.

Engagement – The degree of involvement a person has with the media when using it.

E-procurement – An online, business-to-business marketplace through which participants can purchase goods and services from one another.

Even schedule – The uniform schedule of media advertising over an extended period; also referred to as a continuous schedule.

Event marketing – The process, planned by a sponsoring organization, of integrating a variety of communications elements with a single event theme.

Event sponsorship – The financial support of an event in exchange for advertising privileges associated with that event.

Execution – See **Tactics**.

Experiential marketing (on-site sampling) – A form of marketing that creates an emotional connection with the consumer in personally relevant and memorable ways.

Experimental research – Research in which one or more factors are manipulated under controlled conditions while other elements remain constant so that the respondent's actions can be evaluated.

External publics – Those publics that are distant from an organization and are communicated with less frequent.

Eye movement–camera test – A test that uses a hidden camera to track eye movement to gauge the point of immediate contact in an advertisement, how the reader scans the ad, and the amount of time spent reading.

Feature – Tangible aspects of a product, such as durability, design, and economy of operation.

Field sales force – An organization's external sales representatives who regularly call on customers to pursue orders.

Fixed-response (closed-ended) questioning – Questions that are predetermined with set answers for the respondents to choose from.

Flight – A period of time in which advertising is scheduled.

Focus group – A small group of people with common characteristics brought together to discuss issues related to the marketing of a product or service.

Folder – A direct response sales message printed on heavy stock that can be mailed with or without an envelope; may be several pages in length.

Follow-up – Maintaining contact with customers to ensure that service has been satisfactory.

Format – The type and nature of the programming offered by a radio station.

Free sample – Free distribution of a product to potential users.

Free-standing insert (FSI) – A booklet featuring coupons, refunds, contests, or other promotional advertising distributed by direct mail or with newspapers, magazines, or other delivery vehicles.

Frequency – The average number of times an audience has been exposed to a message over a period of time, usually a week.

Frequency discount – A discounted page rate based on the number of times an advertisement runs.

Frequency distribution – The number of times each answer in a survey was chosen for a question.

Frequent buyer program – See **Loyalty program**.

Game (including instant-win) – A promotional contest that includes a number of pre-seeded winning tickets; instant-win tickets can be redeemed immediately.

Geodemographic segmentation (cluster profiling) – The identification of target markets according to dwelling areas defined by geographic and demographic variables; based on the assumption that like people seek out residential neighbourhoods in which to cluster with their lifestyle peers.

Geographic segmentation – The identification of a target market based on the regional, urban, or rural location of the customers.

Gross rating points (GRPs) – An expression of the weight of advertising in a media schedule; calculated by multiplying reach by frequency.

Head-on positioning – A marketing strategy in which one product is presented as an equal or better alternative than a competing product.

Hit – Each time a server sends a file to a browser.

Horizontal rotation – The placement of radio commercials based on the day of the week (same daypart on different days).

House list – An internal customer list.

Hypothesis – A statement of outcomes predicted in a marketing research investigation.

Image positioning – See **Lifestyle positioning**.

Impressions – See **Ad views**.

Inbound telemarketing –The calls received by a company from consumers whether to place an order, inquire about products or services, or in response to a toll-free telephone number promoted on a direct response television commercial.

Incentive – A free gift or offer included in a direct mail package.

Indirect competition – Competition from substitute products that offer the same benefit as another type of product.

Infomercial – A long commercial (e.g., 10 to 30 minutes) that presents in detail the benefits of a product or service; usually includes a call to action (e.g., a 1-800 number).

Innovation positioning – A marketing strategy that stresses newness (based on a commitment to research and development) as a means of differentiating a company or a brand from competing companies and brands.

In-pack self-coupon – A coupon for the next purchase of a product that is packed inside the package or under a label.

Insert – A preprinted, free-standing advertisement (e.g., a leaflet, brochure, or flyer) specifically placed in a newspaper or magazine.

Inside sales force – An internal group of sellers, often referred to as order takers, who accept orders from customers by telephone or other means.

Instantly redeemable coupon – A removable coupon often located on the package or a store shelf that is redeemable on the current purchase of the product.

Instant-win – See **Game**.

Integrated marketing communications – The coordination of all marketing communications in a unified program that maximizes the impact on the intended target audience.

Interactive communications – The placement of an advertising message on a website, usually in the form of a banner, pop-up ad, rich media ad, sponsorship at a website, or an ad delivered by email.

Interior card – A transit ad in the rack above the window or near the door of a bus or subway car.

Internal publics – The publics with which an organization communicates regularly; can include employees, distributors, suppliers, shareholders, and customers.

Internet – A worldwide network of computers linked together to act as one in the communication of information; like a global mail system in which independent entities collaborate in moving and delivering information.

Internet radio – Listening to radio broadcasts via the Internet.

Key benefit statement – A statement of the basic selling idea, service, or benefit promised the consumer by the advertiser; appears in the creative plan section of an advertising plan.

King poster – An oversized poster attached to the side of a bus.

Leaderboard (super banner) – An ad that stretches across the entire top of a webpage.

Leadership positioning – A marketing strategy in which a product presents itself as a preferred choice among customers.

Leaflet – A one-page flyer that offers relevant information about a direct mail offer.

Lifestyle (image) positioning – A marketing strategy based on intangible characteristics associated with a lifestyle instead of tangible characteristics.

Line rate – The rate charged by newspapers for one agate line or one modular agate line.

List broker – A company specializing in finding or developing lists for direct response purposes; finds prospect lists based on target market criteria established by marketing organizations.

Listing– An agreement made by a wholesaler to distribute a manufacturer's product to the retailer it supplies.

Lobbying – Activities and practices designed to influence policy decisions that will affect an organization or all organizations in a particular industry.

Local spot – Advertising bought from a local station by a local advertiser.

Logo – See **Brandmark**.

Loyalty program (frequent buyer program) – A program that offers consumers a small bonus, such as points or play money, each time they make a purchase; the bonus accumulates and can be redeemed for merchandise or some other benefit.

Mail interview – In marketing research, the collection of information from a respondent by mail.

Mall poster – A form of advertising located inside shopping malls; relies on pedestrian traffic only.

Market development index – See **Category development index (CDI)**. **Market segmentation** – The division of a large market into smaller homogeneous markets based on common needs and characteristics.

Market share – The sales volume of one product or company expressed as a percentage of total sales volume in the market the company or brand is competing in.

Marketing communications plan – A plan that identifies how the various elements of marketing communications will be integrated into a cohesive and coordinated plan.

Marketing control – The process of measuring and evaluating the results of marketing strategies and plans and of taking corrective action to ensure marketing objectives are achieved.

Marketing objective – A statement that identifies what a product will accomplish in a one-year period, usually expressed in terms of sales, market share, and profit.

Marketing plan – A short-term, specific plan of action that combines strategy and tactics.

Marketing planning – The analysis, planning, implementing, and controlling of marketing initiatives to satisfy target market needs and achieve organizational objectives.

Marketing research – A marketing function that links the consumer/customer/public to the marketer through information; the information is used to define marketing opportunities and problems, generate marketing strategies, evaluate marketing actions, and monitor performance.

Marketing strategy – A plan of action that shows how the various elements of the marketing mix will be used to satisfy a target market's needs.

Mass customization – The development, manufacture, and marketing of unique products to unique customers.

Media brief – A document that contains essential information for developing a media plan; used to stimulate discussion between a client and agency.

Media calendar (blocking chart) – A document that shows allocation of a brand's media budget according to time of year and type of medium; shows coordination of various media recommendations.

Media execution – The translation of media strategies into specific media action plans; involves recommending specific media to be used in the plan and negotiating the media buys.

Media kit – A package of relevant information associated with a product or organization that is distributed at a press conference.

Media objective – A statement that outlines what a media plan is to accomplish (who, what, when, where, or how).

Media plan – A strategy that outlines the relevant details about how a client's budget will be spent; involves decisions about what media to use and how much money to invest in the media chosen to reach the target audience effectively and efficiently.

Media strategy – A plan for achieving the media objectives stated in the media plan; typically justifies the use of certain media.

Media-delivered coupon – A coupon distributed by traditional media alternatives such as newspapers, magazines, and direct mail.

Merge/purge – A process in which numerous mailing lists are combined and then stripped of duplicate names.

Micro-segmentation (micro-marketing) – The identification of very small yet profitable market segments.

Mission statement – A statement of an organization's purpose and operating philosophy; provides guidance and direction for the operations of the company.

Modular agate line (MAL) – A standardized unit of measurement used in newspaper advertising equal to one column wide and 1/14" deep.

Modular agate unit – A standardized unit of measurement in which a newspaper page is divided into equal-sized units, each 30 modular agate lines deep.

Monopolistic competition – A market in which there are many competitors, each offering a unique marketing mix; consumers can assess these choices prior to making a buying decision.

Motive – A condition that prompts an individual to take action to satisfy a need.

Mural advertisement – A hand-painted outdoor ad seen on the side of a building.

Need – The perception of the absence of something useful.

Negotiated rate – The rate ultimately paid by an advertiser as a result of negotiations between an ad agency and a particular medium.

Network advertising – Advertising from one central source broadcast across an entire network of stations.

New product development strategy – A marketing strategy that calls for significant investment in research and development to develop innovative products.

Newsletter – A document sent to a predetermined audience that contains news about an organization (e.g., a newsletter sent to alumni of a school or to all employees of an organization).

Noise – Any potential form of disruption in the transmission of a message that could distort the impact of the message; competitive advertising or the clutter of advertising messages in a medium are forms of noise.

Non-probability sample – A sample of respondents who have an unknown chance of selection and are chosen because of factors such as convenience or the judgment of the researcher.

Non-verbal communication (body language) – The expression of thoughts, opinions, or information using non-verbal cues such as body movement, facial expressions, and eye contact.

Objection – An obstacle that a salesperson must confront during a sales presentation.

Observation research – A form of research in which the behaviour of the respondent is observed and recorded; may be by personal or electronic means.

Oligopoly – A market situation in which only a few brands control the market.

Online database – An information database accessible online to anyone with proper communications facilities.

Online selling – Using the Internet to conduct sales transactions.

Online survey – In marketing research, using an online questionnaire to collect data from people.

On-pack self-coupon – A coupon that is printed on the outside of a package redeemable on the next purchase of the product.

On-site sampling – See **Experiential marketing**.

Open-ended questioning – See **Open-response questioning**.

Open-response (open-ended) questioning – A situation where space is available at the end of a question where the respondents can add their comments.

Opinion-measure testing – A form of research yielding information about the effect of a commercial message on respondents' brand name recall, interest in the brand, and purchase intentions.

Opt-in list – A list of people who have agreed to receive messages via email.

Order taking – In retail sales, a floor clerk provides product information and shows goods to the customer who then goes to the checkout counter to pay for purchases.

Outbound telemarketing – Calls made by a company to customers to develop new accounts, generate sales leads, and even close a sale.

Overall goal – The objective of an advertising campaign.

Paid circulation – The circulation of a newspaper or magazine that is generated by subscription sales and newsstand sales.

Partnership selling – A strategically developed long-term relationship that involves selling products and providing comprehensive after-sales service and effective two-way communications to ensure complete customer satisfaction.

Pay-per-click advertising – See **Search advertising**.

Peer group – see **Reference group**.

Penetration strategy – A plan of action for aggressive marketing of a company's existing products.

Perception – The manner in which individuals receive and interpret messages.

Performance allowance – A discount offered by a manufacturer that encourages a distributor to perform a merchandising function on behalf of a manufacturer.

Permission-based email – Email sent to recipients who have agreed to accept email advertising messages.

Personal interview – In marketing research, the collection of information in a face-to-face interview.

Personal selling – Face-to-face communication involving the presentation of features and benefits of a product or service to a buyer; the objective is to make a sale.

Personality – A person's distinguishing psychological characteristics that lead to relatively consistent and enduring responses to the environment in which that person lives.

Picture matching technology (PMT) – A relatively new way to collect television audience data; determines what viewers are watching by periodically "sampling" the video image on their television screens, and then comparing this time-stamped video "fingerprint" with a library of all television sources that are available at that time.

Podcasting – Audio programming that is downloadable to iPods and other portable digital media devices; allows the listener to tune in when it is convenient for them to do so.

Point-of-purchase material – See **Dealer display material**.

Population (universe) – In marketing research, a group of people with certain age, gender, or other demographic characteristics.

Portable people meter (PPM) – A form of electronic observation where electronic metering devices are carried by household members that register what is being watched on television every minute of every day.

Portal – A website that serves as a gateway to a variety of services such as searching, news, directories, email, online shopping, and links to other sites.

Position charge – The cost of requesting a preferred position in a newspaper.

Positioning – The selling concept that motivates purchase, or the image that marketers desire a brand to have in the minds of consumers.

Positioning strategy statement – A summary of the character and personality of a brand and the benefits it offers customers.

Post-buy analysis – An evaluation of actual audience deliveries calculated after a specific spot or schedule of advertising has run.

Poster (billboard) – A common form of outdoor advertising; usually a picture-dominant advertisement with a minimum of copy.

Post-testing – The evaluation and measurement of a message's effectiveness during or after the message has run.

Pre-approach – The gathering of information about customers before actually making sales contact.

Premium – An additional item given free, or greatly discounted, to induce purchase of the primary brand.

Presentation strategy – A plan of what to say to a customer in a sales presentation to identify customer needs, summarize benefits, and prepare for potential objections.

Press conference – A meeting called by an organization to present information to representatives of the media.

Press release – A document prepared by an organization containing public relations information that is sent to the media for publication or broadcast.

Pre-testing – The evaluation of commercial messages prior to final production to determine the strengths and weaknesses of the communications.

Price positioning – A marketing strategy based on the premise that consumers search for the best possible value given their economic circumstances.

Primary data – Data collected to resolve a problem and recorded for the first time.

Primary medium – A medium that receives the largest allocation of an advertiser's budget; the dominant medium in a media plan.

Primary research – The collection and recording of primary data.

Probability sample – A sample of respondents who are known to have an equal chance of selection and are randomly selected from the sampling frame.

Problem statement – A brief statement that summarizes a particular problem to resolve or an opportunity to pursue and serves as the focus of a marketing strategy.

Product advertising – Advertising that provides information about a branded product to help build its image in the minds of customers.

Product as hero – A creative execution technique in which the advertised product is shown coming to the rescue (e.g., of a consumer in a difficult situation).

Product configuration – The bringing together of various products and services to form a solution for the customer.

Product differentiation strategy – A plan of action for communicating meaningful attributes and benefits of a product to a target market.

Product integration – See **Branded content.**

Product placement – The visible placement of brand name products in television shows, movies, radio, video games, and other programming.

Product seeding (buzz marketing) – Giving a product free to a group of trendsetters who promote the product to others by word of mouth.

Profile-matching strategy – A media tactic that involves matching the demographic profile of a product's target market with a specific medium that has a similar target profile.

Promotional advertising – Advertising that communicates a specific offer to encourage an immediate response from the target audience.

Prospecting – A procedure for systematically developing sales leads.

Psychographic segmentation – The identification of a target market according to lifestyle characteristics such as activities, interests, and opinions.

Public affairs – Strategies to deal with governments and to communicate with governments.

Public relations – A form of communications designed to gain public understanding and acceptance.

Publicity – News about an organization, product, service, or person that appears in the media.

Publisher's statement – A statement published by the Audit Bureau of Circulations twice a year that is the authority on which advertising rates are based.

Pull – Demand created by directing promotional activities at consumers or final users, who in turn pressure retailers to supply the product or service.

Pulse schedule – A scheduling of media advertising in flights of different weight and duration.

Pupilometer test – A device that measures pupil dilation (enlargement) of a person's eye when reading; it measures emotional responses to an advertisement.

Push – Demand created by directing promotional activities at intermediaries, who in turn promote the product or service among consumers.

Qualifying (a customer) – Assessing if a prospect needs a product, has the authority to buy it, and has the ability to pay for it.

Qualitative data – Data collected from small samples in a controlled environment; it describes feelings and opinions on issues.

Quantitative data – Measurable data collected from large samples using a structured research procedure.

Rating – Television and radio audience estimates expressed as a percentage of a population in a defined geographic area.

Reach – The total unduplicated audience exposed one or more times to a commercial message during a specific period (usually a week).

Reach plan – Rotation of commercials in various dayparts on radio according to a predetermined frequency.

Rebate– A predetermined amount of money returned directly to customers by the manufacturer after the purchase has been made.

Recall test – A test that measures an ad's impact by asking respondents to recall specific elements (e.g., the selling message) of the advertisement; can be aided (some information provided) or unaided.

Recency – A model that suggests advertising works best by reminding consumers about a product when they are ready to buy.

Recognition test – A test that measures a target audience's awareness of a brand, copy, or of the advertisement itself after the audience has been exposed to the message.

Rectangular ad – A large ad, slightly wider than it is tall, on a webpage.

Redemption rate – The number of coupons returned expressed as a percentage of the number of coupons that were distributed.

Reference group (peer group) – A group of people who share common interests that influence the attitudes and behaviour of its members.

Referral – A recommendation by a current customer of a potential new customer to a sales representative.

Related recall – The percentage of a test commercial audience who claims to remember the test commercial and can provide as verification some description of the commercial.

Relationship selling – A form of selling with the goal of developing a plan of action that establishes, builds, and maintains a long-term relationship with customers.

Reliability (of data) – Degree of similarity of results achieved if another research study were undertaken under similar circumstances.

Repeat transaction – A retail sales situation that involves a relationship between the buyer and the seller; the customer returns to the same store for similar goods and services.

Research objective – A statement that outlines what the marketing research is to accomplish.

Response card – A card filled in, usually at the time of purchase, that collects information about customers that can be added to the organization's database.

Response list – A list of direct mail buyers who have previously bought based on direct response offers.

Retail advertising – Advertising by a retail store; involves advertising the store name, image, location, and the re-advertising of branded merchandise carried by the store.

Rich media – A form of online communication that includes animation, sound, video, and interactivity.

Rifle strategy – A strategy that involves using a specific medium that effectively reaches a target market defined by a common characteristic.

Rotation plan – The placement of commercials in time slots purchased on radio; can be vertical according to the time of day or horizontal according to the day of the week.

Run of network – See **Run of site**.

Run of site (run of network) – Ad rate for placements anywhere on a website.

Run sheet – A schedule of daily events that shows the various dates, times, and locations of activities at an event.

Sales presentation – A persuasive delivery and demonstration of a product's benefits; shows buyers how the product's benefits will satisfy their needs.

Sales promotion – An activity that provides incentives to bring about immediate response from customers, distributors, and an organization's sales force.

Sales promotion plan – An action plan for communicating incentives to appropriate target markets at the right time.

Sample – A representative portion of an entire population that is used to obtain information about that population.

Sampling frame – A list used to access a representative sample of a population; it is a means of accessing people for a research study.

Satellite radio – A radio service that offers commercial-free programming for a monthly fee.

Search advertising (pay-per-click advertising) – An advertiser's listing is placed within or alongside search results in exchange for paying a fee each time someone clicks on the listing.

Seasonal schedule – Scheduling media advertising according to seasonal sales trends; usually concentrated in the pre-season or the period just prior to when the bulk of the buying occurs.

Secondary media – Media alternatives used to complement the primary medium in an advertising campaign; typically less money is allocated to these media.

Secondary research – Data compiled and published by others for purposes other than resolving a specific problem. In advertising, secondary sources are frequently used to gain access to media information that benefits media analysis and planning.

Selective direct mail – See **Solo direct mail**.

Selective spot – Commercial time during a network show that is allocated back to regional and local stations to sell; advertisers buy spots on a station-by-station basis.

Self-image – One's own idea about oneself and one's relationship with others.

Setup – See **Bump-in**.

Seventy poster – A small poster usually affixed to the back of a bus.

Shotgun strategy – A tactic involving the use of mass media to reach a loosely defined target audience.

Single transaction – A retail sales situation where a salesperson spends time with a customer and closes the sale on the spot.

Skip schedule – The scheduling of media advertising on an alternating basis, such as every other week or every other month.

Skyscraper – A vertical box-shaped ad that appears on a webpage.

Slippage – The situation of a consumer collecting labels in a promotion offer but failing to follow through and request the refund.

Slogan – A short phrase that captures the essence of an entire advertising campaign; reflects the positioning strategy of the brand and is shown in all ads in all media.

Social Media – Online tools that people use to share content, insights, experiences, and media itself, thus facilitating conversations and interaction online between groups of people.

Social Media Network – a social website (e.g., Facebook and Twitter) that connects people with different interests together

Solo direct mail (selective direct mail) – A unique advertising offer mailed directly to a target audience by a marketing organization.

Spam – Unsolicited email.

Spectacular – see **Superboard**.

Spiff – An incentive offered to retail salespeople to encourage them to promote a specified brand of goods to customers.

Sponsored email – Email that includes a short message from a sponsor along with a link to the sponsor's website.

Sponsorship – The act of financially supporting an event in return for certain advertising rights and privileges.

Spot colour – The addition of one colour to an otherwise black-and-white newspaper or magazine ad.

Starch readership test – A post-test recognition procedure that measures readers' recall of an advertisement (noted), their ability to identify the sponsor (associated), and whether they read more than half of the written material (read most).

Statement stuffer (bounce back) – An ad or offer distributed in monthly statements or with the delivery of goods purchased by some form of direct response advertising.

Station poster – An advertisement located on the platform or at the entrance or exit of subways and light rail transit systems.

Stickiness (sticky) – A website's ability to keep people at the site for an extended period or to have them return to the site frequently.

Strategic alliance – The combination of separate companies' resources for the purpose of satisfying their shared customers; the companies have strengths in different areas.

Strategic planning (corporate strategy) – The process of determining objectives (setting goals) and identifying strategies (ways to achieve the goals) and tactics (specific action plans) to help achieve objectives.

Strategic selling – A form of consultative selling that involves dealing with each customer as an individual, stressing that in the transfer of product information.

Streaming media – Audio or video delivered online in small, compressed packets of data that are interpreted by a software player as they are received.

Super banner – See **Leaderboard**.

Superboard (spectacular) – Outdoor advertising that is larger than a normal poster and much more expensive to produce; can include extensions beyond borders and electronic messaging.

Superbus advertising – An advertisement painted on the exterior of a bus; the advertiser also has exclusive use of interior cards.

Support claims statement – A substantiation of the promise made in the key benefit statement; appears in the creative plan.

Survey research – The systematic collection of data by communicating with a representative sample by means of a questionnaire.

Sweepstakes – A chance promotion involving the giveaway of products or services of value to randomly selected participants.

SWOT analysis – An analysis procedure that involves an assessment of an organization's strengths, weaknesses, opportunities, and threats; strengths and weaknesses are internal variables, whereas opportunities and threats are external variables.

Tabloid – A smaller newspaper that is sold flat (not folded).

Tabulation – The process of counting various responses for each question in a survey.

Tactics (execution) – Action-oriented details that outline how a strategic plan will be implemented.

Tagline – A short phrase that captures the essence of an advertised message.

Target market profile – A description of a customer group based on demographic, psychographic, and geographic variables.

Targeting request – An ad placed to reach a specific target audience of a website, for which a premium is usually paid.

Teardown – See **Bump-out**.

Telemarketing – The use of telecommunications to promote the products and services of a business; involves outbound calls (company to customer) and inbound calls (customer to company).

Telephone interview – In marketing research, the collection of information from a respondent by telephone.

Test marketing – Placing a commercial, set of commercials, or print ad campaign in one or more limited markets that are representative of the whole to observe the impact of the ads on consumers.

Text messaging – The transmission of short text-only messages using wireless devices such as cell phones and personal digital assistants.

Tip-in – An insert that is glued to a page in the publication using a removable adhesive.

Torture test – A creative execution technique in which the product is subjected to extreme conditions to demonstrate its durability.

Trade allowance – A temporary price reduction that encourages larger purchases by distributors.

Trade promotion – An incentive offered to channel members to encourage them to provide marketing and merchandising support for a particular product.

Trade show – An event that allows a company to showcase its products to a captive audience and generate leads.

Trademark – A brandmark or other brand element that is granted legal protection so that only the owner can use it.

Transit shelter advertising – Street-level advertisements incorporated into the design of the glass and steel shelters located at a bus stop.

Transmission – The sending of a message through a medium such as television, radio, newspapers, magazines, outdoor advertising, Internet, and so on, or through personal selling.

Trial close – A failed attempt at closing a sale; the buyer said "no."

Unique selling point (USP) – The primary benefit of a product or service that distinguishes it from its competitors.

Universe – See **Population**.

Validity (of data) – A research procedure's ability to measure what it is intended to measure.

Venue marketing (venue sponsorship) – Linking a brand name or company name to a physical site, such as a stadium, arena, or theatre.

Venue sponsorship – See **Venue marketing**.

Vertical rotation – The placement of radio commercials based on the time of day (within various dayparts).

Video messaging – The transfer of video messages and other content (e.g., television shows) via cell phones and other personal electronic devices.

Viral marketing – Online marketing that encourages the receiver of a message to pass it along to others to generate additional exposure.

Visit – A sequence of page requests made by a visitor to a website; also called a session or a browsing period.

Visitor – A unique user of a website.

Voice-pitch analysis test – A test that uses a recording of a person's voice response to measure change in voice pitch caused by emotional responses to the communications.

Volume discount – A discount linked to the dollar volume purchased over an extended period; the more volume purchased, the higher the discount.

Washroom advertising – A mini-poster ad located in a public or institutional washroom; usually placed above the urinal or on the back of the stall door.

Webcasting (webisodes) – The production of an extended commercial presented on the web that includes entertainment value in the communications.

Webisodes – See **Webcasting**.

Wordmark – The stylized treatment of the brand name; serves the same function as a symbol.

Word-of-mouth marketing – The transfer of a product message by people (often using technology) to other people.

Index